Land, Power, and Economics on the Frontier of Upper Canada examines Ontario's formative years, focusing on Essex County in Ontario from 1788 to 1850. Upper Canadian attitudes to land and society are shown to have been built on contemporary visions of the cosmos. John Clarke examines the actions of individuals from the perspective of the political culture and its manifestations, doing so within the constraints of geography and the cultural baggage of the settlers. Placing human action in the context of economics and *laissez-faire* capitalism, Clarke shows how almost unbridled acquisitiveness, and its concomitant land speculation, could promote or hinder development.

The prevailing ideology in Ontario at the time was a conservative culture that rejected everything American and attempted to preserve the best of the British world in the new Eden. Those building the state believed that a social and political hierarchy composed of those possessing a "natural virtue" would serve society best. In consequence, a few individuals at the top of the hierarchy, through their access to power, came to control the bulk of the land, the basis of the economy. At the other end of the spectrum from the elite were those transforming the land and themselves through their own labour.

How did the physical environment and government land policy affect the pattern of settlement and the choice of land for a viable farm? What was the price of land, and how common was credit? Did the presence of reserved lands hinder or promote development? How extensive was land speculation and how did it operate? Clarke brings these issues and more to the forefront, integrating concepts and substantive issues through a problem-oriented approach. Blending qualitative and quantitative approaches, he weaves together surveyors' records, personal and government correspondence, assessment rolls, and land records to measure the pulse of this pre-industrial society.

JOHN CLARKE is professor of geography and environmental studies at Carleton University.

Land, Power, and Economics on the Frontier of Upper Canada

JOHN CLARKE

McGill-Queen's University Press
Montreal & Kingston · London · Ithaca

© McGill-Queen's University Press 2001
ISBN 0-7735-2062-7 (cloth)

Legal deposit second quarter 2001
Bibliothèque nationale du Québec

Printed in Canada on acid-free paper

This book has been published with the help of a grant
from the Humanities and Social Sciences Federation of
Canada, using funds provided by the Social Sciences
and Humanities Research Council of Canada.

McGill-Queen's University Press acknowledges the
financial support of the Government of Canada through
the Book Publishing Industry Development Program
(BPIDP) for its activities. It also acknowledges the
support of the Canada Council for the Arts for its
publishing program.

Canadian Cataloguing in Publication Data

Clarke, John, 1943–
    Land, power, and economics on the frontier of Upper
    Canada
    Includes bibliographical references and index.
    ISBN 0-7735-2062-7 (bnd)
    1. Land settlement patterns—Ontario—Essex (County)—
    History–19th century.   2. Essex (Ontario : County)—
    Historical geography.   I. Title.

HD319.05C53 2000   333.3'09713'3109034   C00-900985-X

Typeset in 10/12 Baskerville by True to Type

For my parents, Martha McEvoy and John Clarke, my brother, George, my wife, Vilma Nathaniel, and our son, John Nathaniel Clarke – the core of the community of love where I have been fortunate to find myself

Contents

Plates

Figures

Tables

Glossary

Allometry: a branch of mathematics concerned with the growth of parts relative to the system as a whole.

Abstract index to deeds (AID): abstracted copies of all registered land transactions in an Ontario county. The AID was among the major sources used in this study.

Bargain and Sale (B&S): a legal instrument used to convey title to land, originally so that it could be done secretly. Conveyance is made with all rights and privileges, in return for monetary consideration or an equivalent in goods or mineral and timber rights. These are the most commonly recorded instruments in the abstract index to deeds.

Cadastral: the adjective for the noun "cadastre," a line-by-line survey of property which is usually conducted for purposes of assessing taxation.

Chi-Square (χ^2): a measure of statistical association used when the data available are only for the nominal level of measurement. For example, in this work, it is possible to show that a particular lot had a black-ash vegetation on it but it was not possible to say that the lot was 81.9 per cent black ash. In this instance chi-square is an appropriate test to establish the relationship between the occurrence of black ash and the occurrence of poor drainage.

Coefficient of variation: a relative measure of dispersion used to compare different data sets with different orders of magnitude. Conventionally such standardization is obtained by dividing the standard deviation by the mean.

Co-linearity: a condition in statistics in which one variable is a surrogate for another.

Confidence level: a statement of the probability of the occurrence of some event.

Consideration: the terms of a transaction, most usually monetary.

Deed: a general term meaning a document under seal and including specific instruments such as indentures, deeds of bargain and sale, mortgages, leases, and patents. It is a conveyance of realty between the parties and in this way differs from the term "deed poll" under which only the party making it binds himself to it.

Degrees of freedom: a statistical term used to describe the number of steps that remain before the outcome of a statistical event can be known. It is used in the evaluation of confidence in inference.

Dower: that part of the deceased husband's estate that the law allows his widow for life. Few sought to assert this dower right in Essex and none did so in Malden Township, the area studied to establish the frequency of particular legal instruments. However, where the person acquiring the land sought to purchase the dower right, this was accomplished by paying a standard fee of five shillings to the wife of the "party of the first part."

Easting: a measurement in an easterly direction.

F Analysis of Variance: a statistic used to infer the probablity of the occurrence of a statistical "event."

Fiat: a legal document sanctioning an action, in this work the issuing of a patent.

Gage: a pledge deposited to guarantee an action and subject to forfeiture for non-performance; in origin a "glove thrown down" by a knight to express his willingness to appear in battle to support his assertions. The most common gage in English law is a mortgage.

Grant: an instrument that appears to transfer title and that is similar in effect to an indenture of bargain and sale. The grantor is the Crown; the grantee the recipient.

Indenture: a deed that is "indented" for identification and security purposes. In this sense, all instruments with the exception of deed polls are indentures. The parties generally enter into reciprocal and corresponding obligations towards each other. In some instances there may be a transfer of title without consideration, for example, in the case of a will. Most usually, however, in the Essex records when an indenture is found in the instruments column of the abstracts, this represents a transfer of title between the two parties, for some consideration. There is one limitation in a transfer of this nature, and that is that the wife of the party of the first part retains her dower right.

Inverse distance decay form or function: With distance from some centre the score on some variable decreases. For example, in an economically rational system, grain crops may diminish with distance from the farmer's home. This reflects the human energy available.

Isochrone: a line on a map joining places of equal time or date; the closest analogy is the contour map.

Iterative procedure: the repetition of an action used in cluster analysis to assign particular observations to groups.

Logarithmically transformed: one of several methods for transforming data that are not normally distributed so that they can be analysed using the linear model.

Mean: the "average" in a set of scores. It is related to the size of sample "n." For example, in the series 0,1,2,3,4, the mean is 2.0. In statistics it is written as $\bar{x}$.

Median: the value separating a set of scores into two parts at the half-way point. In a set consisting of five scores or numbers, it is the third score. In the series 0,10,20,30,40, the median (also defined as the fiftieth percentile) is 20.

Mode: the most frequently occurring number in a set of numbers. In the series 2,3,4,4,6,7, the number 4 is the mode. If there is one mode the series is decribed as *unimodal*; where there are two the appropriate term is *bi-modal*; and if more the series is *multi-modal*.

Mortgage: A mortgage is a deed for the conveyance of real or personal property by a debtor (mortgagor) or a creditor (mortgagee) as security for a money debt. Mortgages are recorded in the instrument column of the Essex abstracts as "mortgage" or abbreviated to "mort." Occasionally, mortgages are recorded as indentures, although it is obvious from the context that they are, in fact, mortgages. When this happens the term "mort" is added to the Comments column. If, within a certain time, the debt is repaid, the mortgagee is obliged to reconvey the property. This action is recorded in one of three ways: as a D.M., or discharge of mortgage in the Instruments column; as "disch." in the Comments column; or by a line drawn through the whole of the entry. Where a mortgagee transfers his responsibility to another individual, such action is recorded in the Intruments column as an Assignment or Assignment of Mortgage (A.M.). Where common-law mortgages were not used, property could be placed in the hands of one or more trustees to secure the repayment of a sum of money or the performance of some particular condition. This was accomplished with a deed of trust or trust deed, which, though different in form from a mortgage, had a similar effect. In this instance, instead of a D.M., a deed of release is executed by the trustees to reconvey the property to the grantor. If, on the other hand, the mortgagor defaults on his agreement, an instrument of foreclosure is used to ensure that the land is transferred to the mortgagee. Foreclosures will also be used where the instrument was a bond. A bond therefore appears to be similar to a mortgage, the grantor putting his land as security against the amount of money borrowed in the agreement.

Nearest neighbour statistic: a measure of pattern based on distance measures which are compared to a theoretical norm. The statistic (RHO) varies from 0 (when the data are clustered) to 1 (when the pattern is spatially random) to 2.149 (when the pattern is regular or uniform).

Normal distribution: a set of scores in which the mean, median, and mode are identical; the distribution is "bell-shaped" and its form and underlying probabilities are the basis of much statistical inference.

Northings: a measure of position in a northerly direction; conventionally this is expressed as latitude.

One-tailed test: a statistical means of determining whether something is bigger or smaller than a specified "norm."

Outlier: an extreme value.

Parabolic: a distribution in which the data describe a curve of high degree resembling a parabola. Such a distribution can best be described using a polynomial.

Patent: a legal document recognizing the completion of a set of pre-conditions and entitlement to the possession of land granted by the Crown. It was also entitlement to enfranchisement. Money was never recorded prior to patent because such transactions were grants and not sales. The patentee had full legal title to the property patented, provided the taxes were paid. If this did not happen the property was seized by a sheriff's deed, sheriff's sale, or simply by the sheriff.

Pearson product moment correlation coefficient: a number indicating the degree of association between two variables. The correlation coefficient (r) ranges between zero and 1.0; the closer to 1.0 the greater the association between the variables. Correlation coefficients may have positive or negative signs which describe the direction of the association. Where positive the relationship is direct; where negative it is the inverse, that is, as one variable increases the other decreases.

Polynomial: the expansion of any power in a mathematical expression using many terms. It is based upon the binomial theorem.

Power of attorney: this instrument enables one individual to act for another.

Quit-claim (q.c.): This is an instrument whereby one party gives up all its interest or claims in the land. It may be used to clarify an earlier property description and thus reduce conflict between neighbours, or, indeed, it can be used to settle accounts where a mortgagor has been unable to meet his obligations and foreclosure is imminent.

Range: a statistical term used to describe the limits of a set of data. For example, in the series 1,2,3,4, the range is three.

Regression analysis uses the method of least squares to determine a "line of best fit" which describes the trend in a data set. The "regression line" minimizes the departure of all scores from it.

Scattergram: the presentation of data in diagrammatic form. The data are presented in point form, their location measured along two axis.

Score: a measure of association with a particular variable. For example, the score of someone aged 57 on the variable "age" is 57.

Spearman rho: a measure of association between two variables measured at the ordinal or ranked level. The measure is useful when interval data (continuous measurement on a variable) is unavailable or the researcher can place little confidence in it.

Standard deviate: a recognized (standardized) measure of position with respect to the mean. It allows comparison of the scores on a particular variable and between variables. In the series 0,1,2,3,4, the standard deviation is 1.58 and since the mean of this series is 2.0 the first standard deviate above and below the mean is found at the score of 3.58 and 0.42 respectively. Standard deviates have the property that a known percentage of scores on a particular variable fall within them. For example, in a normally distributed set of scores, 68.3 percent of the scores (values) fall within one standard deviate; 95.45 per cent fall within two standard deviates, and 99.7 within three. Standardization in this form is useful for comparative purposes. For example, in the second set of scores, 0,10,20,30,40, things are clearly of a different magnitude. The mean of 20 reflects this as does the standard deviation of 15.8. However, a positive score of 3.58 on this first variable and one of 35.8 on the second are clearly at the same relative position.

Standard deviation: a measure of the spread of scores around the mean. In the text it is written as sd or σ. It can have positive or negative signs describing position above or below the mean.

Standard error: as used here, a statistic that describes the "fit" of a regression line to a set of data.

t test: This test generates a statistic; this is "Student's t" and was originally devised for use in quality control in the production of batches of Guinness. It is one of several "difference of means" tests used to decide inferentially if differences exist between samples.

Trend-surface analysis: any method by which a set of observations or scores is analysed spatially by dividing the data into two parts – that which is attributed to the regional trend and that attributed to the residual or local component. In this book the method used is derived from the linear, least-squares method and uses the successive expansion of polynomials.

Acknowledgments

That I have been able to devote so much time to a topic says that I, and my generation in our universities, have been enormously privileged. We have been able to take part in "curiosity" research, research simply for its own sake. This is not to say that quality research need be totally without application. Clearly, the space age has seen insights produced in one field applied to another, such as the tinted glasses I wear. In the human sciences, even the work of historians and historical geographers can be applied too, for example, in the resolution of native land claims. Still, a purely pragmatic society whose universities operate hand in glove with the private sector, as is increasingly the case, is one that, in my opinion, must suffer from a peculiar myopia and may even lose its own history.

I am indebted to a large number of people who have given me the benefits of their intellect, their knowledge of particular materials, their money, or their faith that what was engaged in was worthwhile. Among these are my former teachers R.S. "Ben" Lyons, William Kelly, Anthony Q. Stewart, James Paul, and J. "Louis" Lord at Belfast Royal Academy, and Emyr Estyn Evans, Robin Glasscock, and Noel Mitchel at Queen's University, Belfast. In Canada, this group includes Philip Keddie at the University of Manitoba and Harry Taylor, Alan Philbrick, Charles Whebell, and especially my former adviser, W. Robert Wightman, at the University of Western Ontario, who heightened my interest in things Canadian.

I wish to acknowledge the following academics who gave of their particular expertise and/or data during the research phase. I include here Alan Brunger, Bruce Elliott, David Gagan, Roger Hall, Margaret Ogilvie, Fernand Ouellette, Colin Read, Syd Wise, Neal Sargent, and Randy Widdis. At the writing stage I was treated most generously by several individuals who gave of their time and expertise to make this a better volume than it would otherwise. David Brown, a former student, commented upon chapters 1 to 3; Alan Brunger, my fellow graduate student of yesteryear,commented upon chapter 4; Charles Whebell, a former teacher, and I discussed aspects of surveying which appear in chapter 2. Daniel Brock provided biographical advice, as did Frederick Armstrong, a fellow student of the Western District who was one of a number of examiners for my doctorate and who has continued his support over the years. In the final stages, he worked tirelessly on all aspects of chapters 7 to 10, commenting upon structure, grammar, and substance. I thank as well my copy editor, Curtis Fahey, whose touch was light but precise and who guided the book through the publication process; and my editor, Donald Akenson, who accepted the manuscript for McGill-Queen's in 1998 and who provided just the right amount of encouragement and prodding to see the volume through to fruition. In the final stages of the project, the work was coordinated by Joan McGilvray of McGill-Queen's, to whom I am grateful. I also wish to acknowledge the supportive criticism of two anonymous referees who strengthened my belief and faith in the ideals of the academy. It is my duty to record these things but intellectually it is my pleasure to do so because such interaction manifests the ideals of the university, transcending age, discipline, and human quirk: all working to the common end. In the final analysis, the synthesis is mine alone, as is the responsibility. With the penitent I proclaim, *"Mea culpa."*

Work such as this is impossible without the assistance of archivists and map and art curators. At the Archives of Ontario, these have included Christine Bourolias, Raymonde Cadorette, Barbara Craig, Wayne Crockett, Gordon Dodds, John Fortier, Caroline Gray, Sandra Guillaume, Paul McIlroy, Susan McClure, John Mezaks, Roger Nickerson, Alec Ross, Tim Stanford, James Suderman, Larry Weiler, Leon Warmski, and Ian Wilson. At the Archives du Séminaire de Québec, I have especially to thank Mirelle Saint-Pierre. At the National Archives of Canada, one of the world's great archival institutions, the following never failed to help: David Brown, Marc Baisillon, Jim Burant, Marc Cockburn, Edward Dahl, Tim Dubé, Lawrence Earl, Eldon Frost, Robert Grandmaitre, Patricia Kennedy, Betty Kidd, John F. McDonald, Marthe Marlowe, Ghislain Malette, Roanne Mukhtar, Patrick McIntyre, Tom Nagy, Harold Naugler, Bill Russell, Carol Whyte, and Joan Schwarz. Art Armstrong at the Department of Lands and Forests,

Toronto, was among the first to help with this project, as was Anne Sexton and Edwards Phelps from the Regional History Collection at the University of Western Ontario. In Windsor, at the then Hiram Walker Historical Museum, Alan Douglas and Elizabeth Francis were encouraging in these early years. In more recent years I have been grateful for the assistance of Brian Trainor and Anne McVeigh of the Public Record Office of Northern Ireland; Lise Brunet of the Law Society of Upper Canada; Janet Cobban, curator of the Park Museum and the Francis Baby House in Windsor; Geoff Raymond of the Windsor Community Museum; Robert McKaskell of the Windsor Art Gallery; Carol Baum of the Canadian section of the Royal Ontario Museum; Guy St Denis, Regional History Collection, University of Western Ontario; David Fall, McIntosh Gallery, University of Western Ontario; Bob Garcia, National Parks, Fort Malden; Joan McKnight and John Quinsey of the Association of Ontario Land Surveyors; Agnes Malone, Special Collections, University of Windsor; and Robert Lochiel Fraser of the *Dictionary of Canadian Biography*.

At Carleton a host of "support staff" assisted me most cheerfully in typing manuscript and making maps and photographs: Hazel Anderson, Daljeet Atwal, Larry Boyle, Else Broek, Judy Chan, Christine Earl, Elsie Clement, Barbara Farrell, Heather McAdam, Monica Mueller-Ferguson, Callista Kelly, Marc Lewis, Anant Nagpur, Alan Pendlington, Elaine Quehl, Beth Ray, Rita Richard, Pam Ross, Robert Smith, Pete Stanley, and Linda Stewart. Betty Wysse and, most especially, Anne Burgess helped direct me towards money, just as necessary as secretarial and cartographic support. In the final stages, she helped compile the index. Christine Earl deserves special mention here because she has been connected with this project for perhaps twenty years. As a cartographer, she has an unusual gift – a sense of the aesthetic combined with the capacity to execute what she envisions. I am lucky to have had her cartographic services for so long. Towards the end of the project, she was even willing to proofread all of the manuscript.

A series of deans tried in their own manner to assist the project: Gilles Pacquet, John ApSimon, Roger Blockley, Ken McGillivray, Tom Ryan, Tom Wilkinson, Bill Jones, and, most especially, Syd Wise. In differing financial worlds and in periods of great personal frustration, I was granted research time by deans Ryan and Wilkinson. I shall be forever grateful to them for their support and action, as I shall be to the Social Science and Humanities Research Council, its predecessor, the Canada Council, and the Multi-Culturalism Directorate of the Secretary of State. These organizations provided assistance in the form of scholarships, research grants, and leave fellowships, awarded in the days when the granting councils were permitted to support things, as they should. This sort of work requires such support if we are to continue to add to our understanding of Canada and the Canadian experience. To date, private industry has failed to support such aspects of the nation's culture and in the 1990s politicians seem concerned with the needs of private industry to the exclusion of all else.

The book has been published with the help of a grant from the Humanities and Social Science Federation of Canada using funds provided by the Social Science and Humanities Research Council of Canada. I am grateful for this support and for the assistance towards the costs of publication from my own university in the personages of Dean Jones and Vice-President ApSimon.

Barbara Burrows, David Brown, John Buffone, David Broscoe, John Nathaniel Clarke, Marc Cockburn, Lucille Dorken, Andrea Emard, Sean C. Farrell, Gregory F. Finnegan, Charles Hotzel, Riquia Islam, Nana Amankwah, Nehemiah Shadreck Mudzingamyama, Colin Old, Karl Skof, James Trotman, and Jesse Weldon all acted as student assistants for me. They did so for periods of three months to three years and at rates of pay that varied with my capacities to scrounge or to win research grants; some worked for nothing. All gave 100 per cent of their effort, irrespective of their remuneration, for something that we all held to be a worthwhile pursuit. I shall forever be grateful for the enthusiasm and idealism of youth.

Some became my co-authors and I celebrate the contributions of David Brown, John Buffone, Greg Finnegan, and Karl Skof. A special word is also in order for my research associate of the last few years, John Buffone. Though not an Ulsterman, John knows well the value of loyalty, integrity, dedication, hard work, and stubbornness. If he is representative, there are Ulster-men living all over Abruzzo. Without his skills in so many fields, this book might have languished in the great electronic void. The fates and Canada threw us together and the book is the better for it; indeed, without his dedication and loyalty through all sorts of adversity, it would simply not have been completed nor for years to come. The debt to my friend is very great indeed.

Here I must recognize the members of the "Old Brigade" in Geography at Carleton who have been and are my well-wishers: Duncan Anderson, David Bennett, Dennis Fitzgerald, Mike Fox, Peter Johnson, David Knight, Gordon Merrill, Fraser Taylor, John Tunbridge, Ken Torrance, Philip Uren, Iain Wallace, Tom Wilkinson, and Peter Williams. I also include some of my neighbours, Fred, Jenny, and Ben Oxtoby, Suzanne Swan and Brian Davidson, and those who fed and housed me as well as gave me companionship during archival trips to Toronto – Joy and Benoy Biswas, Benita and Bruce Black, Patricia Nathaniel, and Rena Ghose. Patrick MacGahern, the owner of one of Ottawa's most celebrated bookstores, was very helpful. I have been accompanied and supported in the writing stages by Kathleen Battle, Wolfgang Amadeus Mozart, Antonio Vivaldi, and the staff of the Sitar Restaurant, Ottawa's oldest and most celebrated "Indian" restaurant.

This list of thanks is now quite long and there is the danger that someone inadvertently omitted might feel slighted. All I can ask is that, like all those named, they continue to forgive me.

Parts of this book have appeared in various journals. I wish to thank the editors of the *Journal of Historical Geography*, the *Canadian Cartographer*, the *Canadian Geographer*, the *Canadian Historical Review*, *Histoire Sociale/Social History*, and the University of Toronto Press for requisite materials which appear in chapters 1, 2, 4, 5, and 8. I thank my co-authors David Brown, Greg Finnegan, and Karl Skof for their permission to quote from articles we produced in common in a number of these journals. I wish also to acknowledge the use of portraits, plans, and prints provided by the Law Society of Upper Canada, the University of Western Ontario, the principal of Huron College, the Archives of Ontario, the Ontario Association of Land Surveyors, the National Archives of Canada, Fort Malden and Parks Canada, and the National Gallery of Canada. Special thanks go to those institutions that provided such items for a minimum reproduction fee or none at all.

Finally, the book is offered in memory of my parents, John and Martha Clarke. It is dedicated to my brother, George, who for several years gave a large portion of his salary so that I might lead an appropriately wild life as an Irish undergraduate. I also dedicate the book to my wife, Vilma, and our son, John Nathaniel. Both contributed to the volume and my life as a whole in discussion around the family dinner table. They accepted a smaller rice bowl so that what I thought worthwhile might appear. They continue to put up with my shortcomings. Both know, I hope, how much I love and value them and how important they are to me.

Ottawa, March 2001.

Preface

This book is about land and power in its many forms. By extension it is about the ways in which all human history is formed, but it is written specifically about a time when possession of land was central to life and when agriculture was the very basis of it, rather than, as it was to become, something preserved for urban dwellers in eco-museums. In Ireland, my birthplace, this struggle inflamed the passions of its people; nations were embroiled in it and from the struggle over land emerged the Irish nation and a sense of Ulster/British identity. With distance from the main events, a revisionist Irish history is now engaging with the political and economic circumstances of landlordism, as well as with the perspective of the people who experienced it.

The territorial nature of the Irish struggle is well known, but though the pulse may have been more feint and less enduring, it was also a struggle over land that strengthened Upper Canadian identity in the War of 1812 and challenged Upper Canadian values in 1837, the year of rebellion. These early years from about 1788 to 1850, which included the struggle for the northern half of the continent, are the focus of this book. It was in that period that Upper Canadian, and Canadian, ideology was being developed.

Part of that ideology was a conservative culture which rejected all that the United States stood for and preserved the best of the British world, itself in flux, in a North American setting that God had endowed as the new Eden. From the patrician perspective of those building the state, and contributing to its emerging *raison d'être*, it was clear that there was in society a social hierarchy to which they themselves belonged. This virtuous elite served the people, although not in the modern democratic sense, through a constitution held to be superior to all others.

This tripartite constitution limited the powers of the monarch but left the powers of its threefold elements unspecified or to be negotiated. In return for their service to the state, those capable of and therefore charged with the responsibility to serve would receive compensation from the state. Both in Britain and in Upper Canada, a small percentage of people who had access to power came to control the majority of the resources, at least for a while. These people used their social position to augment their economic position and enhance their claim to its base – the possession of land. In the long term, of course, the New World's ability to provide land for all would diminish their importance.

To this point in the historiography of Upper Canada, it has been possible to view such people as "natural" leaders of Upper Canadian society and as the recipients of a "natural" and due reward for their service. It is also possible to conceive of them in Thompsonian terms as predators and the state as their object of prey. This perspective has received less attention. No doubt the motives of individuals were complex but it has to be remembered that Upper Canadians, like Britons in this period, lacked the social-welfare programs of the contemporary state. Individuals had to rely upon self-help in all its forms and had to provide for their families, for the possibility of loss of income, and for their old age. As a consequence, they had to be concerned with relationships of power.

Power may be construed as the capacity to affect the world of others and to influence the outcome of events. It may be overt, as in military conquest; it may be subtle and psychological, as in the capacity to appear authoritative and persuasive; or it may take the form of pressure to conform or adapt to the prevailing economic and social systems. Conversely, freedom or liberty is freedom from the will of others; the individual, who from the perspective of the species is still emerging, is as free as he is the proprietor of "his personality and capacities." Freedom is a function of the possession of what C.B. MacPherson calls "possessive individualism," the idea that individuals owe nothing to society and are the proprietor of their own persons.

Where individual qualities and ties of language, culture, ethnicity, kinship, and marriage influence outcomes, freedom is constrained by the exercise of power. No doubt this has happened in all of human history. Such avenues to power certainly existed in Upper Canada, as a number of works, including that of J.K. Johnson show clearly. These variables should not be ignored and are not ignored in this volume.

Indeed, wherever possible they are highlighted, most especially, the importance of kinship, ethnicity, friendship, and marriage. Yet, while significant in particular cases and circumstances, these are, in the author's view, secondary to the central issue of land in the eighteenth and nineteenth centuries. Access to land was of primary importance, because it was the basis of life and of economic and social prestige.

The period upon which this book focuses was for Upper Canada just as heroic a period of primitive accumulation as was that associated with England some decades earlier. Perhaps this was even more so since the extent of the prize was so much greater and participation so much easier; indeed, that is why one can speak of the "best poor man's country." R.S. Neale, in *Class in English History*, reminds us of the eighteenth- and nineteenth-century antagonism between "property" and "liberty." He points, on the one hand, to Adam Smith's acceptance of financial expenditure by the state in the defence of property and indeed his view that civil government was instituted for its protection. On the other hand, he shows that Tom Paine believed property to be incompatible with liberty and was the illegitimate product of power. Can there be any doubt of the central importance of property and especially, in the New World, of landed property? Kinship, marriage, ethnicity and a myriad of other factors may have been important in providing access to power but the economic and thereby political base of most, if not all, power was landed wealth.

As F.J.C. Hearnshaw notes, Pitt, the British prime minister who sought to enlarge the "political public," maintained that political representation was of property, not of person, and that "in this light there is scarcely a blade of grass which is not represented." John Strachan, leading member of the Upper Canadian oligarchy known as the Family Compact, echoed such views. When speaking of the state and constitution, he asked: What could be stolen if property was secure? For most of the century, especially in a relatively capital-deprived province such as Upper Canada, property was primarily landed property and the link between political ideology, economic philosophy, and, for that matter, the law that codified such relationships was clear. The possession of land meant security, wealth, prestige, and the ability to influence events. To be a member of the elite meant, for most, to be landed; even as Upper Canada moved on towards modernity, property remained important. Later, for instance, prospective members of the Senate of a confederated Canada created by the British North America Act of 1867 were required to meet a property qualification.

At the other end of the continuum from the elite were the people striving through their own sweat to build a new life for themselves. Like their social "betters," they too sought to acquire. With a large family, this goal was unattainable in the Old World but entirely possible in the New. By transforming the land the immigrant family could transform itself. In contrast, in Upper Canada the "gentry" might well be handicapped in a society which required human and animal muscle and required of individuals certain basic skills. So strong is the myth, largely justified, that this was and is the "best poor-man's country" that it has generated an amnesia about the past, a forgetfulness that Canada was also the scene where man's acquisitiveness was manifest and where some sought more than that necessary to sustain life. Like the older visions of Ireland's struggle, this mythology needs revisiting.

Notions of hard work bestowing human dignity upon a rustic populace, and of paternalistic leadership guiding this new garden of Eden, are the hallmarks of a pre-industrial society. This most certainly existed in Upper Canada at the turn of the nineteenth century, although by the 1830s and 1840s there were signs of economic and political change as "pre-industrial" gave way to "proto-industrial." Yet, beneath the surface, all was not well. From a sense of powerlessness and disgust with colonial land policy, a rebellion occurred in even this most loyal province in 1837. Relicts of this event, in my opinion, still persist in the attitudes of its people and the predispositions of its historians.

This book seeks to deal with some of these issues from the perspective of the political culture of an English-speaking world. It views Upper Canadian attitudes not as static but as dynamic (as the realities of the new environment were explored) and built upon existing eighteenth- and nineteenth-century visions of the cosmos. Of necessity, it looks at these views and the experience of the actors from the perspective of the political culture and its manifestation on the ground as Crown, clergy, and Indian reserve land. It does so within the constraints of geography and the cultural baggage the settlers brought from the Old World or more recently from the United States. It places human action in the context of economics and the laissez-faire capitalism which ruled out state intervention. In Upper Canada this meant almost unbridled acquisitiveness and its concomitant, land speculation, against which it might be necessary to intervene, although it was not always clear whether such intervention might help promote or hinder development. In Ireland, the same Smithian philosophy of non-intervention by the state meant that food was exported to the "market" and people starved.

The book looks at Upper Canada not only from the perspective of the prevailing political culture but also from the perspective of the environment and of government land policy. It seeks to answer such questions as: What was the role of the physical environment in the settlement process? What were the mechanisms by which land was acquired? What was the price of land? Where were the Crown, clergy, and Indian reserves and were they, as some historians have argued, more or less developed than surrounding non-reserve land? How can land speculators be identified and how did they behave in terms of what they paid for land, their mode of operation, and their assessment of the physical environment? Did these people actually make money and if so how much? Were the land speculators assisted in their operations by their position in the political power structure, or the military hierarchy of the time? Some of these questions, as they pertain to Upper Canada, have been addressed before but not all have and certainly not for any one specific area. That, it seems to the author, is one of the advantages of the work – it brings together a set of interactions which cannot be observed in isolated thematic studies.

While, of necessity, I have journeyed away from the topic of settlement at the micro-scale, if only to gain perspective or remain sane, I have devoted a large part of the last thirty-five years to this task. During that time, the techniques of data storage and analysis have changed from the cadastral survey to the use of mainframe computers, to the revolution that was the micro-computer, and, most recently, to geographic information systems (GIS). I have, in my office, the "coloured" pencilled maps of yesteryear as well as the the coding forms and punch-cards of the 1960s and 1970s and their contemporary form, the computer disk. All testify to changing technology, but at the same time to an abiding concern with locational aspects of human existence and administration; interestingly, the British record keepers of the 1790s stored their data in data matrices though they referred to them as drawers B2, C5, and F9!

It is also worth observing that, during this same time period, the philosophy of social science(s) has changed and become pluralized. There is now no one valid philosophy but rather a myriad of approaches. This is healthy in itself but it has been another change which practitioners have had to grapple with. Some of these philosophies are more useful than others; some appear to have purely pedagogic value, though that, of itself, is not to be discredited. A number are embodied in this text; two are identified below.

The book claims to be a historical geography because that is the tradition of its author, but it also has elements of economic history, social history, and sociology. That is how, in my view, it should be because it is surely foolish to draw rigid boundaries which can only limit insight. Although contemporary social science seems to wish to distinguish between quantitative and qualitative method, this work employs both perspectives as is appropriate or indeed possible; to do otherwise would also be foolish. The work is empirical and problem-oriented, premised on the notion that there is a real world which is observable. Sometimes this means that the methodology employed is concerned with the observer's perspective and the measurement of parts which are surrogates for a wider set of elements and processes. This is in the tradition of positivist science, the whipping boy of contemporary social science. However, positivism is, in this author's view, something drawn in abstraction rather than observable in any meaningful work in the human and social sciences. There are few historical geographers who would own up to being philosophical positivists, though they might, of necessity, employ such an approach. Rather, most historical geographers would seek to conjoin this approach with other appropriate philosophies, most usually that which has come to be known as the "humanistic tradition," within which authors employ the actor's perspective on events. This is the case here.

If in the ensuing years since this work began as a doctoral dissertation, the philosophy and method of the social and human sciences has changed, and if the technology and methods have been transformed, so too has archival practice. In fact, the notations used by some depositories are utterly changed and what was once sufficient, such as shelf six, box seventy-six, is no longer so. For example, with the addition of expanded funds in the Archives of Ontario, records once classified in this manner have been placed in record groups and maps have been assigned appropriate accession numbers. Maps in the federal jurisdiction, once located by horizontal or vertical files, have now been assigned unique NMC numbers permitting the computer search of databases. Both designations have been used wherever possible in this study. Some holdings have been transferred from one institution to another; for example, many archival boxes formerly held by the Hiram Walker Historical Museum in Windsor were transferred to the provincial archives and new referencing has been assigned. It has been quite impossible to follow the fate of all materials over the years. The most obvious case is that of Ontario's reorganized Department of Lands and Forests (DLF), whose holdings were scattered both to the Archives of Ontario and to the Department of the Environment and several other ministries. It is regrettable that the sources shown in the list of primary documents drawn from DLF cannot be systematically and easily traced; however, DLF markers are undoubtedly still present on the source material and researchers using these sources may be content identifying material used years ago by the author, and others of his kind. In short, if the archival process leaves something to be desired, there is always sufficient information in any citation to allow the material to be traced and retrieved. As far as possible, the citations are those current as of the date of publication.

The volume makes use of extensive quotation. These are reported in their original form, free of editorial punctuation, grammatical correction, or modern spelling. Such authentic reproduction permits the reader to grasp something of the linguistic flavour of the times. Where unconventional spelling is extensive, I have made an appropriate endnote to confirm its authentic form. I have also standardized some names although in the nineteenth century there were many permutations of the same name. Thus, Dupperron or Duperon Baby has been rendered as Dupéront Baby, and Richard Patterson, Paterson, or Pattinson has been rendered as Pattinson except when used in quotation.

All of the substantive matter of this book, because of the inordinate archival work involved, has had to be addressed from the vantage point of a single county. This is Essex County in southwestern Ontario with which I first became involved some thirty-five years ago as a doctoral student at the University of Western Ontario. Essex County is a place in which the Upper Canadian variables are in peculiar combination. It is the most southwesterly part of present-day Ontario. Climatically, it is one of the best endowed for agricultural purposes; edaphically, it originally was one of the poorest areas in terms of the extent of soil suited to agriculture, but, after the implementation of drainage schemes with government assistance in the late nineteenth century, it was utterly transformed. It was one of the earliest settled areas in the province; French seigneurial settlement pre-dated British control and, because of the French presence and the particular history of the area, it was one of the most culturally heterogeneous areas before 1850 and remains so today. Historically, it was on the western frontier of Upper Canada. Nonetheless, the processes of acquisition and settlement can be readily observed in Essex, and while these occur at particular rates, they are generally representative of Upper Canada as a whole. Only more comparative work will modify or negate this claim, a prospect I can only welcome.

Land, Power, and Economics on the Frontier of Upper Canada

1 The Land Revealed: The Physical Background

INTRODUCTION

Essex County (Figure 1.1), the most southwesterly peninsula of southern Ontario, extends some thirty-five miles from east to west and is, at its widest, twenty-five miles from north to south. The only land boundary is on the east; water in the form of the Detroit River on the west, Lake Erie on the south, and Lake St Clair to the north surrounds it on three sides. The county, including Pelée Island, contains, according to the modern soils report,[1] 452,480 acres of land of which the largest part (70.8 per cent) was in its natural condition poorly drained (Appendix 1.1).[2] Today, however, this area contains some of the most productive farmland in southern Ontario, leading to its identification as the "Garden Gateway" to Canada.[3] Perhaps more than any other part of southern Ontario, Essex provides the clearest testimony to the role of technology and collective action in the transformation of landscape. For example, the extensive areas of Brookston Clay which constitute 55.25 per cent of the county[4] are rated by the modern soil scientist as "good" to "fair" for the production of fall wheat but in their natural condition are considered poor.[5] The latter would ring true to the pioneer settler of this area for whom these extensive interior tracts (in the period before government subsidized tile-drainage and society assumed a more collective form to handle the problem) must have seemed formidable barriers to settlement.[6]

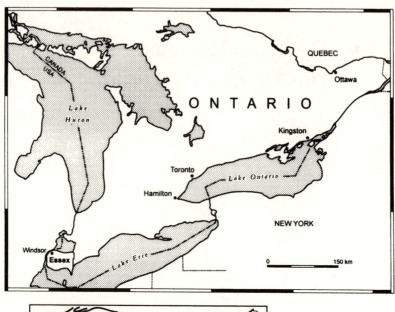

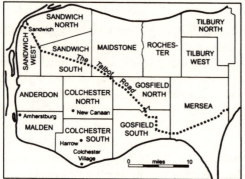

Figure 1.1   Situation and township divisions of Essex County

Nothing illustrates this better than comparison of figures 1.2, 1.3, and 1.4. The first of these, assembled from the surveyors' plans, shows why this part of the Western District was the recipient of such a large proportion of the assistance available for under-draining.[7] Seasonal wetland and swamp is seen to be extensive if fleeting.[8]

However, the map shows an extensive area of open marsh in Gosfield Township. This does not appear in Figure 1.3, which displays crop adaptability under modern conditions. The marsh has been drained and is now part of what Richards, Caldwell, and Morwick, writing in 1949, considered the best farmland in Essex.[9] Similar

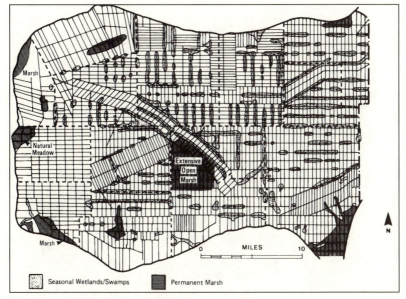

Figure 1.2   Seasonal wet land and marsh
Source: Surveyors' reports

areas in Sandwich, Tilbury, Mersea, and Colchester townships had by the middle of the present century been converted into second-order cropland. The "natural meadow" in Sandwich Township had become prime agricultural land (Figure 1.3). The change in the agricultural fortunes of the county had been dramatic, as a cursory survey of figures 1.3 and 1.4 reveals. Figure 1.4, constructed from the soil survey of the county, depicts the natural or inherent qualities of the soil. The most obvious fact to be drawn from this map is that Essex, in the pioneer period, was dominantly an area of class five soils, heavily textured and poorly drained. In comparison, these same areas are hailed by the modern soil scientist as areas of "good" cropland.

THE SETTLER AND THE ENVIRONMENT

While some of the most innovative would have anticipated this transformation, most of the earliest, agriculturally oriented settlers probably did not. For the majority, the experience of pioneering was an adaptive one in which they learned to read the environment, to test reality against the lore and mythology they had inherited. In the light of that experience, they must have adjusted their search pro-

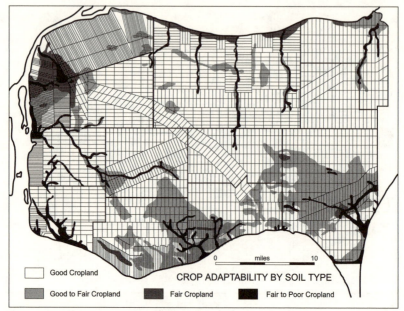

Figure 1.3   Crop adaptability according to soil type
Source: N.R. Richards, A.G. Caldwell, and F.F. Morwick, *Soil Survey of Essex County*

cedures to their ever-increasing knowledge of the physical milieu. Moreover, these procedures and adjustments for sifting the environment likely varied with the cultural background of the settler. While the settlers' origins are known, their attitudes towards the environment are not.[10] Still, these attitudes can be gauged by inference *post facto*. What can be done is to juxtapose a series of axioms against the behaviour *in aggregate* of the settlers and by so doing judge the behaviour of people in general as well as that of the individual.

This behaviour can be tested against four ideas: 1) that the Upper Canadian settler sought accessible land; 2) that the settler, in this period, sought land which could be converted into worthwhile farmland; 3) that topographically there were no hindrances to the use of the land; and 4) that, within the constraints of what was available, settlers sought to find a particular combination of ideas 1 through 3 which, within their cultural tradition, maximized their opportunity. With what obvious tools might this have occurred? The most obvious was their own capacity for observation, again rooted in their culture and individual experiences but assuredly containing the elements of

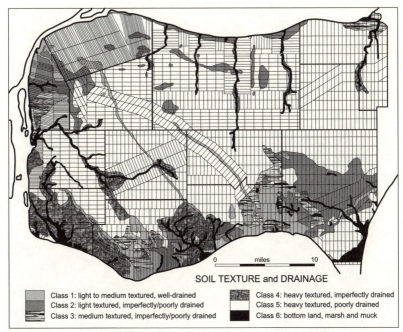

Figure 1.4   Soil texture and drainage
Source: Soil Survey of Essex County

drainage and of forest. The most apparent and pervasive was the forest cover of the county. What was the settler's attitude to forest and what were the ingredients of the Essex forest?

The Forest and Forest Lore

Kenneth Kelly suggests that the settler's attitude to forest was basically one of antagonism. He notes that "settlers stripped the trees from their land as quickly as possible, shrinking only from burning them as they stood. They attacked the forest with a savagery greater than that justified by the need to clear the land for cultivation, for the forest smothered, threatened, and oppressed them."[11]

The conditions portrayed in the accompanying Bartlett print (Plate 1.1) seem to have produced at least in some a boding sense of gloom, termed "forest fever." Finding themselves in "a perpetual gloom of vaulted boughs and intermingled shade, a solemn twilight monotony,"[12] settlers were removed from familiar sounds and experiences

Plate 1.1   A Forest Scene. Engraving by W.H. Bartlett.
Willis, *Canadian Scenery Illustrated*, following page 52.

and their sense of well-being was perturbed. The forest hindered development. Even after sweat and toil had produced a clearing, the settler had to be ever vigilant against renewed encroachment. While the forest provided fuel, food for animals, and shelter for both human being and livestock, it was also the home of lurking predators. Until experience showed that deforestation could produce dire consequences in terms of excess run-off, increased drought and soil erosion, damaged orchards, and diminished fuel supply and shelter,[13] the desire of the farm community would be for a landscape from which all trees had been removed. Which trees would be removed first?

If one assumes that the settlers had the opportunity to make a choice, that they were not politically constrained by government land policy, as many in fact were, was there sufficient information available to allow them to do so?[14] The literate could consult the field notes of the surveyors if indeed these were available soon after the survey.[15] The inferences drawn could, of course, vary with the settlers' levels of education and experience of North America's woodland; moreover, an exclusive reliance upon such written material could produce an erroneous conclusion because the surveyors' notes were restricted to their line of march and did not seemingly concern themselves with the overall vegetation on a lot as a whole. This same limitation would apply to the second source that could be consulted, namely the settlers' guides published in the first half of the nineteenth century. The illiterate would have to rely on second-hand information. In an age that was of necessity more communal, this was not difficult to obtain at local churches and taverns.[16] Aided by personal observation, based upon a host of indicators, prospective settlers could glean a detailed picture of the forest communities in which they might reside. However, as Kelly has pointed out, they might possesses only the most crude image on a broader scale. Two instances of contemporary comment, by Charles Rankin and E.A. Talbot, will suffice to illustrate the prevailing lore. Writing in 1824, Talbot suggested that:

Land upon which black and white Walnut, Chestnut, Hickory, Bass-wood, grow is esteemed the best on the continent. That which is covered with Maple, Beech, and Cherry, is reckoned as second-rate. Those parts which produce Oak, Elm and Ash, are esteemed excellent wheat-land, but inferior for all other agricultural purposes. Pine, Hemlock, and Cedarland is hardly worth accepting as a present. It is however, difficult to select any considerable tract of land, which does not embrace a great variety of wood; but, when a man perceives that Walnut, Chestnut, Hickory, Basswood, and Maple, are promiscuously scattered over his estate, he need not be at all apprehensive of having to cultivate an unproductive soil.[17]

Two years later, Charles Rankin, the deputy surveyor for the Western District, of which Essex was a part, noted: "Good and bad land. The good is known by the quality of the timber. Weeds and shrubbing, White and Red Oak and Brush loamy upland Walnut, Cherry, bass, Sycamore, Wild Plumb [sic], Spice Woods, Prickly Ash a deep soil Small Oak sassafras, black ash, elm Wet and Swampy, Prairies and marshes apart."[18]

How common were these species? Where were they in the county? What was the likelihood that, by using any single indicator, the settler could hope to find suitable land? The answer to these questions requires some knowledge of the source materials used to reconstruct the composition of the forest and some appreciation of the experience of the surveyors.

SOURCES FOR RECONSTRUCTING THE INGREDIENTS OF THE FOREST

The data used for this purpose were gathered from the field notes, maps, plans, and diaries that early surveyors working between 1796 and 1836 compiled in the course of their duties.[19] In discharging these obligations the surveyors were beset by bad weather, financial shortages, lack of instruments, inadequate personnel, and political pressures to have the surveys finished in a very short time indeed. As a result, the records of survey vary in character, especially in the early years when Upper Canada lacked an adequate number of well-trained individuals. Yet, in total, they provide a mass of detailed information which, after careful perusal, seems accurate.

The land-survey records are of considerable value in that they provide a record of the date at which particular townships were surveyed as well as information on the extent of particular surveys and of the vegetation flourishing on particular lots.[20] Additionally, most if not all of the survey records have survived to the present day. As sources for the reconstruction of the physical environment, the records are not flawless. For example, although Figure 1.2, based upon the surveyors' plans and maps, seeks to portray the surveyors' views of wet lands in the county, it does so over almost a forty-year period between 1796 and 1836. The records nonetheless do provide insights into the perception of land quality, at least by the surveyors who, as agents of the administration, issued location tickets to prospective settlers. The surveyors could well have passed on the benefits of their field experience because, at intervals, they recorded information not only about vegetation but also about topography, the occurrence of streams and lakes, bogs and swamps, and the quality of the environment, in terms such as "good land" and "low land." Some idea of what they considered good land can be deduced from the notes they made. The following excerpts, taken from the notes of Mahlon Burwell (see Plate 1.2), will suffice to elucidate the point. In surveying the Talbot Road, west through Gosfield Township (Figure 1.1), Burwell recorded:

lot 256 good land, walnut, chestnut, white oak, maple and bass
lot 257 good cleared land, walnut, chestnut
lot 258 good land, maple, elm and bass
lot 259 maple, elm, beech
lot 260 black ash swamp
lot 261 black ash[21]

In his survey of Rochester Township, he recorded the vegetation in somewhat greater detail, but similar inferences, as to what the vegetation could indicate to the early settler, can be drawn. The following is taken from his survey of the Middle Road in Rochester:

lot 9 at 9 chains – good land, white oak and beech
lot 9 at 20 chains – black ash and elm swamp.
lot 10 at 7 chains – black ash and elm swamp
lot 11 at 23 chains – good land, white oak, beech, maple and hickory
lot 11 at 30 chains – black ash and elm swamp
lot 12 at 24 chains – black ash and elm swamp
lot 12 at 2 chains – good land, white oak, beech, maple and hickory
lot 13 at 3 chains – good land, white oak, beech, maple and hickory[22]

Because the survey of a particular township was frequently conducted at different times and by different surveyors, the value of the land-survey records varies with the responsibility and knowledge shown by the surveyors. Consequently, the survey records do not provide the measures available to and required by the modern botanist; measures, for example, of density, dominance, soil acidity, and soil-mineral composition. Their usefulness also varies with the surveyors' perception of the composition of the forest. If, for example, the surveyor simply recorded the presence of oaks, no distinction can be made between red and white oaks. His perception might also vary according to the year or the time of the year at which the survey was made, since the extent of swamp and marsh could presumably fluctuate and hinder observation. Moreover, it was not until 1859 that the split-line method of recording survey field notes was introduced by Thomas Devine.[23]

Plate 1.2   Mahlon Burwell, Surveyor.
Courtesy of the principal of Huron College, University of Western Ontario

Hence, the early surveyors' plans provide little information on the spatial distribution of particular trees or plant communities, and the field notes, as exemplified above, do not specifically mention the dominant element on any one lot. However, the regularity with which particular species are mentioned might suggest that this is a reasonable inference.

The Experience of the Essex Surveyors

Although early surveys were conducted along the Essex shore by Patrick McNiff and Abraham Iredell in the 1790s, the bulk of the work (with the exception of Anderdon and Malden townships, surveyed by Peter Carroll) was conducted by Thomas Smith between 1805 and 1806 and by Mahlon Burwell, between 1811 and 1836. Indeed, since many of Smith's surveys were subsequently re-surveyed by Burwell one can state confidently that the Burwell surveys were the source of most of the data used here. Burwell's experience as a surveyor was much greater than that of any of the others. By 1836, when he completed his final field notes for Essex, he had completed surveys in at least forty-four different Ontario townships beyond the boundaries of Essex. These stretched from the Niagara peninsula through the modern-day Wellington County, south and west to Middlesex and neighbouring Kent counties. By 1825, twenty-four of the townships had been completed. By comparison, when Iredell came to survey the townships of Colchester North and South in 1796, he had experience of only ten townships. Smith, who was to survey these same townships in 1805–06, had experience of only two townships beyond Essex. Carroll, who surveyed Anderdon and Malden in the 1830s, had been working in seven townships outside the county. In short, not only was Burwell the dominant surveyor in Essex County, he had a wide experience of a variety of landscapes in Ontario as a whole.[24]

THE DATA AND THE METHOD

The surveyors' field notes record 11,763 observations of vegetation. Their location was noted in terms of lot and concession together with those comments which suggest land type, that is, marsh, swamp, meadow, good land, poor land. Counts of the absolute occurrence of some forty-four species were recorded together with their relative frequency expressed as percentages (Table 1.1). For the present study, these data were mapped on a scale of one inch to one mile by working out distance expressed by the surveyors in links and chains. In turn, this working map, in conjunction with tables 1.3 and 1.4, which show the frequency of occurrence of particular species with one another, are the basis of Figure 1.5.[25] On the map each lot is "typed" according to whether any group exceeded 50 per cent of the references.[26] Three regional groups were identified; a fourth, labelled "mixed hardwoods," included those in which various species were in closer equilibrium. Membership in any group was determined by visual inspection of tables 1.2 and 1.3, with reference to Table 1.1 where it is shown

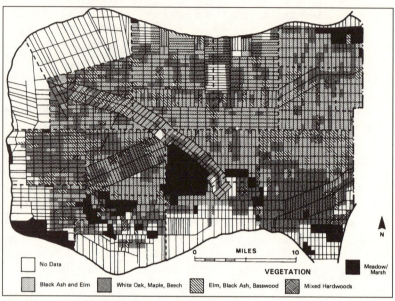

Figure 1.5   Pre-settlement vegetation of Essex County
Source: Clarke and Finnegan, "Colonial Survey Records," 124.

that the classes used included 79 per cent of all vegetation mentioned. Counts of the occurrence of specific trees within each of the surveyors' land qualities, and within soil and drainage classes taken from the county soils report (Figure 1.4), amplified the classification. For example, in figure 1.6a, beech, maple, and white oak show a dramatic decrease through "good land" to "swampy land." Conversely, elm, black ash, and willow rise through the water continuum. A similar dichotomy exists for less dominant species (Figure 1.6b).

RESULTS: PATTERNS OF INTERRELATIONSHIP AND THE BASIS OF SETTLER BEHAVIOUR

The forty-four types of vegetation recorded in the study area contrast with the sixty-eight identified by J.H. Fox and W.S. Soper and the sixty-two recognized by P.F. Maycock.[27] In part, this must reflect the more limited range of possibilities in an area much smaller than southern Ontario as a whole; it also partly reflects the superior observational capacities and technology of contemporary observers over the nineteenth-century surveyors. The early surveyors treated elm, maple, and hickory as specific types; in contrast, Maycock recognized three species of elm, five of maple, and three of hickory. Maycock listed eight types

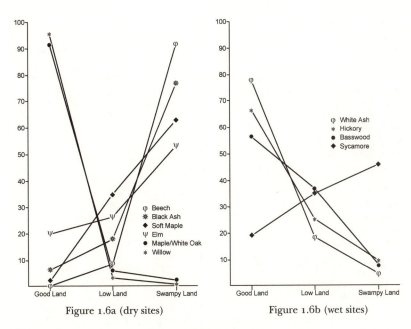

Figure 1.6a (dry sites)   Figure 1.6b (wet sites)

Figure 1.6   Tree species in relation to the water continuum
Source: Clarke and Finnegan, "Colonial Survey Records," 126, 128.

of oak in his sample; the surveyors identified five specific types and a
general category.

Table 1.1 shows the absolute number of observations made, the relative occurrence of each species, the number of townships in which
the species was encountered, and the relative rank of the species. The
most frequently occurring species in the county were elm, black ash,
white oak, beech, basswood, maple, hickory, white ash, red oak, chestnut, sycamore, and soft maple.[28] These twelve constituted almost 95
per cent of all references; all others mentioned did not account for
more than 1 per cent. In addition, these first twelve species were found
throughout the county; the remaining thirty species represent more
unique components, specific to particular sites.

Table 1.2 compares the ranking of the species in Essex County with
those published by Maycock for Ontario and Wisconsin. However, the
reader should note that, while the Essex data are ranked on the basis
of the frequency, the tabulated Ontario and Wisconsin series were
manipulated into regional indices by Maycock. The values, while not
strictly comparable, are nonetheless suggestive. Only the first twenty
species in Essex are recorded, together with their corresponding
values on the regional index. Where the latter suggested a rank lower

Table 1.1   Observations of all tree types in Essex County

Tree Type	Numbers of observation	Rank	(%)	Cumulative percentage	Number of townships in which observed
Elm	2125	1	18.07		9
Black Ash	2118	2	18.00	36.07	9
White Oak	1444	3	12.28	48.35	9
Beech	1328	4	11.29	59.64	9
Basswood (Whitewood)	1253	5	10.65	70.29	9
Maple	1014	6	8.62	78.91	9
Hickory	613	7	5.21	84.12	9
White Ash	404	8	3.43	87.55	9
Red Oak	275	9	2.34	89.89	8
Chestnut	218	10	1.85	91.75	6
Sycamore/Plane Tree	203	11	1.73	93.47	9
Soft Maple (Red Maple)	138	12	1.17	94.64	9
Oak	122	13	1.04	95.68	6
Poplar (Balm of Gilead)	74	14	0.63	96.31	6
Willow	58	15	0.49	96.80	8
Hornbeam (Ironwood)	56	16	0.48	97.28	5
Ash	44	17	0.37	97.65	3
Lynnwood	36	18	0.31	97.96	3
Sassafras	32	19	0.27	98.23	3
Black Walnut	31	20	0.26	98.49	4
Walnut	29	21	0.25	98.74	3
Alder	29	21	0.25	98.99	6
Black Oak	17	23	0.14	99.13	6
Plum Tree	14	24	0.12	99.25	2
Dogwood	13	25	0.11	99.36	2
Witch Hazel	13	25	0.11	99.47	1
Butternut	9	27	0.08	99.55	3
Pepperidge (Black Gum)	8	28	0.07	99.62	1
Swamp Oak (Pin)	7	29	0.06	99.68	3
Prickly Ash	6	30	0.05	99.73	3
Aspen	6	30	0.05	99.78	2
Spice Bush	4	32	0.03	99.80	2
Birch	3	33	0.03	99.84	2
Cherry	3	33	0.03	99.86	2
Mulberry	3	33	0.03	99.89	2
Scrub Oak (Burr)	3	33	0.03	99.91	2
Sugar Maple	3	33	0.03	99.94	2
Blue Ash	2	38	0.02	99.96	1
Hawthorn	2	38	0.02	99.97	2
Cedar	1	40	0.01	99.98	1
Tamarack	1	40	0.01	99.99	1
Hackberry	1	40	0.01	100.00	1
	11,763				

Two other vegetation types were mentioned in the surveyors' notes but cannot be identified using standard references. They are Cranberry (1), Thornberry (1).

Source: Clarke and Finnegan, "Colonial Survey Records," Table 1.

than the twentieth, this is not noted here although it can be identified in the original work. In Ontario and Wisconsin five tree types are found within the ten most recorded in Essex, namely, elm, white oak, basswood, maple, and red oak. As might be expected, an additional three species, beech, hickory, and white ash are ranked similarly in Essex and Ontario. Two species present in the upper half of the table which are not among the highest ranked Ontario and Wisconsin series are black ash and chestnut. In Essex County, black ash was the second most frequently recorded species; in Ontario, it was eighteenth in frequency but not significant as a regional contributor. The difference in frequency is indeed understandable since Essex in its natural state contained such a large percentage of wet lands (figures 1.2 and 1.4). Subsequent nineteenth-century drainage schemes, assisted by government financial subsidies,[29] may well have altered even the Essex proportion of black ash. Chestnut, not included among the top twenty in recent surveys of Ontario and Wisconsin, appears as tenth in Essex. Fox and Soper[30] record that the chestnut has been drastically reduced by fungus infestation; here the historical record provides elegant testimony of the former importance of this species in the forests of the county. The lower-ten-ranked species are numerically few in number and account for only an additional 6.6 per cent of the references to vegetation (Table 1.1). In Wisconsin and Ontario, only willow, poplar, and ironwood assume an importance similar to that in Essex.

How frequently did these species occur one with another in Essex? Tables 1.3 and 1.4, showing the absolute and relative frequencies with which this happened, cast light on the topic. Both tables are ordered in terms of the occurrence of each species with that first mentioned in the surveyors' notes. When white oak was first mentioned, it occurred 663 times in conjunction with beech (Table 1.3) or roughly 73 per cent of the 907 total observations (Table 1.4). Black ash was mentioned first in conjunction with elm 1095 times or 75.8 per cent of the 1444 times that it was dominant. Perusal of these tables shows that, when a specific species was first mentioned more than 200 times, the following relationships were brought to light. When white oak occurred first, beech appeared 73 per cent of the time, maple 40 per cent, hickory 33 per cent, basswood 27 per cent, and red oak 21 per cent. Beech was found in conjunction with maple 72 per cent of the time, basswood 33 per cent, and white oak 23 per cent. Maple first appeared with beech 40 per cent of the time, basswood 39 per cent, elm 36 per cent, and white oak 26 per cent. When elm appeared first, basswood occurred 74 per cent of the time, black ash 32 per cent, hickory 27 per cent, and white ash 16 per cent. In contrast, black ash appears to be of importance only with elm, which appears in 76 per

Table 1.2   Comparison of the rank of particular species in Essex with Ontario and Wisconsin

Tree Type	Ontario	Wisconsin	Essex
Elm	2,16[4]	5,10[7]	1
Black Ash	–	–	2
White Oak	6	3	3
Beech	3	14	4
Basswood	10	7	5
Maple	1,8[5]	1,4[8]	6
Hickory	9,13[6]	19	7
White Ash	4	17	8
Red Oak	7[1]	2	9
Chestnut	–	N/A	10
Sycamaore	–	–	11
Soft Maple (Red Maple)	5	–	12
Oak	–	–	13
Poplar	20[3]	9	14
Willow	14[2]	8[9]	15
Ash	–	11[10]	16
Ironwood	–	18	17
Lynnwood	–	–	18
Sassafras	–	–	19
Black Walnut	–	–	20

Source: Calculations of the author and Maycock, "The Phytosociology of the Deciduous Forests," Table IX.

– indicates a species present in the first twenty as ranked in Essex but absent from the first twenty ranked in Ontario or Wisconsin.

[1] Maycock's seventh-ranked species includes black oak, ranked twenty-third in Essex.

[2] Black cherry ranked fourteenth (with black willow) in Ontario but thirty-third in Essex.

[3] Maycock recognizes cottonwood.

[4] Maycock's second-ranked species was white elm; his sixteenth was red elm.

[5] Maycock's first-ranked species was hard maple; his eighth was silver maple.

[6] Maycock's ninth-ranked species was shagbark hickory; his thirteenth was butternut hickory.

[7] White elm and red elm were ranked fifth and tenth respectively in Wisconsin.

[8] Hard maple and silver maple were first and fourth respectively in Wisconsin.

[9] Black willow is identified in the Maycock study, willow in the Essex survey notes.

[10] Red ash is identified in the Maycock material, ash in the survey notes.

cent of the instances. Where some percentages are exceptionally high (Table 1.4), as in the case of black walnut with white oak, the absolute number of occurrences is small.

Although it is obvious that certain trees do occur with regular frequency in conjunction with others, this is not to say that they occur in any specific order. Indeed, Maycock, whose greater number of interval-measured variables permitted him to investigate the problem of

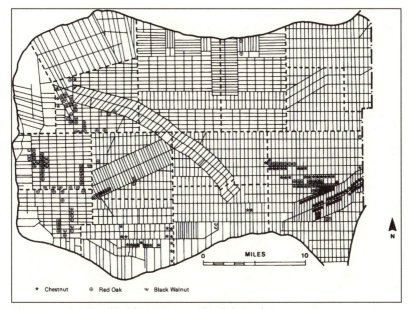

Figure 1.7   Species of local importance on well-drained sites
Source: Clarke and Finnegan, "Colonial Survey Records," 132.

ordination more fully, negates this hypothesis. Nonetheless, the data are suggestive. In a sample of 419 lots designated "good land" by the surveyors and on which white oak, beech, or maple were first mentioned, considerable variation occurred. At least one of these three did not appear at all 40 per cent of the time. Twenty-six per cent of the time, chestnut, basswood, red oak, black oak, walnut, white ash, and elm replaced them. Maple dropped out 44 per cent of the time, beech 33 per cent. White oak was the most stable, dropping only 23 percent of the time. There was considerable geographical variation. White oak disappeared from the records most heavily in Tilbury (86 per cent) and Sandwich (44 per cent) and least in Colchester Township. Beech dropped 81 per cent of the time in Colchester, 48 per cent in Malden, 46 per cent in Anderdon, 31 per cent in Mersea, 22 per cent in Gosfield, and 22 per cent in Sandwich. It did not drop from the good lands association in the wetter, northern townships of Maidstone, Rochester, and Tilbury.[31] A number of phytogeographical factors, operating at the micro-level, would seem to be influential; one identified by Maycock as of prime importance, and treated here, is the role of soil moisture (figures 1.7 and 1.8).[32]

Further insights into the ways in which trees occurred in conjunction with one another and the role of soil moisture can be gained from

Table 1.3 Number of occurences of one species with another, Essex County

	White Oak	Beech	Maple	Elm	Black Ash	Basswood	White Ash	Red Oak	Hickory	Willow	Black Walnut	Oak	Soft Maple	Poplar	Sycamore	Hornbeam	Ash	Chestnut	Sugar Maple	Lynnwood	Walnut	Alder	Swamp Oak	Black Oak	Butternut	Birch	Aspen	Sassafras	Tamarack	Dogwood	Plum Tree	Scrub Oak	Total	Times obs. with others	Times obs. alone
White Oak	119	663	359	165	59	245	145	190	302		15	1	3	25	19	13	8	38	1		1			3									2262	907	29
Beech	55	85	378	39	11	174	42	13	34		4	3	1	1	7	5		11	2		2			2	1		3	3	2				846	524	8
Maple	45	13	22	76	17	84	12	7	4		7		1	2	6	10		3			1			1	1								364	214	0
Elm	14	14	11	1095	140	329	69	6	121	12	24	5	86	12	43	10	4	2	1		13		6	2	2	2		1				2	864	443	1
Black Ash	35	14	16	50	23	143	26	4	80				3		99	3	5	2				3	3	1									1612	1444	242
Basswood	16	11	7	15	8	143	31	14	15	3	3	5	3	3	10			2					1										224	77	1
White Ash	15		2	2	10	17		2	7			1	1	6				3	2														91	43	1
Red Oak	9	6		6	5	13	15		17		3												1	1									81	23	10
Hickory		2	2	3	4	6	6											3	2														41	10	11
Willow				3				3																									11	11	
Black Walnut	5	3	1	5	4	6	5		1							4	1	1		1													33	6	
Oak			8	11	5	24	1		13		2						5	10				3											80	24	1
Soft Maple				2	3	3			1								2																11	3	
Poplar			1	1					1													1											3	3	
Sycamore	2			2			2		2				2																				6	2	
Hornbeam		2		2				1	1								2															1	11	3	
Ash				1				1											1														4	1	
Chestnut	19	19	5	3	2	1			5			2			2																		56	27	
Sugar Maple		2						2										1															4	2	
Lynnwood	4						1		1								5	1															10	5	3
Walnut																																	1	1	1
Alder																																	0	0	2
Swamp Oak																																	0	0	
Black Oak																																	0	0	
Butternut																																	0	0	
Birch																																	0	0	
Aspen																																	0	0	
Sassafras																																	0	0	
Tamarack																																	0	0	
Dogwood																																	0	0	1
Plum Tree																																	0	0	
Scrub Oak																																	0	0	
	33	820	810	1478	291	1045	354	236	605	12	25	48	114	55	186	35	27	72	6	2	17	10	5	6	3	1	6	3	1	2	2	1	6615	3773	301

Source: Clarke and Finnegan, "Colonial Survey Records," Table 2. Obs.=observed.

Table 1.4 Percentage occurence of one species with another, Essex County

	White Oak	Beech	Maple	White Ash	Red Oak	Chestnut	Oak	Black Walnut	Basswood	Hickory	Hornbeam	Lynnwood	Elm	Soft Maple	Black Ash	Willow	Sycamore	Poplar	Ash	Sugar Maple	Walnut	Alder	Swamp Ash	Aspen	Butternut	Black Oak	Sassafras	Birch	Aspen	Dogwood	Plum Tree	Tamarack	Scrub Oak
White Oak	23	73	40	16	21	4		2	27	33	1		18		7		2	3		1													
Beech	26	72	40	8	2	2		1	33	6	1		7		2		1	1										1					
Maple	26	40		6	3	1	3		39	2			36	2	8		3	1								1		1					
White Ash	37	26	16	65	5		2		40	16			35		19		1	14															
Red Oak	65	26	0	65		13			57	74			9		43																		
Chestnut	70	70	19	4					4	19			11		7		1																
Oak	13	33	33	4		42			100	54	67	20	46		21			2	21														
Black Walnut	83	18	17	83		17	5		100	17	4		83	4	67		13				17												
Basswood	45	20	21	40		3	5	30		19		60	65		30								1										
Hickory	90	20	20	60			4	30	60				60		50																		
Hornbeam	67	67								67		20	67						67														
Lynnwood	80	67								20			67						100														
Elm	10	3	5	16	1		5		74	27	2			4	32		10	2		1			1										
Soft Maple									100	33			67		100		1		67	1													
Black Ash	1		1	2					10	6			76	6		1	1	1	67			1											
Willow													27		36		1		9			27											
Sycamore				100									100	100																			
Poplar	33								33	33			33																				
Ash									100	100			100																				
Sugar Maple	100					100																											
Walnut	100				100	100	100																										
Alder							100																										
Swamp Ash																																	
Aspen																																	
Butternut																																	
Black Oak																																	
Sassafras																																	
Birch																																	
Aspen																																	
Dogwood																																	
Plum Tree																																	
Tamarack																																	
Scrub Oak																																	

Source: Clarke and Finnegan, "Colonial Survey Records," Table 3.

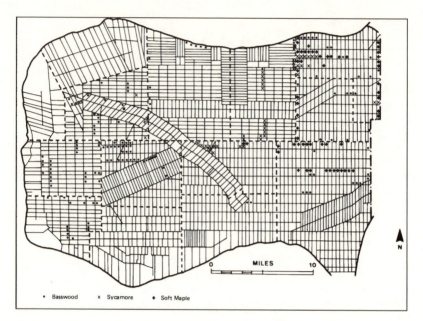

● Basswood   × Sycamore   ◆ Soft Maple

Figure 1.8   Species of local importance on lowland to swampy sites
Source: Clarke and Finnegan, "Colonial Survey Records," 132.

using the terminology by which the surveyor qualified his remarks. The surveyors recognized a number of terms. These included "excellent land", "very good land," "good land," "low land," "wet land," "flats," "bottomland," "swale," "marsh," and "swamp." Cross-classified, these terms have been subsumed into three distinct types, designated "good land," "swampy land," and an intermediate category called "lowland" (Figure 1.9). Tables 1.5–1.8 and figures 1.4 and 1.5–1.8 illustrate the relationship between tree species and land types along the water continuum both for Essex and for its constituent parts. As soil drainage improves so too does the frequency of, for example, beech, chestnut, maple, and white and red oak. As soil drainage deteriorates there are increasing frequencies of willow, black ash, soft maple, elm, and sycamore. Some species are more tolerant of moisture conditions appearing on both ends of the continuum. Examples include basswood and hickory. In short, these results, and Maycock's, seem remarkably congruent. Cross-classification of land types and the six categories of soil-texture and drainage conditions shown on Figure 1.4 and derived from amalgamating classes in the county's soil report substantiate this conclusion. The results are highly significant.[33] Generally, the surveyors' land classification and perception of land quality

Table 1.5:   Number of times species was observed with a specific land type

Tree Type	Rank	Good Lands Abso-lute*	Percent-age	Low Lands Abso-lute*	Percent-age	Swampy Land Abso-lute*	Percent-age	Total Observations of individual Species n
Beech	(4)	1187	96%	40	3.5%	4	0.5%	1231
White Oak	(3)	1209	93%	83	6.0%	25	2.0%	1317
Maple	(6)	900	93%	59	6.0%	6	1.0%	965
Red Oak	(6)	219	85%	36	14.0%	2	1.0%	257
White Ash	(8)	298	78%	70	18.0%	16	4.0%	384
Chestnut	(11)	135	94%	7	5.0%	2	1.0%	144
Basswood	(5)	652	56%	417	36.0%	99	8.0%	1168
Hickory	(7)	387	66%	144	25.0%	55	9.0%	586
Sycamore	(10)	39	19%	73	35.0%	96	46.0%	208
Elm	(1)	412	20%	547	26.0%	1136	54.0%	2095
Black Ash	(2)	114	6%	367	18.0%	1568	77.0%	2049
Willow	(15)	0	0%	5	8.5%	54	91.5%	59
Soft Maple	(12)	2	1.5%	46	35.0%	82	63.0%	130
Black Oak	(22)	11	100%	0	0%	0	0.0%	11
Sugar Maple	(31)	2	100%	0	0%	0	0.0%	2
Oak	(13)	63	80%	11	14.0%	5	6.0%	79
Walnut	(28)	2	67%	0	0%	1	33.0%	3
Black Walnut	(17)	29	100%	0	0%	0	0.0%	29
Ironwood	(16)	38	97%	1	3.0%	0	0.0%	39
Dogwood	(31)	2	100%	0	0%	0	0.0%	2
Sassafras	(23)	6	67%	3	33.0%	0	0.0%	9
Poplar	(14)	37	55%	13	19.0%	17	25.0%	67
Tamarack	(34)	0	0%	0	0%	1	100.0%	1
Ash	(20)	9	53%	3	18.0%	5	29.0%	17
Swamp Oak	(24)	1	12.5%	4	50.0%	3	37.5%	8
Birch	(28)	2	67%	1	33.0%	0	0.0%	3
Butternut	(31)	2	100%	0	0%	0	0.0%	2
Pepperidge	(28)	0	0%	3	100.0%	0	0.0%	3
Aspen	(25)	0	0%	2	33.0%	4	67.0%	6
Prickly Ash	(26)	4	80%	1	20.0%	0	0.0%	5
Spice Bush	(27)	4	100%	0	0%	0	0.0%	4
Plum Tree	(21)	10	83%	2	17.0%	0	0.0%	12
Lynnwood	(19)	8	36%	10	45.0%	4	18.0%	22
Alder	(18)	0	0%	0	0%	27	100.0%	27
Total Observations		5784		1948		3212		10,944
Site References		1748		607		1624		

Source: Clarke and Finnegan, "Colonial Survey Records," Table 4.

*Absolute equals absolute numbers of occurrences

Table 1.6   Number of references to specific species within the good-lands group; Essex Townships

Tree Type	Mai.+ Roc.	Gos.	Mal.	Col.	Mer.	And.	San.	Til.	Total
				Townships					
Black Ash	21	10	2	28	16	12	16	114	114
Elm	29	20	22	108	40	94	59	40	412
Basswood–White Wood	77	25	63	101	62	81	153	90	652
Hickory	59	4	51	78	40	94	45	16	387
Beech	390	48	42	95	112	81	214	205	1187
White Oak	341	49	61	202	165	110	206	75	1209
Maple	201	22	27	99	50	74	219	208	900
Sycamore–Plane	1		9	6	11	10	1	1	39
White Ash	28	10	47	73	40	64	16	20	298
Red Oak			53	2	57	43	67	3	219
Black Oak	3				2	6			11
Chestnut	1	9			119		6		135
Soft Maple		1						1	2
Sugar Maple						2			2
Oak		2		4	9	48			63
Ash					6	3			9
Walnut		1	1						2
Black Walnut		1	6	4		18			29
Ironwood		4		12		18	1		35
Willow									0
Tamarack									0
Alder									0
Swamp Oak	1								1
Poplar		4	2	11	10	10			37
Sassafras					6				6
Dogwood					2				2
Birch				2					2
Pepperidge									0
Butternut		2							2
Aspen									3
Hornbeam							3		3
Prickly Ash						4			4
Spice Bush						4			4
Plum Tree						10			10
Lynnwood		2			6				8
Hawthorn									0
Mulberry									0
Cedar									0
Total Observations	1154	214	386	825	753	786	1000	668	5784
Total References to Good Land	400	71	76	250	235	190	301	225	1748

Source: Calculations of the author

Townships: Mai.=Maidstone; Gos.=Gosfield; Mal.=Malden; Col.=Colchester; Mer.=Mersea; And.=Anderdon; San.=Sandwich; Til.=Tilbury; and Roc.=Rochester

Table 1.7   Absolute number of references to specific species within the lowlands group; Essex Townships

	Townships								
Tree Type	Mai.+ Roc.	Gos.	Mal.	Col.	Mer.	And.	San.	Til.	Total
Black Ash	21	7	37	32	101	80	69	20	367
Elm	97	9	36	53	114	101	101	36	547
Basswood–White Wood	94	9	20	28	79	47	109	31	417
Hickory	35	1	26	18	4	1	43	16	144
Beech	11	9	2		10				40
White Oak	14	6	5	10	29	3	16		83
Maple		5	4	11	36		3		59
Sycamore–Plane	1		14	6	36	7	1	8	73
White Ash	18	4	6	17	14		11		70
Red Oak	9		6	10	1	9	1		36
Black Oak									0
Chestnut				7					7
Soft Maple	1	2		5	27		6	5	46
Sugar Maple									0
Oak	1			3	7				11
Ash				3					3
Walnut									0
Black Walnut									0
Ironwood									0
Willow	1		1	2	1				5
Tamarack									0
Alder									0
Swamp Oak	1			3					4
Poplar		6	2	3		2			13
Sassafras				3					3
Dogwood									0
Birch					1				1
Pepperidge					3				3
Butternut	2								2
Aspen									0
Hornbeam			1						1
Prickly Ash					1				1
Spice Bush									0
Plum Tree					2				2
Lynnwood	4			6					10
Total Observations	302	60	162	197	491	258	362	116	1148
Total References to Low Lands	104	20	38	60	130	102	117	36	607

Source: Calculations of the author

Townships: Mai.=Maidstone; Gos.=Gosfield; Mal.=Malden; Col.=Colchester; Mer.=Mersea; And.=Anderdon; San.=Sandwich; Til.=Tilbury; and Roc.=Rochester

Table 1.8   Absolute number of references to specific species within the swampy-lands group; Essex Townships

	Townships								
Tree Type	Mai.+ Roc.	Gos.	Mal.	Col.	Mer.	And.	San.	Til.	Total
Black Ash	569	96	18	198	131	4	224	328	1568
Elm	423	36	18	131	102	1	137	288	1136
Basswood–White Wood	32	1	2	1	2		32	29	99
Hickory	11	1	8	10	1		16	8	55
Beech		4							4
White Oak		2	1	14	4		4		25
Maple		2	1		3				6
Sycamore–Plane	32	13	6	5	6		6	28	96
White Ash		3		1			3	9	16
Red Oak				2					2
Black Oak									0
Chestnut		1			1				2
Soft Maple				7	12		1	62	82
Sugar Maple									0
Oak				4	1				5
Ash		1		1	3				5
Walnut		1							1
Black Walnut									0
Ironwood									0
Willow	1	7	3	9	25	3	6		54
Tamarack					2				2
Alder	3	7		8	5		4		27
Swamp Oak							3		3
Poplar		3	6	5	3				17
Sassafras									0
Dogwood									0
Birch									0
Pepperidge									0
Butternut									0
Aspen				2			2		4
Hornbeam									0
Prickly Ash									0
Spice Bush									0
Plum Bush									0
Plum Tree									0
Lynnwood		4							4
Hawthorn									0
Mulberry									0
Cedar									0
Total observations	1071	182	63	398	301	8	438	752	3213
Total references to swampy land	575	103	21	208	151	7	232	327	1624

Source: Calculations of the author

Townships: Mai.=Maidstone; Gos.=Gosfield; Mal.=Malden; Col.=Colchester; Mer.=Mersea; And.=Anderdon; San.=Sandwich; Til.=Tilbury; and Roc.=Rochester

agree with the modern surveys. An additional (chi-square) analysis of particular vegetation groupings within the same moisture and texture categories proves equally significant.[34]

There is, therefore, statistical justification for the hypothesis that a knowledge of specific vegetation types would indeed lead the nineteenth-century settler to identify the better-drained areas. As Table 1.5 shows, these well-drained sites, which mainly lie along the Lake Erie shore, carried a high percentage of beech, chestnut, maple, white oak, red oak, and, to a lesser extent, white ash. All drained lands, principally in the interior, carried the highest percentage of willows, black ash, soft maple, elm, and sycamore. These basic relationships are illustrated on Figure 1.5, on which three major areas in which particular tree types occurred in combination with one another are mapped. The three areas are those in which the members of the class accounted for more than 50 per cent of the vegetation mentioned on each lot.[35] A fourth area labelled "mixed" lots included those in which various species were in closer equilibrium. Their hierarchical classification on Figure 1.3 is thought meaningful in terms of the potential usefulness for agriculture, category one having the highest potential. There are obvious similarities between this map and Figure 1.9, the map of land quality. As noted earlier, this is for good reasons.

In addition to the ubiquitous species mentioned earlier and shown on Figure 1.5, there were particular species present in unusually large quantities in particular areas. Figures 1.7 and 1.8 portray these species for wet and dry conditions. Figure 1.7, showing trees seeking richer, well-drained sites, includes chestnut, red oak, and black walnut. Figure 1.8 portrays species more tolerant of wet conditions. Basswood, sycamore, and soft maple are included here. The maps speak for themselves; there is a spatial pattern.

Although Alan Brunger[36] and Kenneth Kelly[37] observe some variation among nineteenth-century commentators on what were considered good and poor indicators of land quality, there was considerable agreement. Kelly states that forest cover was used as an indicator of drainage conditions and that, in Ontario, first-class wheat land would be found under a mixed hardwood cover, including maple, basswood, elm, and beech.[38] Essex County exhibits variance with Ontario as a whole with respect to vegetation indicators. Here the surveyors believed that good land lay under the white oak, beech, and maple found throughout the area. These lands might not have been the first choice in the wider area but they were the best available in the county because of the predominance of ill-drained land. Even within the wider area they were still high-priority choices. While these areas had difficulty accumulating moisture once the humic

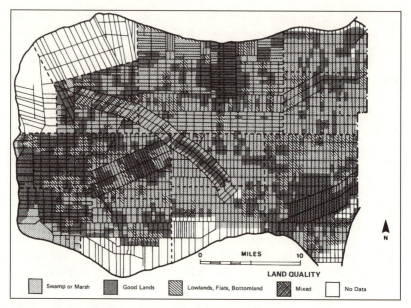

Figure 1.9   Land quality as measured by the surveyors
Source: Clarke and Finnegan, "Colonial Survey Records," 133.

mould had gone from the soil surface, they were readily cleared and settlers with little capital often chose them for their first farm. In fact, moisture deficiency was rarely a problem in Essex.[39] Brunger and Kelly agree that pine, cedar, and hemlock all indicated poor land. Pine and hemlock were absent in Essex; cedar may have been present in small quantities along the Lake Erie shore but is not detectable because the field notes have not survived. In contrast to Ontario[40] as a whole, the poor indicators in Essex are all deciduous, namely, black ash, soft maple, alder, and willow on the wettest of lands, and elm, sycamore, and basswood on moderately wet lands. While surveying in what was to become Anderdon Township in 1792, Patrick McNiff encountered swamp, not for the first time. He reported to the Land Board administering the settlement of the area: "the Timber in those swamps Water ash, and small Elms, the Bottom whole Clay, mixed with sand, if ever they could be drained, the soil is not worth the expence, nor is the timber growing there useful even for fuel."[41]

From the above, it would seem that there was indeed a rich lore that could be used to identify well-drained and poorly drained areas within Essex. Individuals could rely upon individual species or groupings of species.[42] With certain exceptions, single species could

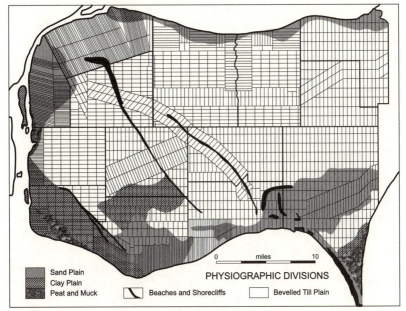

Figure 1.10   Physiographic divisions of the county
Source: L.J. Chapman and D.F. Putnam, *The Physiography of Southern Ontario.*

be used. Indeed, within the literature much credibility is given to the pursuit of the black walnut.[43] Such species would be as infrequent in Essex as elsewhere in Ontario (Figure 1.7), but, as Table 1.4 indicates, single reliance upon beech, chestnut, maple, and white oak would identify well-drained sites. Conversely, single reliance upon willow, black ash, and soft maple would identify ill-drained lands even when personal observation of surface drainage did not permit this.

The contrasts between well-drained and poorly drained indicators, paralleling the physiographic division of the county (Figure 1.10),[44] would generally be apparent to most settlers. A variety of indicators might have been used, including tree profile, leaf type, bark, twigs, and fruit. Misdiagnosis of certain species within a particular genus would not matter. In the case of the maples, however, the uninitiated might not differentiate between hard and red maples and might indeed confuse some with sycamore, if the sole criterion was leaf type. Knowledge of species profile, bark, and fruit would alleviate this problem. Misidentification on whatever basis of red or soft maple with rock or black maple would place the settler on wetter land. Similar confusion and consequences would arise in the case of the hickory family, whose members the surveyors do not distinguish. Even modern authorities have difficulty distinguishing the members of this group, the most reliable criterion being fruit which is observable only at specific times of the year and at close range.[45] Elm, basswood, and poplar, with their greater tolerance of moisture conditions, would prove similarly difficult. In short, it would seem that most prospective settlers, armed with a basic lore and a moderate sensitivity to tree type, could distinguish land quality.

By doing so they could in all probability identify the areas recognized on Figure 1.4. This figure is premised on the variables "texture" and "soil drainage," readily available to the hand and eye. These variables must have been important in all areas and especially in Essex but they cannot have been the only ones. Life for the backwoods settler, however idealized, was not simple, especially when it came to something as vital as the choice of land, on which so much would subsequently depend. A host of variables – slope, aspect, stoniness, elevation, colour and depth of soil,[46] and density of stand[47] must additionally have come into play, their importance related to the experience of the settler. However, Figure 1.4 must suffice as the surrogate for a myriad of such decisions. No doubt mistakes were made. Adjustments would have had to be made based upon personal experience or advice received after church, at the barn-raising bee, or in the tavern. Nonetheless, by such adaptive processes, the pattern of settlement that would evolve in this area would to a large extent come to mirror the opportunities offered by nature. Eventually, through trial and error and transmission in the folk culture(s), the potential of this area would become known.

Environmental indicators played a role in this process, although in an age in which few were literate, or if literate had the time to record their action for modern researchers, extensive support for such claims will be rare. Nonetheless, examination of contemporary newspapers and the Township Papers for the county in the period 1790 to 1850 revealed nine instances in which particular tree types were used to convince people to choose or purchase particular lots.[48] In two instances, individuals seeking to buy land instructed their agents to use the field notes and maps.[49] The number of such references is small but this was the period of initial settlement in Essex when sales were limited because land could still be acquired by patent from the Crown. History is frequently silent on the orthodox wisdom! The conclusion that people not only could select land using vegetation but did so is a reasonable one.[50] In later chapters, the reasonableness of this conclusion will be further demonstrated by inference from the aggregate behaviour of the settlers.

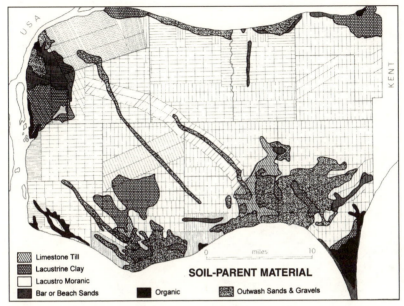

Figure 1.11   Soil-parent material (after Vandall)
Source: P. Vandall, *Atlas of Essex County*

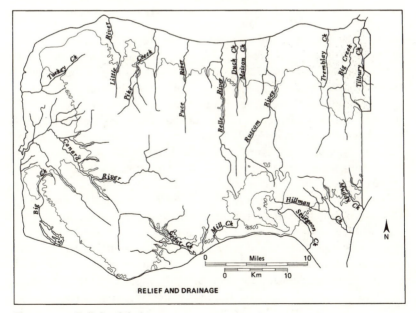

Figure 1.12   Relief and drainage
Source: National Topographic Series (NT), Essex 1:63360, Survey and Mapping Branch [1950].

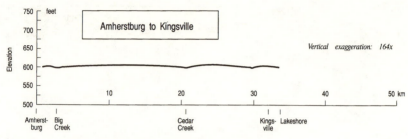

Figure 1.13   Relief profile, Amherstburg to Kingsville
Source: NT, Essex, 1:63360, Survey and Mapping Branch [1950]

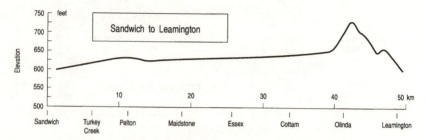

Figure 1.14   Relief profile, Sandwich to Leamington
Source: NT, Essex, 1:63360, Survey and Mapping Branch [1950]

Armed with such forest lore, settlers might very well have been able to distinguish between the habitable coastal areas and the uninhabitable water-laden interior. The contemporary language for identifying these soils (Appendix 1.1) may have captured their origins and qualities, although probably not in the manner of Figure 1.11, which describes the soils in terms of parent material.[51] However, the contrasts between the "warm" soils of the first group in Figure 1.4 (including, for example, Fox Sandy Loam) and the "cold" soils of class six (including, for example, Brookston Clay) would surely have been very apparent. As distinctions blurred (and opportunity for error increased), other terms might have been employed. Reliance upon vegetation, which transcends property lines, must have made many at the local level rue the day they chose a particular lot and thereby soil type, most especially if it disguised one of the nutritionally limited outwash sands. At the level of the county, the division between wet and dry site conditions must have been only too apparent and have led to an emphasis upon the Detroit and most especially Lake Erie shores. As Table 1.9 shows, agricultural opportunity in Essex was limited in this first phase of settlement.

Table 1.9   Summary tabulation of acreage of specific soil classes for Essex County

Class	Characteristic	Acreage	% Total Area
1	Light- to medium-textured, well-drained	28,000	6.19
2	light-textured, imperfectly drained	47,500	10.51
3	Medium-textured, imperfectly and poorly drained	23,000	5.09
4	Heavy-textured, imperfectly drained	33,000	7.30
5	Heavy-textured, poorly drained	304,500	67.37
6	Bottom land, marsh and muck	16,000	3.54

Source: Appendix 1.1.

If this was so, the distribution of cultivable land was such that it was accessible and there were no topographic barriers that limited settlement nor prevented farming. As Figure 1.12 indicates, the area physiographically is a plain of little relief, generally about 600 feet above sea level and rising to 700 feet near the modern town of Leamington. The profiles of the relief (figures 1.13 and 1.14) show that gradients are gentle; nowhere in the county are they likely to have prohibited the use of the plough, even if such usage was widespread.

Baron de Rottenburg surveyed this and other areas in 1855 (figure 1.15). He did so with a military eye, recording the condition of roads, the number of men and horses that could be billeted in particular places, and the accessibility (presumably to American infantry rather than settlers) along the coast.[52] Nothing was recorded along Lake St Clair; presumably the main threat was to be expected elsewhere. From the site of Sandwich on the Canadian shore he reported "steep banks diminishing towards Hog Island." South of this, for a distance of some miles, he reported low banks and a coast penetrated by the Turkey and Canard rivers. Here, some sixty years earlier, Patrick McNiff, the surveyor, had travelled "2 days and part of a third through marshes" and had concluded that passage between Lake Erie and Lake St Clair was impossible because of these extensive marshes.[53] Thereafter, for several miles the coast had steep and difficult banks, which from a military perspective, enhanced the value of the site for Fort Malden. Below the fort the banks were again low and shallow and easily penetrated, but much of the area immediately behind the coast was marsh. While settlement could have been brought about in this area, it would seem more likely (if things were not directed from the west as they in fact were) to have taken hold from Colchester Township east towards the middle of Gosfield Township. Here, from the site of Colchester village, for a distance of almost nine miles, the beaches were low and the potential for agriculture greatest. To the east, banks

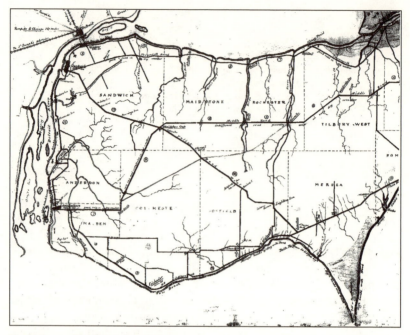

Figure 1.15   The Rottenburg map
Source: NA, NMC 0012437, the Rottenburg Map.

of clay thirty to sixty feet high inhibited accessibility; beyond this, high banks limited accessibility to the cedar swamps of Point Pelée.[54] In an unconstrained world, the Lake Erie shore should have seen the greatest activity but prior settlement by the French would lead, at least in the initial phase, to an emphasis on the Detroit shore.

European settlement, then, took place under certain environmental circumstances involving the human perception and evaluation of resource. However, decisions to settle were also affected by economic and political circumstances. It is to these circumstances that we now turn.

2 Peace, Order, and Good Government: The Organization of a Landscape

INTRODUCTION

In this second chapter the political, social, and economic background to settlement is examined in order to appreciate how these factors, in conjunction with the physical environment, influenced decisions relating to land. Its purpose is to set the scene against which the drama was played. The chapter begins by looking at the prevailing ideology. Some readers may find this unrepresentative of the total political culture of Upper Canada. It might appear to fault the analysis by placing too great a stress on conservative values when in fact these values were in a process of constant evolution.[1] No apology is made for this approach, however, because the present book is not a work of political science per se; rather, its purpose is to describe the dominant ideology of the time so that readers may appreciate how land was obtained and the effects of government policy on the ground. To do so, it uses the work of Professor Sydney Wise, still, in this author's opinion, the most convincing, insightful, and elegant of writers on Upper Canada.[2] The chapter also looks at the organization of the landscape in terms of surveying and the policy of reserving land for particular purposes. Additionally, it examines the evolving infrastructure of Essex which influenced individual decisions.

The chapter has three distinct subsections. These deal with political ideology, its manifestations in the pattern of survey and in the location of the reserved lands, and, lastly, the infrastructure that influenced locational decisions. The topics are geographical, as is the treatment.

Each section culminates in a map which summarizes the spatial organization of the theme. In turn, the maps reflect a variety of source materials such as the survey records discussed in chapter 1 (Appendix 2.1)[3] and cartographic source materials in federal and provincial depositories, the latter being used to assist in the reconstruction of infrastructure[4] or the location of reserved lands.[5] Documentary materials used for the purpose of delimiting the reserved lands included the schedules of the Crown and clergy reserves as well as published statements (Appendix 2.2), the Domesday Books (Appendix 2.3), the patent index, and the abstract index to deeds[6] and the Canada Company registers.[7] Data on the infrastructure were also gained from the assessment rolls and the enumeration returns of the Census of Canada;[8] in a subsequent chapter these same data are used to analyse the price of land. In addition to these primary sources a number of secondary sources were used.[9]

No one of these sources was sufficient in itself but had to be used in conjunction with one another in the manner described by the author and David L. Brown.[10] Nor was there any one method, no special elixir by which the pattern of surveying, the reserved lands, or the infrastructure could be determined. The method used was the conventional one, a systematic checking of sources against each other and the weaving together of a variety of materials to a particular end.

THE PREVAILING MENTALITY OF THE TIMES: ROOTS OF THE CONSERVATIVE CULTURE OF UPPER CANADA

The political culture of Upper Canada, or rather of those who held power for so much of its existence, was based on a deep attachment to "existing social arrangements as a repository of the accumulated wisdom of the past."[11] However, one's view of what constituted wisdom might turn, whether consciously or not, upon developments in Britain more than a century earlier.[12] There, with the restoration of the monarchy in 1660, there began a debate which culminated in the "Glorious Revolution" of 1688.[13] This debate involved, on the one hand, the notion of absolute monarchy, which, in the minds of its advocates, enjoyed extensive scriptural backing. Their interpretation was that absolute familial dominion had been bestowed upon Adam and Noah and had been transmitted patriarchally through primogeniture to various monarchs.[14] An omnipotent God had communicated kingship to his vice-regent; it followed that the King was owed allegiance as a matter of right.[15] Most holding to this view answered at first to the epithet Royalist or Cavalier and later to the label Tory, a term originally attached to Irish outlaws and now transferred to the party of the court.[16] In their attempts to secure their ends, Anglican Tories were not above suggesting collusion between the Whigs, often Calvinists, and those pejoratively labelled Papists.[17] Insecurity about these two groups was to be transmitted to most British colonies, including Upper Canada. It was manifest in the clauses of the Constitutional Act of 1791 which supported a "Protestant" clergy and in, for example, the prohibition on dissenting clergy performing marriages. In contradistinction was the view held by Whigs that "popery" and absolutism were to be avoided and that a sovereign people might depose an arbitrary ruler. These divisions became marked during the Exclusion Crisis of 1679 to 1681, when parliament sought to exclude the future James II from the throne. In the event this failed, but so did James II, who ultimately was forced to abandon his throne and flee abroad. With the Glorious Revolution of 1688, parliament abrogated the principle of absolute hereditary kingship.

Tories[18] finally accepted and adapted to the Revolutionary settlement by accepting the transfer of authority to the three estates of Crown, Lords, and Commons, in a Lockean contractual arrangement that seemed to preserve the best of the "old" and "new" and thereby, it was held, protected all.[19] In words attributed to Edmund Burke, whom Winston Churchill described as "perhaps the greatest man that Ireland has produced,"[20] "the Regal power is that part in the Constitution which being detached from, and superior to, all the local parts, parties and interests in the Nation exerts itself to preserve a constitutional equipoise and general interest in all the parts."[21] The King, who had an interest in the perpetuation of the constitution, called it "the most beautiful combination that ever was framed" (Plate 2.1).[22] Eventually, the wisdom of involving the community in the legislative function of monarchy was accepted. Ultimately, this perspective came to be viewed as "traditional," although as late as 1795 there were writers who appeared to support the old-style absolutism.[23]

This debate was transferred to British America: in the revolting colonies the emphasis upon Lockean liberalism, Puritanism, civic humanism, and republicanism, together with arguments derived from the Enlightenment, particularly in its Scottish form, led ultimately to a break with Britain.[24] In all of this there was perhaps no greater influence than that of Thomas Paine, who argued that monarchy was dangerous, destructive, silly, and contrary to God's law.[25] Those ideologically at variance with such views remained quiet or carried their more conservative ideology to Canada, where they were known as Tories or, after 1775, as Loyalists.[26] Yet even here there was no slavish acceptance of a divinely instituted monarchy.[27] Notions of juridical rights appeared

Plate 2.1   King George III. Engraving by Benjamin Smith from a painting by
Sir William Beechey.
Courtesy of Fulford Gallery, Ottawa.

Plate 2.2 Sir John Beverley Robinson, chief justice of Upper Canada. By George Theodore Berthon. Oil on canvas, 1846.
Courtesy of Law Society of Upper Canada, Fine Art Collection (no. 265).

in Upper Canada in, for example, the personage of that avatar of the Family Compact, John Beverley Robinson (Plate 2.2).[28] This American-born loyalist and chief justice would insist that the oath to the King be taken "in right of Parliament."[29] Yet he and his fellow conservatives, then and now, feared social indiscipline, averred the Petrine recommendation to accept the powers that be,[30] and valued loyalty above all things. Like others, Robinson abhorred revolution, which he had experienced directly, whether it was in what was now the United States or in revolutionary France.

Robinson in many ways epitomizes the two streams of conservatism which Wise, in his seminal work, identifies as converging on Upper Canada.[31] Wise sees, on the one hand, a counter-revolutionary outlook which was a blend of eighteenth-century Toryism with Burkean repudiation of and animosity towards French Jacobinism. On the other hand, though he does not explicitly identify it with Robinson, he sees the emigré sense of loyalty to King and Empire, antagonistic to the United States and possessed of an acute, partisan sense of history. This was so very marked because of the price that had been paid in personal terms and in the loss of property in the territory abandoned.

The new land, the Upper Canada that was to emerge, was in a state of permanent siege if not from American troops then from American ideas.[32] This made "loyalty" the crux of the conservative vision. Loyalty was not just to the Crown but to those beliefs and institutions that set Upper Canada apart from the United States:

To the Tory, American democratic republicanism was the worst possible form of government, since it tempted politicians to play upon the worst appetites of men. The tory was ignorant of such subtleties in the American constitution as the system of checks and balances, or if he was not, considered that their effect was rather to weaken executive government than to check the turbulence inherent in democracy. The deistic founding fathers, in their rejection of the connection between religion and the state, had sacrificed the most effective brake upon public disorder, and paved the way to anarchy. While it was true that men created the institutions under which they chose to live, the conservatives believed quite as strongly that institutions made men and men made nationality. The American, shaped by his secularized and revolutionary democracy, was a being altogether different from the British American; and his society was moving along another road.[33]

That road appeared to be democracy, which was something that, in the Tory view, had so tormented the American mind[34] that it had led to an unnatural break with the mother country. The American Loyalist, Jonathan Boucher, expressed great disapproval of appeals to the people recollecting that "it was thus the people once were cunningly led on to depose a Charles, and make a Cromwell their protector; to intercede for a thief, and to crucify the Saviour of the world."[35] To an Upper Canadian, Christopher Hagerman, democracy was like a serpent "twisting round us by degrees, it should be crushed in the first instance."[36] Upper Canada's first lieutenant-governor, John Graves Simcoe (Plate 2.3), saw the British constitution as of immense benefit, "offering the best method gradually to counteract and ultimately to destroy, or to disarm, the spirit of democratic subversion, in the very Country which gave it existence and growth, and this it is reasonable to believe may be effected, by exemplifying, a better practical system of internal Government, than the separate States of America can possibly demonstrate."[37]

Therefore, in Upper Canada, trappings of democracy such as the township meeting, which recalled memories of similar meetings prior to rebellion in America, France, and Ireland and also of the agitation in England which would culminate in the massacre at Peterloo in 1819, were to be resisted.[38] Terms such as "Democrat" and "Republican" were used as insults. Upper Canada was a place that would preserve the best of the British system. It possessed a "mixed" constitution[39] of limited monarchy represented by a governor who could withhold assent to bills originating in other estates and who could himself be overruled from London. There was an upper house, equivalent to the House of Lords, whose membership was appointed to what was termed the Legislative Council. Initially, this was to consist of at least seven men appointed by the governor for life plus additions as might appear reasonable from those who were ennobled, an event that never actually took place. In the early years, the numbers were small, but the council grew as attempts were made to include representatives of various districts[40] and in the light of growing opposition to its power to broaden its base to ensure greater independence of the executive.[41] Membership on this council frequently overlapped with that on the Executive Council. Appointment to this body was at the pleasure of the government. Roughly equivalent to the English cabinet, which was itself in the process of profound change,[42] this body, unlike its British counterpart, was in no way responsible to the House of Assembly, which by analogy was equivalent to the House of Commons.[43] The structure was therefore similar to what Alan Tully describes for the seventeenth-century American colonies, from which it was in part derived, but the Americans, paradoxically basing their arguments on the importance of English rights, were in the eighteenth century leaving this structure fast behind them.[44] The marked overlap between the two councils – elaborated upon in chapter 9 – and the lack of responsibility to the elected House of Assembly meant that the formal exercise of power was restricted ultimately to the governor although an inexperienced one might be controlled by his

Plate 2.3   John Graves Simcoe, lieutenant governor of Upper Canada.
Courtesy of Toronto Reference Library (JRR, T34632).

council. He appointed the members of the councils. He could withhold assent to bills originating in the legislature. Ultimately, he was
responsible to Westminster although the imperial parliament might
be grateful not to have to exercise its responsibility, if business was
being satisfactorily conducted in Canada. Such silences, including
the fact that the Canada Act was itself silent on the functions of the
Executive Council, simply assuming that such a body was a normal
part of a British colony, were taken to be part of a balanced constitution which was inherently superior.

In the political turmoil that marked the period from 1760 to 1790, the idea of a balanced constitution could never have worked without "those customary responses which formed the civilisation of the age."[45] This civilization developed in Britain but its extension abroad was threatened by a "world turned upside down," by threat of revolution, by war without, and by economic changes presaging the Industrial Revolution. The counter to all of this activity and the ill-disposed dispositions of human beings was to be found in Nature.

Attitudes towards what was natural permeated all aspects of society including the religious and the political. Following the rise of the scientific movement and the ensuing conflicts within religious bodies, supernatural explanations of worldly events proved less satisfactory but this did not lead to the demise of religion as such. Indeed, to the study of the Scriptures was added a second avenue of revelation, that of Nature, the manifestation of the works of God. Increasingly, science pointed to a Great Machine revealing design, order, and law where there had been chaos; its existence presupposed a grand designer. A people both pious and scientific could, in Basil Willey's mind, exclaim with their spokesman, Alexander Pope: "Nature and Nature's laws lay hid in night: God said, Let Newton be and all was light."[46] Such enlightenment came from the explanation of nature and used reason as its vehicle.

An illustration of this view is to be found in the life of David Hume,[47] the Scottish-born philosopher, who, close to death, sought the healing waters of the spa at Bath. He was attacked for doing so by Adam Smith, his fellow Scot, who wrote that "mineral water was as much a drug as any that comes out of an apothecaries Shop and must therefore be an unnatural remedy, occasioning itself 'a transitory disease' and weakening the power of Nature to expel the disease."[48] In fact, the stimulation of the waters was advocated by contemporary medicine, and Hume was only following the latest logic. Nevertheless, Smith's view that the self-balancing power of nature might be upset by resorting to spas was in accord with the current thinking about the nature of the world and of society. It was generally believed that there was a natural order and harmony in human society which could not be reconstituted by human will power. Nature was beneficent, tended always towards balance and stability, and was apparent in the world around. It was clear and simple. People possessed "natural virtue," a condition described in the literature of the time, for example, in Oliver Goldsmith's *Vicar of Wakefield*,[49] whose principal character displays natural virtues uncorrupted by the city. Natural virtue appears here "as a simple-hearted goodwill towards others, a placid acceptance of the orders of society, an absence of torturing ambition."[50] Boswell[51] in his work applauds the style of an Ayrshire ploughboy who is happy as the day is long. Neither author challenges the status of ploughboy or peer; such clear delineation was of the order of nature.

This same thought appears in the political and economic thought of the period, especially in Adam Smith's *Wealth of Nations*,[52] which advocated resisting the institutions of the day for "unnatural interference" with the "normal course of relations between men." The role of government, Smith declared, was to protect against violence, to administer justice, and to carry out projects which were too large for individuals; that was all. Smith's exposition of the "invisible hand" of competition guiding an economic system liberated individual acquisitive instincts in the name of Nature. Individuals were to be free to seek individual profit. The result of this thought, still propounded more than two centuries after the publication of Smith's work, was that private profit produced public wealth; only in times of great upheaval might one think of state intervention. The Middle Ages had condemned "that effort to achieve a continuous and unlimited increase in material wealth which modern societies applaud as meritorious."[53] Now, in the eighteenth century, "God and Nature fixed the general frame, and bade self-love and social be the same."[54] The law of Nature had been transformed into a sanction for laissez-faire; while usury laws might persist in Britain and Upper Canada, the post-lapsarian impulse to acquisitiveness sanctioned reaching out for this world's goods. Property rights became a cherished concomitant of individual rights or indeed, in some circles, of the natural rights of man. Acquisitiveness was sanctioned by these views and was perhaps possible in the New World in a manner unimagined in the Old. Smith must accept a large measure of responsibility for such notions, although their roots can be traced back to the Renaissance. Yet the irony is that, though his ideas were to have such a revolutionary impact, Smith himself valued stability and dealt with social classes as they were; indeed his work is an indication of the stability of eighteenth-century English society.[55]

Even one of the greatest philosophers of the age, Jeremy Bentham, revealed something of the same easy certainty through his iconoclastic work on government and on morals and legislation.[56] His concept of utilitarianism contained much that was revolutionary. A lawyer by trade, he held, unlike Blackstone[57] that the common law did not represent the essence of English life but rather a set of rules to achieve certain ends. When in time the law ceased to be meaningful, it should be altered to ensure the ultimate end of society, which he defined as "the greatest happiness of the greatest number, each counting for one and none for more than one."[58] Each institution should be tested to see if its aim was consistent with the greatest happiness; if not, it could be scrapped. In his use of happiness to explain away moral judgments, and in his logical extremism, Bentham cut at institutions in a radical way, but in fact the mankind he describes is still of the "common sense conventional man of the age." Bentham, says Stephen Watson, "no more than Adam Smith foresees the explosiveness of human beings, for he cannot imagine them released from the straight jacket of the eighteenth century code."[59] Moreover, his principle of "utility" is very like the "law of nature,"[60] which is simple and certain and prescribes a wise permanency in human society.

It was against the background of such thinking that the idea of a "natural aristocracy" developed.[61] Membership at the apex of this hierarchy was usually identifiable by particular social characteristics. Burke, in writing about the revolution in France, had noted that the legislators of ancient Greece and Rome had found benefits in social-ization, which raised people above their naturally base nature. These benefits were associated with particular habits and privileges charac-teristic of different classes: "They thought themselves obliged to dispose their citizens into social classes, and to place them in such sit-uations in the state, as their peculiar habits might qualify them to fill and to allot to them such appropriate privileges as might secure to them what their specific occasions required."[62] Members born into or admitted into such an elite exhibited wisdom and courage, demon-strated virtue, and were imbued with the responsibilities of public service. Used to the exercise of power, they were less likely to be cor-rupted by it; born to the ownership of large amounts of property, they would not stoop to doubtful means in anything.

To be bred in a place of estimation; to see nothing low and sordid from one's infancy: to be taught to respect one's self: to be habituated to the censorial inspection of the public eye: to look early to public opinion; to stand upon such elevated ground as to be enabled to take a large view of the wide-spread and infinitely diversified combinations of men and affairs in a large society; to have leisure to read, to reflect, to converse; to be enabled to draw the court and attention of the wise and learned, wherever they are to be found; to be habituated in armies to command and to obey; to be taught to despise danger in the pursuit of honor and duty; to be formed to the greatest degree of vigi-lance, foresight, and circumspection, in a state of things in which no fault is committed with impunity and the slightest mistakes draw on the most ruinous consequences; to be led to a guarded and regulated conduct, from a sense that you are considered as an instructor of your fellow-citizens in their highest con-cerns, and that you act as a reconciler between God and man; to be employed as an administrator of law and justice, and to be thereby among the first bene-factors to mankind; to be a professor of high science, or of liberal and ingenuous art; to be amongst rich traders, who from their success are presumed to have sharp and vigorous understandings, and to possess the virtues of diligence, order, constancy, and regularity, and to have cultivated an habitual regard to commutative justice: these are the circumstances of men that form, what I should call a natural aristocracy, without which there is no nation.[63]

The words are again those of Edmund Burke, but they might well have come from the mouth of an Upper Canadian high Tory.[64] Robinson gave vent to such views in the discussion in the early 1820s of the union of Upper and Lower Canada and the proposal to abolish the Legislative Council in its then current form.[65] An elected council, he argued, would produce a government "subjected to the anarchic passions of the popular assembly."[66] Only in an appointed council "could gentlemen place honour and duty ahead of their political fortunes."[67] Robinson and others of his ilk[68] shared with Burke the notion that there could be not be a nation without an aristocracy.

It was this idea that would sanction the rise of a group of individuals bound by a similar world-view, common military service, and, frequently, membership in the same religious denomination. Known to Upper Canadian historians as the Family Compact,[69] this body wrote the former lieutenant-governor, Sir Francis Bond Head,[70] in 1839, "is composed of those members in society who, either by their abilities and character" have been honoured by the confidence of the executive government, or who, by their industry and intelligence, have amassed wealth. The party, I own, is comparatively a small one: but to put the multitude at the top and the few at the bottom is a radical reversion of that pyramid of society which every reflecting man must foresee can end only by its downfall."[71] This group was marked by an "accommodative" political culture and, in the words of Wise, "made no high assimilative demands beyond its insistence upon adherence to vital survival values – loyalty, order, stability."[72]

The hallmark of membership in this "natural" aristocracy was property, unequally distributed. Arguably this included women and in the early years it certainly included slaves.[73] The most common expression of patrimony was possession of land; in the British society to which Upper Canada was heir, the punishment for moving a survey post was death. Accordingly, it is totally understandable that the most complete records of this society pertain not to the qualities of individuals but to land. Land was in abundance and everyone wished to acquire it.

This, it was recognized, posed little problem, although the worst excesses of land acquisition, like other societal excesses, should be constrained by law.[74] As Robinson said in his 1836 address to the grand jury of the Western District:

When we behold an indifference to the observance of the Laws and a restless diligence to evade them – a want of reverence to Magistrates & Superiors a disrespect to stations, offices, ranks, and orders of persons ... we may consider these as a symptom fatal to the true liberty of that country – In such cases every little disappointment – every imaginary grievance – every wanton desire of change produces a ferment & threatens the public peace – Everyone carves out his own method of redress, and prosecutes his designs by the dictates of his own corrupt will – To prevent these evils a love of Order becomes necessary by which we are induced to conform to the laws and to promote the welfare of the community.[75]

In Robinson's view, the welfare of the community derived from the Crown and parliament, whose will the courts interpreted.[76] Yet public convenience had to be balanced with property rights: "When it trenches upon private rights of property," then "the interference should go no further, nor be exercised in any other manner, than the legislature has expressedly permitted. Statutes for all public works and objects of this kind, when they authorize depriving individuals of their property, are to be construed upon the principle last mentioned."[77]

Predicated upon such views, and given existing conditions, a "natural" aristocracy could arise without assistance, but it was argued that an unselfish aristocracy might require assistance. To perpetuate a desirable hierarchy, steps had to be taken. In his letter to Lord Stanley at the Colonial Office, Lord Dorchester (Plate 2.4), the governor general, stated that "it may be advisable to reserve in every township of thirty thousand acres, five thousand acres to be granted only at a future day under the King's Special directions; These reserved parcels will enable His Majesty to reward such of His provincial Servants as may merit the Royal favour, and will also enable the Crown to create and strengthen an Aristocracy, of which the best use may be made on this Continent, where all Governments are feeble, and the general conditions of things tends to a wild Democracy."[78]

In contradistinction to democracy and anarchy lay order, essential to tranquillity and the very being of the state in Robinson's view.[79] This could be maintained only by unselfish politics and could best be entrusted to the aristocracy and the gentry. In Upper Canada, in the absence of true aristocracy, the gentry possessed the natural intelligence, education, and property to serve in the role of preserving society from either monarchical tyranny or democratic anarchy: "It is to be remembered that there is in Canada no counteracting influence of an ancient Aristocracy, of a great landed interest or even of a wealthy agricultural class: there is little in short but the presumed

Plate 2.4   Guy Carleton, 1st Baron Dorchester, governor of Quebec, 1768–78,
and governor-in-chief of British North America, 1786–94.
Courtesy of National Archives (c2833).

good sense, and good feeling of an uneducated multitude, (which may
be too much tempted) to stand between almost universal suffrage and
these institutions, which proudly and happily distinguish Britons from
the subjects of other monarchies, and no less so, from the Citizens of
that Great Republic ..."[80] The gentry possessed and valued "independence," which came with the possession of large landed estates.

Landed property thus guaranteed liberty, a view that Robinson shared with his Compact colleague John Strachan (Plate 2.5), who wrote: "Does any person doubt whether the British be the freest nation on earth, let him tell me where property and its rights are so well protected. This is the life and soul of liberty. What shall oppression seize when property is secure? Even a tyrant will not be wicked for nothing; but the motives and objects are removed, and the seed of oppression destroyed, when property is safe. By this, life and liberty are rendered sacred."[81]

Here, then, was a society possessing particular values with respect to monarchy and to a "natural" aristocracy based on the possession of land. It was also by definition an agrarian society and it was perhaps only in such a place, vitally concerned with the possession and acquisition of land, that such values might thrive.[82] Land of itself bestowed virtue through membership in the magistracy or the councils of state, as well as access to a host of revenue-generating jobs. Such virtue could be achieved through patronage! This would add a mechanism of perpetuation through the creation of a clientage system.

Patronage, though of course ancient, was commonplace in Britain at this time[83] and it was used in Upper Canada from the beginning.[84] Even before the American revolution, individuals had been seeking to "establish and fortify local oligarchies in the colonies."[85] Jonathan Boucher, one of the most vocal opponents of the rebellion, wrote that "in the present state of human affairs ... a man has, or has not influence, only as he has or has not, the power of conferring favours."[86] While he wrote from the perspective of those labelled Tory, the view that political and economic power should be in the hands of a wealthy minority was also held by all kinds of Whigs.[87] This was, therefore, a common view shared by both sets of belligerents and would therefore manifest itself in Upper Canada.

Lieutenant Governor Simcoe "used patronage for the explicit purpose of cementing to government the loyalties of the most 'respectable' members of society, whose principles through emulation would then be broadcast throughout their localities."[88] Though Simcoe's political objectives were never lost, motives of private gain became more marked as time went on and control came to rest with officials.[89] Those among them who enjoyed the particular confidence of authority used their position to benefit their relations and friends, a case in point being William Dummer Powell (Plate 2.6), who sought the clerkship of the court over which he presided for his son.[90] As S.J.R. Noel notes, the line between using land as the reward for loyalty and to create social stability, on the one hand, and using it as "unvarnished political patronage" on the other, is "an exceedingly fine

Plate 2.5   John Strachan, Anglican bishop of Toronto and executive councillor. Courtesy of National Archives (C3305).

one."[91] Here the potential for patronage was tremendous "indeed beyond the wildest imaginings of English domestic politics and all because of a fortuitous moment in history that allowed it [Upper Canada], in the span of a few brief decades, to dispose of truly enormous quantities of fertile land. To find a comparable moment in English history it is necessary to go back to the period of the Norman

Plate 2.6   William Dummer Powell, chief justice of Upper Canada, 1816–25.
Attributed to Georges Theodore Berthon. Oil on canvas, 1891.
Courtesy of Law Society of Upper Canada, Fine Art Collection (no. 81).

conquest."[92] Soon it was difficult to make one's way without the necessary connections in the clientage or "interest" system, the chief characteristic of which was that it was enduring and involved reflexive relationships between "client" and "patron".[93] The condition has been
well put by Wise: "As the clientage system ramified, as indeed it was
bound to, since every prominent official at York had at least some jobs

or perquisites in his gift, it hardened into a complex network joining officials at the capital to interest groups in every locality, in a bewildering maze of inter-relationships. As early as the 1820s, and probably well before then, each community had a local oligarchy – in effect, a party machine – through which the provincial government dispensed its favours."[94] The Tory "party" was then, in Wise's view, a coalition of central and local elites united to distribute honours and rewards to the politically deserving; sociologically and geographically it was a nested hierarchy of "interest."

Assistance in creating the desired political culture was to come from the Church of England. In the circumstances of rebellion in this province in 1837–38, Anglican clerics warned that "by the Divine will 'kings reign and princes decree justice' and to their rule we are obedient as to the ordinances of God, for they that resist shall receive to themselves damnation."[95] In the annexation crisis of 1849, A.N. Bethune, in a sermon on *The Duty of Loyalty*, declared that "the question of reverence for those that are in authority, respect for the laws, and submission to the government, is not a mere question of expediency or self, but a duty which ranks high amongst Christian ordinances ... it is something for the neglect or slight of which we shall one day give an account at the general judgement of the world."[96] Thus, the Anglican clergy were engaged in strengthening the imperial tie and in diffusing "those principles of piety, loyalty and obedience for which the Church of England has ever been distinguished."[97] Church and state shared a "reciprocity of interest."[98] The church, by inculcating certain attitudes towards the state and by promoting the welfare of society, was to be a prop of good government.[99] In turn, the state, by creating order and restraint, assisted redemption.[100]

This stood in stark contradistinction to the hostility to hierarchical government that accompanied, or at least flourished in, post-revolutionary America. In the United States, a Christian republicanism held that in a truly Christian republic the regulatory functions of the state would simply wither. This was not the case in Upper Canada, where Christian loyalism viewed evangelical voluntarist approaches as, in essence, republican and even the British Wesleyan Conference attacked the American Methodist tradition.[101] In this view, efforts to make political life more democratic were not Christian since monarchy and the state were part of God's order. In Strachan's mind, while inequality was part of the order and gradation of the cosmos,[102] subordination in the natural world, including within the human species, was not slavish. The parts, the ordered series, were part of an organic whole and as such men should accept their station since each order was an essential support of community. To oppose the order of nature was therefore human folly. Order was the essential attribute of the creation; social gradation worked to that order and human institutions ensured it.[103]

When, in 1828, the Anglican bishop of Quebec suggested that individual congregations might strengthen the church's claim to the clergy reserves by writing to the home government to stress their numerical strength, Archdeacon Strachan argued that the bishop should petition on behalf of the whole church: "This will sustain the dignity of our Establishment," he wrote "and not descend to a measure which would induce every man to think that our retaining the reserves depended on his signature" – "references to the people smells too much of Democracy for me."[104] At least to some, Anglicanism, in which God's providence was most clearly evident, was about order.[105] Indeed, Robinson, as chief justice, reminded the grand jury of the Western District that "order is heaven's first law."[106]

The view that the state ought to favour a particular church,[107] or any church, is one that modern Ontarians find most difficult to consider seriously, but this was not so in the nineteenth century. J.W. Grant expresses this clearly: "Belief in some form of religious establishment came naturally to those who retained something of the older organic view of society."[108] For a millennium and a half, he contends, it had been considered natural for a Christian monarch to promote the welfare of the church and for a bishop to promote loyalty to the state. In England, since Elizabethan times, the established church had rallied national sentiment and in Upper Canada establishment could help keep it British. Strachan believed staunchly in establishment as a mechanism for mission in new territory but also because "nature does not go forth in search of Christianity, but Christianity goes forth to knock at the door of nature, and if possible, to awaken her out of her sluggishness."[109] Without the influence of the Church of England, Upper Canada "was certain to become a moral waste and a hotbed of sedition and discontent."[110] This was particularly clear to some in the circumstances of the rebellion in 1837. The Reverend Thomas Green, an Anglican priest, wrote in a letter to *The Times*:

We see who are the disaffected, and who are the contented. How desirable then by every means to increase the number of the latter and draw off from the ranks of the former. In a word, how all-important is it for the promotion of good order and peace in Upper Canada to look well to the provision existing for the sound religious instruction of the people there in the principles of the Church of England. Can it be doubted that the efficiency of the Church in Canada is important towards quelling existing disorders and promoting a healthier tone of society, harmony among the inhabitants and obedience to the laws? In the disaffected parts of Upper Canada it is evident it must be available to this end.[111]

The political ends are quite clear here, but additionally, the Church of England's decency and good order offered a model for combatting the "enthusiasm" which threatened the very foundations of society. Moreover, and this was especially so in a developing society such as Upper Canada, the provision of adequate facilities for the poor could be best served through a state-supported church. The responsibility to provide for the poor rested, in this view, upon the state, which was remiss if it "failed to put its resources at God's disposal."[112] The church should therefore be endowed with the resources to carry out its ministrations; and, in the context of developing societies such as Upper Canada, this meant land.

The Church of England was not alone in feeling this way; on the contrary, the clergy of the other major churches (Church of Scotland and Roman Catholic) were, according to Wise, instinctively social and political conservatives who distrusted Protestant dissent, especially if it came from the United States: "All believed that churches had a public role to play; and all accepted the principle that churches should support order and government through the promotion of public and private morality and the inculcation of ideas of subordination and of veneration for authority."[113] Moreover, their competition over the clergy reserves not withstanding, there was not a great deal of difference between wealthy Anglicans and Presbyterians, who gravitated towards one another and "met and mingled easily in society and business."[114]

Many in society believed that Upper Canadians were in fact a chosen or "peculiar" people[115] and that behind all that they enjoyed, constitutionally and economically, was the providential hand of God. In individual lives and most especially in the national life, fortune and misfortune, bounty and scarcity, happiness and misery were thought to issue from the loving hand of an omnipresent God who had endowed Upper Canada as a new Eden.[116] Almost thirty years ago, Wise identified the importance of providentialism in confirming the values of the state. Writing of Strachan, he asserted that: "the ruthlessness and intolerance of his political style derived from the absolute belief that the prescriptions he defended in church, state and society were part of the providential order, that Upper Canada had a special mission to preserve them in North America, and that any opposition to them was a sign of the grossest and most blasphemous infidelity, and of a dangerous sympathy for the condemned revolutionary society of the United States."[117] Robinson, too, understood the value of providentialism. In his polemic on the proposed bill uniting the two Canadas, he wrote that "religion is the only secure basis on which civil authority can rest."[118] Later, he would state: "There is a meaning in the moral world no less visible than in the great works of Nature – Order, stability, peace, security the great blessings of social existence ... can be reaped only as the rewards of a religious adherence to what is right and true ... the foundations of a peoples welfare must be laid in public virtue."[119] Religion and society went hand in hand and "order was not only a religious but also a social virtue."[120]

Who were the people who adhered to this state ideal? As is suggested above, conservative values crossed the divide of religion, and in Essex members of the local oligarchy, while predominantly Anglican, included some well-known Roman Catholics such as the Baby family. Nor were all unqualified supporters of the central oligarchy. As Wise argues, the need to respond to local issues and needs, and, in the case of the assemblymen, to be re-elected, tended to dilute high Tory principles. In fact, these Tories were no more united than the Reform opposition and disagreed frequently with positions taken by the official class on many provincial and local issues.[121] They were diverse rather than homogeneous, alliances of various groups with different interests and outlooks.

Toryism was a natural philosophy for those who, by self-ascription or public perception, belonged to the "respectable classes." It was also a natural fit for those landowners who thought of themselves as "gentry" rather than farmers. Direct benefit flowed to those members of the professions who were supporters of the "establishment" and most were, although there were remarkable people such as John Rolph,[122] the Baldwins,[123] and Marshall Spring Bidwell[124] who were not supporters of the government.[125] The bias of the military "was instinctively conservative"[126] but self-interest motivated the larger merchants and businessmen. Most substantial merchants, shipowners, and lumber operators were government adherents and, in turn, "the official class proved reasonably responsive to the interests of the provincial mercantile community, and to the larger needs of St. Lawrence commercialism."[127] All of these people stood to gain in business, in office, and in land from recognition by government.

If society was ordered socially,[128] if Upper Canada had, by divine providence, been placed within the British Empire and constitution, and endowed like no other area, it followed that Upper Canadians, heirs to the Judaic-Christian tradition, viewed their new garden of Eden as equally orderly. God had given mankind dominion over the earth; indeed, the earth's purpose was to serve humanity. If its order was properly understood, nature would respond in a predictable and rewarding manner. What appeared chaotic was "a mere surface attribute concealing an ordered reality that man could discover and profitably exploit."[129] Indeed, this had been the experience of Upper Canadians in other parts of North America. As Loyalists, they had chosen to be newly transplanted into this environment. In their belief in their capacities to transform the physical environment, Upper Canadians differed from their distant ancestors in their "perception of nature as a realm corrupted by the Fall and disfigured by the Flood, terrifying in its hostility and subject to malevolent supernatural forces."[130] They brought this view into every realm of their existence. "Aesthetically, for example, the qualities that came to be most highly prized, in everything from art and poetry to architecture and furniture-making, were those of order, balance and harmony; while what came to be considered most beautiful in nature was that which showed to best effect, the moderating and civilizing influence of man – as in a well-ordered agricultural landscape."[131] Theirs was not an unruly assault on wilderness but rather an orderly progression in which government played a large part, as did the ideology that individuals carried with them. The Upper Canadian mentality combined political ideology, religion, and attitudes to the environment, all interwoven one with another. Ultimately, it affected the form of settlement on the ground; eventually, rejection of the worst effects of these ideas would lead to social outrage and to rebellion. However, for the longest time they were the dominant ideas, and their effects on the organization of territory appeared at an early date.[132]

After the British acquired this land, they set about organizing it according to their concepts of order. First, this involved the peaceful acquisition of land from the aboriginal population. This was accomplished for Essex as part of the McKee treaty of 1790 (Plate 2.7 and Appendix 2.4). Whatever is thought of this and other like surrenders, and there is good reason to believe that the native interest was not well served, it was accomplished peaceably and without the violence that accompanied similar transactions in our neighbour to the south. The territory thus acquired had then to be surveyed since it was a maxim of British land policy (although one not always observed, as the history of the county shows) that settlement should follow survey. In addition, provision had to be made for the location of the reserved lands prescribed by the Constitutional Act of 1791 under which Essex, as part of the province of Upper Canada, would be governed. Finally, government policy would produce a system of roads by which the needs of everyday life and of commerce would be accommodated. To this infrastructure the settler added various institutions, reflecting local conditions and needs. The church, post office, saw and gristmill, the tavern,

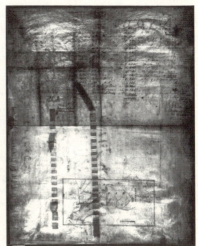

Plate 2.7   The McKee treaty of 1790, showing the signatures of the European participants and the totems of the native ones.
Courtesy of National Archives (IT002).

and the blacksmith's shop were indispensable elements of pioneer life. To understand how Essex was settled, it is necessary to know where these manifestations of government and human activity were to be found on the land itself.

ACQUIRING AND SURVEYING THE LAND

Development in any newly settled area is ultimately linked to the length of time during which colonization has been taking place, to the economic and technological circumstances in which it occurs, and to the cultural baggage of the settlers. The purpose here is, therefore, to describe the surveying of Essex so that the reader can appreciate which areas were open to settlement at particular periods. The section rests upon the documentary and cartographic source materials identified in appendices 2.1 and 2.2.

Since the survey of the area was initiated by members of the establishment such as Lord Dorchester, by the Surveyor General's Office, or by the Land Board responsible for its settlement, the topic of surveying inevitably involved issues of logistics, of government policy, of attitudes to the native owners of the land, and of attitudes to the French occupants whose settlement of this area pre-dated the British occupation by at least forty years.[133] The correspondence of the land boards also shows that effective British control (and survey was a mechanism of this) was threatened or at least impeded by claims to land under Indian grants entered into prior to the legal surrender of this territory to the Crown.

The survey was to be orderly. It was to focus around the township, divided into concessions and lots which described locations that could be quickly transformed into property for individual settlers.[134] The tasks of survey and settlement would go hand in hand and the records that would survive into modern times would not be the records of individual achievements as much as they would be of surveyed property parcels. As Louis Gentilcore points out, the first land-use plan for British Canada included a framework that included the laying out of townships, the reservation of land, and the taking of inventories.[135] Government policy sought to see this land settled but only after it had been legally acquired and surveyed.

This process apparently began for the British[136] as early as 1785 when a tract of land at the mouth of the Detroit River, in what was to become Malden Township, was granted by the Huron and other natives to a number of officers of the Indian Department and an ensign, Phillip R. Fry (Frey), was assigned the task of surveying the land.[137] The evidence is based upon a letter of Lieutenant Governor John Hay of Detroit to Fry in which he asserts that the land had been granted to the King rather than to the particular individuals but that they (captains Bird, Caldwell, Elliott, and McKee), Sir John Johnson (superintendent of Indian affairs, entrusted with the settling of the Loyalists: see Plate 2.8), Hay himself, and a number of others were to become the de facto occupants.[138] In effect, he was according gubernatorial recognition to an action that he had earlier thought doubtful and had so informed his superior, Governor Frederick Haldimand (Plate 2.9).[139] The deed remains unlocated and so it is uncertain if de jure transfer was made to the Crown, but it was certainly made to the King's friends. Haldimand's advice to Hay was that the Indians meeting in council had to make the tract over and that "their deed must be transmitted to Sir John Johnson to be properly confirmed by the governor of the Province when regular grants will be given to the persons who are to be proprietors of the Land."[140]

If the deed was in fact made, it preserved the process of acquisition (however doubtful the arrangement) preceding survey. The survey, completed in 1785, was the earliest British survey in this part of what was to become Upper Canada and later Ontario.[141] North of it, in what came to be known as Anderdon Township, was a seven-square-mile tract at the Rivière aux Canards acquired on 15 May 1786 by Colonel

E.Bartolozzi.R.A.

Plate 2.8   Sir John Johnson, superintendent and inspector general of the Six Nations, 1782–1830, "friend and fellow warrior" of the Indians, heir to 200,000 acres. Courtesy of National Archives (c2847).

Alexander McKee for the Crown and known as the Huron reserve.[142] McKee subsequently sought this land for his own use but withdrew his request within a week of negotiating a much bigger deal, one that, with the exception of two small reserves (one at the Canard for the Huron and the other at the Jarvais or Knagg's Creek), involved:

a certain Tract of land beginning at the mouth of Catfish Creek, commonly called Riviere au Chaudiere on the North side of Lake Erie, being the Western extremity of a Tract purchased by his said Majesty from the Messesagey Indians in the year One Thousand seven hundred and eighty Four and from thence running westward along the border of Lake Erie and up the Streight to the mouth of a River known by the name Channail Ecarté and up the main branch of the said Channel Ecarte to the first fork on the South side, then a due east line until it intersects the Riviere a la Tranche, and up the said Riviere a La Tranche to the North West corner of the said cession granted to his Majesty in the year one Thousand Seven Hundred and Eighty Four, then following the western boundary of said tract being a due South direction until it strikes the mouth of Catfish Creek or otherwise Riviere au Chaudiere being the first offset ...[143]

While the members of the Land Board were aware of McKee's responsibility in matters relating to land surrenders by the Indians, they were unaware of his progress towards completion of a treaty. In its final form, they were dismayed at its terms, most especially the concession of lands already surrendered by the Indians. William Robertson of the Land Board expressed his dismay at the way things had been handled.[144] McKee believed the retention of these lands by the Indians essential to the accomplishment of the larger objective. The achievement was indeed formidable.[145] The surrender, for the sum of £1200 Quebec currency, constituted no less than the territory of southwestern Ontario! A real-estate transaction of this magnitude required such solemnity and care that it was witnessed and signed by twelve regular officers, three militia officers, an officer of Indian Affairs, five civilians, and thirty-five Indians representing the Ottawa, Chippewa, Pottowatomi, and Huron. In effect, it empowered the British administration to proceed with the business of settlement and British surveyors set to the task.

British Surveys: Pre-1800

Unlike the detailed surveys that were to follow, the initial surveys were exploratory. Their purpose was to describe for the authorities the possibilities for settlement, in general situational terms, as well as reporting on the feasibility of implementing the various plans which the Surveyor General's Office had devised to meet the political expediencies of government. For Essex, they were undertaken by the Irish-born Patrick McNiff[146] and, to a lesser extent, the American-born Abraham Iredell.[147]

Within a month, McNiff, under the orders of Patrick Murray, the commandant of the British post at Detroit, proceeded to make a

Plate 2.9   Sir Frederick Haldimand, governor of Quebec, 1777–86.
Courtesy of National Archives (c3221).

coastal survey of the north shore of Lake Erie from Long Point westward.[148] His report was phrased in terms of accessibility, quality of the
vegetation and its association with soil quality, and prior existing settlement hindering development. Good land behind Long Point and
running northeast, from Point-au-Pins carried bass, black walnut, hard
maple, yellow and white sand, stands of chestnut, and scrubby oak.

Plate 2.10   McNiff's survey.
Courtesy of National Archives (NMC 16,996).

The sand banks from Point-au-Pins to Long Point precluded settlement, there being no harbours where even light boats could enter
except the rivers Tonty and à la Barbue. Westward for thirty-seven
miles towards Point Pelée, a bank fifty to a hundred feet high limited
accessibility. From here, for some sixteen miles of Essex shore to the
New Settlements being established for the disbanded Loyalists, accessibility to the lake was limited by a twelve-mile-long high bank or, on
the east side of Point Pelée, by marshy conditions (Plate 2.10).[149] In
spite of this, the Lake Erie shore of what soon would be designated
Essex County was assessed as "Good." Within it, however, prior settlement would prohibit the implementation of the schemes[150] devised by
government for the settlement of its new territory. Additionally, property rights accorded individuals before the McKee purchase would
prescribe the proper location and size of a town suitable for promoting settlement.

    Either the instructions of the board were not sufficiently clear (as
McNiff claimed) or the deputy surveyor simply could not or chose
not to understand them, but it was not until August 1790 that he

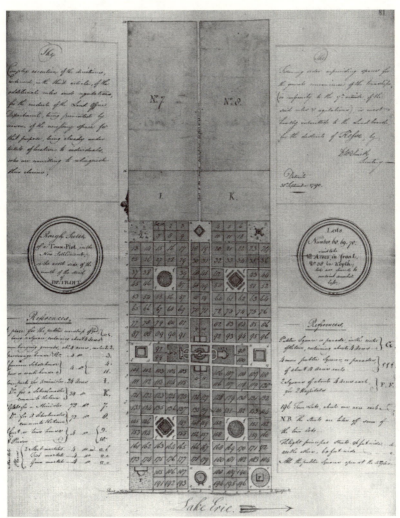

Plate 2.11   Town plot of Colchester. An early example of Canadian urban planning,
it made provision for public squares, a church, a burying ground, a prison, a schoolhouse, and a parsonage. The ideal was not totally realized.
Courtesy of National Archives (c144947).

began to lay out what became the Township of Malden[151] and the
"New Settlement". The latter, subsequently designated the "Two
Connected Townships," were to become the townships of Colchester
and Gosfield.[152] The board reported to Lord Dorchester that these

had been surveyed by October (although not completed in terms of the land regulations),[153] submitting at the same time a rather grand plan for a town (Plate 2.11) as was required by the government's land regulations.[154] It also noted that, owing to the surveyor's indisposition, the surveys of the Thames River, although requested, had not been completed. By May 1791, no single survey had been fully completed. The board seized the opportunity to complain that the lack of progress in this district was the fault of the Surveyor General's Office and its representative, McNiff. It noted that "my Lord Dorchester cannot expect from this board any progress towards the Settlement of the District, until enabled to do it by the proper aids from the Surveyor-General's office and its deputy. The board has not only no general plan of the district, but has no official delineation of any portion of it in which to grant allotments agreeable to the additional instructions."[155]

Meanwhile, since the members could not form themselves into a quorum, the Land Board did not meet and so was unable to respond to requests that McNiff twice made for the stationery needed to put down his surveys.[156] When it did meet on 7 December 1790, "the Board took the same into consideration and after deliberating thereon, do not find themselves warranted to take measure for the furnishing of the required stationary, not having any special or general direction on that head and wishing to avoid any interference between the Surveyor's Office and its Deputys, which would seem the most natural channel, for equipments of the above nature."[157]

Following this complaint, McNiff hastened to record the results of his surveys in 1789 and 1790[158] and complete the bearing of the La Tranche (Thames) for seventeen and a half miles.[159] Both parties continued to complain of one another, to protect their respective interests, to issue minor threats, and, above all, to seem to defer to higher authority in the form of the Surveyor General's Office or the governor. In his surveys north from Lake Erie to Lake St Clair and from the Canard eastward in August 1791, McNiff's progress was hindered by extensive marsh and swamp. In spite of several attempts to circumvent the marshland, he concluded that, in the light of it, and given the authorized mode of survey, extensive settlement in the interior was not possible. He therefore decided to extend his earlier work in the New Settlement to a second concession and to extend the survey of the Lake Erie shore to Point Pelée.

Finding myself unable after various attempts and many days' hard Labour, to effect the object of my Instructions, and rather than return immediately with the party, thought it best while here, to lay out the land in front, from my last Survey East ward to the bottom of Point aux Pele, as also the front of the second Concession and last Survey where the land would admit of it. But this being no part of my Instruction, still I flatter myself, from my own Knowledge of the wishes of the Land Board to promote the Interests of the Crown, in forwarding Surveys of the Country, I will be held Blameless. My late Surveys, etc. I am ready to lay down, and deliver for use of the Board as soon as the Board will enable me to do it, by furnishing me with drawing paper and Led pencils for that purpose.[160]

His efforts were of little avail to him; the complaints continued, the board laying responsibility for the lack of settlement at the door of the Surveyor General's Office and McNiff and "seeking the support of two, or more, active and willing Surveyors for at least one Season."[161] In the absence of a favourable response, the board again turned to McNiff in the spring of 1792, using his services to assist in sorting out conflicts arising over title to lands. The front and side lines of L'Assomption, along the Detroit River, were, the board admitted, "in great Confusion and irregularity." The inhabitants were to register their deeds and his survey here and along the St Clair to the mouth of the Thames was to be the mechanism by which "the differences and deviations between the usurped and the ceded ones will be ascertained."[162] Upon its completion,[163] he was then ordered to Petite Côté to mark out road allowances along the northern boundary of the reserve at the Canard, and to lay out the second concession. This was to satisfy the inhabitants who had requested an extension of their lands in the front of Sandwich Township.[164] This he attempted to do, but he was prevented from completing the second concession by marshes associated with the Canard which were impassable on foot or in a boat. Although he found several families, he concluded that "this concession can only be deemed useful for the wood on it, the land being of no value."[165] His comments on the third and fourth concessions of Petite Côté, which he attempted to survey seven months later in the winter of 1792, were just as negative. He encountered swamps and a beaver pond, both unfrozen, where "the timber was water ash and small elm, the bottoms white clay, mixed with sand, if even they could be drained, the soil is not worth the expence, nor is the timber growing thereon used for Fuel ..."[166]

By January 1793 he had extended the division line between the Huron reserve and the church lands in L'Assomption and measured the third concession (the first of a new township to be formed, that is, Sandwich South). Here he again encountered the Grand Marsh, which he showed on his plan as an extensive tract.[167] Proceeding east because of the volume of water, he examined the land for almost twenty miles to the sources of the Belle and Ruscom rivers. Now, in what would become Maidstone and Rochester townships, he reported that "the land at different places in that distance is exceeding good, but much cut in pieces with small marshes and Swamps at the Sources of those Rivers, the timber on the good land, Maple, Bass and Button-wood, the soil black and deep, but am of the opinion that in many parts of the Country Water will very difficult to be procured in dry seasons."[168]

In February, he was back in this area at the instigation of a board dis-appointed at his initial findings (and at the manner in which the survey was executed),[169] examining the Peche, Puce, Belle, and Ruscom rivers. He reported them navigable for between two and six miles. He recommended changes to the established order of survey to accommodate the optimum number of farms.[170] He repeated his by now familiar comment on the swampiness of the land, in this instance, the third, fourth, fifth, and sixth concessions of Sandwich. The third concession, perhaps the most accessible and therefore the most likely part of the nine-mile stretch which he surveyed to be settled, was found to be "chiefly low wet land few lots fit for culture."[171] Within a month, he was reporting on his survey of the Thames River[172] in neighbouring Kent County,[173] but his career as a British surveyor was fast drawing to a close. He had lost the support of Colonel Richard England at Detroit and Lieutenant Governor Simcoe thought him incompetent and impractical. Even as he reported to England on set-tlement on the Thames, Petite Côté, and L'Assomption in the fall of 1794 he had been declared redundant[174] and the dissolution of the land boards in November ensured his demise.[175] He was refused further employment in Essex, and after England marched his troops out of Detroit in July 1796, he opted for the United States,[176] from where he continued to offer his services for land in Essex as well as Michigan.[177] He had already been replaced in June 1795 by Abraham Iredell, who was to complete the survey of the coast of Essex before others carried survey and settlement into the interior.[178]

Iredell, who was middle-aged when he began the task of surveying in Essex, had considerable experience as a deputy surveyor near Philadelphia and in New Brunswick before moving to Newark in 1793.[179] He was soon engaged in a number of surveys in the Niagara peninsula and in the western country. Like McNiff, he, too, was to become embroiled in controversy in this area, charged, in his role as surveyor, in assisting the fraudulent acquisition of land by known speculators.[180]

It was Iredell who completed the survey of Malden ordered by Simcoe on 8 January 1793 and awarded to the Indian Department officers. By 17 April 1796, he had resurveyed the area with which Fry had originally been involved in 1785, adding to the nineteen lots along the river front an additional eighty-four.[181] That same year, he completed his work along the coast in what were to be Maidstone and Rochester townships,[182] the front in Gosfield Township,[183] and part of Sandwich,[184] where he was stopped by the Indians who claimed not to have sold the land beyond the Canard (Figure 2.1).[185] He extended official knowledge into Mersea with whose east coast he was again to become acquainted in 1798.[186] Between January and July 1797, he was checking on McNiff's work in Sandwich[187] and surveying the Indian reserve.[188] He was to return here in December of the following year to survey the town plot after the Indian reserve had been purchased from the Huron[189] and again in 1799.[190] In 1797 he was at work in Colchester Township as well as Tilbury and Dover and Raleigh in adjoining Suffolk and Kent counties.[191] Iredell was the first to survey Tilbury West,[192] laying out nine lots as part of his survey of the Lake Erie shore in 1798, and his extension eastward into Mersea completed the British knowledge of the coastal areas of Essex.[193] Quite how spatially extensive his surveys were is not certain because of incompleteness of the cartographic and documentary record. He is known to have been responsible for the completion of the second and third concession of L'Assomption between 1797 and 1799, although, of course, McNiff had penetrated at least part of the way.[194] He completed the survey of Malden Township,[195] but Carroll would rework lots 64 to 94 in 1831.[196] He completed the first concession of Mersea Township in 1798, including its subparts A to D, leaving the more northerly concessions to be finished by his successor, Thomas Smith.[197] Because of the circumstances of his appointment and the official distrust of the work of his predecessor, he reworked the latter's surveys in Colchester, Gosfield,[198] Sandwich, Maidstone, and Rochester townships. On the basis of the cartographic evidence, it could be argued that Iredell established the Gore lots and concessions two to five of the western part of Colchester,[199] five concessions in Tilbury West,[200] and south to the Middle Road in Rochester and Maidstone townships.[201] However, in his letter to Chewett and Ridout in 1803 concerning surveys in the larger Western District, Iredell remarked, "You mentioned that the front and rear boundary lines have already been established; it is not the case in some of the Townships in this District i.e. Chatham, Rochester, Colchester from the Reserve to Gosfield East and West, Mersea, Romney, Raleigh, Harwich and Howard on Lake Erie, there has been no second Concession Lines run."[202]

This provides the necessary limits in all but Maidstone and Roch-

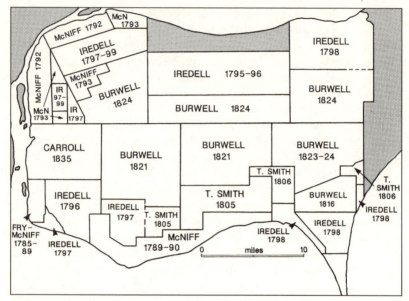

Figure 2.1   Lands known to be surveyed and available or occupied, Essex County
Source: AO and DLF Surveyors' plans. Notebooks,and Letters.

ester townships where the precise extent of the Iredell survey remains
unclear. It is portrayed as such on Figure 2.1, which seeks to show
where lots were first demarcated on the ground. In these townships, if
two concessions are interpreted as the "distance of two concessions"
from the coast, then the available lots (if not already pre-empted prior
to official survey) lay within the possible limit, which in turn must
largely correspond with the limits of the earlier McNiff survey in the
area. In other words, neither the McNiff nor Iredell survey reports or
plans permit the precise location of the lots they surveyed. Still, it
seems certain that by 1796 at least the coastal parts of Rochester and
Maidstone were open to settlement. Indeed, as a result of the exertions of these men, all of coastal Essex had been opened up. In Sandwich Township the British had resurveyed the lots which, at least theoretically, had been settled under seigneurial tenure beginning in
1749. Here they proceeded to resolve property conflicts and to extend
the French long lots into the second and third concessions.

British Surveys after 1800

After the initial surveys of the 1790s, the work of completing the survey
was carried out by Thomas Smith[203] between 1805 and 1806 and in the

1820s by Mahlon Burwell. By the turn of the century, surveying was becoming more institutionalized; surveyors were having to complete more detailed accounts, diaries, and field notebooks. Smith's records provide insights into the problems that surveyors faced. These may be summarized as: 1) problems of supplies in the form of paper and pencils (in this respect both Iredell and Smith tended to be much less vocal than McNiff had been, presumably because they faced fewer problems); 2) problems of hiring and retaining the services of survey crews, especially given better opportunities in the market (it was perhaps for this reason that many of the surveys were conducted in the spring when the cost of labour was lower and the potential labour pool greater); 3) dishonesty – many, given money and supplies as retainers, simply did not honour their commitment or return the advances made; 4) illness. There can be little doubt that the work was demanding, involving long hours of tedious toil conducted in forest and swamp accompanied by rain or mosquitoes and blackflies, but the clauses in their agreement permitting them two days' supplies to return to the place of commencement may have hastened the onset of illness.

Smith's survey of Colchester and Gosfield townships, conducted in 1805 and 1806, is indicative.[204] Having advertised for eight men and offering "generous wages," he found that none would work for less than six shillings per day and a full ration of provisions. However, on 13 April, he managed to engage five men at half a dollar per day (41.6 per cent of the amount demanded above) and full provisions (not to be weighed or measured) and half a pint of whiskey per day. The ingredients of the ration were not specified but they commonly included one pound of pork at a cost of two shillings, biscuit at six pence per day, flour at two and a half pence per day, and the whiskey. In that spring of 1805, he had to pay two individuals (James Lockhart and John Quick) four and six shillings respectively per day, presumably including rations. He quickly discharged them after searching in the adjoining township for cheaper labour, but when he came to assemble a party for the upcoming season he found that in addition to the "normal" terms he had to agree to larger rations of flour and an advance of one month's wages to each member of the party, one of whom immediately disappeared with it. His agreement of 21 April 1806 provides more information on emerging labour relations in the backwoods.[205] It required the men, all illiterates, to "hold themselves in readiness and to set off on the service aforesaid on the first notice, and to continue in the same until regularly discharged. To have particular care of provisions, axes, kettles, tents, bags etc. so that nothing be lost, wasted or destroyed. and to be faithful, diligent and obedient in all which they may be commanded."[206]

The new contract provided for a pay increase to 3 shillings and three halfpence of provincial currency, or five shillings York, per day, to the men in general, although chainmen would receive a half shilling (six pence) extra per day. Rations were to consist of one pound of pork per day, two pounds of flour, and a half pint of whiskey. Additionally, there was to be one month's advance in wages.[207] Interestingly, the contractor was worse off than some of his employees. Smith claimed to have made £9.15.7½ Provincial[208] for three months' service, which works out at two shillings and four pence per day or the equivalent of three shillings and six pence York. His chainmen enjoyed five shillings and nine pence York per day and the signing fee of one named Laplante had been six pounds, in advance! Gains for labour included a provision of one day's pay in the event of sickness and sufficient rations to get home. A managerial gain amounted to a performance bond; errors by the chainmen would result in the loss of wages and rations although the arbitrator of this was to be the surveyor general and not the deputy surveyor. In spite of these enhanced provisions, Smith had problems hiring. In June 1806 he was unable to hire at all because he could not compete for the services of harvest labourers who were then enjoying the equivalent of five shillings (presumably Provincial) per day plus provisions.[209]

Smith had difficulties with personnel; the circumstances of survey did not protect him or his employer, the surveyor general, from abuse. On 4 May 1805, having discharged John Quick owing to illness, he noted that "I find it inconvenient if not impossible to follow the Surveyor-General's Instruction in the case of Quick or any other discharged in the Field where it may happen that no respectable witness may be had to witness the pay lists within 20 miles – and – if such persons should have received money in advance to purchase necessaries (which generally is the case) – the surveyor may not see them both again, and therefore loses the money paid in advance and the ration."[210]

Thus, one Langavin (more probably Langevin) deserted him with a sixteen shillings' advance in April 1806 and J. Voisin did the same on 6 June. Drunkenness was a frequent problem and on one occasion he removed his crew from town, presumably to minimize the consequences. It rained constantly and there were complaints of foot problems. There was a constant effort to replace those who were ill or had deserted. Between 13 April and 21 May 1805, he hired fifteen people but by the 21st he had discharged seven of them. During the survey season of 1805 and 1806, he was replacing a man every seven days on average. On occasion, it could be the whole crew that was replaced, and on other occasions it was impossible to hire a single individual.

Even Smith himself tired; on 28 May 1805 he noted on his survey of Gosfield: "Rain. The party having 5 days like the two former, are unwilling to serve any longer – no appearance of another party coming to relieve. The Chain men having sore feet and wore out with fatigue. The excessive bad weather which the Chain and myself have endured since the commencement of the survey. The woods full of water-marsh not passable and provisions scarce. I came to a determination of quitting the survey until a more favourable season."[211]

That came in 1806 and by June of that year he reported the completion of his work in the three townships of Colchester, Gosfield, and Mersea, finding no more than a third habitable. The account he gave offers further evidence of the difficulties he and his kind faced in conducting their business but his report was hardly conducive to the promotion of settlement. He found "extensive swamps and marshes, perilous places in thickety and the water throughout stagnant and verminous. The surveyor has not been able to keep a party two weeks complete for sickness. McNiff and a party of Soldiers of the 5th Regt. attempted to run a line from Lake Erie to Lake St. Clair about the year 1790. Some of the men died in the woods; others afterwards in Hospital. himself [sic] never recovered to perfect Health and without affecting the business."[212] This is a much more empathetic view of McNiff than the one of him held by the members of the Land Board or the administration in general.

Smith carried the task of survey inland from the coast.[213] His efforts would seem to have satisfied the demands for land in the interior until the 1820s when the task of expansion was entrusted to Mahlon Burwell.[214] Burwell, who in the closing years of his life was to be a politician of considerable import, began his career as a surveyor, a profession that allowed him to be recompensed for his services with a percentage of the land in the townships he surveyed. His bid was invariably 4.5 per cent and by this method he is known to have received at least 39,759 acres, not including compensation for eighteen surveys on which the record is silent.[215] In 1821 he began a marked association with the townships of Essex, where he was to receive 11,494 acres for his efforts.[216] As a result of this experience, and similar work elsewhere, he was by 1825 perhaps the most experienced surveyor of the time, having completed the survey of all or part of twenty-four townships in southwestern Ontario. By 1834, he was to have completed an additional twenty-five for a total of forty-nine surveys or re-surveys.[217] This was a remarkable accomplishment and the basis of considerable wealth.[218] Yet, the work was physically demanding and stressful because of bad weather and insufficient resources to pay, shelter, and feed his men. These hardships would take their toll on Burwell, who

Plate 2.12   The Hon. Thomas Talbot, Anglo-Irish soldier and aristocrat, *c.* 1852.
By James B. Wandesford. Watercolour.
Courtesy of McIntosh Gallery, University of Western Ontario (gift of Judge Talbot
MacBeth).

would develop such severe rheumatism that he would eventually ask to be relieved of his duties.[219]

According to a newspaper report in 1833, Burwell had not much more than twelve months of schooling, and when he decided to take up surveying he had little formal training in it.[220] He failed to meet the provincial requirements as a surveyor in 1805, the year in which Smith was beginning his work in Colchester.[221] However, he acquired the necessary skills to use a circumferentor and the Gunther chain.[222] Because of his personal connection with Colonel Thomas Talbot (Plate 2.12) he was employed by the provincial government in 1809.

Beginning in 1811, he surveyed the Talbot Road, long considered the best road in Upper Canada and an enduring testimony to his skills as a surveyor.[223] Work on this was interrupted by the War of 1812, during which he served as a lieutenant-colonel, and it was not until after the cessation of hostilities that he completed its survey through Mersea Township.[224] Ultimately, he would carry this road north and west through the interior of the township, following, at least in part, an earlier Indian trail and an even older beach line, and in 1824 he reached Sandwich.[225] The Talbot Road, which disrupted the neat pattern of survey in several of the townships, was the main artery of communication throughout the period studied here and indeed remained so into the present century. The Mersea portion constituted the first of Burwell's work in Essex. In February 1823 he reported that he had established the rear boundaries of Sandwich, Colchester, Gosfield, Maidstone, Rochester, Tilbury West, and Mersea. Using this as a governing and proof line, he had run the township lines except for the Colchester/Gosfield line, where he was stopped by a large and deep marsh. He finished the Middle Road that same year and, as he wrote, he had two parties in the woods exploring for the Middle Road from Raleigh (Kent County) to Tilbury and the same road through Rochester and Maidstone.[226]

His work was characterized by devotion to detail in spite of the trying circumstances under which it was completed. The survey notes of interior Sandwich, Rochester and Maidstone,[227] Tilbury, Colchester, Gosfield,[228] and Mersea – created between 1821 and 1824 – are meticulous and his plans set a new standard for accuracy, clarity, and completeness. This represented the last of Essex to be surveyed for some years since Anderdon Township, as it would become, was still an Indian reserve. With its surrender and survey, the task of surveying Essex was effectively finished although some tasks remained to engage others.[229] The survey of Anderdon Township, in 1835, was entrusted to Peter Carroll since Burwell was, by his own admission, no longer physically capable.[230]

Figure 2.1 shows that Burwell surveyed more than any other surveyor in the county. In fact, his work was even more extensive because the purpose of the map is to show which parts were first available for settlement. Areas that he surveyed are attributed on this map to earlier surveyors who first laid down lines on the land. Indeed, the history of survey in this and other areas of Upper Canada is one of continuous reworking, consequent upon human disaffection, simple error, administrative inefficiency, and the trying circumstances in which these enterprises were conducted.[231]

Burwell appears to have acted with great propriety although engaged in a business where large fortunes stood to be made. In 1826 and 1828, finding several individuals stealing lumber, including white pine, he posted notices warning of the punishments that would befall such persons upon conviction and made an inventory of those he considered legitimate settlers.[232] Although required by Executive Council resolution,[233] such devotion was commendable when others might have taken advantage of the situation. His predecessor, McNiff, himself a land speculator on what became American territory, did not hesitate to denounce the "extravagant claims" of the members of the local elite.[234] There is the suggestion that even Iredell may have been corrupted by members of the Land Board, acquiring lots for them under various *noms de plume*.[235] He certainly acted on behalf of John Askin in this regard, as will be shown later. In these instances, the image of the King's surveyor is not without tarnish but Burwell appears, in the words of his first biographer, as "a modest and faithful servant, and as a dignified and highminded man."[236]

Problems of Maintaining the Grand Design

Even as the surveyors began their work, they discovered that the best-intended plans designed by authorities remote from the field were difficult to implement on the ground. The plans of the Surveyor General's office, requiring the creation of townships of a particular geometry, were designed to assist in the organization of the new territory but they changed through time as the nature of that territory became apparent.[237] Initially, Haldimand, the governor general, believed townships of six miles square to be ideal and his instructions specified the acreage to be granted and the size and number of lots per concession. He wrote, "I propose to grant to each Family, vizt.120 acres, of which six are to be in front, which will make 19 chains in front and 63 Chains and 25 links in depth – so that every Township will have 25 lots in front and four Chains 75 links will remain for a Road by which Distribution each Township will contain 175 lots of 120 acres."[238]

The idealized plan envisioned in remote Quebec could not always be met in the light of the physical realities of Upper Canada. There were frequent departures from this plan and its most frequent variants were the "interior" model, calling for a township of ten by ten miles, and the "coastal" model, a rectangle nine by twelve miles (Figures 2.2 and 2.3).[239] In Essex, only two townships followed any of these models with respect to size, namely, Colchester and Gosfield; all other township dimensions were irregular. Similarly, the plans to establish the reserved lands, required by the Constitutional Act of 1791, according to sets of mathematical tables and the various locational models of D.W. Smyth, the surveyor general, had often to be modified to allow for the fact that settlement sometimes preceded survey, no matter how undesirable this was.

The word "special" in Appendix 2.6 testifies to the fact that in Essex changes were made to the established order so frequently that the "approved" systems, the single- and double-front systems of the 1790s and 1820s, were less regularly found than the deviant or modified subsets. These plans called for different numbers of lots per concession and side roads at different spacing. In the single-front system, the township was to be six miles square, seven concessions deep and twenty-five lots wide. The lot dimensions were to be roughly either 19 by 63 chains or 19 by 105 chains, yielding respective acreages of approximately 120 and 200. In Maidstone and Rochester townships, the base line of the early surveys was run along the interior of the Lake St Clair inlet rather than following the Lake St Clair shore. This permitted the use of the then prevailing single-front system, and the lots along, for example, the Pike, Puce, Belle, and Ruscom rivers have at least one dimension equal to what was required by this model. Some of the north-south running concessions adhere to both dimensions. However, only Rochester meets the requirement of seven concessions (Maidstone has nine); these are of different sizes and run orthogonal to the coast. Moreover, the lot dimensions are sixty-six by thirty chains, dimensions diagnostic of the double-front system, hardly surprising since that is what Burwell instigated when he surveyed here and neighbouring Maidstone in 1823–24. The Middle Road, which runs through both townships, and the Talbot Road, running north and west through southern Maidstone, further complicate the survey pattern and ensure that no single label can be applied to describe the survey type in these townships. Additionally, Maidstone is ten miles from north to south and 7.7 miles wide; Rochester is six miles wide and, along its eastern boundary, nine miles long. In size terms, both Colchester and Gosfield meet the stipulation that coastal townships be approximately nine by twelve miles, and in their northern extensions,

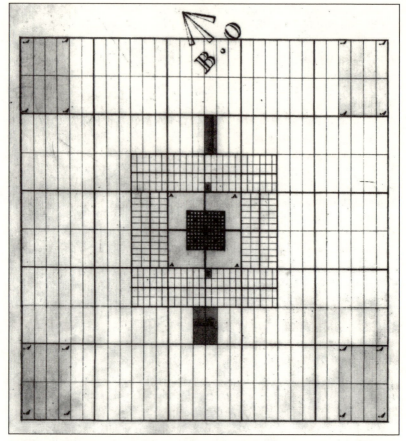

Figure 2.2   Plan of a town and township of ten miles square
Source: NAC, NMC–276.

with the exceptions of the Malden[240] and Talbot Road South, their lots conform to the almost sixty-seven by thirty chain dimensions of the double-front system. However, their administrative history, along with the need to adjust to the physical environment while surveying and to accommodate prior locations, earned for these otherwise "double front" townships the epithet "special." Sandwich Township (Figure 2.4) with its relics of French seigneurial tenure in the long lots, more regular lots characteristic of later British surveying practice, a special survey for the Talbot Road, and a gore laid out to accommodate different orientations in survey, epitomizes this deviance. In fact, in Essex as a whole, there are more exceptions to the rule of order than there is adherence.

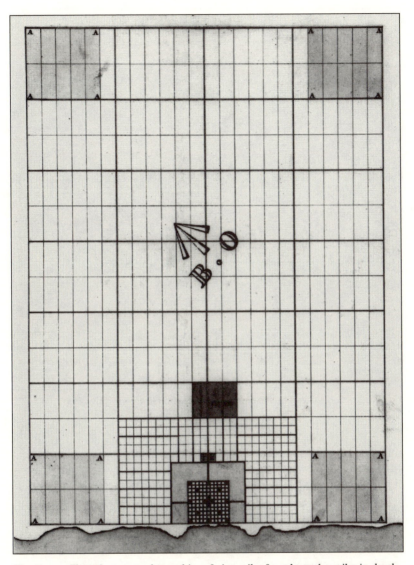

Figure 2.3   Plan of a town and townships of nine miles front by twelve miles in depth
Source: NAC, NMC–272.

Yet all of this was of little consequence to the settler who arrived
after about 1800 when single- and double-front systems were in vogue;
prior to this date, the French seigneurial form in Sandwich and its
extension into coastal parts of Colchester and Gosfield Townships had
promoted a greater propinquity. The size and shape of the lots pro-

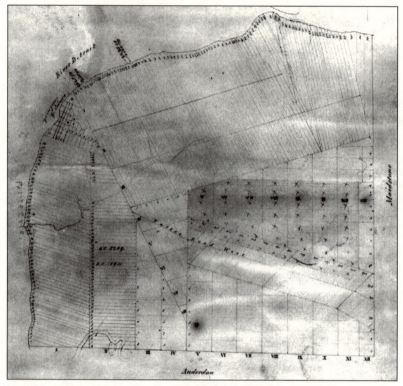

Figure 2.4   Thomas Parke, "Survey Grid, Showing the Reserves," July 1843.
Source: AO 4815, C277–1–365–0–5

duced in the second period seems to have provoked no controversy whatsoever. This was not so of the reserved lands, which were a continuous source of social and political aggravation throughout the first half of the nineteenth century. Even their establishment on the ground was fraught with difficulty.

Part of the problem of surveying and settling this and other areas was the relative newness of the administrative structure and the geographical remoteness of the executive and the Surveyor General's Office from the surveyor in the field. In the abstract scheme of things, the distance problem was to be overcome by the institution of land boards, but until their authority and role was fully known, indecision was inevitable. The surveyor referred a problem to the members of the Land Board, who, when unable or unwilling to resolve the issue, referred it to higher authority in Quebec. Quebec, for its part lacking local familiarity, supposedly the advantage of the Land Board, referred it back to the local area. These problems, characteristically colonial, were compounded (or at least appear to have been compounded) by deference to authority and human frailty. The "pencil and paper" affair is illustrative. Quebec, concerned at the lack of progress in settlement, pressures the Land Board of Hesse. The board blames the surveyor (McNiff) and the Surveyor General's Office for its lack of direction.[241] McNiff blames the board for its failure to provide the necessary materials. The board, denying that its role is to provision the surveyor, refers the matter to Quebec. In the ensuing delays, many potential settlers left the area for the United States; pencils and paper were presumably available in Detroit!

Other problems stemmed from centralized planning, including, in the atmosphere of centralized control, the absence of a plan. The Land Board complained of this in October 1790.[242] On Friday, 3 June 1791, it required McNiff to explain why the survey of the Thames River, authorized on 11 and 12 August 1790, had not been conducted in accordance with the "General Plan of Survey, explained by the 9th and 10th articles of the Rules and Regulations of 17 February 1789, and the additional Rules and Regulations of 25 August same year."[243] In his reply McNiff reported how he had been ill but had in fact submitted his survey on 23 January 1791. In the first of these townships, he had found problems occasioned by the physical environment and prior occupation: "If the Land Board would even admit of carrying the present Standing order of Survey into execution, it could not be done without the Ruin and Removal of all the Inhabitants, already settled in that Space but had there been no inhabitants there, the standing order of Survey could not possibly be carried into execution, as there is scarcely one place in that Space, where 40 chains of dry Land can be had." In the second township, McNiff, "finding the River taking a much more Southerly direction ... could not take upon him to make a Change without the order of the board, and his Provisions being expended, found it requisite to decline the Survey, and returned to the Garrison."[244]

For similar reasons, McNiff was sceptical about implementing the survey plans of Quebec in the those parts of Sandwich, Colchester, and Gosfield upon which he reported in August 1791: "From the various traverses that I have made in that part of the Country, am of the opinion that in 3 townships that there will not be found 6 farm Lots in the 2nd Concession, if laid out agreeable to the Present mode of Surveys; still many good Farm lots might be had there, provided the Method of now laying out such lots could be dispensed with and settlers permitted to make their pitch where the land projects out in different angles into the marshes."[245]

This situation the board accepted even if it did not acknowledge his repeated request for "drawing paper and Led pencils."[246] In the same way, the deviation from the general rule of survey, which McNiff recommended for the St Clair shore in March 1793 so as to accommodate "half as many more settlers," was accepted by the board.[247] This resulted in a different orientation of the survey and the classification of the townships of Maidstone and Rochester as "special."

If these adjustments to the physical realities of the county did not produce much controversy, the establishment of the various categories of reserved land did. As early as 1791 McNiff identified this requirement as one of several reasons why the pace of settlement in this region had been slower than expected.

Another cause which at present greatly impedes the settling of this country [the District of Hesse] is the present standing order of survey for townships situated on navigable rivers and lakes; by that order of survey there are so many reserves made that only two farm lots can be granted in the front, two in the second and twelve in the third concession, a plan of survey in its nature so injurious to new settlers that none will consent to settle in the back concession and leave so great a quantity of woodland in their front through which they would at a greater expense and labour than new settlers can bear, have to make roads.[248]

In the townships surveyed by him on the Rivière la Tranche, he had found twenty-eight families settled in the front who had made considerable improvements and "should the present order of survey be carried into effect there it will remove every one of them from these Improvements."[249] The board recognized this problem and pointed out to the Legislative Council's land committee the speed with which a township could be surveyed if the land regulations were revised.[250] McNiff reiterated his comments in September 1791 when speaking of the need to locate the reserved lands of Malden and Sandwich in such a manner as not to conflict with the rights of settlers already located.[251] By the spring of 1792, this had become such an issue as to prompt the president of the board to examine its powers to dispense with the necessity of having reserves for town plots.[252] Problems of prior occupation concerned the board greatly and it recommended that:

The reserves and Restrictions of the present standing order of Survey, and an unwillingness to digress from it without authority, have prevented this board from being able to pay attention to the numerous petitions before it for Land, and we do not scruple to declare that unless it is dispensed with, the appointment of a Land Board in this District is almost negatory – for the people will not settle with rear Concessions, which for the most part are very swampy, while there remains any unlocated lots in the front – and they have made a pitch even on these reserves and improved thereon, from whence the board knows not how to remove them, could even such a measure be recommended.[253]

The Reserved Lands

The result of these remonstrations was the removal of the need to provide for town plots, which henceforth were allowed to emerge spontaneously from the circumstances of settlement, and the granting of permission to adjust the locations of the reserved lands to allow for local conditions.

What and where were these reserved lands whose establishment caused such difficulty? Basically, they bore three epithets – Crown, clergy, and Indian reserve. The controversy surrounding the existence of the first two in the early nineteenth century is reflected in the attention which the subject has received from historians. Both types of land have been the subject of numerous studies;[254] the authors of the two important works concerned with general land policy in Upper Canada have, of necessity, devoted considerable space to this topic[255] and Alan Wilson's scholarly work is expressly entitled *The Clergy Reserves of Upper Canada.*[256] The Indian reserves, as the name implies, were areas set apart for the use of the aboriginal signatories to treaties with the Crown;[257] in the present context, these were the Huron reserves specified in the McKee treaty. The effects of Indian reserves in the settlement process have, by contrast with the roles of the Crown and clergy reserves, been largely ignored, probably because of their limited occurrence in the landscape of Ontario and the lack of much material about them.

The authority for the creation of the clergy reserves, which Wilson has described as a Canadian mortmain,[258] was embodied in the Constitutional Act of 1791[259] whereby the governors of Upper and Lower Canada[260] were authorized to set apart an amount equal to one-seventh of the land granted at any one time for the support of a Protestant clergy. Following medieval precedent and more recent North American experience, these lands were regarded as inalienable, their benefits to the secular world being indirect in that they provided a source of revenue which would allow the church to continue its ministrations.[261] Thus the clergy reserves were truly locked as in a dead hand.

Under an instruction of 1791,[262] the lieutenant-governor of Upper Canada was authorized to create Crown reserves equal in number to

A PROCLAMATION,

To such as are desirous to settle on the lands of the crown in the Province of

UPPER CANADA;

BY HIS EXCELLENCY

John Graves Simcoe, Esquire;

Lieutenant Governor and Commander in Chief of the said Province, and Colonel
Commanding His Majesty's Forces, &c. &c. &c.

BE IT KNOWN to all concerned, that his majesty hath, by his royal commission and instructions to the governor, and in his absence the lieutenant
governor or person administering the government for the time being, of the
said Province of Upper Canada, given authority and command to grant the lands
of the crown in the same by patent under the great seal thereof; and it being expedient to publish and declare the royal intention respecting such grants and patents, I do accordingly hereby make known the terms of grant and settlement to be:

First.—That the crown lands to be granted be parcel of township: if an inland township, of ten
miles square, and if a township on navigable waters, of nine miles in front and twelve miles in depth, be
run out and marked by his majesty's surveyor or deputy surveyor general, or under his sanction and
authority.

Second.—That only such part of the township be granted as shall remain, after a reservation of one
seventh part thereof, for the support of a protestant clergy, and one other seventh part thereof, for the
future disposition of the crown.

Third.—That no farm lot shall be granted to any one person which shall contain more than two
hundred acres; yet the governor, lieutenant governor or person administering the government, is allowed and permitted to grant to any person or persons such further quantity of land as they may desire,
not exceeding one thousand acres, over and above what may have been before granted to them.

Fourth.—That every petitioner for lands make it appear, that he or she is in a condition to cultivate
and improve the same, and shall, besides taking the usual oaths, subscribe a declaration (before proper
persons to be for that purpose appointed) of the tenor of the words following, viz. " I A. B. do promise and declare that I will maintain and defend to the utmost of my power the authority of the king
in his parliament as the supreme legislature of this Province.'

Fifth.—That applications for grants be made by petition to the governor, lieutenant governor, or person administering the government for the time being, & where it is advisable to grant the prayer thereof a warrant shall issue to the proper officer for a survey thereof, returnable within six months with a plot
annexed, and be followed with a patent granting the same, if desired, in free and common soccage, upon
the terms and conditions in the royal instructions expressed, and herein after expressed.

Sixth.—That all grants reserve to the crown, all coals, commonly called sea coals, and mines of gold,
silver, copper, tin, iron, and lead; and each patent contain a clause for the reservation of timber for the
royal navy of the tenor following: ' And provided also, that no part of the tract or parcel of land here-
' by granted to the said   and his heirs, be within any reservation heretofore made and
' marked for us, our heirs and successors, by our surveyor general of woods, or his lawful deputy; in
' which case, this our grant for such part of the land hereby given and granted to the said
' and his heirs forever as aforesaid, and which shall upon survey thereof being made, be found within
' any such reservation, shall be null and void, any thing herein contained to the contrary notwithstanding.'

Seventh.—That the two sevenths reserved for the crown's future disposition, and the support of a
protestant clergy, be not severed tracts, each of one seventh part of the township, but such lots or farms
therein, as the surveyor-general's return of the survey of the township, shall be described as set apart for
these purposes, between the other farms of which the said township shall consist, to the intent that the
lands to be reserved may be nearly of the like value with an equal quantity of the other parts to be granted out as afore-mentioned.

Eighth.—That the respective patentees are to take the estates granted to them severally free of quit
rent and of any other expences, than such fees as are or may be allowed to be demanded and received by
the different officers concerned in passing the patent and recording the same, to be stated in a table authorized and established by the government, and publickly fixed up in the several offices of the clerk of
the council, of the surveyor general, and of the secretary of the Province.

Ninth.—That every patent be entered upon record within six months from the date thereof, in the
secretary's or register's offices, and a docket thereof in the auditor's office.

Tenth.—Whenever it shall be thought advisable to grant any given quantity to one person of one
thousand acres or under, and the same cannot be found by reason of the said reservations and prior grants
within the township in the petition expressed, the same, or what shall be requisite to make up to such
person the quantity advised, shall be located to him, in some other township, upon a new petition for
that purpose to be preferred.

And of the said several regulations, all persons concerned are to take notice, and govern themselves
accordingly.

Given under my hand and seal, in the city of Quebec, the seventh day of February, in the thirty-
second year of his majesty's reign, and in the year of our Lord, one thousand, seven hundred
and ninety-two.

John Graves Simcoe.

BY HIS EXCELLENCY's COMMAND,

THOMAS TALBOT, Acting Secretary.

Re-printed at Newark, by G. Tiffany, 1793.

Plate 2.13   The Royal Proclamation of 1792.
Courtesy of National Archives (RG1, E3, vol.87)

the Clergy reserves for the express purpose of raising "by sale or otherwise, a fund to be hereafter applied to the support of Government."[263] In this way, it was held, the continued allegiance of Britain's remaining colonies in North America could be assured.[264] Taxation had been a prime cause of the American revolution, and by guaranteeing the colonial government a continued source of revenue, the Crown reserves would remove a potential source of discontent.

Acting on these authorizations, Lieutenant Governor Simcoe issued a proclamation on 7 February 1792 (Plate 2.13) which defined the size of townships and of lots and specified the fees payable for land,[265] as well as the procedures to be followed in applying for land. Its second and seventh clauses, specifying that the Crown and clergy reserves should not be "severed Tracts each of One Seventh Part of the Township, but such Lots or farms therein ... between the other farms ... to the Intent that the Lands so to be reserved may be nearly of the like Value with an equal of the other parts to be granted,"[266] were not sufficiently exact prescriptions for the location of the reserves. It was left to the Surveyor General's Office primarily in the personage of the newly appointed D.W. Smith,[267] to establish the reserves on the ground in accordance with the various sizes and shapes of township that had been created or envisaged. Smith's personal inclination to meet the requirement of reserves was to produce six-mile-square townships designating each fourth and seventh township as Crown or clergy. This was not accepted, nor was his plan for a township containing twenty-eight lots, the Crown reserving 5, 6, 17, and 18, the clergy 11 and 12, 23, and 24 throughout the twelve concessions of a river township or the eleven of an inland one. This adaptation of the "garter parallelogram," which would have created two Crown and two clergy bands or garters in each township and which was already adopted in Lower Canada, was rejected.[268] There upon, Smith dutifully produced a scheme that, among other qualities, included the required scattering of lots. This was the now famous chequered plan (Figure 2.5), adopted on 15 October 1792.[269]

Had the land regulations sanctioned a morphology that mathematically permitted a multiple of seven, Smith would have had little trouble. This was the case in the scheme for twenty-eight lots which he had proposed (no doubt with the reserves in mind) but which had been rejected. It was also the case in the townships on the north side of Lake Ontario governed by older regulations than those issued in Lower Canada in February 1789. Here, the thirty-five lots in a concession produced a simple division into sevenths, without fractions.[270] Where, however, this was not the case – as in Colchester and Gosfield townships, which most closely resembled the nine-by-twelve-mile ide-

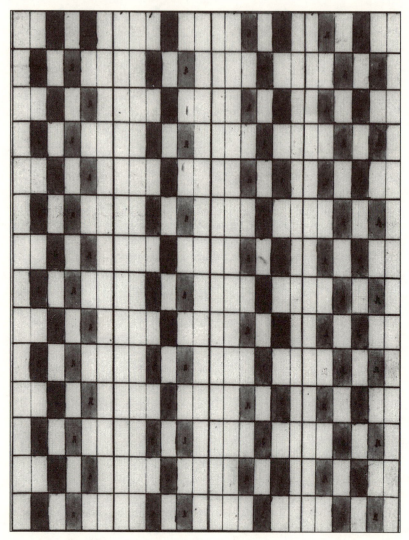

Figure 2.5   The chequered plan
Source: NA, NMC 286.

alized model of fourteen concessions and twenty-four lots (Figure 2.5)
– Smith had problems that he had to resolve. He did so by exceeding
the stipulation. In such circumstances:

comprehending 336 Lots; The two seventh parts of which, are 96 Lots which
is 6 Lots and 6/7th of a Lot in each Concession. But for the sake of uniformity,

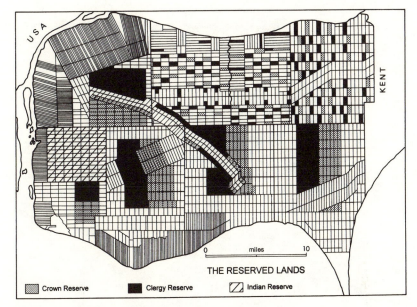

Figure 2.6   The reserves as established for Essex County
Source: Compilation of author, based on his "Documentary and Map Sources," 77.

as well as to sent too great a Subdivision, it was approved to be seven Lots in each concession thereby giving an additional Reserve of two Lots, in the whole Township more than what is required by Act of Parliament, which may be disposed of (in any situation before the specification is made up) should it be the interest or inclination of Governement so to do.[271]

His chequered plan (Figure 2.5) met the requirements that the reserves be offset with respect to each other either in the same or in the next concession, ensured that lots 1 and 24 were free of reserves so that the pattern could be maintained over a number of abutting townships, and maintained access via the concession roads which the survey planned every six lots. However, as a result of creating these avenues of "free" lots, the reserves had to be placed in ribbons in a combination of four, three, three, and four lots. This had the effect of leaving lots, which theoretically were available to settlement, cut off as oases in a sea of reserves. The net result might well be to inhibit development, but, given the conditions established by central government, it was perhaps the optimum solution.[272] Smith produced a set of "proof" tables to demonstrate the reasonableness of his solution and a set of polymetrical tables by which future surveyors completing even part of a township could assign reserves.[273]

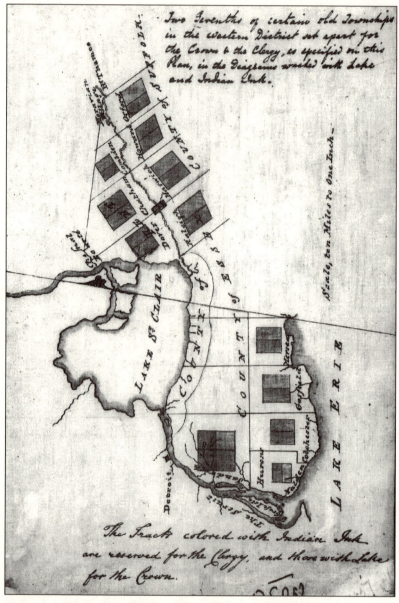

Figure 2.7   Two-sevenths of certain old townships

Source: NA, NMC 121271.

As Figure 2.6 shows, there was considerable difference between the orderliness envisaged in the Legislative Council and what was possible on the ground. Only in the three northern townships of Maidstone, Rochester, and Tilbury, where population was as yet negligible, was it possible to scatter the reserves and then, for a variety of reasons, only in a manner approximating the chequered plan.[274] Such irregularly surveyed areas were, in Smyth's own words, to "have their reserves as near as circumstances will admit upon the principles of the chequered plan."[275] In fact, in these areas the reserves fell short of the 28.56 per cent of the township upon which the chequered plan was premised.[276] Prior occupation negated the possibilities of establishing reserves according to the surveyor general's scheme unless the government was willing to accept the alienation and loss of large numbers of faithful subjects. In Lincoln County, the clergy reserves of eighteen townships were set apart in a single block behind Beverley and Flamborough townships.[277] Similar adjustments were to be made in the Home, Eastern, and Midland districts where reserves were to be located "partly in the rear Concessions of the Old Townships and partly in Bulk."[278] In the interests of consolidating settlement in the Western District, McNiff's advice was heeded and blocks of reserved land were also created as Crown and clergy Reserves in Sandwich, Malden, Colchester, Gosfield, and Mersea townships.[279] Figure 2.7 is a reproduction from the original report.[280]

INFLUENCES OF INFRASTRUCTURE: THE CONTEXT OF SETTLEMENT

Settlers entering Essex or any other part of Upper Canada had, as we have seen, to contend with government policy which made certain lands available only following surrender and survey or which withheld certain lands from the settler to support the prevailing political ideology. Additionally, they had to create the necessary infrastructure of roads and functional institutions to support their activity in pursuit of a livelihood. In Essex, as elsewhere, this was done by a mixture of private and government enterprise. Government provided the normal institutions of the state, the courthouses, jails, registry offices, post offices, and, most important, roads; individuals provided the buildings and fixtures required by their occupations. As such, they would not only experience the economic and social landscape but would ultimately play a role in its creation. The process was dynamic and not static but at least initially the settler had to view the environmental context in which decisions were to be made about the location of a farm, tavern, or blacksmith's shop (all termed establishments here) in

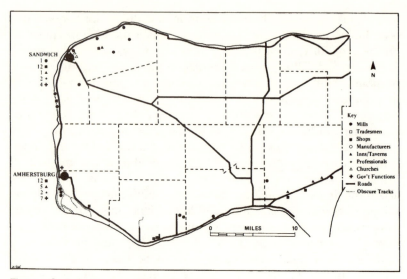

Figure 2.8   Infrastructure of Essex County, 1825

Source: J. Clarke and D.L. Brown, "Pricing Decisions for Ontario Land," 171–2.

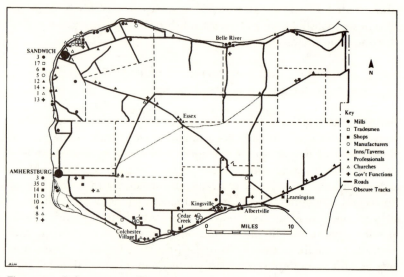

Figure 2.9   Infractructure of Essex county, 1845–52.

Source: J. Clarke and D.L. Brown, "Pricing Decisions for Ontario Land," 171–2.

static terms. Ultimately, adjustments might be made. Figures 2.8 and 2.9 respectively show the elements of the infrastructure that might influence such decisions as they existed at two points for which data are most readily available, namely, 1825 and 1847–52, including, within the latter, the census year 1850–52.[281]

The figures indicate that, by 1825 and continuing to mid-century, the largest concentration of establishments was in the towns of Amherstburg (Plate 2.14) and Sandwich. By 1852, these two towns would account for 167 of the 200 urban enterprises located in the county. Between 1825 and 1852, the number of establishments located in Amherstburg increased from 27 to 91. These 91 enterprises provided goods and services for a population of approximately 1000 people. Conversely, in the town of Sandwich, where there was a population of 500 people, there was a total of 76 different establishments. Obviously, the degree of concentration per unit of population was much higher in Sandwich than in Amherstburg. Generally, the period from 1826 to 1851 saw an increase in government functions in Sandwich; in Amherstburg government functions remained stable. This was also true of professional establishments: Sandwich gained thirteen establishments and Amherstburg two. It is interesting to note as well the parallel growth of taverns in Sandwich relative to professionals, though this is interpreted as association rather than causation!

Beyond Amherstburg and Sandwich, the distribution of establishments in both periods was similar. While by 1825 their numbers had increased markedly, their distribution remained coastal and tied to the road network. As appendix 2.6 illustrates, Windsor, with a population of 500 people, was the third most important centre. Demographically as important as Sandwich, the range and number of functions it provided was more limited, in a period in which it awaited the phenomenal growth of the late nineteenth and twentieth century. Ultimately, Windsor was to absorb Sandwich but in 1851 it was a relatively new centre, as effectively were all the others. The population of these villages or hamlets was small and the number of establishments in each never more than half a dozen. In 1851 Kingsville contained 100 people; Albertville, a few miles to the east, had another 100. While the population of the other centres is unknown, Rottenburg recorded that in Leamington 50 men and 10 horses could be billeted, in Colchester village 100 men and 25 horses, and in Essex Village 40 men and 10 horses.

There were three orders of centre in 1852. The first order included the towns of Sandwich and Amherstburg; the second order included Windsor, Colchester village, Cedar Creek,[282] and Kingsville; and the third order included Albertville, Essex, Belle River, and Leamington.

Plate 2.14   A view of Amherstburg. By Margaret Reynolds, daughter of Thomas Reynolds, commissariat officer at Detroit and Amherstburg.
Courtesy of Parks Canada, Fort Malden Historic Site.

All of these were important in the lives of a farm community and Essex remained in 1851 an overwhelmingly rural place, but they were also places to which one might resort infrequently to acquire a new dress or plough. However, it might well be that proximity to rural service in the form of the mill, the blacksmith's shop, or the church was as or more significant in everyday life.

SUMMARY

The settlement of Essex County took place under particular environmental, social, and political circumstances. Notions of social and political order were carried in the eighteenth-century Anglo-American culture to which Upper Canada was heir. These included the idea that society was ordered with respect to a monarch who was not absolute but who was nonetheless worthy of respect as part of a "balanced constitution" which had emerged from seventeenth-century struggle. There was an enduring natural order, or hierarchical structure, and a natural aristocracy or virtuous elite which could and should rule on behalf of the majority. To meddle with this was, in this conservative tradition, to provoke calamity and bloody revolution, as those who had lived through events in the United States and in France knew only too well, and as Scripture warned. It was the reciprocal responsibility of the church and the state to support one another. To this end, the Constitutional Act of 1791 recognized the role of the established Church of England, and that church was to be endowed with land to enable it to continue its traditional ministry to the sick, the poor, the uneducated, the dying, and those in need of salvation. Mankind was both a part of nature and set apart from nature by the capacity to reason, which invariably revealed the underlying order of creation. As a free spirit, man was acquisitive, and personal acquisition might be considered the mark of virtue; if not, the virtuous elite and those who had served the state might be endowed by the state with land, the essential basis of life and wealth. This was all part of the natural order.

Some of the ideas about the state are brought together in the following quotation from William Dummer Powell. He speaks of benevolent monarchy, loyalty, environmental endowment, the guidance of providence, human nature, the pretentiousness of Toronto, and the curse of elections:

When the mild and beneficent Government of the King of Great Britain was expelled from the Colonies of Great Britain in 1783, His Majesty devoted to the consolation of his loyal adherents the superb Territory of Upper Canada first in Climate, first in Soil, first in Water, of the habitable Globe. Providence seemed especially to protect its new population and render it the toast of the World, until the exalted feeling of its Legislature could no longer brook the diminutive Epithet of York, given to its Capitol by the Monarch's first Representative in grateful memory of what England was and shrinking from all of her glory have urged to the Seat of the King's Govt. the wild and terrific sound of TORONTO entailing upon its miserable Inhabitants the Annual Curse of a popular Election the power to call forth all the bad passions of human Nature.[283]

Beginning in 1785, Essex was systematically surveyed. The process was a lengthy one because European exploration of the area was just beginning and the landscape was not totally predictable. While there is little local relief (Figure 1.13), the surface was obscured by forest and fluctuating water levels meant that the early surveyors never knew when they might end up in swamp and their work terminated. Not only was much of this land being surveyed for the first time, but the interrelationships between the surveyor in the field, the Land Board for the District, and the Surveyor General's Office in Quebec City were also being established. The task was also complicated by human insecurity, by logistical and labour problems, and by the time lag involved in communicating with a remote administration. As a result, parts of several townships had to be surveyed a number of times by different surveyors. Yet, while this was costly in time and money, comparatively little error resulted. Given the rudimentary instrumentation, the nature of the terrain, and the physical regime in this area, it is incredible what was achieved here and elsewhere in the province.

By the end of the 1790s, all of coastal Essex had been surveyed by McNiff, Smyth, and Iredell. In Malden and Sandwich townships, survey had been extended well beyond the coast into interior concessions; even in Maidstone and Rochester, survey may have proceeded farther than is shown on Figure 2.1, which is cautious on the achievement of this period. After 1800, the work of survey was effectively completed by Smyth in the first decade of the century and by Burwell in the second and third. After 1826, when Burwell completed his work, only the Indian reserve in what would become Anderdon Township was unsurveyed and this was accomplished by 1835.[284]

In surveying these lands, every attempt was made to adhere to land regulations which specified the form of survey and the pattern of the reserved lands, but these theoretical requirements had to be altered in the face of the circumstances facing the surveyors. Because of prior occupancy in Sandwich, Colchester, and Gosfield townships, these areas contained a number of "special" surveys. Similarly, because of hydrological circumstances in Maidstone and Rochester, the earliest lots there had to be oriented differently to the "normal" pattern. In fact, in Essex there are more "special" circumstances than there are "normal" ones. In short, surveying in Essex came close to approaching the prescribed model but never achieved it; things were "orderly" but not wholly "ordered." It follows that, if none of the townships fitted the "coastal" or "interior" models perfectly, then the pattern of reserved lands could not follow the ideal model either. The chequered plan was itself a compromise and in Essex it was not perfectly implemented because of local circumstances, most especially prior occupancy which necessitated the creation of blocks of Crown and clergy reserves.

The reserves had been established to generate revenue. The first attempts to raise revenue came with the introduction of a system of leasing, initially proposed in 1795 and finally introduced in 1802. The reserved lands were to be leased for twenty-one years and the lease renewed every seven years, at which time the rent was progressively increased. In fact, little interest was shown in leasing the reserves, except initially by speculators who had no intention of improving the land, simply seeing these lots as sources of valuable timber or as desirable locations from which they might hope to profit as land values rose.[285]

Owing to dissatisfaction with the results of the leasing policy, the British government's refusal after 1817 to continue its support of the colonial government,[286] and the desire to end the controversy surrounding the existence of the Crown and clergy reserves,[287] the government in 1824 decided to sell the reserves once and for all to a newly established speculative corporation, the Canada Company. The clergy reserves, included at first, were subsequently removed from the agreement. They remained in the hands of a government body, the Clergy Corporation, until thrown open to purchase by an act of the imperial legislature in 1827.[288] The clergy reserves were attacked on the sectarian ground that they were designed for the support of a church whose numbers did not justify the privilege it enjoyed, and both they and the Crown reserves were described as undeveloped parcels of land that hindered the successful settlement of the province. By 1827, however, the sale of the Crown reserves to the Canada Company and the instigation of a sales policy for the clergy reserves meant that, at least in theory, these lands could no longer be regarded as effective barriers to settlement, although they might remain locally an irritant and for the state a political and religious issue. In fact, little is known of their fate in specific areas such as Essex. Almost a quarter of a century after Gates and Wilson produced their seminal work in this area, little is known of the impact of the Crown and clergy reserves on the ground. This, as several historians have suggested, is the ultimate test of whether or not they frustrated settlement. Who acquired them? Were they acquired at the same time as other properties and, if they were, did they develop at the same or slower rates? Were the lots closest to the road system, the urban centres, and the rural infrastructure taken first? These themes are addressed in a subsequent chapter, where the maps of the infrastructure in 1825 and 1852 (figures 2.8 and 2.9) prove useful in evaluating land prices and the relationship between surveying and settlement.

3 Acquiring Indian Land in the Era of the Land Boards

INTRODUCTION

The purpose of this chapter is to describe one mechanism by which land was acquired in this and other parts of Upper Canada in the early years of settlement. The chapter describes the difficulties involved in the acquisition of land from the native population, a process that in this area was old indeed, stretching back well into the French jurisdiction. Much of the chapter is based upon the records of the land boards established by the British administration. The records are not complete. They are scattered in a number of depositories[1] and transactions with the Indians cannot therefore be quantified in the way that other records allow. What is clear, however, is that land acquisition and speculation was frequent and extensive from the earliest times in Essex although the acreage involved remains uncertain. In qualitative terms these records permit insights into British views of the aboriginal population and its rights, at least in the geopolitical circumstances of the 1780s and 1790s. They also allow some judgment to be made on the consistency of the application of policy upon the privileged and more marginal of society, although it is assumed that these official records have in fact been cleansed of obvious prejudices. Finally, sufficient material has survived for the District of Hesse, of which Essex was a part, to gain substantive insight into the conflict between emerging British colonial policy and its implementation.

BRITISH POLICY AND INDIAN LAND

In 1763 a Britain that had newly acquired Canada was only too aware of problems with the Indians. The tribes of the Ohio and upper Great Lakes had broken out in rebellion both to ensure the survival of the "ancien regime" and as an act of desperation to preserve their lands and culture against the advance of the frontier.[2] The uprising began in May 1763 when the pro-French chief Pontiac besieged Detroit[3] and it soon spread to the Iroquois, traditional supporters of the British against the French. The British in 1763 were indeed worried. Their policy henceforth was to be one of placating the Indians and of forging the "Covenant Chain"[4] to ensure, in Robert Allen's words, "the preservation and defence of Canada through the use and assistance of His Majesty's Indian allies."[5] The initial phase of this centred around a general plan for the management of Indian affairs and trade through a series of imperial regulations. The first of these, the Royal Proclamation of October 1763, was the most significant and has become the "Magna Carta" of Canadian-Indian relations.[6] It was proclaimed by Sir William Johnson, the superintendent of Indian affairs, who since 1756[7] had been responsible for all matters relating to Indian policy in the American colonies.[8]

Johnson was acting upon the King's command and upon a letter of the "right honorable lords commissioners for the trade and plantations." The route of the King's command is significant. The expressed purpose of the proclamation was to create jurisdictions for newly acquired territory in Quebec, East and West Florida, and Grenada. In turn, these were to permit "our loving subjects" to "avail themselves, with all convenient speed, of the great benefits and advantages which must accrue there from to their commerce, manufacture and navigation."[9] The relationship was not one-sided because from the earliest contacts trade had been an important element in maintaining relationships between Amerindian and European. Indeed, trade had arguably given birth to military alliance.[10] Certainly, this had been the case with respect to British relationships with the Iroquois upon whom so much had and would rest in the struggle for the continent as a whole and Canada in particular. Johnson's secretary recognized this when he wrote, "Trade was the foundation of their Alliance or Connexions with us, it is the chief Cement which binds us together. And this should undoubtedly be the first Principle of our whole System of Indian Politics."[11]

This view was manifest in the Royal Proclamation. Having described the geographical boundaries of the "new territories," the document went on to reassure the King's subjects that representative institutions would be established "as near as may be agreeable to the laws of England." It also sought to ensure the active support of the military by rewarding service with land according to rank.[12] The remainder of the text, almost one-third of the document, was concerned with Indian matters. It sought to secure the continued friendship of the Indians by establishing limits on European expansion and securing a land base for the indigenous societies because "it is just and reasonable and essential to our interest and the Security of our Colonies that the several Nations or tribes of Indians with whom we are connected, and who live under our protection, should not be molested or disturbed in the possession of such parts of our Dominions and territories as, not having been ceded to, or purchased by us, are reserved to them or any of them as their hunting grounds."

Governors and commanders-in-chief were explicitly forbidden to make grants beyond the limits of their jurisdiction and "any lands whatever, which not having been ceded to or purchased by us as aforesaid, are reserved to the said Indians or any of them." The proclamation established a frontier between Indians and whites. It prohibited settlement where the native "interest" had not been "extinguished" and required those who had "wilfully or inadvertently seated themselves" upon Indian land to "remove themselves from such settlements." It prohibited private purchases of Indian land and required that all purchases be made by the representatives of and in the name of the King at a public assembly. All trade with the Indians was to be "free" although subject to the granting of a licence for which securities could be required. Essentially, the proclamation sought to reassure the Indian allies of the Crown, guarantee the conditions of trade, and allow the imperial "interest" room for expansion.[13]

In 1768 the Lords of Trade acknowledged the wisdom of limiting encroachment upon Indian land and dealing with abuse by traders. In doing so, they revealed the motives behind the proclamation as ones of immediacy and political necessity, acknowledging that the "necessity which appeared in the then State of our Interests with the Indians of making some immediate Provision against these two Causes of their Discontent induced the Proclamation of 1763."[14] Yet they could still envisage the extension of colonial control into the interior of the continent to promote population and the consumption of British goods, to secure the fur trade, to protect the old colonies from the Indians, to reduce the expense of presents and supplies, and lastly – presumably because the occupants were mainly French – to protect those already there.[15] The three most important posts in the interior were Detroit, Michilimackinac, and Niagara and of these "that at Detroit which is the great Center of Indian Commerce, situate among many numerous Tribes of Indians, and where a considerable Number of French remain under the Faith of the Treaty of Paris, does appear to us to be far the most important Object, not being confined merely to Convenience of any particular Colony but embracing every Advantage upon which the safety & Extention of our Indian Commerce do depend."[16] Within a few years the boundary between Indian and white had been extended to the Ohio.[17]

The demand for Indian land grew in defiance of royal authority[18] and reached such an extent that General Thomas Gage, the British military commander, felt the need in April 1778 to reiterate government policy, stipulating that all grants made by British commanders are "null and void; and of no value" and that Indian purchases made under the French regime were similarly invalid unless approved by the governor general of Canada. He also authorized dramatic and effective action against those in violation of this policy.

I am now to require of you, as soon as this is received annul and make void by Public Act every Concession made by Monsr. Bellestre [the French commandant at Detroit[19]] in the year 1760, every Grant made by any British Commander, without exception, and all Indian Purchases whatever or Indian Deeds, not obtained by the King's Permission and Authority – And that you do not suffer any Settlement to be made with the above Titles or any new Settlements to be begun on any Pretense whatever, and that you will pull down as fast as any Person shall presume to build up. And that you do seize and send down the Country all Persons who shall be endeavouring to settle among the Savages.

I imagine the Indians will set upon to talk to you upon these Subjects you will answer that the King is tender of their Property & has made regulations to prevent their being cheated and defrauded; That His Majesty has been induced to make these Rules upon the frequent Complaints of the Indians against the White People who have defrauded them of their Lands by making a few of them Drunk, & getting them in that Condition to give away their Country to the great Disgust of the rest of the Nation, and that by such means the Indians have represented that the White People have taken a great part of their hunting grounds. This has happened to many Indian Nations, and unless you stop it in the beginning at the Detroit, the same thing will happen here.[20]

And so, even in the year of capitulation, the process of making Indian grants was continuing. Henceforth, it was to cease but of course it did not. There are only a few recorded instances of such grants being made on what was to become the Canadian shore.[21] Although one of the most celebrated (the Schiefflin case) involved all of the worst ele-

ments of which Gage prophesied, namely, fraud and alcohol, the practice of securing land on Indian grant seems to have been sufficiently
common to require Lieutenant Governor Henry Hamilton in 1778 to
reassure Governor Haldimand at Quebec that British protocol was
being observed. Nonetheless, he had felt it necessary to grant temporary occupancy to some while asserting that "any buildings or fences
they should raise would be destroyed or removed whenever it was
thought necessary."[22] These words were seemingly sufficient to
quieten the governor, who himself on several occasions experienced
difficulty in reconciling official policy with local needs. In one
instance, where the procedures employed to secure land would not
have been upheld by the official protocol, he encouraged continuing
occupation and improvement by Indian officers with whom he must
have felt a common identification as "one who had served." By 1784,
Lieutenant Governor John Hay at Detroit felt moved to send a list of
those holding land under Indian grants. He had been advised to dis-
countenance these grants but the directive had come too late "to have
any effect since almost all the land between Lake Erie and Huron on
both sides the streight is claimed and a great part settled upon and
improved." Several had already built and improved these lands "who
have no other pretensions than the Indians' consent." Perhaps in an
effort to establish the full extent of the predicament, to unload the
problem and at the same time ingratiate himself, he reported that
"Captains Bird and Caldwell are of the number, at a place they call
Fredericksburg."[23] The problem was extensive.

The historian David L. Farrell, is of the opinion that along the
Detroit frontier the rules were bent to fit existing or desired condi-
tions. He estimates that, between 1763 and 1796, over 400 families
settled on Indian grants. In the area as a whole, the Ottawa alone had
granted 65,750 acres by October 1780. Some individuals had done
exceedingly well although little actual settlement had taken place.[24]
Patrick Sinclair, marine officer and later lieutenant governor of
Michilimackinac, had acquired 4000 acres on Lake St Clair,[25] William
Macomb in 1776 received some 6000 acres on the islands of Grosse
Isle and Stoney Island, Colonel Abraham DePeyster received 6000
acres,[26] James Abbott obtained a tract of nine leagues,[27] and Jacques
Dupéront Baby (Plate 3.1),[28] the father of Jacques or James Baby
(Plate 3.2), who would play a significant role in Essex and the province
of Upper Canada, would eventually accumulate 57,600 acres on grants
from Indians.[29] Most of this was not, of course, on the Essex shore.

Had this all led to actual occupation of land, the British might not
have been upset because it would have made a de facto case for continued control of a territory which de jure had been surrendered to

Plate 3.1   Jacques Dupéront Baby, soldier of France, fur-trader, and member of the District Land Board.
Courtesy of the National Archives of Canada (c941).

the Americans at Paris. However, it had not, although people had been actively encouraged to settle at Detroit.[30] At the same time, the potential for explosion was high. Until the Vincennes Treaty of 1792, nego-

Plate 3.2   James (Jacques) Baby, a French-Canadian, Roman Catholic member of the
"Family Compact."
Courtesy of Windsor Community Museum, Windsor, Ont.

tiated after American defeats in 1790 and 1791, American policy was that the Amerindian had no "right of soil" following the British cession. The United States had by January 1786 dictated three treaties to the Indians of the "Old Northwest" based upon the philosophy that the land was American by right of conquest and accordingly the United States could draw boundary lines allowing for American expansion.[31] The Indians were determined to overthrow these treaties. While they were disillusioned with the British, who had not thought fit to consider their Indian allies' needs in the Treaty of Paris in 1783, they were strengthened, in their determination to resist, by the fact that the British had now decided to hold on to the western fur posts.[32] This, in spite of the fact that the creation of the border placed these posts clearly on the American side. Detroit was the most important of the posts, and it would not be abandoned until Jay's Treaty of 1796.[33] Even afterwards, this region would feature in frequent British-American sabre-rattling as "the American frontier ... moved in upon a *de facto* British Imperial protectorate on American soil,"[34] and the resulting tensions would contribute to the outbreak of hostilities with the Americans in 1812.[35]

CREATION OF THE LAND BOARDS

In 1788 Governor Dorchester visited the western settlements and was impressed by the problems that the Loyalists were encountering from the lack of authority to allocate land to them. Returning to Quebec, he sought to articulate their grievances and began the process of decentralization.[36] He created four districts: Lunenburg, Mecklenburg, Nassau, and Hesse.[37] Each was given a land board, which was to function as an intermediary between the governor and the governed. Hesse was the largest of the districts, being the residue after the needs of all others had been met.[38]

The boards were to run until May 1791. Their number was increased to seven in October 1792 and they were permitted to allot land in thirteen of the nineteen counties into which Upper Canada was divided. Their life was extended until November 1794, when the new lieutenant governor, Simcoe, abolished them and transferred the power to grant land into the hands of the magistrates, many of whom had been members of the county and district boards.[39] The role of the boards was to receive petitions to the governor in council, examine into the loyalty and "pretensions" of the petitioners, and administer oaths of allegiance and fidelity to the King.[40] If a board was satisfied with the qualifications of an applicant, it issued a certificate to a deputy surveyor or to the Surveyor General's Office. Within two days of contacting the surveying authority, a certificate (location ticket) valid for one year had to be issued for a 200-acre lot. Those seeking more than 200 acres had to have their petition forwarded by the Land Board to the Land Committee of the Executive Council. This committee functioned as a sort of court of appeal and reported to the Executive Council per se. The process required that applicants go twice through the cycle between the Land Board and the Executive Council. When it was complete the attorney general was instructed to issue a patent.[41]

Throughout the seven-year history of the Land Board of Hesse, there were thirteen members.[42] Four of these, majors F. Close, Patrick Murray, and John Smith and Colonel Richard England,[43] were professional soldiers and appeared on the board during the years they commanded the garrison at Detroit. Similarly, the officer of engineers at Detroit, Robert Pilkington, appeared as a member of the board.[44] There were also nine civilian appointees during its years of operation. Initially, the board consisted of Major Close, the fur trader and commissary officer Adhemar St Martin,[45] the Indian agent and fur trader Alexander McKee,[46] the Indian trader and Indian Affairs officer Jacques Dupéront Baby,[47] the merchant William Robertson,[48] the businessman Alexander Grant, (Plate 3.3)[49] and Judge William Dummer Powell.[50] Until May 1791, any three could serve as a quorum; thereafter, five were required. New members were added. These were the fur trader and militia officer Jean-Baptiste-Pierre Testard Montigny de Louvigny,[51] and the merchants George Leith[52] and John Askin Sr (Plate 3.4), Grant's brother-in-law.[53] The admixture of soldiers, Indian officers, and members of the judiciary was what might be expected given the history of the area, the trade policy of the government, the need for defence, and the closely related need to administer the affairs of the Indians. Clearly, the merchant class was the dominant influence from the outset and it remained so even after additions were made to the board in 1791, especially since Powell was unable to attend because he was in Quebec seeking to defend himself from attacks on his character.

William Robertson never attended after 1790. By 1791, Baby was dead, Adhemar St Martin was residing in Michilimackinac, and Alexander Grant had become a member of the executive and legislative councils and ceased to attend. By 22 July 1791 the board was reduced to only five members. In these circumstances, Quebec was requested to permit once again a quorum of three and it was under this rubric that John Askin, Montigny de Louvigny, and George Leith conducted so much of the board's business after 1792, with either Smith or England in the chair. Earlier, the members had had wider

Plate 3.3   Alexander Grant, administrator of Upper Canada, 1805–06, seen here
in nautical attire as commodore of the lakes.
Courtesy of Toronto Reference Library (JRR408, T15065).

responsibilities than the purely local: McKee for Indian affairs, Baby,
Grant, and Robertson for the executive and legislative councils, Powell
for the administration of justice. Now the members who could or
would attend had predominantly local interests. Montigny, Askin, and
Leith were merchants, leaving England, the board's president, as
the only member without specific interests.[54] Askin's influence
with the board must have been great, as great perhaps as Powell's had
been earlier. Like some on other boards, he was among the largest

Plate 3.4   John Askin, Sr, one of the largest land speculators in the Canadas. Either
portrait painters were in short supply in the back country or Askin placed little value
on their efforts.
Courtesy of Hiram Walker Museum, and of James Askin, Windsor, Ont.

landowners in the province and would soon own more than 11,300
acres in Essex.[55] If attendance correlates with influence, his was the
best of all in percentage terms. He attended 88 of the 92 meetings
(95.6 per cent) for which he was eligible, surpassing Montigny's attendance and that of England. Only Powell, when he resided in the district, came close to equalling Askin's dedication. To all intents and
purposes, Baby, Close, Adhemar St Martin, and McKee were, in terms
of attendance, inactive and probably ineffective members of the
board, although Mckee attended when Indian affairs were a specific
issue.[56]

Membership on a land board was one of the paths to prominence in
what was to become Upper Canada or, at least, it enhanced a profile
that was already marked at the local level. Success in obtaining membership on a land board permitted creative interpretation of policy
directives from Quebec. The Land Board decided who would become
landowners and thereby determined social status. It also gave access to

a great deal of information which could be beneficial to one's own business. David Moorman, who has examined the land boards as a whole, has identified an image in the local community, prior military service, and demonstrated loyalty as essential elements in appointment to the Land Board.[57] Apart from the professional soldiers, several members had been active in the service of the Crown. McKee, Grant, St Martin, and Louvigny de Montigny had seen active service. So had Baby, who, having fought for France, had come to the British colours during Pontiac's insurrection. In 1777 he became a captain in the Department of Indian Affairs, and the year before his appointment to the Land Board he was serving as a colonel of militia. Askin was to become a militia colonel and in the War of 1812 would have no fewer than seventeen of his immediate family in arms.[58] Powell and McKee were born in the revolted colonies; Powell's maternal grandfather had been the lieutenant governor of Massachussets.

This was one of the chief virtues required of the justices of the peace, whom Frederick H. Armstrong[59] sees as essential building blocks of the administration. Being a JP led to probable membership on the Land Board and to appointment on the Heir and Devisees Commission, charged to a large extent with dealing with problems created or permitted by the Land Board. Grant received a commission as a magistrate two years before his appointment to the Land Board in 1788, Baby became a JP in 1784, and Adhemar St Martin followed suit in 1788. In that same year, Baby, McKee, and Robertson were all appointed justices of the Court of Common Pleas, although Baby declined. Askin became a JP in Detroit in 1789 and a member of the Land Board in 1791. Only Leith and Louvigny de Montigny were not JPs at this time but they would become so, in 1796 in the case of the former[60] and in 1808 (in Lower Canada) in the case of the latter. Powell, who had been appointed first judge of the Court of Common Pleas in 1789,[61] was appointed to the Heirs and Devisees Commission in 1797, Askin and Grant in 1798. Several of the members of this particular board went on to prominence beyond the local level. McKee became the deputy superintendent of Indian affairs in 1794 and the member of the Legislative Assembly for Essex in 1800. Grant and Robertson were to become, within four years of their appointment to the Land Board, members of the executive and legislative councils. Powell would become puisne judge of the Court of King's Bench within the lifetime of the board. By 1808 he would be a member of the Executive Council and in 1816 he was to become chief justice of Upper Canada. Of all of them, Grant appears to have achieved the most although he could neither read nor write and, according to William Robertson, signed his name in a most mechanical manner.[62]

In 1799 he was appointed lieutenant of the county, supervising all the magistrates, and in 1805 nothing less than administrator of Upper Canada!

These were people whom the system trusted. When it was suggested that the board be expanded to include "two or more proper persons, being Loyalist, U.E.," the board responded that such people could not be found within sufficiently close proximity to be useful and even if geography was not a factor there was no one "suitable for the trust." The board was then empowered by the Land Committee to waive the new regulation. Moorman, who records these developments, makes the following points: that those recommended had already begun to establish their positions in the social hierarchy either through prior military service or acquired wealth or both; that they were right-minded and had proven themselves committed to British colonial society; and that the process of selection reflected the personal, hier-archical character of the society. Names were passed up for authoriza-tion but "the qualifications passed down did not require that the persons be specifically competent or experienced in land administra-tion, only that they be recognized as part of the family so to speak."[63]

This was a most powerful body of people even within the lifetime of the board and in 1794 it must have been apparent that its members would achieve even more because they were well connected in Quebec. Indeed, several members were part of the councils that ran the whole colony. It was not a body to be taken lightly; those who sought to challenge it would do so with difficulty. However, being a member of such a board was also not an easy task.

As earlier recounted, the Constitutional Act required the establish-ment of reserved lands according to a pre-ordained plan. This was a problem to be resolved, at least in part, by the board. Similarly, there were difficulties in locating settlers upon land that had not yet been surrendered by its owners, the native population. This was especially so in light of the Royal Proclamation, which explicitly protected the interests of the indigenous people. Given the provisions of this procla-mation and a central administration far removed from the local area and often unaware that the land it "controlled" had not been legally acquired, there were problems meeting the needs of would-be settlers. Authority for many actions had to be sought in distant Quebec, if local action was not to be illegal and local sanctions were not to be rescinded. The land boards seem to have wanted to take few decisions or perhaps their terms of office were not sufficiently clear; in any event, their records show a most deferential respect to central author-ity, characteristic, one presumes, of the ways in which British colonial systems operated at the time. Local advice could be rendered; solutions might be pointed to but never explicitly taken. Such decision making took place in distant Quebec or even more remote London. In such circumstances, the central authority might criticize the ineffectiveness of the local authority, little realizing that the problem lay in its own immediate purview. The local authority, unable to proceed without official sanction, had to bear the criticism.

In the Western District, the board was accused of doing little to populate the area; the board's answer, never explicit, might have been that action was impossible until land was available and policy clarified. The problem was compounded by the fact that land transactions between the native population and the Europeans had been going on for many years in ignorance or violation of central government. A board that refused to recognize such actions was one that might precipitate a political crisis or lose settlers in an area where they were so very necessary; hence, a lot of its time was taken up with investigation and de facto recognition of earlier actions. This is the benign interpretation and possibly the correct one, but there were accusations that members of the Land Board acted not just in the interests of the state but indeed of themselves. In these circumstances, such tension was to be exploited, as was the delay between submission of a request to the central administration and the requisite answer. In this, the view of Thomas Smith, the first clerk of the board, a number of those acting in this way were major speculators using their position to advance their private concerns.

The Board and Thomas Smith

What follows illustrates the fate of those confronted with power. It is based upon Smith's records. Smith is writing to complain and to defend himself, not to Lieutenant Governor Maitland directly, but to Major George Hillier who, as his secretary, officially held no power whatsoever but who was, in the words of his biographer, "the majordomo of the Maitland administration."[64] What is most interesting is that Smith is writing fully thirty-seven years after the first of the incidents which he relates. His motive would seem to have been directed at clarifying the record and perhaps at obtaining revenge on W.D. Powell, who, as judge in the then District of Hesse, must have had a major role in his censure by the Land Board. It was certainly possible to challenge the board in the circumstances of 1828. Powell, the chief judge and member of the Executive Council and speaker of the Legislative Council, had been retired for three years and the embarrassment he had caused Maitland was such that Smith's message had greater hope of being heard.[65]

Abraham Iredell,[66] who had replaced Patrick McNiff as deputy sur-veyor after the elimination of the land boards and the demise of the District of Hesse, was said by Smith to have been part of a consortium or as he termed it "confederacy," designed to look after its own inter-ests while appearing to serve the larger public good. In particular, he reported on 10 April 1828 that the lands selected by Ebenezer Allan, as agent for settlers who had been induced to come to Upper Canada from the Genesee area of New York, had been entered in the names of those with whom he was in cahoots. The evidence for this, he claimed, had been established by Indian Affairs official Prideaux Selby. Selby had searched the office of the attorney, Walter Roe, after his death.[67] This evidence, which took the form of articles of agree-ment, had been transmitted to Lieutenant Governor Francis Gore's office but could not be found when required in 1818. Smith believed the explanation for this to be simple: it had been destroyed by some of the actors in the drama – members of the Land Board for Hesse who had been promoted to various offices in York. In his first letter to Major Hillier, Smith is careful not to specify exactly who might have done this either because he did not know or, more probably, because he was unwilling to name specific members of the Land Board since some of these individuals were the lieutenant governor's personal friends or, like Alexander Grant and Jacques Baby, had been appointed to the Executive Council. He was willing to identify unspecified members of the board as part of this "confederacy" as well as Iredell and Matthew Dolson, who, he argued, maintained a canteen in order to acquire the lands of disbanded troops. The asso-ciation was one "that tarded the settlement of the Country, by a monopoly of the prime lands under different names – a conspiracy that sprung out of the Land Board; and which served to strengthen the credibility of other extraordinary events that had, and were about emerging."[68]

In the years before Major Murray and Colonel McKee resigned, the Land Board met in the home of William Robertson, and he (Smith), as clerk, was excluded. These years were characterized by him as years of inaction during which the development of the area was retarded; in frustration, the "disbanded troops and loyalists from the long delay became disgusted, many sold their claims for little value, went off, and never returned. This gave advantage to those who bought up the claims."[69]

The suggestion at this point is that things were purposefully ineffi-cient and that he (Smith) had been falsely accused of personal gain in order to discredit him since he was clearly not willing to participate in doubtful schemes. The justification for his replacement as clerk of the board was that he had issued a receipt to a Joseph Beauchamp for 100 pounds of flour "a compte de le bureau or the same thing, pour les honoraires de le Bureau."[70] This innocent receipt, he argued, had been the reason for the "libel" against him. "By an ungenerous quibble on the word 'Bureau,'" it was wilfully construed that "the Clerk was taking money in the name of the Board and three of the members, to wit, Mr. Wm. D Powell, William Robertson his Creditor and select friend; and Major [John] Smith (who had relieved the Gallant Murray in the Command) having an interest in the event, clandestinely, without calling the clerk to answer signed the Report; and poor Grant as a matter of course made the fourth subscribe."[71] Both Powell and Major Smith, he suggested, had personal reasons to replace him. Both sought the office for one of their own; John Smith's son, David, got it. The basis of this action, the "evidence," had been locally removed from the official record but was available to the lieutenant governor, who should make it available to the public. Smith added: "Why was there occasion to mutilate the Record if the charge was true? The very glimpse of the imposture is too evident, that the Clerk would never have given a receipt out of his hands to stigmatize himself was there any thing to be concealed – it would be contrary to moral order."[72] This slight – although it was clearly not slight in his mind since he devoted much greater space to it – was minor compared to the design of removing the French inhabitants from the area, which, he implies, was the intention of at least some of the board.

In a second letter that he wrote to Hillier on 19 April, Thomas Smith sought to explain why he had not been included on a list of magistrates although it might have been expected that he should have been. This, he felt, was because he had opposed the acquisition of woodland by Prideaux Selby[73] in an area in which timber was in short supply for the French-Canadian settlers. A delegation of the most intelligent was sent to Judge Henry Allcock "but could have no access; for the Judge did no business before Breakfast, then he went to Court, and after Court he was so attached to the enjoyment of the table, that business was out of question, however important."[74]

After pressure from French-Canadian representatives in his court, Judge Allcock had promised that he would advise that this resource should be divided up among the inhabitants. In point of fact, he had represented Thomas Smith as an agitator and a seditious speculator to the lieutenant governor. Selby got the land, a source of continuing agitation, and the lieutenant governor sought to ensure that Smith did not receive a commission of the peace. Although he later relented, after Smith had been elected to the House of Assembly, it was too late; Smith's constituents would not have understood.[75] Moreover, in the house, Smith had in conscience opposed the extension of the full rigour of the law of England, which was ill suited, he believed, to a country in the early stage of development.[76] As a result, his reputation in the lieutenant governor's eyes deteriorated further:

After this business I was yet more out of favor – I was cast into the obscure ground and made subject to many vexations and degrading circumstances; even in the Court of King's Bench, among a throng of strangers, and many of my friends, my name was hurled down to the tail of the Jury; Some of whom I disdained to associate with. This insult was so pointed, that I declined further attendance; and at the same time threw up my rank in the militia: and every other station at that juncture, that might subject me to further mortification ... the manifold Injuries I sustained from time to time, through the collusion of bad men.[77]

Eventually, things improved. Lieutenant Governor Peter Hunter apologized indirectly and awarded him some townships to survey.

Whatever the reason for the third letter, which he wrote on 2 May 1828,[78] its contents are most interesting because it raises the spectre of treason. Smith indicates that someone, whom he believed to be attorney Walter Roe, had delivered a letter by Governor Dorchester into American hands at a time when a French frigate was in the St Lawrence and attempts were being made to incite the French Canadians to insurrection. He suggests that high officials in Quebec may have been involved and therefore the contents of the letter, which reported upon strategic conditions on the western frontier, were critical. The letter spoke of the imbecility of the commanding officer at Detroit, reported the strength of the garrison, indicated that a frigate was to be built for service in this area, and pointed out the importance of the Indians to the British military and their vulnerability to disease. Smith claimed that "this was the period the old members of the Land Board endeavoured to drive the Indians from their villages (for the purpose, as it appeared, of granting those lands to themselves) on whom the safety of the country principally depended – and was one of the reasons Colonel McKee and Major Murray would not sit at the Board."[79]

It is hard to conceive of a more sensitive report than this falling into enemy hands and a military tribunal was established to investigate the embarrassment. It did so in the most minute detail, examining the colour of ink and the quality of paper used. Smith had been away at this time and did not have access to Major Smith's correspondence; indeed the major had complained of him to the governor general. Given this, the matter of the ink and paper, and the fact that W.D.

Powell, as a member of the Land Board, may have had access to the appropriate records and requisite materials and was known to have been visited by an American officer, the evidence seemed to point to Powell although Smith in his letter remained unconvinced. Powell kept twelve stands of arms with fixed bayonets in his home and never left home without pistols. Powell's "bustle" that Smith was the informer was construed to be a "pretence" and he was, in Smith's view, sent to Lower Canada as a state prisoner. However, because of Powell's association with Isaac Todd and James McGill (Plate 3.5), powerful economic interests in Montreal, with William Robertson, and with Chief Justice William Smith of Quebec (prior to the division into Upper and Lower Canada), the affair was, in Smith's opinion, "hushed up." In his letter he reported the views of a contemporary newspaper on the power of Chief Justice Smith and the dangers inherent in having so much power exercised by someone whom his detractors thought to be an American sympathizer.[80] The chief justice's influence[81] and that of Powell's creditors (Todd, McGill, and William Robertson) saved Powell. Thomas Smith believed that he and the clerk of the Navy Department had lost their positions because of this and that an attempt had also been made to replace the clerk of the Indian Department.[82] All of these people, it is implied, stood to thwart the success of the "confederacy": "my enemies no doubt, have traduced me behind the curtain, but openly they take me by the hand."[83]

In his letter of 13 May, Smith reveals other difficulties he had with the power structure of the time. He had written to Selby, who had sought his opinion of Powell supposedly for the benefit of Lieutenant Governor Gore. Gore had shown Smith's comments to Powell, an action that Smith interpreted to mean that future relations with the lieutenant governor would be difficult. Indeed they proved so. In a second incident, he had refused to surrender the papers of Charles Wyatt, the surveyor general, who had a law case pending with the lieutenant governor. He had also refused to sign an address to Gore when invited to do so by the landowner and merchant Robert Nichol and the lawyer James Woods. In the second instance he refused because he had, with others, been appointed a commissioner of interrogation with respect to this particular case and saw the possibility of conflict of interest. This action likely did not endear him to Gore, who may have placed entries in the records of the Executive Council which were transmitted to the Colonial Office, although this had been denied by John Small, the council's clerk. After the war he had surveyed city lots in Detroit and this may have been held against him even though he had sought and received official sanction. Again he was perceived as

Plate 3.5   The Hon. James McGill, philanthropist, businessman, land speculator, and associate and friend of John Askin.

Courtesy of National Archives (c2873).

one who had not volunteered during the recent war, but in fact he had offered his services on several occasions during a particular action.[84] His conclusions to all this were understandable. He wrote: "Taking the detached narratives together, they will exemplify in a great degree, that no Individual, if he has not some friend in power, can withstand the intrigues of party – what one suggests another will aver. This is the result of experience, tho' I hope there are many exceptions."[85]

In the final letter in the series, dated 18 August 1828, Smith reiterated many of his charges and added some more (Appendix 3.2).[86] He identifies Powell as, in his position of judge, "sole arbiter of real and personal property without the intervention of a Jury; or any other check," labels Robertson a "keen speculating merchant" who had refused a seat in the executive and legislative councils for political reasons, and casts doubt upon Alexander Grant's loyalty or at least his wisdom. Robertson and his associates had sought to purchase the upper peninsula of Michigan and his agent had been charged with seeking to corrupt some of the members of the American Congress. Iredell, the surveyor, had either been part of a co-partnership or had accepted bribes to enter fraudulent names to secure land for Robertson and Dolson and had hypocritically charged Ebenezer Allen, the agent of the Genesee settlers, with bribery. Smith himself had been defrauded of land by Iredell, and though his claim to it had been recognized by the Executive Council, it was rejected by the Colonial Office. He suggests that this happened through the efforts of Powell, then in London. The land was subsequently acquired by Robertson. Attempts had been made to remove the Indians from their villages and to replace the storekeepers in the navy and Indian departments.[87] At the same time, attempts were made to remove the French Canadians, who were in debt over their property. Additionally, an unnamed judge threatened an individual[88] who had purchased an anchor from the military stores with what might happen to him under the law. In this way the judge would have secured a property worth $12,000 for himself but for the intervention of the military commander, Major William Ancrum.

To point out all the Intrigues, subterfuges and swindlings of the first Members of the Land Board of Hesse would take no little time, but the person who may take the pains to examine their conduct throughout – and the pitiful change in the Land Board Book, which detects its own infamy, he will discover its inconsistency as well as the imposition practised on Lord Dorchester – an old man under the influence of another [likely Chief Justice Smith] and a fitter subject to colour their untruths than the noted cantineman Matthew Dolson their copartner, could not be found perhaps in His Majesty's dominions.[89]

Of course, much of what Smith had to say was correct. Powell was the sole arbiter; he did practise without a jury[90] and, as today, there were few checks on judges. He was in London at several points and may have spoken against Smith's claim because he believed him corrupt. Robertson was a speculator and investor and did seek to buy a significant part of Michigan in association with others. He would not have denied this but, in fairness, both he and Baby seem to have been possessed of principle. Robertson and Baby had been offered positions as judges of the Court of Common Pleas for the District of Hesse in 1788 but had declined.

We are plain merchants, unacquainted with the forms of courts of Judicature, unacquainted with the general principles of law, unskilled in the complex system of Canadian Jurisprudence and extensively interested in the trade of this circuit. To delegate therefore to us, under these disqualifying circumstances, the administration of laws which affect the rights and property of our fellow Citizens, which interest might seduce, or ignorance betray as to misinterpret would be reposing in our hands, a dangerous authority; which we could neither exercise with satisfaction to ourselves nor to the Public.[91]

Attempts were indeed made to remove the Indians because the location of their settlements was in demand from the perspective of the development of the county as a whole, although there can be no doubt that particular individuals would have benefited from this action. Powell was no friend of the Huron and is on record as such; he supported their removal. Powell and Major Smith did seek to advance their own childrens' futures by securing their employment in the navy and Indian departments but this was not uncommon at the time.[92] If, as Thomas Smith reports, Powell was in debt to Robertson and to Todd and McGill, he is also known to have been in debt to Edward Ellice and to James Monk of Montreal.[93] These were all powerful individuals and they may indeed have had Powell in their pocket but there is no direct evidence; all else is a matter of interpretation.

Certain items remain unproven. There is no proof of the corruptibility of Iredell in this instance, although it will subsequently be shown that he behaved with partiality towards John Askin, a major speculator. Nor can it be demonstrated that he acted for the co-partnership of Robertson and Dolson together with other members of the "confederacy." There is no evidence of a systematic attempt to remove French Canadians and none whatsoever of the treason of Powell. If Powell, American-born with property still to be recovered in the United States, could escape such a charge in these most sensitive political times, he could most certainly escape any other charge. He did.

Many years later, in trouble with the administration he had served, Powell sought to justify his life by writing a volume entitled "The Story of a Refugee" in which, among other things, he describes the trauma of the accusation of treason made soon after he assumed the role of first judge for the District of Hesse.

I had not attained this state of Trust and authority without jealousy or Envy, although the general Population and the class of my Equals did me the Honor to profess this highest esteem and Respect; but it has happen to me before and since, where I had rendered services, which I could not add to, that Inability was the Signal for Complaint, and in proportion as my Services had been useful the reward, in Evil was proportionate – Two immediate Dependants, whom I had brought from Montreal, on public service conspired to destroy me, in hope to share the Spoils and fabricated a forged Correspondence, with the American minister of war, whose army was then advancing, on the Native Allies of GB; suggesting the most inhuman Means of destruction, as from me, and the Villainy was so artfuly contrived and executed, as to expose my life to the resentment of the Indian Tribes.[94]

This letter, purportedly written to Major-General Henry Knox, the American secretary of state,[95] must have upset many with its contents but none more so than the indigenous population because it recommended the deliberate inoculation of the Indians with disease. Their angry reaction was predictable. Charles Smith,[96] who would replace Thomas Smith as clerk of Powell's court but was then a clerk in the trading house of William and David Robertson, provided a sworn testimonial that no less a person than Joseph Brant (Plate 3.6) had visited his place of business and, in a manner suggesting he expected it to be conveyed to Powell, had declared that he and his companions "having been informed that the Judge did not like to see American Scalps and having procured three from the Shawnees they had approached the Judges home on their way to Detroit from the Miamis made an unusual noise and Holloworing on purpose to mortify the Judge who had better let the Indians alone and mind his own business."[97] Powell's wife and children were frightened in mock Indian ambushes. Fearing for his life and that of his family, he took the family to England where the children were placed in school.

Whatever greater motive (if any) lay behind this attempt to discredit him, Powell attributed his immediate tribulation to the base motives of Roe and McNiff. What Roe had done is unclear[98] but, as shown in an earlier chapter, McNiff as surveyor had incurred the wrath of the board and been replaced by Iredell. Moreover, in an earlier phase in the New Johnstown district, while still a government employee, he had

Plate 3.6   Thayendanegea (Joseph Brant), *c.* 1807. He insisted on the right of the Six
Nations to dispose of their land on the Grand River and many, including Samuel
Street and his portraitist, William Berczy, were willing to oblige him. By William
Berczy. Oil on canvas.
Courtesy of National Gallery of Canada, Ottawa (acc. 5777).

begun to establish a political party almost single handed,[99] and had organized against the officer corps,[100] which he felt excluded him from various actions and benefits and which he claimed was guilty of peculation.[101]

Fortunately for Powell, "Providence interfered by dementing these Traitors, who exposed themselves by their Expectation, to Governor Simcoe, who although prepared not to be my friend most honorably spared me all doubt, as to these wretches, who became intemperate, and soon ended their Carrer (sic), one, in an American Dungeon at Detroit, and the other suffocated, on the River while stooping to assuage the fever of Intoxication."[102]

On the receipt of the letter to Knox, Powell had little choice but to forward it to headquarters.[103] If he believed McNiff and Roe to be its authors, he also believed that Thomas Smith had to be involved since, as his clerk, Smith would have been able to provide examples of his handwriting. When he had spoken with Smith, the latter had pointed to McNiff's capacity to forge and had related "frequent instance of his [McNiff's] malevolence and threats."[104] Powell had on two occasions visited McNiff with witnesses, accusing McNiff and Smith of acting against him in this matter. On the first of these visits it seemed to him and to his witness, Charles Smith, that both McNiff and his wife had known the specific contents of the letter before the interview.[105] On the second, which took place a fortnight later, he had again accused McNiff in the presence of George Meldrum, William Robertson, and Prideaux Selby.[106] Afterwards, he sought confirmation from Meldrum, Robertson, and Selby of McNiff's implicit admission of intervention in the business of the Land Board, but the record is silent on whether this was forthcoming.[107] However, he did manage to obtain sworn affidavits, one from Charles Smith testifying as to what had been said[108] and another from Mathew Dolson, at whose tavern a purported draft of the letter to Knox had been exhibited in McNiff's presence.[109] "A thousand other minute circumstance support the evidence that Mr. McNiff was the Author and the whole Indian Department except Colonel McKee affected to believe it mine and to publish it to the Indians as I was assured by Adam Brown the Huron or Wyandot Chief."[110]

McNiff had, of course, alienated Powell by attacking the board in a letter to the Land Committee in Quebec. In this letter he had charged that the board, which was expressing dissatisfaction with his survey work or, more accurately, his lack of work, knew little of surveying. He had also insinuated that people in commerce should not be appointed to such boards because of conflict of interest. The Land Committee had rejected McNiff's hypothesis and the board would soon reject him[111] because, among other things, he felt no need to report to it, claiming that his responsibility was to the Surveyor General's Office alone and that, if the board needed his report, it should obtain it from Quebec.[112] Powell had written and moved a rebuke of McNiff's behaviour and it had been officially recorded in the minutes of the board.[113] On occasion, McNiff denied receiving the board's instructions[114] or claimed not to understand them[115] or to have received inadequate instructions[116] or materials.[117] Powell must have seethed but the tone of the official record is of parties dissatisfied with each other but playing "games" within strict bureaucratic and defensible limits. Criticism of McNiff continued even after the membership of the board changed[118] and Powell departed for England, but there can have been little love between the two, which may have manifested itself in accusations of treason, especially after McNiff had vowed "the most implacable revenge" for a legal judgment rendered against him by Powell.[119] Powell cannot have had a direct hand in McNiff's dismissal but must have rejoiced when he was dismissed on 27 January 1794 on the recommendation of Colonel England and the concurrence of Lieutenant Governor Simcoe.

Although McNiff might be regarded as having personal animosities towards Powell,[120] he showed another side of himself in the meeting with Powell, Meldrum, Robertson, and Selby which took place on the 20 April. He claimed that Powell had deliberately misled the Land Board and had assured its members that the Loyalist claims had to go for approval to Quebec. Powell, he argued, had long acted against the Loyalists and the settlement of the area.[121] McNiff was not alone in this view. John Cornwall would swear that in speaking to Captain Caldwell of Indian Affairs about land for his son, he had been told by Caldwell that he was a fool to seek land in the province. If he was to persist in this foolish thought he should leave out of his petition all mention of loyalty "for it was not the fashion now when such men as the Chief Justice and the Judge of the District of Hesse were employed and such as judge".[122] Here are traces of opinion about Chief Justice Smith that McNiff shared with Thomas Smith. Edward Hearle would swear, his oath witnessed by William Macombe, that Captain Caldwell had declared in the presence of a Mr Stockwell and a Mr Robert Denison that "Mr. Powell first judge of the Common Pleas had it in his power to procure Provisions for the disbanded Soldiers but that being himself a Rebel and inclined to favor the Americans he uses his interest to prevent the granting provisions except to a few who have never served and also to parcel off the granting of lands in order to procure Dissatisfaction among the people and engage them to favour the Americans and disquiet them against the actual Governement."[123]

In his defence, Powell would also cite his loyalty and his efforts to discourage those who sought to alienate by denying genuine settlers the resources of government and seeking to preserve the Indian lands whose acquisition they wished legalized. Certainly this is how he wrote to Lord Dorchester at the time although he was careful not to name names.

From an early day after my arrival in Detroit, it became evident that any Instructions of the regular Administration of distributive justice was obnoxious, and in proportion to the probability of that Instruction operating a Check on abuses of the Crown Interest which from the first Settlement of the Colony had been subjected to the most unbounded spirit of speculation – Some Communication at the Land office board soon evince that a Change was to take place in the business of Indian purchases and I was considered as an enemy to that unjustifiable Traffic.[124]

He went on to report how he was accused of using his influence on the Land Board to prevent the Loyalists from obtaining land and provisions, thereby disposing them to favour invasion from the United States.[125] He had attended most of the meetings of the Land Board and had seemingly alienated many of the Indian and military officers. He experienced great opposition from this quarter "from my Activity at the land Board to sustain the Instructions under which it sat ..."[126] Both groups, at too great a distance from headquarters to be themselves controlled, were accustomed to their own way. They resented the intervention of newcomers.[127] They were upset by his "necessary rejection" of Indian deeds "as decisive of points in controversy."[128] An independent judge was "subject of very general disgust in those Departments, which being alarmed forgot their jealousness of each other, and made common Cause against the new Authority."[129]

Powell escaped all of this accusation either because his personal qualities were such that it was patently absurd or because he was recognizably part of the establishment. As noted earlier, he was a Loyalist icon, descended directly from the colonial establishment in Boston, trilingual, and privately educated. A friend of Lord Dorchester,[130] he had organized against the revolutionary party in Massachusetts and had borne arms against the Americans. His word was clearly to be taken over that of McNiff, the Irish-born troublemaker who had signed "one Rebel Association"[131] and who had accused gentlemen of land speculation while engaging in it himself.[132] Thomas Smith, a former captain in the Indian Department, a militia officer, and a future member of the Legislative Assembly for Kent,[133] was perhaps more worthy of attention. However, as secretary to the board, he seems to have used his position to further his own interests and had been caught at it. In 1790 Powell and the board had sought to dispel the rumour that special application forms were needed and had sent model application forms to all militia captains in both English and French.[134] Smith, it appears, had told settlers that he alone could draw up applications for land in the approved format, had refused to reveal this format, and had charged £2 for each application, this on the evidence of Mathew Dolson who had paid him £14. In April 1791 Powell had instigated an inquiry into "reports that have reached him respecting extortions by Mr. Thomas Smith."[135] Moreover, he had demonstrated incompetence in his recordkeeping and Powell had proceeded against him.[136] As a result of all this, Smith had lost his job, although officially he resigned to pursue his business as a notary public.[137]

The truth is uncertain because those in power could find as they would and they found for Powell. Soon after the business of the letter, he was in Quebec to secure his position and was presented to the Duke of Kent, a sure sign of approbation.[138] Moreover, on his own evidence, in a private conversation, Simcoe had supported him when they first met. William Osgoode, the chief justice at the time,[139] testified that Simcoe believed in his innocence "for he put the letter into my hand and forestalled my opinion upon it as a weak and infamous forgery."[140] Simcoe declared that "the behaviour and conduct of Mr. Powell, as far as lies within my knowledge, has been in every respect such as becomes the station he holds" and similar reassurances were given by the home secretary, Henry Dundas.[141] With such support, in 1794 he was made a puisne judge of the Court of King's Bench and in 1797 he was appointed to the Heir and Devisees Commission, where, according to S.R. Mealing, he displayed fairness.[142] He seems to have the strength of conviction and personal fortitude to hold out in a matter of law against four chief justices and three attorneys general.[143] He became a member of the Executive Council in 1808 but remained sufficiently independent to cross Lieutenant Governor Gore on matters of principle and law. Yet Gore remained his friend. In supporting Powell's nomination as a legislative councillor, Gore declared him a "gentleman who has discharged the duties of his important office with probity and honour for upwards of twenty years."[144] By 1814 such was the confidence placed in Powell that he was appointed commissioner for treason charges, and an appointment as commissioner for war losses followed in 1815. Soon he was speaker of the Legislative Council. Finally, in October 1816, he received his much-desired appointment as chief justice of Upper Canada. If official approval was ever required this was it. Clearly, the charges of treason and of self-gratification while a member of the Land Board had come to nothing.

Some evidence in support of his integrity can be found in the fact that in Essex County, the most developed part of his judicial District of Hesse, he owned only one lot.[145] His influence by 1795 was now great. As he grew older he began to make mistakes disclosing confidential information on financial matters relating to Lower Canada[146] and in two pamphlets, prompted by the "Spanish Freeholder" affair,[147] discussing differences he had with Lieutenant Governor Maitland and his secretary, George Hillier. His behaviour was such that it was unbecoming in a chief justice and member of the Executive Council and he lost the support of the latter body, which he had hitherto chaired.[148] His resignation was requested because his conduct had been "prejudicial to the harmony and respectability of the Government."[149] His enemies sought to deny him a pension. Lieutenant Governor Maitland had refused to assent to it,[150] yet such was his influence that he received a pension of £1000 in the same year that he resigned.[151] Others might simply have slipped away and enjoyed the rewards of a long career but he claimed that it was his legal rectitude which had earned him Maitland's enmity. Six years into retirement and at age seventy-six, he still sought an investigation into the affair.[152]

In short, there appears to be no substantial evidence[153] to support the accusations of either McNiff or Smith, both of whom can be made to appear disgruntled, self-serving individuals caught with their own hands in the till. This may actually have been the case but there can be no doubt that the social and power gradient between them and their accusers ensured the outcome. How, then, were the Indians treated by the board and how were those holding land under Indian grants treated by a system that at least theoretically disapproved of such grants?

The Board and Indian land rights

That there were problems regarding land in the District of Hesse had been recognized from an early date. Major Robert Matthews, the former secretary to General Haldimand and in 1787 the commandant at Detroit, wrote Haldimand almost as soon as he arrived in Detroit:

Individuals possess immense tracts of Land upon General Grants, sell it out in detail to poor wretches for, 100 for three acres in front and forty deep, for which the farm is at the same time mortgaged, the settler labours for a few years with only half his vigour, paying and starving all the time: & ultimately from debts on every hand is obliged to give up his Land ... In Trade the lowest of the profession resort to these obscure places, they are without education or sentiment & many of them without Common honesty – these are perpetually overreaching one another, knowing that they are too distant for the immediate effects of the Law to overtake them. The only resource in all matters in dispute, is the commanding officer, for our Justices of the peace, it seems, are not authorized to take cognizance of matters relating to property ... It is so much to be wished that some mode for the prompt & effectual administration of Justice were established, for the want of it is a temptation to many to take advantages & commit little chicaneries disgraceful to society distressing to trade & Individuals.[154]

He had spent so much time in arbitrating such affairs that there had been little left for his professional duties and the legal consequences of his actions were unknown. He sought help. No doubt partly in response to this, a Court of Common Pleas was established under Powell and the Land Board created in 1788. On arrival, Powell was quick to perceive the importance of the question of Indian grants. So great had the purchase of Indian lands been that many purchasers had "in contemplation princely estates" and he advised Lord Dorchester that this warranted early intervention by the legislature. His advice was that "whatever may be the true point on these purchases," if harm was not to be done to those who had acquired land subsequent to an Indian purchase, then the occupiers had to be given deeds "without the least animadversion to the Indian purchase." In this way he argued "the view of the Jobber will be defeated, the Industry of the Laborer rewarded and the Settlement released from the Shackles of a projected Monopoly."[155] Of course, the practical effect of this would have been to recognize and legitimate acquisitions hitherto unsanctioned by the Crown. Henry Motz, Dorchester's secretary, refused to act, recognizing that the "grasping individual, attempting to engross the waste lands of the crown by unauthorized Indian purchases, ought not to reap any benefit from his transgressions to the public detriment." The Land Board, it was held, was best suited to make the necessary judgments.[156]

The Land Board began the task, reporting that in fact, on the information of McNiff, the surveyor, and McKee, the deputy superintendent of Indian affairs, there was no land in their jurisdiction that did not belong to the Indians or been parcelled out by them on Indian grants. The letter of 28 August was particularly telling in that it described the full extent of the problem spatially, pointed to concerns where "the right of soil is subject to discussion," and echoing Judge Powell's point (he was a member) about the problems of litigation, described the inevitable delay in achieving the administration's objectives.[157]

... none of the Lands within the limits of this District have been purchased from the Indians for the Crown, although they have been parcelled out in large grants to individuals by the Natives, so as to leave none unclaimed from Long point on Lake Erie to Lake Huron ... We are so sensible of the Insufficiency of these claims, by Individuals whose acquisitions have not been authorized by the Crown, that of themselves they would not be an obstacle to our progress; but by presuming on the constant practice of the Crown, to purchase the right of soils, by contact with the Natives, as well as your Lordships sentiments expressed to us relative to the lands opposite the Island of Bois Blanc, we think it cannot be your Lordship's intention that any settler should be planted by us, where the right of soil is subject to discussion ...

It is with true regret that we announce to your Lordship a delay in the execution of your Lordship's Wishes, but are satisfied that your Lordship must approve our Caution in a measure which might involve the first Settlers in Disputes, and eventually retard the progress of settlement more than the actual delay.[158]

Dorchester's answer, penned some five days later, was direct. The board was to consider what was needed to ensure the necessary land was available to accommodate immigrants. Alexander McKee would negotiate it under instructions from the superintendent general of Indian affairs. The board had to seek McKee's advice because of his knowledge of the Indians in "ascertaining what extent of Country it may be proper to treat for with them for the present, consistently with their comfort." No grants could be made until *the whole* had been surrendered; and where individuals without authority had purchased land from the Indians, the board had to advise Quebec. Otherwise the board could authorize certificates to actual occupants.[159] Having expressed his views directly to the board, Dorchester sought to strengthen his position (if it needed strengthening) by involving the Indians through Sir John Johnson, superintendent general of Indian affairs:

His Lordship is informed that the greater part, if not the whole, of that Country is now claimed by Individuals, under pretext of purchases or Grants from the Indians, in which claims they are understood to acquiesce. If so, any Interest of their own seems to be out of the Question, and their objections must be founded on misconception. they should be reminded, that all Bargains of Individuals with them respecting Lands are totally void, against Law and can never be acknowledged by the Crown, that whatever lands are wanted for the settlement of the King's Subjects, the King has made it an invariable Rule to apply to the Indians and to satisfy them, for the Cession therof, and afterwards to distribute such lands among his Subjects according to Justice and their deserts, that this Law is for the comfort and Security of the Indians, as well as for the maintenance of due order among the King's Subjects, and can never be departed from.

That all the King's Subjects know very well that they cannot be protected in the possession of any lands without his authority and therefore the less excusable in setting up claims under pretext of Grants or purchases from the Indians contrary to Law.[160]

It took the Board until 7 December to produce a description of the territory to be acquired; a meeting one week earlier had to be postponed because of Powell's absence.[161] In the interim, the members returned to the theme of those holding land under Indian grants and the difficulty with the clause that required actual occupation. Clearly there were local needs that had to be met and the board sought to serve them, presenting its case to Dorchester in terms that he might appreciate. The board had offered land to Quakers although it had been claimed under Indian grant. Adherence to the principle of occupation would be embarrassing because "they had pledged themselves and the faith of Government." An inability to keep their promise "cannot but be injurious if not for some time *fatal* to the great view of settling the Colony." Finally, the board stressed the importance of local input and control.

However desirous it may be to act under specific Instructions and to avoid that Responsibility to which any latitude might subject us, yet we cannot forebear to observe to your Lordship, that the Difficulty of communicating on every doubt being so enhanced by our remote situation; it may be requisite, to effectuate you[r] Lordships Views, that the Board, in Cases where the Difficulty shall have evidently escaped your Lordships animadversion, & delay be hurtful to the progress of the Colony, may be permitted to proceed on the Guidance of their own Judgement influenced by the general Spirit of your Lordships Instructions ...[162]

Dorchester sanctioned this approach while reminding the board how it should act towards both the Indians and the white settlers.[163] He also sought to constrain the board by reiterating that no other Indian purchase was anticipated than that made by the Indian officers in June 1784 in what, in the future, would become the Township of Malden. Given this, "you will find scope for your trust to operate in every *other* part of the district. You will, therefore, be very particular in your minutes, if you shall see cause in the exercise of your discretion to give hopes to persons that indulge expectations under such Indian Grants, as were not made agreeable to the Royal Instructions, nor have yet had the Countenance or approbation of Government."[164]

Dorchester's remarks perhaps reflected the frustrations that Quebec was experiencing in this most remote part of its jurisdiction. Powell was certainly frustrated: "I have not the doubt, but am sorry to say that I believe strong actions were made to create confusion which may protract the settlement of the Waste Lands ... all the Claimants of large tracts under Indian Deeds are interested to continue as long as possible in Confusion which will benefit them and they continue to sell lots of two Hundred Acres for, 100."[165] In January 1790, well after the establishment of the board, Motz at Quebec, in an effort to determine exactly what was happening, demanded a report.[166] The request seemed simple and logical enough. An accurate map of the district was needed as well as a map of locations made by the acting surveyor. The board should transmit the names and descriptions of all occupants, the acreage they held, the basis of all land claimed, and a reference system for the map. No funds were made available for this task and, given the system established for land granting whereby the board recommended but the Land Committee in Quebec sanctioned, an up-to-date inventory was hardly possible. There were not sufficient surveyors to tackle the most basic tasks and the one they had was a difficult person. Moreover, the full extent of Indian grants was not known since no system of registry had been required, although the board in October 1789 had posted notices requiring claimants on Indian deeds to inform it of "their Titles and pretensions."[167] In the absence of such a system, all that could be done was to post warning notices. This was done along the Thames, at highly desirable locations where people were continuing to occupy without official sanction.[168]

Dorchester's letter of 2 September 1789 had set in motion the process of negotiating a land cession from the Indians. The only official cession to this point was that of a seven-square-mile tract, on the east of the strait, made in 1786 and adjoining the grant made earlier to the Indian officers.[169] A greater amount of land was now required and the letter written in September opened up an issue that was to be of some importance in the years to come. This was the need for a site for a town to serve local needs, perhaps in anticipation of an eventual British withdrawal from Detroit. The letter recognized the importance of the island of Bois Blanc as the potential site of such a town but authorized the selection of other sites if justified. Obviously, the selection and location of such a site was critical for the infrastructural development of the area, but it was also critical for the private futures of those owning the site or land adjacent to it. The extent of the emotion can be gauged from the following comment made by Powell in a letter to Motz. Describing Captain Caldwell, one of the holders of land by Indian grant, as a "madman" and a "dangerous Character," he reported on a visit he made to the area together with Commodore Alexander Grant and a Mr Smith, presumably Thomas. At Captain Elliott's home they were joined in the evening by Captain Caldwell, who thought they were planning a town and who "with every indecent threat used his Endeavours to Deter us," including "prophecies of Indian War and the total extirpation of the English by the natives."[170]

On the 21 May 1790 McKee informed the board *post facto* that he had completed the cession from the Indians.[171] The sale covered a huge area of southwestern Ontario but, to the ire of the board, two reservations had been kept by the Indians. One of these was the old Huron reserve between the Huron church and the Jarvais (Gervais) River; the second was a tract beginning at the Indian officers' land and running up the strait to where the French Canadians were settled.[172] McKee had effected this cession as superintendent of Indian affairs without informing the board of which he himself was a member! His action so enraged Powell that he wrote directly to Lord Dorchester to express his discontent both at the contents of the document and the manner in which McKee had behaved.[173] Powell's arguments were that land was being returned to the Indians which had already been surrendered; that the manner of the transfer was improper in that the Land Board was not represented and the formal procedures of acknowledging the tenor of the deed had not been followed; that the new reserve, north of the Indian officers land, was the only site on which a town could be built on the east side of the strait; that the reserve at the Canard frustrated communication; that it was poorly chosen in that its true owners, the Ottawa and Chippewa, did not plant, hunt, or camp on it;[174] that without outside advice the reserve would be sold for a "trifling consideration"; that the Huron, the new owners of the Canard reserve, had no claim on this land when it was transferred in 1786; and that the Ottawa and Chippewa were astonished at what the Huron had received (Plate 3.7). Finally, this usually most calm of individuals seems to have become emotional on the subject of the Huron, apparently unable to see that their objectives might be different from his own. The Huron, he argued, were "inimical to the King's government." At the treaty of Fort Harmar, they had betrayed the British and claimed American support for land held by the Shawnees who had supported the King: "Acquainted with their general odious Character and their particular Conduct at the American treaties, it is perplexed to account for the unmeasured favour shewn to this contemptible people, which seems to grow with their insolence, and finally sacrifice to their Caprice (for it cannot be called accommodation) the Convenience and ease of a whole settlement, at the same time that it leaves to them, the exclusive occupation of a spot

Plate 3.7   Indian dance at Amherstburg, *c.* 1825–28. This painting, an oil on canvas, is by William Bent Berczy, himself a resident of Amherstburg from 1817 to 1832. The buildings on the left may be those of Matthew Elliott.
Courtesy of National Gallery of Canada, Ottawa (WBB5; acc. 30860).

which may truly be called the Key of Detroit as it commands the Channel."[175]

These proceedings were all so astonishing to Powell that he believed there must be some agreement between the Huron and the government that had had to remain confidential. If this was not so and the Canard reserve was to be disallowed, the facts should be confirmed by accurate investigation because "I have to combat the resentment of a very powerful faction in this place the holders of large Indian grants." Clearly, he did not want to be identified as the cause of this change. He was thought of as "their principal enemy" and he had been accused by one of them of "promoting discussion of his title to land by extra judicial opinion."

The board objected to the reservations on 22 May, sending a copy of its minutes to McKee.[176] McKee's response justifying the reservations was that the reserves had to be made both because the tribes did not wish to cede them and to achieve a number of goals, namely to demonstrate continued good faith towards the Indians, to ensure their comfort, to cement their loyalty to government, and to avoid trouble with the whites. Finally, McKee, feeling the need to support the Huron and his action, made the following personal testimony: "The body of the Hurons have been well known for their attachment to government by their Bravery and Services during the late War having lost, many of their principal Men, when acting in Conjunction with the King's troops, to which I was a witness – Altho' it may be possible there may be some discontented Amongst them, yet in general no nation have been more attached."[177]

A more official statement of the Land Board on 28 May 1790 was written by Powell, who reiterated officially what he privately believed and had expressed to Dorchester already. He had one new thought: the possibility of treating with the Indians for the waste land near the Huron church, "reserving to them a Building for retirement when they occasionally attend public worship." Otherwise, the official state-ment presented the same arguments as before but its impact must have been diminished by the fact that the military commandant, Patrick Murray, dissented from the whole and Alexander Grant dis-sented from specific parts. Murray believed the matter to be the busi-ness of the Indian Department, whose officers, he thought, were per-forming well in the interests of peace and harmony and were not responsible to the Land Board. Grant objected to two paragraphs which dealt with Indian matters and the attitudes and loyalty of the Huron. This left two of the four members (Powell and Robertson) sup-porting the whole document and a third (Grant) supporting parts, including the last paragraph, which emphasized the difficulty of the situation.

To express to his Lordship how truly interested this Board is to support by their individual and joint exertions the glorious Character of the nation for Humanity and Justice, but at the same time to represent the expediency of repressing the Insolence of the Indians by a steady and firm support of the Lands within the settlement without discrimination, and to avoid any Submis-sions to their caprice which may indicate apprehensions of their Power to injure, and in presuming thus to hazard advice on a Subject whose connection with the appointment of this Board may not be immediately obvious to state to his lordship the Impossibility of continuing with any satisfaction towards the establishment of the Country while the settlers under its sanction are exposed to Insult and rapine without redress.[178]

Much of the emotion on this issue stemmed from the fact McKee had kept the Land Board in ignorance about the progress of the negotiation right up to the last minute so that "the Clerk of the Board,[179] who, without its Sanction was employed to draw the Deed, informed some of its members, that it contained no Reserves and the Evening before the Council [was] drawn, the present deed containing the reserves which was not completed more than an hour before it was brought into Council."[180]

This was especially alarming because the board had before it for consideration a request from McKee for exclusive ownership of land at the Canard, as well as one from McNiff which had been declined.[181] McKee had claimed that he sought the land not for his own use but to place loyal subjects upon it. Loyalty was the basis of McNiff's claim.

... if Loyalty be the Criterion which justifies the conferring such favors, on Individuals, I think that in that point I have no right to give way to any one claimant in the District, not even to Captain Mckee himself, or if long and faithful service, and that of the most labourious kind under the Crown can be deemed meritorious, or an essential qualification in obtaining such grants, I presume I ought to be ranked among the first favourites, but in that case I should conceive to be receiving the land from His Majesty, and not from captain McKee, nor would I on any other consideration have any part of it.[182]

Was McKee acting on his own behalf or, as he claimed, that of the Indians? Powell claimed that, when McKee had learned of McNiff's request, he declared that if he or his friends could not enjoy the land, he would give back the deed to the Indians.[183] McKee's interpretation, presented on 25 May, was different. He had received the grant to serve the Indian interest but as an act of faith would be willing to surrender it. His action was, of course, different, but arguably he had served the Huron interest and indeed that of the larger society by agreeing to the reservation.

With the remonstrations of Powell and McKee and the intransigence of the Huron,[184] expressed in August to no less a figure than Sir John Johnson, the whole issue came to the attention of the Land Committee in Quebec. A committee was struck in October to investigate this issue and the larger question of what was hindering the development of the area and of a district town. The committee was to correspond with the Hesse Board, with Sir John Johnson, and with any others deemed appropriate to seek satisfaction for the Huron. All testifying were to be informed that their communications were to be placed on the public record of the Executive Council.[185]

William Robertson, member of the Hesse Board, appeared to give evidence orally in front of a committee consisting of Hugh Finlay, the chairman,[186] John Collins,[187] and Alexander Grant, member of the

Hesse Land Board as well as the Land Committee. His remarks were wisely restrained; there was no comment on the character or loyalty of any particular group. He recognized the problems with extensive speculation in Indian grants. He denied that the reserve was necessary for the "comfort" of the Indians, who had, in fact, pressed it upon McKee in May 1786. He argued that the surrender of Crown territory would impede the settlement of the area since the territory in question was "Key to the Upper Country, were it Ceded. the Chain of Settlement would be broken where it ought obviously to be the Strongest."[188]

The Land Committee also heard the evidence of Patrick McNiff, never content to restrict his activities to surveying.

In the next place the various and almost unlimited Claims made by Individuals to Tracts of Land by virtue of Indian Grants has been a great cause of keeping the Country unsettled and will so long as they are suffered to Exist, when settlers came from the States of America at the Instigation of Government, Instead of being placed on the waste lands of the Crown without delay they were told that such and such particular Tracts of land as they may have pitched upon was the property of Individuals by virtue of Purchases made of Indians and that the King had no land in this Country, the consequence was that Numbers of those Intending to settle on King's land returned again to the States & others of them for want of Money to take them back were under the necessity of purchasing Land perhaps of those persons Claiming large Tracts under Indian Titles, at the enormous price of £100 for 100 acres of wild land; In order to continue this practice of settling land and prevent Government from settling the Country it has been reported at Fort Pitt through the instigation of some persons here, Inimicable to the Interests of Government and perhaps principal Claimants that all the land in the Country was claimed by a few Individuals and that the King has no Land here, however as Government has disapproved of such grants, it is to be hoped every obstruction to the settlement of the Country arising from such Claims will in future cease.[189]

Sir John Johnson saw the causes and impediments to settlement as resting in the following: that land was not perceived as vested in the Crown; that there had been a failure to permit settlement on lands ceded to the Indian officers prior to the creation of the land boards; that the surveyor was not qualified to act; that, exasperated with a delay of sixteen months, potential settlers had returned to the United States; and that the survey plans for navigable townships, which required reservations on the front concessions, inhibited development.[190]

In their report the commissioners rejected McNiff's assertion that members of the Land Board of Hesse engaged in commerce or with family connections to it "are unfit for a Seat at that Board, insinuating that they may be activated by apprehensions that the settlement of the country might affect the interests of people in Trade."[191] This outcome was probably to be expected. Collins had likely engaged in trade, Grant most certainly had, and Finlay was to seek to use his position as chairman of the committee to obtain no fewer than twenty-four townships.[192] The report acknowledged the Indian officers' possession of the land ceded in 1784 which included the site of the proposed town of Georgetown. It found the reason for the departure of potential settlers to rest in the lack of rations and farming utensils.[193] It acknowledged that the survey regulations may have hurt settlement possibilities, and it noted that land was owned by the Indians in 1789 and that none had been purchased by the Crown before 26 May 1790. Given the lack of land, there could be few location certificates issued. The committee also found that McKee believed himself authorized to make the reservation at the Canard in order to acquire the larger territory. In fact, the committee concluded that the Huron had surrendered their interest in 1786 to prevent encroachment by the settlers in the neighbourhood. It authorized Sir John to set in motion events that might lead to the removal of the Huron to the Chenail Ecarté in adjacent Kent County.[194] Sir John may have known that this was unlikely.

The board was still remonstrating in May 1791. There was, it was argued, no other unimproved land on the east side of the strait for a town, "the whole being settled either under the Grants of the french King or private purchases from the Indians *countenanced by the Several Commanding Officers and Lieutenant Governors of Detroit, who had received the rents and fines on such speculations, as well as upon Lands possessed under the Sanction of the french Crown.*"[195]

The board could see no good reason for reserving a waste in the heart of the settlement and thereby disrupting communications, and finally it advanced the argument that the reserve contained a most valuable resource – a limestone quarry.[196] Its views had no direct effect: the reserve at the Canard was created and remained in existence until 1835 when it became Anderdon Township. However, on 10 August 1799, the Indians would grant to the Crown sufficient space for roads westward to the garrison town of Amherstburg and northward to settlements of Sandwich Township. They would also sell the Huron Church reserve for £300 Quebec currency.[197]

With the McKee treaty of 1790 and the Huron Church reserve soon to be surrendered, it might seem that a sufficient land base had been assembled to meet the needs of the District of Hesse and that the problem with Indian purchases might finally have been resolved. At the meeting of the board in March 1792, Major Smith, the board's president, went so far as to stress actual occupation rather than just ownership.

... and the Major proposes to the Board the necessity of making known and discouraging by every means possible the idea of rights to those claiming large parcels of land, not actualy occupied by themselves, under Indian deeds: The Act of Parliament which has given a Constitution to Upper Canada, having most expressedly reserved and guarded the ancient privileges of the Crown – And he trusts that no petitioners will be allowed by the Board to avail themselves of this wanton aggression on His Majesty's rights, or receive their Sanctions for the Recommendation of a larger Location than they can actually occupy, or to which they may be entitled under any of the existing Instructions.[198]

However, there were two major areas where things were still not finally resolved. These were in the New Settlement – the future townships of Colchester and Gosfield – and along the strait in the future Malden Township. Both had been festering for some time. The resolution of these issues showed how power was used in this time and place.

POWER AND THE INDIVIDUAL

After the Revolutionary War, in the winter of 1783–84, the Wyandot (Huron) and Ottawa agreed to cede a seven-mile-square tract of land at the mouth of the Detroit "in love and affection" to a group of Indian officers and interpreters who had served with them. There would seem to have been genuine bonds of affection and respect among these people, whose life together had involved them in a most precarious existence and indeed outright danger. Among the Europeans who shared this camaraderie were Henry Bird, William Caldwell, Matthew Elliott, Alexander McKee, and Simon Girty.[199] These were Indian fighters, many of them with "Scotch-Irish" origins and along the American frontier their very names shook fear into men, women, and children. This was especially so of Girty, "the white savage." Elliott had fought against the Indians of the Ohio, fled Pittsburg with McKee and Simon Girty about 1778, and "settled" in Detroit. Elliott, Girty, and McKee served with Bird in Kentucky in 1781. In 1782, Caldwell defeated the Americans under Crawford near Sandusky. Elliot and Girty took an active part in this action. Additionally, Caldwell's Rangers dealt a crushing blow to the Americans at Blue Licks, where again Elliott was present. These men were themselves part Indian or had lived with the Indians. McKee's father was Irish-born but his mother seems to have been Shawnee; he had married a Shawnee woman. Caldwell, Irish-born, fathered a mixed-blood child. Elliott, born in Donegal, had lived among the Shawnee and a Shawnee woman was the mother of two of his four sons. Girty, born in Pennsylvania, had lived as a child with the Seneca. These people had fought together and had organized the tribes to resist American military expansion and demand for land. They had served, and it seemed not inappropriate to some that they might now live together once again. However, they were threatened in their ambition for a while by the action of a single individual, one Jacob Schiefflin, who, like them, had served in the Indian Department but in an inferior station. This is the Jacob Schiefflin who served as secretary to Governor Henry Hamilton and held the rank of lieutenant in the British army. He lived in Detroit until 1783 and subsequently in Montreal and New York. His relative, Jonathon Schiefflin, fought with Bird in Kentucky in 1780 and acted in conjunction with Askin and others, to secure twenty million acres of land in Michigan. Reconciled to the new American government, he served in the Assembly of the Northwest Territory.

On 11 October 1783 Alexander McKee, who (with others of the Indian Department) had personal designs upon land opposite to Bois Blanc, the most desirable location in Essex for a town, reported that Schiefflin had, with the aid of drink, obtained a deed to this location from a series of chiefs.[200] McKee held that Schiefflin's intent was to sell this property. It was claimed that he had acted knowing full well that unnamed officers and Loyalists were in the process of acquiring the land, which they intended to settle. McKee wanted the sale stopped because it would cause trouble between the Indian nations and had written to Sir John Johnson to that effect. The land had been ceded on the 13 October[201] but this had only been discovered by accident.[202] Two days later, Schlieffin wrote McKee. Schlieffin had known of his competitors' plans for acquiring the site of a town and had determined to become their neighbour but would surrender the land he had acquired if he became a joint proprietor.[203] Presumably McKee chose not to act on this offer. However, it would seem that, had he sought to be a part of the consortium of Indian officers and addressed his letter to Henry Bird, he might have been included.[204] He was, after all, of the Indian Department. Schlieffin's greed, it would seem, would cost him dearly because the Indian Department men would now use all their influence to deny him. Meanwhile, Johnson had written to Haldimand, who ordered that Schiefflin be fired from his position if in fact he had registered the deed.[205] Haldimand also authorized the calling of an assembly of Indians to voice the government's disapproval of such action, thus setting in motion the steps by which the grant would be negated. Schiefflin seems to have been "the more culpable, having in the course of his duty been witness to Lt. Gov. Hamilton's displeasure on a similar occasion and his positive commands against any practice of the kind ..."[206] This would not deter Schiefflin in this particular instance nor in the future.[207]

The council that Haldimand authorized was held between 18 and 22 October 1783. On the 18th, Equshaway,[208] the Ottawa chief, describing himself as "loaded with grief and sorrow" and perceiving the danger of conflict between the tribes, argued that if land was to be given away it would only be after deliberation and to those who had fought with them.[209] The birds, he said, "sing bad notes already" and if, with the assistance of Sir John Johnson and the commander-in-chief, the deed were not destroyed, it "will be the cause of much Mischief among us."[210] At the meeting on the 20th, McKee reported that he had been unable to get Schiefflin to surrender the deed or attend the council meeting.[211] On the 21st, those in attendance included Alexander McKee and captains Caldwell, Elliott, and La Motte as well as John McComb. There were three interpreters and twelve Indian chiefs, only one of whom was Chippawan. The Indians complained of Schiefflin's behaviour, affirmed McKee's belief in the dangers of war among them, and requested the destruction of the deed. McKee, as Indian agent, reassured the chiefs that the commanding officer would obtain it and informed them that their complaint would be transmitted to Sir John Johnson.[212]

By the next day, McKee had been joined by the commandant, Lieutenant Colonel DePeyster, the "gentlemen of the garrison," and seven additional Chippawa chiefs.[213] There are a number of things that are interesting in the transcriptions of these meetings. One is the language used. The Indians are addressed as "Children" and McKee as "Father". Significantly, the spokesman on both occasions was Syndoton of the Huron, who had not been represented at the initial council meeting. Schiefflin is accused of being a "deceiver" who should be hanged for his deceit. In the course of his speech, Syndoton reveals the attitudes of the native towards the land. Land is for the use of people; Schiefflin had been given land before and he had sold it. If he is given land again he will sell it and leave the country. The Indians want the deed destroyed, and indeed Schiefflin would on 20 October deliver it to the commandant but not to the Indians, a distinction that he made much of.[214]

In the interim he tried to survive by appealing to Sir John Johnson. He had been informed by Captain Bird and others that there was a plan for a town for the accommodation of Loyalists. Captains McKee, Bird, and Caldwell, McKee's son,[215] and three others would be the sole proprietors.[216] He had sought to accommodate them and would have joined them as a proprietor but they sought the whole for themselves. It was clear that "the zeal these gentlemen express for the accomodating the Loyalists springs more from a principal of self Interest, as they can receive the Land from me on terms as advantageous as from them."[217] Alcohol had not been involved and the Indians as *allies and not subjects of the King*[218] were, he thought, entitled to dispose of their land as they pleased. His justification for this view was that Colonel DePeyster had accepted such a grant from the Pottawatomi, as had James Baby, William Macomb, and one Williams (likely Thomas), the former as deputy agent of Indian affairs, and the last two as JPs. Indeed, it was because so little remained in the possession of the Indians that he had to act to ensure the land promised him as a government servant since one-quarter of the district was now in the hands of these three individuals. The council's purpose was to invalidate his deed, for "I am well aware that Indians may be induced by the interposition of presents to retract any thing they have ever done, or said, especially as several of the principal chiefs are now absent who have assented therto, upon learning that McKee, Captains, Bird, Caldwell and others interested were displeased at my acquisition."[219]

On the 24th, in another letter to Sir John, Schiefflin reiterated that the purpose of the council had been to frighten him, adding that the Indians present were unrepresentative of their people, that they were not genuine chiefs, and that the minutes of the meeting had been kept by McKee. He proclaimed that "it is not the value of the land that I avoid to sacrifice but the consequent acknowledgement of having done wrong in accepting it when so many superior to me in fortune, and in power, have set the example." Why was he not as entitled to land as McKee, McComb, DePeyster, and Williams?[220] If he had failed to get the commanding officer to approve his action, he found it strange that he had not had a trial since in DePeyster he faced both accuser and judge. However, he would accept Sir John's impartiality if the case was submitted to him.

In holding the councils, McKee, on Haldimand's orders, had been observing the necessary proprieties. Haldimand was soon to remind Lieutenant Governor Hay of this fact.

It is also necessary to observe to you that by the King's instructions, no Purchase of Lands belonging to the Indians, whether in the name or for the use of the Crown, or in the name or for the use of Proprietaries of Colonies be made, but at some general meeting at which the Principal Chiefs of each tribe claiming a proportion in such lands are present: and all tracts so purchased must be regularly Surveyed by a Sworn Surveyor in the presence and with the assistance of a person deputed by the Indians to attend such survey, and the said Surveyor shall make an Accurate Map of such Tract, describing the Limits, which map shall be entered upon the Record with the deed of conveyance from the Indians.[221]

Effectively, these instructions laid aside the claims of Schiefflin "even had he obtained it by less unworthy means than he did."[222] In the same moment that he gave expression to these words, Haldimand anticipated and perhaps encouraged an application for land from those who had served with the Indians, warning Hay that such application would have to follow the appropriate route, that is, via McKee and Sir John Johnson.[223] Haldimand, a soldier, was part of a military culture and as governor, he had the power to so influence the outcome of events. He believed in the "indispensable need" of maintaining alliances with the Indians to safeguard the "pays d'en haut";[224] this would come from supporting those who had served and who had built solid relations with the Indians, that is, the Indian officers.[225] In this dispute they would be catered to and Schiefflin disregarded.

Perhaps in response to Haldimand's "invitation," Captain William Caldwell had, in the names of the Indian officers, renewed their application to settle. Haldimand, in his letter of the 14 August 1784, recognized that the Indians wished the lands granted to be speedily settled by the Indian officers, for emotional and political reasons. Yet, though he was unable to grant these lands since they were surrendered to the individuals and not the Crown and were therefore illegal, he did encourage the Loyalist officers to continue their improvements until McKee could obtain a surrender to the King in the appropriate manner. In all of this the routing was circuitous; at each point on the route additional weight seems to have been added to a predictable outcome. Initially, McKee informed Johnson who wrote to Haldimand. Haldimand made his views known to Mathews, the commander at Detroit, who informed Johnson, seemingly *de novo*. Johnson presumably closed the circle with a letter to Haldimand. In this way the texts empowered the participants and informed the desired outcome. In writing to Sir John Johnson to "order" that the Loyalists receive tools and rations to assist them, Major Mathews noted that land transfer based on Indian deeds "has been practiced at Detroit beyond all Bounds of Reason, in so much that except the Hurons there is not a nation in that neighborhood that has any property remaining." Clearly, the treatment of the Indian officers was very different from that of Schiefflin. Halidmand wrote:

I consider the intended Settlement as a matter that may prove of infinite utility to the Strength and Interest of this Province, and wish to give it every Encouragement in my power ... In the mean time ... they shall carry on their Improvements with every diligence in Their Power, until the Land can be laid out & granted agreably to the King's Instructions ... Mr. McKee should explain to the Indians the nature and intention of the precautions the King has granted to prevent their being iniquitously deprived of their Lands, and that they formally, in Council, make over to the King, by deed, the Tract of Land in question, for the purpose they wish. Their deed must be transmitted to Sir John Johnson to be properly confirmed by the Governor of the Province when regular Grants will be given to the Persons who are to be the proprietors of the Land. The Intended Settlement being at the entrance of the River and by Capt. Caldwell's Report, a Place where it may hereafter be necessary to establish a Post, I would have two thousand yards from the center of such Place on all sides reserved for that purpose.[226]

Mathew's postscript, which he offered as his own, seems to have been directly plagiarized from Haldimand's letter.[227]

As I look upon the Settlement mentioned in this Letter to be in some degree a Military one, in so much that it is to be composed of Persons, who have served in the course of the War together, and considered by the Indians as connected with them, for their mutual Strength and Safety, You will be particular in not permitting little traders and interested Persons from creeping into it, and admit those only whose services and undisputed Attachment to Government shall recommend them to the principal persons of the Settlement.[228]

His recommendation that "petty traders" be kept out was taken to heart. Lieutenant Governor Hay instructed the surveyor to provide for twelve individuals who were named. Not surprising, all were of the Indian Department; the land remaining after these were satisfied was to go to other Indian officers! The largest grants went to Caldwell, McKee, and Elliott but provision was to be made for Sir John Johnson and Hay, the very person who authorized the survey![229]

Yet the issue of these lands had still not been resolved in 1789 when the Land Board of Hesse met to discuss the creation of "Georgetown," ordered by Motz's letter of 15th June. After reciting the history of the area, including the extension of the frontage from six to forty arpents under the authority of Lord Dorchester, the board thought fit to observe that it "is too sensible of His Lordship's uniform attention to Humanity and the rights of Individuals to suppose that he would countenance the dispossession of men who made their improvements under such reiterated approbation of persons having authority, without first causing an estimate to be made of the Injury such individuals must sustain by the loss of Their Improvements."[230] They also determined to do nothing about Georgetown until the larger issue had been resolved and forwarded their minutes to Dorchester. At this point the Indian officers had de facto as opposed to de jure recognition of the land but circumstances were to change. In September 1789 Dorchester gave his permission for a site for a town other than the one opposite Bois Blanc.[231] The Indian officers, for their part, recognized that although the original grant had been for an area of seven miles square, they did not want to insist upon this if it meant the removal of settlers already established. Most had not been settled and the Indian officers effectively surrendered little for the subsequent recognition they would be accorded. This came in the fact that the board decided to commence its survey at the eastern edge of the original Indian grant, a tacit acknowledgment of their right to the land.[232] The Indian officers' position was strengthened when the Land Committee acknowledged the history of events from their perspective.[233] After 1791 the new government of Upper Canada proved willing to compromise on this earlier claim in order to ensure the development of a town opposite Bois Blanc. Caldwell represented the Indian officers. A new township, to be called Malden, was created in 1793 with space for a government fort and for the required Crown and clergy reserves. McKee, Elliott, and Caldwell would be the main patentees of the township with the right to exercise their quotas as military officers within its boundaries.[234]

This compromise and the McKee cession of 1790 effectively ended another problem that had occurred. In August 1787 Major Robert Mathews reported to Haldimand that his "good intentions have been frustrated and Your orders not attended to by the late Gov. Hay." Haldimand, it seems, had intended to have Caldwell's Rangers settled within the area that would become Malden but Caldwell had given much of this land to others and instead had obtained another tract "six leagues upon the lake where Mathews was to locate sixty 'fine fellows.'"[235] The initial "owners" of this land may have been Caldwell, Alexander McKee, Charles McCormack, Robin Emphleet, Anthony St Martin, Matthew Elliott, Henry Bird, Thomas McKee, and Simon Girty.[236] Ninety-seven lots were laid out by Thomas Smith on the authorization of Mathews, apparently with Dorchester's consent. In this way de facto recognition was given to the action of squatters. A second concession was added consisting of fifty-two lots in 1788 and in 1790 another twelve were added east of Mill Creek. This was the "New Settlement," so-called to distinguish it from the old at Petite Côté and L'Assomption. Subsequently, it became the "Two Connected Townships" and, ultimately, the townships of Colchester and Gosfield.

In the circumstance of 1787 this, too, was strictly illegal and Caldwell had apparently acted independently. Haldimand, it seems, had come to accept this *fait accompli* although he never actually recognized it as legal. The settlers were Loyalists who had served under fire and it would be difficult to dislodge them if there was any intention to do so. In any event, it is unlikely that Haldimand would have required this. One of the earliest acts of the disbanded Rangers was to seek and secure parity in compensation with that allotted the members of the 84th Foot.[237] Of the 121 people to be settled in the New Settlement, in the summer of 1790 only three were not Loyalist or military personnel. The board behaved reasonably to those who had no time to prepare the necessary petitions, or indeed had lost their certificates, if they appeared on the approved lists of Mathews or Close, and it issued warnings to those who might lose their land because they had not occupied it.[238] Perhaps this was only reasonable since the board was under pressure to see the area settled,[239] but it must have been eased in its decision by the fact that it was dealing with the military and Indian officers. Yet things proceeded slowly and not all developments were good for those involved. Enquiries were launched at Quebec in 1791 and in 1792 the petition for this land was turned aside on the ground that: "the claims are for lands usurped under Indian purchase, grant or Concessions; and not binding in any respect whatsoever, on the contrary the subject who presumes to claim rights on such Tenure is not only guilty of a misdemeanour but acts in apparent defiance to all authority, and repeated orders to the prevention of such Traffic."[240]

However, it would seem that an adjustment was worked out in the same way as occurred in Malden to the west.[241] Thus, the Indian officers had achieved over a period of nine years what at first appeared difficult or impossible. Perseverance and connection would seem to have carried the day.

Yet there were others possessed of such qualities who did not fare so well. One such individual was the Indian woman Sarah Ainse.[242] Although she once claimed to be a Shawnee, she was probably an Oneida[243] and, like other women in matrilineal native societies, was a vocal champion of her legal rights. She had been brought up on the Susquehanna and had lived with several white men. By 1759, she had become a trader. Between 1775 and 1785 she was active in the Detroit area. She engaged in business with many well-known merchants, such as John Askin, William Macomb, and Montague Tremblay. In 1781 her account with Tremblay was for £2620[244], in 1783 she did business with Askin to the extent of almost £3000,[245] and in 1787 her account with Angus Mackintosh was for slightly more than £685.[246] In Detroit she owned two houses, cattle, horses, and four slaves. She was, by any standard of the day, a person of substance.

In May 1787 she moved to the Thames River and took up residence in Dover Township. In 1788 she completed the purchase from local Indians of a 150-square-mile property which ran from the mouth of the river to the forks where the city of Chatham now stands. Part of her land, a parcel 300 acres in width by 33.3 in depth, lay within the territory purchased by McKee in 1790. She asserted, and was supported in her assertion by a number of Indian chiefs, that her lands were exempt from the treaty.[247] McKee said that the chiefs had spoken to him but that he had agreed to do only what he could.[248] As part of her argument she submitted deeds dated 1780, 1783,[249] and 1788, all included in the register of Detroit and clearly pre-dating McKee's purchase.[250] Supported by Louvigny de Montigny, who was present at the negotiations in his individual capacity rather than as a member of the Land Board, McKee denied that such an exemption had been intended[251] and the board decided against her. On 23 August 1793, Ainse was back at the board with an order-in-council dated 17 October 1792. The Executive Council, prompted by John Graves Simcoe, had approved her application for eight lots on the first concession of the first township on the Thames.[252] The board saw need to justify its action. It had simply acted within its instructions, which prohibited sales by Indians to individuals, and had exercised its discretion in awarding these lands to discharged soldiers of the British army. Anxious to comply with the Executive Council's order, the board advertised for these people to assemble to see if a compromise could be effected.[253] Arbitration produced nothing.[254] In November 1793 Littlehales wrote from Quebec: "If any person continue to persevere in their occupation of these Lots granted to her by the Council, they will be prosecuted to the utmost rigor of the Law, by the King's Attorney General, at the same time if Sally Ainse thinks proper to compromise matters with any people who are settled upon her property, she will be perfectly at liberty to do so, but it must be fully explained to her, that this depends totally upon herself."[255]

Ainse's letter of March 1794, undoubtedly written by someone else since she usually signed with her mark, conveys the spirit of the woman.[256] She is writing to a person of some import, perhaps even Simcoe himself.

I received yours by the Express and am sorry to say it afforded me but very little satisfaction, & Dear Sir, as this is the last time I intend to write to you upon this Subject, I shall take the liberty to explain my Sentiments as freely & in as Concise a manner as I can. I therefore hope Sir, you will recollect that twas your promises, time after time, that induced me to be so easy in this affair, depending so much on your promised friendship, I really thought, that you sympathised with me in the injustice which I was likely to suffer, & which has come to pass; – I find D. Sir I am greatly deceived. You heard the Declaration of the Indian Chiefs, You saw (I presume) thro' the Deceit & I may say, Villany, that was carried on by the opposite party – You must remember Sir, that you yourself said, before Colo.l Brant & many others at the same time that my Land should not be granted, until the affair was entirely settled, & sure enough it is now settled in an unjustifiable manner.

Though I am an Indian Woman,(& guilty of a great indecorum in presuming to write to you in this manner,) I see no reason why I should be openly plundered on my property; of what cost me dear; which I could prove in the sight of God; but as it is allowed, for some Gentlemans word to be taken. & to overthrow the Oaths of Eighteen to twenty Indian Chiefs – I have poor chance to go to Law; but I confide in the judicious Character of His Excellency Lord Dorchester, whom I expect, to visit this Summer & I doubt not, but to be recompensed, for my land & trouble.

I shall not trouble you Sir, with any more of my Letters, but shall take it very kindly, if you deign to answer this ...[257]

In June 1794, under pressure from Simcoe, Sir John Johnson, and the Mohawk war chief Joseph Brant,[258] Ainse was ordered to receive 1673 acres or 1.7 per cent of what she had originally petitioned. But she had received nothing by 1796[259] and the Executive Council denied her in 1798.[260] In short, she received neither land nor compensation. She little deserved such treatment because she had worked hard both in the native and in the British cause.[261]

CONCLUSION

That all was not well in the state of land administration in the District of Hesse and the future Essex County cannot be denied. In spite of repeated statements by the colonial authorities in London and their representatives in Quebec that Indian land was inviolate and guaranteed by the Royal Proclamation of 1763, continued inroads were made into this resource without due recognition of the Crown or its procedures. The merchants of Quebec, English and Scots, who had come as army contractors after the conquest, stayed on to monopolize the fur trade.[262] As Donald Creighton has observed, they hated the Proclamation of 1763, which had limited the boundaries of the province and made "an Indian reserve out of Canada's rightful inheritance in the west."[263] They actively sought to change this and would succeed in doing so with the passage of the Quebec Act in 1774, by which the massive territory between the Ohio and the Mississippi was restored to the colony.[264] In the interim Quebec merchants would continue to monopolize the trade of the area and seek to acquire land within it. They were abetted, interestingly enough, by the Indians themselves, although, in fairness, the historical record that has survived is European in its bias.

The McKee Treaty appears to have been amended without the agreement of the Land Board. Robertson's disclaimer that it was not the treaty he had signed earlier casts doubts on the public face of the procedure even if it does not affect its legality. In the case of Treaty 12, which created the Huron Church reserve, Thomas McKee agreed that not all the chiefs need be present to participate in the formal cession since they had to hunt. Part Indian himself, he must have known when the hunt took place and might have arranged another time, but as he himself said, he wished to proceed with speed. In short, procedures were not as orthodox as they should have been. Even though interpreters were present at negotiations,[265] it is difficult to accept that the transcriptions of proceedings conveyed anything other than the spirit of the event, and the detailed geographical descriptions of the property transferred is surely the language of the European surveyor rather than that of the Indian.[266] When McKee spoke to those with whom he had served, did he really speak as "father" and did his "children" answer as such or was this how the European mythology wished it to be? Certainly W.N. Fenton indicates that forest protocol was sanctioned by ritual. While McKee would have been aware of this, and of appropriate forms of address including the use of symbolic metaphor, these forms might not mean what they did in Europe.[267]

As in many colonial situations, what the colonized thought is rarely recorded; history is written by the colonizer. Can such paternalism really have flourished in this most violent of times and in an area where the fates of the Indian and the whites were so obviously interdependent when it came to facing a common American foe? These records tell us little of what the Indians actually thought, including what they thought about the land.[268] However, there are places where their values seem to appear through the otherwise European structure of the documents, for example, in the Schiefflin case. Schiefflin is condemned not just because he is a deceiver but because in the past he had sold what he had been given.[269] It would seem, on the basis of this one piece of evidence, that the Indian concept of surrender or cession was more a licence to occupy and use than an irreversible transfer of ownership. Their "gifts" were to support those who had supported them, that is, the Indian officers and the military with whom they had fought and with whom by now they had ties of blood and language. Their vision of the use of land seems to have stood in sharp contradistinction to European values. On the other hand, the Indian emphasis on use may have been fabricated by the obviously European draftsman of these documents to stress the fact that use was intended and to bolster the image of settlement when the document reached British headquarters in Quebec. Be this as it may, the Indians were clearly still willing to give land to those with whom they had served.

If the Indians were prepared to allow their land to be used, the Europeans,[270] including the officers of the Indian Department, were only too willing to accept whatever they were offered.[271] As Schiefflin pointed out, many of them, including the commanding officer DePeyster, had accepted such land, and one has to assume that they knew full well what official policy was because they had been the recipients of periodic charges, for example, from General Thomas Gage at New York or Haldimand at Quebec. In this regard, Schiefflin's point – that he, like the King's representatives, was able to receive land from Indians who were his Majesty's allies rather than subjects – must have been both galling and telling. Yet, in spite of this, the outcome was almost predictable because those in authority in Quebec seem to have shared a common culture with those whose task was to run the system at the local level. As the King's prime representative, he could not lay aside the sanction against the purchase of Indian lands but he could adjure the officers to bide their time. He did, while the same time warning them to guard against the action of "petty traders."

Was it that Haldimand saw his brother officers of the Indian Department and military simply as suitable recipients of privilege? Were such rewards so much part of the system that had evolved that they were not even consciously recognized as privilege but rather as the price of blood? This was part of the charge that Captain Caldwell had laid against Powell – "that he uses his Interest to prevent the granting provisions except to a few who had never served."[272] Certainly the officers regarded the lands they received as gifts and not as government's recognition of their service because they demanded both.[273] Was it that Haldimand was simply a realist? This area had to be defended. With stretched resources, Haldimand could call upon the experienced Indian officers and the Indians they commanded. The choice between them and Schiefflin may have been easy in such circumstances but it must have been eased by Schiefflin's purported modus operandi; allegedly, he had got his deed by deceit and with the use of alcohol. It may also have been eased by a fact never mentioned in the official documents. Schiefflin, on the evidence of Dupéront Baby, was a Jew.[274] As such, even in 1784 he was not a suitable recipient of the King's bounty, which officially was restricted to Christians[275] although where need be this stricture could be circumvented.[276] Clearly, Schiefflin was not to be part of the privileged; indeed, he stood in their way and conse-

quently had to be removed. In other circumstances, one might hope
to avoid condemnation by authority. William Hands, later a sheriff and
judge in Essex and the Western District, had, with others, occupied
land on deeds from the Indians within the Huron Church reserve.
When this was surrendered to the state, he sought the right to keep his
480 acres or be compensated for it. Although he recognized the
fragile nature of his claim in law, he pointed out that "most of the
Farms of L'Assomption were first settled in a manner similar to that of
your Petitioners."[277] He was about to "remove from the american to
the British side of the Detroit purely from principles of loyalty and
attachment to the British Government" and this no doubt assisted the
outcome. The Quebec Land Board's decision, made in 1798 before
the formal surrender, stated: "The board cannot confirm purchases
made by the King's Subjects from Indians, Subsequent to His Majesty's
proclamation of 1763. But in consideration of the Expense of the Petitioner in improving the land he lives on the prayer of his Petition is
granted to the extent of his improvements provided the lots of the
Town within Mr. Hands Farm have not [been] appropriated for which
reference is to be made to the Surveyor General and provided they do
not extend beyond the end of the line marked out Pajos Boundary
line."[278] The case continued into the first decade of the century, the
board recording its opinion that "the petitioner is in a similar situation
with many other Persons at Sandwich who have had the like application acceded to." Of course, the circumstances were different than in
the Schiefflin case but so was the man and the solution.[279]

The protocols followed by the Indian officers to secure their success
bear all the marks of a playlet. The paternalistic language used seems
to be employed to signify power and control in relationships. Councils
are called, initially by the victims of the purported deceit (the
Indians), in keeping with the specified protocols. Representatives of
all the tribes are present at a public meeting. Over a series of meetings
the spokesmen of the important tribes hold forth. McKee, as deputy
agent, stresses the various steps that can be taken to retrieve the illegal
Schiefflin deed and the hierarchical links of commandant, the superintendent of Indian affairs, and, ultimately, Dorchester, the governor
general. He is connected to all of these people and will secure the
interest of the natives. Schiefflin is asked to surrender the deed and
when he does so the commanding officer who receives it has his status
with the Indians enhanced. When Schiefflin denies that drink was
used, a chastened chief confesses that he was drunk in his canoe. The
Indians declare they would have hanged him had they the white man's
law and his actions threaten the peaceful relationship of the tribes. All
of this seems not so much a report on what happened but a justifica-

tion of what was to happen: the Indian officers here and in the neighbouring townships of Colchester and Gosfield would have their way. Schiefflin would not and probably he should not have, but it is difficult to see the predisposition towards the Indian officers in other than social terms.

This may also be the case with Sarah Ainse. Clearly, she was guilty of nothing other than defending her right to some of the most desirable locations in the district. Vindication of her claims would negate the aspirations of those who hoped to benefit from land on the Thames after it had passed into the hands of the state. Brant, the Iroquois war chief, had supported her and would continue to do so. His words written in support of her claims seem to capture the particular injustice to her and the broader approach to the lands of the indigenous: "Since, it has been promised in presence of the Five Nations several times to be restored to her, and it is not restored yet, notwithstanding. I really must confess that I begin to think it too hard to see our friends the English so very strict about Indian lands ... It grieves us to observe that it seems natural to Whites to look on lands in the possession of Indians with an aching heart, and never to rest till they have planned them out of them."[280] Certainly this what is happened here. Under the McKee Treaty, the Indians had, to the European mind, parted with much of southwestern Ontario for £1200 Quebec currency or 0.19 pence per acre, but in parts of this territory settled by the French, farms were selling for 300 to 500 pence per acre.[281] Although the figures are not strictly comparable, the differential between "upset" price and development costs has to have been considerable. There can be little doubt that, while the surrender was legal, European society and specific individuals stood to appropriate a considerable benefit. This occurred here, at this time, because both the British and most of the Indians needed one another's help in their contest with a common foe in a most vulnerable theatre. However, within a few years the British would be eager to keep the tribes apart, to divide and rule, to inculcate clientage,[282] to foment jealousy,[283] so that "connection" and concomitant power would be difficult[284] and the price of land could, in this way, be kept low.

This would seem to have been a vital strategy for an economy that as yet produced little agricultural surplus and little in the way of commercial or industrial infrastructure. If the mother country was unwilling to provide funds beyond immediate defence costs, this had to come from somewhere. Indian land acquired cheaply and parted with even for fees was a source of such capital.[285] Hence, there was a need to sow dissent among the tribes and to establish posts at different locations so that the Indians would not congregate where they might inform one another.[286] There was also a need to control the influence of Joseph Brant,[287] who, as the agent of his own and other tribes, would soon raise the asking price to an unprecedented level.[288] Indeed, the government had been coerced under implied threat to permit the sale by the Indians of a tract of Iroquois land, and the Mississauga had refused to cede land for less than 40 pence per acre. The person who reported this was appalled that the chief justice had had to be protected by a military guard while on Mississauga land. He was also appalled by the fact that, in the past, land had never cost more than two pence per acre and in a recent sale had fetched only five cents. The reporter who decried the sudden rise in land prices requested by the Indians was someone familiar to the inhabitants of the District of Hesse – William Dummer Powell.[289] That it was expected that Indians should part with their land base for little or nothing may explain why the price in Essex seven years earlier had been so low. Powell's attitude merely anticipated, reflected, or informed what would soon become government policy. That policy was expressed in the minutes of the Executive Council, meeting at York in 1798. The council was aware of the changing Indian attitude to land in the light of European acquisitiveness:

It is no secret ... that the Aborigines ... are beginning to appreciate their lands ... by the value at which they see them estimated by those who purchase them ... But if this were doubtful now, when the lands purchased from the Indians are distributed among His Majesty's Subjects, at a Fee hardly exceeding the prime cost of them, it cannot possibly remain so when the Indians discover as they unquestionably will, that the purchases made from them are to be converted into a source of wealth to ourselves ... In order therefore to exercise that foresight which our Indian neighbours are but beginning to learn, and in which it certainly cannot be our interest to promote their improvement, we submit to your Honor's consideration the propriety of suspending the promulgation of the plan which has been laid down for us until we can make a purchase sufficiently large to secure to us the means of extending the population and encreasing the strength of the Province, so far as to enable us before our stock is exhausted to dictate instead of soliciting the terms on which future acquisitions are to be made – For we are satisfied that the purchase of 50 or even 100 Townships if made now, will cost us less than the purchase of ten after the promulgation of the Governor-General's plan.[290]

Given this, the indigenous owners of Essex land had been taken advantage of, however much individuals in authority or who had fought with them valued their courage, fortitude, and service.[291]

If the Indians fared poorly, some Europeans did very well indeed. Even if the testimonies of McNiff and Smith are discounted as disingenuous, there was clearly something wrong in the District of Hesse. There may indeed have been a person or persons who stood to benefit from accumulating Indian land, prior to effective British control, and then subsequently having it recognized. These persons may or may not have been members of the Land Board or of the military establishment.

Powell, accused by Smith, seems to have exhibited a remarkable independence of character even prior to his arrival in the district. He had defended certain individuals charged with libelling the judges of Montreal and had secured the introduction of habeas corpus into Lower Canada. As a judge, he had warned Lieutenant Governor Hunter that he had no authority while outside the province, an act that won him little applause.[292] He seems to have been falsely accused of treason and was in fact exonerated. He rose through the system and reached the social and political pinnacle as a member of the Executive Council, something that seems unlikely to have happened had he clearly been acting on his own behalf or that of some patron. However, he did argue pragmatically for recognition of Indian deeds, a predisposition that can also be interpreted as evidence of guilt. McNiff testified that Powell was to secure the Indian title to land. Powell was also in debt to a number of people, including the Montreal firm of Todd and McGill. He sought the removal of the Indians from Essex and was supported in this by William Robertson.

Robertson was a fellow member of the board, who had with Askin been involved in the Cuyahoga purchase, a massive land speculation on the south shore of Lake Erie. He was also involved with Todd and McGill.[293] When Robertson returned to England, he joined the creditors of Todd and McGill, the British firm of Phyn, Ellice and Inglis.[294] Yet he and Jacques Dupéront Baby (who rarely attended board meetings) had both refused appointment as judges, although the cynical may argue that acceptance of this office was incompatible with accumulating large acreages. Also, in the larger district, as opposed to Essex County, both men did accumulate land. John Askin came later to the board but he had been associated in business with Robertson and was the Detroit agent of Todd and McGill, who treated him generously when he became bankrupt.

These people include three accused named by Thomas Smith, that is, Powell, Robertson, and the commandant at Detroit; if Askin, Robertson's associate, is included, there are four individuals, all of them members of the land board. At some unknown date, presumably about the time of his retirement, Powell decided to commit to paper what he had described in general terms in his letters to the authorities in Quebec. These drafts were never incorporated in the memoirs that he published. He writes of public plunder, of extensive claims on Indian grants, and how large fortunes had been made during a war in which no enemy had been within 500 miles: "In addition to the immediate participation in public Plunder many individuals had acquired from the Indians extensive Grants of Land which the Law did not recognise and the whole Tribe of Indian grantees were added to the Friends of disorder."[295] Never explicit, he names those who found benefit in a coalition: the commander of the garrison of Detroit, the commander of the navy, and the superintendent of the Indians! If he is writing of events before the discovery of the letter to Knox in April 1792 (and he was understandably obsessed with this event), he has identified Major John Smith,[296] Commodore Alexander Grant, and Colonel Alexander McKee. Only one of these people, the commandant at Detroit, is also on Thomas Smith's list, but the significant point is that, in all instances, these were members of the Land Board. The chance of collusion between Powell and Smith seems remote indeed.

There is, of course, no way to be absolutely certain of any of this but the perception was clearly that there was widespread corruption.[297] Certainly costs were high. On 6 July 1780 Haldimand complained to Major DePeyster of the costs associated with his command. He attributed what were for the times staggering sums (more than £64,000) to the amount and types of trade goods and gifts. The Indians, for example, had been provided with English saddles, no doubt by some astute purveyor who helped create the market and establish the price. He also remarked upon the deleterious effects of government officials also serving as merchants.[298]

In 1781 Haldimand accepted a further demand for £35225.13s.6d.[299] and in 1782 one for £17917.1.6.[300] Moreover, this may have been an enduring feature for some time. Major Robert Mathews,[301] formerly military secretary to General Haldimand and soon to be aide-de-camp to Lord Dorchester, had reported problems of this nature to Haldimand in 1787. Bribery was practised and Captain Robertson at Michilimackinac had made a fortune;[302] it was, Mathews said, assumed that he, like all commanding officers, could be purchased or "rolled in a beaver blanket."[303] He had disabused this unidentified speaker of the idea and stood ready to clear up other problems of order as well.[304] There had been a shameful abuse of the provision and Indian departments and the seigneurial *lods et ventes* had been purloined by Lieutenant Governor Hay and Major Ancrum, then commanding the garrison. Moreover, little had been done to correct these practices by those in charge and indeed Haldimand's correspondence on such matters disappeared. It was perhaps to this period that Powell was referring, rather than to a second round five years later, this time involving Smith or England. Yet peculation may have continued within the Indian Department; Matthew Elliott, superintendent of Indian Affairs for the District of Detroit, was suspected of it and was dismissed in December 1797.[305] Elliott had also acquired four boats, one of them from John Askin. He was not in a hurry to pay. In complaining about this in a letter to Robertson, John Askin felt publicly constrained by his position but made the following private observation: "Have little more to say. I am of the land Board and as in your time we receive Petitions but give no Grants. The Land, the Surveyor, The Country and many of the Pepole are crooked and yet the Instructions are to make all Square and Strait, until the world gets an other Shake as in Noahs time these Orders cannot be Executed."[306]

None of these men acquired Essex land from the board during the time they were on it, as a search of the land records has revealed, but perhaps this is all that might be expected since, under the law, land transactions did not have to be registered. They could, of course, have acted for others; power need not be overt. A better question might be how much land they might potentially have converted by legal process if Indian land grants had been recognized.

Tables 3.1a and 3.1b show the owners of land in this area who owed in excess of £50 under *lods et ventes*, the seigneurial dues.[307] It is not possible to say how much land was owned nor to distinguish land held under French grants from that held under Indian deeds. This limits the usefulness of the data, although, strictly speaking, only land held *en seigneurie* was subject to *lods et ventes*.[308] However, the tables provide some suggestion as to where the pressures on the military commandants and the members of the Land Board might have come from in the two time periods. William Brown, about whom little is known, was clearly important in both periods, as were the merchant firms of Macomb and Macomb, and Macomb, Edgar and Macomb. None of these was a member of the Land Board, although William Macomb was in fact first a magistrate and then one of the two members of the House of Assembly representing Kent.[309] Indeed, if Father Edmund Burke was correct, Macomb acted clearly in his own interest. In 1795 he had successfully sought to prevent a meeting of the tribes which would have been useful to the British interest. With the use of rum, he had portrayed the British as seeking to promote the interests of some tribes over others and had prevailed on some tribes to meet with the American, General Anthony Wayne. The real purpose of this was to preserve his own property. Burke, showing a pastoral concern and perhaps even an obsession with the drink, reveals the power and influ-

Table 3.1a   Those owing more than £50 in *lods et ventes* in the Detroit area, 1775–82

	Name	Amount
1	John Askin	£88.18s.1d.
2	William Brown	£210.4s.10d.
3	James Casely	£122.4s.5½d.
4	Thomas Cox	£100.0s.0d.
5	Joseph Drouillard	£55.11s.1d.
6	Patrick Drouillard	£66.13s.4d.
7	Pierre Drouillard	£53.3s.10d.
8	George Leath [Leith] & Co.	£50.0s.0d.
9	George Lyons, Lyons & Wright	£120.16s.8d.
10	George McBeath	£50.0s.0d.
11	Macomb & Macomb; Macomb, Edgar and Macomb	£211.13s.11¼d.
12	Jacob Schiefflin	£77.15s.6d.
13	Louis Tremblay	£50.0s.0d.
Total *lods et ventes* due		£3619.18s.8¼d.

Table 3.1b   Those owing more than £50 in *lods et ventes* in the Detroit area during Colonel De Peyster's Command, dated 30 April 1783

	Name	Amount
1	John Askin	£123.11s.8d.
2	William Brown	£269.13s.9½d.
3	Thomas Cox	£100.0s.0d.
4	Antoine Dequindre	£52.15s.6¾d.
5	Pierre Drouillard	£186.3s.2¾d.
6	George Lyons	£58.6s.8d.
7	Joseph L'Enfant	£88.15s.7d.
8	Louis Tremblay	£50.0s.0d.
9	Macomb & Macomb	£250.11s.0¾d.
10	Jacob Schiefflin	£55.11s.1d.
Total *lods et ventes* due		£2972.11s.9½d.

Source: NA, RG1, L4, vol. 2, "Lods and Ventes."

ence of this man and two others, Sharp and McIntosh, also merchants, who had been appointed as magistrates. He writes:

I think him one of the most dangerous subjects in this Province. Wealth no matter how acquired, gives him influence, a stock of self-sufficient pride, the necessary result of ignorance in affluence, emboldens him to undertake, and a sort of cunning, a substitute to common sense, enables him to rule the peasant and the Indian. He has moreover a couple of tools at command.

Sharp and McIntosh, both magistrates famous for supplying the Indian with rum. As this junto rules the bench in Detroit his Excellency's appointment of an officer to prevent the sale of spirits, and the whole train of concomitant and consequent evils, is rendered totally ineffectual.[310]

No doubt Macomb did act to preserve his own interest and this may have included testifying against Powell, but there are other candidates for the powerful interests who are alleged to have pressured and abused the system locally. George Leith, a founding partner in the merchant house of Leith, Shepherd and Duff, was a member of the Land Board, as was John Askin after 1792. Askin was to become a major landowner in Essex. Even more significant, he was a major speculator in what was to become Michigan,[311] where he and his fellow speculators, who included William Robertson and Jonathon Schiefflin, expected to obtain twenty million acres.[312] In northern Ohio he claimed 5,294,120 acres.[313] In Essex, he was the most active member of the Land Board. If the records of the board make little explicit recognition of Indian deeds, Askin's actions in Michigan in having his Indian deeds recognized after the British withdrawal from Detroit suggest his economic circumstances and lack of sympathy with official British policy.[314]

If Askin was the representative of any group, it was probably a commercial one that perhaps linked local groups to powerful interests in Montreal and Quebec. His name appears in association with that of Dupéront (Duperron) Baby and others on McNiff's map of "Extravagant Claims" to land, which McNiff presumably used to support his arguments against the Land Board.[315] With the exception of Essex per se, where he identifies the Indian officers Schiefflin and Caldwell as claimants, the names include Alexander Grant for land in what is now Lambton County and Williams, Macomb and Baby for land in what was to become Michigan. All were merchants. Interestingly, little commotion is made in the record at all about Baby, whose holdings were the most extensive of all and whose family connections stretched to the seat of government in Quebec. With the exception of the military, the board was representative of the commercial interest and British policy dictated that this be so. However, there was a second group the Indian officers: the Caldwells, McKees, Elliotts, Birds, La Mottes. They too had their connections to the power structure and, as demonstrated earlier, their connections ensured their welfare. Others who lacked their service or social cachet, such as Schiefflin or Sarah Ainse, would be left in the cold.

It is impossible, two hundred years later, to identify exactly the major players in this area who sought not the welfare of the native or

Table 3.2   Number of grants made, acreage granted and percentage of total within size categories by district, Upper Canada, 1799

Size	Home District			Midland District		
	No. Grants	Acreage	% Total Acreage	No. Grants	Acreage	% Total Acreage
100 or less	235	1621	0.2	37	225	0.1
101–500	1221	278901	31.9	447	93487	51.5
501–1000	144	106666	12.2	46	32798	18.1
1001–2000	84	112313	12.8	22	26335	15.6
2001–3000	9	24389	2.8	3	6900	3.8
3001–4000	1	3450	0.4	1	3263	1.8
4001–5000	3	14170	1.6	1	16543	9.1
5000+	6	33245	38.0	–	–	–
Total	1703	873755	–	557	181551	–

Size	Western District			Eastern District		
	No. Grants	Acreage	% Total Acreage	No. Grants	Acreage	% Total Acreage
100 or less	6	6	-	54	3533	1.0
101–500	296	68989	30.7	1152	244620	67.6
501–1000	52	42239	18.9	65	45829	12.7
1001–2000	61	86389	38.5	28	41279	11.4
2001–3000	6	16355	7.3	3	7500	2.1
3001–4000	1	3600	1.6	4	14169	3.9
4001–5000	–	–	–	1	5000	1.4
5000+	1	7000	3.1	–	–	–
Total	423	224577	–	1307	361930	–

Source: NA, RG1, L6 B, vol. 25, 971, 6 January 1801

that of the embryonic state but rather their own self-interest. However, it is possible to gain a measure of the effects of their activity. Table 3.2 is based upon data taken from the auditor's docket books.[316] It pertains to the districts into which Upper Canada was divided at the close of the eighteenth century. The Western District, the successor to the District of Hesse and a larger unit than Essex County, had by that date fewer grant applications approved to patent. This was no doubt a reflection of its more remote location and more politically tenuous circumstances in comparison to more central locations in the province, such as the Home District. However, it may also have been due to the fact that a minority of individuals anxious to garner the fruits of their efforts had succeeded in discouraging the settlement of the majority. With the exception of the Home District, where the demands of official grantees were also satisfied, the largest percentage of land is to be found in the category 1001 to 2000 acres in the Western District. The acreage accounted for in this category is not as impressive as in the Home District, where six grantees account for 332,245 acres. Yet, in absolute terms, there are many more grantees in the Western District enjoying acreages well in excess of the 200 acres commonly allowed by the Land Board. Indeed, 38.5 per cent of the acreage distributed lay in the under-2000-acre category. Some of the people holding these grants had presumably received them as rewards for service with the military and the Indian Department. Impatient with the land boards, including that in Hesse, Simcoe had often ordered large grants himself.[317] Some received these as merchants, some as public officials,[318] but undoubtedly many had received them from the Indians in "love and affection." In this, Essex was presumably no different from other parts of what was to be Upper Canada, although its particular history and vulnerability may have made for greater impact. Yet the years after 1794 and the abolition of the Land Board would see the structure of landholding in this district and in Essex County transformed significantly as the land began to fill.

CONCLUSION

In an age of acquisitiveness, Upper Canadian land offered almost unprecedented opportunity. What was needed was the fast cession of land from its original owners to be accomplished in a peaceful and orderly manner, especially as the native population became increasingly aware of the true value of land to the European. This was accomplished by the McKee treaty, by which a large part of modern southern Ontario passed to the British Crown. Thereafter, a land board was created in Essex in order to ensure the orderly distribution and development of the land acquired. There is the suggestion that there were powerful interests in Essex who actually sought to retard the settlement of the area until they could complete the private acquisition of land. The identity of those who might have acted in this way remains uncertain though they may have included members of the Land Board. These people saw their private interests as pre-eminent over the orderly settlement of the area and the needs of the native population or indeed of the Crown which they purported to serve.

A social gradient operated here as it did in the British society to which Upper Canada was at least formally attached. As was shown in the disparate treatment of Sarah Ainse, Schiefflin, and the Indian officers, the outcome of events was often predicated upon who one was or one's connections. This was understandable because Upper Canada was little different from Britain. Self-interest, social connection, and power relations were closely related in both societies. In Essex, all three factors operated from the beginning of British settlement and probably in the French era as well. In the final analysis, this was because of the vulnerability of the individual in an age lacking the social-support institutions of the modern state. It was also because of the opportunity to acquire land at domesday prices. It is to this theme, so central to life in the nineteenth century, that this book now turns.

4 European Land Acquisition after the First Land Board

This chapter focuses upon the theme of land acquisition and views it as part of the larger process of settlement. It seeks to answer the following questions. When was land legally acquired or patented in Essex County? By whom was it patented and what influenced the timing of patenting for particular categories of land? In what townships was land acquisition most rapid and why? What was the role of accessibility and the physical environment in the decision of individuals to acquire particular pieces of property? Given these objectives, it is important to understand the rules under which patents were conferred in Upper Canada and Essex, and considerable space is therefore allotted to the theme of colonial land policy. Later in the chapter, the discussion turns to the temporal and spatial patterns apparent in the land-acquisition data.

INTRODUCTION: APPLICATION OF THE RULES OF THE COLONIAL LAND SYSTEM

Although the Land Board of Hesse had been established in 1788, the first land patent or legal title to acquisition was issued in Essex only in 1796. No doubt McNiff might have viewed this development as more than accidental, given his views on the effectiveness of the board's members in developing the territory. Some of the elements of the land-acquisition process that had evolved during the time of the Land Board continued to operate afterwards and others grew from experience with the circumstances of settlement and social conditions in the country. The petitions of William Dummer Powell and John Askin may be illustrative. In 1797 Powell petitioned the Executive Council for 1200 acres for his wife and seven of his children "in consideration of the Petitioner's actual Station in the Province & ten years care and labour to promote its prosperity & happiness as also a life of unceasing loyalty to the King and constitution."[1] He met with a positive response: "The Council unanimously accede to the prayer of this Petition as the Petitioner was one of the first American Loyalists who adhered to the Unity of the Empire, & from a conviction of the propriety of their distinguishing the high & important Office which the petitioner holds in the Province, & of marking their sense of the ability & zeal with which he has conducted himself in it for several years."[2]

Askin, describing himself as a "firm Loyalist" and "praying for such Quantity of Land as the Council may think proper," was ordered to receive 1200 acres.[3] Each of his seven children was ordered to receive 600 acres,[4] but when he applied on 26 July 1799 for land obtained on magistrates' certificates, the Land Committee ruled that the original holders had to apply in their own rights.[5] The petitioning process, then, continued to be used as the initial step both to recognize recipients worthy of favour and to control abuse. One still petitioned for land to the Executive Council. The process could begin there or at the local level with the magistrates who replaced the members of the district board in examining into the character of the applicants and administering the oath. In fact, the board members and the JPs were generally one and the same; most members of the land boards were magistrates and vice versa. The change was Simcoe's and was instituted as part of his plan for the establishment of an aristocracy.[6]

Basically, in the early years, the system was one whereby the Land Board or magistrate, after examination and administering the oath of allegiance, recommended to the lieutenant governor in council the issue of a grant to a petitioner. The order-in-council authorizing the grant was taken to the receiver general's office and the appropriate fees paid. The receipt for fees was returned to the Executive Council office and an order-in-council issued the grantee, who took it to the attorney general's office. The latter issued a *fiat*, which was taken to the surveyor general's office for a ticket of location and description of the lot issued. This description was forwarded to the principal secretary and it was the authorization and guide for engrossing the patent. Upon completion of the conditions of this certificate, a patent was issued. The procedures were changed after the more universal application of settlement duties in 1818. Thereafter, a successful petitioner received a warrant addressed to the surveyor general, who issued a location ticket. Upon completion of the settlement duties, an affidavit to this effect was filed in the Surveyor General's Office. At this stage the fees were paid and a *fiat* was sent from the attorney general to the Surveyor General's Office, where a description of the grant was prepared. This was forwarded to the provincial secretary, who prepared the patent.[7] The terms varied over time and from place to place and took many years to complete. For some this was too much.

Problems with the System: Squatting

Part of the problem in land matters in the early years was that the steps for acquiring land were cumbersome and involved considerable personal inconvenience. Some, disillusioned by the process or having no intention to acquire land legally, simply squatted upon it. In fact, this was an important process in the settlement of Upper Canada. It was also an ephemeral one which left almost no trace in the land records though not in the political realm.

Throughout much of the first half of the nineteenth century, the term "squatter" had an ambivalent meaning because land titles on the frontier were often unclear and many "settlers" started off life as what would legally be described as "squatters." Government reports recognized this, distinguishing between the "deserving" and "undeserving squatter,"[8] the latter knowingly and illegally occupying frontier land to denude it of its resources in quick order. Nowhere was this distinction clearer than upon Indian land in the Grand River valley. A report of 1844 noted that action against the farm-oriented "squatter" (the deserving) might be postponed because by their improvements such people had "given a sort of security for their ultimately making to the Indians full compensation for their temporary usurpation." A second class, those selling liquor and "disseminating the vices into which the Indians, so easily fall" (the undeserving), were to be acted against promptly.[9] On the other hand, it was not possible to protect Indian land per se in the Grand River area. Sydney Harring points out that in 1840 a European squatter population equalled in size that of the Indian population and occupied 20 per cent of the land.[10] These people could have been quickly punished for violating the Royal Proclamation of 1763 and General Brock's proclamation of 1812, both designed during particular exigencies to protect Indian rights and to secure Indian loyalty. They were not. Rather, in 1841 the Indians, under pressure from a government unable to protect their interests, surrendered much of their land in the valley, retaining a smaller portion which in theory could be protected against the action of squatters. As Harring points out, it was not. It might seem that the less agriculturally oriented owners of this land were in fact less "deserving"![11]

Clearly, government policy saw development and orderly progress in agricultural terms. Indeed, Lillian Gates has acknowledged that, apart from government assistance itself, "squatting" was the prime element promoting settlement.[12] In contradistinction, she sees the creation of privileged grants, which, in altered form, continued until 1851 as detrimental to the settlement of the country. Some of these clergy reserves, Crown reserves, Crown land, and Indian and private land were occupied by squatters. Pre-emption privileges were subsequently allowed them and in some instances they successfully petitioned for legal possession of the lots they occupied.[13]

An increasing incidence of conflict, the use of "professional" squatters to assist land speculators in pursuit of profit rather than social goals,[14] the dilapidated appearance of neighbouring property, and the exhaustion of soil by an insecure, impermanent group of people finally led society to turn against squatters. In 1852 Chief Justice John Beverley Robinson was asked by John Macaulay[15] of the Legislative Council for his assistance in drafting a bill to afford occupants of private land what in custom they had enjoyed but in law had never received. He agreed to assist but warned Macaulay that he (Macaulay) might not control nor appreciate the outcome of the process he had begun. The chief justice advanced his own personal opinion:

I have no sympathy with the genus squatter ... I would [allow] no preemption right to be [given those?] who have gone upon land to which they well knew they had no ... claim ... but would give them plainly to understand that so far from the impudent act of trespass giving them a claim they might be satisfied that whatever other persons might get a grant of land they certainly never should – on any terms.

I think the favour that has always been shown to squatters has a democratizing tendency and leads to confusion in the notions of *meum and teum*.[16]

Robinson, however, was himself a land speculator and squatters often employed such people as their agents. Furthermore, one suspects that in spirit, if not in law, he would have exempted those servants of the Crown, the Indian officers, who, in defiance of the Royal Proclamation of 1763,[17] had "squatted" upon land in Malden. He was no doubt pleased to see the privilege of pre-emption ended in 1859 and the Crown Lands Department dispose of land held in this way in Essex and elsewhere in 1861.[18]

In fact, the government of Upper Canada had from an early date required its surveyors to report the phenomenon and warned squatters that they should vacate on pain of being denied a regular grant.[19] In the Western District, Burwell had complied, reporting on those he found along the St Clair River in 1826. Thereby he provided one of the more extensive sets of data for this area and a valuable glimpse into a fleeting phenomenon.[20] Here and elsewhere, squatting was regarded positively. Individuals petitioning for land to the Crown Lands Department in the 1840s and 1850s would cite the improvements they had made, confidently expecting a grant to be made to them.[21] Occasionally, the records contain revealing pieces of information. Joseph Richard, writing from Sandwich to the Crown Lands Department in 1846, commented on problems with the central bureaucracy. He had been told to see a surveyor and had done so. He had been told to petition the governor. He had done so. He had improved the land. He had a verbal agreement of 30 pence per acre but the demand had now doubled. He would like to know what he had to do for the agent: McMullin "says he would sell the said lot at 5/- and I am already on it ... Please let me and McMullin have a final answer about the matter."[22] This is hardly the expression of a supplicant but rather one convinced of the strength of his cause. Others expressed a similar conviction. In 1839 one J.B. Lucien (presumably Jean-Baptiste) agreed to buy the north half of lot 2, north of the Middle Road in Colchester, adjoining his property. He had been unable to pay until now, now being twenty-five years later![23] Joseph Giniac was similarly willing to pay but could not remember how long he had been there.[24] Vidal Vermieux claimed occupancy rights under a deed from one of the Baby family, a transaction that, while not strictly legal, carried social respectability for Vermieux and one presumes the Crown Lands Department.[25] In fact, the department would most usually be only too pleased to agree to make such an occupation legitimate.

Indeed, the usefulness of squatters in opening up new country was long admitted and the squatter came to be thought of as "equitably entitled to compensation for his improvements if he were dispossessed."[26] Given the slowness of the process by which land was obtained from the governor in council,[27] in the era before the establishment of the land boards, squatting was thought to be a reasonable response. If Major Smith, the president of the Land Board, is not thought the disingenuous agent of a commercial cabal, he believed that squatters deserved compensation. Some individuals had petitioned for lots on the Thames but had conformed to the Land Board's order to resist occupation; others had squatted and had made improvements "almost through self-defence." He maintained that "should the original petitioner be invested with the certificate: and the actual occupant thereby dispossessed, a Reasonable equivalent for the labour of the latter merits investigation, by the Claimant, perhaps making good to the Occupier, the value of the improvement, extending the value of the Enjoyment."[28] The larger grants made to the privileged meant that there was a constant shortage of surveyed land, and with the introduction of a sales system in 1825 there would no longer be agents in the local area to provide information or to issue location tickets. Given this, vacant land held as United Empire Loyalist, militia, Crown and clergy, or Canada Company grants might be regarded as legitimate targets by a community sympathetic to genuine, if impermanent, farmers. Such a view would appear justifiable to any potential squatter but doubly so to an American, out of sympathy with a monarchical system which treated him as an alien who could never receive a grant.

Squatting or "pitching" occurred for all of the reasons stated and because there have always been people prepared to take advantage of opportunity.[29] The sales act instituted in 1825 extended credit to purchasers and since no deposit was required many individuals would outbid their competitors at auction and simply fail to complete the purchase, counting on the fact that by the time of the next auction those prepared to pay would have disappeared.[30] Unsold or unleased clergy reserve lands seem to have been a particular target since the majority of people were unsympathetic to benefits bestowed on a particular church. Moreover, the rules of the Clergy Corporation, charged with the management of the clergy reserves, did little to change these predispositions. If one submitted an application form, pre-emption rights were bestowed and this continued even after the auction system came into effect and indeed was continued until 1836.[31] Purchases could then be made on ten years' credit and at auction, where little else than the upset price could be obtained.[32] Of course, if substantial clearance had taken place, the squatter would exercise his pre-emption right at the value of unimproved land and receive compensation for improvements. The regulations of 1841 limited this compensation to 25 per cent of the purchase price but recognized squatters of five years as having equity considerations if they paid back rents at 35 shillings (420 pence) per year and applied to purchase. What was most telling was that the provision for purchase was at 75 per cent of current valuation, not the original valuation. This put pressure on squatters on clergy land as never before.[33] Regulations such as these might well explain Richard's predicament and Giniac's amnesia!

In March 1846 pre-emptions were again recognized with a purchase deadline line of 1847. This, together with the offer of credit for purchases of clergy reserves, did affect the sale of such land. Indeed, 1847 was the most active year for sales to that point[34] although not all of this was because of pre-emptions. However, pre-emptions in Upper Canada were sufficient to suspend sales of clergy reserves in 1839. The point here is that, until the late 1840s, there was little incentive for squatters on clergy land to become purchasers. One might use the land for some years and if "caught" receive recompense for improvement while at the same time avoiding taxes which the more legally minded brought down upon themselves. The benefits of "pitching" simply outweighed the expenses of legitimate ownership until the later decades.

This was also true on Crown land and even for a time for Canada Company land, the former Crown reserves sold to the company in 1826. In 1828 government and the company came to an arrangement whereby ten-year squatters on land which was to become company property would receive land at an arbitrated price for wild land. They would also receive benefits for their improvements.[35] Of course, where they could not prove ten-year residence, they had to buy at company prices or lose their improvement. The famous Durham report recommended that squatters on Crown land should be granted a pre-emption and compensation for improvements made to private land.[36] The Land Act of 1837 allowed the governor-in-council to permit private sales of Crown land at a valuation to lessees and occupants who would suffer injury if they could not buy a specific lot. This provision was maintained in the Act of 1841 but squatters never received a *right* to pre-emption and were still petitioning for favour in Essex in the late 1840s and 1850s. Yet squatters were treated leniently by the Crown Lands Department; they were informed of their pre-emption privileges and urged to apply if a request to purchase their lot was received. Even after they had received the appropriate order, they were given three months to purchase, subject to interest. Lots with valuable improvements could not be sold without reference to the department.[37]

Robinson's opinion notwithstanding, it would seem that there were no serious strictures against squatting until the fourth decade of the century, presumably because squatting was seen to be a social good. It may also have been recognized as such by speculators, especially if a cordial arrangement could be arrived at to compensate for improvements because such improvements made the property more desirable. There can be no direct measure of this for Essex and probably for few other areas in Upper Canada because of the nature of the process; however, given the attitude towards squatting, it must have been fairly common. It was only when the process was abused, when the intent was not to derive direct benefit from the land itself but a subterfuge and a mechanism for extensive land speculation, that conflict arose. This happened more towards mid-century in "new" areas such as Huron County[38] where controversies over squatting led to its curtailment.[39]

What can be learned of the qualities of squatters from the Burwell inventory? The range of time spent as a squatter could be from 0.4 to 22 years but ten of the twenty-one families had been squatting for less than five years, at least in the Western District. While the size of family was small for the times, averaging less than six persons, nine of the twenty-one were under four persons but three contained twelve individuals. With respect to acreage improved, this could vary from effectively nothing to sixty acres. The average was 21.1 acres but the distribution was multi-modal, with modes of one, seven, twenty-one, and sixty acres, and the mean and standard deviation were not useful measures. In this as in other qualities, there were a variety of conditions, yet overall there was a relationship between these qualities and the extent of improved land. Pearson correlation coefficients were most strongly associated with the length of time ($r=0.72$),[40] with the number of males ($r=0.59$),[41] and with total family size ($r=0.57$).[42] Eleven of the twenty-one heads of household bore obviously French-Canadian names. Seven had come from Michigan, including Detroit and the Grand Portage within the term; four had come from Montreal and the remainder originated in Upper Canada. With the exception of J.B. Nantais and John Bury, both of whom were newly arrived, all lived in substantial log homes averaging 409 square feet[43] and nine had built log or frame barns[44]. All had either made the improvements themselves or in two cases had inherited the property from their relatives. One was the widow of an Indian Department interpreter who had been promised three hundred acres of land. All were farmers, including François Bertrand, who operated as a blacksmith, and Francois Pelet, whose mill and residence was 572 square feet. James Henderson and Robert Ballinté declared that they were the tenants of one Campau. Asked who had encouraged them to settle, one cited Francis Baby of Malden, one the priest, Father Crevier; six reported the Indians to whom they were paying rent. John Bury, newly arrived, had settled on "mere fancy." John Courtenay, who had been there for twenty-two years, reported that Lord Dalhousie had told him to "work away"; if his lordship had forgotten, Courtenay had not but presumably it suited him. Two individuals had vacated their land between 1807 and 1812, returning in 1815 and 1820 after hostilities had ceased; presumably Americans, they had gone into the Michigan Territory for a time.

*Land-Acquisition within the Rule of Law: Problems and
Resolution*

Those accustomed to an existence of greater security and wishing to
secure their investment of labour and money sought this within the
legal framework of the state. Like those who became squatters, they
might be frustrated with the slowness of procedures. Many contented
themselves with the possession of a certificate either from the Land
Board or from the principal secretary rather than possession of a land
patent. These certificates became the basis of subsequent sale and
transfer, although the patent was the most secure legal instrument and
the final statement of possession. For those seeking to enter the world
of farming and seeking permanency, this was no problem. However,
there were others whose acquisitive nature required constant trading;
for these people, strict adherence to the steps required in British colonial land policy could hinder their rise to prosperity and aggrandize-
ment. Already by the time of the abolition of the land boards, there
had been considerable dealing in land outside this framework; the
extent was described by Richard Cartwright, who, as a major
landowner himself, had an interest in seeing the certificates and other
instruments he possessed recognized as the equivalents of patents. In
1795 he declared:

Ten years had thus elapsed before any Preparation for granting Patents were
in forwardness, and such have been the Mutations of landed property, or to
speak more correctly, of the Rights to landed property, that almost every
Inhabitant of the Province is more or less interested in them. That Patents
were not issued agreeable to the Assurances held forth in the Certificates was
certainly not the fault of the People; and if they should now be delivered to
the Original Holders of the Certificates the whole Country will be thrown into
Confusion. The strongest Temptations will be held out to Fraud and avarice,
all mutual Confidence between the People destroyed, & such Heats & Animosities kindled as may be attended with the most pernicious Consequences
– For although, on complying with the Terms of the Certificate, the Holders
had in justice, the entire and Compleat property of the soil, to be disposed of
as he should see fit, yet in the technical Precision of the law, the delivery of the
patent will entirely overturn every prior Sale or Exchange, even those Sanctioned by the Land Boards perhaps not excepted, will invalidate every Mortgage and give a power to the Party, his heirs or subsequent assigns to eject the
Person who may have made a Bona Fide purchase, and who may have
expended in Improvements more than Twenty fold the original value of the
soil.[45]

Cartwright proposed that, where the conditions of occupation, transfer, sale, and mortgage had been met as subscribed to by two witnesses and the deeds registered within one year of the proposed act, no subsequent patent would be considered as annulling prior claims. The document was transmitted to the Colonial Secretary without comment by Simcoe, who had little sympathy for, and indeed felt he had been humiliated by, the merchant class whom Cartwright epitomized.[46] Nothing came of this proposal directly nor of the attempt by Cartwright's partner, Robert Hamilton, to suggest that the failure to allow for the clergy reserves in the patents necessitated a provincial act which would render certificates valid. The agitation was considerable, however, and resulted in a different solution which passed the legislature in 1797.

This was the Heirs and Devisees Commission, created to resolve issues involving the original nominees of the Crown and their heirs, devisees, and assignees.[47] Appointed commissioners were empowered to determine ownership and to authorize the issue of patents; in the case of mortgages, certificates were issued which, when registered, were to have the effect of treating the land as under patent at the date the mortgage was made. The act creating the commission was passed before the Colonial Office became aware of it. It gave the merchants what they wanted, although, in fairness, it did provide a route to the resolution of difficulties in land proceedings in Upper Canada. However, as William Dummer Powell, who had an alternative scheme stated, much depended upon the attitude of the commissioners.[48] Lillian Gates notes that men deeply interested in a lax interpretation of the law were appointed to the commission. Merchants who had enjoyed contracts to provide for the British army in Upper Canada, who had acted together, and who were land speculators all served; John Askin, Richard Cartwright, and Robert Hamilton vetted each other's certificates.[49] Powell had sought greater adherence to the law of England, although, arguably, the particular circumstances of Upper Canada might have justified a different solution.[50] His scheme included provisions for a jury which would have avoided what he predicted might happen. At first Powell refused to sit on the commission but he later played his part. He was frequently out-voted in a situation where a majority in a commission of three carried the day. Askin, whose own son served on the commission that decided in favour of his father's requests, complained that Powell sought stricter evidence than was required by the act which established the commission.[51] He also sought proof of a nature which, after the event, required a considerable expenditure of money. The chief justice, John Elmsley, was less stringent in his

Table 4.1   Extent to which land certificates had been acquired
by speculators, 1797–1805

Name	Acreage
John Askin	9600
The Baby Family	13400
Hon. Richard Cartwright	9700
William Dickson	5350
Hon. Richard Duncan	5100
Jacob Farrand	10000
Joseph Forsyth	9800
R.I.D. Gray	9700
Robert Hamilton	40645
John McKindlay	15520
Robert McAulay	4050
William Raddish	4750
Livius P. Sherwood	3900
Samuel Street	8800
William Robertson	6800

Source: Gates, Land Policies, 60

demands and Askin Looked forward to his tour of Essex and the Western District.[52]

Gates, using five of the ten books of the records of the Heirs and Devisees Commission in conjunction with the minutes of the Executive Council, demonstrates the extent to which land certificates had passed into the hands of speculators or merchants. Her figures for *some* of the larger holders exclude unlocated lands; if these had been included, the magnitude of holding would have been even greater.[53] Presented in Table 4.1, the holdings include the names of prominent individuals familiar to the reader, including Askin and Robertson. Both men were members of the Land Board and Askin, as noted, was a commissioner of the Heirs and Devisees Commission.[54] Others related to Askin, as Robertson was, were William Dickson and Robert Hamilton and then there was the Baby family, also with Essex connections. These men had received province-wide prominence, as their appointment to the commission recognized.

Two points to be made here are relevant to the chapter and the volume as a whole. The first is that members of the power structure used their positions to sanction their own acquisitiveness, a theme of chapter 9. The second is that clearly these were instances where acquisition of the patent, important to the individual, need mean nothing in terms of the actual settlement of the land. Yet, in the majority of instances, the Heirs and Devisees Act did protect those who had only a few claims to submit for land legitimately acquired by inheritance, purchase, or exchange. In terms of the meaning of the patents, legitimate settlers or speculators, having obtained a favourable interpretation of their claim, might not proceed to complete their title by acquiring the patent. In part, this could explain why many patents in the land records occur after transactions have occurred even when the grantors and grantees are clearly of the same family. As Gates points out, in some instances, the third generation of the original Crown nominees had to apply to the commission a second time. Also for these reasons, the life of the commission was successively extended to 1911, although, in Gate's opinion, most of its work had been accomplished by 1805.[55]

Grants, Sales, and the Patent

In Upper Canada and Essex in these years, those whom the system chose to recognize might acquire one of two basic types of grants. "Normal" grants were of the order of 100 to 200 acres, "privileged" grants of a greater magnitude. The latter were made to those who had served as members of the military,[56] to provincial servants who were to be rewarded for service (for example, Baby or Grant) or to strengthen an aristocracy,[57] or to those who bore the "mark of honour" as United Empire Loyalists and their descendants. As was shown in the last chapter, merchants could sometimes be included among the "privileged." Both groups received patents conferring ownership but under different circumstances. The privileged received their land as suitable recipients of the King's bounty; the former, the "normal" or common grantees, received it upon completion of the settlement duties specified in their location tickets. Before 1825, the system was one of grants subject to survey and administrative fees. Various officials, including the governor himself, derived revenue from these fees.[58] There was, therefore, always a conflict between the need to see the land properly developed and the temptation to derive immediate benefit by reducing the settlement duties to mere tokens or the time allowed to patent.

After 1825, the grant system was replaced by a sales system[59] but those acquiring land by sale still received a patent since this was a fundamental part of property law. It also conferred the right to vote under the system of manhood suffrage. Clause four of Simcoe's proclamation of 1792[60] recognized petitioners as "he or she" (Plate 2.13) but in practice this was almost always as the wives or widows of men. There were women who successfully obtained patents in their own right; Sarah Ainse is an example.[61] But, generally in this period, the doctrine of marital unity entailed the suspension of the independent existence of the wife and "an absorption by the husband of the woman's person and all her belongings."[62] The point is well illustrated by Constance Backhouse in her account of one Hannah Nolan (née Snider) of Colchester Township whose father had sought to provide for her in 1824 with a life interest in fifty acres of land. Her husband, Henry Nolan, even after he abandoned her, continued to enjoy his interest in the land until he sold it in 1856. Nothing could be done until 1864 when he died. The courts then ruled that her life interest reverted to her and she got it back.[63] The situation of Catherine De Cou was worse. She petitioned Peter Russell (Plate 4.1), as President administering Upper Canada, to split land awarded to her mother who had remarried. Her petition is sufficiently succinct to merit reproduction here both to illustrate the form of petitions and to point to the particular concern, De Cou's insecurity. It read:

That she is the only child of the late Frederic Dockstader by Elizabeth now the wife of William Van Every – that upon the Petition of the said Elizabeth as Widow of the said Frederic in Behalf of herself and Child, an Order was made that twelve hundred Acres of land should be surveyed for her and her Son, whereas she had then no son or other Child than your petitioner, who therefore prays that your Honor would take into Consideration the Remises and direct that the said land be divided between your Petitioner and her said Mother & several Deeds for the same be issued in their respective Names, and Your petitioner as in Duty bound will ever pray etc.[64]

The seemingly obsequious form of this petition, with its assurances of duty required, was common enough in the time. Signed for her by her husband, John, it sought to preserve her interest from her mother's new husband but failed to do so.[65] The patent, dated 17 May 1802, was put in the name of Mrs Elizabeth Van Every but was issued to her husband William who, as head of family, received Dockstader's entitlement both metaphorically and in fact.[66] The record is silent on why this happened, although it is perhaps difficult to see how the outcome could have been otherwise without causing social disruption in the larger society. Arguably, the purpose of the grant had been met in that it was awarded to the widow Dockstader to provide for herself and her child. Adequate provision had indeed been made until the girl could marry but even so, there cannot be any doubt that Dockstader would have wished his child to receive the bounty of his entitlement rather than some unknown man. Though it might be that eventually Catherine and her offspring would benefit, the fact that the land was in Van Every's hands made this far from sure.[67]

Plate 4.1   The Hon. Peter Russell. The son of an improvident Irish army officer,
he was the administrator of Upper Canada from 1796 to 1799.
Courtesy of Archives of Ontario (s2168).

After 1825, this system of grants existed side by side with a sales policy; the patent or instrument of legal entitlement issued upon completion of a cash or credit transaction.[68] The patent must therefore be seen as being different things in the period before and after 1825, although in the final analysis it represents simply the date of legal acquisition from the government.

Colonial Land Policy: The Context of the Patents

Although the origins of Upper Canada's land policy can be traced in the first instance to Quebec, of which it was a part for so long, its roots lie in the British administration in Florida, New York, New Hampshire, the Carolinas, and Georgia. From Governor James Murray's instructions of 1763 through to the institution of sales in 1825, policy fluctuated. It did so in response to the philosophy, resolve, and determination of the home government, the opportunities for immigration and development of the colony, the condition of the treasury, and, since fees paid by settlers constituted an important source of individual wealth, the personal predispositions of successive administrators, and their personal avarice.

Murray's instructions were the first pronouncement on land policy for the province of Quebec, a jurisdiction that included within it the territory that was to become Upper Canada and that therefore guided development in Essex. These instructions remained in force until altered by Sir Guy Carleton, who re-established the traditional seigneurial system in 1771. Murray's scheme introduced a township of 20,000 acres modelled on the New England system of township planning, containing reserves for military and naval purposes, a town site, and lots for a church, a cleric, and a schoolmaster. To prevent rampant speculation, grants were to be limited to those who would cultivate them and to 100 acres plus 50 acres for each member of a household. After two years these grants would be subject to a quit-rent[69] of two shillings for every 100 acres. Settlement duties were required of the grantee. However, while provision was made for registering proof of performance, it was not required before obtaining the patent or legal entitlement to the property, unless a second grant was sought.

A second element in the design called for rewards for those who had served the cause of Empire by serving in the King's forces. Reduced officers and disbanded men who had served in North America during the Seven Year's War and were resident in the colony were to receive lands commensurate with their rank. For example, those of field rank were to get 5000 acres, non-commissioned officers (NCOs) 200 acres, and private soldiers 50 acres. Moreover, the troops, unlike civilians, were to be exempt from quit rents for 10 years.

These two elements, of a grants policy for civilians and a rewards scheme for those who had served the military and civilian establishment, became an abiding part of British colonial land policy for many years to come, although the details changed at particular points in time. Thus, the Royal Instruction of 16 July 1783 rewarded field officers with only 1000 acres, captains with 700 acres, and subalterns, staff

officers, and warrant officers with 500 acres unless they had served in
the 84th Foot. This particular regiment had been disbanded, and
those of its members who chose to settle in Upper Canada would be
available to muster when called upon to do so. As shown in chapter 3,
these people, if of field rank, would receive 5000 acres; captains, 3000
acres; subalterns, 2000 acres; NCOs, 200 acres; and privates, 50 acres.
After agitation this was extended to all reduced personnel, without distinction of corps. A number came to be settled in the New Settlement,
along the Erie shore, as was shown in the last chapter. This same
instruction restored Murray's grants of 100 acres to the family,
together with the provision that each family member would receive 50
acres. However, this was soon restricted to those who had entered the
province before 1787. Under the 1783 terms, all grants were to be free
of survey and patent fees, provisions that were to cost the state's treasury dearly since so much of the business of government turned upon
the land business. A third element in the Murray instructions, a provision to sell up to 1000 acres for £5, anticipated a condition which a
number of officials fought for, including Robert Prescott (Plate 4.2) in
1798, but which, for various reasons, was never implemented for more
than sixty years.

In 1768 Murray was succeeded by Sir Guy Carleton, later Lord
Dorchester.[70] It was he who commenced to decentralize the administration by creating land boards, among them that of Hesse. As noted
in the last chapter, this board could grant 200 acres immediately;
larger acreages and family acreages could be obtained on application
to a land committee in Quebec which in turn reported to the Executive Council. Such control was necessary because of interpretations
being placed upon the bounty extended to Loyalists, that these people
were entitled to land for themselves and their children as a "mark of
honour," irrespective of the time of arrival. It would seem that it was
the governor's intention to restrict such largesse to the daughters
(upon marriage) and to the sons (upon reaching the age of majority)
of "families who had adhered to the Unity of Empire and joined the
Royal Standard in America before the Treaty of Separation in the year
1783."[71] Given the difference of definition, control was essential.

Before the creation of the land boards in 1788, all grants were made
under the instructions of 1783 and 1786 and were subject to a quit-
rent of one half-penny per acre. They were made in seigneurial
tenure, a stipulation that may in part explain the morphology of lots
in the New Settlement, where long narrow lots still run back from
Lake Erie. Though surveyed in British times, they mimicked the form
of the French seigneurial grants in Sandwich Township. None of this
pleased the Loyalists, many of whom sought the abolition of both the

Plate 4.2   General Robert Prescott, governor-in-chief of British North America, 1796–99. He sought to prevent land speculation in Upper Canada. Mezzotint of a painting by William Albrecht Ulrich Berczy, Sr.
Courtesy of National Archives (c12562).

rent and seigneurial tenure. In both objectives they were successful. Quit-rents were remitted for ten years and the seigneurial system was effectively abolished in the new territory.

The Constitutional Act of 1791 which created Upper Canada was proclaimed by Simcoe in 1792.[72] It simply provided for grants in "free and common soccage" (clause five of Plate 2.13) and allowed those holding certificates of occupation to receive fresh grants. Clause four of the proclamation specified that land was to be granted only to those who could show they could improve it, but the extent of the improvement needed to pass to patent was not specified. The maximum grant available under clause three was interpreted to be 1200 acres and all grants were to be free of expense, other than the fee for the patent itself (clause eight). This and the provision in the second clause for Crown and clergy reserves, designed to obviate the need for taxation, was part of the method by which Simcoe hoped to show Great Britain's rebellious colonies the benefits of the imperial connection. Paradoxically, the imperial government increasingly favoured a revenue system; a manifestation of this was that, after 1796, all grants carried survey fees unless, of course, made out to Loyalist or military claimants.

The proclamation of 31 October 1798[73] established a change of fee to six pence an acre, exclusive of the expenses of survey of one pound, seven shillings, and six pence (330 pence). This proposal had been accepted because it increased revenue, raised the value of the land of existing owners (including officials), and ensured that those who had struggled earlier now benefited. The survey fee and half the patent fee had to be paid when the warrant was taken out; the balance was due when the patent was issued. If a grantee wanted more than one patent, he was to be charged the full fee for every patent except the largest, and the land covered by any one patent had to lie in the same township. If not, several patent fees would be needed. The patent fee, which had been £2.18s.8d. (704 pence sterling), was now raised to £5.0.0 (1200 pence), of which £1.2s.2d. (266 pence) went to the officers of the Crown Lands Department. The last figure represented 22.2 per cent of the total but was still regarded as inadequate by those who administered the system. This period, which was one which saw a serious attempt to increase revenues and, concomitantly, fees, witnessed other adjustments. In November 1797 military claimants were limited to 1200 acres so that land would be available for those capable of paying. On 15 December 1798, a proclamation restricted Loyalists to 200 acres free of charge if resident before 28 July 1798 but allowed these people to employ an agent rather than attend at York and to have the claim certified at the Quarter Sessions.

After Simcoe's departure in 1796 and his subsequent resignation in 1798, and before the appointment of General Peter Hunter in 1799, Upper Canada was administered by Peter Russell.[74] He, like Dorchester and Simcoe, was of the view that property added to one's dignity and influence, and that maintenance of the social distinction found in older societies was a safeguard against the democratic and republican influences emanating from the United States. To that end, he made land grants of 1200 acres to magistrates, barristers, and "old merchants," 600 acres to "young merchants," and 400 acres to merchants' clerks. The wives of barristers and members of the House of Assembly received 600 acres. The children of Loyalists, who would normally have received 200 acres, received several times this according to their father's rank. Senior officials received as much as 8400 acres and the wives and children of legislative councillors 1200 acres. Russell justified his action: "The Consideration which has induced us to join in this Request ... is the Propriety, if not the necessity, which we conceive to exist that all the Servants of the Crown in this Province should in their separate Stations support the Honor and dignity of His Majesty's Government by adopting as large a plan in their domestic establishment and their manner of living as their Incomes will admit."[75]

The argument carried the day and in this instance former councillors were awarded 6000 acres each. The award was justified in terms of the expenses involved in removing from Newark in the Niagara peninsula to York, the precursor of modern Toronto and the new seat of government. In this way, the oligarchy in power rewarded itself with the resources of the state.

No doubt Russell initiated the change because he subscribed to Loyalist values, but he also personally welcomed the fees and was disappointed that he was obliged to share them with his predecessor, Simcoe. His successor, Hunter,[76] declared that Russell was so avaricious that he would have admitted the devil and his family as Loyalists so long as the appropriate fees could be paid.[77] This pattern continued. In 1802 survey and patent fees were both required within three days of the order-in-council, effectively rendering the requirements and benefits of settlement duties null and void. In 1803 patent fees had to be paid in sterling rather than Halifax currency; the effect was to raise revenue and, concomitantly, fees by about one-ninth. By 1804, the fees on a 2000-acre lot, including survey and patent, totalled £8.4s.1d. or 1969 pence. That same year grants unlocated by 26 June were considered void unless all fees were paid at the *new* rate within three days to ensure immediate receipt of the patent fee and its less immediate disbursement to officialdom. Also, to ensure that those privileged grantees, the children of United Empire Loyalists, would not procrastinate until a sale was imminent, their agents were required to take out patents immediately their claim was recognized. Between 1802 and 1804, Hunter struck off 900 names from the list of Loyalists entitled to free grants.[78] After 1804, all grantees were allowed to forgo settlement duties if they paid the 1804 fees (in most cases higher than originally required) and appointed an agent to sue out the patent.

Hunter, appointed lieutenant governor on the 10 April 1799, sought to maximize his personal return.[79] He issued patents in the names of the original grantees even though the registration of ownership may have changed and the legality of the transaction was under consideration by the requisite body, the Heirs and Devisees Commission. This way, two fees were possible if not certain, and the return was much faster. Hunter, in due course, received his share of the fee; the legal uncertainty made work for his successor who was not recompensed for it. Hunter's years saw 7800 patents pass, a rate unequalled again until 1824[80] when the threat of the inception of the sales system provoked an appropriate response. In part this was because he engrossed patents on a production schedule, with the expenses of the materials borne by his secretary. William Dummer Powell wrote that "by this singular Course of Tyranny the Lieutenant Governor was enriched and the secretary was beggared."[81]

Particular circumstances could, of course, change things. During the War of 1812 and immediately thereafter, grants were made to the military, free of fees. Enlisted men received 100 acres, officers initially 200 acres to ensure compact settlement near their men and then additional land commensurate with rank. Both enlisted men and officers also received provisions for one year and farm implements. Civilians from the United Kingdom received 100 acres, as did their sons at majority. These people got tools at less than cost, as well as rations free for six months and then at cost until the harvest was in. To guarantee attachment to the colony, a deposit of £6 was required for a male and £2 for every female. This was refundable in two years.

Common or ordinary applicants could get 100 acres and paupers 50 acres from land boards, re-established in the local district so that immigrants need not attend at York. By 1819, with the return of more normal circumstances, fees were again escalating. In that year they doubled on lots greater than 100 acres and in 1820 they doubled again. This was the work of Lieutenant Governor Maitland and it proceeded without the sanction of the United Kingdom government. The effect was that a 200-acre lot in an older township cost three shillings (36 pence) per acre or £30 in total, although there were still areas where government policy was such that it was possible to obtain land for less than the prevailing fees.[82] In light of this, Lillian Gates believes that the process of converting to a land-purchase system began well before 1825.[83] In fact, as will be shown later, in 1825 the recommended "upset price" in many areas was four shillings per acre.

In the period before the institution of a formal sales policy, settlement duties varied through time and over space. The land regulations of 1763–71 made provision for registering proof of performance of these duties but this was not required before patenting. Indeed, registration was not required at all unless the grantee wished a second grant on the same terms as the first.[84] Lord Dorchester required improvements within twelve months and instituted a requirement that additional grants to the military or Loyalists be granted only after improvements had been made on initial grants.[85] Yet in fact it has been shown that, although required as early as 1763 and regarded as an integral part of the settlement process, the requirement for improvements could be set aside totally if it suited officialdom, which could thereby collect its fees more expeditiously. While land was granted under the Constitutional Act in free and common soccage, it was understood that it was granted on condition of cultivation but no precise terms of improvements were inserted in the patents. Simcoe's instructions were that land was to be granted to those who could improve it. This obligation was to be expressed in the patents but, since it was never expressed specifically, this was of little effect.[86] In the early years it was not required that people would reside on their lot; it was assumed that they would reside in the province, although even here exceptions were made. Settlement duties were enforced in a piecemeal manner. Generally, after 1791, it was necessary to build a house of sixteen by twenty feet, clear half the roadway in front of the lot, and clear and fence five acres. These were what was known as "Yonge Street" conditions after the area where they were first instituted.

As seen earlier, the Executive Council had by 1802 required survey and patent fees to be paid within three days of a grant being made and the patent had to be sued out within three weeks. The effect was to abandon settlement duties, replacing them with a stipulation of three years' residence. In remote areas there was little prospect of checking this and, in any case the patent was out! In 1804, except along Yonge and Dundas streets, the main north-south and east-west axes, it was permitted to ignore the settlement duties if the fees introduced in that year were paid within twelve months. With the exception of the Talbot settlement, where actual residence on the property was required, where clearance demands were twice the provincial norm, and where an eccentric and autocratic Anglo-Irishman, Thomas Talbot, super-vised his "principality," these duties became increasingly token.[87] Beyond Yonge Street, Dundas Street, and the Talbot settlement, given that the duties could be dispensed with for a fee, the only restriction on grants was the provision inserted in the patents since 1803 which required three years' residence.[88]

Plate 4.3 is illustrative of settlement requirements away from the Talbot Road in these years. It shows a patent issued to John Askin for 140 acres of lot 95 in the 1st concession of Colchester Township.[89] This occurred under the seal of Peter Hunter on 7 December 1803 and, no doubt in the expectation of fees, was endorsed by Russell

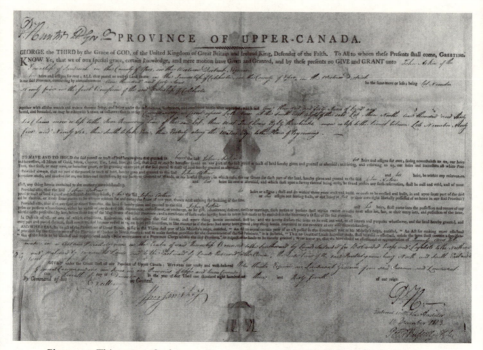

Plate 4.3   This patent, for lot 95, 1st concession, was issued to John Askin by Peter Russell on 15 December 1803. It allowed the transfer of the land before the settlement duties were complete!
Courtesy of Archives of Ontario (F474, MU13, John Askin Papers).

within eight days! The patent reserves all gold, silver, tin, lead, iron, coal, and white pine for the Crown. It specifies that twenty acres had been set against it to meet the requirements of the Crown and clergy reserve policy and notes that, if a reservation had been made for it by the surveyor of woods, the grant was null and void. In this very condition is an indication that the administration of lands was far from perfect. Among the other conditions, those placed upon the patentee lay in the future, again a prescription for abuse. Askin was to have a "good and sufficient building" erected within three years and to live or have someone live on the property for one year. He could dispose of the property within twelve months by gift, inheritance, or sale, provided that he took an oath before a magistrate and registered a certificate. Within five months he had done so. On 1 April 1805 he and his wife Archange acknowledged receipt of the final instalment of £180 New York. They endorsed the reverse of the patent, an act witnessed by Charles Askin. Presumably, this was then surrendered to the purchaser. Presumably, also, Askin had met all the requirements of the patent. Here is the very process that Cartwright described earlier. Askin would seem to have behaved within the letter of the law and his only fault may have been the common one of acquisitiveness. Insights such as this are relatively rare because few of these patents issued to the settler have survived, but it is clear that a stipulation of settlement conditions, in the form permitted by Hunter, would not be conducive to the development of any area. Indeed, it would seem that settlement duties had been all but abandoned.

By 1818 they were enforced with some vigour.[90] In a belated effort to control speculation and absenteeism, a wild land tax was introduced and a system of settlement duties adopted and enforced. On 4 October 1818 public notice was given that a habitable house and five acres in every hundred was to be cleared as part of the settlement duties. These were Yonge Street conditions although they had already been applied in Essex to the Talbot Road. Henceforth, they were to apply to all new grants. A change was that these specific duties had to be completed before patenting was possible. Moreover, unless a certificate testifying to the completion of these duties was made within twelve months and the patent taken out, grants made prior to April 1819 were to be rescinded. In the light of these stipulations, there seemed no reason to prohibit sale until three years after patent and this requirement was abolished. In 1818 it appeared that for the first time there was a genuine prospect of ensuring the systematic development of the territory. However, the certificates of completion were obtained from newly constituted land boards or local magistrates on the witness of two individuals and upon taking the oath. There seems to have been much fraud.[91]

The new regulations were constantly adjusted in an effort to set a balance which would allow genuine settlers to proceed to patent and which would keep out land speculators. The term "habitable house" stipulated in the settlement duties was indefinite and differed from "inhabited house." Following complaints about the severity of the terms, the amount of clearance required was reduced to clearing half the road and cutting down timber for one chain in depth from the road. The amount of time permitted was extended from eighteen to thirty months.[92] The regulations of November 1830 offered prospective settlers a choice. They could either clear half the roadway and reside on the property for two years or clear the road and the lot itself to one chain back (sixty-six feet) from the road. If they chose the second option, they could forgo residence. A certificate of performance had to be filed within two years; the patent would follow after five. Earlier locators could chose either the old or the new ways; presumably, speculators chose the second route since they could not be omnipresent on the great number of lots they held. Perhaps because of this, there was a swing back to the requirement of residence, although the requirement as stated was that only part of the property need be resided upon.[93]

For a short while, residence was also required on the privileged Loyalist and military grants. However, so great was the agitation by these people and the speculators who had been accumulating such grants that in 1834 Colborne reverted to the rules of 1832.[94] By 1835 the government had succumbed to pressure. Anticipating the need for election support in 1836, it permitted location free of settlement duties on both Loyalist and military grants. A wave of settlement on paper followed. As Gates points out, in Upper Canada between November 1818 and October 1835, 2,078,489 acres of land were patented, but in the three years between 1 July 1835 and 4 October 1838, 1,162,300 acres were patented.[95] A report made for Lord Durham stated that, by September, Loyalist and militia claims amounted to 3,937,698 acres, of which 275,176 acres were as yet unpatented and unlocated lands totalled 526,282 acres.[96] The extent of the problem accounts for the bitter opposition to Lieutenant Governor John Colborne's attempts to uphold settlement duties on these lands. In the three years from 1835 to 1838, Gates shows that 917,013 acres were claimed by these privileged groups and, as the present author has demonstrated elsewhere, in 1836 alone 54,536 acres were claimed in the Western District, most of them in Lambton County.[97]

How did all this apply to Essex County? Little is known. Along the Talbot Road, the Executive Council, at the instigation of Thomas Talbot,[98] instituted demanding settlement duties.[99] Here and on the other land in Maidstone, Rochester, and Tilbury which Talbot supervised, settlers had to erect a "good and sufficient building" of at least sixteen by twenty feet, to be occupied by the owner or a "substantial tenant." Ten acres had to be cleared and fenced within two years, half the road had to be cleared in front of the lot, and no trees were to be left standing within 100 feet of the road. If the cost of the survey exceeded the revenues from the survey fees, the additional costs were to be carried rateably, that is, as taxation on the grantee.[100] These were demanding terms indeed but they were limited spatially. Elsewhere in Essex, in the majority of the county, one presumes that the general conditions applied. However, examination of the certificates of completion of settlement duties held in the Archives of Ontario produced a zero return for the Western District; this was not so for other areas.[101] Clearly, the survival of such records is subject to all sorts of processes, including chance, but it is also possible that given the physical conditions in this area and its remoteness from government control, little attention was paid to settlement requirements. This interpretation is perhaps congruent with the views of Benjamin Springer, the surveyor. While not addressing Essex townships specifically, as late as 1833 he could write that "measures should be taken to check the vile information practised in regard to the performance of settlement duties on land in the Western District."[102]

Institution of a Sales Policy

Increasingly, land policy had to be viewed in revenue terms. To raise revenues and to reduce criticism of the operation of the Crown Land Department, it was decided to instigate a sales policy in 1825. The impetus for the sales policy lay ultimately in the needs and desires of the British government to reduce expenditures. However, there were those in Upper Canada who recognized the need for revenue and thought that it might also flow to provincial rather than imperial coffers. There were also in government, to say nothing of Upper Canadian society as a whole, capitalists who argued philosophically that a more revenue-oriented policy would benefit the colony and hasten development. They were probably not averse to the benefits that might accrue to themselves and their families from such a change.

Much of the impetus for the change in land policy came from outside and from a Colonial Office seeking to settle the responsibility for growth and for defence upon the shoulders of the colonies themselves.[103] To that end, the Colonial Office's under-secretary of state, R.J. Wilmot Horton, had been preparing a vast imperial sales scheme which would emerge by 1825 as the New South Wales System (NSW). In July 1825 the colonial secretary, the Earl Bathurst, relayed the NSW rules for land granting to Lieutenant Governor Maitland and his Executive Council.[104] He was, in fact, soliciting opinion about the suitability of the scheme to Upper Canada. In particular, Bathurst was seeking the advice of his friend, John Beverley Robinson, whom he had introduced to British society and who was in England at the time. As a former attorney general and solicitor general and the leader of the government party, Robinson was well acquainted with the Upper Canadian circumstances[105] and with the constant threat of economic collapse and depression in the post-War of 1812 era. With little industrial or mercantile development, Upper Canada was to a considerable extent dependent on the disposal of land as the basis of its economy.[106]

The NSW model contained twenty points; two, related to the use of convicts in achieving remittance of the original purchase price and (in the case of a grant of land) of redemption of quit-rent credits, were without meaning in Upper Canada. Robinson suggested the addition of legal interest for instalment buying, and proposed that the scheme be administered through the Upper Canadian township, which would be exactly twice the New South Wales parish, that is, fifty square miles. He also recommended the addition of the Upper Canadian practice of reserving mines, minerals, and white pine, and the reduction of the maximum size of grant from 2560 acres to 1200 and the minimum from 320 to 100 acres. Basically, he accepted the proposal that purchases by individuals be limited to 10,000 acres dispensed in quantities of 100 acres; the NSW conditions allowed 9600 acres in lots of 1920. The Upper Canadian insistence on smaller grants presumably reflected a more grain-oriented economy than that of New South Wales.[107]

After pointing out the peculiar circumstances of Upper Canada which resulted from its relationship to the United States, and the need to provide for military claimants and Loyalists, Robinson saw fit to support the proposal.[108] The Executive Council acknowledged Robinson's insights and on 29 October 1825 relayed a positive recommendation to the lieutenant governor. The council[109] found that the proposed system would not mitigate against emigration, since land could still be obtained on grants against a quit-rent of 5 per cent per annum; that the system offered "an advantage to Capitalists," for "a commerce in lands may be gradually opened highly beneficial to the Province, and married Men be induced by a fair prospect of gain to Settle among us"[110]; and that, given the base population and the rate of natural increase, natural reproduction would put pressures on a diminishing land base even without emigration. In sum, "the Same reasons for promiscuous grants do not now exist, that may have induced them heretofore."[111]

This policy, adopted officially in January 1826[112] and effectively in July of that year,[113] put into place a dual system of land grants and sales, the latter advocated as early as 1798 by Governor Robert Prescott and most recently for the Crown reserves by Robinson.[114] Application for grant or purchase had to be made on a prescribed form at a prescribed fee and all correspondence had to go through a single office. No one was to receive a grant of over 200 acres unless the government was satisfied of his ability to expend a capital equal to half its estimated value; grantees under 200 acres had to reside upon and improve their property. Proof of meeting these stipulations was required and the land was to be forfeit if they were not met. The terms for grants were to be a quit-rent of 5 per cent per annum, redeemable within the first twenty-five years for a sum of twenty times the quit rent.

Thus, to use a hypothetical example, the purchaser of 100 acres at four shillings per acre would agree to pay £20 but would pay nothing for seven years after which the annual quit-rent would be one pound. This could be paid anytime within twenty-five years from the date of the sale or "grant."[115]

If the same person wanted another grant he had to pay the quit-rent on it from the beginning. Those who sought to buy could pay in quarterly or annual instalments but a 10 per cent discount was to be offered for "ready money." On final payment, a grant in fee simple would be issued to the purchaser at government expense. Those seeking purchases of more than 10,000 acres could apply to the secretary of state. Compensation would have to be offered to those officials who had lived by the older system of grants.[116] To make the plan operational, the land had to be evaluated before being sold at advertised auctions to the highest bidder; if the assessed value was not met, no sale would occur.

In 1825 and the early part of 1826, the government asked the members of the legislature, the district land boards, the surveyors, the grand jurymen, the magistrates in Quarter Sessions, and Colonel Thomas Talbot[117] to evaluate the townships in their respective districts. These people were to assess land in terms of soils, situation, previous cash, and credit sales based on instalments in the last five years and how much they thought the land was worth. Where townships had not yet been surveyed or open to location, it was recommended that the value fixed upon by the legislature in 1811[118] as the basis of assessment be used for a minimum price. In such circumstances, it was thought expedient to admit forty or fifty settlers at two shillings (twenty-four pence) per acre; from their interaction, a future price might be fixed. Such action would absorb those emigrants who had come presuming the old circumstances still applied. This would occur before the change would be known in the chief recruiting area for settlers, namely, the United Kingdom. Not to dampen emigration, the price in the new townships should be set at less than the average valuation so as to encourage sales of government land rather than purchases from individuals. Population could be used as a surrogate for land value "when positive evidence is wanting."[119] In the older townships, after ascertaining the general value of land, a price could be fixed and the land sold at public auction to the highest bidder.[120]

The result of this inquiry was a report made to the Colonial Office using the township as the basis of evaluation.[121] Three variables were reported for price: previous cash sales or "ready money", credit sales made by instalments, and the individual's personal view on a fair price for land. In Essex, the respective "upset" values were between 33 and 96 pence per acre for credit sales and 31 and 75 pence per acre was the personally assessed value.[122] It is not known exactly how many sales were made under these terms; however, the number of patents issuing in any one year is known and will be discussed below.

Summary

In the period before 1825 there were effectively two groups of individuals for purposes of granting land, that is, the ordinary or common individual and the privileged or official grantees who might receive an amount of land commensurate with their service to the state or their perceived status and "respectability." There was nothing accidental about the process; it was a deliberate part of colonial land policy to permit a cash-strapped society to reward those who had served it and to pay in a currency that *all* valued. Lieutenant Governor Simcoe also saw this process as the mechanism by which an aristocracy might be created. It, and the provisions to support the ministrations of the Church of England and to endow the state with land so as to obviate the needs for taxation, were some of the ways in which Simcoe sought to demonstrate the benefits of the British connection to the rebellious American colonies which had broken "unnaturally" with the mother country. The second group of individuals who received their land free of survey and patent fees, became increasingly part of what S.J.R. Noel calls a "clientage" system; as such, its members had to return time after time to the source of its benefits and were increasingly bound to one another and the central structure.[123]

This was the basis of the charges of "privilege" and favouritism levelled at colonial land policy by the Reform party in the House of Assembly. It was something to be addressed by those in government who sought change, but the historical legacy was strong and "faithfulness" would have to be accommodated in whatever sales policy was instituted. Those who sought to redesign the system would be compromised at the outset by the decision to operate the civil establishment on land resources. This had resulted in a system of fees, in pursuit of which certain officials had been willing to continue to revise the regulations within legal limits to ensure greater revenues. The greatest beneficiaries were the Loyalists who were forever seeking a more beneficial interpretation of their inheritance; when, in 1837, they were allowed to secure their land without settlement duties or fees, a virtual land rush occurred. The need for fees to finance the system and its officials, especially those officially exempt from such fees as privileged grantees, was so great that it compromised other elements of the system itself, namely, the settlement duties. These had never been universally applied; they provoked much criticism from all elements of society – the Loyalists, the ordinary settler, and the land speculator or developer. At various points they were not enforced, to allow land to pass to patent; at others, they were removed if one was willing to pay the appropriate fee. As a result, development was sabotaged; those acquiring land all received a patent, but, in terms of development, the patent might have no meaning other than the right to occupy subject to the normal conditions of life such as taxation. Theoretically, the year 1825 represented a divide between the policy of grants and that of sales but of course the privileged could exercise their rights to secure land at any time when they believed conditions best suited them; for the Loyalists, this was in the circumstances of 1836 and 1837 when settlement dues and fees on these lands were abolished. For government, forgoing the appropriate fees could not even bring the satisfaction of knowing that these lands were being actively settled. Freed of restriction, these parcels became highly desirable to speculators and were grabbed in a veritable land rush. "Common" settlers willing to pay increased fees of a particular period were also able to escape settlement duties; again the issue of patents guaranteed little in developmental terms. Talbot knew this and managed to exempt the area that he supervised from the sales policy.[124] Indeed, all that can be said is that the process became increasingly commercialized with time and the form by which patents were obtained changed from grants subject to fees to sales. Inevitably, in older townships, government sales came to outnumber grants at some point after 1825.

THE PATENTS AS SOURCE MATERIALS FOR ANALYSIS

Patent information is available in a number of sources, namely, the patent index in the Ontario Archives, the abstract index to deeds in the various county registry offices, and the Domesday Books maintained for many years by the Department of Lands and Forests of the government of Ontario. These sources yield information on the names of the grantees, the location, the date of the grant, and its registration. They can and have been used to determine the spatial pattern of land acquisition as well as the timing of land acquisition in the county as a whole. They have been used to identify particular categories of land such as the Indian, Crown, and clergy Reserves, although identification of Talbot's land requires independent sources, in this case, his maps. The timing and spatial pattern of speculative holdings can be derived if defining cri-

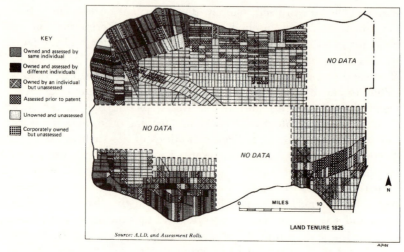

KEY

- ■ Owned and assessed by same individual
- ■ Owned and assessed by different individuals
- ▨ Owned by an individual but unassessed
- ▨ Assessed prior to patent
- ☐ Unowned and unassessed
- ▦ Corporately owned but unassessed

NO DATA

NO DATA

NO DATA

0   MILES   10

N

LAND TENURE 1825

Source: A.I.D. and Assessment Rolls.

Figure 4.1   Tenure conditions in Essex, 1825

Source: Abstract Index to Deeds, Census of Canada, 1850–52, and assessment rolls for Essex County.

teria can be agreed upon. Although patents cannot be used without qualification, they and other documents relating to land have survived where other information has not. For example, information on natives, women, and the ethnic origins of the people of Upper Canada is much more scarce than these land records. It is presumably because of this, and the greater availability of the patent data and subsequent legal instruments compared to, for example, the tickets of location, that these data have been widely used by a number of researchers such as C. Wood,[125] L. Wood,[126] K. Kelly,[127] J. Clarke,[128] A. Brunger,[129] L. Johnson,[130] B. Osborne,[131] R. Widdis,[132] J. Weldon,[133] D. Akenson,[134] G. Lockwood,[135] J. Duncan,[136] D. Gordanier,[137] D. Watt,[138] and S. Hannon.[139]

How useful are the patents as an indicator of actual settlement? Clearly, as discussed earlier, there cannot be complete agreement between patenting and actual settlement because of changes in the requirements through time, the existence of the "privileged" who were not required to reside on or develop their property, and the intentions of individuals such as land speculators. This problem of patent reliability is critical to Ontario historiography but it is one that has been largely ignored because of the incredible amount of work needed to address it in a systematic way.

A number of attempts are made here to come to grips with this issue of reliability. The first of these turns upon the spatial portrayal of patented land and comparison of this with occupied land. Figures 4.1 and 4.2 show tenure conditions in Essex cross-sectionally for 1825 and

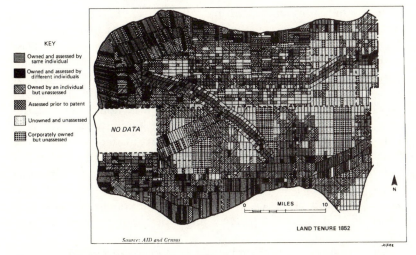

KEY

Owned and assessed by
same individual

Owned and assessed by
different individuals

Owned by an individual
but unassessed

Assessed prior to patent

Unowned and unassessed

Corporately owned
but unassessed

NO DATA

MILES
0   10

N

LAND TENURE 1852

Source: AID and Census

Figure 4.2   Tenure conditions in Essex, 1851–52.

Source: Abstract Index to Deeds, Census of Canada, 1850–52, and assessment rolls for Essex County.

1851–52. Each and every lot was examined for these years and the
name of the owner(s) determined by following the logic of the
abstract index to deeds. This was then compared with the name
assessed for the property on the assessment rolls of the county and the
results cross-classified.[140] Three classes were recognized. The first consisted either of land identified as occupied in the assessment rolls or
land in the process of being patented.[141] The second class consisted of
patented but unoccupied land; and the third, unpatented and unoccupied land. Two points might be made here. One is the sheer amount
of unpatented land in 1825 and even later, at mid-century. This must
contrast with other areas of Upper Canada settled at the same time. A
second point is that, in both periods and most especially in 1850–52,
the second category, that is, patented but unoccupied land, was quite
extensive. Patenting clearly ran ahead of actual settlement in the bulk
of circumstances, perhaps because of changing regulations which
encouraged more rapid patenting or because of the need to provide
for progeny or the activities of land speculators. However, the maps,
while interesting, provide no direct measure of the relationship
between settlement and patent.

A gross measure of patent reliability is provided by counts of the
frequency with which there are "problems." If the patent is the final
step in a system of acquisition, exactly how orderly was this administrative system? How extensive were the problems to which Cartwright
alluded in his argument to recognize duly witnessed legal transac-

tions as the equivalent of the patent? In Essex between 1796 and 1916, patents were issued for 3156 properties but there were 112 lots which, for whatever reason, never received a patent or at least about which the records are silent. In fact, many of these were in Sandwich Township. Here, continued occupation from the days of the French regime must have constituted sufficient title in itself. An additional 219 lots were found to have transactions ahead of the patent. While the 219 are problems in an administrative, bureaucratic, and legal sense, they are not, of course, in an economic sense. Nonetheless, the 219 represent 6.7 per cent of the cases of patent. In 136 of the 219 instances these reflected "normal" economic transactions of the "Bargain and Sale" variety, of which there were 108; there were also twenty-eight mortgages. Additionally, thirty instruments of "indenture" and "deed" might be so interpreted although with less certainty.

The remaining 53 consisted of wills, powers of attorney, deed polls, quit claims, leases, bonds, and other instruments and sheriffs's deeds. These 53 deeds reflect actions which either were independent of the patentee or constituted the justification for the final assignment of the patent, for example, in the case of a sheriff's deed. A sheriff's deed on land being sold for back taxes could be the justification for a seemingly tardy patent. Some problem with legal description might also retard the issue of a patent until the necessary quit-claim was issued.[142] On the other hand, it is clear that leases did not affect the patent date. If the 53 are removed from the calculation, problems amount to only 5.05 per cent; if the 112 properties without patents are added, then problems amount to 8.5 per cent. If all 331 are included, then "administrative disorder" constitutes 10.1 per cent of the cases.

Exactly how extensive such problems were in Upper Canada is not known – the work has simply not been done – but, in Essex, they ranged from 3.4 to 6.1 per cent of the cases. This last figure is remarkably congruent with that obtained in a second sample drawn to establish the lag between date of patent and first sale. Of the 1003 observations included, 107, or 10.7 per cent, of the cases proved negative, meaning there was some sort of activity on a lot prior to patent.[143]

Ultimately, what is required is to cross-check such sources with the time of first occupation in such documents as the assessment rolls. Essex County and in particular Malden Township have an unusually rich set of extant assessment rolls compared to other Upper Canadian areas but lack the annual runs needed to make precise judgments. Moreover, the census of Malden in 1847 which has survived and which asked the date of entry for the non-British and non-natives comes too

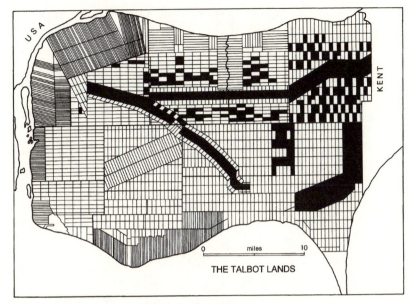

Figure 4.3   Areas "controlled" by Thomas Talbot
Source: J. Clarke, "Mapping the Lands," 13.

late to provide any meaningful amount of information.[144] Yet, for the wider Western District, of which Essex formed a part, and for a sample of 399 property parcels, this writer suggests that the lag between purchase or location and date of patent may have been of the order of six to eight years.[145]

Again, as in the matter of settlement duties, the areas controlled by Talbot proved deviant (Figure 4.3). Such was the power and influence of this benign Anglo-Irish despot, who as early as 1809[146] was charged with supervising 204,743 acres in the Western District, including at least 44,035 acres in Essex, that few rushed to patent after having received his "blessing." Indeed, by 1836, only 400 acres of Talbot-supervised land had been patented in Essex, although de facto ownership was undoubtedly greater than de jure (Table 4.2).[147] Talbot's requirements were stringent. People were offered the possibility of complying or "otherwise they will all be turned off."[148] If they were to be evicted, their names were simply erased from the township maps, on which he had recorded their location. Talbot was sufficiently confident to advise the surveyor general that he should also insert names in pencil[149] in his plans to await the latest of the colonel's adjustments. Given this extraordinary system of record keeping, it was critical that Talbot's records be available to the state but they were still in the

Table 4.2   Frequency of locations made by Colonel Thomas Talbot within Essex County 1811–1849

Date	Township						Total
	Gos.	Mai.	Roc.	Mer.	San.	Til.	
1811	0	0	0	1	0	0	1
1815	0	0	0	1	0	0	1
1816	0	0	0	1	0	0	1
1817	0	0	0	1	0	0	1
1818	0	0	0	14	0	0	14
1819	0	0	0	1	0	0	1
1820	0	0	0	1	0	0	1
1830	0	1	1	1	0	3	6
1831	0	1	0	1	0	1	3
1832	0	8	5	16	4	15	48
1833	0	5	11	4	0	17	37
1834	0	20	16	1	1	20	58
1835	0	28	10	2	5	59	104
1836	0	11	28	25	2	77	143
1837	0	2	5	15	0	5	27
1838	0	2	3	1	0	1	7
1839	0	4	2	2	2	0	10
1840	0	1	1	2	0	0	4
1843	0	1	1	2	0	0	4
1849	0	1	0	0	0	0	1
Sub Total	0	84	82	92	14	198	470
No data	21	43	16	42	36	32	190
Total	21	127	98	134	50	230	660
Percentage Western District	1.5	9.1	7.0	9.6	3.6	16.4	47.2

Source: Clarke, "Mapping the Lands," Table 2.
"Gos." = Gosfield; "Mai." = Maidstone; "Mer." = Mersea; "Roc." = Rochester; "San." = Sandwich; and "Til." = Tilbury

colonel's possession when he died on 5 February 1853.[150] Until that date, Talbot's word and certificate had almost the force of law. While one eventually needed a patent for conveyancing purposes, the need was not immediate.

Given the process whereby Talbot recorded the date of location of those who were successful, and the subsequent recognition of this success by the state, it is possible to obtain lag rates for a larger number of Talbot lots than non-Talbot lands, since few actual location tickets have survived the ravages of time. In fact, it is theoretically possible to obtain such comparative data for 1401 lots in the Western District, although poor script, frequent erasure of the pencil entries, and archival preservative (which obscures the text) make the task difficult. In all, the date of location and of patent for 885 lots were recovered, of which 461 were in Essex. Based upon this sample, the average lag between location and patent on Talbot land was 20.53 with a standard deviation of 8.78 years. This was greater than in neighbouring parts of Elgin and Middlesex counties, the "core" of his "principality."[151] Presumably, proximity to Talbot produced greater haste. Yet in 1830, John Richards, an imperial lands commissioner, reported that only 785 of the approximately 6000 families that Talbot claimed to have established had taken out their patents. If one was certain that Talbot would not simply erase one's name from his map and thereby one's livelihood, one need not rush to patent or to throw away money on fees that might be spent elsewhere.[152] In fact, in 65 per cent of the cases on Talbot land in Essex, the lag was between 11.75 and 29.31 years. In one instance it was 44 years. Clearly, Talbot land was atypical in terms of the lag between location and patent.

On non-Talbot land, there are fewer observations by which to gauge the lag between location and ultimate ownership, and studies by which one might establish a comparison with this or other areas are not abundant. Yet, if Talbot land is theoretically removed from the equation, it would seem that there was a genuine relationship between patenting and actual settlement of the order of six to eight years. This is the same magnitude that Gregory Finnegan established for Fitzroy Township[153] and which John I. Little recorded for Winslow Township in Quebec, where more than 55 per cent of owners of "free-grant" land took between five to nine years to receive their patent.[154] It is clear both to this and many other authors that there is not a perfect relationship between patenting and settlement both because of legal complications and because of the widespread operation of land speculation. There were indeed many instances where patenting preceded settlement and vice versa but until more studies are available it would seem that a lag of nine years is not unreasonable and in Essex it was even less. Yet, even if it could be shown that the relationship between occupation on the ground and patenting was far from perfect, this would in no way lessen the value of patents as a comment upon legal land acquisition.[155]

ANALYSIS OF THE TIMING OF PATENTING: CLASSIFICATION AND METHOD

Details of 3156 patents were gathered and the frequency of occurrence was recorded for all of them and for particular subsets or classes.

Clearly, there was no problem in recognizing Crown, clergy, or Indian lands since these were nominal specifications but it was necessary to define "land speculator." It was decided that anyone holding over 400 acres should be considered as such. While this figure might not be as useful in the latter part of the century, when the settlers acquired the financial resources and technology to handle large tracts of land, it provides a "rule" for the whole period and allows for the possibility of an individual and his son of the same name acquiring land. There is some debate about the arbitrariness of the definition; this will be discussed in greater detail in a later chapter.

The patents taken out in any one year were accumulated for each township and expressed as a percentage of the number in the final year of patenting. The rate of land acquisition in each township was then analysed using the logistic growth or s-shaped curve[156] to describe changes in the accumulated percentage of land patents with time, the independent variable. The model has a basis in theory.[157] It assumes an s-shaped growth from an initial starting position through a time of more rapid growth to a final stage, characterized by a flattening of the curve, as all available land is taken up by the settlers/patentees. In effect, the fact that land is finite dictates the *general* form of the curve. The model, transformed into an equation for a straight line, allows for evaluation in terms of degree of fit to a line (the correlation coefficient) and for comparison of slopes of acquisition by township (the beta coefficients of the respective equations).[158] Before turning to the specific results of this particular analysis, it is useful to consider the acquisition of land in more general terms.

The Temporal Acquisition of Land in the County as a Whole

As might be expected, there was a direct relationship between the amount of land patented in nineteenth-century Essex and the population. This increased in an almost linear manner from about 2347 in 1805 to 5297 in 1820, 17,817 in 1851, 32,697 in 1871, and 55,545 in 1891.[159] Moreover, particular decades of especially marked population growth were accompanied by significant increases in land patenting. This is reflected in Figure 4.4, which identifies two major periods of land acquisition separated by the end of the Napoleonic Wars in 1815. With Napoleon in captivity and hostilities with the United States ended, immigration to Upper Canada began to increase and was indeed promoted by the government. The return to peaceful conditions prompted increased land granting, a fact reflected in the histogram where the number of patents taken out in each five-year period increases markedly until 1870 when decline set

Land Acquisition 1790-1900

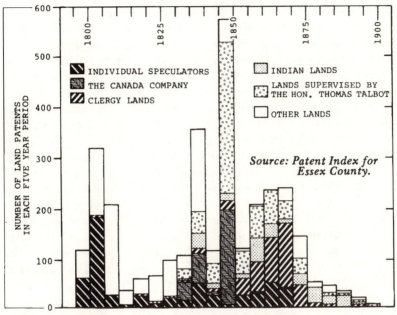

Figure 4.4   Land acquisition: two major periods of acquisition separated by the end of the Napoleonic Wars

Source: J. Clarke, "Aspects of Land Acquisition," 106.

in. Within the second period, the quinquennial 1836 to 1840 and 1846 to 1850 were of particular note. The decades 1830 to 1850 were periods of especially marked population growth. Between 1830 and 1840 the population of the county increased by 73.2 per cent. Between 1840 and 1850, when Upper Canada as a whole was experiencing the effects of the Irish Famine emigration and Essex County's isolation relative to the rest of the country was breaking down, it increased by 94.1 per cent.

Population increase must therefore explain much of the rapid acquisition of land in these years, but the increase in patenting was also affected by the institution of sales and the reduction in settlement duties discussed earlier. Again, in 1836, the government sought to buy votes by issuing patents, the basic requirement of enfranchisement. In 1837 it decided to allow the Loyalists to acquire land free of settlement duties.[160] These and similar changes of land policy in the 1840s directly affected the rate of acquisition in Essex County. In 1839 lands located prior to 1832 and still unpatented by 1840 were threatened with forfeiture; similarly, an 1846 decision that those located after 1832 and unpatented in 1847 would be confiscated produced a land-patenting rush in Essex.[161] In 1846 alone, 245 patents were taken out in Essex County. This can be contrasted with 139 taken out in 1836 and the 18 taken out in 1809, when the future of this area appeared most secure because of its proximity to the proposed capital for Upper Canada at what is now the city of London.[162]

The years to 1815 were those in which the future of this area seemed particularly promising and, consequently, speculation by individuals was most rampant.[163] In the period from 1800 to 1805, 57.3 per cent of all the land patented was acquired by speculators, more than by any other category (Table 4.3). Thereafter, the number of active land purchasers patenting declined. However, the number of patents held for speculative purposes remained high because of the activities of the Canada Company which had acquired the former Crown reserves.[164] Charged with withholding land from patent to avoid the tax on wild land, the company was castigated by a select committee of the House of Assembly in 1835. It responded rapidly: within three years, almost half of its holdings in Upper Canada had passed to patent.[165] In the years 1831 to 1835 and 1846 to 1850, the company patented 35.8 and 33.1 per cent of all lands patented in the county (Table 4.3). By 1838 the company had patented 30.4 per cent of its property parcels in Essex, and by 1846, when it felt similarly threatened by the latest government land policy, 98.7 per cent of its land had been patented.

The 1846 decision also threw some urgency into those locating on the lands whose settlement had been entrusted to Colonel Thomas Talbot.[166] Having satisfied that eccentric Anglo-Irish aristocrat of their suitability as settlers, these individuals normally postponed the required visit to York to pay their patent fee, but in the period from 1847 to 1848 alone, 247 patents were taken out.[167]

The decades 1830 to 1850 also saw the patenting of the former Indian reserve (Anderdon Township) and the sale of clergy reserves reached some pitch. The clergy reserves, which, like the Crown reserves, constituted one seventh of the land granted in each township, were a constant source of political embarrassment. Their removal as sources of discontent began with the introduction of a sales policy in 1827 and was continued by acts of 1840 and by the introduction of a ten-year credit system in 1846, culminating in the Clergy Reserve Secularization Act of 1854.[168] In Upper Canada as a whole, the decade 1845 to 1855 was the most important time for the disposal of these lands; in Essex it would seem to have been somewhat later. The most important period was from 1866 to 1870, when Clergy

Table 4.3 Percentage of patents in particular quinquennial periods, Essex County, by category, 1791–1900.

Period	Indian Reserve	Canada Company	Clergy Lands	Thomas Talbot	Individual Speculators	Other Patentees
1791–95	–	–	–	–	–	–
1796–00	–	–	–	–	52.9	47.1
1800–05	–	–	0.9	–	57.3	41.8
1806–10	0.5	–	–	–	13.0	86.5
1811–15	–	–	–	–	16.6	83.4
1816–20	–	–	4.0	–	41.6	54.4
1821–25	–	–	–	6.3	15.9	77.8
1826–30	–	–	–	19.0	21.9	59.1
1831–35	0.9	35.8	1.9	18.0	15.2	28.2
1836–40	8.4	15.6	2.8	11.7	13.9	47.6
1841–45	8.7	12.0	2.6	33.7	12.2	31.6
1846–50	2.3	33.1	3.5	52.3	0.5	8.3
1851–55	6.0	–	29.0	47.0	11.9	6.1
1856–60	24.9	0.5	29.2	32.0	12.9	0.5
1861–65	11.5	–	38.0	29.8	21.7	0.0
1866–70	3.4	0.4	52.7	16.0	15.2	12.3
1871–75	18.4	–	30.5	21.5	–	29.6
1876–80	65.4	–	7.7	13.5	–	13.4
1881–85	42.2	–	6.7	4.4	–	46.7
1886–90	74.2	–	–	6.4	–	19.4
1891–95	33.3	–	11.1	22.2	–	33.4
1896–00	25.0	–	–	–	–	75.0

Source: Clarke, "Aspects of Land Acquisition," Table 3

Reserve sales made up about 53 per cent of all sales. Sales continued strongly at least until 1875 (Table 4.3).

A cursory glance at Figure 4.4 might suggest that there was little activity by smallholders after about 1841. This is not so, however; for, while there is evidence to suggest that some of the former clergy lands were acquired by speculators, most were not. The Indian lands were purchased by smallholders, and the lands supervised by Colonel Talbot were without question acquired by genuine settlers. So, too, were the former Crown reserves surrendered to the Canada Land Company. Most of these, as will be shown later, ended up in the hands of individuals rather than in corporate hands. Thus, those acquiring holdings equal to or under 400 acres were proportionately at least as numerous in the latter period as in the earlier. Indeed, if anything, increasing demand commensurate with increased immigration in the 1840s and 1850s, together with increased subdivision as a response to economic difficulty, produced proportionately more smaller holdings.

Rates of acquisition in the Townships of Essex

Patenting began in all but three of the fourteen townships before 1810 – that is, before the War of 1812 and its aftermath slowed the process because of the uncertainty of the times and the post-war restrictions on American immigration. These three were Tilbury North, first patented in 1825, Sandwich South, patented first in 1826, and Colchester North, patented first in 1834. In spite of start-ing later, land acquisition was more rapid in these townships, the process taking an average of fifty-seven years. Though there is little difference in date of first patent within the other eleven townships, there is considerable difference in their achievement rates. Thus, Malden (in 1803), Sandwich North and East (in 1806), Colchester South (in 1808), Sandwich West (in 1817), and Gosfield South (in 1818) all passed the 50 per cent mark before 1820. In contrast, Rochester (in 1847), Maidstone (1847), Tilbury West (in 1848), Mersea (in 1847), Gosfield North (in 1846), Colchester North (in 1845), and Sandwich South (in 1847) took almost thirty years to reach these levels, and Anderdon (in 1862) and Tilbury North (in 1861) took another forty years. Those in the pre-1820 achievement category possessed locational advantages in both the French and British periods with respect to the settlements at Detroit. The early patenting in Sandwich in fact resulted from British recognition of the validity of the older French settlement dating from 1749. In addi-tion, these areas enjoyed an initial advantage in that the Indian offi-cers in Malden had been allowed to have their Indian deeds recog-nized. Moreover, the political decision to establish British ex-regulars in this politically sensitive area (Gosfield and Colchester townships) had assisted settlement. By 1842, Gosfield and Colchester had sur-passed the 75 per cent mark; this was not achieved by the other "early" townships until the 1860s, and in the case of Anderdon (an Indian reserve for a long time) not until 1880. In most of the town-ships, 75 percent of the land had been taken up by 1865. In the county as a whole, the process took 103 years, and in the townships, on average, it took about eighty years.

All Essex townships experienced a period of lag when little patent-ing activity was taking place (Table 4.4). This varied in its duration but generally had passed by the 1840s. It endured least in the town-ships closest to Detroit and Michigan and is well illustrated in the cases of Rochester and Gosfield North townships (Figure 4.5). Minimal patent activity stemmed partly from the action of specula-tors in discouraging people from settling in the area, and partly from the locational disadvantages of the region. Forty years before, this

Table 4.4   Land-acquisition data, Essex County townships
(Sorted by Duration of Lag Period)

Township	Date of First Patent	Year in Which 50% Was Patented	Year in Which 75% Was Patented	Years to Completion	Number of Lag Years	Date
Roc.	1798	1847	1859	97	41	1804–45
Mai.	1797	1847	1857	85	32	1806–37
Til. W.	1801	1848	1864	83	27	1811–24
						& 1828–40
Mal.	1797	1803	1831	65	28	1803–30
Mer.	1801	1847	1864	94	26	1806–31
And.	1836	1862	1880	64	24	1809–32
San. W.	1797	1817	1834	72	17	1804–20
Til. N.	1825	1861	1865	71	16	1825–40
Gos. N.	1806	1846	1862	80	14	1810–23
Gos. S.	1797	1818	1831	98	8	1809–16
Col. N.	1834	1845	1855	55	9	1838–46
Col. S.	1796	1808	1838	77	9	1812–16
						& 1825–29
San. S.	1826	1847	1857	58	8	1826–33
San. N. E.	1800	1806	1833	99	6	1810–15
Essex County	1796	1846	1859	103	29	1808–36

Source: Clarke, "Aspects of Land Speculation," Table 4.

"And." = Anderdon; "Col." = Colchester; "Gos." = Gosfield; "Mai." = Maidstone; "Mal." = Malden; "Mer." = Mersea; "Roc." = Rochester; "San." = Sandwich; and "Til." = Tilbury. "N." = North; "W." = West; "S." = South; and "E." = East.

region had been one of considerable promise. Lieutenant Governor Simcoe, had planned to establish the capital of Upper Canada nearby at London and a naval dockyard at the site of Chatham. Neither of these plans came to fruition. Moreover, the situation was exacerbated by the British abandonment of Detroit, by the decline of the Indian trade, and by the realization that the quality of land was better elsewhere in Upper Canada. The area stagnated and the focus shifted from the Detroit area eastwards towards the new capital at York. The Western District and Essex County were off-centre with respect to this development.[169] However, with the opening of the Erie and Welland canals, the further development of the road network, and the fact that "saturation" of the central areas forced newcomers westward and northward, this area experienced renewed patenting activity on a larger scale than ever before. The results are

Representative Profiles of Land Acquisition

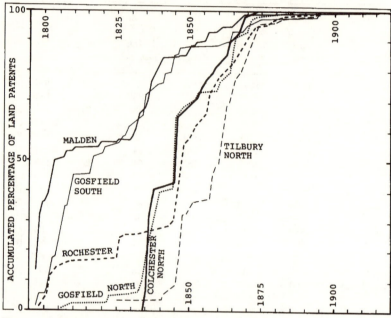

Figure 4.5   Land acquisition: Essex County and its townships
Source: J. Clarke, "Aspects of Land Acquisition," 110.

reflected in the graphs which swing markedly upward after 1840 (Figure 4.5).

The usefulness of the logistical growth curve as a tool of analysis is indicated by Table 4.5, where the correlation coefficients are seen to be high.[170] The beta coefficients, describing the overall rates of change, were ranked and tested for differences between them. Eight groups were recognized. Of these, five included more than one township (Table 4.5). Throughout the nineteenth century, the slowest overall rates of development were found in the townships of Malden, Gosfield South, Sandwich North and East (all of which had sufficiently similar coefficients to be classed as one group), and Colchester South and Sandwich West. These were townships that had enjoyed an initial advantage in terms of accessibility and in terms of proximity to the embryonic urban centres of Amherstburg and Detroit. They were also townships that contained a large portion of well-drained land in an area that was on the whole poorly endowed. As a result, they experienced a fair amount of land-acquisition activity by land speculators and the friends of the government in the early

Table 4.5   A table of correlation coefficients and of township linkage by similarity of beta coefficients

Group	Township	Correlation Coefficient	Beta Coefficient*
8	San. N. and E.	0.97	0.059
8	Mal.	0.91	0.061
8	Gos. S.	0.96	0.064
7	Col. S.	0.87	0.068
6	San. W.	0.95	0.075
5	Roc.	0.96	0.083
5	Mer.	0.96	0.092
4	Til. W.	0.93	0.083
4	Mai.	0.94	0.094
3	And.	0.98	0.126
3	Gos. N.	0.97	0.130
2	Til. N.	0.98	0.138
2	Col. N.	0.95	0.144
1	San. S.	0.98	0.155
	Essex County	0.95	0.086

Source: Clarke, "Aspects of Land Acquisition," Table 5

*Significant at the 0.001 level.

"And." = Anderdon; "Col." = Colchester; "Gos." = Gosfield; "Mai." = Maidstone; "Mal." = Malden; "Mer." = Mersea; "Roc." = Rochester; "San." = Sandwich; and "Til." = Tilbury. "N." = North; "W." = West; "S." = South; and "E." = East.

years. This in turn rendered the profiles of townships in groups six through eight more parabolic than might have been expected in more normal circumstances. Townships in groups four and five experienced higher overall growth rates even though they were located in areas that were more poorly drained. Their growth profiles were more characteristically sigmoidal, indicating a period of slow growth in the initial period during which time the more southwesterly townships were being taken up. This continued into the 1830s and 1840s when the county's isolation from the eastern hub of the colony increased. Thereafter, their growth rates increased markedly as a result of the spreading effect from the eastern core. The highest rates of growth occurred in the townships of Anderdon and Gosfield North, which are grouped together on Table 4.5; in Tilbury North and Colchester North, townships that also had sufficiently high beta coefficients to form one group; and in Sandwich South, where the growth rate was the highest of all fourteen townships. These townships, relatively inaccessible and with much poor soil, were among the last to begin the process of patenting. An analysis of the size of the beta coefficients against the date of first patent supports this observation, yielding a positive correlation of 0.86. The period of regional isolation over, these townships experienced rapid land-acquisition rates, which reflected not only the movement of population westward from Toronto but also the decisions to end the existence of the Indian reserve in the west and to create Anderdon Township, to pressure the Canada Company to make available Crown reserves, and to sell the clergy reserves.

In three of these "back" townships there were unusually high amounts of reserved land. The reserved lands of Sandwich Township had been allocated in what became Sandwich South Township and as a result almost 80 percent of this township consisted of Crown and clergy reserves. Similarly, the reserved lands of Colchester North and Gosfield North constituted approximately 47 per cent and 68 per cent respectively of the townships. The result of these political decisions, and of other ones threatening forfeiture against the non-reserved and unpatented lands and offering land free of settlement duties to those holding militia and United Empire Loyalist rights, was to produce a land-patenting rush and to raise the beta coefficients for the townships. In Sandwich South, the percentage of land acquired increased from 5.9 per cent in 1834 to 41.6 per cent in 1840 and from 45.2 per cent in 1845 to 66.2 per cent in 1850. In Gosfield North, the respective figures were 6.5 per cent to 38.0 per cent and 41.9 per cent to 69.0 per cent. Between 1845 and 1846, the figure increased from 41.5 per cent to 65.0 per cent! In Colchester North, the change was from 0.5 per cent to 41.4 per cent between 1835 and 1840, and 42.7 per cent to 69.1 per cent between 1845 and 1850. In this township, all of the Canada Company lots were patented in 1846. The company was, of course, anxious to patent its land because its contract with government was drawing to a close and criticism of its activities was loud. The high rates of acquisition in these townships were not, therefore, a result of their superior natural endowment but rather testify to the operation of the political process.

ANALYSIS OF THE SPATIAL PATTERN OF ACQUISITION

Figure 4.6 shows the pattern of acquisition for every lot in Essex. Mapped to the level of the fifty-acre parcel, the pattern is shown here to the level of the half-lot, or approximately 100 acres in most instances. The map appears to emphasize the southwest township of Malden as the core area for land acquisition. There is a large measure of truth to this in the British era. However, the reader will appreciate

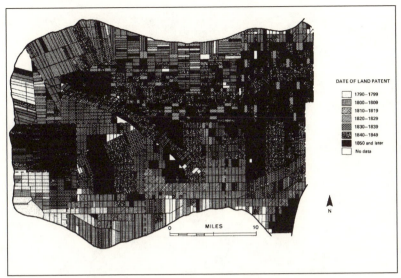

Figure 4.6   The spatial pattern of acquisition: Essex County
Source: Abstract Index to Deeds, Essex County.

that the oldest settlement was actually in the northwest in what became Sandwich Township. Here, the recognition by British patents of a French settlement in Petite Côté and L'Assomption which preceded the creation of the land boards by forty years creates a false impression of the origins of settlement. Elsewhere, things are more reliable and it is clear that the acquisition of land reflected accessibility, the more remote and less accessible lots being generally taken up later. It is also clear that the area of earliest settlement was more extensive along the south shore of Lake Erie than northward along Lake St Clair, reflecting, as described in the first chapter, the distribution of better-drained soils. Accessibility along the Talbot Road was also of importance but only in a relative sense because, generally, patenting became progressively later as one moved into the interior.

That said, accessibility and soil conditions were obviously not the only factors because there are large compact blocks and scattered lots which together represent the political process in action. Anderdon Township was clearly acquired later. There, Robinson gave voice to a widespread frustration over having an Indian reserve command such an important location. Elsewhere, the extensive blocks patented in the 1840s and 1850s coincide with the pattern of Crown and clergy reserves identified in chapter 2 or with the scattered pattern of the reserves in Maidstone and Rochester townships.

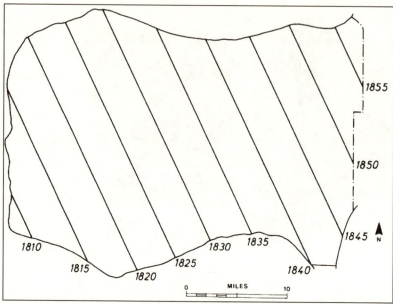

Figure 4.7   Trend-surface analysis of Essex: the linear surface
Source: J. Clarke, "Aspects of Land Acquisition," 113, 116, 117.

Accessibility and the role of the physical environment were significant factors in the settlement of Upper Canada and indeed of any newly colonizing area. Their relative importance is difficult to assess in descriptive form. However, there are explictly spatial techniques for partitioning each map observation into two parts. Trend-surface analysis, developed in geology and using the mathematics of polynomials, is one such approach which has been applied to problems in the natural sciences and also to the spread of population and settlement.[171] The approach uses the least-squares linear model and subsets of increasingly more complex equations to predict trends in a dependent variable (Figures 4.7, 4.8 and 4.9) from a knowledge of spatial location[172]. In this instance, the dependent variable is date of land acquisition and the extent to which an observation cannot be predicted exactly constitutes the extent of the local effect plus error in measurement. These residuals identify areas settled or behind the dominant trend (Figures 4.10) established by equations which provide surfaces of "best fit" to the data. The technique is, in this sense, diagnostic in that areas of extreme residuals can be shown to be spatially coincident with other phenomena, for example, political processes, conditions of the environment, or social circumstances.

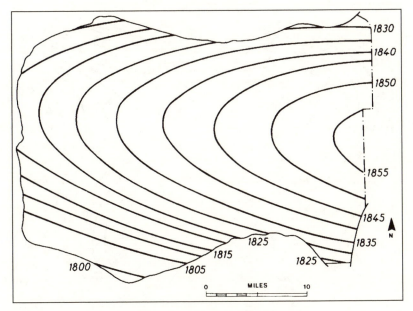

Figure 4.8   Trend-surface analysis of Essex: the quadratic surface
Source: J. Clarke, "Aspects of Land Acquisition," 113, 116, 117.

Moreover, the approach allows one to answer the question, "What if"? What if certain types of patent were rejected from a sample? What would the surface of acquisition look like if the atypical lots were removed from the analysis. For this reason, the result of such analysis is often spoken of as a "response surface" and it is in this manner that the technique is used here.

Accessibility and the Environment in the Choice of Individual Lots

In order to answer the question, "What was the role of accessibility and the physical environment in the decision of individuals to acquire property?" two samples were taken and subjected to trend-surface analysis. The first of these was a stratified sample of 516 lots and included representative data points from the Crown, clergy, and Indian reserve lands as well as those held in speculation. The second was a sample of 327 from which all four categories had been removed since they obscured a more fundamental pattern of land acquisition, that of the smallholder, and made the evaluation of the importance of the physical environment more difficult. In both cases, the cubic

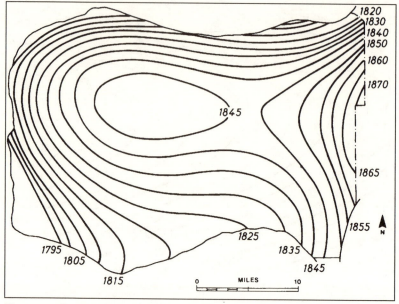

Figure 4.9 Trend-surface analysis of Essex: the cubic surface
Source: J. Clarke, "Aspects of Land Acquisition," 113, 116, 1

surface was deemed the most appropriate and proved significant at the 99.9 per cent confidence level. The surfaces were remarkably similar, and because of this, only the surface from the second smaller sample has been presented here (Figure 4.9). The residuals, plotted to identify factors of local rather than regional importance, were those greater than one standard error. These were of two types: negative residuals, where patenting was generally ahead of the general trend of acquisition; and positive residuals, where lots were acquired later than the overall trend. Figure 4.10 shows the extreme residuals from the first sample of 516 lots.

In at least five instances, the extreme departures from the trend (residuals greater than one standard error) reveal the clergy reserves of Essex, and a sixth group reveals the former Indian reserve in Anderdon Township (Figure 4.10). As shown in chapter 2, the establishment of these reserved lands was among the first tasks faced by the surveyors of the area. The reserves were to have been scattered with respect to one another and to those in adjacent concessions in accordance with Smyth's chequered plan.[173] As noted earlier, implementation of the plan in one of the earliest settled parts of Upper Canada would have required the removal of settlers.[174] Since this was not

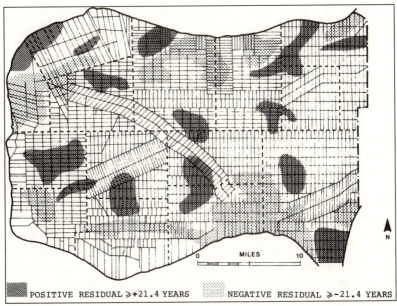

Figure 4.10   Extreme residuals from the first sample of 516 lots: cubic surface
Source: J. Clarke, "Aspects of Land Acquisition," 113, 116, 117.

desirable in a strategically sensitive area, it had been decided to allocate the clergy and Crown (later Canada Company) reserves in blocks
in Sandwich, Malden, Colchester, Gosfield, and Mersea townships.[175]
In Figure 4.10, all of the clergy blocks appear as areas of positive
residuals. The areas of negative residuals, acquired earlier than the
general trend, are in part those where land speculation by individuals
was particularly marked. In Maidstone and Rochester townships, the
area of negative residuals corresponds with lands patented by the
Askin family, which, as will be shown later, placed its priority on
compact accessible holdings rather than land quality.[176] In Malden
Township, the officers of the Indian Department had acquired large
quantities of land at an early date but, in this instance, the negative
residual areas also correspond with an area of fairly well-drained soils.
Elsewhere, the extreme negative and positive residuals appear to
identify environmental conditions. In Mersea Township, the extreme
positive residuals in the extreme south correspond to an area of
known swamp; along the Lake Erie shore, a band of extreme negative
residuals reveals the well-drained soils of this part of the county. The
role of the physical environment becomes clearer with the removal of
the Crown, clergy, Indian, and speculative holdings from the sample.

The generalized linear surface for the smaller sample of 327 points (R=0.17) indicates that the land acquired earliest was in the west of the county, in Sandwich and Malden townships, and that settlement took approximately forty-five years to reach Tilbury Township in the northeast (Figure 4.7). The quadratic surface explained an additional 8 per cent of the variation and took the form of a west-to-east rising ridge (Figure 4.8). The basically concentric pattern of land acquisition represented by the cubic surface (R=0.31) is obviously related to overall access by water and via the Tecumseth, Talbot, and later Middle roads (Figure 4.9). However, the distance between isochrones would seem to emphasize the particular importance of the well-drained soils of the Lake Erie shore along which land was rapidly acquired. In a given five-year period, larger amounts of land were taken up in this area than in other parts of the county. This was particularly true of the period from 1820 to 1825, when larger amounts of land were patented in Colchester and Gosfield townships than along the Lake St Clair shore in Maidstone and Rochester townships. As Figure 4.6 shows, the earliest patents occurred in Malden, the latest in Tilbury and Mersea townships. The decade 1835 to 1845 was one of considerable importance in the Essex area. This is reflected in the generalized surface of land acquisition.

The map of extreme residuals from this cubic surface (Figure 4.10) clearly suggested the importance of soil-drainage conditions as a local factor affecting land acquisition. Drainage characteristics were summarized as poorly drained and well-drained categories.[177] A chi-square test was run between these two drainage classes and the sign of the residuals greater than one standard error. It was expected that there was a significant association of well-drained soils and negative residuals and, conversely, of positive residuals and poorly drained soils. A χ^2 value of 14.9 confirmed the hypothesis at the .01 level. A second chi-square analysis was performed to investigate the relationship between timing and the dominant type of vegetation since vegetation has been thought to have been used as a guide to good land.[178] This second analysis was conducted in Gosfield, Rochester, and Mersea townships. The vegetation was classified into an oak-hickory, chestnut group and a black ash and elm swamp group. The value of χ^2 was greater than that required for significance at the 0.001 level and with one degree of freedom.[179] The null hypothesis was therefore rejected. The hypothesis that the early settlers may have used the type of vegetation as an indicator of soil quality is seen to have statistical validity.

CONCLUSION

Within Essex County there were two distinct periods of land acquisition separated by the War of 1812 and its aftermath. In the first period, which lasted until about 1815, large tracts of land were acquired by capitalists who at any one time could acquire more than 50 per cent of all the land taken up by patentees. Defined in this chapter by scale, these speculators controlled a diminishing proportion of land patented in the second period but their place in the hierarchy of patentees was taken by the Canada Company, a corporate speculator. The effects of government land policy were most marked in this later period. Faced by the threat of the House of Assembly recommending forfeiture to the imperial parliament, the Canada Company rushed to patent its lands. Similarly, Thomas Talbot endeavoured to have the lands he supervised patented. In 1850s and 1860s, most of the lands being patented were former Indian reserves and Clergy reserves, reflecting the government's desire to rid itself, at least in the case of the clergy reserves, of a constant political sore.

The analysis at the township level showed that by 1865 most of the lands of Essex County had passed to patent. All townships had on average been patented within eighty years and several much sooner. The townships that were patented fastest were the back townships of Sandwich South, Colchester North, Gosfield North, and Tilbury North. This reflected neither their superior physical endowment nor their accessibility, but rather the fact that they contained large amounts of reserved lands which for political reasons were patented rapidly. Moreover, they had begun to be acquired at a time when the region as a whole was beginning to orient itself towards the more rapidly growing eastern urban centres of Toronto and Hamilton. Those townships that contained well-drained soils, that were more accessible either by road or from the coast, and that were close to the village centre of Amherstburg in Malden Township or the town of Sandwich (modern Windsor) experienced an initial advantage, but the advantage was lost when development shifted to the Toronto-Hamilton area. A period of lag resulted and lasted to 1840, during which there was little or no increase in patenting. While rapid recovery took place thereafter, this resulted in lower overall acquisition rates.

Use of trend-surface analysis at the lot level pointed to the importance of overall access and identified the Indian and clergy reserves as areas that were anomalous in terms of the date of their acquisition. Whether or not they were also anomalous in terms of their actual

Plate 4.4   Samuel Street, Jr. American-born, Street was one of the wealthiest men in Upper Canada when he died in 1844. With Thomas Clark, his fortune was made in land speculation, mortgaging and mortgage foreclosures, money lending to the powerful and as a financier.

Courtesy of Toronto Reference Library, J. Ross Robertson Collection (SRR 1280, T17056).

development is another issue which, together with the activities of land speculators, is addressed elsewhere in the volume. The analysis of the extreme residuals from the trend surface showed that these were associated with soil-drainage conditions, the earliest patentees acquiring well-drained, lightly textured loam and sandy loam soils. Differences in soil were in turn reflected in differences in vegetation, which could well have been used as a guide to soil conditions. Certainly there is a statistical association that lends support to this supposition but a search of the township papers and contemporary newspapers [180] produced little documentary evidence. In fact, there were only nine instances in which particular tree types were used to convince people to choose or purchase particular lots. This need not diminish the argument since the prevailing mythology supports the notion that settlers were aware of the physical environment, and prevailing mores attract little overt commentary. Knowledgeable individuals in the land business such as John Prince, Charles Askin, and Samuel Street (Plate 4.4) used the field notes and the surveyor's maps to their benefit and that of their clients. [181]

5 The Market for Land: Sales in Essex to Mid-century

INTRODUCTION

This chapter places an emphasis upon the economic factor in the settlement process.[1] Until recently, it seemed as if settlement had taken place in an economic vacuum; however, the work of W. Norton,[2] W. Marr and J. Paterson,[3] D. McCalla,[4] D. Gagan,[5] J. Clarke and D. Brown,[6] D. McCallum,[7] M. McInnis,[8] E. Gray and B. Prentice,[9] and R. Ankli and K. Duncan[10] has done much to rectify this impression. In fact, as Douglas McCalla has shown, even the subsistence farmer was an economic being, requiring capital to acquire land and for the means of production. The commonly applied epithet "self-sufficient" was rarely appropriate in Upper Canada; most had to borrow for supplies to maintain their farm operation until a surplus was available. Indebtedness was, therefore, a logical strategy necessitated by the settler condition,[11] a topic that receives separate treatment for Essex in the subsequent chapter. From the outset, all were involved in risk taking. Unless a member of the privileged few, a settler was limited to a two-hundred-acre grant. If acquisitiveness or visions of self-worth or desire to provide for one's family were important to a person, this meant acquiring land by purchase, often secured by loan. Yet little is known about the price of land, the frequency of transfer of land, or the frequency of indebtedness in the first half of the nineteenth century.

The prime purpose here is to establish the price of land for Essex for its own sake and so that the behaviour of individuals and groups can be placed in local context. The terms "price of land" or "land price" are used throughout even though it has not been possible to deflate the value to allow for the costs of a residence or out-buildings that may or may not have been included in the transactions upon which the inference of price is based. Arguably, this might make a case to refer to these observations as "farm- price per acre" rather than "land price per acre." Yet even this would be unsatisfactory in that it would refer only to the fixed elements of farming. A second purpose is to describe and "explain" the operation of the land market and to provide comparative data for later work on this topic. In this last respect it is anticipated that Essex prices will be lower than those in other parts of southern Ontario, most especially the Toronto area. However, as yet, the full parameters of land prices are not known and cannot be until more attention is devoted to the topic.

The chapter looks at the chronology of sales and compares this to the chronology of patenting. It discusses the price of land through time and seeks to relate this to developments in the Upper Canadian, American, and British markets. It accords a special place to wheat as the staple which was long thought to have driven the Upper Canadian economy. The chapter stresses the role of the local economy, although links to the outside world, British government expenditures, and monies brought and invested by immigrants were clearly important. As McCalla concludes, the prime objective of the settler must have been to build wealth in the form of a farm. In the long term, this would produce income and its capital value could be expected to grow with the economy.[12]

The chapter ends with an analysis of local infrastructure and its effects upon the price of land. All of this, and subsequent discussion in later chapters on mortgaging, land tenure, and land speculation, is largely based upon data sets created primarily from the abstract index to deeds. This source is therefore discussed at some length before the substantive results of the research are presented.

SOURCES

As is implied in the title, the abstract index to deeds[13] contains abstracts of original deeds, copies of which were retained by the lawyers of the parties and by the registrar for the county in which the transaction had taken place. These deeds were transcribed into "copy books," many of which have survived the ravages of time and the destruction of the originals. The origin of the "abstracts" lies in the legislation of 1865[14] which required the county registrars to abstract the detailed information contained in the registrars' copy books and to prepare indices for each county.[15] While the specific data used in this study came primarily from these abstracts, the general form of the deeds followed the law of England, modified to meet the "American" experience.

The system was provided for in the Constitutional Act of 1791. Unlike the notarial system in use in Lower Canada, it offered the potential purchaser or lender greater protection for a particular property than was available in that colony.[16] In Upper Canada, the fact that registration had to be in the county in which the transaction occurred increased the protection of the purchaser. So too did the fact that a registered deed took precedence over an unregistered one; the status of a property was immediately available for a small fee, as seen in the following quotation: "Registration in Upper Canada gives publicity to every deed or encumbrance on land, and a prior instrument, not registered, would not affect a subsequent one which is registered, so that a prudent man in Upper Canada can always ascertain whether he is secure, which in Lower Canada he cannot do."[17]

Though essentially voluntary, registration was in the legal interest of both parties to an agreement. While it is possible that some deeds were not registered, and while there are clear gaps in the Essex records, the registration of deeds became widespread in Upper Canada. W.H. Merritt, witness to the committee investigating the civil government of the Canadas, noted that the registration system "is universally approved of; there is not a person in the country who does not feel the benefit of it."[18] Increasingly, deeds contained the stipulation that they be registered. Arguably, by offering legal protection, registration increased the availability of credit. It was probably to encourage this, as well as to cater to the cultural predisposition of British settlers in Lower Canada, that the Canada Tenure Act of 1826 had been passed. This permitted conversion from seigneurial tenure to "free and common soccage" with its concomitant system of British Common law and registration.[19] Interestingly, in Upper Canada, agreements were sometimes registered even when it might not be expected that they would be, for example, in the case of the intergenerational transfer of land. In some instances, as David Gagan has shown elsewhere, security in old age was assured by a mortgage in the family.[20]

In the abstracts, data are presented in a succinct manner, as Table 5.1 shows. Nine types of information are given, and all but the first two are self-explanatory. The first, the instrument number, is a device to allow the registrar either to locate the original or, by noting the date of registration, to obtain the exact terms of the original in the copy books. The "Instrument" heading of column 2 indicates the particular legal device or instrument used in a given transaction. In the excerpt chosen to illustrate the process, there are six different types of instrument, of which four (the patents, the indentures, mortgages, and the bargain and sale) occur most frequently. Definitions of the most significant of these terms is given in Appendix 5.1; in terms of the transfer of land, the most important are instruments of "bargain and sale" and "indentures," although this last instrument can be used for a variety of transactions including mortgaging. However, in the context of the abstracts, this should be apparent from the sequence of events. Table 5.2 shows the frequency with which these various instruments were used in Malden Township to mid-century. In terms of sales of land, "Bargain and Sale" (321 out of 624) constitute slightly more than half of all instruments suggesting transfer. The addition of 106 indentures might raise the level of transfer to slightly more than 68 per cent were it not for the fact that this instrument need not always transfer title (Appendix 5.1). In Essex most did.

In Table 5.1 no fewer than fifteen legal instruments pertaining to the history of this particular lot (lot 30 in the 3rd concession of Malden Township) are summarized without recourse to the extant originals. Use of the abstracts hastened the compilation of the data required to analyse the frequency of sale, the price of land per acre, and the identification of owners over a wide geographical area. The abstracts provided an invaluable short cut in the analysis of a huge volume of deeds which otherwise would have had to be dealt with in a study of more than 3500 lots in the county over more than sixty years.

Additionally, the chronological organization of the abstracts allowed the tracing of events. Following the rules of conveyancing allowed conclusions to be reached as to who owned what when. While counts of the frequency of transfer and calculations of price per acre were relatively easy to obtain, determining ownership was the most time-consuming aspect of accumulating the data. Knowledge of the owner of a property was necessary to deduce tenure condition: the name of the owner was compared to that of the occupant, with assessment rolls and the enumeration returns of the census of 1851–52 as the source of information. Figures 5.1 and 5.2 show the result of this process for Malden Township in 1825 and 1852. Figures 5.3 and 5.4 can be used to gauge how much time this involved. These figures illustrate the steps necessary to establish ownership on two properties, lot 3 in the 1st concession and lot 24 in the 2nd. In the records, these properties are closely intertwined with two others, the Bell Farm and the so-called Caldwell Grant between Lake Erie and Big Creek.

The abstracts have a number of advantages and disadvantages. Among the former, as indicated above, is the relative speed with which data can be gathered; among the latter are the limits imposed by the

Table 5.1 Malden Township, Lot 30, 3rd concession

Instru-ment No.	Instrument	Its Date	Date of Registry	Grantor	Grantee	Quantity of Lands	Consideration of Money	Remarks
A15	Patent	6 Mar. 1798	5 May 1798	Crown	Mathew Elliot	Among other lands	–	Lot No. 30
c115	B & s	8 July 1811	9 July 1811	Mathew Elliot	James Rouse	100 acres	Not mentioned	S½ of Lot30
155	Mortgage	8 July 1811	9 July 1811	James Rouse	Mathew Elliot	100 acres	–	S½ of Lot30 Mort.
d140	Mortgage	13 Mar. 1819	1 Oct. 1819	James Rouse	Robert Reynolds	100 acres	£140	S½ of Lot30 Mort.
F44	B & s	24 Sept. 1822	8 Aug. 1831	Mathew Elliot	Pierre Beniteau dit Labadaine	100 acres	£37.10s.0d.	N½ of Lot30
A244	B & s	19 Jan. 1840	20 Jan. 1840	Jeanne Beniteau	Jean [] Beniteau		Natural Love	See Description of Consideration
i186	Will	22 April 1814	2 Sept. 1843	Mathew Elliot	See Will	–		
A119	Q.C.	26 Mar. 1850	26 Mar. 1850	Thomas Bain	Michael Malone	–		–
120	Will	5 Jan. 1827	30 Mar. 1850	Pierre Beniteau	See Will of	–	5/-	Lot No. 30
121	Q.C.	8 Mar. 1850	30 Mar. 1850	Clement Beniteau	John [] Beniteau	Among other lands	£37.10s.0d.	Lot No. 30
143	Q.C.	24 April 1850	20 Aug. 1850	William I Little	Théodore Washington Little	–	£20	Lot No. 30
144	Indenture	17 July 1850	20 Aug. 1850	Théodore Washington Little	Michael Malone	100 acres	£30.5s.0d.	in the [] of Lot 30
146	B & s	8 Aug. 1850	17 Sept. 1850	James Rouse	John O'Connor the Younger	100 acres	£50	S½ of Lot 30
176	B & s	8 Mar. 1851	8 Mar. 1851	Thomas Bain Junior & W.	Michael Maloney	100 acres	£75	S½ of Lot 30
220	B & s & Q.C.	21 Oct. 1851	21 Oct. 1851	John O'Connor Jun. & W.	Michael Maloney	100 acres	£25	S½ of Lot 30

Source: Clarke "Land and Law," Table 1. B&S=Bargain and Sale; Q.C.=Quit-Claim

Table 5.2   Malden Township: frequency of recording of particular instruments, money, and acreage

Instrument	Number Recorded	Number Recorded with Money	Number Recorded with Acreage
Deed	17	17	17
Bargain and Sale	321	274	135
Indenture	106	88	81
Deed Poll	6	4	2
Dower Right	0	0	0
Mortgage	88	76	77
Assignment of Mortgage	16	6	7
Discharge of Mortgage	4	0	1
Deed of Trust	5	4	1
Deed of Release	8	7	3
Lease	1	1	1
Foreclosure	0	0	0
Sheriffs' Deed	4	4	3
Bond	0	0	0
Deed of Gift	10	2	10
Deed of Confirmation	2	2	0
Deed of Partition	3	0	0
Agreement	3	2	0
Power of Attorney	13	0	0
Grant	3	2	2
Quit Claim	14	11	9
Total	624	500	349

Source: Clarke, "Land and Law," Table 2.

N.B. Since money is never recorded for patents or wills in the abstracts, these instruments have not been included in the table. There were 65 wills registered and 199 patents in Malden Township in the period up to 1852.

abstraction process. The most precise geographical descriptions are to be found in the original deeds but, for most purposes, those of the abstracts are adequate. When a sale involves not one but a multitude of properties, this will be signalled by "among other lands" (Table 5.1 and instrument A15). In such instances, exact locations will not be given although these *may* have been available in the original. Important information such as the inclusion of the "old gray mare" within the transaction and the cost of borrowing are not available to the researcher who does not use the original deeds or their transcribed equivalents. The occupations of the parties to the transaction and their status as farmer, yeoman, or gentleman was not abstracted. Nor was place of residence, so important to the understanding of emerging credit facilities and frequently recorded in the copy books. Multiple transactions are often reported in the abstracts as "among other

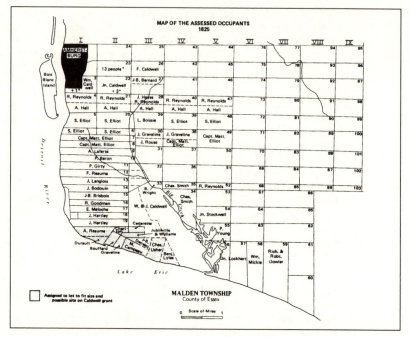

Figure 5.1   Land ownership, 1825, Malden township
Source: J. Clarke "Land and Law," 486.

lands" but the actual deeds may specify the locations.[21] However, a careful tracking of the parties, the cost for "consideration," and the date can overcome this problem and the spatial extent of the transactions can be determined. Further, intention can occasionally be discerned in the deeds; it will never be discerned in the abstracts although it may be inferred from the use of additional sources, for example, the existence of a mill, tavern,[22] or industrial equipment.[23] These were not abstracted in such a way as to show such features.

Most important, a sale with immediate conveyance of title, using an instrument of "bargain and sale," cannot be distinguished from a credit arrangement between purchaser and vendor unless the registrar made appropriate comments, adding "Mort" to the "Comments" column. In fact, this is de facto as opposed to de jure recognition of the status of the transaction. In the absence of this notation or of a second convention whereby the registrar drew a line through a discharged mortgage which was not explicitly recognized as such, the context will help separate a mortgage from a sale. Thus, if the names are the same on two agreements but in reverse order on the second and if the date is identical, one can with safety deduce a mortgage.

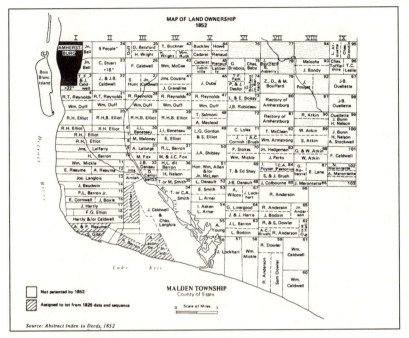

Figure 5.2   Land ownership, 1852, Malden township
Source: J. Clarke "Land and Law," 487.

Similarly, where the location is the same, the date different, the "consideration" different, but the parties identical, a credit relationship most probably exists. A single entry of a "bargain and sale" indicates a simple conveyance. These procedures of inference were used here and estimates of sales and mortgages in any one year gauged by deduction from the sequence of events, including instruments of indenture and bargain and sale as well as the mortgage per se.[24] This is the main shortcoming of the procedures employed; the outcome of the decision-making process is probabilistic and an unspecified error can exist.

Yet frequently this abstracted information is the only material that has survived; the original deeds have simply disappeared. While this was not true in the Essex case, the "originals" in their copy-book form did "disappear" for quite a few years, only to reappear at a later date. In the interim, sole reliance had to be placed upon the abstracts. When the microfilmed copies of the transcribed originals were found once again, they were used to test the usefulness of the abstracts and the method of inference. In both instances, the results were sound.[25]

Some 4800 extant instruments for the years 1788 to 1836 were examined. The results of this were to add three mortgages to the list

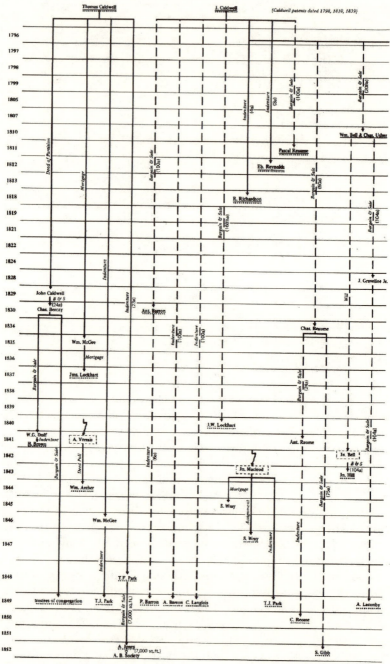

Figure 5.3   Lot 3, 1st concession, Malden

Source: J. Clarke, "Land and Law," 488–89.

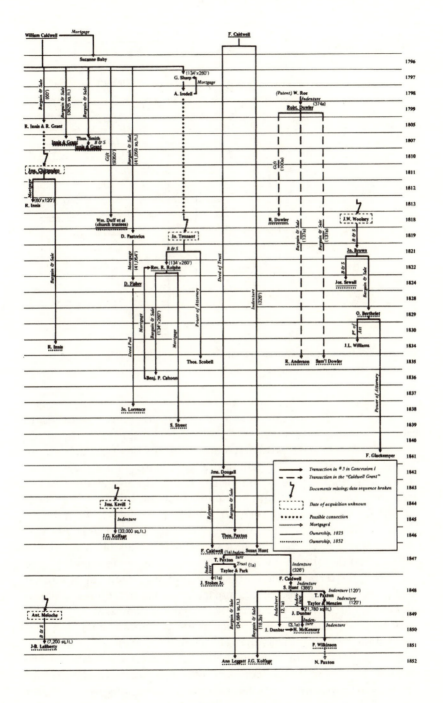

William Caldwell — *Mortgage*

Suzanne Baby

F. Caldwell

1796
1797
1798
1799
1805
1807
1810
1811
1812
1813
1818
1819
1821
1822
1824
1828
1829
1830
1834
1835
1836
1837
1838
1839
1840
1841
1842
1843
1844
1845
1846
1847
1848
1849
1850
1851
1852

(134'x260')
G. Sharp
Mortgage
A. Iredell

(*Patent*) W. Roe
Indenture
(374a)
Robt. Dowler

R. Innis & R. Grant

Innis A Grant
Innis A Grant

Thos. Smith
B & S

Gift

Jms. Chippawa

R. Innis

(80'x120')

Bargain & Sale (60')
Bargain & Sale (5825 sq. ft.)
Bargain & Sale
Gift (8060')
Bargain & Sale (41,050 sq. ft.)

Wm. Duff et al (church trustees)

D. Pastorius

Jn. Tennant

B & S

(134'x260')
Rev. R. Rolphe

D. Fisher

Mortgage (41,050')

(134'x200')

Deed Poll
Mortgage
Bargain & Sale (134'x200')
Mortgage
Power of Attorney

R. Innis

Thos. Scobell

Benj. P. Cahoon

Jn. Lorrence

S. Street

Gift (100a)

R. Dowler

Bargain & Sale (137a)
Bargain & Sale (137a)

Deed of Trust
Indenture (326')

J.W. Woolley

B & S

Jn. Brown

B & S

Jos. Sewall

Bargain & Sale

O. Berthelot

Pr. of Att

J.L. Williams

R. Anderson   Sam'l Dowler

Power of Attorney

F. Glackemyer

Jms. Dougall

Jms. Kevill

Indenture

J.G. Kolfage (33,000 sq. ft.)

Release
Bargain & Sale

Thos. Paxton

F. Caldwell (1a) *Inden-ture*   Susan Hunt
T. Paxton   *Trust* (1a)
Inden-ture   Taylor & Park
(1a)
J. Stokes Jr.

F. Caldwell
S. Hunt (386')
Indenture
T. Paxton
Taylor & Menzies   *Indenture* (120')
(21,780 sq. ft.)   (120')
J. Dunbar   *Inden-ture*
(3.1a)
J. Dunbar ➤ H. McKenney   *Indenture*
P. Wilkinson

Ant. Meloche

B & S

J-B. Laliberty (7,200 sq. ft.)

Bargain & Sale (24,684 sq. ft.)
Bargain & Sale (18.2a)

Ann Leggett J.G. Kolfage

N. Paxton

Legend box:
→ Transaction in #3 in Concession i
⇢ Transaction in the "Caldwell Grant"
⚡ Documents missing; data sequence broken
▢ (dashed) Date of acquisition unknown
•••• Possible connection
⋯⋯ Mortgaged
≈≈≈ Ownership, 1825
▪▪▪ Ownership, 1852

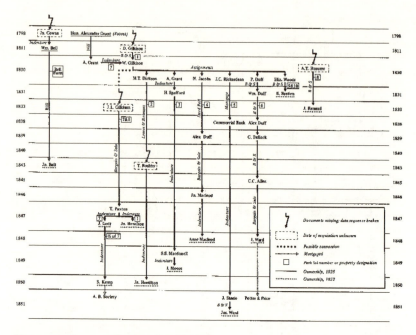

Figure 5.4   Lot 24, 2nd concession, Malden
Source: J. Clarke, "Land and Law," 490.

of those identified by inference from the abstract index to deeds, to add forty cases to the derived variable "length of time to mortgage discharge," and to make possible computation of "price per acre" in an additional eight cases.[26] Again, of the 649 records of mortgages identified in Essex, 414 were without the financial consideration or the acreage. However, subsequent examination of hundreds of deeds points to the omission of such variables in the original; the information in the originals was faithfully compiled and abstracted. This search also showed that, in the case of instruments of "bargain and sale," when the phrase "by way of a mortgage" or some similar phrase was used, the terms of the mortgage included a statement of interest and a schedule for repayment. In each instance, the inference drawn from the chronological pattern was sustained. Similarly, a search of "bargains and sales" omitting such phrases demonstrated that they contained no terms whatsoever. The sample size used in this instance was a 10 per cent of all instruments in a particular quinquennial period. In all, the sample consisted of 488 instruments. The results showed that, without exception, these were sales giving the purchaser immediate title. In short, when counts of the frequency of "bargains and sales" and straight forward "indentures" are classed together, the new category would seem to include all transfers of land between individuals for an immediate consideration, which was most usually cash. When "mortgages" and "bargains and sale by way of a mortgage" are added to form a single class, that class would appear to contain the overwhelming majority of credit transactions.

This chapter is concerned with transfers of property as "sales." In calculating the number of sales and the price of land, legal instruments such as wills, quit claims, mortgages, agreements, leases and releases,[27] and sheriffs' deeds[28] by which property was seized were ignored. So too were "in family" transactions where conveyance was made "in love and affection" or for the sum of five shillings, the sum required for legal purposes. However, "in family" transfers where the "consideration" appeared to be for a reasonable sum of money within the existing price of land were included in a data set established to reflect economic realities rather than ties of family and kin.

THE SALE OF LAND

While land was initially acquired by grant from the state or by the state's sanction of purchase from the Indians or recognition of the prior existing French regime, the sale of particular parcels of land took place from the beginning. Table 5.3 lists the number of patents and the number of sales or transactions in each year from 1798 to 1852 and coincidentally the number of mortgages. A transaction is defined here as a sale subsequent to initial acquisition from the state; it could, in fact, be thought of as a re-sale since after 1825 the method of acquisition of the patent was a sale by the state to an individual. The net result of the decision to exclude "in-family" may have been to diminish the number of sales in any one year and to have reduced the measure of demand. However, it is clear that there is a sufficient number of "deeds" and "indentures of bargain and sale" to suggest the existence of a genuine market from the beginning, increasing over time.

In all, between 1798 and 1852, there were 4751 sales of land, 2091 patents, and 798 other legal transactions registered in rural Essex. Figure 5.5, a graph of the number of transactions, shows that the modal class was the class of one to five transactions and contained the mode (one), the median (three), and the mean ($\bar{x}$) of 4.11 and a standard deviation (σ) of 4.2. If the median is used as the measure, 50 per cent of the lots changed hands at least three times in fifty-four years or slightly more than once per generation. However, there were several parcels in Malden Township where

Table 5.3 Number of patents, transactions, and mortgages, with price in pence per acre: Essex County, 1798-1851

Year	Price per Acre	Number of observations on which price is based	Total number of transactions*	Total number of patents	Total number of mortgages
1798	392	21	35(60.0)	63	2
1799	342	5	25(20.0)	21	6
1800	306	5	18(27.8)	11	11
1801	903	2	10(20.0)	74	5
1802	423	4	26(15.4)	74	7
1803	–	–	41(–)	63	4
1804	127	8	35(22.8)	83	5
1805	122	3	24(12.5)	29	8
1806	135	7	52(13.5)	72	7
1807	124	12	61(19.6)	31	10
1808	267	27	60(45.0)	60	7
1809	251	17	52(32.6)	18	6
1810	145	17	44(38.6)	27	5
1811	337	11	32(34.3)	20	8
1812	344	3	27(11.1)	6	7
1813	232	12	30(40.0)	8	2
1814	127	3	9(33.3)	0	0
1815	293	10	27(37.0)	2	3
1816	186	20	44(45.4)	10	6
1817	500	23	48(47.9)	5	11
1818	455	34	77(44.1)	37	5
1819	229	15	39(38.5)	8	3
1820	292	27	58(46.6)	3	10
1821	173	9	32(28.1)	7	6
1822	266	23	49(46.9)	8	3
1823	634	29	66(43.9)	13	12
1824	462	28	74(37.8)	17	7
1825	246	26	49(53.1)	18	7
1826	362	35	56(62.5)	60	9
1827	295	29	65(44.6)	4	9
1828	297	34	79(43.0)	16	3
1829	314	28	62(45.2)	2	0
1830	577	44	101(43.6)	14	3
1831	294	55	94(58.5)	11	7
1832	410	55	105(52.4)	14	10
1833	274	47	101(46.5)	7	14
1834	316	82	117(70.0)	23	10
1835	264	48	103(46.6)	50	18
1836	455	93	209(44.5)	155	19
1837	632	111	166(66.9)	64	6
1838	597	84	107(78.5)	63	26
1839	587	93	136(68.4)	35	14
1840	566	115	176(65.3)	63	18
1841	646	93	128(72.7)	26	15

Table 5.3   (continued)

Year	Price per Acre	Number of observations on which price is based	Total number of transactions*	Total number of patents	Total number of mortgages
1842	427	95	147(64.6)	19	18
1843	324	77	114(67.5)	25	14
1844	407	89	137(65.0)	19	17
1845	480	86	141(61.0)	29	12
1846	489	94	163(57.7)	246	18
1847	403	127	180(70.6)	95	35
1848	504	126	186(67.7)	171	22
1849	639	170	261(65.1)	21	28
1850	427	147	215(68.4)	42	33
1851	439	182	268(70.5)	29	45

Source: Clarke and Brown, "The Upper Canadian Land Market," Table 1.

*Figures with brackets are sales with money as a percentage of total sales.

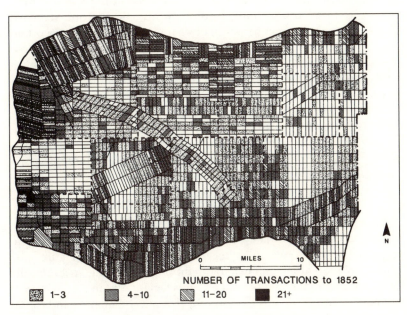

Figure 5.5: Number of transactions per lot in Essex County to 1852
Source: Abstract Index to Deeds, Essex County

Table 5.4   Descriptive statistics of the number of transactions per lot in Essex to 1852

Township	No.lag Years	Max.	Med.	Mode	$\bar{x}$	σ	n
Sandwich	6	20.0	3.0	1	4.60	3.80	499
Colchester	9	20.0	4.0	3	4.40	3.40	294
Gosfield	14	29.0	3.0	1	3.90	3.60	291
Tilbury	16	14.0	3.0	1	3.38	3.59	114
Anderdon	24	10.0	3.0	2	3.88	2.19	40
Mersea	26	16.0	3.0	1	3.23	2.68	226
Malden	28	87.0	5.0	5	7.27	11.38	95
Maidstone	32	39.0	3.0	1	3.92	3.98	201
Rochester	41	14.0	2.0	1	3.40	3.01	137
Total	29	87.0	3.0	1	4.11	4.20	1873

Source: Calculations of the author based on AO, Abstract Index to Deeds, Essex County.
"Max." is the maximum number of transactions and "Med." is the median number of transactions.

demand was so great that the number of transactions on them exceeded the number of years between the establishment of the Land Board of Hesse in 1788 and the mid-century mark (Table 5.4). Malden was clearly a place where land was in demand because of its location on the strait and its access to Amherstburg. As Table 5.4 also shows, the median here was five transactions and the $\bar{x}$ and σ were 7.27 and 11.38 transactions; in other words, 68.26 (one standard deviation from the mean) per cent of the lots could have recorded up to nineteen sales in this time frame.[29] This township had three lots with forty-five, sixty-two, and eighty-seven sales! There was obviously a relationship to location and to the length of time that patenting had been going on with the number of transactions. A Spearman rank-order correlation coefficient confirmed this.[30] Yet, before the introduction of a "sales policy" in 1825, only the most desirable properties, possessed of some particular locational advantage or particular resource, would produce repeated demand and intense competition because of the attractiveness of "free" land.

The spatial pattern of first sales

Figure 5.6 shows the date of first sale on lots in Essex. Clearly, the pattern has to be related to the map of land patents (Figure 4.6) shown in the earlier chapter. By definition, a lot had to be legally acquired before it could be sold and this legal status, in all but a small number of instances, was bestowed by patent. The map, by indicating the date of first sale, says something about the desirability of particular areas; obviously, accessibility was important to purchasers. In the

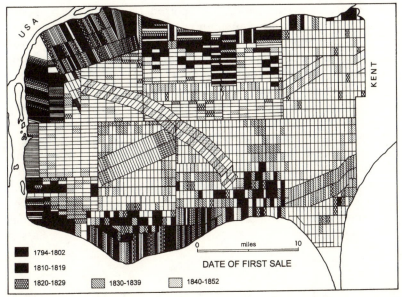

Figure 5.6   Date of first sale
Source: Abstract Index to Deeds, Essex County

earliest period, accessibility to coast was valued most. Later, as coastal areas were patented, accessibility to interior lands via the road network of the time (Figure 2.9) became more important. The linear pattern is far from perfect. For example, it is broken in Anderdon Township. Here, because of the presence of the Huron reserve, the land was unavailable until after 1835 and first sales did not occur until the 1840s and 1850s. It is broken in Colchester, Gosfield, and Mersea townships, where blocks of Crown and clergy reserve remained largely inviolate, although sales had commenced. The linear pattern is perhaps best developed in Malden Township and Petite Côté in Sandwich Township. North and east, in Sandwich East Township, the pattern is more punctiform. Along Lake St Clair in the townships of Maidstone, Rochester, and Tilbury, the timing of sales appears dichotomized. An early pattern of sales before 1810 stretches further inland than in the county, coincident with the realization that the streams and rivers of the area provided the best land in a poorly endowed wet area. The later pattern, of lots sold in the 1840–52 period, corresponds with higher elevations and with the developing road network. Overall, the pattern is thought to reflect demand because there was a market for land in the county, although it was perhaps not as strong as elsewhere.

Yet each sale has to have reflected personal decisions taken in conditions unknown to the contemporary observer. An early sale could reflect poor choice of land or simply an unusual opportunity, for example, the wealthy immigrant who arrived without experience of the country but was willing to pay for a "developed" farm. The farm sold towards mid-century could reflect a poorly endowed property which the patentee had to wait to sell until diminished opportunity forced the immigrant of the 1850s to accept. Conversely, there must have been cases in Sandwich where a settler was at least satisfied and perhaps even so happy with his lot that only old age, diminishing muscle power, or lack of family would prompt sale of the property. In short, an absolutely linear pattern of sale is as unlikely as an absolutely linear pattern of initial acquisition. Each decision was a judgment of local site factors, environmental circumstances, and indeed personal well-being.

Length of time to first sale

Tables 5.5a and 5.5b show the distribution in the time lag between first sale and initial acquisition, measured in terms of the date of patent. Table 5.5b reveals that 107 of these sales preceded patent, a total representing 10.4 per cent of all 1,033 observations for which it was possible to obtain both dates. The remaining 926 are shown on Table 5.5b as positive, that is, first sale came after the "normal" order or the date of patent. In 188 cases, as Table 5.6 demonstrates, there was no difference between the two dates, that is, they were sold within the year. In an additional 447 cases, 61 of them negative and therefore preceding patent, the sale took place within four years. So, in 61.5 per cent of the cases in Essex, transfer took place within four years; in this respect, as will be shown later, it is interesting that most instruments of bargain and sale which contained credit arrangements were written for three years! An additional 13.9 per cent exceeded the patent by up to nine years; 12.4 per cent, or 128 cases, did so by twenty years. Eighty lots took more than twenty years after the patent was issued to sell, and in half of the ten townships (subdividing Sandwich) the maximum lag exceeded forty years. In Sandwich South and East, it was forty-eight years; Sandwich West held the record for a transaction, exceeding the patent date by sixty-three years, but no doubt this was a legal anomaly as well as a statistical one. If the county average within the classes zero to minus and plus four was 61.5 per cent of the cases, the newer townships exceeded this. In Maidstone Township, 70.2 per cent lay within these classes, in Anderdon it was 72.0 per cent, in Mersea 77.9, in Rochester 82.7, and in Tilbury 84.0. In the older settled townships,

Table 5.5a   Descriptive statistics of time between patent and first sale, Essex County, 1794–1852, by quinquennial periods

Date	n	Minimum	Maximum	$\bar{x}$	σ
1794–1800	68	–1	40	11.0	11.0
1801–1805	217	–7	48	8.7	12.0
1806–1810	144	–10	39	6.8	9.8
1811–1815	22	–8	23	5.5	8.9
1816–1820	34	–7	26	7.4	7.9
1821–1825	42	–26	12	0.5	7.8
1826–1830	49	–32	21	1.1	11.0
1831–1835	62	–5	17	4.6	4.2
1836–1840	223	–12	16	2.8	4.5
1841–1845	47	–29	7	0.6	6.5
1846–1850	116	–15	6	1.5	2.5
1851–1852	9	–63	1	–10.0	20.0
Total	1033	–63	48	4.9	9.3

Table 5.5b   Revised descriptive statistics of time between patent and first sale, Essex County, 1794–1852, by quinquennial periods

Date	n	Minimum	Maximum	$\bar{x}$	σ
1794–1800	66	0	40	11.35	10.66
1801–1805	182	0	48	10.97	11.61
1806–1810	133	0	39	7.91	9.42
1811–1815	17	0	23	8.06	8.45
1816–1820	32	0	26	8.13	7.47
1821–1825	30	0	12	3.30	3.95
1826–1830	39	0	26	5.28	6.45
1831–1835	60	0	17	4.83	4.04
1836–1840	212	0	16	3.19	4.16
1841–1845	42	0	7	2.38	2.61
1846–1850	107	0	6	1.98	1.68
1851–1852	6	0	1	0.17	0.37
Total	926	0	48	6.24	8.42

Source: Calculations of the author.

the respective figures, in descending order, were Colchester (58.1 per cent), Sandwich (54.6 per cent), Gosfield (53.0 per cent), and Malden Township (44.8 per cent). In Essex as a whole, the average lag was 4.9 years with a σ of 9.3 years. If those cases in which sales preceded patent are regarded as administrative and legal anomalies and removed from the sample, the $\bar{x}$ and σ for the reduced sample become 6.24 and 8.42 years respectively. One may debate the legitimacy of either including

Table 5.6   Descriptive statistics of time between patent and first sale, Essex County, 1794–1852, by township

Lag	And.	Col.	Gos.	Mai.	Mal.	Mer.	Roc.	SE.	SW.	Til.	Tot.
N20+	–	–	1	1	–	–	–	2	6	–	10
N10–19	–	1	–	–	–	–	–	2	3	1	7
N5–9	1	3	2	–	1	3	2	5	10	2	29
N1–4	–	8	6	1	–	–	6	11	23	6	61
0	3	47	25	14	4	22	6	20	29	18	188
P1–4	15	53	58	58	26	52	36	42	28	18	386
P5–9	2	36	35	18	12	6	5	15	14	1	144
P10–19	4	22	27	7	14	9	2	27	16	–	128
P20+	–	16	14	5	10	3	1	14	13	4	80
Total	25	186	168	104	67	95	58	13	142	50	1033

Source: Abstract Index to Deeds, Essex County; calculations of the author.

The following abbreviations are used: positive (P); negative (N), Anderdon (And.), Colchester (Col.), Gosfield (Gos.), Mersea (Mer.), Maidstone (Mai.), Rochester (Roc.), Sandwich East (SE.), Sandwich West (SW.), Tilbury (Til.).

or excluding such observations, but the results of either action appear little different. In the former instance, 68.26 percent (one σ) of the cases occur in no more than 14.2 years; in the latter, 14.7. In older townships such as Malden, it could take between nine and twenty years from the patent for a sale to occur.[31] How these figures compare with other parts of Upper Canada is, as yet, unknown.

Table 5.5b indicates a steady decline in the years to first sales commensurate with increased demand, which the institution of a sales policy had been specifically designed to facilitate. The number of years to first sale dropped from 11.35 years between 1794 and 1800 to 1.98 in the quinquennial period from 1846 to 1850. At first sight there appears to be a linear quickening of demand but analysis of the internal variation shows it to have been a more step-like decline. A series of t tests revealed four distinct groupings, the first including the years of establishment of the British jurisdiction down to 1805, the second the period 1806 to 1820, the third the years to 1835, and the last from 1836 to mid-century.[32]

The first of these periods witnessed the establishment of the administration. During this time, the population was small and the demand for re-sale was low since almost all efforts were concentrated upon initial acquisition. The second period was one of wars, rumours of wars, and the aftermath of war. This part of Upper Canada witnessed invasion by American troops during the War of 1812. Considerable destruction ensued. Nonetheless, it was a time of considerable pros-

Table 5.7   Summary table of number of mortgages, sales, and price per acre within specified periods, Essex County, 1798–1851

Date	No. Mortgages	No.Sales	Pence/acre
1798–1800	18	78	346.66
1801–1805	30	136	393.75
1806–1810	35	269	184.40
1811–1815	20	125	266.60
1816–1820	35	266	332.40
1821–1825	34	270	356.20
1826–1830	26	363	369.00
1831–1835	56	520	311.60
1836–1840	83	794	567.40
1841–1845	75	667	456.80
1846–1850	136	1005	492.40
1851	45	258	439.00
Totals	593	4751	365.52

Source: AO Abstract Index to Deeds, Essex County.

perity for the province and presumably for Essex as well. For a variety of reasons, these were years of increasing supply problems and the government prohibited both exports and the use of wheat for alcohol. However, it was also a period of as yet unprecedented prosperity during which, in Essex, the speed of property transfer quickened somewhat.[33] Moreover, in the aftermath of war,[34] great things were anticipated and land prices per acre continued to rise (Table 5.7). However, depression followed in the 1820s and the price of wheat fell throughout the province.

It would be convenient to view the 1820s period as one when most people "unloaded" land as fast as possible[35] and a few chose to "ride" it out. Yet this view is simplistic, because Essex land prices improved modestly in the 1820s (Table 5.7). They continued to rise after the financial crisis of 1837. Expansion returned in 1838. Although all Western economies experienced a deep trough in 1842 to 1843, the onset of the Irish Famine led to increased prices for grain. In the last period, which included the Famine, land prices continued to rise and it is tempting to tie this to the increased demand for grain. However, as McCalla has shown, world supplies of grain "proved surprisingly elastic"[36] and the price of wheat became so volatile that, in Toronto, the price doubled between late summer 1846 and July 1847. By September, the price was off by a third.[37] It would therefore seem that, while there is some relationship between land prices and known events and known fluctuations in the econ-

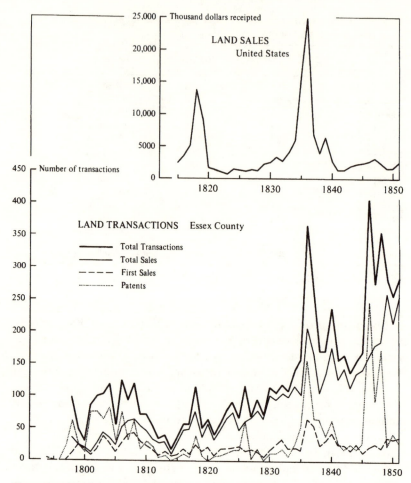

Figure 5.7   Land transactions in Essex and United States

Source: J. Clarke and D.L. Brown, "The Upper Canadian Land Market," 229.

omy, it is not possible to link these things precisely. Yet the overall trend was one of decreasing intervals between patent and first sale, commensurate presumably with a predominant trend of sustained growth.[38]

Figure 5.7 was reconstructed from frequency counts of the total number of transactions, total sales, the number of first sales, and the number of patents issued in any one year. What is interesting about this figure is the general similarity in form of its various components, although clearly the number of patents and first sales are of a lower order than "total sales" and "total transactions." Clearly, there can be only one first sale, most usually following the issue of the patent, but as was shown in the earlier chapter, sales could in fact precede the patent. Again, unless there was some legal difficulty necessitating the re-issue of a patent following, for example, a decision from the Heirs and Devisees Commission, there can be only one patent. For this reason and because land in any area is finite, the trend of patenting and of sales must diverge. In Figure 5.7 this happens in 1807, when the absolute number of sales exceeded patents for the first time. Thereafter, the number of sales exceeded the number of patents except for particular years, such as 1826, when they were almost equal, and 1846, when patents exceeded sales. The importance of patenting in 1826 is thought to reflect the beginning of recovery after a period of depression which ran from 1819 to 1822. Indeed, John McCallum has suggested that Upper Canada experienced generally depressed conditions until 1827.[39] However, the numbers here have also to be linked to the fact that, with the institution of a sales policy, the meaning of a patent changed. After 1825, the issue of a patent on land acquired by sale no longer signified the completion of settlement duties or of actual occupancy. The subsequent transaction might in fact be justifiably termed a re-sale as much as a sale although the first-sale terminology has been retained here. Freed of fees, and with the only barrier to acquisition now money, the number of patents might be expected to increase.

Patenting was affected not only by demand but by social and political pressures. For example, the increase in patenting in 1836 is partly attributable to the government's desire to secure suitable electors by issuing the appropriate patents to those who by their possession became enfranchised. However, it was also due to government pressure upon the Canada Land Company, which, as it was shown earlier, had acquired the Crown reserves. In 1846 this same company was threatened with a loss of its land unless the land was developed. The company responded appropriately by patenting lots in Essex that same year! The effect is shown in Figure 5.7. Yet this may be too simple an explanation, because, as Arthur Cole has demonstrated, 1836 and 1846–47, but most especially 1836, were years of considerable land acquisition in the United States. The increase in patenting at this time may have been a response not to local administrative decisions, but to wider economic forces. In any event, these waves of acquisition surpassed the earlier one that lasted from 1798 to the commencement of hostilities with the Americans in 1812.

The pattern of sales closely reflects the trend of patenting to 1812. Thereafter, with the exception of the years already discussed, it departs from the trend in patenting, culminating in a high volume of sales in the 1840s and 1850s. In part, the increased activity in the sales market for land can be attributed to the fact that fewer patents could be issued by this later period, given the availability of land. Since the number of patents represent a finite market for land, one should expect to observe increased activity in the sales market through time; indeed, since there is theoretically no limit to re-sale, this could and did happen repeatedly.

Undoubtedly, improvements to the local road network made the region more accessible and, as a result, more attractive to potential newcomers from other parts of the province and abroad. In turn, these developments in infrastructure were at least in part the manifestations of reduced possibilities of grants and concomitant price increases in more centrally located areas. By the 1840s, as Gagan has shown for Peel County[40] and Johnson for the Home District,[41] these areas were approaching satiation at a time in which there was still a considerable amount of land available in Essex. In fact, in 1841, 55.2 per cent of Essex remained unpatented.[42] Of course, the processes of patenting and purchase are closely related, as is, by definition, the pattern of first sales. A regression of total sales and patents, and of first sales and patents, yielded statistically significant Pearson correlation coefficients of 0.47 and 0.37 respectively. Obviously, patenting and sales are related to development generally. The surrogates used here are Essex and Upper Canadian population and Upper Canadian land cultivation. The respective 'r's were 0.48 and 0.59 for Essex's and Upper Canada's population and 0.74 for land cultivation.[43]

Changes in the price of "land" through time

Figure 5.8 shows the change in price throughout the period as a plot of mean prices and as a generalized trend of five-year running means.[44] The values given are the prices agreed upon at the time the bargain was struck between individuals, although, as will be shown later, in the minority of instances where a mortgage or a "bargain and sale by way of a mortgage" were used, title might not be conveyed until some three or four years later. In such instances, the explicitly identified or implicitly identified instrument would not be used in the calculation of land price although the original transaction would. Transactions "among other lands" and in "love and affection" were also excluded. So too were those sales which yielded such extraordinary prices that they appeared suspicious. If, for example, such values were found to correspond with the occurrence of a mill or retail establish-

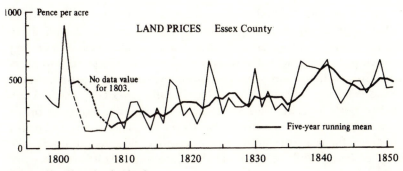

Figure 5.8 Changing land prices
Source: J. Clarke and D.L. Brown, "The Upper Canadian Land Market," 230.

ment on maps of infrastructure, they were removed from the analysis. In these instances it might well be that the price of the building and the "good will" of the business was included within the final price.[45] The inclusion of such observations within the analysis might well have resulted in marked abnormalities and on this basis their removal is justified. Yet it still has to be remembered that, in the majority of instances, the land prices may well have included the price of a house and adjoining out-buildings.[46] The price may also reflect a level of development which cannot be identified from the source material, although clearly, for example, the amount of land cultivated has a direct bearing upon the price. While the analysis of price through time must depend upon average price rather than prices corresponding to particular developmental stages, this issue is attended to later in the chapter and applied to two cross-sections.

The graphs serve both to identify a series of cycles within a steadily upward trend and, by comparison with one another, to identify periods of relative increase and decrease.[47] Comparison in this way points to a correspondence with known events. A period of political instability and sabre-rattling led to lower prices between 1804 and 1807.[48] Tables 5.3 and 5.7 show that, as confidence grew in the British and Canadian cause, as money was pumped into the Upper Canadian economy, and perhaps also as a result of inflation, the price of land rose again throughout the war years, reaching almost 267 pence per acre. Yet within the period there were lows. The Americans held Detroit, Fort Malden, and the surrounding area from October 1813 until the end of the war.[49] In 1814 there were few sales in Essex, and if three sales with money can be indicative, land prices declined to the levels of 1804 and 1807 when the threat of war was imminent, that is, 124 pence per acre.

In the period that followed, recovery set in but the years 1819 to 1822 were again years of depression in Upper Canada and Essex County. Booming land prices followed in 1823 when land sold for 634 pence per acre. Prices diminished somewhat in 1824[50] and then re-established themselves to more modest levels until 1830, when wheat exports were at a peak in Upper Canada and Essex land reached 577 pence per acre. The years 1834 and 1835 experienced lower prices since Upper Canada was in a major depression. Thereafter, land prices boomed for ten years until 1845 when they stabilized at a generally higher level. While these oscillations are attributable to particular events, including particular combinations of land placed on the market in any one year, there is no doubt that, throughout the period, the general trend was upward, a tendency that became more marked after 1852. As Table 5.7 shows, Essex land could be bought for as low as 184.4 pence per acre between 1806 and 1810 and 567.4 in the dying years of the third decade. In particular years, one could pay less or more.

This was the range of prices for "normal" rural land in Essex, albeit that in any one year there would be considerable geographical variation in price. However, in themselves, these prices as averages dampen a range that one might pay to pursue particular initiatives. For example, in 1852 and 1853, the Great Western Railway started to acquire land in Maidstone, Rochester, and Sandwich to gain access to the town of Windsor. Prices rose closer to Windsor. The parcels sold were small (3.8 acres on average in 1852) and grew smaller until, in 1853, the railway was purchasing 1.93 acres on average. However, the prices were high relative to rural land, especially after people in these townships knew the railroad was coming and realized they had a "captive" market. In 1852 the average price was 12,766 pence per acre, and in 1853 it was 20,994. This was rural land in process of conversion to non-farm usage but it was not within a city and the prices obtained were markedly different from the "typical" rural price of 419 pence at mid-century.[51]

Individuals learned to bargain with the railroad and seemed to receive in proportion to their endurance. In 1853 a J. Langlois and a J. Lafoilet received identical sums of money per acre for parts of lot 135 which they owned in the 1st concession of Sandwich Township. In the same year, the Ginas brothers accepted 29,455 pence and 25,716 pence per acre for two parcels of 0.55 and 1.65 acres on lot 111 in the 1st concession. More dramatic were the transactions involving lot 153 in the 2nd concession. A group of people, recorded in the abstracts as Carron et al., sold 1.3 acres for 19,695 pence per acre, but a F.

Duchene held out for more and received 42,000 pence per acre for a parcel measuring only 0.05 acres. Whether there was division among the Carron group or whether the Duchene property was the critical piece in the assemblage is not known. The learning curve appears rapid. In 1852 two acres were transferred by one Montreuille for 33,000 pence per acre; in 1853, 0.05 acres were sold for 192,000 pence per acre, a dramatic increase even if there was a major building on it and there is no evidence of this.

This, of course, was for developed farms although the extent of development is unknown.[52] The "upset" price, the price at which government would part with undeveloped or "wild" land, was much lower. Forty-seven Crown properties advertised in 1839 were purchased for an average of 113 pence. However, the mode and median was 96 pence, far below the 587 pence obtained in 1839, the 566 of 1840, and the 646 pence obtained in 1841 for developed land in the county.[53] Government policy enunciated in 1852 set the upset price of wild land, west of Durham and Victoria counties, at 90 pence per acre;[54] as late as 1861 such land could still be obtained for an average 144 pence, still a fraction of the price of developed land in 1841.[55] Land set aside and controlled by the Clergy Corporation was also cheap by comparison, and it too, like Crown land in this period, could be paid by instalment. The sale of fifty-two clergy lots in Essex beginning in 1833 was reported in 1841.[56] Fifty per cent of the cases lay above and below 120 pence per acre, which was also the mode or most commonly occurring value.[57]

The cheapest land of all, then as today, was that which came from the misfortune of others. This was land appropriated for indebtedness to individuals or to the state for failure to pay taxes. Under legislation introduced by Lieutenant Governor Maitland in 1824, land in arrears for eight years could be sold after having been advertised and its owner given one year to pay the back taxes and a premium of 20 per cent. Such land could be disposed of for very small sums indeed. Very often it was sold to individuals known to be investing or speculating in land – in fact, the very people who had fought the passage of the legislation.[58] On average, in Essex, such land sold for 21 pence per acre and, in 95 per cent of the cases, it could run as high as a total of 117 pence per acre (2 σ), but good land, as Table 5.8 shows, could be obtained in Essex for between six and just under fifteen pence per acre. Moreover, this was not raw land but rather developed land and the lot might include a house and out-buildings. Such opportunity was rare, however, and most had to pay the "going" rate.

Table 5.8   Land price in pence per acre for properties acquired on sheriffs' deeds, Essex County 1831–52

Tnp.	Price per Acre		Deeds with Money	Total Deeds
	$\bar{x}$	σ		
And.	–	–	–	–
Col.	6.04	4.43	8	14
Gos.	33.55	331.10	15	16
Mal.	–	–	–	4
San.	4.45	0.22	4	6
Mai.	36.94	32.15	18	22
Mer.	7.06	5.28	14	23
Roc.	16.43	14.73	7	8
Til.	14.47	22.13	5	13
Essex	21.17	47.90	71	106

Source: AO, Abstract Index to Deeds, Essex County. Abbreviations as in Table 5.6.

*If an outlier is removed, the mean and standard deviation become 7.22 and 4.19

Essex Prices in the Context of Upper Canada

How did this "going" price compare to prices elsewhere? Alas, there are few studies of land prices in Upper Canada. Where such data sets do exist as a price series, they do not always overlap with respect to time. Gagan, working on the five townships of Peel County, reported data on land price between 1840 and 1870 and thus shares a decade with the present study.[59] Edward Gray and Barry Prentice provide continuous annual observations on price between 1836 and 1981 in three townships of Wellington County but they share only fifteen years with the time-frame of the present study.[60] Daryl Watt's work begins in 1784 but, from the perspective of comparison with Essex prices, ends prematurely in 1844.[61] Alan Brunger's cross-sectional analyses are limited in their time-frame although useful inferentially in that measure of central tendency and size of sample are available.[62] Ennals's estimates of average provide neither the standard deviation nor the sample size on which the mean was based for the years he reports.[63] Moreover, the number of observations upon which the price is based in any one year can, through no fault of any of these authors, be small, with marked consequences for reliability.[64] Additionally, the method for gathering data, for its inclusion or exclusion, is not known.[65] It was perhaps because of this that regressions of the series by Clarke, Gray and Prentice, Watt, and Gagan yielded statistically insignificant results, except

Table 5.9   Price of Upper Canadian land in pence per acre, 1840–1845

Researcher	Years	Location	$\bar{x}$	σ	n	Comment
Gagan	1841–45	Peel County (5 twps)	1347.1	1474.8	n/a	c.v. 1.09; Agg.ann+; oconnv$
Gray and Prentice	1842–45	Nichol Twp.	244.0	49.8	7	c.v. 0.2; Agg.ann+
Brunger	1841–45	Duoro Twp.	272.9	199.6	63	c.v. 0.73; direct calculation
Clarke	1841–45	Essex County (9 twps)	456.8	119.7	440	c.v. 0.26; Agg.Ann+
Palmer	1843–45	Ramsay Twp.	241.7	292.8	21	c.v. 1.14; direct calculation
Watt	1841–44	Fredericksburg Twp.	774.0	481.5	54	c.v. 0.62; Agg.ann+
Ennals	1840–44	Hamilton Twp.	504.0	n/a	n/a	Agg.ann+
Read	1842–45	Townsend, Windham, Charlotteville, Walsingham Twps.	810.3	595.0	12	c.v. 0.73; Single Family++

Source: Compilation and calculations of the author.

+ statistics based upon aggregated annual value (Agg.ann+); converted at four dollars
to the pound (oconnv$). c.v. is the coefficient of variation.

++ relates to purchases and sales of the Culver family only.

in the case of Peel and Essex, where a statistically significant correlation co-efficient of -0.63 was obtained.[66]

Thus, there are shortcomings in the data which themselves may mask considerable variation, although, where the mean and standard deviation are known, one presumes the variability is succinctly captured. Indeed, there was considerable variability in price. Tables 5.9 and 5.10 show the respective means and standard deviations for the periods for which comparable data can be obtained. The following, written about the Perth area in 1833, was applicable to all of Upper Canada: "The price of land varies to its quality and situation. Within a mile of this town, it is worth from £10 to £50 an acre while, 5 or 6 miles off it could be purchased for as many shillings, and, thirty or forty miles back in the woods, can still be had from one dollar to two dollars an acre."[67]

Ennals, who reports an average price of 53 shillings or 636 pence per acre for Hamilton Township in the period from 1845 to 1849, also observes that wild land could be obtained for 216 pence per acre but

Table 5.10   Price of Upper Canadian land in pence per acre, 1846–50

Researcher	Years	Location	$\bar{x}$	σ	n	Comment
Gagan	1846–50	Peel County (5 twps)	861.4	335.4	n/a	c.v. 0.39; Agg.ann+; oconnv$
Gray and Prentice	1846–50	Nichol Twp.	503.6	91.4	21	c.v. 0.18; Agg.ann+
Brunger	1846–50	Duoro Twp.	290.1	230.3	61	c.v. 0.79; direct calculation
Clarke	1846–50	Essex County (9 twps)	492.4	92.1	664	c.v. 0.19; Agg.Ann+; 10
Ennals	1845–49	Hamilton Twp.	636.0	n/a	n/a	Agg.ann+
Read	1846–50	Townsend, Windham, Charlotteville, Walsingham twps.	579.4	503.2	20	c.v. 0.87; direct calculation

+ statistics based upon aggregated annual value (Agg.ann+); converted at four dollars to the pound (oconnv$). c.v. is the coefficient of variation.

that in 1845 one gentleman had offered £1500 for 175 acres, payable with £900 down and the remainder over nine years.[68] This amounted to 2057 pence per acre, almost 3.25 times the average price of developed land and ten times the price of "wild" land.

As Tables 5.9 and 5.10 show, such variability was characteristic of all parts of Upper Canada for which data are available. The coefficients of variability indicate that this was especially so of Peel County in the years from 1841 to 1845. Even though the variability in Peel was reduced in the five-year period that followed,[69] the county remained second to Duoro Township, which in both time-frames exhibited considerable variability. Essex remained unchanged in terms of its variability between the two time periods; it was second-lowest in a field of six in the earlier period and occupied the same position in a reduced field in the later period. It also showed a statistically significant but modest increase in price from 456.8 pence per acre to 492.4 pence per acre;[70] clearly, these were years of relative stability in Essex. This was not so of Nichol Township near Peel. Here the coefficient of variability indicates little change. Yet, in relative terms, the price of farm real estate in Nichol soared, in a location becoming increasingly central with respect to a developing economy.[71] In Peel, some twenty miles east of Nichol, the price of developed land was the highest in both periods.[72] It exceeded by almost a factor of two its nearest competitor, Fredericksburg Township, which also enjoyed proximity to a major urban centre, in this case the town of Kingston. Since Essex was geographically removed from Montreal, and lacked a centre of the order of Toronto or even Kingston, its prices were intermediate, in both time-frames, between these more central, established areas and less developed townships such as Duoro and Ramsay.[73] In 95 per cent (two normal deviates) of the cases, a developed farm in Essex towards mid-century would cost between 308.28 and 676.52 pence – less than £3 – per acre.[74] At the lower limit the idealized 200-acre farm would cost £257; at the upper limit, considerably more £564. In fact, the average farm in Essex at mid-century was, as the census enumeration returns show, eighty-three acres. The actual outlay for developed farm real estate was therefore considerably less, between £107 and £234. This was still much more than the outlay on "wild" land, which could be acquired in 1839 for eight shillings per acre or £33 for a typical farm of eighy-three acres.[75] If its transformation was to be produced by the sweat of the settler's body, all was well; however, if others were to clear the land, this was an expensive proposition. Land cleared professionally could cost as much as £4 per acre, and in Essex at mid-century the "average" farm had twenty-five acres cleared.[76] This route, together with the purchase price of £33, would mean a total outlay of £133, without including the prices of livestock and farm equipment which might cost another £100.[77] At this rate a prospective farmer might be advised to consider a developed farm because his total outlay was now approaching that of developed land.

What set the price of land in Essex?

Apart from the particular ability of the individual to bargain (a capacity that grew with experience) and the opportunities that came with sales to the railroad or purchases from the economically disadvantaged, what affected price in these years? To answer this question, a number of variables were gathered to augment the data on land price, the number of patents, and the number of mortgages. These included the number of Crown sales in Upper Canada from 1824 to 1851;[78] the volume of emigration from the United Kingdom;[79] the volume of land taken up in the United States as a whole as well as particular American states between 1814 and 1851;[80] the population of Essex and Upper Canada;[81] the extent of cleared acreage in Essex and Upper Canada;[82] the amount of the land resource remaining in Essex;[83] British and American interest rates;[84] the acreage sold and the price of land in Britain;[85] the price of British wheat in pence per quarter;[86] the volume

Table.5.11a   Essex land prices in the context of the county, 1804–51

	r	Sample
Number of sales/year in Essex County	0.65*	n=48
Number of first sales/year in Essex County	0.34*	n=48
Number of mortgages/year in Essex County	0.46*	n=48
Price of mortgages	0.18	n=48
Population of Essex County	0.48*	n=27
Amount of cleared acreage in Essex County	0.05	n=12
Number of leases/year in Essex County	0.0005	n=48
Amount of Essex land resource remaining (unity minus accumulated number of land patents)	–0.62*	n=46
Number of patents/year in Essex County	0.25*	n=52

Table.5.11b   Essex land prices in the context of Canada, 1804–51

Canadian wheat prices in denier/minot at Montreal	0.16	n=38
"Western" Canadian wheat prices in pence per bushel	–0.19	n=26
"Central" Canadian wheat prices in pence per bushel	–0.17	n=40
Amount of Upper Canadian population	0.59*	n=20
Number of Crown sales in Upper Canada	0.32	n=28
Amount of cultivated acreage in Upper Canada	0.74*	n=17
Number of Ohio sales	0.33*	n=38
If five year average of price	–0.78*	n=42

Table 5.11c   Essex land prices in the British context, 1804–51

British wheat prices in pence/quarter	0.34*	n=48
Amount of acreage sold in Britain/year	0.02	n=48
British wheat imports from Canada	0.01	n=12
British land prices	0.04	n=48
The annual average for British interest rates	0.26	n=51
United Kingdom emigration	0.17	n=37

Table.5.11d   Essex land prices in the American context, 1804–51

The annual average for United States interest rates	0.27	n=21
Number of Ohio sales	0.33*	n=38
Number of Michigan sales	0.01	n=34
Number of sales in the United States	0.002	n=37

y = annual mean of Essex land prices in pence per acre

*statistically significant at the 95 per cent confidence level.

Source: Clarke and Brown, "The Upper Canadian Land Market," Tables 2–5; McCalla, Planting the Province.

of British wheat imports from Canada;[87] and the value of Canadian wheat both at Montreal[88] and in Upper Canada.[89]

Tables 5.11a–d report the results of a series of statistically significant regressions for the years from 1804 to 1851, a time-frame selected because of the suitability of the linear model and the relatively few reliable observations available for the period down to 1804 upon which to base an inference. At the outset, it was suggested that land prices might be influenced by three interrelated elements: the local Essex market, the Upper Canadian market, and the British market. However, because of the geographic proximity of this region to the United States as a whole, and to Ohio and Michigan in particular, it was decided to consider those elements of the American economy for which information was available.

Six of the nine variables listed on Table 5.11a proved statistically significant at the 95 per cent confidence level. The highest correlations were with the volume of sales (r=0.65) and inversely with the percentage of Essex that remained to be settled with the passage of each year (r=-0.62). Both of these are measures of demand and their signs are appropriate. The relationship to population was also strong, as in the case of the Upper Canadian variables, where a correlation coefficient of 0.59 was recorded. Interestingly, because of the small number of observations, land cultivation was not significant among the Essex variables. However, when price was regressed against Upper Canadian cultivated acreage, the correlation coefficient was 0.74 (Table 5.11b).

The Wheat Staple and Land Prices

None of the measures of Canadian wheat prices, using either the Montreal or the McCalla "Upper Canadian" series,[90] proved statistically significant.[91] In fact, the overall trend of wheat prices was downward, running counter to the trend in land;[92] an "adjusted" data set of five-year running means produced a significant 'r' of 0.58 with an inverse sign.[93] Presumably, the price of wheat was dropping both because the war had ended and various financial crises had passed and also because of economies in production. At the same time, Essex land prices showed a positive relationship to wheat prices in the British market, although the correlation coefficient of 0.34 is perhaps not as high as expected. That the signs of the correlation coefficients are different is explicable in terms of the different scale of analysis, the different needs of the two economies, British desires to protect their own agriculture from overseas competition via a shifting tariff and changing freight rates. As elsewhere in Upper Canada, wheat was undoubtedly an important element in the farm economy and an export commodity. Yet, if it was a significant factor, it did not, in itself, set the price of land in Essex. Presumably, Essex land prices were affected by the dual effects of the market and government policy which released land via the sales and patenting process. Thus, the agreement between Canadian or British wheat prices and Essex land prices need not be exact since the economy was not wholly a market economy or indeed a total wheat economy.

This is also the position of a number of economic historians whose recent work has done much to reassess the notion that wheat was "king" and that the Upper Canadian economy was one driven by a single staple.[94] These people regard the single-staple theory as rather naive.[95] Expansion of the economy continued in the 1830s and the British market on which, according to the conventional view, so much depended was not open to Upper Canadian wheat until the 1840s. Using the evidence of thirteen stores scattered across the province, McCalla has shown that indebtedness was met by wheat only in 10 to 45 per cent of the cases and that, in specific places and specific times, this could be as low as 3 per cent. The crops second in importance for discharging debt – barley, tobacco, ashes, and corn in the Essex case – show there was a local trade in products other than wheat.[96] McCalla employs the records of twelve farmers to demonstrate that while, wheat was central to a farm's earnings, in all but one case there was a second commercial crop or livestock.[97] As the basis of estimates of household consumption and of seed-yield ratio, and assuming a wheat-fallow-wheat rotation, McCalla argues that after 1821 less than a quarter of the land under culture was required for wheat produc-tion.[98] This increased over time, especially from the 1840s to 1852, which were years of markedly increased production and export. But it would be wrong to think of the fifty years preceding 1840 as in any way similar to the decade of the 1840s in wheat production.[99]

McCalla claims that Upper Canadian agriculture was "always a mixed-farming system with wheat as a substantial element in much of the province."[100] Similarly, R.M. McInnis, in seeking to measure net output per farm as a measure of "agricultural performance," con-cludes that "in the circumstances of the middle of the nineteenth century even a pronounced emphasis on wheat was built upon a diver-sified base of general farming."[101] This base included an animal hus-bandry which, although not yet specialized, was at least as important as wheat.[102]

The analysis here would seem to bear out the notion that the Essex and Upper Canadian economies were more complex than staple theory prescribes. In short, to cite McCalla: "It does not seem possible that one could say that given certain conditions in the wheat market,

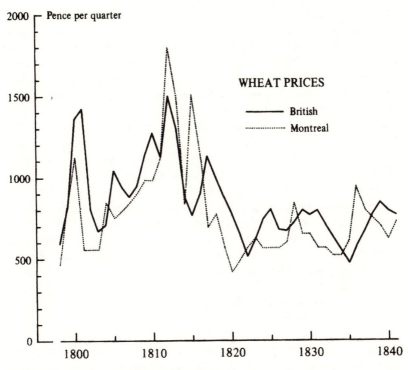

Figure 5.9   Canadian and British Wheat Prices
Source: J. Clarke and D.L. Brown, "The Upper Canadian Land Market," 233.

certain consequences necessarily have followed,"[103] in this case the land market. Yet wheat remains the only variable in the series of British variables that proved significant. Figure 5.9, which presents both Canadian and British wheat prices in a common metric – that is, pence per quarter[104] – demonstrates the expected relationship between Canadian and British wheat. A correlation coefficient of 0.66, significant at the 0.05 level, confirmed this statistically. What is especially interesting is that there are twelve years when Montreal prices exceeded British wheat prices. These were the years 1795, 1804, 1812, 1813, 1815, 1816, 1822, 1823, 1828, 1835, 1836, and 1837. These were years of poor harvest, war, or economic depression. Interestingly, neither British nor American interest rates, which are among the surrogates for the development of the economy, proved significant (Table 5.11c and 5.11d). Perhaps this reflects problems with variables which do not account for inflation and are not therefore "real" interest rates. Moreover, in the British and Canadian cases, the variable reflects the operation of the usury laws.

That sales in Ohio did appear significant is to be expected because of the proximity of this state to Essex and its greater development compared to Michigan.[105] The Ohio variable is essentially a local one like other Essex variables. Other than local factors, only British wheat appears statistically important in determining Essex land prices. That said, the form of the waves of land acquisition and sales was rather like that which Arthur Cole has described for the United States.[106] Troughs occurred in 1814, in the first few years of the 1820s, in 1842 in the United States, and in 1843 in Essex. Peak years in Essex and the United States were in 1818, 1836, and 1846–47. Whether or not the United States had a similar wave to that which Essex experienced between 1800 and 1810 cannot be determined from Cole's data. Yet clearly there were cycles in prices commensurate with broad cycles in other geographic areas; when to this is added the results of McCalla's analysis of commodity prices, it becomes clear that prices were set in a "wider economic universe and not directly and exclusively determined by local supply and demand."[107]

Cross-sectional analysis of the determinants of price in 1825 and 1850–52

Locally, how was the price of land set? What factors established the price of land within the county? To determine this, sales data were manually linked to data on the extent of cultivation obtained from the assessment rolls and the first census of Canada and analysed via simple and step-wise multiple regression. In what follows, the data are described cross-sectionally for two periods, that is, 1798 to 1825[108] and 1826 to 1852, to ensure that the spatial pattern is in fact apparent.[109] However, the multivariate analysis of land price presented here is based upon a narrow range of years in order to ensure more representative prices than would otherwise be obtainable; specific values for the years 1820 to 1826 and 1841 to 1845 were used.[110]

Figures 5.10 and 5.11 and Tables 5.12 and 5.13 show that the highest prices in the period to 1825 were in the townships of Sandwich, Colchester, Gosfield, and Mersea. This is to be expected since price reflects demand and these townships also had the greatest number of transactions (Figure 5.12). Moreover, while some change did occur between then and 1852, the overall pattern remained basically unchanged; these same four townships still accounted for the largest percentage of transactions in the second quarter of the century and for the majority of lots in the higher price ranges (tables 5.12 and 5.13). Statistical comparison of the relative rank of the townships in each of the periods, in terms of their average land prices,

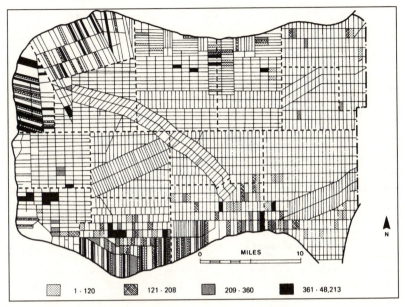

Figure 5.10 Average land prices in pence per acre, 1798–1825.

Source: J. Clarke and D.L. Brown, "Land Prices in Essex County," 309.

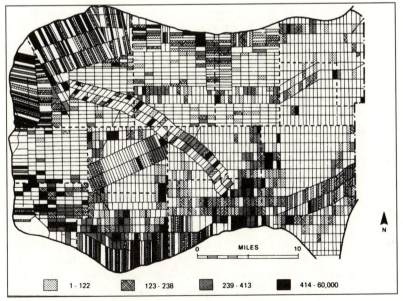

Figure 5.11 Average land prices in pence per acre, 1826–52.

Source: J. Clarke and D.L. Brown, "Land Prices in Essex County," 309.

Table 5.12   Average land prices, 1798–1825, and number of sales (with money) in each township

Prices	And.	Col.	Gos.	Mai.	Mal.	Mer.	Roc.	San.	Til.	Tot.
699 or less	2	75	38	13	16	19	11	42	18	234
700 or more	1	2	1	0	3	1	1	15	0	24
Totals	3	77	39	13	19	20	12	57	18	258
Rank	9	1	3	7	5	4	8	2	6	

Source: Clarke and Brown, "Land Prices in Essex County," Table 1.

*And. = Anderdon Township; Col. = Colchester; Gos. = Gosfield; Mai. = Maidstone; Mal. = Malden; Mer. = Mersea; Roc. = Rochester; San. = Sandwich; and Til. = Tilbury Township.

Table 5.13   Average land prices 1826–52 and number of sales (with money) in each township

Prices	And.	Col.	Gos.	Mai.	Mal.	Mer.	Roc.	San.	Til.	Tot.
699 or less	15	180	142	84	53	159	56	173	36	898
700 or more	6	20	14	6	10	1	0	55	3	115
Totals	21	200	156	90	63	160	56	228	39	1013
Rank	9	2	4	5	6	3	7	1	8	

Source: Clarke and Brown, "Land Prices in Essex County," Table 2.

*And. = Anderdon Township; Col. = Colchester; Gos. = Gosfield; Mai. = Maidstone; Mal. = Malden; Mer. = Mersea; Roc. = Rochester; San. = Sandwich; and Til. = Tilbury Township.

yielded a Spearman rho value of 0.88, suggesting a strong relationship between price and number of transactions. This proved significant at the 0.01 level[111] and testified to the fact that, in terms of distribution, the first fifty years of the nineteenth century were a period of stability.

Generally, the highest prices in both periods were located in townships that experienced high rates of initial acquisition, for example, Sandwich and Colchester.[112] Because these townships incurred an early influx of settlers and demand for land, lot improvements were quicker to develop (Table 5.14 and 5.15). This undoubtedly affected the price obtained for individual properties. Unfortunately, the data have not survived for Gosfield in the earlier period; however, Sandwich and Colchester townships ranked first and second with respect to the total number of lots and were either totally or partially cleared. In the later period, Sandwich, Gosfield, and Colchester townships ranked one to three

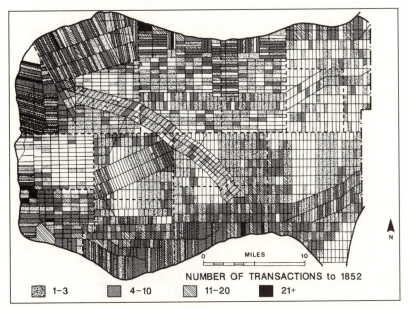

Figure 5.12   Spatial pattern of land transactions in essex to 1852
Source: Abstract Index to Deeds, Essex County

respectively in terms of the total number of lots that were partially cleared.

Another factor that appears to be influencing the spatial distribution of land prices within the county is the proximity of lands to the central places of the time and most especially the major urban centres. Figures 5.13 and 5.14 illustrate that land prices decline with distance from the towns of Sandwich and Amherstburg for both time periods.[113] As might be expected, prices increased through time. As tables 5.16 and 5.17 illustrate, the most dramatic changes occurred in two areas; within four miles of Sandwich and Amherstburg (the major economic centres of the county), and beyond nine miles of each (within the area which in the earliest period was relatively unsettled or deliberately withheld from the market as Crown and clergy reserves). The reader will note that in Table 5.16 the most significant change in the number of sales occurs for lands over 2000 pence per acre and within four miles of Sandwich Township. Beyond nine miles, the largest percentage increase was in the lower-priced lots. A deviation from this pattern is the 100 per cent increase in lots valued in the 700-1999 pence range. This zone, lying twelve miles from Sandwich, is the zero-to-four-mile zone of Amherstburg, which itself records the highest change (Table 5.17).

Table 5.14   Number of lots sold, 1798–1825, and extent of cleared acreage

| | Acres cleared | | | | | | |
Twp.	0–19	20–39	40–59	60–79	80–99	100+	Totals
And.	–	–	–	–	–	–	–
Col.	31	41	13	0	1	1	87
Gos.	–	–	–	–	–	–	–
Mai.	10	1	2	0	0	0	13
Mal.	22	4	8	2	0	5	41
Mer.	40	24	0	1	0	0	65
Roc.	20	1	0	0	0	0	21
San.	98	43	37	14	11	6	209
Til.	–	–	–	–	–	–	–

Source: Clarke and Brown, "Land Prices in Essex County," Table 3. Abbreviations as in Table 5.6.

Table 5.15   Number of lots sold, 1826–52, and extent of cleared acreage

| | Acres cleared | | | | | | |
Twp.	0–19	20–39	40–59	60–79	80–99	100+	Totals
And.	–	–	–	–	–	–	–
Col.	42	38	38	21	7	22	168
Gos.	77	52	32	12	8	10	191
Mai.	95	27	7	0	1	1	131
Mal.	32	26	20	8	3	7	96
Mer.	32	37	28	10	3	4	114
Roc.	69	22	6	0	0	0	97
San.	121	97	66	35	14	19	352
Til.	57	15	2	1	0	0	75

Source: Clarke and Brown, "Land Prices in Essex County," Table 4.

Differential growth in any system is only to be expected. In this particular circumstance it reflects the overall history of the area. For example, during the 1798–1825 period, land acquisition and sales in the interior of these townships were undoubtedly limited by the rudimentary condition of the road network, by the political decision to create the Crown, clergy, and Indian reserves,[114] and perhaps by a realization of the difficulties of farming the wetlands of the area (Figure 1.4). The importance of roads is illustrated in tables 5.18 and 5.19; clearly, in both periods, there was a propensity to purchase land close to the nearest road. With increased development of the road network,[115] the release of the former Crown reserves by the Canada

Company after 1826, the institution of similar policies by the Clergy Corporation, and the opening of the Anderdon Indian reserve in 1835, these undeveloped regions experienced more activity than the higher priced areas.

By 1852, as was shown earlier in chapter 2, a number of embryonic centres were emerging in the county, and they had the effect of increasing land prices within their immediate vicinity (figures 2.9, 5.13, 5.14). Furthermore, whereas in 1825 Amherstburg and Sandwich were the dominant centres in Essex, by 1852 they were beginning to lose their economic predominance. The town of Windsor was their chief rival; other centres that were developing included Albertville, Belle River, Cedar Creek,[116] Colchester, Essex, Kingsville, and Leamington.

In 1852 these lower-order centres were still relatively small. For example, no centre performed more than thirteen independent functions, whereas the towns of Amherstburg and Sandwich performed ninety-one and seventy-six different functions respectively. Obviously, Sandwich and Amherstburg were still, from the perspective of the county, the dominant centres. Yet, while this was so, these may well have been places that one resorted to infrequently, except of course for those whose livelihood was obtained within them. Given the self-sufficient life styles of the time and the difficulties of communication via a still primitive road network, the majority of rural dwellers sought more regular contact with the local blacksmith, saddler, store, school, and tavern. Two or more of these functions, conducted in close proximity to each other, no doubt constituted what is recognized here as a "node" of activity, one of several focal points of human activity organized hierarchically. Obviously, Sandwich and Amherstburg were still places of joy and excess to which one might resort frequently.

In this study, it was assumed that settlers were knowledgeable and rational and so would frequent the closest local node, hamlet, or village (for example, Albertville or Kingsville) to fulfil immediate wants and needs. A variety of routes were identified to each of these locations, and it was assumed that the shortest path to the destination selected would be used. Price, it was held, would be inversely related to these nodes and to the human energy involved; it would fall in an inverse distance-decay form. Scattergrams for regression analysis showed that this was so in both time periods. The correlation coefficients were inverse at -0.21 and -0.35 respectively.[117] These measures of "minimal" distances to the coast, the road network, and the rural "nodes" were included as independent variables in a data set which, because it included the variable "cleared acreage" and was for a shorter time span, was now reduced from 156 and 1071 to 50 and 447 observations in the respective time periods.

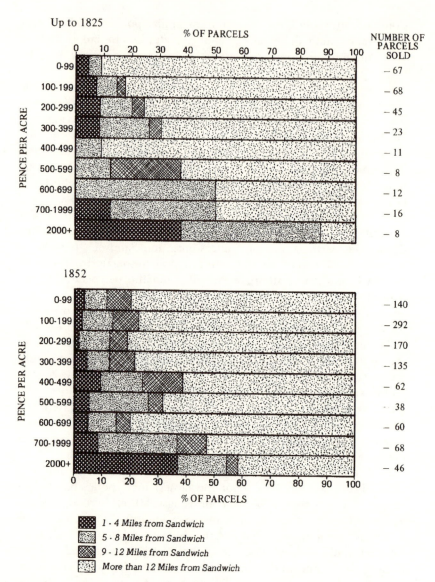

Figure 5.13   Distribution of prices and distances from Sandwich: (a) to 1825, (b) in 1852.

Source: J. Clarke and D.L. Brown, "Land Prices in Essex County," 311–12.

The data were plotted cumulatively through the price continuum. Examination and empirical investigation suggested that maximum order might be revealed at above and below the 700 pence per acre level. This may have been the effective boundary between farm and

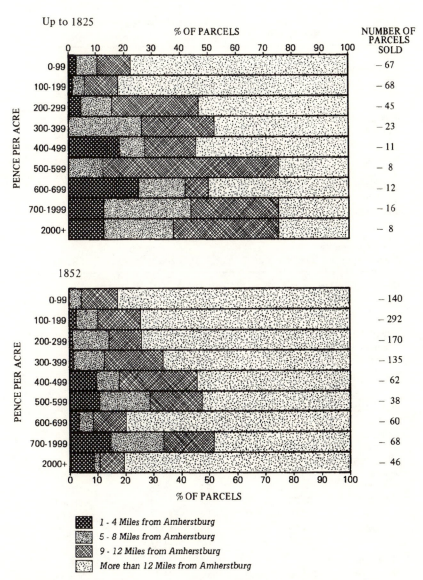

Figure 5.14   Distribution of prices and distances from Amherstburg: (a) to 1825, (b) in 1852.

Source: J. Clarke and D.L. Brown, "Land Prices in Essex County," 311–12.

non-farm properties in much of Essex. Two groups of prices were recognized above and below this level. Logarithmically transformed,[118] these data were entered into stepwise multiple regression analyses. The dependent variable was land price in pence per acre. The inde-

Table 5.16   Relative change in the sale of lands with money and within particular distances of Sandwich for the two periods

Price Category (price in pence per acre)	Distance				County-level percentage change within particular price ranges
	0–4 miles	5–8 miles	9–12 miles	12+ miles	
0–99	10.53	22.86	171.43	25.89	28.30
100–199	15.79	77.14	357.14	85.79	86.82
200–299	–5.26	37.14	128.57	52.79	48.45
300–399	21.05	20.00	157.14	45.69	43.41
400–499	31.58	22.86	128.57	14.21	19.77
500–599	10.53	20.00	0.00	10.66	11.63
600–699	15.79	0.00	42.86	21.32	18.61
700–1,999	21.05	37.14	100.00	14.21	20.16
2,000+	73.68	11.43	28.57	9.14	14.73
Change in county distance zone	194.74	248.57	1114.29	279.70	291.86

Source: Clarke and Brown, "Land Prices in Essex County," Table 5.

Table 5.17   Relative change in the sale of lands with money and within particular distances of Amherstburg for the two periods

Price Category	Distance				County-level percentage change within particular price ranges
	0–4 miles	5–8 miles	9–12 miles	12+ miles	
0–99	–15.39	3.33	19.23	39.26	28.30
100–199	46.15	66.67	71.15	98.77	86.82
200–299	0.00	56.67	11.54	62.58	48.45
300–399	15.39	30.00	42.31	48.47	43.41
400–499	30.77	13.33	30.77	16.56	19.77
500–599	30.77	20.00	3.85	11.04	11.63
600–699	–7.69	3.33	11.54	25.77	18.61
700–1,999	61.54	26.67	13.46	17.79	20.16
2,000+	23.08	–3.33	1.92	21.47	14.73
Change in county distance zone	184.62	216.67	205.77	341.72	291.86

Source: Clarke and Brown, "Land Prices in Essex County," Table 6.

pendent variables were the land-patent date for each lot, the amount of development on a lot measured in terms of the total acreage sold by an individual and the extent of the acreage cleared, the distance from the centre of a lot to the coast, the distance to the nearest road, the

Table 5.18 Land prices and proximity to nearest road, 1798–1825

Prices (pence per acre)	Miles from nearest road			
	0–2.5	2.6–5.0	5.1–7.5	7.5+
699 or less	206	27	1	0
700 or more	20	4	0	0
Totals	226	31	1	0

Source: Clarke and Brown, "Land Prices in Essex County," Table 7.

Table 5.19   Land prices and proximity to nearest road, 1826–52

Prices	Miles from nearest road			
	0–2.5	2.6–5.0	5.1–7.5	7.5+
699 or less	804	90	2	0
700 or more	113	1	0	0
Totals	914	91	2	0

Source: Clarke and Brown, "Land Prices in Essex County," Table 8.

distance to the nearest node, the distance to the nearest mill,[119] and the frequency with which a particular lot changed hands. These are discussed within three classes of land, namely, that held by resident owners and tenants, by non-residents, and by speculators. The expectation here is that, as members of a mostly farm community, the owners and tenants would exhibit similar characteristics with respect to acreages held and cleared. The combination of these would be different from that of speculators and this might be reflected in different prices paid.

The analysis, within tenure conditions, presupposes that the respective tenure classes can be identified. However, the condition of early-nineteenth-century records does not permit rapid and easy identification of the members of each class. Obviously, speculators did not voluntarily identify themselves as such, and census enumerators could not and did not always distinguish between farm owners and tenants. In the absence of such clear labels, inferences had to be drawn from the marriage of the abstracts, the township assessment rolls, and census-enumeration returns in the manner described earlier.[120] For example, where the abstracts and the census were identical, a resident owner was deduced; where they were different, a tenant was inferred. Where a lot was owned, but

Table 5.20 Regression results of land prices in Essex County, 1821–26 and 1845–52

Equation for land prices	n	r^2	F
1 Land prices 1821–26 $*Y = 3.91 + -0.59 \log X_1$ $+ -0.20 \log X_5$ $+ -0.20 \log X_2$	50	0.75	19.54**
2 Land prices 1845–52 $Y = 3.95 + -0.67 \log X_1$ $+ -0.16 \log X_2 + -0.06$ $\log X_5 + 0.11 \log X_3$ $+ -0.05 \log X_4$	447	0.82	176.48**

Source: Clarke and Brown, "Pricing Decisions," Table 2.

*Where Y = log Essex land prices; X_1 = acreage sold; X_2 = distance to nearest node; X_3 = absolute cleared acreage; X_4 = distance to mill; X_5 = distance to coast; X_6 = distance to nearest road; X_7 = total number of transactions; X_8 = patent date.

**Significant at the 95 per cent confidence level.

Table 5.21 Regression results of land prices in Essex County subdivided by tenure categories

Equation for land prices	n	r^2	F
3 Land prices 1821–26, resident owners and tenants $*Y = 4.73 + -0.78 \log X_1$ $+ -0.48 \log X_5 + -0.58 \log X_6$	21	0.86	16.18**
4 Analysis of non–resident owners 1821–26, possible speculators	n/a		
5 Land prices 1845–52, resident owners and tenants $Y = 3.94 + -0.68 \log X_1$ $+ -0.16 \log X_2 + -0.05 \log X_5$ $+ 0.09 \log X_3 + -0.05 \log X_4$	388	0.82	153.04**
6 All land prices 1845–52, non–resident owners (possible speculators) $Y = 3.73 + -0.68 \log X_1$ $+ 0.14 \log X_3 + -0.11 \log X_5$	45	0.82	27.90**

Source: Clarke and Brown, "Pricing Decisions," Table 3.

*Where Y = log Essex land prices; X_1 = acreage sold; X_2 = distance to nearest node; X_3 = absolute cleared acreage; X_4 = distance to mill; X_5 = distance to coast; X_6 = distance to nearest road; X_7 = total number of transactions; X_8 = patent date.

**Significant at the 95 percent confidence level

Table 5.22   Regression results of land prices in Essex County subdivided by tenure categories, 1845–52

Equation for land prices	n	r^2	F
7 All speculative holdings $*Y = 4.01 + -0.95 \log X_1$ $+ 0.25 \log X_3 + -0.17 \log X_2$ $+ 0.12 \log X_4$	54	0.91	62.19**
8 Speculative holdings prices over 700 pence per acre $Y = 4.07 + -0.69 \log X_1$	14	0.75	15.27**
9 Speculative holdings, prices equal to or less than 700 pence per acre $Y = 2.55 + 0.23 \log X_3$ $+ 0.11 \log X_4 + -0.31 \log X_1$	40	0.60	6.82**
10 Non–speculative holdings $Y = 3.94 + -0.65 \log X_1$ $+ -0.14 \log X_2 + -0.07 \log X_5$ $+ 0.10 \log X_3 + -0.07 \log X_4$	392	0.80	141.36**
11 Non–speculative holdings, prices over 700 pence per acre $Y = 4.02 + -0.49 \log X_1$ $+ -0.18 \log X_2$	75	0.72	37.79**
12 Non–speculative holdings, prices under 700 pence per acre $Y = 2.79 + -0.22 \log X_1$ $+ 0.09 \log X_3 + 0.04 \log X_5$ $+ -0.06 \log X_2$	317	0.34	8.23**

Source: Clarke and Brown, "Pricing Decisions," Table 4.
*Where Y = log Essex land prices; X_1 = acreage sold; X_2 = distance to nearest node; X_3 = absolute cleared acreage; X_4 = distance to mill; X_5 = distance to coast; X_6 = distance to nearest road; X_7 = total number of transactions; X_8 = patent date.
**Significant at the 95 per cent confidence level.

unoccupied, a speculator was surmised. Non-residence was considered prime evidence of the "classical speculator" waiting on rising land values to sell his "barely developed property." In the event that non-residence did not provide an exhaustive description of the category "land speculator," recourse was made to a list of individuals whose history as speculators was known from experience and whose scale of operation was such that they could be included in a sample of speculators.[121]

Tables 5.20–5.22 show the results of a series of multiple regressions. While eight variables were used in each regression, only those that were statistically significant have been allowed to enter the analysis. Two variables, namely, the "total number of transactions" (included initially because it was thought to reflect demand for land) and "patent date" (included as a measure of time and perhaps achievement), were excluded by the multivariate procedure. As was shown earlier, patents have not always been viewed as the best measure of length of settlement and, in the first time frame examined, their definition changed. Moreover, one might question whether the number of times a lot had changed hands would have influenced willingness to pay in either of these two periods, in fact, given the restricted time-frame and the length of time between patenting and first sale, the probability of frequent sale of any property was not great.[122]

The results presented here (Table 5.20) indicate the pre-eminence of parcel size. As equation 1 on Table 5.20 shows price varied inversely with acreage sold; the smaller the parcel the larger the price per acre. This is, after all, the prime factor after initial decisions on location are taken; accessibility is still seen to have been important in both time periods though it is defined in terms of accessibility to the coast (x_5) and to the nearest node (x_2). Interestingly, since distance to the coast is an absolute quantity and the number and nature of nodes can change over time, the importance of these two measures shifts. In the earlier period, accessibility to the coast is seen to be the most important, in part because there was little else. In the second period, the coast is literally less accessible to those who have settled in the interior. Given the developing nature of the county, these results are understandable.

In statistical terms, the R^2 values, indicating the percentage of the variation "explained," are high in both periods and the results are statistically significant. In the second period, when the equation (equation 2) is shown to have accounted for 82 per cent of the variation, this is in part because two additional variables have been permitted to enter the analysis. That they were able to do so does, however, say that they were not just of statistical significance but of meaning in the lives of the people. By the middle of the century, sufficient human effort had been spent in Essex for there to be some variability in achievement, in a way in which there could not be in the earlier period. Now prices varied not only with accessibility but directly with the fourth variable to enter, absolute acreage cleared (X_3). Associated with this, in a grain economy, was distance to the mill. Mills were twice as common as before and more accessible.

A plot of the residuals showed them to be approximately normal, a requirement of the general linear model in statistical analysis. All the extreme residuals, greater than one standard error, were mapped, and their association with particular individuals, particular soil types, and the economic infrastructure was determined. Residuals had been used in this manner in an earlier published paper. Their use as a diagnostic tool had in fact led to the restructuring of the analysis of land prices to include tenure category. In this instance, no particular pattern was detected and no additional variable for inclusion in subsequent analysis was diagnosed.[123]

Table 5.21 shows the data divided by time period and for the two tenure subsets, resident and non-resident. In the case of the former, composed of both resident owners and tenants, this group of people displayed characteristics similar to the total population from which it was drawn (comparison of equations 1 and 3, 2 and 5). Also, the data appear to reflect a changing emphasis upon those variables considered to be measurements of development. In fact, for the period 1845–52, not only does the magnitude of the coefficients of variation appear identical, but the order in which the variables appear in the multiple regressions is also identical. However, the non-resident tenure group seems to display characteristics somewhat different from those of the total group (comparison of equations 2 and 6). For 1845–52, non-resident owners appear to place greater emphasis on cleared land. If non-resident owner tenure actually reflects the actions of speculators, then cleared acreage was of greater importance than one might expect of a group that classically has been portrayed as purchasers of cheap land. In fact, it is quite probable that the term "speculator" for non-resident owner tenure is a misnomer.

In order to verify this supposition, the data for 1845–52 were analysed and cross-tabulated with a list of known speculators. In this instance, speculators were defined as those individuals owning more than 400 acres of land and those who were known to have been playing in the land market. Of the 1071 observations (transactions) for this period, 103 were definitely associated with known speculators. However, 66 of these were included within resident-owners and tenants, and only 37 occurred where they should, that is, among non-resident owners. Consequently, it would seem that the non-resident group included a variety of people. These included the newly established pioneer, who had time to register his ownership but was not included in the tax-assessment lists; the established farmer, resident on an adjacent lot and cultivating adjoining fields; and the classical speculator, waiting on rising land values and seeking to avoid the tax gatherer. It was not an exclusively speculator group. Speculators probably operated in a variety of tenure conditions and with a variety of strategies; probably there was no one mode of behaviour.

If this was so, we might well expect that the prices paid for land would be little different between the two groups, and indeed a difference-of-means test showed that this was the case.[124] On the basis of the criteria mentioned above, 54 of the 447 observations for which all variables were available were determined to be in the speculator group. They were subsequently analysed in a fashion similar to that for the data by tenure group. The results of this, and of an analysis of 392 observations on lands purchased by non-speculators, appear on Table 5.22. This table, in essence, summarizes the differences between the farm community and the speculators with respect to what the two thought were important factors in establishing price.

Were speculators and farmers looking for the same things when they purchased land? Did market forces operate in such a way that people of different intentions responded in similar ways? That is to say, were those who were able to pay large sums of money for the more accessible locations in Essex (Figure 2.9) looking for the same things, whether farmer or speculator? Table 5.22 suggests that the difference between the two groups, irrespective of price, was insignificant. Over 700 pence per acre, speculators and non-speculators placed their emphasis on the acreage sold in the more developed parts of the county. The speculator purchaser of land under 700 pence per acre placed greater emphasis on cleared acreage than did the farmers, whose first priority presumably, because they had the capacity to transform it, was the quantity of land sold. Presumably, the threshold for economic viability was larger for the former than for the speculator.

CONCLUSIONS

In Essex and elsewhere in Upper Canada, there were sales from the beginning of the British jurisdiction, just as there had been in French times. Although there were parts of the county such as Malden Township where, because of location and demand, land transfers on particular lots could exceed one per year, more commonly land was conveyed about three times in fifty-four years or slightly more than once per generation. One suspects that this was less frequent than in more central locations near Toronto, but as yet little is known because the research remains to be completed. First sales mirrored first location and the pattern therefore generally followed that of patenting. Of course, each decision was an individual judgment of location, local site, and environmental condition weighed in the light of money.

In slightly more than 10 per cent of the 1033 observations reviewed, sales preceded patent. This was at once a measure of demand, of the "illegal" or ill-advised acquisition of land contemporaneous with setting up the apparatus of the state, of the belief that clear title in the French regime guaranteed title in its successor, and of contentedness with the certificates issued by the Land Board or the government surveyor. With respect to this last issue, there has been a supposition in Ontario historiography that a sale prior to patent is in fact evidence of some scurrilous behaviour. No doubt this was so in some instances but, as the Askin patent demonstrates, the land could in fact be transferred immediately by registering a statement and this in the period preceding the formal adoption of a sales policy in 1825. Overall, a sale took place within four years on average but, if the 10 per cent are removed from the sample, the $\bar{x}$ and σ change to 6.24 and 8.42 years respectively.

So, in slightly more than 68 per cent of the cases, a sale occurred within about fifteen years. The situation was likely different in other parts of Upper Canada. In the most central parts of southern Upper Canada, in the 1840s and 1850s, the speed by which land sold or, for that matter, was granted must have been much greater than in more remote Essex or in the eastern part of the province. Yet, even in Essex, the pace quickened, presumably as this most south westerly region became more integrated with an emerging provincial economy; between 1846 and 1850, land was being sold within two years of legal acquisition.

Throughout this period, there was a relationship between land patenting and the number of first sales. Both were affected by government policy or government's preoccupation with the war. By instituting a sales policy in 1825 which altered the interpretation of the patent (although not its legal import) and by threatening the activities of that corporate speculator, the Canada Land Company, colonial land policy literally sent waves of human energy through Essex. Ultimately, the paths of sales and of patenting had to diverge since land has a finite limit and could be patented but once. Yet there were common pulses as, for example, in 1836, when the number of sales and patents were unusually high, or again in 1846 and 1848. It is tempting to attribute all of the action in 1836 to the political exigencies of the government to secure votes in the forthcoming election or to attribute the 246 patents issued in 1846 solely to pressure upon the Canada Company, but in fact these pulses are also reflected in similar cycles in the United States and related to economic events and human suffering in Europe. Upper Canadian events were clearly important but there was also a link to the Atlantic economy.

Given all of this, it is not surprising that there were oscillations in land prices. Yet an upward trend was still identifiable. Generally, the price of land (439 pence per acre) was at least twice in 1851 what it had been in 1825 (246 pence per acre). Although opportunists could still "make a killing" by buying low at tax sales or selling high to the railroad, for most people things were much less dramatic and still not beyond their reach even at mid-century. If, of course, their intent was to acquire non-farm property in the most developed parts abutting the strait or the urban centres, this was a different matter. The Essex price for developed land was comparable to prices in Wellington County and significantly different from those in Peel County, where such land cost £3 per acre, or Hamilton Township, where it cost four and a half pounds per acre. So, too, was the price of "wild" land, which could still be obtained for eight shillings per acre (96 pence) compared to thirty shillings (360 pence) in Hamilton Township. Strict comparison between a single centrally located, well-endowed township and the more physically diverse townships of Essex is difficult. It would seem, however, that "wild" land in Essex was 27 per cent of the Hamilton price and "developed" farm real estate was 41 per cent of what had to be paid in Hamilton Township near Toronto and surrounding the town of Cobourg.[125]

Though, in absolute terms, Essex land would seem to have been a "good deal," the figures are unsatisfactory because they are unrelated to the capacity to pay. Some insight can be gauged from the work of Leo Johnson, who argues that in this area the income of a skilled labourer (£112 per annum) could be obtained from 36.0 acres devoted to wheat.[126] In 1851 this would have cost £66.18s.9d., given the prevailing price of 439 pence per acre for developed land. Even if expenses at 33.3 to 50 per cent are allowed (for capital costs, taxes, draught animals, and seed) the total outlay would range between £88 and £99.[127] In other words, for this sum of money one could hope to continue close to the top of the economic hierarchy for a very long time.[128] The most logical candidate for a "respectable" farmer of this kind was an agricultural labourer. Could he, in fact, afford the investment? In Upper Canada in the 1840s, such a person could command an average of £30 per year but in the Western District, where labour was scarce, he commanded a premium of £7.[129] More than farm labourers elsewhere, then, he could afford the investment. Generally, the food and accommodation costs of such an individual were met by the farmer for whom he worked. Even if it were not, the evidence is that such costs were a diminishing part of wages. These remained stable for twenty or thirty years.[130] In short, with less than three years of saving, such a person could transform his situation, especially if he could use the labour of others; he could do so for a much smaller outlay using his own labour, as was most usual. If this same labourer chose not to purchase in the market but rather to acquire land by patent from the state, the price could be as little as a quarter of the price mentioned and it was payable over time.[131] By 1851, at least 45.2 per cent of Essex land was still available in this manner.[132] By these standards, even if one had to borrow, Essex was among the best parts of the "best poor man's country."

It is clear that the price of land in Essex in the first half of the nineteenth century was largely determined by local Essex and wider Upper Canadian factors. It is also clear that, while Canadian and British wheat prices were related, the price of wheat in the Canadian market fell progressively throughout the first half of the century while Essex land prices increased. These events were probably largely independent of one another because of economies achieved in wheat production as the century wore on and because Essex, like other parts of Upper Canada, was never a monoculture wheat region. Rather, as McCalla and McInnis have both suggested, Upper Canada from early on was a mixed agriculture economy. This was especially true of Essex. In a sample of 1324 properties drawn to examine the relationship between cultural origin and cropping, it was found that 555 Essex farmers did not grow wheat.[133] Even so, wheat was important in the county. Figure 5.15 shows that wheat was normally distributed and this, together with the higher values of mean and mode for wheat, indicates that this was the major crop in Essex. Further, Table 5.23 indicates the average farm had 40.5 per cent of its cropland in wheat and the modal value was 50.0 per cent. In all, 435 out of 1324 farms had between 21 and 50 per cent devoted to wheat; another 136 properties had between 51 and 75 per cent of their land in wheat, and for 34 farms wheat was a monoculture. Given these figures and the fact that wheat occupied 9234 acres of Essex,[134] it can be argued that wheat in Essex was indeed king but the absolute acreage was small. While the average acreage lies within a reasonable magnitude of what McInnis has shown to be characteristic of the wider Ontario area a decade later,[135] at 8.76 acres it was small indeed.[136] Yet, if wheat was the pre-eminent cereal, it was not the only one in Essex. Figures 5.16 and 5.17 and Table 5.23 show that corn and oats were also important. Indeed, there were actually more corn growers than wheat growers, a fact reflecting the climatic suitability of this area to Indian corn. As in the case of wheat, the respective acreages devoted to corn and oats were not great, although the difference between them was statistically significant.[137] It is clear that wheat was indeed an important element

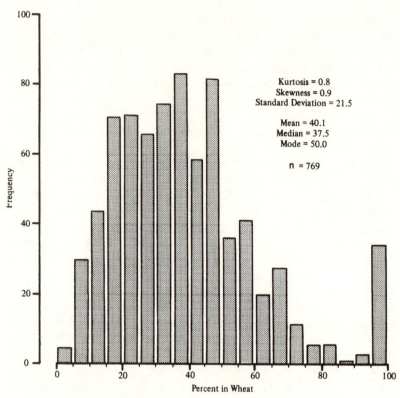

Figure 5.15   Statistical distribution of land in wheat
Source: Enumeration returns, Census of Canada, 1850–52.

Table 5.23   Specific cereal crop as a percentage of the land in crop, Essex County, 1850–52

Crop	n	$\bar{x}$	σ	Mode	Median	Min.	Max.
Wheat	769	40.50	21.51	50.0	37.47	2.0	100.0
Corn	846	32.51	26.14	19.0	24.70	1.0	100.0
Oats	708	28.88	21.16	33.0	24.60	2.0	100.0

Min. = minimum; max. = maximum

Source: Census Enumeration Returns, Census of Canada 1851–52, Essex County.

in the grain economy. Essex land prices were shown to be associated with wheat prices in the British market but the latter were not the only element in the farm economy, which might explain why the correlation coefficient was not higher.

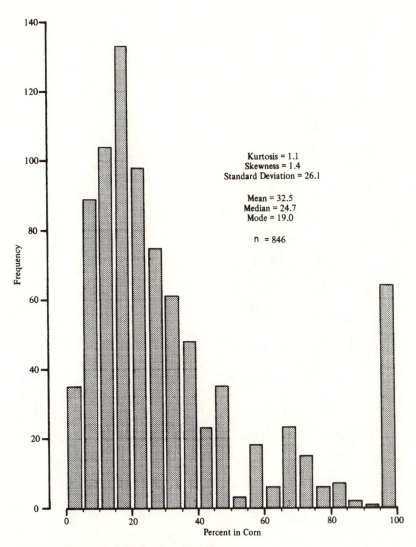

Figure 5.16 Statistical distribution of land in corn
Source: Enumeration returns, Census of Canada, 1850–52.

Turning to the analysis of land prices at the respective cross-sections, it would seem that the purchasing power of the pound was of more importance than accessibility to urban centre or the rural infrastructure, a point that may need emphasizing given the emphasis on the importance of the urban dimension in the existing literature on development. This was found consistently. The importance of "cleared

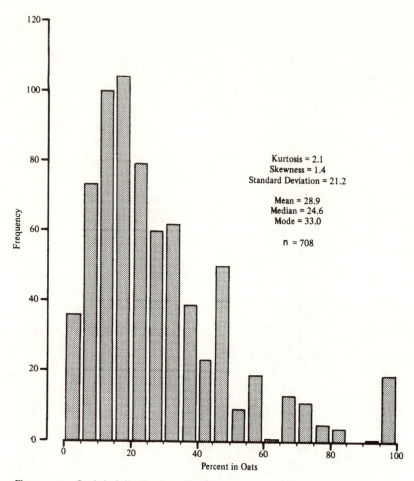

Figure 5.17   Statistical distribution of land in oats
Source: Enumeration returns, Census of Canada, 1850–52.

acreage" was more prominent with respect to land selling at or below 700 pence per acre; these lots were less accessible to the coast, the roads, or rural establishment. Above this, the variable never appeared in any of the sub-sets analysed. This lends credence to the idea that in Essex the boundary of the farm community was possibly around the 700-pence-per-acre level, although there were farms that commanded higher prices. In the earlier period, the era of a more subsistence agriculture, when land was readily available from the state and more outside the monetary economy, the relative lack of emphasis is totally understandable. By mid-century this situation had changed. Yet a word of caution is necessary. It may not be absolutely correct to assume that those lots selling above 700 pence per acre were, of necessity, less rural. They may or may not have been. The potential speculator might well have operated in both or any one of these areas. So might the potential tavern keeper, apothecary, lawyer, or industrialist. Much depended upon intention and, as today, upon "self-image." All had to make a choice, a choice conditioned in the final analysis by ability to pay.

From a methodological perspective, it was assumed at the outset that a marriage of assessment rolls with the abstract index would identify non-resident owners and that creation of this class was de facto recognition of the speculator category. The analysis here suggests that such simple variable description is naive, although non-residence may still be one of several important descriptors of the category. Speculators were shown to operate in a variety of tenure conditions, as resident owners as well as non-residents. They undoubtedly rented their land to tenants as a strategy for survival. The fifty-four speculators identified here were recognized by their case histories and by the scale criterion, that is, they were included if they held over 400 acres of land and made frequent sales. These speculators appear to have looked for the same qualities in land as society as a whole, although they placed greater emphasis on cleared acreage when purchasing land at under 700 pence per acre.[138] Given that they would ultimately dispose of this land to the larger society, their attitudes were sensible. The farmers' stress on size of holding under 700 pence per acre related to their greater need for land under conditions of extensive agriculture. At about the 700-pence level and in the more developed and probably less farm-oriented areas, speculators and non-speculators both sought large acreages as their first choice. Depending on their circumstances, they could command larger or smaller acreages in prime or more remote locations; as today, some chose to borrow to optimize their investment strategy.

6 Buying on Credit: The Upper Canada Dilemma

INTRODUCTION: THE CONTEXT OF CREDIT

Although the received wisdom has been that Upper Canada was a subsistence economy until some unspecified date in the first few decades of the nineteenth century, McCalla has argued that even as early as 1800 "this was not, properly speaking, a subsistence economy, given its dynamic growth, its net immigration, its ability to survive harvest and market downturns, its capacity to build up and hold appropriate stocks of relevant commodities, and its apparent responsiveness to changing market conditions."[1]

Household production and domestic exchange and investment, together with external financial links, were the components that fostered provincial development.[2] Farmers produced wheat at levels beyond subsistence from the beginning and, because of their needs for capital and credit on what was a commercial frontier, could never retreat into absolute self-sufficiency even in times of extreme difficulty and hardship.[3] If this was so with respect to the economy as a whole, it was certainly so for that subset which was concerned with the acquisition of land and with the maintenance of a farm as a functioning entity. Though it was possible to rent land,[4] and indeed it will be shown later that this was a common practice, the ultimate goal of most seems to have been to own it. Those who received the bounty of the state might conform to the duties assigned them and for little outlay of money, though not of sweat, acquire the means to a farm-life. The need for credit was certainly minimal before 1825, because, although there was a system of settlement duties and a schedule of administrative fees, such grants were effectively free. Indeed, in this early period, the attractiveness of "free land" may have militated[5] against the purchase of land, the development of a market per se, and the need for mortgages. Yet those investigating the establishment of a sales policy in 1825 asked questions designed to elicit answers about the cash and credit value of land.[6] In 145 instances they received answers which showed that, on average, the cash price was at least 16.52 and perhaps 26 per cent lower than the credit price.[7]

The actual figure is not as important here as the fact that, as early as the mid-1820s, credit was theoretically available as was a "discount" for cash. Even if the basis of the actual land transaction was cash, bringing that land into production might require a credit-outlay for seed and for necessary tools. By 1833, given that legal rights to ownership were commonly withheld, credit was so available that Patrick Shirreff saw it as a deficiency in the land-settlement system. Shirreff believed that it did not encourage responsibility either on the part of the settler, who might abscond, or on the part of the owner, who stood to gain from the labour spent by the settler.[8] The agricultural economy and the commercial system were essentially interrelated and built upon an integrated chain of connection stretching back to New York and indeed to England. Such connections tended to be personal at the outset or soon became so.[9] When either American or British markets went into contraction and demanded immediate payment, "the resultant liquidity crisis highlighted the economy's reliance on credit for its ordinary and routine functioning by temporarily interrupting that credit."[10]

It was not until after the administrative decision to institute a sales policy in 1825, in turn related to the development of the economy, that a genuine market for land developed, fuelled in part by increasing immigration. As has been shown, while patenting exceeded sales until 1812 and continued as a legal formality even after the institution of a formal sales policy in 1825, sales were well under way by that date. The new policy allowed people to acquire land by a series of instalments. A successful bid generated a patent as before but the new and critical dimension was the institution of a credit system on Crown land.[11] With access to these vast resources, the need to purchase in established areas was greatly reduced for many, especially the poor. This was especially so in newly developing areas where prices were lower although greater numbers might *in aggregate* generate more mortgages. Elsewhere, in older and often better endowed areas, land carried a premium price and had to be obtained not from the state but by purchase from someone who might have been the original patentee. Essex was certainly older but its physical endowment was dichotomized; the best land had been rapidly acquired and therefore for some this might necessitate borrowing in the private sector. Here as elsewhere in Upper Canada, there were those who were prepared to lend. Indeed, for some, investment in mortgages was even more secure than investing or speculating in land. Catherine Parr Traill could write:

My husband and friends, conversant with the affairs of the colonies, say, lend it on mortgage, on good landed securities, and at a high rate of interest. The purchase of land is often a good speculation, but not always so certain as mortgage, as it pays no interest; and though it may at some future time make great returns, it is not always so easy to dispose of it to an advantage when you happen to need. A man possessing many thousand acres in different townships, may be distressed for twenty pounds if suddenly called upon for it when he is unprepared, if he invests all his capital in property of this kind.[12]

This chapter, like the study as a whole, focuses upon the security of rural land; urban mortgages were deliberately eliminated from the data set used here. It uses data drawn annually but summarized by five-year periods and cross-sectionally for 1825 and 1850-52. The chapter examines the frequency and extent to which credit was extended by mortgage and by vendor/purchaser agreements. It also examines the mechanisms that drove the mortgage market, the question of second mortgaging, the level of mortgage indebtedness in Essex County, the length of time between purchase and mortgage indebtedness, the time taken to discharge credit agreements, and the sources of capital available to mortgagors. Relatively little is known about these subjects, especially before 1835, the year chosen by David Gagan as the starting date for his seminal study of such credit mechanisms.[13]

METHODS OF TRANSFER AND THE LAW

Historically, credit mechanisms have varied from society to society; within particular societies they have taken on different forms, some oral, some recorded.[14] Varying forms have accorded varying rights to creditor and debtor.[15] In common law, when two parties agree to the conditions, the property is simply transferred when the terms (not always monetary) have been fulfilled. In a monetary economy, the vendor, in order to "close" a sale, may agree to accept payment over time with or without interest. This is in fact a credit transaction, usually established by "an indenture of bargain and sale." Where the parties are less secure, or where the legal culture requires it or more likely where credit is advanced by a third party and the need is to secure the loan rather than acquire land, there may be insistence upon more legally comforting instruments than the simple deeds, indentures, and bargain and sales by which conveyance was often effected. In common law, this device is the *mortgage*, the legal instrument by which a property interest is transferred by a debtor (mortgagor) to a creditor (mortgagee).[16] In a society such as Upper Canada, where land was so central to the social and economic well-being of the individual, it might seem obvious that mortgaging might be a common part of the land-acquisition process. This presupposes that there were legal benefits to the process of mortgaging (*sensu stricto*) that outweighed the shortcomings, that there were mortgages to be had, and that societal attitudes sanctioned credit and countenanced the use of mortgages.

While common law was introduced into Upper Canada by 1794,[17] no immediate provision was made for equity, that branch of English law which serves to add to and "correct" limitations in common law. For various reasons, a court of chancery was not created until March 1837.[18] However, as Elizabeth Brown has shown, in a territory where default was common, the common law courts were prepared to practise their "own variety of equity cloaked in the language of the common law"[19] and the legislature was prepared to pass specific acts to provide equitable relief in extreme cases. Nonetheless, until 1837 at common law, a mortgagor conveyed conditional title to a mortgagee in return for a sum of money; if money was not repaid, the mortgagee's title would become absolute.

John Weaver sees these "peculiar conditions" of Upper Canadian law as at variance with the laws of England from which they were derived and as severely disadvantaging mortgagors while posing little problem to mortgagees.[20] Indeed, in Thompsonian vein, he argues that in Upper Canada "law can be seen to mediate and legitimate existent class relations,"[21] pointing to the potential advantage to men of landed wealth and of capital[22] as well as to members of the judiciary such as Chief Justice John Beverley Robinson, whose self-interest, he argues, may in part have ensured procrastination in the creation of an equitable jurisdiction.[23]

In contradistinction to common law, the laws of equity permitted an "equity of redemption" whereby the mortgagor would be permitted a set time to repay the money after the due date and have the land re-conveyed. Equity recognized the right of the mortgagee to foreclosure but this was impossible to secure until 1837, nor, in practice, could mortgagors avail themselves of their "equity of redemption."[24] For some, potential mortgagees, the situation prior to 1837 was unsatisfactory in that debtors could simply walk away from their responsibilities, leaving the mortgagee in possession of title but with issues of equity still unresolved. These responsibilities were sufficiently cumbersome and onerous that Daniel Bilak has concluded that "the mortgage was a prohibitively restrictive mechanism" for the rural vendor of land.[25] In contrast, the "bargain and sale" mechanism necessitated little if any capital on the part of the purchaser. Where the transaction was a cash one, conveyance was immediate; where terms were included, the bargain-and-sale instrument became a credit instrument by the addition of a payment schedule and/or statements of interest charges. Such an instrument also offered the vendor adequate protection since default ended the contract. Until 1837, those defaulting but desiring their "equity of redemption" to be acknowledged were similarly frustrated by the absence of a court of chancery. However, the act of 1834 concerning real property, while henceforth limiting claims for an interest in land to twenty years, also anticipated the establishment of an equitable jurisdiction and permitted claims until five years after the establishment of Chancery, that is, effectively until 1842.[26]

In short, before and after 1837, both instalment purchase contracts and mortgages existed in Upper Canada and were used to varying degrees. Bilak suggests that *mortgages* were mainly a means of facilitating capital investment in manufacturing and commerce and as such were largely restricted to urban communities. On the other hand, the work of David Gagan[27] and the author[28] would seem to suggest that mortgages on rural land were not uncommon, but the literature on this matter is thin. Given the willingness of common law courts to extend equity protection to vendors and purchasers[29] and the shortage of long-term capital in the province, "the law of mortgages was a cumbersome method by which to transact land sales for both vendors and purchasers."[30] It is therefore to be expected that, in Essex County, instruments of bargain and sale extending credit to the purchaser would outnumber mortgage instruments (Table 5.2). While legal historians might appreciate information on the frequency of the two types of instruments, both instruments describe credit agreements. The legal differences between them are inconsequential for purposes of the present study. In any case, the line between mortgage and bargain and sale was often fine.

The following excerpt from an "Indenture of Bargain and Sale by way of Mortgage," signed by Edward Butler on 12 January 1846 with the Amherstburg merchant Thomas F. Park, is illustrative of the form of such agreements. In tone it is so solemn as to support the notion that people might be threatened by the very act of "mortgaging."

Whereas the said Edward Butler is indebted unto the said Thomas F. Park in the sum of one hundred and twenty two pounds, two shillings and six pence ... hath granted, bargained, sold, alienated, transferred, conveyed and confirmed unto the said Thomas F Park ... his heirs, executors and administrators and assigns for ever. Provided always ... that if the said Edward Butler his Executors or administrators or some one of them shall and will well and truly pay or cause to be paid unto the said ... the full sum ... with interest from the date of these presents ... Then this indenture and every clause Matter or thing herein contained shall cease and be null and void ... and that if default shall happen to be made ... it shall and may be lawful to and for the said Thomas F. Park his executor, administrator or assigns to enter into and upon and to Have, Hold, use, occupy, possess and enjoy the said Messuage, hereditament and premises with their appurtenances, and that until such default it shall and may be lawful for the said Edward Butler to occupy, possess and enjoy the said Messuage and premises with their appurtances and to receive the rents, issues and profits thereof, to his own use.[31]

The land was actually conveyed by this instrument; Park was taking no chances that he might be engaged in subsequent litigation or that by foreclosing on a genuine mortgage he might lose the land to the highest bidder at a public sale or his right to sue if the asset fetched less than it had been mortgaged for. The land was lost unless redeemed! Butler had, of course, the right to "occupy, possess and enjoy" and "to receive the rents, issues and profits thereof, to his own use," but this was ultimately to be to Park's benefit if Butler failed. The instrument used in the Butler\Park agreement is not a mortgage per se but, purposefully, a memorial "by way of a mortgage." This usage may explain why, as will be discussed later, foreclosure was almost unknown in Essex. Park wanted a contract rather than a discussion of equity or a debate on his right of foreclosure! Though the law of the time did not require it, the document did, strengthening Park's claim in the event he reneged.

Similarly, the agreement entered into in April 1800 between John Baptiste Barthe and the merchant house of Leith, Shepherd and Duff was simply described as an indenture rather than an indenture of bargain and sale or as a mortgage. However, its effect was not lost upon the registrar of the county. When Richard Pollard registered the instrument, he indicated that a "Memorial of this Indenture of this Mortgage" had been recorded on 29 May 1800 as Liber A, folio 94 and 95. When the terms were met he added to the document itself, "This mortgage discharged." Whatever the form, this was clearly a mortgage. The terminology of the document was slightly different; the elements provided for were more all-encompassing and greater security against prior debts and mortgages was offered the mortgagee in this document than in many others of the time. Barthe had to confirm that the premises and its parts "now are and be ... and shall ever be, remain and continue free and clear, from all former and other Gifts, Grants, Mortgages and encumbrances whatsoever." Leith, Shepherd and Duff were to have occasional access to check on the property and absolute access "without the let, suit, trouble, molestation ot interruption" upon Barthe's default. There are those who would argue that this document was drafted in a superior and legally more elegant manner than other instruments of the kind, but it was nonetheless a mortgage. Certainly, its ultimate intention was clear:

That until Default, shall be made in payement of the aforesaid sum, with interest as aforesaid, according to the time above limited for payement thereof, it shall and may be lawfull to and for the said John Baptiste Barthe, his heirs and Assigns, peaceably and quietly to have, hold, occupy, profess and enjoy, all and singular the said Premises – above granted and released, and to have, receive, and take the rents, issued and profits, thereof to his and their own particular use and benefit, anything herein contained to the contrary notwithstanding.[32]

This agreement, which contained a provision for interest at 6 per cent, was to run for one year and was in fact discharged, presumably within the legal time-frame.

The very tone of these documents, particularly the Park and Butler agreement, is appropriately solemn and threatening, reminding the parties of the importance of the agreement they were entering into. For many, of course, such documents were nothing more than the legal instruments needed to bring about desirable ends, the enhancement of personal fortune and the development of society as a whole by guaranteeing the capital needs of individual entrepreneurs. David Burley has demonstrated the importance of credit and debt in the transition to industrial capitalism in an urban setting; increasingly, qualities of character and personality were of less importance than wealth and the capacity to encumber property.[33] Not so, one suspects, in the countryside, where an inherent conservatism among farmers must have allowed such values to survive longer. This is not to say that rural society was idyllic and free of acquisitiveness[34] and even avarice. It was not. In a society in which landed property was worshipped, Gagan has shown that what distinguished families was not just capacity to own and cultivate land but to accumulate capital via the security which it offered. Citing Catherine Parr Traill's advice that mortgages, not land, were the best security in the long run, Thomas Conant's image of the successful farmer as one who had built his security on

Plate 6.1   Mortgaging the Homestead. By George A. Reid. Oil on canvas, submitted to the Royal Academy of Arts in 1890.
Courtesy of National Gallery of Canada Ottawa (acc. no. 86).

loans and mortgages in the neighbourhood,[35] and the eagerness of Canadians to accept twenty-one year indentures with annual interest payments ahead of cash,[36] Gagan distinguishes between the rural capitalist and the ordinary farmer.[37] The former actively sought capital. The latter, imbued with Victorian notions of prudence and living in an agrarian society in which land was literally life,[38] may well have entered most hesitantly into a formal mortgage. In a society that venerated the Bible, the possible consequences of mortgaging must have been known to many from the story recorded in Nehemiah. Seeking support to rebuild Jerusalem, Nehemiah received a negative answer because the land of those whom he asked had been mortgaged to purchase corn. The consequence was that "we bring into bondage our sons and daughters to be servants ... neither is it in our power to redeem them, for other men have our land and vineyards."[39]

This biblical "truth" must have been only too apparent in the everyday life of many Ontario farmers and must have strengthened their resolve to avoid mortgaging at all costs. Mortgaging, for this group, was not to be entered into lightly. Indeed, according to one observer, "a mortgage on the home carried about the same connotation as illegitimacy in the family."[40] It is this attitude that George A. Reid captured so well in his famous painting "*Mortgaging the Homestead*" (Plate 6.1), which spoke to Ontarians even in the last decades of the century[41] Here, the mother contemplating the seriousness of the action looks away; the son resignedly accepts his future; the grandparents reflect upon their accomplishments and their needs in old age.[42] Another painting, Reid's *Foreclosure of the Mortgage*, struck such a cord that the artist tired of hearing it discussed to the exclusion of his other work and had it put into storage.[43] We shall never know the extent to which Edward Butler shared the anxieties which Reid captured but his agreement with Park was to run for thirty-six months and he discharged his obligations in four![44]

The Literature on Mortgaging

In the Upper Canadian rural context, the literature on mortgaging is sparse, consisting of the published work of David Gagan and the unpublished study of James Kennedy.[45] These authors deal with areas remote from one another; they also concentrate on the period 1835 to 1881 whereas this study focuses on the dying years of the eighteenth century and the first half of the nineteenth. Both examine mortgaging in the formal sense and show that it was of a low frequency but increased through the time period studied. In Toronto Gore in 1851, mortgaging involved 24.4 per cent of proprietors; in Marlborough, the comparable figure was 8.69 per cent. In both areas in 1851, indebtedness, measured as a percentage of the value of a sale, was high, in excess of 80 per cent. In absolute terms, the average debt was the equivalent of £337.18s.0d. in Toronto Gore[46] and £499.6s.0d. in Marlborough.[47] Secondary mortgages were frequent in both areas, constituting 54 per cent of indentures in Gagan's area and 66 per cent in Kennedy's,[48] and so were likely for purposes other than the primary acquisition of land. The bulk of these mortgages were covered by non-resident, private lenders and relatively few by institutional lenders. In Toronto Gore, private lenders held never less than 83 per cent of all mortgages; and while the equivalent figure in Marlborough was 79.95 per cent, in 1851 it was 100 per cent.[49] Farmers and the social elite were major sources of capital and the merchant class was comparatively insignificant. Kennedy reports that 40 per cent of lenders were farmers, 21.6 per cent were "gentlemen or esquires," and 9.2 per cent were merchants; the rest consisted of widows, spinsters, professionals, manufacturers, and tradesmen. Gagan is less explicit but acknowledges that widows, housewives, "gentlemen," farmers, and merchants accounted for 80 per cent of the mortgages and within this grouping "merchants ... the traditional source of rural credit, fall well down the list."[50] The time taken to discharge a mortgage was, by the standards of today, very short, that is,

2.5 to 6 years. How by comparison did Essex fare on these measures in the earlier period?

Readers will recall that the main source of information on this topic, as on the matter of sales, is the abstract index to deeds, discussed at some length in the earlier chapter. Little need be added here except some observations from a qualitative perspective. Interestingly, agreements were sometimes registered even when it might not be expected that they would be, for example, in the case of intergenerational transfer of land. In some instances, as Gagan has shown elsewhere, security in old age was assured by a mortgage in the family.[51] These were exceptional uses of the mortgage instrument, interesting in themselves but excluded from this study, which concentrates upon the market economy. More usually, as in the present, mortgages were used to transfer land between parties having no emotional ties to one another or a relationship other than the purely fiscal.

An additional facet of mortgaging revealed in the deeds was that, in a minority of circumstances (perhaps 1 per cent), the terms of the mortgage were satisfied in produce rather than specie. Thus, Jean Baptiste LaFramboise agreed in 1810 to accept 2000 minots of wheat in fifteen annual instalments beginning in 1812 from Pierre Girard for lot 23 in the 1st concession of Petite Côté, Sandwich Township.[52] That same year, Richard Pattinson of Sandwich and William Duff of Amherstburg agreed to accept wheat or flour from one J. Pardons against lot 75 in the front concession of Colchester Township and "the penal sum of £100 Upper Canada."[53] The practice seems to have continued for some time. In 1821 Veronique Drouillard accepted payment of £10 in flour, £10 in cyder, and £10 in farm produce to allow J. Drouillard to discharge the mortgage he had signed in 1818.[54]

Of some interest, at least to legal historians, is that in at least three situations the term of the mortgage could be very long indeed. Thus, the Girard/LaFramboise mortgage discussed above was written for a term of 1000 years; the L'Husier/Park mortgage of 1802 was written for a term of 500 years,[55] as was the Rouse/Reynolds mortgage of 1819.[56] All three contained provisions for earlier discharge and these provisions were exercised.

Though inherently interesting, such instruments were few in number. The legal draftmanship varied with lawyers and presumably with the particular circumstances, but mortgages and their equivalents, "indentures by way of a mortgage," follow a basically similar form which would, as the century moved on, become "standard." Both types of instrument were counted as a mortgage for the purposes of this chapter; the reasoning is that a mortgage represents a credit transaction between people no matter which instrument was used.

MORTGAGING IN ESSEX: WHAT DROVE THE SYSTEM?

In the final analysis, of course, the decision to mortgage was an individual decision made in the expectation of enhanced profit, to secure a loan, or initially to acquire land. However, no one lived in a vacuum and each decision was taken with respect to prevailing economic conditions. Part of that context was that the potential mortgagor might be affected by prevailing interests rates or by the cash crop most important to the economy at that time, namely, wheat.[57] As in the previous chapter, therefore, a series of correlations were run against British and American interest rates in the absence of a Canadian series. These produced statistically insignificant results, a fact that is perhaps not surprising because of the operation of the usury laws.[58]

Interest rates, as recorded in the copy books, ran between 4.5 and most commonly 6 per cent or were expressed, in keeping with the usury laws, as "legal interest." There was little variation in the official interest rates although various devices such as finders fees, designed to subvert the law, may have been in place in Upper Canada. On these, which may have been the real basis of decision making, the official record is silent. One has to wonder what Catherine Parr Traill meant by "a high rate of interest." R.E. Ankli, citing the evidence of prominent individuals reporting to the colonial government in the 1840s, concludes that everyone realized that the legal interest rate of 6 per cent was "only honoured in the breach."[59] Thomas Rolph, author of the *Statistical Account of Upper Canada, 1836–1842*, acknowledged that more was demanded. Thomas Saunders from Guelph reported that the figure was between 10 and 15 per cent, and A.B. Hawke, the chief emigration agent for Upper Canada, admitted that money carried a premium because of its scarcity. A bonus was often paid, which increased the rate to 10 to 12 per cent. This was the range that the agent of the Canada Company gave as well when he described the existence of such bounties or "other well known means," designed to circumvent the lending of money on such "easy" terms as the legal limit of 6 per cent permitted by the usury laws.[60]

Where money was scarce, such limits were evaded. Sherriff Dunbar Moodie, for example, pointed to bank stocks yielding more than 8 per cent. Of course, banks stocks carried more risk; individuals might also be unreliable but land secured by a mortgage was immutable. Yet it was clear that more than 6 per cent was needed for some to invest in mortgages; double this amount seems the "normal" expectation. Conant, writing of Upper Canada in the dying years of the nineteenth century, describes what an unknown number of credit-purchasers faced in dealing with some mortgagees: "This money and the accumulated earnings of years he lent to his neighbours at a maximum rate of twelve per cent, with discounts and drawbacks and many other dark and mysterious ways of figuring – so mysterious, indeed that in many instances the loan netted him twenty to twenty-five per cent, per annum ... Floods, disasters, deaths, fires – nothing seemed to stand in the way of the steady tick of interest and accumulated wealth."[61]

Interest of this magnitude, if it was common, must surely have deterred all but the most foolhardy or desperate. It may also explain why interest rates are rarely mentioned in the records at all. It is, of course, possible that there was no need to mention them; there may simply have been two prices, one for cash and one for credit, as the designers of the 1825 imperial inquiry anticipated and the respondents returned. A $100 loan at 6 per cent would over four years, commonly the length of an Essex mortgage or purchase agreement, produce $126.24; in this way, one might envisage the $26.24 profit as carrying charges. The credit price exceeded the cash price by this magnitude in 59 out of 145 townships, not including the 18 cases where credit seems to have been actively preferred to cash. Although the data are somewhat skewed, the $\bar{x}$ was found to be 26.07 and the σ was 14.57 per cent. This places the class limits of the normal deviate at 11.5 and 40.64 per cent. Even if these figures were never achieved – if, in fact, this was only the expected differential that the respondents to the government inquiry of 1825 anticipated – the latter's expectation must have been reflected in credit arrangements somehow. The simplest adjustment was to add it to the price for those buying on credit. The evidence is circumstantial and care must be exercised with the statistics, but the lower limit comes close to the 12 per cent commonly anticipated and the mean exceeds the solid return that Conant's investor desired and created for himself. Given such rates, it is quite apparent why there can be little relationship between official rates and the performance of any portion of the economy; "real" mortgage rates cannot be known and official rates are simply irrelevant.

Since the Upper Canadian economy was linked to overseas markets, it might seem logical that its health would be reflected in what was appreciated overseas, namely, wheat. A good performance in the British market to which Upper Canadian wheat was directed might lead in subsequent years to investment in additional land and a concomitant mortgaging. In fact, the correlation coefficient for this relationship was also low, at 0.34, though statistically significant.[62] An earlier study produced similar results for the price of land through time; the relationship between price of land and number of mortgages produced a correlation coefficient of 0.46. It would seem that mort-gaging, as part of the larger system of land economics, was affected not so much by international conditions, nor even Upper Canadian con-ditions, as by local circumstances.[63] If there was no local resistance to mortgaging, then the price of land was such that mortgaging was not widely required or else economic opportunities were as yet limited.

As population increased in Essex (from 4199 in 1820 to 16,817 in 1851),[64] so did the demand for land and for mortgaging. Yet the rate of mortgaging per thousand people remained relatively stable, aver-aging 1.78 throughout the period but rising towards the end.[65] The best single measure of mortgaging through time was found to be the number of sales, which produced an r^2 of 0.67. The largest residuals, with normal deviates greater than 2.0, were found for the years 1837, 1838, 1847, and 1851[66]. In 1837, a year of stem rust, poor crops, and rebellion, the number of mortgages was understandably smaller than was expected by the author. For 1838, the sign of the residual was pos-itive, indicating a greater than "normal" number of mortgages and signs of recovery from the previous year. In 1847, the greater number of mortgages than was expected is perhaps to be explained in terms of the repeal of the Corn Laws in Britain in 1846 and the expectation that this might prove beneficial to Essex farmers[67] or, as in any other year, for security of debts previously incurred.

How frequent was mortgaging?

Figure 6.1 shows the frequency of mortgaging in Essex County from 1798 to 1852. It would seem that, until about 1825, the number of mortgages rarely exceeded ten in any one year. Thereafter, as the economy of this county and Upper Canada improved, mortgaging increased; in 1839 there were twenty-seven mortgages and in 1847 there were thirty-five. Basically, this figure shows graphically the statis-tical relationship demonstrated above. However, it is noticeable that the number of mortgages is always much less than the number of sales transactions, a term that includes all conveyances except those by gift, intergenerational transfer, or patent from the government. What per-centage of people mortgaged their land? Did this increase over time and if so why?

Table 6.1 records that new mortgages as a percentage of sales within particular periods never exceeded 25 per cent in Essex County; they came closest to this figure in the first two quinquennial periods. Although, as noted earlier, French settlement had begun as early as 1749 in this area, these were the formative years for European settle-ment. Consequently, at this time land acquisition from government

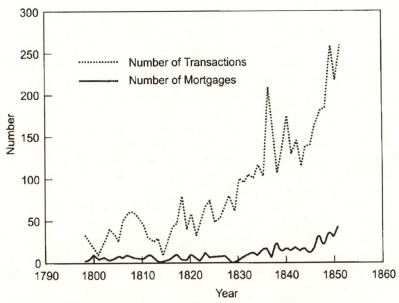

Figure 6.1 Essex County: number of mortgages and transactions, 1798–1852
Source: Abstract Index to Deeds.

Table 6.1 Mortgaging activity, Essex County, 1798–1852

Date	No. Mortgages	No. Trans- actions	Mortgages as Percentage of Sales	Date	No. Mortgages	No. Trans- actions	Mortgages as Percentage of Sales
1798–1800	18	78	23.1	1826–1830	26	363	7.2
1801–1805	30	138	21.7	1831–1835	56	528	10.6
1806–1810	35	280	12.5	1836–1840	83	737	11.3
1811–1815	20	125	16.0	1841–1845	75	667	11.2
1816–1820	35	266	13.2	1846–1850	136	1005	13.5
1821–1825	34	270	12.6	1851–1852	100	570	17.5
Total	172	1157	14.9	1798–1852	476	3870	12.3

Source: Calculations of the author.

exceeded that by purchase (Figure 5.7). There was abundant land available, even allowing for the legal requirement to provide two-sevenths of the surveyed area for Crown and clergy reserves[68] and a political climate that permitted extensive land speculation.[69] As a result, there was less need for purchase from private individuals. When a sale did occur, it was because a large amount of land was being assembled by someone other than an official grantee, that is, someone sanctioned to receive the bounty of the state, or because the property being acquired was already owned and especially desirable of itself or had been developed and contained, for example, a grist mill. Special purchases of this kind or on this scale might require the security of a mortgage and generate an inflated statistic for these years relative to the later period. For instance, for the period down to 1812, mortgages as a percentage of sales were 26.3 per cent; if these numbers are calculated as a percentage of *all* transactions including patents, sales, and mortgages, the statistic would be 12.73 per cent. Yet mortgaging relative to sales is the requisite statistic and over the fifty-four year period mortgaging averaged 14.6 percent of sales with a σ of 10.6. The median was 12.0 and the mode 14.3 per cent of sales.[70] If comparison is made to overall figures and not just sales, the $\bar{x}$ is 8.39, the σ is 4.83, and the median 7.66. These figures suggest that mortgagors and mortgagees, in a nineteenth-century society that emphasised thrift,[71] either possessed enough capital or were unwilling to hold or unable to obtain large mortgages.

Comparison with other areas is possible only for a restricted time frame. Gagan has shown that, for an area with access to the major urban market of Toronto, mortgaging in any decade was never more than 37 per cent and for the decade 1841 to 1851 it was 24.4 per cent.[72] James Kennedy, in his study of Marlborough, an area with accessibility to the Rideau Canal linking Kingston and Ottawa but poorly endowed, has shown that mortgagors in this same decade constituted 8.69 per cent of all proprietors. In Essex County, mortgages as a percentage of sales were 12.8 per cent. With the exception of newly settled Anderdon which until 1835 had been an Indian reserve, this same statistic ranged for the remaining nine townships from 3.6 per cent in Maidstone to 14.5 per cent in Malden.[73] Given the superior location of Toronto Gore Township, and assuming that higher rates of mortgaging is indicative of economic investment (it may not be so), these figures are understandable.

An interesting feature of Table 6.1 is the U-shaped form obtained when mortgaging is expressed as a percentage of total transactions in any one period (Figure 6.2).[74] Obviously, mortgaging decreased in relative if not absolute terms down to 1825 only to increase thereafter. A number of factors may explain this, including the possibility that in the early years more land was acquired by patent than by sale. As the years went on and the better lands were taken up, more people had to resort to purchase rather than acquisition from government. The greater choice in the early years may therefore affect the form of the curve.

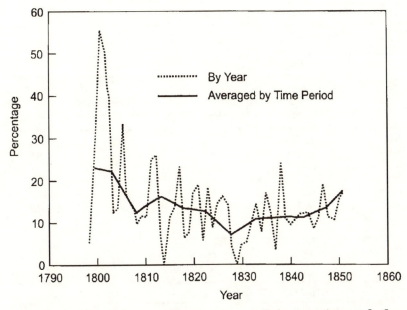

Figure 6.2   Essex County: mortgaging as a percentage of sales transactions, 1798–1851
Source: Abstract Index to Deeds.

Another factor that may have been involved was the new patent system instituted in 1825, which, by permitting instalment payments to the state, reduced the need to acquire land in the private sector and the probability of having to secure it with private credit. Moreover, following initial enthusiasm over the prospects of Essex County, development may have passed it by for more central locations in Ontario. The years from 1800 to 1825 were a period of potential instability and little or no growth in land acquisition in the townships of the county. It was only afterwards that, in keeping with the general growth of the Upper Canadian economy, increased confidence in Upper Canada's political system, and the exhaustion of suitable lands in the central core, land acquisition by patent or sale began to increase markedly.[75] Mortgaging exhibited a similar tendency but always at a lower rate; even in the quinquennial 1846–50, when mortgaging was greatest in absolute terms, it was proportionally less than in the period of initial settlement (Table 6.1).

Table 6.2 treats the number of mortgagees and mortgagors in each of two developmental phases in Essex County, that is, prior to 1825 and between then and mid-century. In each phase the mortgagors and mortgagees are classified according to the number of mortgages held or granted. By 1825, 82 people had mortgaged their land; by the end of the second period, 284 had; mortgaging had increased by 348 per

Table 6.2   Characteristics of mortgagees and mortgagors in Essex County, by class

Mortgagees

	1798–1825				1826–1852			
Class	No. Mort- gagees	% Total Mortgages	No. Mortgages Trans.	Class as % Mortgages	No. Mort- gagees	% Total Mortgages	No. Mortgages Trans.	Class as % Mortgages
6+	6	10.3	65	38.0	9	3.8	112	24.2
5	5	8.6	25	14.6	6	2.6	30	6.5
4	3	5.2	12	7.0	10	4.3	40	8.6
3	6	12.1	18	10.5	10	4.3	30	6.5
2	14	24.1	28	16.4	51	21.7	102	22.0
1	23	39.7	23	13.5	149	63.4	149	32.2
Total	54		171		235		463	

Mortgagors

	1798–1825				1826–1852			
Class	No. Mort- gagees	% Total Mortgages	No. Mortgages Trans.	Class as % Mortgages	No. Mort- gagees	% Total Mortgages	No. Mortgages Trans.	Class as % Mortgages
6+	3	3.7	27	15.8	4	1.4	48	10.3
5	3	3.7	15	8.8	6	2.1	30	6.4
4	5	6.1	20	11.7	11	3.9	44	9.5
3	9	11.0	27	15.8	16	5.6	48	10.3
2	20	24.4	40	23.4	46	16.2	92	19.8
1	42	51.2	42	24.6	201	70.8	201	43.2
Total	82		171		284		463	

Source: Calculations of the author.

cent. In contrast to mortgagors, potential mortgagees had increased to a greater extent by 405 per cent, that is, from 58 to 235. Fifty-one per cent of those mortgaging their land in the earlier period were mortgaging one property; by the end of 1851, 70.8 per cent of mortgagors were mortgaging only one property. While the absolute number of mortgagors increased, in all categories greater than one, the percentage of those mortgaging more than one property declined. Thus, in the period ending in 1825, only 3.7 per cent of the mortgagors sought mortgages on six or more properties; after 1825, this declined to 1.4 per cent. Presumably, this is explicable in that over time a larger proportion of a larger population was satisfied, at least temporarily, with a single property or farm; the earlier period contained either a more financially substantial body of individuals or a greater proportion of investors. As perhaps might be expected, there was greater inequality in the number of mortgagees compared to mortgagors since the objective of the former was to secure an investment rather than the means of production. In both periods, the class "5 or more mortgagees" was much greater than the equivalent class of mortgagor. In the earlier period, mortgagees in these classes constituted 18.96 per cent of the totals; among mortgagors the figure was 7.4 per cent. In the second period, the respective figures were 6.4 and 3.5 per cent. In short, there were people both among mortgagors and mortgagees whose goal was to become something other than an Upper Canadian backwoods farmer. Indeed, some already had.

Secondary Mortgages

Gagan argues that, while Toronto Gore was not a society of chronic debtors, secondary mortgages accounted for more than 54 per cent of mortgages entered into but less than 42 per cent of the township's indebtedness in the years from 1841 to 1891. Unlike primary mortgages, which averaged 80 per cent of the value of a farm, secondary mortgages averaged 47 per cent. Kennedy reports figures of a similar order; secondary mortgages were two-thirds of all mortgages and worth half of the per-acre price of primary mortgages. Acquiring land, Gagan concludes, produced the most burdensome debts but the main cause of indebtedness was maintaining and improving a farm.[76]

The results for Essex are stark by contrast. In a sample of 261 drawn from the abstract index to deeds for which both price and acreage were available, only three mortgages were secondary; in a second sample of 129 drawn from the copy books and pertaining only to the more financially demanding years from 1847 to 1851, ten were secondary mortgages.[77] Whichever figure is used, secondary mortgaging never reached the levels of Toronto Gore. Obviously, the times were different as was the location. In this early phase of settlement, the focus in Essex was upon acquisition. The price of land was significantly lower in Essex so that the need to encumber the property a second time was less.[78]

How soon was indebtedness necessary and how long until it was discharged?

How long did it take for people to mortgage their land after purchase? Analysis of 252 mortgages suggests that mortgaging was almost immediate in most cases, and over the long term, the elapsed time until a

Table 6.3   Mortgaged price per acre, sale price in pence per acre and price as a percentage of sale

Years	Mortgaged Price per Acre		Mean as a % sale		Mean Price
	$\bar{x}$	σ	$\bar{x}$	σ	
1798–1800	319.0	15.1	100.0	n.a	346.7
1801–1805	207.7	175.7	146.7	46.4	393.7
1806–1810	171.5	103.1	122.3	37.2	184.4
1811–1815	120.0	n/a	75.0	25.0	266.7
1816–1820	686.3	945.7	71.6	38.5	332.4
1821–1825	740.6	1002.0	47.3	42.0	356.2
1826–1830	884.0	897.4	72.8	37.5	369.0
1831–1835	349.5	320.8	97.1	144.5	311.6
1836–1840	292.6	333.7	115.7	107.6	567.4
1841–1845	268.8	343.2	67.6	40.9	456.8
1846–1850	528.1	1235.3	100.7	191.9	492.4
1851–1852	519.9	836.8	155.1	239.7	n.a

Source: Calculations of the author.

mortgage was paid shortened. There were particular periods when the interval was unusually long. For the quinquennial 1801–05, the $\bar{x}$ and σ for the time before mortgaging were 4.17 and 3.08 years; for the period 1821 to 1825, this lengthened to 8.22 and 7.21 years. Overall, the respective figures were 2.31 and 4.49 years. By the quinquennial 1846–50, the average length of time had shortened to 1.56 years and 66 per cent of the cases were within one standard deviation or 4.58 years. Presumably, this occurred in response to higher purchase and capital costs in establishing a farm. In simple terms, 152 of the 252 cases took place immediately, 26 within a second year and a additional 13 within three years. Thus, almost three-quarters of the land which would be mortgaged was mortgaged within three years, a not unexpected result.[79]

How long was it until people discharged their obligations? Here one has to rely upon inferences drawn from the copy books, since it is rare for the date of discharge to be recorded in the abstracts. Inferences can be made only for a short period and for a small sample. Moreover, in a voluntary system of recording, the date of discharge frequently occurred only many years after the actual discharge; this has the effect of reducing the sample further. In this way, ninety-two mortgages were available for examination. The $\bar{x}$ for the period 1845–51 was found to be 2.96 years with a σ of 2.08 years. The median and mode were two years! Since mortgages were commonly written for two and five years and on average for 3.27 years, people in Essex completed well ahead of schedule.[80] What percentage of mortgagors failed? We shall never really know because of the practice of conveying subject to specific conditions. This totally negated the need and dangers of foreclosure, a solution that was not even available until after 1837.[81] However, examination of 129 mortgages drawn from the copy books and checked for their subsequent fate in the abstracts, suggests that failure was low. Success is here defined as completion of the mortgage within the specified time or early completion ensuring control of the resource. The fate of eighty mortgages is unknown; of the remaining forty-nine, forty-four were successful. This view is supported by the statistics on indebtedness associated with sheriffs' sales. Of the 101 sales made by the sheriff in the years from 1818 to 1851, only 15 were directly connected to a prior mortgage.[82] Of necessity, one must be cautious but it would seem that there is reason to rejoice in the ability of Essex mortgagors to redeem their property.

How indebted were people?

If this is so, what did mortgagors face? What was the extent of indebtedness? Three measures are available, namely, the price per mortgaged acre, the percentage of a transaction that had to be mortgaged (Table 6.3), and the average value of a mortgage (Table 6.4). Table 6.4 shows how the percentage mortgaged changed over time, dropping in the years of difficulty during the war and the years of depression and bad harvests that ensued. It would seem that mortgagees proceeded more cautiously in these years than at other times, although the mortgaged price per acre was at its highest then and far outstripped the price per acre being paid for land. In fact, with the exception of the decade 1806–15, the price of land continued ever upward (Table 6.3) but bore no relationship to the mortgaged price which exhibited a more cyclic pattern. As noted above, this cycle was highest in the years between 1815 and 1830, mortgaging presumably being one response to wartime and post-war difficulties. What was the average indebtedness? Table 6.4 shows it to have been about £190[83] – and going down – but declining too was the size of the mortgaged property as land regulations changed, more and more people arrived, and subdivision proceeded. Still, even when this is taken into account, the net direction was downward, especially after 1835 as the ratios of average debt to average size of mortgaged property show (Table 6.4) and as the analysis of length of time to successful termination of mortgage confirms. For the quintile 1846–50, the average debt was £158.4s.5d., low by comparison with Toronto Gore where it was the equivalent of £337.3s.7d.[84]

Table 6.4   Price of the average mortgage and size of mortgaged property

Year	Number of Mortgages	Price (£.s.d)		Property Sizes (acres)	Ratio
		$\bar{x}$	σ		
1798–1800	6	425.5.7	363.1.1	154.33	2.75
1801–1805	8	224.4.2	204.0.10	209.50	1.07
1806–1810	4	80.7.9	54.12.7	108.75	0.73
1811–1815	2	100.0.0	—	150.00	0.66
1816–1820	14	233.0.10	325.13.1	134.38	1.73
1821–1825	11	170.3.4	168.18.9	8.16	2.50
1826–1830	10	233.0.10	267.1.10	128.57	1.81
1831–1835	26	228.2.0	354.15.9	124.18	1.84
1836–1840	27	191.16.7	168.2.10	143.54	1.34
1841–1845	35	87.2.7	70.6.1	102.29	0.85
1846–1850	62	158.4.5	268.8.7	98.38	1.61
1851–1852	60	144.13.4	168.17.0	91.72	1.58

Source: Calculations of the author.

Who mortgaged and with whom?

As Table 6.2 shows, 82 people mortgaged their property in the period up to 1825; 284 thereafter. In all, 634 mortgages were negotiated; in the second period, 463. Were the mortgagors in the earlier period the same people? In fact, only 4 people acted as multiple mortgagors out of 55 and only 8 of the 58 parties who were mortgagees were the same persons. Were they the same type of person? In a society in which, compared to today, few mortgaged their land, this is an important question. An analysis of all individuals involved as one of the parties to a mortgage showed that, until 1825, eleven out of twenty major mortgagors were merchants or traders (55.0 per cent of mortgagors). They mortgaged 59.5 per cent or fifty-three of the eighty-nine mortgages negotiated by the major borrowers. Angus McIntosh, a merchant, distiller, and shipowner associated with the North-West and Miami companies, is one example. One of his transactions concerned 500 acres in Sandwich Township, mortgaged to secure £25,428.18s.0d of Lower Canadian money, a sum that apparently necessitated the involvement of mortgagees from beyond Essex.[85] So, too, is John Askin, who in 1803 mortgaged five lots in Essex totalling 1000 acres as well as his property in Detroit and Sandwich;[86] in that same year, Thomas McKee mortgaged 675 acres of Essex and 620 acres of adjoining Kent County to the Sandwich merchants Alexander Duff and James Leith.[87] As Table 6.4 shows, all three of these transactions were for acreages much greater than average. In the second period, only ten out of thirty-seven major borrowers (mortgagors) were merchants (27.0 per cent) and they negotiated a smaller percentage (27.2 per cent) of the mortgages obtained by the major borrowers. One of the trading companies, McDonnell, Holmes and Company, mortgaged as many as eighteen properties in this period. Among major lenders of three or more mortgages, the importance of the merchant class decreased in a similar way through time. Until 1825, thirteen of the twenty-seven mortgagees (48.1 per cent) of three or more properties were merchants or traders (fourteen if D. Pastorius, innkeeper, is included). In the second period, thirteen out of thirty-nine mortgagees were merchants, including, among others, the London and New York partnerships of Wildes and Pickersgill; local merchants such as T.F. Park; the Indian trader Richard Pattinson; the Amherstburg merchant and legislature councillor James Gordon, who had been John Askin's partner in Albany; Colonel Matthew Elliott, partner in the trading firm of Elliott and Caldwell; McTavish and McGillivray (merchants and fur traders); the trader George Meldrum; and William McCormick, a merchant in Colchester.[88] Before 1825, these merchants held 82 out of 129 mortgages (63.6 per cent); after 1825, the percentage was 36.9.

Lending money on mortgages would seem to have run in families. Among the major mortgagees there were three Askins, John and his sons John and Charles; three Babys, James, Francis, and Jean-Baptiste; two Elliotts; and the Park brothers. At least six mortgagors and at least seven mortgagees had been involved in the fur and Indian trades. Obviously, as opportunities for profit declined in these areas, renewed opportunities for investment were found in land.[89]

As the importance of the merchant class declined over time, so too did that of the "members of the establishment," defined here as anyone who held any office or position within the government of the day. Before 1825, seven of these people were involved in forty-one mortgages or 46.1 per cent of the cases involving three or more mortgages; after 1825, eight of these major mortgagors borrowed in 20.2 per cent of the instances. Before 1825, 60.5 per cent of the loans were made by mortgagees who were connected to government. These included Pattinson, Gordon, and Elliott, all members of the House of Assembly; JPS William Park, George Meldrum, William Duff, and George Jacobs.[90] Additionally, Meldrum was a member of the Land Board for the district, and Duff was a commissioner of customs.[91] In the second period, the proportion of mortgagees with government connections declined to 25.8 per cent. Before 1825, of the fourteen mortgagees, twelve were both merchants and members of the "establishment" and these provided 56.6 per cent of the mortgages; after

1825 eight out of ten members of the establishment group were merchants and they provided 18.4 per cent of the loans.

Did success in borrowing and lending money in the mortgage market lead to success in political life or was it vice versa? Both and neither are the conventional answers to this question. Beyond the fur traders, merchants and officeholders, few others were involved in mortgaging or mortgage lending. Among the mortgagors, there was an attorney (James Woods), a miller, a millwright, and two municipal officials; the mortgagees included that eccentric and sad attorney and entrepreneur, John Prince, lawyer James Woods, land speculator/investor A.J. Robertson, and Peter McGill, a bank president and chairman of a railway company. Interestingly, three of the individuals involved as mortgagees, John Askin, Jr, William Duff, and J.G. Watson, had all been collectors of customs in the area, a post that is held to have been lucrative and that was perhaps the source of capital.[92] There was, as might be expected, considerable overlap between those dealing in the land market itself and those prepared to lend on mortgages.[93] Also interesting is that three of the mortgagees were women: a Margaret MacDonald; Sarah Elliott, widow of Matthew Elliott; and Susan Hunt, the former Susan Caldwell, who had married Theobold "Wolfe" Hunt, nephew of General Wolfe. One presumes that all three were widows securing their future through investment in mortgages.

How many of the mortgagees were from the county itself, or alternatively, to what extent was Essex land financed by outside capital? For the years from 1847 to 1851, the copy books again provide the sample and show that fourteen individuals from as far away as Detroit, Goderich, Barrie, Toronto, and Montreal were operating in this area. In 5 of 113 instances of private lending, both mortgagor and mortgagee were from outside the county; an additional nine mortgagees were also. In other words, towards mid-century most of the private capital was still being generated from within but at a lower level than in Peel County.[94]

In the second period, a new dimension emerges: institutional as opposed to individual lending. The investment company of William Pickersgill and Company began providing loans, and so did new building societies, a British innovation that was in its early years in Canada. The first of the Canadian societies was founded in Montreal in 1845; the movement was given the protection of law with the passage of a bill in May 1846.[95] Given the exclusion of the chartered banks and savings banks from lending using mortgages as security, other building societies were soon established. Four were operating in Essex within a few years. The Chatham Building Society processed its first Essex mortgage in 1848 and three others followed in 1849. The Essex Building Society offered its first mortgage in Essex in 1850 and negotiated an additional seventeen in the next two years; similarly, the Building Society had entered into eleven mortgages by 1852, when a certain PPB Society – identity unknown – processed two mortgages. Since those societies' do not seem to have survived it is not known whether they were short-lived or more enduring although the former is presumed. An entry against the Amherstburg Building Society in the abstracts includes the names of McLeod and Menzies parenthetically;[96] the copy books indicate that the president of the Chatham Building Society was one Alexander Douglas McLean and that the president of the Essex Building Society was John Prince, later judge of the Algoma District.[97] In these years, building societies provided 21.6 per cent of the mortgages in Essex County.

Whatever the origins and structure of the building societies, they performed differently from the private market. For comparative purposes, two samples of building-society mortgaged prices and non-building-society prices were drawn, the latter from locations comparable to the former. By any measure, the sample of building-society lots exhibited greater variability and a greater range of prices than mortgages held by individuals. Moreover, the prices were generally higher, as a test of difference of means demonstrated.[98] These differences seem to suggest that lending institutions had greater confidence than individual lenders. A second measure of this difference is provided by comparison of a series of ratios contrasting the mortgaged price per acre with the actual sale value per acre for the building societies, and a group drawn to reflect comparable location and land quality. While the samples were small, the results are significant. In twelve of the sixteen cases, the building-society ratios exceeded unity, the point where sale value equalled mortgaged value; the mean ratio for this group was 2.42. In contrast, in only three of sixteen instances did the ratios for individual lenders exceed unity and the mean ratio was calculated at 0.57. The differences are striking; they point to the building societies providing funds for more than the cost of land; in three instances the transactions were urban, presumably involving urban functions and appropriate premises, such as, for example, a bakery.

When funds were loaned by individuals rather than institutions, did origin play a part as it seems to have done in the case of the purchase of land?[99] For the years 1847–50, the origins of both parties in a mortgage transaction were recorded. For a sample of 144 mortgages in the years 1847–51, the personal schedule of the Census of Canada was used to determine the origins of the parties involved. Complete data were avail-

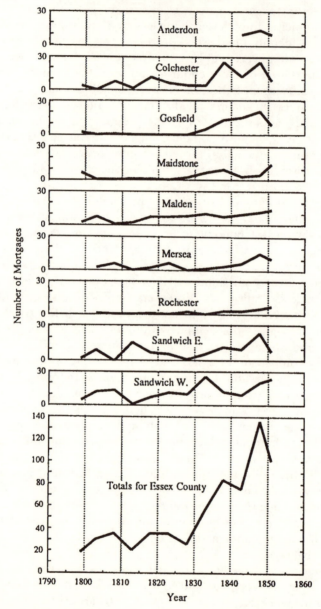

Figure 6.3   Essex County: number of mortgages by township averaged over five-year periods, 1798–1852

Source: Abstract Index to Deeds.

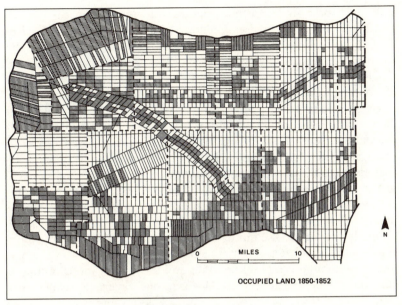

Figure 6.4   Occupied land in Essex County, 1850–52

Source: J. Clarke, "Geographical Aspects of Land Speculation."

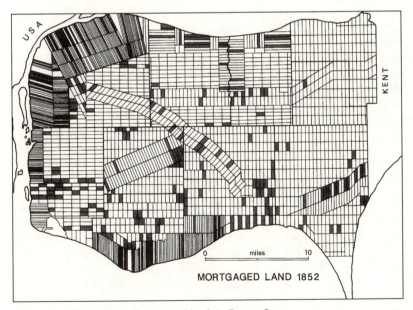

Figure 6.5   Distribution of mortgaged lands in Essex, 1852

Source: Abstract Index to Deeds.

able only for forty transactions because of omissions in the census, death, out-migration, or non-residence. Most of these involved French-Canadian (seventeen) or "English Canadian" mortgagors (ten). Of the former, the mortgagees were English (five), French Canadian (five), English Canadian (four), American (two), and Irish (one); eight of them were in Sandwich Township. Geography played a greater role than origin, it would seem; presumably, the French dealt wherever they did best, which, interestingly, was more among non-French capitalists than among their own. An additional twelve mortgages involved American mortgagees, five of them in Colchester Township. Only one of the mortgagors was American, although an unknown number of "English Canadians" may have been born of American parents. The picture is not wholly clear but it would seem possible that it was proximity and opportunity rather than affinity which assisted these transactions.

Finally, we turn to the timing and the spatial pattern of mortgaging. Sandwich and Colchester were the townships in which mortgaging was the most common in absolute terms and in which it was common in all time periods (Figure 6.3). All townships experienced increased activity after 1831, most especially in Colchester and Gosfield as the back concessions were opened up. Malden was perhaps the most steady of all. As a comparison of figures 6.4 and 6.5 shows, mortgaged land was found within the band of "occupied," that is, owned or rented land, at mid-century. However, there were areas in Anderdon Township and in the interiors of Colchester and Gosfield townships where mortgaged land did not correspond with actual settlement. In these few instances, the mortgage may have been used as a vehicle for speculation; in this way, John A. Macdonald (Plate 6.2) subsequently the first prime minister of Canada, came to control much of the land in the hinterland of what would become Essex village in northeastern Colchester. More usually, mortgaging was part of the lot of the Upper Canadian farmer!

CONCLUSION

It would seem that, in all but a few instances, mortgages using either mortgage instruments (*sensu stricto*) or "bargains and sales by way of a mortgage" were used to acquire land rather than to secure an investment, at least in this time and place. This is not in keeping with the interpretations of David Burley, Daniel Bilak, and John Weaver but they write about urban circumstances of a later period during which the transition to industrial capitalism was more marked than in Essex. Mortgaging, including vendor/purchaser agreements within that term, was most affected by the demand for land, best measured in

Plate 6.2   The future Sir John A. Macdonald looking pleased with himself. He had
just sold his Essex land in a few short years!
Courtesy of National Archives (c3813).

terms of number of sales transactions, that is, total conveyances minus
gifts, mortgages, and patents. Land was acquired in this way in no
more than 25 per cent of the cases, leading to the suggestion that
credit was usually not necessary, perhaps because land was plentiful
and prices were low. Potential settlers entering Essex had a lot of land

available to them for the price of the government "fee." Even after the institution of a sales policy in 1825, they could pay for this government land by instalments. On the better-endowed lands of the Lake Erie shore, credit was probably necessary to acquire land which commanded a premium price.

Here, as elsewhere in the county, the most common instrument used was not the formal mortgage instrument but rather the "bargain and sale by way of a mortgage." This was because it was legally less complicated than the former instrument and because capital, scarce in Upper Canada, was not required. Of course, agreements might have been reached informally, and, if so, no amount of record analysis will recover the true extent of credit. In whatever form, credit as payment over time was probably essential to disposing of land in an area where mortgagees were hard to find and where, for much of the first half of the century, adverse drainage conditions curtailed the demand for land. Yet, here as elsewhere, credit was probably necessary for both parties to the transaction.

In a recent and fascinating econometric exercise, Frank Lewis and M.C. Urquhart, using a series of simulations, show that "for a potential settler, making a farm in the absence of a well-functioning credit-market would not have been in his long-term interest."[100] A young man whose alternative income was only 30 per cent of what he might receive on a fully cleared farm would receive "insufficient compensation" over his working lifetime. This would be the case in spite of the fact that he would have had to save for thirteen years and even after starting would have to be satisfied with low consumption for an additional three years. The model assumes an economic rationale which potential settlers might not have been fully aware of, but even if they were, sources of credit were available from merchants and other individuals. Such transactions turning upon supplies of seed, farm equipment, and foodstuffs do not usually appear in the land records; nor, of course, does income generated as potash and timber or as cash from winter work.[101] Credit in the form of supplies needed to generate such income does not appear in the formal records, although, of course, details of the credit transfer of land do.

What the records do show is that in Essex, in these years, mortgaging frequency varied from 3.6 to 14.5 per cent depending upon the township. Such figures are low presumably because of the paucity of mortgage funds, the availability of land via a patenting process which permitted instalment buying, and the widespread use of legal instruments which allowed this in the private sector. The existence of such instruments may explain why there are no records of mortgage foreclosure in the land records, although, of course, this is more likely in the case of urban than rural properties and urban properties were deliberately excluded from the analysis here.[102] In the county as a whole, the number of mortgagees increased steadily between the two time periods, more than quadrupling from 57 to 235; yet the rate of credit buying per thousand people remained almost constant except towards mid-century when it began to increase. A mortgagor, in the period after 1825, had a great choice over where he might give his business in that mortgages were less concentrated in a few hands. In the earlier period, years of marked land speculation, 38.0 per cent of mortgages were in the hands of individuals who held six or more mortgages. In the second period, only 24.2 per cent were held by this class. At the other end of the continuum, 13.5 per cent of mortgages were held by mortgagees with only one mortgage before 1825, compared to 32.3 per cent later when single mortgages constituted 63.4 per cent of all mortgages. Much of this "broadening" was brought about by vendors offering purchasers mortgages as a condition of sale, but the facts are that they could afford to do so and that mortgagors in the second period had a greater choice of financiers. Effectively, this involved credit extended by the state but after 1845 Upper Canadian banks were permitted to deal in mortgages and building societies were becoming more prevalent.

The low incidence of mortgaging might also suggest that the need for a mortgage was low, given that the price of land in this area was not high. Unfortunately, there is little comparable data. In Essex at mid-century, the price of land/farm real estate was 439 pence per acre;[103] in central Wellington County, it averaged 495 pence per acre;[104] and in Toronto Gore township, it sold on average at 720 pence per acre.[105]

Those who had mortgages were able to discharge them in a very few years. This must point to their capacity to pay and perhaps their abhorrence of indebtedness. Indeed, although empirically unverifiable, this element may well have been one of the most important factors in keeping the mortgage rate low. In the period before legislation sanctioned institutional involvement in this market, all mortgages were personal transactions. This would soon diminish as banks acquired the right to secure loans with land and as building societies came into existence to ensure access to a more communal credit. As yet, the majority of mortgagees still lived within the boundaries of the county. Credit lending was primarily a local, personal business, but in spite of this there was little association with ethnicity. More and more, as population increased and as institutions were transformed, the local credit upon which Essex had hitherto depended became less significant and was gradually integrated with provincial and international markets.

Secondary mortgaging was uncommon in Essex compared to what Gagan discovered in Toronto Gore because the times, location, and economic circumstances were different. However, the fact that not all mortgages were taken out immediately (although most were within three years) might suggest that when sale and mortgage were of the same date, the goal was to secure a capital investment and not just the land itself. Most conveyances involved cash and were immediate. Examination of 488 cases stratified through time showed that *none* of these instruments contained conditional agreements permitting payment on time or interest. This was the dominant form. Most people in Essex got land from the state or could afford to pay for it in the re-sale market.

Where credit was involved in land purchases, most discharged their obligations within two years. The average debt was about 47 per cent of what it was in Peel in the same period. Merchants were significant as mortgagors and mortgagees[106] both before and after 1825. Askin was involved in ten, as was Thomas McKee; the Park brothers loaned on seventeen; and the biggest mortgagee of all was Richard Pattinson, who advanced money on twenty-three mortgages. In fact, Pattinson loaned money on almost anything; when he died, he owned 14,869 acres in the Western District and his estate listed 435 debtors whose qualities were described as "good," "doubtful," and "bad."[107] Like "members of the establishment," merchant lenders were a declining element. In geographical terms, mortgaging was a normal accompaniment of settlement, although mortgaged land preceded actual residence in a few instances.

7 Who Were the Speculators and How Extensive Was Speculation?

INTRODUCTION

The purpose here is to identify the speculators operating in Essex and by so doing determine the extent of speculation. Two routes are used to this end: a simple summation of the acreage held by each individual, and an inference drawn by reconstructing the tenure status of each lot in 1825 and again in 1851–52. Both measures establish possible limits to the extent of a phenomenon which, if symptomatic of Upper Canada and not just Essex, was, by any measure, remarkable.

The method used is systematic in that the activity of every individual who ever owned, or at least registered, land was examined for possible inclusion on the list of speculators. Using a scale criterion and a number of behaviourial indicators, a typology of players in the emerging land market is produced. It is used, in conjunction with the written record, to examine the activities of individuals and of groups whose characteristics they shared.

The chapter begins with a review of the historical record to describe the nature and extent of speculation in Essex and elsewhere, describes the characteristics of subgroups or classes of speculators, and ends with measures of the amount of speculation in the county as well as with its spatial impact in Essex.

The settlement of Crown land was perhaps the most important problem that faced the government of Upper Canada in the early years. The government was forced to sail a course between Scylla and Charybdis, since on the one hand it sought to see Upper Canada effectively settled, and on the other hand it was obliged to use land as payment for services and Revolutionary War losses. As Johnson has shown, many who received land in this way viewed it not as the means to an agricultural life but rather as unrealized capital, from which they hoped to gain at some distant date when profits could be maximized.[1] As was seen earlier, this was certainly the case in Essex. Here, from the beginning, individuals began accumulating large amounts of land on Indian grants and actively sought to discourage settlement, presumably so that they could continue to accumulate.

Within the literature pertaining to Upper Canada, there is a minor controversy on the routes to the identification of land speculators; the precise nature of this controversy is perhaps relatively unimportant but its implications are far-reaching since its resolution probably determines the extent and nature of the phenomenon.

That land speculation took place, given the operation of laissez-faire capitalism, can simply be assumed a priori. In fact, the phenomenon was identified and its worst effects decried by contemporaries.[2] One person who remarked upon it was McNiff in 1791, although he too engaged in it.[3] In July 1795 Colonel England, the commandant at Detroit, reported to Simcoe in circumspect terms that "land-jobbing seems to be the rage at present" and went on to report how the "adventurers" had set out for the meeting at Greenville to have their acquisitions ratified by the American general Anthony Wayne.[4]

Matthew Elliott reported to Colonel McKee that "a parcel of land Jobbers" had deliberately kept the Indians intoxicated so as to prevent their meeting with Joseph Brant. They had been successful and Brant had returned. Elliott was prepared to name those who had gone to Wayne's meeting – "the Principle are John Askin Jun, J Beaubien and young Beaufit."[5] Worse still, from the British perspective, was that "many on this occasion have shewn their want of attachment to the interests of Great Britain, and some of them servants to Government." Among these was the notary Askwith, who was "an intimate of that infamous fellow, Mr. McNiff."[6] Brant's concern, expressed in a letter to his confidante John Butler, with whom he had served in the Revolutionary War, was understandably different in tone and perspective:

There is a swarm of Land Jobbers at Detroit I mean the Kings Subjects buying lands from the Lake Indians, giving them rum which made those Indians continually drunk and not doing any business with them, many of these Land Jobbers are now gone with the Indians to Wayne with their Deeds to get them confirmed by him, and a great many other old Deeds besides the new ones are also sent as I was told. The first people at Detroit are the Chief Traders in this Land Affair, Sir you see the poor Indians must lose their Country at all Events

– Colonel England cannot interfere with the people of Detroit. Colonel Mckee is gone from there so the Indians are entirely left to themselves.[7]

Quite who these "first people" were is not clear, although the comment recalls the accusations about the members of the Land Board. However, so great was the speculators' momentum that they sought to call a council of the different Indian nations, a prerogative hitherto reserved to government.[8] In an atmosphere of mounting excitement and of danger of war between the Americans and the British, Prideaux Selby wrote to the Secretary of Indian affairs in April 1796:

The Indians are at present very numerous in this Town owing to the Land Jobbers sending them speeches of invitation in order to obtain sales of the Indian Country, some Millions of acres have been sold to them for little more than a keg of Rum, but the Misfortune does not end there, for their clamours for provisions must in some measure be complied with – and unless some strong steps are taken to prevent the traders from holding Councils and Calling the Indians together whenever they have formed a scheme to defraud them, the Indians of their lands, we can expect nothing but uproar, Confusion and Expense.[9]

Such was the extent of the uproar and of concern with the political repercussions of the actions of speculators that it engaged the attention of Simcoe.[10] The lieutenant governor was anxious to preserve the improved relations with the United States following the conclusion of Jay's Treaty in 1794 and Britain's evacuation of the posts ceded to the United States. He sought to avoid conflict from any source, including land speculators. The particular event that made Simcoe anxious in 1796 was the examination by Congress of two land jobbers, Charles Whitney of Vermont and Robert Randal of Philadelphia. These men were partners with John Askin, Jr and Sr, William and David Robertson, Robert Jones, and Richard Pattinson of Detroit, which at this time still lay within British territory. Whitney and Randall had declared that they possessed enough influence with the Indians to obtain a vast tract of land in Michigan, where the young United States had ambitions. Randall had been arrested for attempting to bribe members of the House of Representatives. There was considerable danger here, in the testy circumstances of 1796, and it moved Simcoe to communicate with the King's consul general at Philadelphia. Simcoe believed that "this Government is not answerable for the expressions of individuals, nor does it seem practical to coerce a liberty of speech which breaks not out into action; but I can easily conceive that the language of these jobbers may be detrimental to that harmony which I trust will daily increase between the two countries, and gradually improve into the most cordial confidence and alliance."[11] The danger of this particular controversy, which involved almost twenty million acres, was allayed, but it does point to the extent and consequence of land speculation in Detroit and its immediate hinterland.

With the British withdrawal from Detroit, the nature of the threat posed by land speculation changed, although the problem remained. Peter Russell, who became administrator of Upper Canada in 1796, after Simcoe's departure for England, was acutely aware of this. Russell's predisposition towards personal benefit is well known.[13] Indeed, he confessed an inability to control speculators and land jobbers[12] even as he claimed virtue in requiring a half fee when land was transferred from privileged grantees to others, including known speculators. Otherwise the state would have had to pay for the issue of deeds taken out in the names of the original grantees. In this way, he was, of course, acknowledging and permitting the action of speculators while personally enjoying a portion of the fee which would flow to the treasury, although he presented it as a savings accruing to the public. Russell put his case this way:

The Council and myself are exceedingly happy that your Grace appears to approve of the Steps we have taken to get rid of the pernicious System of settling the Waste lands of the Crown by appropriating large Tracts to associated Companies, and our determination to proceed in future in making Grants to Individuals only. But even in the latter Case it has not always been in our Power to counteract the Schemes of Speculators and land Jobbers who are constantly practicing a thousand different arts to evade our Vigilance – particularly by purchasing the rights & claims of U.E. Loyalists and Military Claimants to whom the faith of Government has been pledged for Specifick quantities of land – The transfers of which to bona fide Purchasers having been permitted by the Land Boards under the Sanction of Lord Dorchester's Regulations cannot be annulled. We have contrived however to draw advantage from this Evil by obliging those who ask Deeds for such Transfers in their own Names to pay the half Fee for each Right so transferred, which would have fallen on the Treasury had the Deeds been taken out in the Names of the original grantees – by which Means a considerable saving may accrue to the public.[14]

Russell favoured the sales policy proposed by the governor-in-chief, Robert Prescott, and offered his advice on its implementation, seeking to guard against abuse by speculators. There was little need because by 1798 Prescott was in conflict with members of his own governing council, whom he suspected of using their official positions to acquire large tracts of land for themselves.[15] Like Russell, he believed in a deposit (one eight of the price) such "that we do not think any man ought to offer himself a candidate for purchase of the Waste lands who cannot command it. Those persons who have that presumption are speculators only who depend wholly upon their subsequent sales for their payments, which if they should fail in, you will hear no more of them. Five Years we also think are ample to accommodate the Convenience of Men of real property, who are the kind of settlers we should principally wish to introduce into these provinces by Purchase."[16] Robert Gourlay, banished from the colony in 1818 for his "radical" views, identified land speculation as a major cause of instability and political agitation.[17] Susannah Moodie wrote evocatively of the results of speculator activity, addressing the deliberately invisible directly: "O ye dealers in wild lands – ye speculators in the folly and credulity of your fellowmen – what a mass of misery and of misrepresentation productive of that misery have ye not to answer for."[18]

Fred Landon, citing contemporary evidence, claimed that Upper Canada became a paradise for speculators who were able to enlist the help of civil servants at York.[19] Indeed, when the government departments were investigated after the Rebellion of 1837, the Surveyor General's office was castigated for a "system of partiality, favouritism and corruption" which had begun early in its operation and continued thereafter.[20] If favouritism was a factor, so too was the existence of credit. Patrick Shirreff described the extent of speculation in Upper Canada in 1833 and tied it to the ready availability of credit:

Much land is held by absentee proprietors, or the members of the party who sway the councils of the province. It is commonly in the hands of agents empowered to sell. The prices are generally higher than crown lands and credit unlimited ... There is never any hesitation in selling to a man without capital, as the rights are withheld. Every tree which is cut down enhances the value of the property which is unproductive while they are standing. When a settler absconds after some years residence, a case by no means rare, the proprietor derives great advantage from its operations ... In almost every district people are found anxious to sell land, and small farms may be bought on cheaper terms than land belonging to the Crown, Canada Company, or large proprietors, more especially if cash is paid. Indeed the necessities of many people are so urgent, and credit so general, that an individual with cash in his pocket may drive a good bargain at all times ... The whole system of settling land in Canada has been bad for many years.[21]

In 1839 Charles Rankin, chief agent for immigration in Upper Canada, who was familiar with Essex and the Western District from his days as a surveyor, remarked on the dire consequences of speculation from the perspective of settlement in the colony as a whole: "These blocks of wild land place the actual settler in an almost hopeless condition; he can hardly expect during his lifetime, to see his neighbourhood contain a population sufficiently dense to support mills, schools, post-offices, places of worship, markets or shops, and without these civilisation, retrogrades. Roads under such circumstances can neither be opened by the settlers nor kept in proper repair, even if made by the government."[22] Additionally, modern historians have documented the prevalence of the phenomenon, and one, Lillian Gates, has suggested that, by 1825, 62 per cent of the land granted in the province to that date was in the hands of speculators.[23]

The problem is not to convince people of the existence of speculation, then, but to find a means of identifying speculators within particular areas so that a series of questions can be answered in this and subsequent chapters. How did speculators behave with respect to the changing economy? Did these individuals make a profit on their investment? Were they all looking for the same thing? Were they aware of differences in the physical environment? Did they belong to discrete groups with distinct behavioural patterns or were they simply groups of opportunists willing to invest in that which appeared lucrative?

ORIGINS AND NATURE OF LAND SPECULATION

The origins of land speculation are ancient but extensive land speculation was most marked during the nineteenth century[24] when the physiocrats argued that land was the only source of wealth and the key to rapid economic development.[25] Indeed, as J.K. Galbraith notes, until the Industrial Revolution all economics were agricultural economics. With industrialization, land had to be turned into a commodity owned by those impelled by self-interest and profit.[26] Opportunities existed in Europe and its colonies overseas during the nineteenth and twentieth centuries,[27] but Europeans were also content to "share the whiteman's burden" and impose their values on subject peoples of markedly different cultural backgrounds.[28]

In Australia, New Zealand, and the United States, early settlement was accompanied by land speculation which often ran ahead of the settled area. Writing of pre-revolutionary British North America, the American historian Bernard Bailyn sees land speculation as everyone's work, not just the initiative of the few, "for it was a natural and rational response to two fundamental facts of American life: the extraordinary low ratio of people to arable land, and the strong likelihood that the ratio would change quickly and radically as the population grew."[29] In North America as a whole, the conflict between European and native values with respect to land was marked and often bloody, although the Upper Canadian experience is at variance with the statement.[30] In Upper Canada, speculation could occur because of a government policy that rewarded the faithful with large quantities of land and that after 1825 instituted land sales.

The very term land speculator is emotive and the image of the land speculator is not very pure.[31] The social advantages and disadvantages of the "speculator," "jobber," "absentee owner," or, to use the contemporary term, "developer," is something that is as much debated today as it was in the past.[32] Yet, as L.C. Gray has pointed out, speculation is a part of the larger issue of the advantages and disadvantages of private property in land and capitalism as a whole.[33] In the rural context, prospects of a speculative profit have stimulated pioneer settlement, mineral prospecting, and exploration. Numerous pioneers might never have succeeded but for the credit facilities of the speculator. In Upper Canada, D'Arcy Boulton recognized the role of speculation in agricultural development.[34] On the other hand, the same process has resulted in an extended farming frontier when rising land prices have stimulated the occupation of submarginal lands later abandoned. Again, rising land values and concomitant taxation out of all proportion to potential farm income have often resulted in depressed agriculture, an increased amount of mortgage indebtedness, and an increase in farm tenancy.[35] The question is therefore not a simple one, since it strikes at the very heart and experience of traditional Western society. Land speculation, and speculation in general, was and is part of our social structure and only its excessive manifestations are deplored.[36]

Raleigh Barlowe, a student of land economics, has defined land speculation as "the holding of land resources, usually in something less than their highest and best use, with primary managerial emphasis on resale at a capital gain rather than on profitable use in current production."[37] Advisedly, Barlowe speaks of "primary managerial emphasis" because, as a group, economists have sought to distinguish philosophically between the investor in land and the speculator in land, the distinction being one of emphasis. The former acquires land as a factor in production, the latter in hope of profiting from an increase in its value. In practice, however, the investor must often assume risks of changing values and the speculator may have to engage as a producer in the development of a property as a condition of ownership or to promote the increase of value sought.

Initially, an individual may be moved by both objectives. The distinction is therefore not a sharp line but a broad zone,[38] a fact that, at least in the American experience, was recognized by the pioneers who included within the term not only the absentee landowner of agricultural land but also the dealer in timberland, the corporate speculator, the moneylender, the purchaser of town lots, and the renter of farms in shares.[39] This has inevitably led to a discussion of typologies, not all of which agree with one another or are meaningful in particular places at particular times. One has been offered here; none has been so broad as the definition of Horace Greeley, nineteenth-century editor of the New York *Tribune* and a long-time land reformer, who argued that a speculator was "anyone who had purchased raw land with no intent to farm it or who acquired more land than he could expect to develop."[40] Under such a definition, almost everyone, even those who simply wished to farm, qualified as speculators.

Since, in the final analysis, a land speculator can be considered as someone who owns ten acres or ten thousand acres, motivation is the crucial element in the identification of a speculator.[41] It is, however, a condition of the business that few are willing to own up to the title, though some will accept the less pejorative "developer." In the case of nineteenth-century Essex County, the Buell Papers in the Archives of Ontario provide some limited insights into the secretive nature and extent of speculation.[42] On 2 December 1853 Alexander Cameron, lawyer and businessman,[43] wrote to his father-in-law, Andrew Norton Buell,[44] that he did not think he would accept an offer of five thousand acres because "the newspapers are making a free use of my name and I think they might employ their talents to a better purpose."[45] In Essex, Cameron intended to purchase 15,000 acres, a speculation whose worth he had confirmed by the interest of one of Upper Canada's most heavily capitalized speculators, Thomas Clark Street of Niagara (Plate 7.1).[46]

I wrote to John Bell offering the lands in Mersea and Gosfield at nine shillings per acre. I also wrote to three other persons upon the subject. Mr — has not returned from Montreal but as soon as he does I shall finally decide what quantity of land we shall take up and the course to pursue. I think if we want the lands at all it will be much better to take them at the regular prices which about averages 7/6 rather than have them put up at auction. I feel perfect confidence in the scheme. I have the best assurance that if these lands are put up for public competition that Street of Niagara will buy every acre good and bad and give 10/. I myself am convinced that every acre in this Western County will be worth $10 in the course of ten years. Now with this conviction I am loathe to abandon any portion of these lands. The whole amount of the first instalment fee for the 15,000 acres in this county will not amount to more than £550 or £600.[47]

Plate 7.1 Thomas Clark Street left an estate of $3 to $4 million, earned in commerce, mortgage lending, and land speculation.
Courtesy of Toronto Reference Library (JRR1280, T17055).

Ten dollars was the equivalent of 50 shillings or 480 pence – a long way from the purchase price of 90 pence! Four years later, having made purchases at land sales in Windsor, Chatham, and Sandwich, Cameron could write: "I shall add this year nearly 10,000 acres to my present stock and then I will close the business and retire on my lands."[48]

IDENTIFYING LAND SPECULATORS

Where the researcher has access to material such as the Buell Papers or the even more voluminous Askin Papers,[49] a judgment can be made regarding motive. In the absence of such records, one has to rely upon inference. If land speculation lies along an economic and acreage or size continuum, the task is to trace this empirically, to identify types and their associated qualities.

The earliest answers, offered in the work of Clarke, Brunger, and Gagan, relied on a scale approach. Understandably, there was not complete agreement upon the entry level to the class "speculator," Clarke employing a "cut-off" of 400 acres,[50] Brunger[51] and Gagan one of 500 acres.[52] Widdis's contribution to the Upper Canadian literature was to stress the importance of motivation, although even he, in seeking a method that recognized speculation at all scales, proposed a 400-acre criterion.[53] Other researchers, wishing to allow for accumulation by family members, suggest raising the barrier to 1000 acres.[54] All of these figures are, of course, arbitrary. Of themselves, they have no particular validity. How could they since even those who directed the Upper Canadian land system were unsure of the level appropriate to sustaining agriculture and limiting speculation? In 1798 the Duke of Portland, writing to Governor Prescott, suggested that "the most effectual way of guarding against speculators and land jobbers who have no intention to settle or cultivate will be to dispose of the lands in allotments not exceeding 5 or 600 acres at the most." For his part, Prescott believed that lots should not "exceed 5 or 600 or at most 10 or 12000 acres."[55] From a pragmatic point of view, as Figure 7.1 shows, use of any indicator other than Prescott's upper limit provides a manageable sample permitting discussion, although not complete conviction that all so identified were in fact speculators.

The earliest work conducted in this manner was univariate and based upon examination of a single source, the patent data; this was a limiting condition that did not permit analysis of behaviour based upon not one but a series of events. That envisaged by Widdis and others correctly claimed that complete identification required the use of a number of variables – among them, profit, length of time between purchase and subsequent transaction, acreage held, acreage cleared, tenure conditions, participation in land sales, and capitalization – and recognized that these might have to shift from region to region because of the incompleteness of the extant data.[56]

In Widdis's instance, because of the availability of the assessment rolls at regular intervals, he was able to employ a combination of cultivated acreage with absolute acreage held. Using these variables in conjunction with a ranking procedure, he sought to distinguish large and small speculators and produced a typology that recognized two main elements. The first of these was designated the *Classical Speculator* and was characterized as a non-resident with large but poorly developed acreage which over time was disposed of; the second was the *Land Banker*, dealing in land as some might deal in stocks and bonds and either clearing or at least acquiring lots with considerable cleared acreage since cleared acreage and concomitant return was the primary objective. This would seem to approach the first of the classes in the typology developed by Bill Shannon. From the land records of thirteen individuals Shannon recognizes three classes, the *Land Broker*, the *Investor*, and the "quick-flipper" or *Speculator*.

The land broker, of whom there is only one (and it is therefore difficult to generalize), seems to have operated not for the settlers but for himself and for other large landowners. He was aware of his inventory of "stock" and employed an agent. The "investors," characterized by selected transactions of four individuals, purchased land early and held on for a long period of time (34.3 years on average), producing a low annual rate of return.[57] They resemble the "classical speculators" in the Widdis scheme, although the terminology is obviously different. In contradistinction, the land flippers or "true speculators," in the Shannon scheme, held their land for only 8.25 years on average but were able to dispose of it quickly because they bought in a rising market. Unlike the "investors" who did not discriminate, Shannon believes that this group selected land which had the highest potential for profit, that is, mill sites and town sites.[58] In essence, although the variables used to define the classes are different, as are the labels used, there is considerable overlap. Are these the classes one is to expect from an empirical examination of land holdings in Essex?

Defining the Speculators: The Data and the Method

In an ideal research design, one might examine every land transaction ever made in Essex and simply classify individuals according to the extent of their speculative activity. The task, which would be overwhelming, would obviate the need for operational definitions of speculators in the manner employed by Clarke, Brunger, Gagan, and others. Some variables might appear more diagnostic than others given that motive is the primary differentiator of speculator, settler, and investor. Of itself, scale is not the sole determinant; but it is important, especially in a work emphasizing power and economic influence. Moreover, since profit is something that all speculators seek, it is hardly prescriptive since many may fail to obtain it. Again, given the records for Essex, the variable is not readily available. Nor are data on acreage of land cultivated continuously available. If they were, some case could be made for their inclusion. Such an argument might be based upon the stereotypical image of the speculator as one holding on to an unimproved acreage. However, as noted earlier, there may well be instances and circumstances when the speculator must become an investor. More significant is the amount of time during which a property was held, especially if one follows Shannon in conceiving of speculation as a short-term process.[59] Equally significant is the number of transactions. This variable is not only available, like all others from the abstract index to deeds, but it can be qualified by the instruments by which property was obtained, that is, patent, bargain and sale, indenture, gift, mortgage, and sheriff's deed. In this way the methodology assumes an appropriate behaviourial form and it is possible to distinguish speculators taking advantage of colonial land policy (for example, the patents) from those operating within the market economy. Such an approach, combining number of transactions with length of time in the market and total acreage owned at some point in time, should permit examination of points on the speculator/investor continuum, including the mechanisms used.

These variables were derived in the following manner. The abstract index to deeds was searched to determine exactly who owned property in Essex between 1788 and 1852. The work was incredibly time-consuming since it involved following every recorded legal transaction which took place in rural Essex in this period. A decision was made to examine the acreage owned and the name of the owner at each of two cross-sections, 1825 and 1851–52. Though it was not possible to identify all the owners (especially in the French-Canadian areas, where illegibility was a greater problem than elsewhere), 478 and 1604 owners were enumerated in 1825 and 1852 respectively,[60] together with the acreage owned. The method is systematic in that everyone who registered a piece of property could be included in the analysis. However, the data set was limited to those who possessed 400 acres at one or other cross-section, or to what was gauged, in the absence of precise reporting, to be its equivalent, that is, three properties of an unspecified acreage. The reason for limiting it in this way was that, following identification of the individual, the data set had to be re-entered in order to establish the nature of the instruments used, the length of time land was held, and the sum of money involved. In short, the manual nature of this operation and the length of the period being studied demanded that limits be placed on the search. Four hundred acres was a practical datum for limiting the search and it was uncommon in Essex, as Figure 7.1 shows. It was in fact more land than could be dealt with by an individual in a lifetime, although, of course, several generations of the same family might rejoice in the astuteness of its progenitor in acquiring such an amount. At the other end of the continuum, there must have been individuals, most especially in an urban context, who speculated on a few acres. However, the focus of this book is upon rural land and the social consequences of control of a few acres would not usually be as marked as that which stemmed from control of hundreds or even thousands of acres. Yet the records do not always permit precise identification of acreage.

The three-properties limit, or three transactions "in lieu of" or in addition to acreage per se, ensured the inclusion of genuine players in the market. For example, appendix 7.1, which lists those identified as speculators, includes a number of individuals whose acreage alone would not justify their inclusion in a list of speculators. William Duperon Baby is a case in point. He is shown to have owned only 108 acres in 1852, although he also held two properties of unspecified acreage. He was included because he engaged in eleven transactions. Similarly, Francis Baby might not have been included because he owned only 150 acres in 1825 and 225 in 1852, but, significantly, he was involved in thirty transactions. The same is true of three individuals who epitomized the Family Compact and who operated as a group, John Strachan, William Allan, and John Beverley Robinson. The group did not meet the acreage requirement in either category but had twenty-four transactions and so was included too. John Cowan falls into this category as well, although the number of his transactions is closer to the critical limit. Roswell Mount, the surveyor, with zero acres held in either period but thirty-two transactions, is another case.

The acreage presented in Appendix 7.1 has to be interpreted as minimal because the record of many individuals included properties of unknown size. Most usually, such acreage could not be "corrected." Occasionally, it was possible to adjust the acreage, using internal evidence within the abstract index to deeds or other sources. This point can be illustrated in the case of Edward ("Bear") Ellice. The records show that Ellice had acquired 547 acres in Essex by 1825; thereafter, he obtained another 58 acres. By 1852, these same records show that he had sold 1947 acres, more than he owned. This seems an untenable proposition until it is realized that he had also acquired twenty-seven properties in the earlier period. Clearly, he owned a much larger acreage than is recorded here. It was possible in this instance to adjust the figures and Appendix 7.1 shows him owning 3200 acres in 1852. Scale alone is not enough to identify a speculator because there are thirty-one instances in Appendix 7.1 where no acreage could be determined for both 1825 and 1852 but the number of transactions was

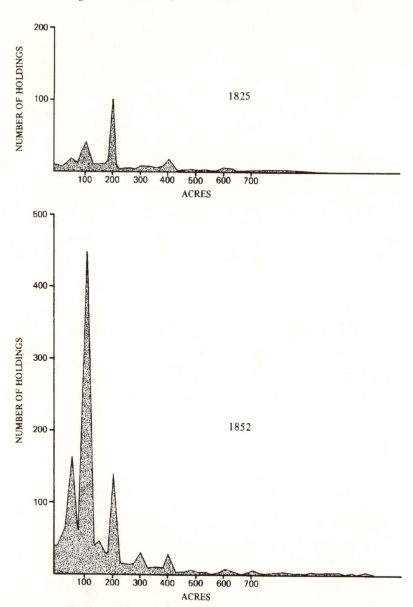

Figure 7.1   Size of holdings: Essex county (excluding Sandwich), 1825 and 1852
Source: Abstract Index to Deeds, Essex County.

high. The merchant C.C. Allen, who engaged in thirty-five transactions, is a case in point. Others genuinely had no acreage because they had successfully unloaded it, had died, or were active in the business in only one of the two periods.

Initially there were 175 potential speculators. However, because of failure to meet the criteria of acreage (or its surrogates, additional properties or number of transactions) and the requirement that most transactions be beyond the family, thirty-one individuals were removed. For the remaining 144 individuals who met the criteria, the following variables were collected or derived: the legal instrument used in the transaction; the length of time between acquisition and disposal; the acreage assembled during these years; the acreage disposed of in these same years, which was included as an indication of intent or at least opportunity; the total acreage owned in 1825 and at mid-century; and the total number of transactions. With respect to the first variable, a "patent" was considered different from a "bargain and sale," "indenture," or "deed." A patent is a manifestation of colonial land policy, a bargain and sale is an instrument of conveyance, and the last two, depending upon context, can be indicators of genuine sales in the market economy. An agreement of bargain and sale between family members for the legally required sum of five shillings is hardly indicative of a commercial transaction; an indenture or deed following quickly after an acquisition by bargain and sale and for a reduced sum of money is probably a mortgage. Instruments such as gifts and leases were ignored for purposes of analysis but sheriffs' deeds were retained in the data set since they indicate a mechanism by which land was obtained.[61] In the actual analysis, each instrument was calculated as a percentage of all commercial transactions.

The instruments of variable one were expressed as percentages of total commercial transactions for purposes of standardization. Deeds, bargains and sales, and indentures were combined in one group of instruments that reflect the operation of the market. Patenting and mortgaging were treated as separate entities. In the case of the patent, this was a manifestation of government policy; in the case of the latter, it is not known if title was actually conveyed or indeed what the exact purpose of the mortgage was. All such instruments were treated separately as qualities of the groups defined rather than as defining variables. So was "non-residency," held by some to be a defining variable. Given a perspective which acknowledges that, in the culture and economy of the time, all those possessing more than is necessary to sustain life are speculators, this is permissible. Non-residency may be an indicator of speculation but is not, in this view, a requirement. Not all would agree.[62]

Even though the instrument "gift" had been removed from the data set, there were several instances where conveyancing took place between members of the same family. In some instances, these transactions were qualified by such terms as "in love and affection"; in others, the remarks column would simply say five shillings (5/- or 60 pence), the legal fee for a transaction but hardly an indicator of a real monetary transaction. These were removed. Among the remaining "within family transactions," the decision was taken to drop them from the data set where their frequency exceeded 25 per cent of all transactions. Fourteen individuals were removed because of this "rule." These included seven members of the Wigle family. Two of the three, J. Wigle, father and son, had sixty-seven transactions to 1852 but twenty-four were within the family. Wendel Wigle conducted twenty-eight transactions but again ten were with members of his family and he was excluded. Similarly, Charles Askin, who is shown in appendix 7.3 to have been among the most prominent, was excluded from the list of speculators because eleven of his twenty-seven transactions were within the Askin family.[63]

The remaining observations were analysed using length of time between acquisition and disposal, total number of transactions, and total acreage accumulated at the end of the period in a hierarchical cluster analysis. This placed the data into groups iteratively and by a process of agglomeration. It is worth stressing that the algorithm used observations on people who owned at least 400 acres at some time during the period up to 1852. Added stipulations included the requirement that the number of transactions exceeded three and that, as noted above, no more than 25 per cent of the transactions were within the family, a stipulation that may have diminished the possibility of selecting French Canadians.[64] Of the 144 cases selected in this way, only 70 were active in 1825 and only 100 in 1852. This is in fact only a portion of those who initially met the scale criterion. In 1825 there were 93 known owners of more than 400 acres and in 1852 there were 135. The actual variables used in defining the groups were the acreage owned in 1852 – that is, the acreage acquired minus the acreage disposed of – the number of transactions in which the individual was involved, and the length of time between acquisition and sale. Other variables, for example, the legal instruments used, were considered qualities of the groups.

At the outset, the procedure considered the number of groups as being equal to the number of observations; at each subsequent step the number of groups was reduced until, ultimately, all observations were contained within a single cluster. Membership in the groups was determined on the basis of a distance matrix of similarity, the particular measure being a distance coefficient; observations with the largest similarity were merged first. At a critical level, indicated by a

Table 7.1   Characteristics of the speculative groups with respect to time held, acreage in 1852, and number of transactions

Sub-Group	Time Held (Years) $\bar{x}$	σ	Acreage Owned in 1852 $\bar{x}$	σ	Number of Transactions $\bar{x}$	σ	n
Cluster 1	7.8	5.5	303.7	312.0	19.5	13.8	124
Cluster 2	3.4	–	523.5	–	188.0	–	1
Cluster 3	8.7	9.1	1802.0	613.8	118.5	13.4	2
Cluster 4	17.0	9.2	2299.9	604.1	40.9	24.2	7
Cluster 5	29.9	5.2	364.9	570.0	20.5	22.0	8
Cluster 6	8.6	3.6	0.0	–	95.0	29.7	2
Total	9.5	7.8	422.2	575.9	24.2	25.2	144

Source: Calculations of the author.

Table 7.2   Characteristics of the speculative groups with respect to legal instruments of acquisition

Sub–Group	Patents Percentage $\bar{x}$	σ	Bargain and Sale Percentage $\bar{x}$	σ	Sheriff's Deed Percentage $\bar{x}$	σ	Mortgages Percentage $\bar{x}$	σ	n
Cluster 1	12.54	16.78	72.37	21.30	2.09	7.48	2.6	3.7	124
Cluster 2	39.89	–	54.79	–	–	–	10.0	–	1
Cluster 3	34.19	44.46	61.22	37.97	0.46	0.65	4.0	5.7	2
Cluster 4	8.13	13.65	75.94	30.67	11.39	28.10	1.4	2.3	7
Cluster 5	32.79	37.86	60.36	34.70	–	–	2.6	3.9	8
Cluster 6	0.43	0.61	69.93	7.17	–	–	24.5	2.1	2
Total	13.77	19.24	71.48	22.60	2.36	9.26	2.9	4.5	144

Source: Calculations of the author.

marked change in the distance coefficients (Figure 7.2), an optimum number of relatively homogeneous clusters emerged. In this study the number was six; their characteristics are outlined on Table 7.1 and associated qualities on Table 7.2. The names of those included within particular groups appears in Appendix 7.2. The qualities of the groups were then examined in terms of their awareness of the physical environment and the legal instruments they used to acquire land.

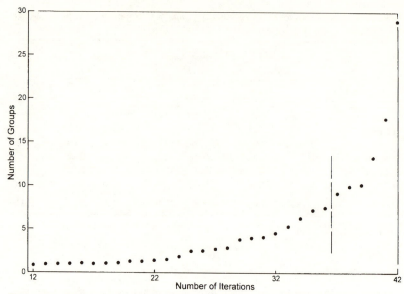

Figure 7.2   Plot of relationship between number of clusters and interative procedure: critical value indicated by dashed line

Source: Calculations of the author.

RESULTS: THE NATURE OF THE CLUSTERS

Cluster 1, constituting the majority of speculators, was a group that, as a group, held less land than the average speculator at mid-century (303.7 acres compared to an overall average of at least 422.2 acres).[65] In fact, there was, as is only to be expected, considerable variation within the group. Twenty individuals owned 600 or more acres in 1852, down from the twenty-four who met this criterion in 1825; four, including Charles Baby (1626 acres), Jean-Baptist Baby (1124 acres), Hercules or Hannibal Burwell (1240 acres), and the estate of Thomas Clark (1000 acres) owned substantially more (Appendix 7.1). Thirty-seven individuals, allowing for the inexactitude in the measurement of the final acreage, seem to have reduced their holdings in 1851 to zero acres. Among them was Prideaux Girty who disposed of the 1139 acres he had acquired, one year before his death in 1853. In fact, it was often their estates that had sold their property; thirteen of those with zero acreage are known to have been dead in 1852.[66] Others may well have been.

Among those who would otherwise appear unnoteworthy by the acreage they held in 1852, was C.C. Allen, who had actually acquired

1149 acres in the second period ending in 1852. The same status would apply to a number of others, such as William Berczy, who still, in 1852, owned 507 acres of the 1307 he had acquired after 1825! If this was the elder Berczy, he had been dead for thirty-nine years! More likely this entry in the land records refers to the son of Von Moll Berczy, the painter, William Bent Berczy. Alternatively, this may indeed have been the estate of the older Berczy; it may say something about the propensity of registrar's clerks to enter not "the estate of" some individual but rather the name of the individual, saving time and money. It may also say something about the speed of legal probate and the fact that the effect of probate need not appear in subsequent transactions until many years afterwards. Yet there are also grounds to think that estates can and could be kept open for many years by various legal devices.[67] One presumes that there were benefits to be gained from such practice in nineteenth-century Canada, just as there are most obviously now. This may explain why Thomas McKee, who died in 1814, might still own 984 acres in 1852. It might answer the puzzle of how Thomas Clark would still possess 1000 acres of Essex after, one presumes, securing a less earthly paradise in 1835! This pattern occurred among other groups; at least eight within the four remaining groups continued to convey after their deaths.

This first group engaged in less dealing than speculators as an overall group, averaging 19.5 transactions,[68] and was in the market for a relatively few years, as were groups three and six.[69] The $\bar{x}$ length of time between acquisition and sale was 7.8 years with a σ of 5.5 years, indicating that 68.26 per cent of the transactions took no more than 13.3 years. Cluster 1, although not different in a statistical sense, patented less than the group as a whole and specific groups.[70] This group of people was not significantly different than all others with respect to acquisition by sale[71] or by their involvement with the mortgage market.[72] As the largest group, they encompassed a variety of experiences. If the average number of transactions was 24.2, those with more than 35 transactions included some well-known individuals, such as Charles Baby (61); Jean-Baptist Baby (36); John Gowie Watson (63); Thomas McKee (52); the merchants William McCormick (44), Angus McIntosh (53), the Park brothers (77), the Duffs (93), Matthew Elliott (37);[73] and John Fulmer (40). The entrepreneur John Prince, acting with others, was involved in 40 transactions, and Thomas Smith, the surveyor, in 51. The sheriffs W.G. Hall (41), William Hands Junior and Senior (52), and R.T. Reynolds (53) engaged in a high number of transactions. Many of these transactions were conducted in the sherriffs' official capacity as agents of the Crown disposing of land for failure to pay taxes.

Table 7.3   Summary statistics for absolute acreage by cluster group

Sub-Group	Acreage Owned 1825		Acreage Owned 1852		
	$\bar{x}$	σ	$\bar{x}$	σ	n
Cluster 1	283.4	531.5	303.7	312.0	124
Cluster 2	2255.0	n/a	523.5	n/a	1
Cluster 3	4302.0	3255.2	1802.0	613.8	2
Cluster 4	2281.1	3074.7	2299.9	604.1	7
Cluster 5	421.4	430.3	364.9	570.0	8
Cluster 6	1060.5	1499.8	–	–	2
Total	468.5	1077.9	422.2	575.9	144

Source: Calculations of the author.

Cluster 2 is composed of a single individual, John Askin.[74] In 1852 Askin's estate owned an amount of land that might very well have been characteristic of the first cluster, where 68.26 per cent of the holdings were between 303 and 615 acres (Table 7.3). His acreage in that year was 523.5 but in 1825 he had held 2255 acres in Essex and indeed his holdings may once have equalled 18,877 acres.[75] He held his land for less time than the speculators as a whole, most of whom retained their properties for upwards of seventeen years. The number of his transactions exceeded that of all others. With dealings in 188 parcels of land, Askin was literally in a group by himself.

Moreover, he was also heavily involved in the mortgage market, although not to the same extent as Pattinson and Pickersgill of cluster 6 (Table 7.2 and Appendix 7.2). Less than any one else, he obtained his land by purchase, 54.79 per cent compared to an overall average of 71.48 per cent (Table 7.2). More than any other cluster, this one acquired land by patent, because Askin had declared for the British early, had been in the land business from the beginning of European settlement in the region, and had served the administration (through, among other things, his work on the Land Board). Of the fourteen individuals who had more than 50 transactions,[76] only Burwell, the surveyor, approached the magnitude of his transactions (128), the percentage acquired by patent and the speed of sale. The purpose of the two men was quite different. For Burwell, land acquisition came in lieu of salary. To survive he had to sell fast; for Askin, this was a speculative venture, where maximum return might be achieved by a fast turnover. In this respect, Askin exhibits characteristics of what Shannon would term the "quick-flipper" or "speculator." Given his other involvements, however, he could wait if necessary.

In general terms, cluster 3 might be added to this characterization, because its members had the second-highest number of transactions and on average disposed of their land faster than the speculators as a whole. Yet it has to be remembered that an average for the group hides the differences between its two members, who held land in one instance for 2.2 years (Burwell) and in another for 15.1 years (Woods).

The two individuals included here were Mahlon Burwell, the surveyor, and James Woods, an opportunistic lawyer. The fact that they both held larger amounts of land at mid-century may not indicate a predisposition to the building of estates, although the heroic names Burwell bestowed on his sons (Alexander, Hannibal, Hercules, Isaac Brock, and Leonidas) might suggest otherwise. Burwell got his land in compensation for his surveying activities; hence the large percentage of patented property (65.63 per cent or 84 of his 128 acquisitions). He had to draw for it by lottery. Woods, ever the opportunist, got land wherever he could but as a lawyer acquired it by purchase. The pattern of these men's holdings was scattered and both held a disproportionate amount of poor land. They and their estates may unavoidably have been encumbered with undesirable land.[77] Burwell (who depended on sales to live) and later his executors tried to unload property as fast as possible. Yet at mid-century Burwell's holdings were actually slightly larger than they had been in 1825, which has to be interpreted as problems in measurement given no real evidence of continued acquisition. As noted above, Woods could wait longer to unload. Between 1825 and 1852, he successfully reduced his inventory from 6604 acres to 1368 acres; the effect on the characteristics of the cluster is apparent in Table 7.3.

Clusters 4 and 5 represent a different end of the continuum. As people who held land the longest, they represent that element which Widdis calls the "Classical" speculator and which Shannon designates "investors," that is, those who sat tight. In the latter's study, a much smaller group of people, in more northerly and more recently settled Collingwood Township, took an average of 25.2 years to unload their land.[78] In Essex, 68.26 per cent of cluster 4 held their land between eight and twenty-six years, averaging seventeen years;[79] the equivalent percentage of cluster 5 held between 24.7 and 35.1 years. Their average was 29.9 years.[80] If these were people who held on to their land, they also possessed a large acreage. In both periods these people averaged more than 1800 acres (Table 7.3).[81] Individuals, such as James McGill and Edward Ellice, son-in-law to the British prime minister, owned 7317 and 5615 acres respectively. By 1852, their holdings or, in the case of McGill, his estate, had been reduced to 2214 and 3200 acres.

In terms of the membership of cluster 4, it is worth noting that the Caldwell and Fox entries refer to more than one individual. It proved impossible to separate both the lands of James and William Caldwell and of James, Jacob, and J. Fox. Had this been possible, it might have been necessary to remove these individuals from cluster 4, characterized by relatively high acreage and number of transactions, to some other group. The remaining four individuals would then share some common characteristics, non-residence in Essex, substantial holdings, and, for at least three, the honorific "Honourable"[82] and a presence in the market beyond Essex.

The title "Honourable" might seem to imply access to patronage but it is worth pointing out that members of the Baby family who had been similarly recognized were placed in the first cluster by the agglomerative algorithm used. This family, and most especially Francis and James, had greatest access to the system and yet made relatively few transactions in total in Essex. Nor was the acreage of these individuals especially large. James, a central figure of the Family Compact, owned 641 acres in 1825 and his estate had disposed of all of it by 1852. Francis owned 150 acres in 1825 and increased his acreage to 225 by 1852. He generally did so by purchase rather than by patent, thus avoiding even the appearance of conflict of interest.[83]

The best-known of the four members of the group being discussed here was John A. Macdonald, who would later become Canada's first prime minister. He bought all but two of his twenty Essex parcels in 1852. These had been assembled for him by W.C. Pickersgill from land they had purchased in turn from the firm of McDonnell, Holmes. While out of office, but just before becoming attorney general for Upper Canada in the coalition government of Sir Allan Napier MacNab[84] and Augustin-Norbert Morin,[85] he disposed of seventeen of them in one year at a profit of 98.5 per cent. The two properties he held in Gosfield Township took twenty-four and thirty-two years to dispose of, and brought the Macdonald average for time held to 3.7 years (Appendix 7.1). However, the mode for disposal of his property in Essex was one year, and he was, in Shannon's terms, a "quick-flipper" of 2905 acres in this county. Macdonald's activities as a speculator were not confined to Essex; he bought and sold land throughout the province in parcels as large as 9700 acres at a time.[86]

Arthur John Robertson, described in the abstract index as the "Honourable," engaged in sixty-seven transactions (Appendix 7.1).[87] In 1840 this man was the chairman of the British North American Colonial Committee, an association of British peers, landlords, and investors who sought to promote emigration to specific areas and thereby promote their own interests. Among other lands he owned a tract of unspecified acreage in Indiana which he had obtained from Richard Pollard and which in 1833 he was willing to dispose of for one dollar per acre.[88] In the Western District he had 30,000 acres. He employed a George Jacob, marital relation of John Askin, as his agent and Askin's son Charles as his lawyer[89] and was willing to give away small parcels of fifty acres, presumably to promote and sell alternate ones.[90] Fifty-three of these properties were acquired between 1830 and 1833 from Richard Pattinson, the American-born merchant, investor, entrepreneur, investor, and parliamentarian.[91] Pattinson died a rich man in 1818 but his heirs and executors continued to convey thereafter. He sold in his own right and on behalf of Mary Ann Robertson.[92] His role was rather akin to that of Pickersgill, the second member of group six. With Pickersgill, he and his estate assembled land which was disposed of to members of the fourth cluster.[93] An earlier customer purchasing land in 1809 and 1810 was Edward Ellice.[94] "Bear" Ellice, as he was known, was a general merchant and fur trader in Europe, North America, and the East and West Indies and *the* spokesman for the "Canada Trade" in Great Britain. It was Ellice who, through "behind the scenes legerdemain," produced the necessary legislation to restructure the Canadian fur trade in 1821. His father-in-law, Charles Grey, had defeated Wayne in 1777 and subsequently become British commander-in-chief in America. His brother-in-law, also Charles Grey, was, as noted earlier, prime minister of Great Britain and the architect of the Reform Bill of 1832. Ellice was his chief whip. He was a powerful man who invested in land – as the powerful did. He became the seigneur of Beauharnois though he never lived there. In Canada and the United States he held 450,000 acres, properties that he visited only twice in his lifetime. Part of this included 5615 acres which he held in Essex in 1825; his holdings were still considerable (3200 acres) at mid-century.[95]

So, too, were those of James McGill[96] whose estate still owned 7317 acres in 1825, almost twelve years after his death. By mid-century his holdings had been reduced to 2214 acres. McGill's fate was tied up with that of his fur-trading partners, especially the Irish-born Isaac Todd (*c.* 1742–1819);[97] at one point the two were the largest shareholders in the North-West Company and increasingly, through participation in the Miami Company and the Cuyahoga purchase, their affairs became entangled with that of John Askin. Askin's indebtedness to McGill and Todd was amicably resolved,[98] leaving Askin in possession of his house, called "Strabane" after his home in the north of Ireland, and the partners in possession of much of his land in Essex and adjoining Kent. These transfers "signalled McGill's entry into systematic land speculation"[99] and he began to acquire land methodically. His biographer, J.I. Cooper, reports that in 1801 alone he acquired 42,400 acres in Lower Canada and began to purchase land near York and Kingston in the upper province.[100] These were also years of growing political influence. In 1792 he had been appointed to the Executive Council of Lower Canada and he was returned for Montreal West in 1800 and for Montreal East in 1804. He gradually withdrew from the fur trade and cautioned Askin to do likewise; increasingly, his wealth accumulated in land and mortgages.

The last of these four is Samuel Street, Jr, nephew of Samuel Street, Sr, who was a judge, MHA for Lincoln, and speaker of the House of Assembly. Unlike his uncle, who engaged little in commerce, the younger man eschewed politics and government service, though he became a magistrate in 1796 and was to serve as deputy registrar for Niagara. Instead, he engaged in business as a miller, helped finance various development projects including part of the Welland Canal, and became lender to many members of the ecclesiastical, legal, and political establishment of the province. Few in the province matched the capacity of Street and his partner, Thomas Clark, as land speculators. He owned land in almost every part of Upper Canada, acquiring it by purchase from individuals and by tax and mortgage default. He maintained agents in every area, including Charles Askin in the Western District,[101] and sought the advice of local cognoscenti, including, in Essex, Sheriff William Hands. In Essex he owned 1648 acres in 1852. In all he made sixteen purchases, twelve of them on sheriff's deeds from Hands. Indeed, this was characteristic of this fourth cluster as a whole. As Table 7.2 shows, this fourth group of people made an unusual use of sheriff's deeds to acquire land (11.39 per cent on average) and had the largest percentage of sales. They also received the smallest percentage of all as bounty from the state (8.13 per cent on average) – one presumes from lack of opportunity to patent rather than aversion.

Cluster 5, whose holdings were on average smaller in both periods than the members of cluster 4, contained a number of individuals who were in fact Loyalists or descendants of United Empire Loyalists.[102] However, it would be a mistake to label Loyalism the essential characteristic of the group because *all* other groups included such people among them. For example, Robert Herriot Barclay Elliott's father, Matthew Elliott, fitted this category. He, his son Francis Gore Elliott, and his wife Sarah (née Donovan) all surpassed Robert[103] with respect to the number of transactions in which they engaged, and his father had owned much more land. In terms of acreage held and the number of transactions, this group was most like group or cluster 1, to which the rest of the Elliotts belonged. What distinguishes them from all other clusters is the length of time in which they held on to the land. Clusters 4 and 5 proved significantly different from one another in this respect and from the average of all groups.[104]

In terms of time held, they stand at marked variance with clusters 1 and 3, which in relative terms turned land over much more quickly. However there are differences. Cluster 4 bought and sold more in the market and by means of sheriffs' deeds; cluster 5, with on average 20.5 transactions, dealt only slightly more than cluster 1 in the market[105] and had in 1851–52 only an average or less-than-average amount of land (364.9 acres)[106] – which was substantially less than cluster 4 possessed (Table 7.3).[107] Its members had received a substantial amount (32.8 per cent) of their land by government grant. In capitalist terms they had wasted their talent. Not so their colleagues in cluster 4.

Who were the members of this fifth cluster? Mary Cornwall was the daughter of John Cornwall, Loyalist, prominent landowner, and member of the House of Assembly. She had married William McCormick, militia officer, magistrate, collector of customs at Amherstburg, and storekeeper and deputy postmaster in Colchester Township. John Cornwall acquired mortgages and land on mainland Essex. These ventures were profitable and his biographer reports that between 1820 and 1839 he realized £2770 from land which had cost him approximately £900.[108] In 1815 he leased Pelée Island from Alexander McKee and in 1823 purchased the lease.[109] McCormick actually owned much more land than his daughter in 1825 (1918 acres compared to 600 acres) and engaged in eleven times her number of transactions. However, Mary was placed here rather than in cluster 1 because of the greater length of time she held the land.

This was also the case with R.H.B. Elliott, separated from his brother, the Reverend Francis Gore Elliott, who held 845 acres in 1852, and his father, Matthew Elliott, who had 4429 acres in 1825. His father and brother have been placed in the first cluster on account of the length of time they possessed this land; Robert Herriot Barclay was placed in cluster 6 because he held on longer. The John Jackson of cluster 5 is presumably the West Indian-born merchant who settled in York in 1806.[110] Lieutenant John Maule was a Loyalist who acquired 1200 acres by patent and sat on it at least until mid-century.

These first four members of the fifth cluster had fewer transactions than many members of almost any other group; not so the remaining five persons. Alexander McKee is already well known to readers. Angus Mackintosh, chieftain of clans Chattan and Mackintosh, had come to

Table 7.4   Absolute count of different tenure conditions in Essex for which cross–tabulated data were available in 1825

Twp.	Own/occ.	Ten.	Own/unocc.	Irre.	Sub-total	Can. Co.	Unpat.	Total
Colchester	77 (2)	26 (9)	65 (34)	2	170	n/a	53	223
Malden	46 (12)	24 (13)	29 (26)	0	99	n/a	43	142
Maidstone	21 (15)		47 (42)	7	74	n/a	192	267
Mersea	9 (1)	3 (3)	56 (38)	25	93	n/a	118	211
Rochester	12 (6)	3 (2)	32 (29)	9	54	n/a	113	169
Sandwich	158 (18)	67 (4)	82 (27)	61	368	n/a	223	591
Total	323 (54)	123 (31)	311 (196)	104	860	n/a	742	1603

Source: Calculations of the author.

No data available for Tilbury, Anderdon, and Gosfield townships

(n/a) applies to the Canada Company because it was not established until 1826

Owner/occupiers (Own/occ.) make up 37.6 per cent of subtotal; tenanted (Ten.) constitute 14.3 per cent; owned but unoccupied (Own/unocc.) land constitutes 36.2 per cent; irregular (Irre.) lots are 12.1 per cent; unpatented (Unpat.) land 46.3 per cent of *all* land.

N.B. values in brackets are the number of properties held by the sample of 144 speculators.

reside in Detroit during the American revolution. With John Askin and others, he had been involved in the Miami Company, acted as the agent for the North-West Company in Detroit and later Sandwich, and speculated in land purchases in neighbouring Harwich Township and in Michigan and Ohio. He returned to Scotland in 1827.[111]

George Benson Hall, an Irish-born officer in the Royal Navy, served as commodore of the Provincial Marine, became in 1816 a justice of the peace, and in the same year was elected as one of two members for Essex in the House of Assembly. He acquired 1200 acres in Colchester and Aldborough townships but, as Appendix 7.1 shows, he had disposed of his Essex property by 1852.[112] He served also as a merchant, as did Meldrum and Park, the remaining members of cluster 5. As indicated earlier Pattinson and Pickersgill assembled land parcels for others; the former to a considerable extent and the latter to an even greater extent.

Table 7.5   Absolute count of different tenure conditions in Essex for which cross–
tabulated data were available in 1852

Twp	Own/ occ.	Ten.	Own/ unocc.	Irre.	Sub-total	Can. Co.	Unpat.	Total
Colchester	121 (6)	78 (2)	166 (1)	35	400	52	69	521
Gosfield	166 (0)	47 (2)	110 (27)	18	341	59	95	495
Malden	84 (19)	47 (17)	71 (33)	11	213	0	10	223
Maidstone	104 (4)	36 (4)	143 (47)	41	324	17	82	423
Mersea	101 (10)	29 (8)	113 (39)	25	268	47	118	433
Rochester	87 (2)	11 (3)	73 (34)	44	215	18	79	312
Sandwich	178 (11)	217 (38)	251 (43)	38	684	26	39	749
Tilbury	58 (0)	21 (3)	80 (28)	18	177	23	162	362
Total	899 (52)	486 (77)	1007 (252)	230	2622	242	654	3518

Source: Calculations of the author.

No data available for Anderdon Township.

Owner/occupiers (Own/occ.) make up 34.3 per cent of subtotal; tenanted (Ten.) constitute 18.5 per cent; owned but unoccupied (Own/unocc.) land constitutes 38.4 per cent; irregular (Irre.) lots are 8.8 per cent; unpatented (Unpat.) land 18.6 per cent of all land.

N.B. values in brackets are the number of properties held by the sample of 144 speculators.

Structural aspects of speculation: Its spatial pattern and extent

Figures 4.1 and 4.2 and tables 7.4 and 7.5 summarize the tenure structure of the county in 1825 and 1851–52. The maps, as indicated in Chapter 4, were constructed by comparing those who owned the land at the requisite period with those who were assessed for it or were enumerated at the first Census of Canada in 1851–52. Mapping was conducted to the level of fifty acres, and the maps might therefore underestimate the amount of any one category appearing on the tables. It is also important to note that measurement is at the nominal level rather than the interval level, and again this may lead to under-estimation of, for example, the amount of tenancy or of owner/occupancy. As the tables show, six categories of tenure were recognized. The first of these was the category "owner/occupier." This was inferred when the names on the abstract index to deeds and the assessment rolls or the census were in agreement. When the names were in disagreement, a tenant was inferred. When land was shown to be owned but not occupied, this was considered to be land either held by a speculator or so newly acquired by a settler that there was insufficient time for it to have been included in the tax rolls or the census. Unpatented land[113] or land patented by the Canada Company was simply that. In fact, until the final sale was effected, many years after initial purchase, Canada Company land was effectively tenanted land, although it was held from a corporate entity rather than an individual. "Irregularly" held land included that which was occupied prior to patent. This was because it was held under certificates of location, or ownership had still to be sanctioned by the Heirs and Devisees Commission, or it was under some legal sanction or indeed was occupied by a squatter!

What is interesting is that in both periods patented but unoccupied land came close to equalling the absolute number of occupied properties. In 1825 there were 311 unoccupied property parcels in Essex at a time when occupied land totalled 323 parcels and tenanted properties numbered 123.[114] In 1851–52 there were 1007 unoccupied parcels and a total of 1385 tenanted and owner-occupied parcels. At the same time there were townships where patented but unoccupied land exceeded occupied and patented land. These included Maidstone, Rochester, and Mersea townships in 1825; by mid-century Rochester had just ceased to be a member of this group but an expansionary Sandwich had joined it. In both periods the tenure structure of the area remained similar in relative terms though the total number of identified properties increased from 1603 to 3518.

Expressed as a percentage of total owned, tenanted, owned and unoccupied, and irregular (the subtotal column of the tables), the percentage owned showed a slight decrease from 37.6 to 34.3 per cent. The percentage owned but unoccupied went up to 38.4 per cent from 36.2 in 1825. So did tenancy, which in the private market amounted to 18.5 per cent by mid-century. If, however, corporate tenants were included and the Canada Company properties included, tenancy would amount to 20.7 per cent of the 3518 properties in 1851–52. The percentage of occupied properties held in tenancy was 22.6 on average ($\sigma = 12.17$) in 1825 and 30.53 ($\sigma = 13.01$) in 1851–52.[115] On this basis, tenancy might appear to be on the increase, but in fact, statistically, these figures are little different from one another.[116] In gross terms, however, the grand mean for Essex suggests figures of 38 per cent and 54 per cent for the respective periods.

Such figures exceed Gagan's figure of 25 per cent for Peel County in 1835.[117] There are more comparable with the tenancy rate in Chinguacousy Township in 1842,[118] with Catherine Wilson's estimate of Upper Canadian tenancy at 45 per cent in 1848,[119] or with Malden Township in 1847, where Johnson reports that 50.26 per cent of farm heads of household were tenants.[120] The latter figure is based upon direct measurement of tenancy using a unique census.[121] Unfortunately, this is the only document that identifies tenants as such. Had there been others it would have obviated the need for inference of the kind employed here. Based upon the unique census, it would seem that scores on other variables might be reasonably accurate, although it has to be pointed out that the Malden statistic refers to a period five years earlier and in Upper Canada tenancy could change markedly. For tenants, this was a highly mobile society in which status or at least location could change, most usually within two years.[122]

The properties held by the 144 speculators numbered 281 in 1825. As a percentage of the three primary tenure classes, this amounts to 32.6 per cent, much higher than in 1852, when the respective figures were 381 out of a total of 2622 (Table 7.5) or 14.4 per cent of properties. By this measure, speculation in rural land was on the decrease over time and the decrease occurred in all of the three primary categories but less so in the owner/unoccupied category. In 1825, 6.7 per cent of occupied land, 25.2 per cent of tenanted land and 63.0 per cent of owned but unoccupied land was held by the speculator group. In 1852 the respective figures were 5.8, 15.8, and 25.02 per cent. In keeping with a more equitable distribution of property as the century proceeded (though not necessarily with revenues), the speculator as a whole controlled less of each category; in relative terms and as a group, however, speculators held a greater proportion of the owner/unoccupied land than of other tenure classes, although this might have been the result of their activity rather than the cause.

In absolute terms, only in Colchester and Gosfield townships, the best-endowed and most agriculturally oriented, did the number of owner-occupied properties come close to the number of owned but unoccupied. This was presumably because the members of cluster 1, who dominated here, were themselves closest to the farm community and sought to prepare for future expansion of their own or their children's futures, either as farmers or as beneficiaries of their investment. Indeed, the high number of owner-occupied properties is in part a shortcoming of the procedures employed, which identify properties but not owners. In almost all cases the properties were on contiguous lots. In one instance, no less than ten such properties were owned by a single individual, Matthew Elliott. However, in two instances, the pattern of ownership of these owner-occupied lots was spatially disparate; this was so of John Askin, who held nine such parcels in Maidstone, and of James Woods, who owned three in the same township and an additional six in Rochester Township in 1825. Clearly, in these instances, owner-occupier really translates as purchaser and taxpayer. What is of particular interest in all this is that speculators found it necessary and beneficial to operate in all tenure zones. While fewer properties were owned and rented by these people, some were; not all chose to confine their activities to the more spatially remote outer areas where they would simply await the day when profit would come to them. The management or promotion of their enterprise might mean renting land until circumstances permitted its sale either in more remote locations or indeed closer to the agricultural core.

This is clear in figures 7.3 and 7.4, which show the distribution of the groups. Comparison of these maps with those of occupied lands (figures 7.5 and 6.4) and cultivated land (figures 7.6 and 7.7) show that the largest of these groups, cluster 1, was to be found both in 1825 and in 1851–52 in close proximity to other settled lands. This was especially so along the Lake Erie shore in 1825, although along the Lake St Clair shore and in Maidstone and Rochester townships the members of classes one and four held land in advance of settlement in both time periods. The same held for the area south of the Talbot Road in Mersea Township. Of course, the overall association with developed land is to be expected since the speculator sought to benefit from such proximity and indeed to unload to people who wished accessibility to road and amenity. Interestingly, the Talbot Road, running north and west towards Sandwich and Windsor, did not attract a lot of speculator attention in 1851–52, although as Figure 7.7 shows, it was an artery by which farming goods were carried into the interior.

Yet elsewhere, by mid-century, as settlement moved into the interior, there were those who were prepared to follow or perhaps even anticipate the movement. This is particularly apparent in northern Colchester, where members of clusters 1 and 4 took up available land abutting on the edge of the reserve lands. It is also clear in Gosfield Township where speculators took up land between the 6th and 9th concessions on the western edge of the township and extended their activity along the eastern boundary. One presumes that the dream was one of cheap land which might be quickly converted to prosperous farm real estate. Yet it is clear that John A Macdonald and Jean-Bap-

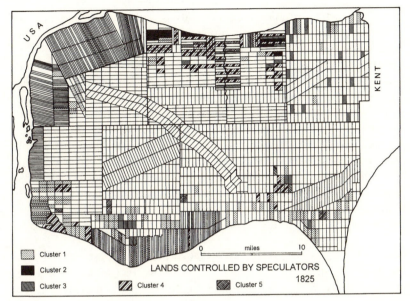

Figure 7.3   Spatial pattern of speculator clusters, 1825

Source: Calculations of the author.

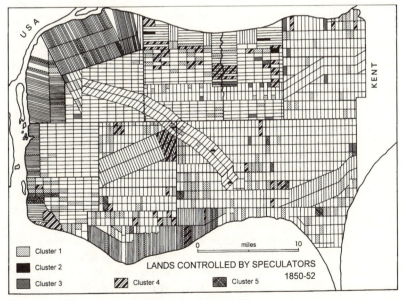

Figure 7.4   Spatial pattern of speculator clusters, 1850–52.

Source: Calculations of the author.

tiste Baby, who purchased in these areas, either possessed or had access to sufficient capital to invest in potential urban land at the embryonic site of Essex village.

Askin's investments are, for reasons that will be discussed, found almost exclusively in Maidstone and Rochester townships. The holdings of Burwell and Woods were predominantly northern. In the case of Burwell, the pattern was associated with his surveying activity, and in Wood's instance with opportunism, although again one suspects that his purchases in Colchester near Harrow were particularly purposeful. In the case of cluster 4, the concentration in Rochester and Maidstone townships is associated with either the fortunes of Askin, and his financiers Todd and McGill, or with those of others such as Street, who sought to take advantage of the distress of these individuals when their properties came up at tax sales.

How extensive and developed were these properties?

As the discussion above indicated, speculators operated in both developed and under-developed areas. The speculator operating in an already developed area might seek and manage to purchase raw land at a low price, but he might also have to develop this land in order to achieve a maximum return. Elsewhere, raw land might remain undeveloped until the settlement "frontier" arrived. Were there in fact differences within the categories of speculators with respect to development and between the speculators and others? Table 7.6 speaks to this issue for 1851–52, when the first census of Canada permits some insight into the question. However, it has to be stressed that the table does not provide an absolutely unequivocal result because of the method employed.

The census yields information on the amount of land held and cleared against the name of the occupant. It does not indicate the head of household's tenure status. It is to be expected that a sizeable number of speculators will be absentees even in class one, those most closely related to the land itself. Even here, the owner may be recorded as absent on a particular property but resident on an adjacent property, or indeed totally absent from the county altogether. Moreover, if, as was suggested earlier, tenancy could run as high as 38 to 54 per cent, the probabilities of linking a particular tenant to a particular owner need not be high, even though it is possible, in conjunction with the abstracts, to indicate at the level of the lot or half-lot the tenure status of the property. This is what was accomplished here. The variables "land held" and "cleared" were aggregated to the level of the lot, and the amount of land held or cleared was attributed to

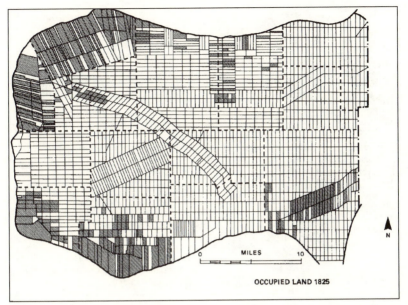

Figure 7.5 Occupied land in Essex, 1825

Source: Assessment rolls for Essex County.

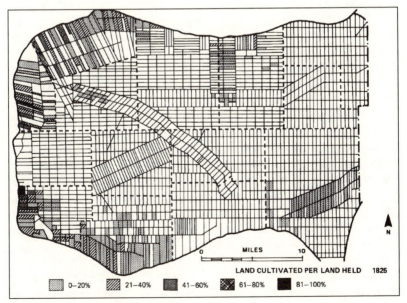

Figure 7.6 Cultivated land, Essex county, 1825

Source: Assessment rolls of Essex County.

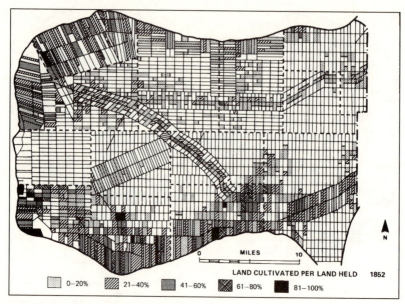

Figure 7.7   Cultivated land, Essex County, 1852.
Source: Assessment rolls for Essex County.

lots where a speculator was absent, or alternatively, where such an individual might have shared part of the lot with a resident owner farmer or a tenant. The point needs recalling in the light of the interpretation of the results which are reported in tables 7.6 and 7.7.

Although the absolute acreage held is understandably higher than the acreage cleared, there might appear to be differences in cleared acreage between the townships (Table 7.6). Statistically this was not so, as a series of ranked values subjected to *t* tests revealed. Differences were, however shown to exist in percentage terms, the division being between Sandwich, Malden and Gosfield townships and the rest of Essex. Normally, this division between "developed" and "developing" Essex might have been expected to include Colchester within the former. However, it would appear that the activities of speculators in acquiring land in the northern part of Colchester had the effect of driving down the cultivated acreage here. Colchester was in fact found to occupy the boundary between the two parts.[123]

Table 7.7 shows the relevant statistics for properties within five of the six clusters; the sixth had no acreage in 1852, though it had at other points in time. With respect to the acreage held, there were no differences in absolute acreage between the groups nor indeed between the speculators as a whole and the non-speculators.[124]

Table 7.6   Acreage held and cleared on speculator properties in Essex townships, 1851–52

Sub-Group	Acres Held $\bar{x}$	σ	Acres Cleared $\bar{x}$	σ	Acres Held %	Acres Cleared %	n
Col.	71.87	65.19	26.41	22.98	44.90	27.35	44
Gos.	78.40	113.82	21.72	25.35	57.87	38.19	86
Mai.	101.69	38.23	7.44	6.14	7.07	5.81	16
Mal.	71.93	57.53	35.46	34.68	62.43	32.54	36
Mer.	98.88	66.31	28.00	18.63	39.75	26.39	8
Roc.	78.75	28.03	11.13	9.74	11.96	9.07	8
San.	64.76	54.53	35.20	36.89	66.24	33.73	51
Til.	76.33	24.74	17.33	12.35	22.61	15.67	6
Essex	75.70	80.77	26.03	28.91	34.39	51.92	255

Source: Calculations of the author.
"Col." = Colchester; "Gos." = Gosfield; "Mai." = Maidstone; "Mal." = Malden; "Mer." = Mersea;
"Roc." = Rochester; "San." = Sandwich; and "Til." = Tilbury.

Table 7.7   Acreage held and cleared within speculator groups in Essex, 1851–52

Sub-Group	Acres Held $\bar{x}$	σ	Acres Cleared $\bar{x}$	σ	Acres Held %	Acres Cleared %	n
Cluster 1	72.31	64.35	26.60	28.96	55.53	36.11	204
Cluster 2	75.00	25.00	2.50	0.50	4.00	2.00	2
Cluster 3	86.11	24.24	14.44	11.07	15.01	9.88	9
Cluster 4	120.67	184.05	27.90	38.20	23.13	29.70	21
Cluster 5	57.57	50.70	25.84	20.28	60.28	33.60	19
Cluster 6	n/a	n/a	n/a	n/a	n/a	n/a	n/a
Speculator	75.70	80.77	26.03	28.91	51.92	36.17	255
Non-Speculator	80.81	67.06	21.26	25.35	38.24	33.73	1652

Source: Calculations of the author.

However, the absolute acreage owned by speculators could vary considerably, as Table 7.7 shows. In Essex in 1825 and 1852, the twenty top speculators averaged 1592 acres in 1825 and 2281 in 1852,[125] little different, it would seem, from what was achieved in Peel County. The statistics reported by Gagan are of a similar magnitude though the time frame is somewhat different.[126] Yet, while an acreage of 7317 could be held by James McGill and 5615 by Edward Ellice in 1825, the average was more modest.

As Table 7.3 shows, this was 468.5 acres for the 144 constituting the group as a whole, but higher for the smaller number who actually held acreage in that year. In fact, the holdings of these seventy individuals constitute the relevant statistic for comparison with the only other study directly comparable, that is, Widdis's study of Elizabethtown Township in eastern Ontario. The $\bar{x}$ of this Essex group was found to be 963.8 acres with a σ of 1387.04. Using Widdis's data, one arrives at the comparable statistics of 520.65 and 485.2, based upon twenty-nine observations of Elizabethtown Township in eastern Ontario.[127] Clearly, Essex exceeded Elizabethtown – perhaps simply because it was by far the bigger territory and presented greater opportunity. What is apparent is that speculator holdings could commonly have upper limits of 1000 to 2000 acres. In contrast, but again as was only to be expected, the property parcels of non-speculators were much smaller in the same period. In Elizabethtown, scores within one standard deviate ranged between 52.77 and 822.77 acres.[128] In Essex County, the comparable figures were 40.55 acres and 302.83 acres.[129] In 1825, Essex was by comparison a more extreme place but how it fared relative to other more central areas awaits further work. By 1852, the size of speculative holding in Essex had fallen; for the 100 speculators identifiable at this time, it was on average 608.01 acres ($\sigma = 604.2$ acres).[130] For most, this still meant large holdings compared to non-speculator holdings of about 118 acres.[131]

Application of the same method to the absolute values of land cleared produced a threefold classification which placed classes four, one, and five in one group and three and two in statistically separate groupings.[132] A modified permutation of this appeared when "percentage cleared" was used in the analysis. This is perhaps the more useful variable and application of a series of sequential tests produced four statistically different groupings with subgroups five and one included in the same group.[133] Interestingly, subgroups five and one, alike in their acreage and the number of their transactions, were also alike with respect to their acreage cleared. What is also interesting is that speculators as a whole had a greater percentage of their property cleared than did non-speculators; 51.92 per cent on average ($\sigma = 36.17$) compared to 38.24 ($\sigma = 33.73$).[134] While the statistical conclusion is incontrovertible given the size of samples employed, the substantive meaning of the results can in fact be debated. Perhaps the results reflect inadequacies in measurement, although it would be hard to structure the analysis differently. Alternatively, significant quantities of land were being acquired in the most developed part of the county. There, what was acquired was already developed land or land that had to be developed to meet expectations in terms of price. In this respect, the speculator presumably had an advantage over the backwoods farmer in his access to the capital needed to have a property transformed, or indeed used tenant-farmers as the vehicle of change. Given the absence of formal agreement and a tenantry predicated on sharecropping for a year at a time, it was possible to have large numbers of tenants transform land in a short time.

CONCLUSION: THE EXTENT OF SPECULATION IN ESSEX AND UPPER CANADA

This chapter has shown that, in an age of laissez-faire capitalism, land speculation was endemic to Upper Canada as no doubt it was elsewhere. This was inevitable, given a system whereby the state rewarded its servants from its bounty and the most plentiful commodity available for this purpose was land. Land was not only the basis of life but the mark of social prestige. Consequently, the problem was one of finding the appropriate balance so that the natural aristocracy, thought to be so essential to the proper governing of society, might spring into existence, while at the same time the state could guard against excess so that Upper Canada might be effectively developed.

Speculation is part and parcel of capitalism. Though there is nothing inherently wrong with it since it is tied to risk taking and thereby development, problems become acute when a few come to monopolize all or most of the resources of the state. Essentially, that is what began to happen in the early years in Essex and Upper Canada. The documentary record points to the early emergence of the phenomenon. There is clear evidence of speculating in land, both in the French period but most especially in the British era, when British control and the resumption of peace permitted the exploitation of an unimaginable resource base.

How much land did speculators actually control? The answer, of course, varies with one's definition of speculation. If the 400-acre criterion is used, then one can say that, by 1825, 81,994 acres in a county in which 129,259 acres had been patented were in the hands of speculators.[135] This means that as much as 63.4 per cent of the land had been patented to such people.[136] This figure is not out of line with what Lillian Gates has suggested was the provincial norm by 1825. She argues that, by 1825, when a sales policy was instituted and measures taken to establish a more monetary-based society, 62 per cent of all land in the province was already in the hands of large-scale speculators. Her figures obviously include appropriate figures for Essex.[137]

A second measure, one obtained by following the rules of conveyancing, is to determine how much land was owned by people fitting the 400-acre criterion. Inspection of the abstracts and reconstruction of all registered and conveyed land suggests that, in 1825, 74,893 acres were held out of a total of 130,405 acres.[138] By this standard, speculation was of the order of 57.43 per cent. By 1852, the total acreage owned was 199,286.6 acres, of which 68,273 acres was controlled by people holding over 400 acres.[139] While down from 1825 this would still mean that 34.26 per cent of the land in Essex, not counting the two-sevenths at the disposal of the Canada Company and the Clergy Corporation, was in the hands of speculators.

Some support for this figure is provided by the fact that "owned and unoccupied" land, within which speculative holdings were most likely to be found, constituted 36.2 and 38.4 per cent of all holdings in 1825 and 1852. However, it has to be remembered that the measurement used here is at the nominal level, that this category might have included the newly settled, and that, as was shown, speculators were also to be found in the owner/occupied tenure category. In fact, within this last category there were few names that were unknown to the author after a long acquaintance with the area. If there were new persons acquiring land here, they were relatively few. Even these people may, too, have been speculators. It is indeed possible that speculators controlled upwards of 50 per cent of the Essex total.

Such figures are marked and may seem "unrealistic" to some. Speculation is, in the final analysis, an attitude of mind and not just a matter of scale. However, in the absence of "self-identification," it is difficult after the event and without a special crystal ball to get into the minds of particular individuals to determine their intentions. Moreover, the social consequences of owning a thousand acres are in general greater than owning one acre unless that one acre is critical to the development of a city or the site of a critical resource. If, as has been argued in the literature, Upper Canada was from the beginning other than a purely subsistence economy, then land had a potential value to be realized and was for *all* a matter of speculation. While not all owners of 400, 500, or even 1000 acres – the "cut-off" recognized for purposes of discussion by Clarke, Brunger, Gagan, Johnson, and Widdis – may have been speculating, it seems to this author that in an age of acquisitiveness most were. Few can have been indifferent to the future of land upon which ultimately life depended, then and now.

Those unhappy with scale as the sole mechanism of identification – and, ultimately, that must be all serious researchers – may be more content with the extent of speculation identified using the cluster analysis employed in this chapter. The present study used a measure of scale in the form acreage owned. This was supplemented by number of transactions, length of time in the market, and limitations upon transactions within the family. In this way the number of speculators was reduced by thirty-one from the potential number available on the scale criterion alone. This procedure permitted insights into the behaviour of six subgroups with respect to their means of acquiring land and of holding it. These groups mirrored elements of the typologies suggested by Widdis and Shannon. John Askin and John A. Macdonald were seen to possess the characteristics of a speculator or, in Shannon's parlance, "quick-flipper". The members of groups four and five exhibited the characteristics of the "classical speculator" in Widdis's scheme. Though some such as Askin had an unusually large number of transactions in the period, the overall average ($\bar{x}$ of 24.5 and a σ of 25.2) was sufficiently high to warrant thinking of them as different from the "normal" farmers. Moreover, the spatial pattern of their holdings, which will be discussed in the next chapter, gives added strength to the conviction that these people were not seeking to consolidate their land, as "maximizing" farmers might, or necessarily creating "estates" for progeny close to the family progenitor. This approach identified 144 persons who in 1825 controlled 35,145 acres or almost 27 per cent of settled Essex, and who in 1852 controlled 37,656.3 acres or 18.9 per cent of the county's deeded land. These figures are even more considerable when it is remembered that they do not include lands held by the Canada Company or by the Clergy Corporation and that such lands could add as much as two-sevenths of all land to the calculation.

Yet, to this point, there are few statistics with which to compare these results. The structure of landholdings presented earlier for the early part of the eighteenth century would seem to suggest that the Western District had a head start in this regard, although that is again to equate speculation with size of holding (Table 3.2). Johnson's work on the Home District is suggestive. He points out that, in the first five years of settlement (1795–1800), 55.4 per cent of the lands patented went to recipients of more than 500 acres. He is careful to speak of these absentee "official" grantees as "likely speculators" but some of their names appear in Essex![140] Gagan, in his study of property owners in more central Peel County, points to the fact that, in 1820, 85 per cent of large property owners were absentees and that 75 per cent still were in 1840. In 1820 and 1840 such people were 3 and 1 per cent of all proprietors respectively but held 27.4 and 10.8 per cent of the alienated acreage.[141] To the east in Elizabethtown, Widdis's figures suggest that in 1825 speculators controlled 17.3 per cent of the township. Of themselves, these figures are not indicators of anything other than the unequal distribution of property, but the absentee status of speculators changes the interpretation for this author and hopefully the reader![142]

A number of points emerge from all this. In Essex, the period leading up to the instigation of a sales policy in 1825, was *the* period for speculation. In fact, the absolute acreage changed little between the two periods. Nor was the distribution of holdings within the group of 144 significantly different between the two time periods, as Table 7.3 shows.[143] However, the table reports the figures for the respective groups and the 144 speculators as a whole. If only those with acreage are used, the figures are different; by this standard, speculators owned on average not just some 400 acres but something more like 2000 acres, substantially greater amounts of land than normal.

In Essex, then, as in Peel County and other parts of Upper Canada, landed wealth was not equally distributed. In the period prior to 1825, 14.1 per cent of the people (those with acreages greater than 400 acres) who would acquire land in the area by patent would come to control as much as 63.4 per cent of the resource; the top ten individuals, or 1.9 per cent, held 28.5 per cent of the land in patent, even more imbalanced than the situation in Peel County.[144] In terms of the most conservative estimate of speculative activity, 77 of the 144 identified speculators active to 1825 commanded 27 per cent of the resource. The 77 amounted to 14.9 per cent of all owners at this time. By 1852, the number of speculators active in Essex was 88 and they constituted 7.1 per cent of all owners.[145] This minority controlled 18.9 per cent of the land which was not reserved in one form or other. Clearly, settlement in Essex had grown. Land was now more equitably distributed, at least qualitatively. Nonetheless, the extent of speculation was still remarkable whatever the figure used.

Speculators are seen here to have operated in the three primary categories of land tenure, and in no one exclusively, though they owned less of the owner/occupied land than the tenanted category and much less than the third category here designated "owned but unoccupied." As in the present, this must have been a response to opportunism and an adaptive strategy for survival in difficult times. Much of this third class of land, though not all, lay at some distance from the coast of Essex or roads and amenities. It must also have been cheaper land in its natural state and presumably less developed, although, as was pointed out earlier, speculator holdings were generally more cleared than others because speculators seeking to unload to non-speculator society must have bought where things were developed as well as in a state of nature.

Part of the problem is that individuals can behave differently from the aggregated category to which they are assigned. There were those such as Askin and Macdonald who behaved as "quick-flippers," those such as Samuel Street who operated via agents in all parts of Upper Canada, and those members of group five who operated locally and, holding on for long periods of time, earned for themselves the title of "classical speculator" and "investor" in the Widdis and Shannon typologies.

Most speculators were locally resident in the county and operated within it. Yet there were those such as the merchants J. and R. Park and William Duff and, most notably, John Askin and James Baby who acquired large acreages in other parts of Upper Canada or, in Askin's case, in parts of the United States. Moreover, there were many from beyond the boundaries of Essex and indeed, in the case of Edward Ellice, even beyond Canada who acquired Essex land. These included quintessential members of the Family Compact such as Bishop Strachan, William Allan, and Sir John Beverley Robinson, the three acting as a small consortium. They included people such as James McGill and Isaac Todd, drawn into Essex affairs because of their involvement with the fur trade and with John Askin. They also included individuals such as Thomas Clark, A.J. Robertson, Samuel Street (uncle and nephew) and Thomas Clark Street. The activities of this last group seemed to increase as time went on and as land was exhausted in more central locations. Yet they were among the biggest land speculators in Upper Canada and operated ubiquitously throughout the territory. The total extent of their holdings is as yet unknown, but the point is that Essex offered opportunity for these large players in the land market.

How these individuals, whether large or small, conducted their business must have been a matter of personal predisposition. Each must have used strategies that responded to personal circumstances and the larger condition in which they found themselves. These strategies are examined in the next chapter.

8 The Strategies of Speculators

This chapter examines the behaviour of the 144 individuals identified as speculators in the previous chapter. It seeks to examine the strategy of these people both as individuals and as groups. The questions asked include: Were these people purposeful with respect to the physical environment, that is, did they chose the better soils and drainage conditions required by an agricultural economy? If the purpose of the overwhelming number of people was to become farmers, did land speculators know how to select suitable land? Were particular patterns of location pursued by individuals to maximize opportunity? Was there a particular geometry sought or was the pattern of speculative holding wholly fortuitous? How did particular individuals behave with respect to particular political and economic circumstances? Were some time periods more prone to speculation than others? Were there particular strategies used by speculators to acquire land?

LAND SPECULATION AND THE PHYSICAL ENVIRONMENT

Table 8.1 shows the summary statistics for the 1640 properties owned by the speculative groups relative to the physical environment. Good and imperfect land is shown to have constituted 6.2 and 22.9 per cent of the county respectively but speculators acquired 17.25 and 29.7 per cent of their lands within these classes. While they had more property (Table 8.1) on poorly endowed land, in relative terms they fared better, seeking and obtaining proportionately more of the better lands

Table 8.1   Distribution of properties by environmental quality and speculator groupings

Name	Good		Imperfect		Poor		Very Poor		Total
	$\bar{x}$	%	$\bar{x}$	%	$\bar{x}$	%	$\bar{x}$	%	
Cluster 1	223	19.6	365	32.0	534	47.0	17	1.5	1139
Cluster 2	0	0.0	10	12.5	70	87.5	0	0.0	80
Cluster 3	6	4.6	21	16.0	104	79.4	0	0.0	131
Cluster 4	27	15.9	57	33.5	81	47.7	5	2.9	170
Cluster 5	25	27.4	25	27.4	41	45.1	0	0.0	91
Cluster 6	2	6.9	9	31.0	18	62.1	0	0.0	29
Total	283	17.3	487	29.7	848	51.7	22	0.0	1640
Essex County	n/a	6.2	n/a	22.9	n/a	67.4	n/a	3.5	

Source: Calculations of the author.

in the county. In a county in which 29.1 per cent of land was classed as "good" or "imperfect," these people had 48.0 per cent of such land. In short, they would seem to have known what they were after, although, of course, every decision must have been weighted in financial terms. At least in their minds, an extremely low price and limited endowment might well have been traded against an anomalously high asking price but well-endowed property.

Again, if what was sought was not the capacity to farm but quick profit from cedar, this might explain seemingly irrational actions on the parts of some individuals such as Matthew Elliott, who acquired several properties in poorly drained Mersea (Figure 8.1). As in all things environmental, decisions were taken in the context of opportunity, intention, and costs. The result of all of this machination and cerebration was that speculators, with the exception of those in cluster 3, did well environmentally. In fact, the 131 properties in this class belonged to two individuals identified earlier as having little choice over location or choosing some factor above another. Burwell's choice was dictated by the lottery system by which he was recompensed for his services (Figure 8.2), Woods by the locations of the clients with whom he dealt (Figure 8.3).

The high percentage of poor land in cluster 2 reflects the fact that John Askin chose compactness over land quality (Figure 8.4); this factor has also affected the counts in other clusters. For example, in cluster 6, friend and agent Richard Pattinson received much of Askin's property and could not exercise a lot of choice. Only Askin was free to choose and he chose compactness rather than land quality.

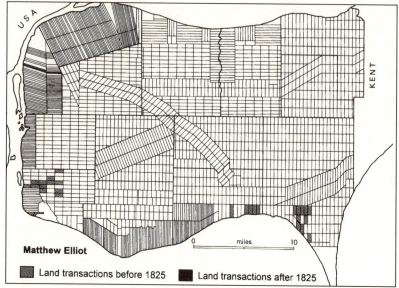

Figure 8.1   Matthew Elliott's holdings

Source: Abstract Index to Deeds.

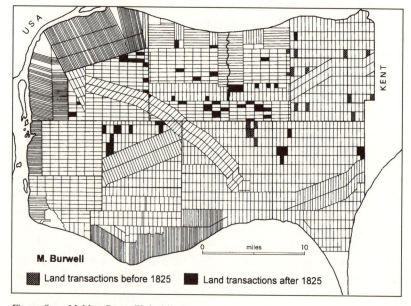

Figure 8.2   Mahlon Burwell's holdings

Source: Abstract Index to Deeds.

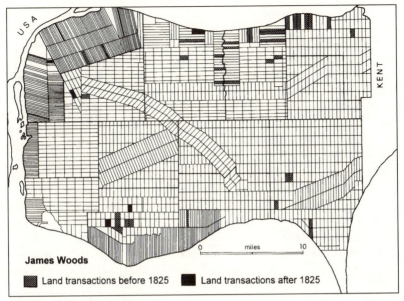

Figure 8.3   James Woods's holdings
Source: Abstract Index to Deeds.

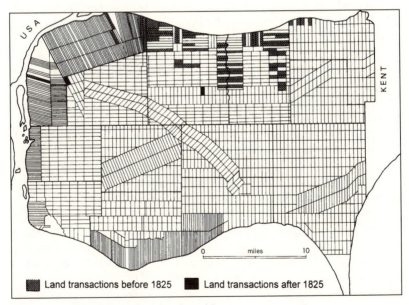

Figure 8.4   Holdings of John Askin, Sr and Jr
Source: Abstract Index to Deeds.

Patterns of Acquisition

Maps of all the holdings of 144 speculators were prepared to gauge the capacity of these individuals to determine environmental conditions, and also to establish whether they followed a particular strategy within Essex. In only thirty-two cases were holdings confined to one township; in thirty-five instances, speculators restricted their activity to two townships and in thirty-two instances to three. In the remaining forty-five cases, these people risked their resources in four or more townships. The overall pattern was one of scatter (figures 8.5–8.8), reinforcing the idea that these were genuine speculative ventures rather than additions made to secure the future prosperity of children. This was the most common pattern, found throughout the groups with the possible exception of the last. Among this fifth group (with the exception of Meldrum and Park), the members concentrated on adjoining lots, obtained their lands by patent or purchase, made the least number of transactions (mean equals 18.4) throughout the period ending in 1852, and held their land for an average of 32.9 years. Among this group were Mary Cornwall, the French royalist and merchant Quetton St George, Robert H.B. Elliott, John Jackson, and Lieutenant John Maule. With properties abutting on one another and fewer than six transactions, these people were probably closer to the "farm" end of the speculator continuum. The merchants Hall, McKee, and McIntosh averaged thirty transactions but for business reasons still concentrated their holdings.

Table 8.2 shows summary statistics for the fifteen individuals who had at least fifty transactions in Essex in these years. The table provides an idea of the distances involved. Fifty is thought to be a sufficiently large number of transactions to support the argument that these events took place with an intent to support more than the family, that is, they were undertaken primarily for the benefit of the individual. The average distance between properties for these people was found to be 1.2 miles, the range 1.74 miles. The table reports the level of clustering evaluated by *rho*, the nearest neighbour statistic. This technique, based upon the work of the plant ecologists Philip Clark and Francis Evans,[1] compares the mean distance between plants or people to that which might be expected if the observed distribution was ordered randomly. Obviously, the closer the statistic is to zero the greater the clustering since the distance between individuals is minimized. An upper limit of 2.149 indicates that the distribution is uniform, a condition not expected in the present context; an intermediate value of 1.0 is interpreted as spatial randomness, although, one hastens to add, not purposelessness.

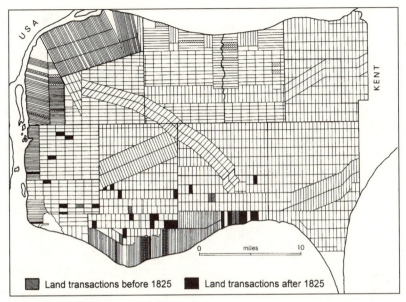

Figure 8.5   Holdings of T.F and J.R. Park.

Source: Abstract Index to Deeds.

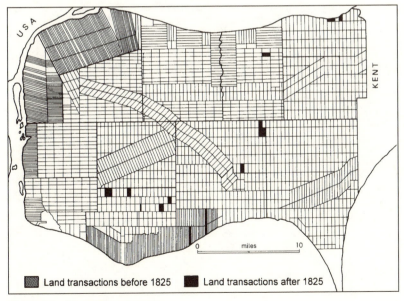

Figure 8.6   Samuel Street's holdings

Source: Abstract Index to Deeds.

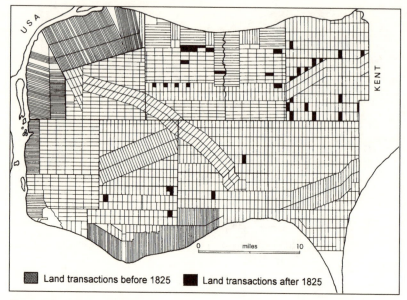

Figure 8.7 T.C. Street's holdings

Source: Abstract Index to Deeds.

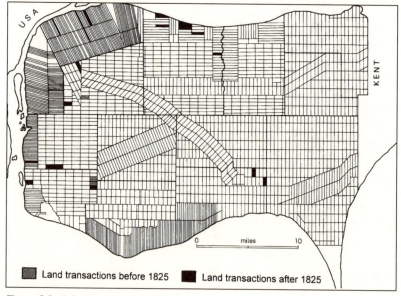

Figure 8.8 J.G. Watson's holdings.

Source: Abstract Index to Deeds.

Table 8.2   Distance between speculative holdings in miles: Value of the nearest-neighbour statistic (Rho)

Name	$\bar{x}$	σ	n^*	Rho
C. Baby	2.16	1.79	21	0.75**
W. Duff	1.10	0.90	33	0.48**
A. McIntosh	0.42	0.20	13	0.11**
T. McKee	1.21	1.43	21	0.42**
R. Reynolds	0.89	0.53	16	0.27**
T. Smith	0.95	1.58	22	0.34**
J.G. Watson	1.43	0.90	21	0.49**
J. Askin	0.63	0.42	71	0.44**
R. Pattinson	1.27	1.21	33	0.55**
M. Burwell	1.11	0.79	85	0.77**
J. Woods	1.48	0.90	39	0.69**
J. McGill	1.06	0.79	38	0.49**
A.J. Robertson	1.95	2.38	21	0.68**
G. Meldrum & W. Park	1.43	1.85	24	0.53**
W. Pickersgill	0.47	0.25	28	0.97**

Source: Calculations of the author.

* equals the number of lots not transactions

** significant at 0.001

Obviously, some individuals showed a greater tendency to concentrate than others and some others appeared to tend more to a random pattern, for example, Mahlon Burwell (rho = 0.77) and James Woods (rho= 0.69: see figures 8.2 and 8.3).[2] Since the former drew for his lots and the latter was the quintessential opportunist who was willing to deal with either the local elite or the less noteworthy if the price was right, there is some comfort to be derived from these particular statistics. Presumably, Robertson (rho = 0.68) operated in a similar mode to Woods, although in his case there is an overlap with Pattinson from whom he acquired a sizeable proportion of his property (Figure 8.9).

Even within families there could be individual differences. Figure 8.10 shows Baby acquisitions to 1852. Francis, Jean-Baptiste, and James Baby showed a greater tendency to concentrate in particular areas most especially Sandwich, where the family home still stands, than did Charles Baby whose rho value approaches randomness. At the other end of the continuum, Angus McIntosh is one individual who acquired all of his land in a single township (Sandwich) and whose rho value indicates an especially clustered pattern (Figure 8.11). In fact, McIntosh was mainly interested in various properties bounded by lots 91 to 96 in the 1st and 2nd concessions. The abstract index records a mortgage for £25428.18s.8d. made between McIntosh

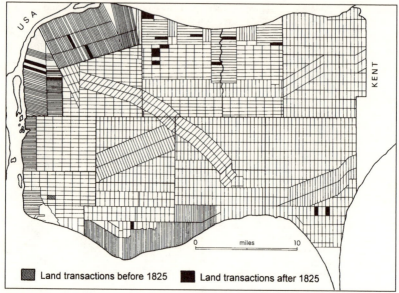

Figure 8.9   A.J. Robertson's holdings

Source: Abstract Index to Deeds.

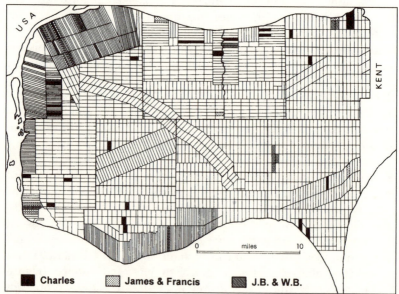

Figure 8.10   Holdings of the Baby family

Source: Abstract Index to Deeds.

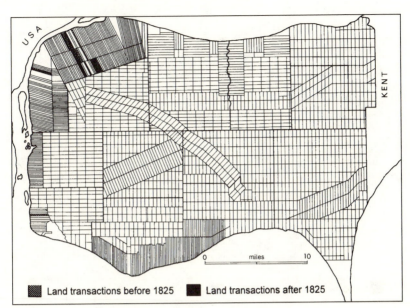

Figure 8.11   Angus McIntosh's holdings
Source: Abstract Index to Deeds.

and the Montreal firm of McTavish and McGillivray in 1812 for these lots, a considerable sum at the time. Much of the land was obtained from an Alexis Maisonville, who is known to have operated an inn on lots 93 and 94; lot 96 contained a windmill.[3] McIntosh was obviously in pursuit of other than wilderness to be transformed into homestead, although, as the entries in the abstracts show, he did engage in the sale of parcels of varying size.[4]

People with intermediate values include, among others, John Askin (0.44), James McGill (0.49), and Richard Pattinson (0.55). Askin is on record as seeking compactness in his choice of locations; when he collapsed financially he was "rescued" by his great friend McGill (Figure 8.12) and to a lesser extent by his son-in-law Richard Pattinson (Figure 8.13). Thirty-six of McGill's land transactions were made with Askin between 1803 and 1807; ten of Pattinson's deals were with Askin, his wife, or daughter in the period 1800 to 1809. Askin's choice of land obviously determined at least in part the pattern of McGill and Pattinson. These two people were unable to assess the land from an environmental perspective; that judgment was made by Askin. Askin was able to acquire land in Rochester and Maidstone because of his early initiative. Given the allocation of Crown and clergy reserves and the wet conditions of the area, the compactness of his lots meant that new-

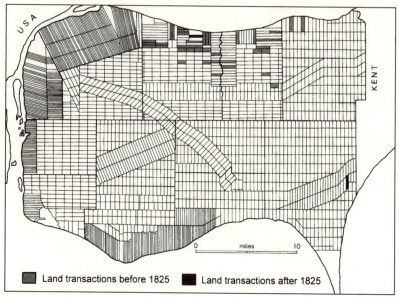

Figure 8.12   James McGill's holdings

Source: Abstract Index to Deeds.

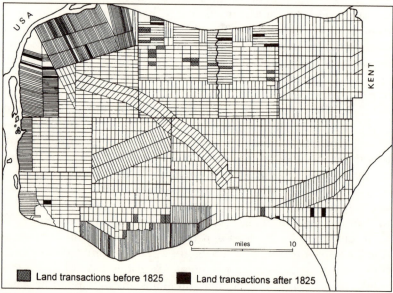

Figure 8.13   Richard Pattinson's holdings

Source: Abstract Index to Deeds.

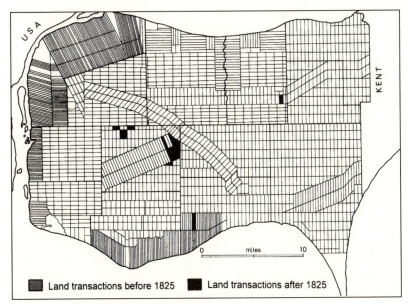

Land transactions before 1825   Land transactions after 1825

Figure 8.14   John A. Macdonald's holdings
Source: Abstract Index to Deeds.

comers had to deal with him. There were better areas for farming but he may have been more interested in timber. When he was embarrassed financially, his friends and relations came to his aid; his determination of areas for investment became theirs by default.

We are fortunate that Askin left records of his activity. Otherwise, we would have to rely upon inference from pattern. The pattern and his records suggest that location was determined by a variety of circumstances including knowledge of the environment, intention, the mechanism by which land was acquired (for surveyors the lottery), and chance opportunity. For some, locational decisions would seem to have been purposeful; but for many, the process would appear to have been *spatially* random although the intention may have been to maximize profit by benefiting from neighbouring developments. Even when lots were clustered this may not indicate design on the part of the purchaser especially if, as in the case of John A. Macdonald (Figure 8.14), he was acquiring the land as part of a larger package.

It is tempting to see the clustering of Macdonald land as anticipation of an embryonic urban structure in the village of Essex in the centre of the county and of the possibilities of enhanced value through improved transportation as rail came to Essex. Perhaps this is true but the evidence points not to Macdonald's awareness of the future but rather to the acumen of William Cunliffe Pickersgill and his Montreal agent, John Rose, who purchased land belonging to a bankrupt merchant house at auction.[5] In fact, this was part of a 9700-acre assemblage scattered over twelve townships and stretching beyond Essex. Macdonald was anxious to unload fast, and though he did not succeed in an attempt to sell to a fellow politician, Malcolm Cameron – "Offer open till Saturday next"[6] – within five months, he wrote to inform Rose of his success in selling to John Ewart, Toronto land agent,[7] and George Lount, the Simcoe County registrar. In doing so, he displayed his active interest in real estate: "Buy property in Montreal to any extent. It will be a fortune to you. Let me in."[8]

THE RELATIONSHIP BETWEEN SPECULATION AND TIME

Figures 8.15 to 8.20 summarize the activity of these individuals throughout the period. If patenting is included within the term, it is clear that the most active period for these people was in the earliest years of the British regime when British-sanctioned settlement was commencing in the county. As noted in an earlier chapter, the years 1805 to 1809 marked a period of sabre-rattling with the Americans. Speculators were not immune to such anxiety and adjusted their behaviour. They reduced their purchases and continued to do so into the war years 1810 to 1814, when their sales actually exceeded their purchases in the area (Figure 8.15). Although recovery began after 1815, the years 1815 to 1822 were ones of depression. If Burwell's patenting (Figure 8.16), undertaken to secure income from his surveying, is excluded from consideration, the number of purchases never reached pre-war levels again until 1830, and then quickly dropped again as Upper Canada entered a major depression in the mid-1830s and experienced rebellion in 1837.

The profile of acquisitions and sales seems complementary (Figure 8.15). True, particular profiles, for example, that of James Woods (Figure 8.16), appear asymmetrical. Quite why this was so for Woods, who died in 1828, is not clear – perhaps there was some particular difficulty in selling the lands he had acquired. This also seems to apply to the estate of James McGill who died in 1813, though sales continued in his name or that of his estate until mid-century. However, in a general sense, the profiles of acquisition and sales, no matter how long or short, appear symmetrical; Burwell (Figure 8.16), McCormick and Pattinson (Figure 8.17), Duff and McKee (Figure 8.18), Askin

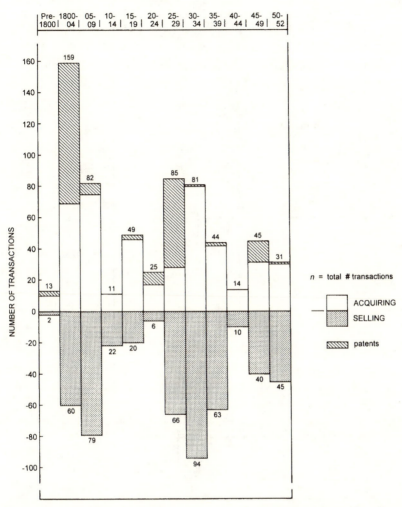

Figure 8.15   Summary of pattern of acquisition and sale for speculators with at least fifty transactions

Source: Abstract Index to Deeds.

and Baby (Figure 8.19), and J.G. Watson (Figure 8.20) are cases in point. The objective of this most active group seems to have been to unload as quickly as it acquired. Many of these people stayed in the land-speculation business in Essex for a great number of years, either through necessity, as in Burwell's case, or by choice as in most other instances; indeed once in, it seems that they stayed as long as they could.

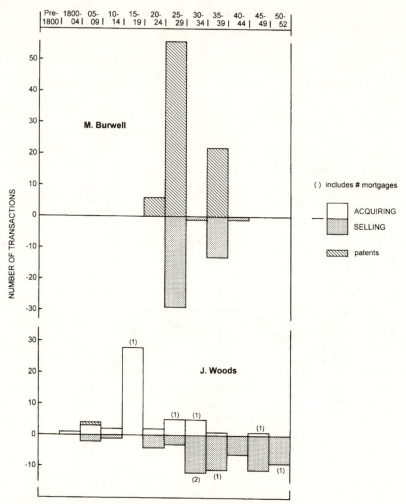

Figure 8.16   Patterns of acquisition and sale by Mahlon Burwell and James Woods
Source: Abstract Index to Deeds.

Only John A. Macdonald, who invested late in Essex, exited early but he continued his speculative business elsewhere.[9] Acquiring his land from Pickersgill, who had, in turn, assembled it at auction from a bankrupt firm in which one James Holmes was a partner, he sold it in 1853. The merchant William Duff was in the market for fifty-two years; John Gowie Watson bought and sold land for forty-five years and not only in his capacity as sheriff; Angus McIntosh was active for twenty-

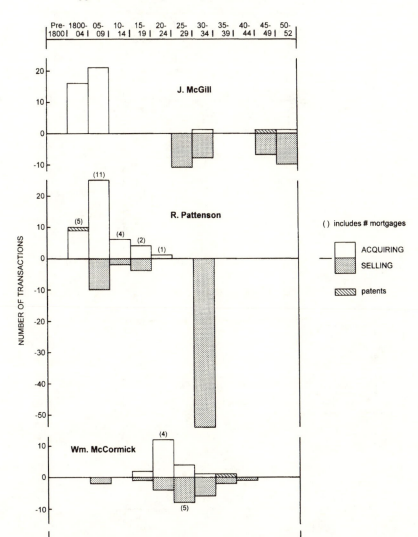

Figure 8.17   Patterns of acquisition and sale by James McGill, William McCormick, and Richard Pattinson

Source: Abstract Index to Deeds.

nine years and William McCormick for thirty-six years. The average duration in the market for twelve of these people was 27.7 years. Some started early in life, McCormick at age twenty, Woods at twenty-two, Pattinson at twenty-seven, but the average age of nine whose bio-

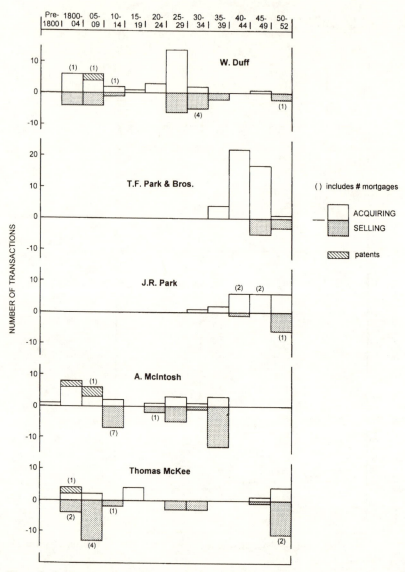

Figure 8.18   Patterns of acquisition and sale by William Duff, T.F. Park and Bros., J.R. Park, Angus McIntosh, and Thomas McKee

Source: Abstract Index to Deeds.

graphical sketches are known was 39.3 and George Meldrum, John Askin, and James McGill were sixty-three, sixty-one, and fifty-six when they began to acquire Essex land, having hitherto had their assets tied

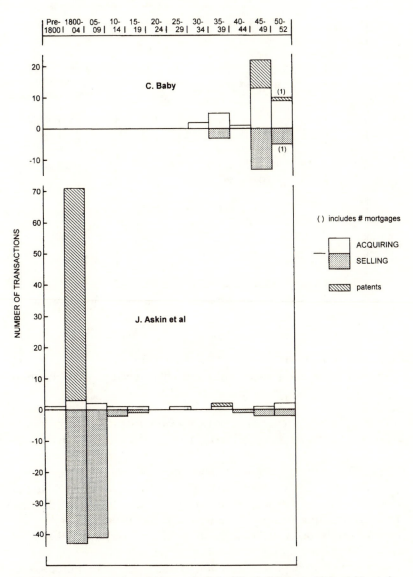

Figure 8.19   Patterns of acquisition and sale by C[harles] Baby and John Askin et al
Source: Abstract Index to Deeds.

up in furs, the Indian trade, and general merchandise. McGill, of course, was dragged into the business of land speculation by Askin's indebtedness to him, and though he became an avid convert for a time, he soon came to realize its dangers and shortcomings.[10]

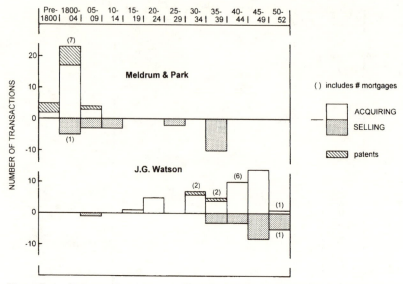

Figure 8.20   Patterns of acquisition and sale by Meldum and Park and J.G. Watson
Source: Abstract Index to Deeds.

This is all that one can say in general about the group; no doubt individual lives manifested individual characteristics. The question must therefore turn to the matter of profit.

THE ECONOMICS OF LAND SPECULATION: WAS SPECULATION PROFITABLE FOR INDIVIDUALS?

Did the speculators make money on their investment? Table 8.3 displays the price (by five-year periods) paid by speculators relative to the general price series. It suggests that they probably did. Until 1841 the price paid by speculators was always lower than the general sale price and a correlation analysis of these data produced a coefficient of 0.57.[11] After that year it would seem that speculators were prepared to pay more than average for a commodity that was itself on the rise. Presumably, as demand for land increased in the decades of the 1840s and 1850s as a result of heavy immigration, increased in number, speculators were prepared to pay a premium. Wealthy immigrants would in turn be willing to pay for a resource located in older, more settled townships rather than establish themselves in more remote, less developed areas. Buying low, they presumably made profits, but because of the condition of the records and the paucity of both purchase and sale price, one can only infer profit from a small number of cases.

Table 8.3   Five-year averages of land prices (pence per acre) in Essex
for the population as a whole and for the subgroup land speculator

Period	Speculator price	n	General price	n
1798–1800	141.00	2	306.00	31
1801–1805	118.21	5	393.75	17
1806–1810	146.19	28	184.40	80
1811–1815	177.02	10	266.66	39
1816–1820	277.41	24	332.40	119
1821–1825	274.70	22	356.20	115
1826–1830	274.27	16	369.00	170
1831–1835	184.31	62	311.60	287
1836–1840	509.56	69	567.40	496
1841–1845	520.93	50	456.80	440
1846–1850	737.44	67	492.40	664

Source: Calculations of the author.

Of all the individuals speculating in land, it is possible to compute
annual returns on only fifty-eight individuals in this time period and
then not from all of their transactions. In order to allow for the effect
of time, an annual rate of return (based upon an equivalent investment in a compound form) was calculated.[12] For the limited range of
data for which returns were available, seven individuals were shown to
have lost money, some dramatically. Thus, R.T. Reynolds, acting in his
private capacity rather than as sheriff, lost in one year 68.75 per cent
of his investment of £200 in lot 5 in the 2nd concession of Mersea.
This did not include legal disbursements, taxes, or improvements on
which for this, as for all other properties, the record is silent. In one
year (1843) the Fox family lost 58.3 per cent of their investment in
Mersea Township. One individual with the heroic name of Horatio
Nelson lost 29.3 per cent per annum on fifty acres purchased in Gosfield in 1836 and sold four years later. In Sandwich, Jul. (Julien?) Langlois lost 20.9 per cent per annum on the 116 acres of land he had
acquired for £400 and disposed of two years later, that is, in 1818.
Other losses occurred over a longer period of time and were not so
dramatic. Charles Berczy lost 15.1 per cent per annum on land in
Malden, selling for £52.10s.0d. in 1841 what he had purchased eleven
years earlier. Four others lost less than 3 per cent per annum for
between four and thirteen years.

Gains could be equally dramatic; indeed, three of the fifty-eight
speculators identified here made annual gains of 50 to 100 per cent,

Table 8.4 Variations in returns per year for particular individuals and properties

Name of Individual	Twp	Location Lot	Location Con.	Purchase Date	Purchase Price (pence)	Sale Date	Sale Price (pence)	%/Year Return
Asa Wilcox	Mal	55	5	1827	36000	1839	36000	0.00
Asa Wilcox	Mal	67	6	1836	12000	1836	15000	25.00
C. Baby	San	10	2	1849	30000	1849	30000	0.00
C. Baby	San	5	2	1835	12000	1835	27000	125.00
C. Baby	Mer	9	Bf A[1]	1834	480	1836	6000	253.55
C. Stuart	Mal	23	2	1818	5064	1826	5400	0.81
C. Stuart	Mal	23	2	1818	1272	1826	2736	10.05
C. Stuart	Mal	23	2	1818	10104	1824	18900	11.00
E. Ellice	Mal	67	6	1808	7500	1833	15000	2.81
E. Ellice	Mal	67	6	1808	7500	1830	15000	3.20
E. Ellice	Gos	21	FCW[2]	1810	12000	1834	26748	3.40
Hy. Whaley	Gos	9	3	1840	6000	1848	18000	14.72
Hy. Whaley	Gos	9	3	1840	6000	1848	30000	22.28
J. Woods	Til	12	Bf	1811	24000	1825	24000	0.00
J. Woods	Mer	11	BfA	1815	24000	1835	27000	0.59
J. Woods	San	4	5	1807	12000	1820	18000	3.17
J. Woods	Gos	5	4	1811	2400	1840	96000	13.56
J. Strong	Mer	11	1	1840	18000	1846	15000	−2.99
J. Strong	Gos	9	3	1837	48000	1846	48000	0.00
J. Strong	Gos	9	3	1837	48000	1846	48000	0.00
J. Strong	Gos	262s	TRW[3]	1840	21600	1848	30000	4.19
J. Strong	Gos	23	5	1837	24876	1838	28800	15.77
J. Strong	Gos	262s	TRW	1840	2400	1848	18000	28.64
W. McCormick	Col	60	Frt[4]	1825	36000	1838	36000	−3.07
W. McCormick	Col	56	Frt	1822	42000	1828	42000	0.00
W. McCormick	Col	60	Frt	1825	36000	1840	36000	0.00
W. McCormick	Mer	18	1	1820	6000	1833	10800	4.63
W. McCormick	Mer	19	1	1820	6000	1833	18000	8.82
W. McCormick	Mer	21	1	1820	6000	1826	12000	12.25
W. McCormick	Col	60	Frt	1825	36000	1836	19200	16.44
W. Duff	Col	20	Gore	1825	24000	1826	48000	100.00
W. Duff	Col	51	Frt	1806	14637	1825	12000	−1.04

Source: AO, Abstract Index to Deeds, Essex County.

[1]Broken Front
[2]Front Concession West
[3]Talbot Road West
[4]Front

three others between 100 and 200 per cent, and six more than 200 per cent. One L. Montreille, who in his earlier ventures in Maidstone Township had made only 5 per cent per annum, acquired eighty acres of lot 106 in the 1st concession of Sandwich in 1850. He unloaded 1.16 acres in 1852 for a figure exceeding the purchase price of his

Table 8.5   Rate of annual return (Percentage) within size classes

Class (acres)	Number Properties	$\bar{x}$	σ
0–50	36	24.95	66.10
51–100	55	11.46	24.92
101–150	11	11.12	36.79
151–200	117	14.93	44.03

Source: Calculations of the author.

original investment, netting an annual return of 862.6 per cent, a most astute sale to the railway company then arriving in this area. A less spectacular but nonetheless impressive investment was made by an R. Boyle, who in the two years 1850 to 1852, transformed his investment in 0.5 acres near the burgeoning village of Harrow into a 207 per cent annual increment.[13] James Askin produced a return of 398.01 per cent per annum for a two-year investment in 113 acres in Sandwich Township,[14] having purchased it on a sheriff's deed, and John McDonnell achieved a 400 per cent return on a less than one-year investment in Maidstone. Charles Baby made 253.5 per cent per annum on lot 9 in the broken front of Mersea, land he purchased in 1834 and sold in 1836. He also made 125 per cent on lot five in the 2nd concession of Sandwich, purchased and sold in the same year. With lot 10 in the same concession, acquired in 1849, he was less successful, unloading it the same year for the purchase price alone. Nonetheless, by spreading the load he produced an average profit of 126.18 per cent per annum! These individuals did better than most but for speculators as a whole returns were considerable, averaging 28.4 per cent per annum.[15]

The variability for individuals could be considerable (Table 8.4); some fared poorly while others did extremely well. For the group as a whole, the average return for the speculators was 33.24 per cent per annum,[16] which at a time when interest in excess of 6 per cent was regarded as usurious, would have provided an incentive to invest in land. What is also apparent in this table and in the larger data set is that the rate of return varied inversely with the length of time held. Shannonian "quick-flippers" such as Montreille, Boyle, McDonnell, and Baby had the highest annual returns; the long-term investor had the lowest, although, of course, in absolute terms, things may have been different.[17]

Throughout the period the returns varied throughout the size continuum (Table 8.5);[18] the smaller the properties involved the greater the return. Presumably, this reflects an intensity of use and perhaps proximity to urban centre. Eight of the twenty-four cases in the smaller size category were properties that were close to Amherstburg or Harrow or included a shop or mill and potashery or were simply on the Talbot Road. One of the highest returns was for a half-acre on lot 12 in the Gore of Colchester, bought and sold within two years for an annual return of 207.15 per cent by one R. Boyle. Boyle bought low and sold high, the traditional route to profit.

Land Speculation, Land Price, Taxation and Indebtedness

How could cheap land be obtained? One of the surest ways to profit was to buy for a song what others had been forced to relinquish for tax failure. Such land could be obtained by speculators watching tax sales, by having agents watch, or by acting aggressively against debtors. As noted earlier, mortgage foreclosures do not appear in the land records per se, presumably because prior to the creation of a Court of Chancery in 1837 there was no real possibility of foreclosure. Equity was pursued under the common law and the form of the legal instruments used included a default whereby title was granted to the mortgagee. Yet, in the 1830s, there were individuals who built businesses and did not hesitate to foreclose or force sales where indebtedness in whatever form was involved. How extensive this was in Essex is not known but two of the most celebrated cases involved people active in speculating in the county.

The first of the cases involved Robert Randal, whom readers will recall had been involved with John Askin, William Robertson, and others in the attempted purchase of the southern portion of Michigan. As their American agent, he had been imprisoned following investigation by the Congress and this may well have affected the later attitude of the Upper Canadian judiciary towards him. He subsequently acquired an interest in a superb iron-working site on the Ottawa River at the Chaudière Falls as well as a source of iron in the same area. Samuel Street, Jr, and Thomas Clark had purchased the share of his former partners. Clark visited Randal in prison in 1812 in an attempt to force him to sell the business and managed to keep him in jail in an age when creditors still possessed such power. Randal languished in jail until 1815; in fact he spent six and a half years in jail for debt.

Two juries upheld Randal's position against Street and Clark. Traditionally, this was sufficient to end such a matter. However, his property was sold at a sheriff's sale at less than market value, in fulfilment of a judgment brought against him by his own lawyer and creditor Henry John Boulton[19] (son of Justice D'Arcy Boulton),[20] though as a debtor he had not been informed of the impending action. At a fourth hearing in 1817, Randal represented himself because Boulton would not. He was opposed by John Beverley Robinson,[21] the pre-eminent lawyer of the time. The judge, William Dummer Powell, threatened the jury with a writ of "attaint," or disciplinary action, if they rendered a verdict contradicting the evidence unless they had private knowledge that contradicted it. Randal was refused another trial by the Court of King's Bench though this would have been "normal" in the circumstance. He lost his property, purportedly to the defendant Elijah Phelps but in reality to Clark. His Chaudière property, an estate of 1000 acres, was sold at auction by the sheriff at much less than market value. Indeed more of it was sold than was needed to meet the debt. The sheriff who seized Randal's property was the brother-in-law of both his lawyer Boulton and one of the co-purchasers of the property, Levius Sherwood of Brockville. Subsequent attempts to reopen the case between Randal and Boulton in the Court of King's Bench were inconclusive because two of the members of the court, D'Arcy Boulton and Levius Sherwood (now elevated to the bench), had an interest in the issue.[22]

With respect to the property that Randal had owned in the Niagara peninsula, this was sold at auction to Thomas Clark after a judgment obtained by Clark against Randal: 1200 acres were obtained by Clark for £40 and Clark then pursued Randal for the remaining £400 owed him. He was also charged with perjury for describing the properties taken from him in this way as his property qualification to stand for the House of Assembly. The charge was laid by Attorney General Robinson upon information given him by Clark and Street! In a similar manner, Clark and Street plotted against a Joseph Pell, importing Pell's nephew to oppose the uncle, paying his legal fees, and agreeing to split the proceeds. Romney's judgment that provincial justice was a "system run by the rich for the rich" would seem justified.[23]

Besides using indebtedness to obtain judgments against individuals, speculators also watched tax sales for opportunities. This could arise when individuals ran foul of the existing tax system. Taxation was not something that speculators cared for since it limited profits; most generally they sought to hide from tax collectors until it was absolutely necessary in order to secure a sale.

There was in Upper Canada a dialectic with respect to land, whereby taxation could not be set so high that it discouraged the cultivation of land, nor so low that it permitted the speculator to keep land off the market and out of cultivation. Taxation, then as now, was a vehicle of social engineering, epitomized in the Upper Canadian context by Edward Gibbon Wakefield's attempts in the 1830s to set government land prices and taxation levels in such a way that a genuine market for

land would be developed and a sufficient pool of labourers maintained to work it.[24] If taxation was too stiff, speculators might be
obliged to sell so rapidly that the land market would be depressed. In
these circumstances, labourers could afford to become yeoman
farmers, thus depleting the labour force. If, on the other hand, the
price of land was set too high, this would be to the ultimate benefit of
speculators and in these conditions there might well be an exodus to
the United States. Land price, taxation, and the development of the
colony are seen here to be most intimately associated. In establishing
the relationship between these elements, the powerful organized
through their political representatives to oppose taxation or to effect
designs that would secure their personal interests. Their goals might
well be different from those of actual occupants, who, for example,
might wish to see roads built through undeveloped properties. Several
individuals in Essex were engaged in the debate over taxation and
many others from and beyond the county came to use the provisions
for tax sales to accumulate to their own benefit.

Between 1798 and 1803 there were several attempts to initiate tax-
assessment legislation in Upper Canada but they met with opposition.
An 1803 Act, enacted after six years of controversy, barely passed, with
the speaker casting the deciding vote. This assessed cultivated land at
one pound per acre and wild land at one shilling.[25] Its opponents
ensured that wives and infants would be exempt and the legislation
allowed non-residents of the province to escape taxation altogether.
Edward Ellice, who held land in Essex, was but one example. In spite
of this and the fact that it permitted people to pay in the township in
which they resided rather than where their land was, this act was re-
enacted in 1807 and again in 1811 when the rate for wild land was
established first at two shillings and later at four. Although the landed
interest was losing ground, it ensured that the legislation applied only
to residents of the province and no means were provided to ensure
that wild land would in fact be reported.[26]

This circumstance changed with the acts of 1819, and 1824. Land
had to be reported only for the township in which one lived. The taxpayer's word was no longer accepted but had to be verified, and the
surveyor general was required to furnish lists of all who had been
granted land. The rate of assessment was raised to four shillings for
wild land and twenty shillings per acre for cultivated land.[27] Yet the
penalties remained weak. It was true that chattels and goods could be
seized fourteen days after demand was made but a non-resident had
nothing to seize. Although interest accumulated and the rate rose with
the length of time in arrears, many simply hoped that the Acts of 1819
and 1824 would be repealed.

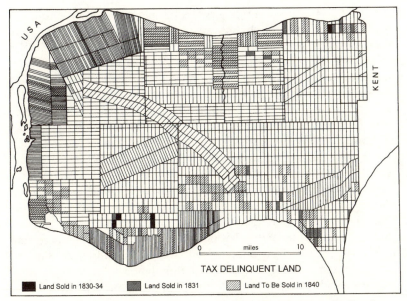

Figure 8.21   Land disposed of in 1831 and 1830–34, and to be disposed of in 1840
Source: AO, F378, HWHM, 20–248.

In fact, these acts, which were scheduled to expire in 1828, were made permanent. Land in arrears for eight years, on which no distress could be found, could now be sold. The original owner was to have one year in which to redeem it, subject to a 20 per cent premium.[28] Opposition to the passage of this legislation came from the leading land speculators, notably William Dickson[29] and Thomas Clark, operating both in Essex and across the province. James (Jacques) Baby, long associated with the area, and now on the Executive Council, and William Dummer Powell, first judge for the area voiced opposition. The last, because of his legal position, did so quietly.[30]

Their arguments included appeals to the oft-proclaimed rights of widows and orphans, the need to recognize the role of investors, the inherent unfairness of a flat-rate system, the adverse effects of the existing acts upon operation of the market, and the importance of establishing an aristocracy. Despite their rhetoric and vehemence, they were successfully opposed by Lieutenant Governor Maitland. The first sales were set to occur in the spring of 1830. The average price would be 6.25 pence per acre and one million acres in Upper Canada would be put up at auction.[31]

Figure 8.21 shows the distribution of lands disposed of in 1831 and between 1830 to 1834 for two different tax periods and lands to be sold in 1840.[32] This land in Essex was but part of a larger amount of tax-delinquent land purchased not by farmers but by capitalists who already possessed thousands of acres. Thomas Clark informed John Galt of the Canada Company that he, in company with his partner Samuel Street and William Dickson, were the principal purchasers throughout the province.[33] Clark was in fact so well known that his name does not appear in full in the records of land sold for back taxes; instead, it was abbreviated to "T.C." Between June and September 1831, 16,542 acres were sold in this way in the Western District.

Thomas Clark bought 2446 acres, Chris Arnold 1200 acres, Charles Askin 590,[34] Alexander Berlett 550, John Hands 460, and Samuel Street, acting through his agent William Dickson, himself a large spec-ulator, 9009.[35] To put this in relative context, at a time when the Canada Company was offering the former Crown reserves at ten shillings and three pence halfpenny (123.5 pence) per acre and Crown land was fetching between four and fifteen shillings (48 to 180 pence), these men bought this tax-delinquent land at between four pence and a half pence and five and a quarter pence per acre.[36] The purchase of these lots was clearly a sound financial investment! The Quebec *Mercury* reported that "the speculator who purchases at these sales knows that he may keep them for eight years without paying any tax, before they can be forfeited and sold for arrears and he cannot employ his capital in any more profitable way than in buying for 4d an acre land which he may hold up the next day at 5s. per acre, and for which in the course of eight years he has every chance of getting 10s."[37] A return of such proportions, 120 pence per acre on an invest-ment of 4 pence, would not come every day!

Clearly, it was the policy that permitted redemption which explains why these early sales are spatially less extensive on this map than those lots which were to be sold in 1840.[38] Were it possible to re-create the pattern of lands to be sold for taxes in the 1830s, the pattern would no doubt have been spatially more extensive, as in 1840 (Table. 8.6). In fact, of the 258 properties disposed of in 1840, only 8 are actually known to have changed hands although an additional 13 might have; in most cases (91.9 per cent) the property was saved for the individual or the family.[39]

In effect, these lands had escaped taxation for seven years. These 258 properties were owned by 147 people; most of them were single parcels owned by 115 individual owners who were unable to pay until threatened by confiscation and sale or who found no compulsion in the existing legislation, which allowed them to hide from revenue offi-cials. Thirty-two owned two or more properties; ten appear on the list of speculators identified in this study. The estate of Matthew Elliott

Table 8.6   List of tax-delinquent land in Essex County

Twp	Land sold for the tax period 1820–28, in 1831 (acres)	Land sold for the tax period 1824–32, between 1830 and 1834 (acres)	Land to be sold in 1840 (acres)
Colchester	1,252.00	464	2930
Gosfield	293.00	–	8455
Maidstone	189.00	–	9199
Malden	–	–	10162
Mersea	1,374.00	–	4670
Rochester	400.00	–	6258
Sandwich	203.75	–	3455
Tilbury	813.00	228	7325
Total	4,524.75	692	52454

Source: Clarke, "Geographical Analysis," 123.

owned nine such properties and that of James McGill owned thirteen. No doubt these estates were in process of being settled and would eventually bear the burden of taxation; but James Woods, the lawyer, was alive and active and he owned thirteen tax-encumbered lots. Clearly, withholding taxes was a mechanism practised by all since at one-fifth of a penny the tax on wild land was insufficiently high to warrant action. Among the 147 in arrears were 40 land speculators who appear in Appendix 7.1 and who between them owned 38 per cent (83 lots) of the land in tax arrears. Given the existing law of the time, such action was not illegal; it was financially rational. The list included a number of well-known merchants such as Matthew Elliott, William Duff, and John R. Park, members of the executive and legislative councils such as James McGill and John Richardson, and notorious speculators such as John Askin and Samuel Street.[40] As noted, three of these people, Matthew Elliott, James McGill, and John Askin, were actually deceased; presumably their executors operated on behalf of their estates.

Some of these people had actually acquired their land in this manner at an earlier date. For example, Samuel Street acquired lot 13 in the 5th concession of Rochester by sheriff's deed in 1831; Charles Askin bought lot 12 in the 3rd concession of the same township in 1832, William Duff acquired lot 12 in the 3rd concession of Colchester by such means in 1823; and William McCormick bought lot 24 in the 4th concession of Mersea at such a sale in 1832, as did Charles Berczy who acquired lot 14 in c concession in 1832. These people must have been well aware of the dangers in their situation but were able to avoid the consequences that befall those from whom they had acquired their properties.[41]

Appendix 8.1 lists sales by sheriff's deeds which are to be found within the abstract index to deeds for Essex for the years to 1852. The abstracts are the most systematic source of information on these deeds, whose survival otherwise is quixotic. There were 38 purchasers of such land before 1852; 23 of them were included among the 144 speculators discussed here.[42] The appendix lists the current purchaser and the parties to the preceding transaction. A number of the speculators occur among the prior transactions also. Thus, William Hands, acting as sheriff, sold lot 14 in the 1st concession of Tilbury to Samuel Street for 78 shillings in 1831. This 213-acre lot had ten years earlier been sold by Jean-Baptiste Baby to James Baby. There were only 9 such recorded sales before 1831[43] but 47 of the 106 took place in 1831 and 1832 and 10 in 1847. Clearly, there were few such sales in the early years when the assessment acts were only being established, but a mounting number in the third and fourth decade as the legislation took effect.

Of these 107 sales, 71 were accompanied by money. Table 8.7 shows the prices paid in the townships of the county for the period as a whole. The period in which the purchase of these lands was most active was in the years 1831 and 1832. In these years the average price per acre for such land was 5.27 pence per acre with a standard deviation (σ) of 1.49 pence. Yet land in this time-frame was being sold at 311.6 pence per acre (Table 8.3). Speculators were accustomed to paying less but even they must have been struck by their acumen and good fortune.[44] Even if the average for the whole period is taken (21.17 pence per acre), purchasers at these sales did exceedingly well, although there was some variation by township.[45]

Given these prices, speculators were keen to acquire such land. In fact of the 38 individuals who purchased this type of land between 1818 and 1852, 23 were on the list of 144 identified for analysis. These people owned all but 16 of the properties purchased; as noted above, the largest buyers here, as in Upper Canada as a whole, were Samuel and T.C. Street and Thomas Clark, a threesome linked by kinship, common interest, and partnership.[46]

These same people sought to ensure that their taxes were up to date, to protect their interest. Paying taxes was not only desirable to preserve property, but could be used to secure it in the first instance, as Charles Askin, acting for William Robertson, noted in 1804: "There is also a charge for Land tax on yours at Grosse Point both of which my Father thinks it is right I should pay for it's not for your interest to

Table 8.7   Prices paid for tax–delinquent land

Twp	$\bar{x}$ (pence)	σ (pence)	Deeds with money	Total (n)
Colchester	6.04	4.43	8	14
Gosfield	33.55	98.57	14	16
Malden	n/a	n/a	n/a	4
Maidstone	36.94	32.15	18	22
Mersea	7.06	5.28	14	23
Rochester	16.43	14.73	8	8
Sandwich	4.45	0.22	4	6
Tilbury	14.47	22.13	5	13
Total	21.17	47.90	71	106

Source: AO, Abstract Index to Deeds, Essex County.

N.B. No data for Anderdon Township.

be on a bad footing with the surveyor and paying taxes gives you a better title."[47]

What follows provides some insight into how decisions might be taken to acquire or retain land and in the context of the present discussion to pay taxes. It is an excerpt from a letter of Leonidas Burwell to his brother in which the former is evaluating their inheritance, the lands acquired by their father, Mahlon Burwell. The letter is interesting because of its stress upon relative location, change, and land and timber quality,

I visited nearly all our lands in Sandwich Rochester Maidstone and the Tilburys and had in some cases to go several miles in the woods on foot. I found them of a better quality than I expected with a fair prospect of increasing in value owing to their situation being in the neighbourhood of the line of rail Road and also to other improvements in roads and drainage.

The country has been heretofore very wet but it can and will all be drained. It is generally quite unsettled but it can not much longer remain so. The middle road passing through those townships was well graded by the Government and will no doubt before long be gravelled or planked. [B]y looking at the Map you will see that the road runs nearly parallel with the rail road at a distance of nearly four to seven miles from it. The facilities must tend to open up the country in a short time. Many of our lands are heavily timbered indicating a strong rich soil. They resemble very much the land in the immediate vicinity of Chatham. [P]erhaps in some instances they are a little wetter. Upon the whole I cannot do other than recommend that the taxes should be paid on all our land excepting perhaps the three lots in Colchester which are situated in a swamp and which are valued so very low by the assessor. These lots I did not visit but was told that they are not worth much besides they are situated in a place that will not improve for a long time. From what I have seen of our lands and taking into account the improving state of the country I should be willing to pay 3/9 per acre for them and pay the taxes besides and then be sure of making something pretty good by waiting a few years. This being the case I cannot but recommend that they should be kept and the taxes paid upon them. I have no doubt but that father thought them almost valueless as there had been nothing done to improve the country until recently and formerly it was thought to be almost covered with water.

Mr. Bullock told me that they would not be sold this year but that he was engaged in making out a list to be advertised which will mean some additional expense unless we pay the taxes before long...[48]

In the final paragraph is the threat of loss via Mr Bullock, who no doubt was the tax assessor. This was something that the Burwells clearly sought to avoid.

A celebrated case of loss in Essex was the land of Richard Pattinson, abruptly sold for taxes (Figure 8.13). Sixteen hundred acres of this were "knocked-down" to A.J. Robertson, perhaps through the negligent behaviour of James Gordon, though he denied responsibility.[49] William Hands, whose son, John, had lands beyond the Western District[50], on which assessments were due, seems to have discharged his obligations in a responsible manner, writing to those whose land was threatened and posting notices of tax delinquency. Some recognized his power; others expressed their power over him. Some seemed to view him as their employee rather than the representative of the state, offering him money for information from which they might gain. This he supplied either because as a multiple office holder[51] he depended on the support of the prominent, or because he was genuinely moving land on behalf of the government, although at the prices paid this cannot have been too onerous a task.

No doubt chastened by his experience with the Pattinson debacle, James Gordon was anxious to pay the arrears on the estate of James Dunlop.[52] One man, an M. Meredith, in a letter to Hands in 1833 acknowledged his debt of £33.10.0, but he went on to explain that "owing to having embarked on another speculation it would be rather inconvenient to find that sum at the instant." However, he would be willing to pay to avoid having his name appear in print.[53] Clearly the appearance of respectability was important because upon it credit would depend. Meredith could and would pay and it is this capacity and veneer that permitted many of the speculators to ignore the taxman until discovered. Thomas Clark knew enough of the system to respond to Hands's initial approach with the value of his purchases and of the deeds for seventy-four properties, a total of £87.16s.5d. "which I will on Monday pay into the Upper bank for your account." No doubt this was acceptable not only because of the speed of payment but also because of the additional comment: "I hope you received the letter I wrote you some time ago from here on the subject of your Memorial for a pension and can only again say, that I am sorry after every enquiry and interest I could waken that I was obliged to write you as I did."[54] Such potentially powerful support was not to be squandered!

That Clark would pay into Hands's account, rather than into an explicitly state depository, is revealing because the individual and the public personage were almost indistinguishable. When Angus MacIntosh was leaving the country, he wrote to Hands. In his letter he recognized that he owed taxes; but though they had agreed to a settlement, which included his tax debts, he had re-examined his books and now claimed a balance in his favour.[55] Mahlon Burwell was another individual whose private and public business relations with Hands were interlocked. In May 1834, he received a letter from Hands informing him that he owed £52.6s.5d. In reply he pointed out that he had a credit of £33.4s.5d. with Hands. This should be "put against it" and Burwell would remit the balance within five days.[56] The relatively poor could not respond so fast. John Dauphin saw his debt in personal terms: "About the money I am owing you I am very sorry I have not got it at present but as soon as I can satisfy you I will do it which I think it is of no yous [sic.] for you to put me to any cost for I am not expecting any money before January."[57]

In contrast, it was Charles Richardson's agent, Robert Grant,[58] rather than Richardson himself who replied to Hands. Richardson had not replied because he had been occupied the past fifteen days in securing his own election![59] In fairness, Richardson, of Forsyth, Thain and Richardson, was, at least with respect to Essex taxes, a solid citizen. He paid his taxes promptly and actually anticipated further payment. For instance, in May 1825, he had supplied Hands with a list of lots which he owned. He had requested details of his assessment so that now that the Assessment Act of 1819 had become permanent he might pay in the future.[60] If he paid promptly he expected no less of others. It would seem that Hands had sold Captain Hall's property to one Wilson who presumably had borrowed from Richardson or perhaps Richardson had re-sold to Wilson. Wilson had not paid, a not uncommon strategy of those speculating. His letter of April 1824 advising Hands of how to proceed with the matter ended with a polite command to: "have the goodness to write us at your earliest convenience."[61] By June they were permitting an extension to August of half the purchase money plus interest: "We shall expect him to be punctual in August, else the measures usual in such cases should be adopted – if purchaser's here at Sheriff's Sale do not fulfill the conditions the property is sold again at his risk and if it goes lower, he is responsible for the deficiency. We hope that coercion may not be necessary but we cannot agree to a longer term for the first half than was proposed by himself."[62] In 1828 they had a writ issued against Wilson.[63]

Hands seems to have been willing to provide information to people active in the land business, some of it of a purely factual kind, such as the taxes on a particular lot or whether it had been sold.[64] Other letters suggest a different relationship. The speculative firm of Clark and Street wrote to Hands in 1835: "You will be so good as to let us know by return post who is the grantee of lot F, 9 Concession, Gosfield, 200 acres and what you know or can easily learn of its quality, situation and value. It is offered to us at 7/6d currency/acre."[65]

Another example is Hiram Jackson's enquiry about a lot sold for taxes in 1830; his offer was quite explicit: "please write to me by the next mail and the number of acres that was sold. And I will satisfy you for your trouble as soon as I receive an answer by mail.[66] It may be that it was for such reasons that it was commonly believed that there was collusion between the larger speculators and the sheriffs, who failed to advertise adequately to avoid competition in the bidding.[67]

Figure 8.22 illustrates the steps that historical geographers some-times have to go to obtain their objectives. The map is based not on properties that were assessed for taxation but rather on statements of lands not included in the assessment returns for 1846 and 1847. These were compiled, one presumes, as a matter of routine to guide assessors in their attempts to identify non-residents who were seeking to avoid taxes or to determine the amount of land still legally available for settlement. No records have survived for Rochester and Tilbury townships but sufficient evidence exists to relate the avoidance of tax-ation not just to the category "land-speculator" but also to society as a whole.

What is interesting here is that, in the townships along the strait, almost all property owners had been included in the assessment rolls and had paid their assessment. The picture is perhaps more dramatic than was the reality, because in the former Indian reserve, in what was now Anderdon Township, a considerable element of the population remained Indian. Indians were not liable for taxation and could not therefore be expected to be included on lists of tax delinquents. The contrast between the three townships of Sandwich, Anderdon, and Malden and the rest of the county is striking, although here again it has to remembered that a considerable part of these lands was in fact

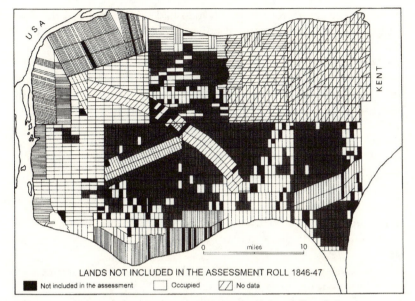

Figure 8.22   Lands not included in the assessment rolls for 1846 and 1847

Source: AO, F378, HWHM, Schedule of lands not inserted on the assessment rolls.

unpatented. Much of this, the blocks in Colchester, Gosfield, and Mersea townships, were in fact Clergy Corporation land. The adjoining blocks and similar scattered parcels in Maidstone were the former Crown reserves, now the property of the Canada Land Company. Neither the Canada Company nor the Clergy Corporation were liable for taxes, a fact that caused excitement and resentment among other owners of wild land who were liable.[68] Leased clergy reserve was taxable, as was Canada Company land held by an individual under the promise of fee simple.[69] However, most of the land shown on this map was not taxable since few leases had been issued by 1846 and 202 of the 242 properties which the Canada Company would come to control would only be patented in that year. Of course, the company had owned these lands since its establishment in 1826, but whatever anyone might think, legally it was not directly liable. Beyond these townships, in Sandwich and Malden townships, the Canada Company and the Clergy Corporation had, by 1847, succeeded in passing on the responsibility for taxation to the persons who had begun to purchase "corporate" land.

What is astonishing here is the extent of land liable for taxation whose ownership was unknown to the assessors, or at least not identified by them.[70] These lands included properties as yet unpatented or owned by the Canada Company, which had legally acquired them as early as 1826 but which some twenty years later had still not paid the taxes on them, presumably on the ground that it was not liable until the patents had been received. The names of the owners of each of the properties in 1847 were identified by following normal conveyancing rules through the Abstracts. In the case of individuals, these were checked against the land speculators identified by cluster analysis. There were 247 of these individuals whose land was not included in the assessment rolls and they owned 423 properties. Sixty-five of these people were included in the list of 144 used in the cluster analysis and they owned 184 of the properties.[71] Thus 26.3 per cent of those unknown to the township assessors and therefore tardy in their tax-paying were responsible for almost 43.5 per cent of such delinquent properties. Moreover, if they were negligent with one property they were more likely to be negligent with a number, as a chi-square analysis showed.[72]

Were there differences in the length of time that properties had been held among those individuals not included in the assessment returns for 1846 and 1847? Arguably, this might be so. Both speculators and new owners intending to farm might be expected to be included in such a document. Presumably, potential farmers had insufficient time to be included in the assessment roll; land speculators might purposefully seek to avoid identification for as long as possible. A test of difference of means showed that this was so. The known speculators had acquired their land on average 14.05 years before, with a σ of 11.58 years. The "others" or the "remainder" or the "non-speculators" had, on average, taken 8.48 years to this point; their σ was 9.54 years.[73] The difference between the two may be little more than the fact that the "speculators" had obtained their land earlier, but it is clear that none of these people rushed to pay their due. The law permitted eight years before tax-delinquent land could be sold and even then warning had to be given. One might never have to face the problem, especially if the land could be sold before the sheriff caught up with the owner. At that point one either had to have or be able to raise sufficient funds to ensure that this never happened. Since these were prominent individuals in the area, this would be little problem. Prominence could protect one's acquisition even if one was tardy in paying, and it could also overcome errors in law for some.

Samuel Street was one of the wealthiest and most powerful of men in Upper Canada and a frequent purchaser of land at tax sales. He had acquired one property, lot 21 in the 1st concession of Gosfield, for £3.15s.5d. Unfortunately, its owner was some distance from the sale and his agent unaware. The land was duly sold and there the matter might have rested because Street possessed resources and contacts that few could equal. However, the non-resident owner was no less a figure than Edward Ellice, one of Her Majesty's principal secretaries of state and a brother-in-law of the British prime minister! In the circumstances, Street acknowledged that an error in law had occurred. He expressed his willingness to permit recovery for the same sum of money and thus exited graciously from what was potentially a most embarrassing situation. Clearly both parties recognized each other for the gentlemen they undoubtedly were; this brings us to the issue of the exercise of power.[74] However, before turning to this theme, both below and in a subsequent chapter, it is worth considering one final issue, that of the acquisition of Loyalist land.

These were lands intended to reward Loyalists and military personnel for their service to the state, but they soon became prey to speculators, especially after settlement duties were abolished. Incompleteness in the records has meant that estimates of the extent to which these lands had been taken up by 1818, when settlement duties were imposed, can vary between 28 and 96.9 per cent.[75] Estimates for Essex[76] indicate that 49 out of 163 grants or 30.1 per cent of these same holdings were taken out before 1818 and that, as in Upper Canada as a whole, the years between 1819 and 1829 were ones in which relatively few privileged grants were processed. Towards the close of Maitland's administration, complaints about settlement duties on these privileged grants were rekindled, perhaps because they had been acquired by speculators and were regarded as a social evil, or because the speculators themselves wished to remove the stipulations which had driven down the price of these lands.[77]

The regulations of 1832, which required residence upon part of a lot, was not welcomed by speculators. They circumvented them by having someone reside on part of a lot with a bond posted to ensure that no more than a small acreage was assigned and the remainder transferred as soon as the patent had issued. Large acreages were built up in this way by members of the House of Assembly and indeed the Executive Council.[78] However, in November 1833, it was decided that only the original grantee could locate these lands. The effect was to make them virtually valueless. Some, including Allan MacNab, who was himself speculating in Essex, believed that the purpose of this order was to make particular individuals rich when it was subsequently repealed.[79] It may have been because of this, and earlier legislation imposing settlement duties, that the size of transactions in these rights would appear to have dropped over the years. Samples reported by Gates were used to test this hypothesis. The first was for the years before 1818; the second for the years 1835 to 1840. The mean for the earlier period was found to be 17,463.2 acres (σ 15,031.7) compared to 7,816.1 with a standard deviation of 12, 388.6 acres. The results confirm that there was indeed a significant difference between the two periods.[80]

Attempts by Colborne to control speculation in these lands were thwarted by members of the Surveyor General's Office.[81] Indeed, it was the action of someone in this office in assisting the holders of 100,000 acres in the Western District[82] to secure their land which prompted Colborne to cease issuing location tickets and to seek a method to prevent the trafficking in these rights.[83] Gates points out that in 1839 J.B. Spragge, a clerk in the Surveyor General's Office who had himself obtained 52,662 acres, had testified that his superior, John Radenhurst,[84] had acted as a private land agent while still a public servant. He had located his clients' lands in older townships where land was supposed to be sold rather than granted. He had in fact acted as if he were a judge interpreting provisions of the land acts which affected policy![85] Radenhurst had been supported in his application for the post of surveyor general by members of the two councils and by forty-five members of the assembly, who, it is suggested, had received benefits from him in that he located Loyalist rights for them.[86]

Clearly, if one was thwarted in the operation of government policy by departments of government, and pressured by politicians in the assembly, the prospects of maintaining existing policy seemed doomed. Colborne seems to have known this, and so he took steps in 1834 to ensure that provision be made in specific townships to accommodate those claiming Loyalist rights.[87] By 1835 Colborne and his Executive Council were aware that the assembly, dominated by Reformers,[88] had passed a bill to abolish settlement duties on such lands, thus infringing on an area hitherto reserved for the executive. Presumably as a matter of strategy, the Legislative Council took no action and the Executive Council abolished the duties on Loyalist and militia claims already located.[89]

The effect was immediate even though only those grants already located were affected. Gates reports that in the eighteen years from 1818 to 1835, 2,078, 489 acres of Crown land were patented but that in the three years from 1835 to 1838 an additional 1,162,300 acres were patented. While not all of this can be attributed to privileged grants, the effect of the changed regulations is clear.[90] In a second calculation, Gates gauges the three-year gain in Loyalist and militia claims as 917,013 acres.[91]

The 1835 action by the Executive Council had left the fate of future claims still uncertain. Increasingly it was thought that the issue should be determined by the House of Assembly. In that fatal year 1837, with the blessing of the Colonial Office, the assembly passed an act which allowed land speculators to locate their claims anywhere not specifically reserved. This and the fact that patents could now be issued in the names of assignees, that settlement duties were no longer required, and that individuals could receive a credit of four shillings per acre in lieu of land represented a triumph for the speculators. These people could now purchase Crown or clergy lands even in the old districts settled before 1824. Many did so, purchasing clergy reserves where terms and conditions were especially favourable; this may have been the case in Essex.

It is, however, possible to say that the timing of these grants in Essex followed that of Upper Canada as a whole: 1818 was a year of action, anticipating the imposition of settlement duties, and the other period of marked activity was the 1830s. This was particularly true of 1832, when eighteen claims were made in Essex, anticipating the strict regulations of that year, and again in 1834 when Colborne's resolve was weakening and fourteen claims were settled. In 1835 and 1836, when settlement duties were abolished, fifty-six claims in Essex were resolved. Together, these three years account for 43 per cent of all claims on Loyalist and military grants. Of course, the absolute numbers are small as is the county's percentage of the Upper Canadian whole. The 163 grants issued in Essex may have equalled 32,600 acres; if so, this is a mere 0.083 per cent of all such grants issued by 1838.[92]

This may reflect the fact that, until the last few years (probably after 1835) the Essex townships were not open for location. Speculators, of course, sought to locate in townships where rapid expansion by an immigrant population would produce concomitant returns; but in Essex, most townships were already well settled and the remaining land was of a relatively poor quality. Even so, it is clear that, by any standard, Essex had no special claim to the "social evil" of acquiring such grants by land speculators. Yet, here as elsewhere, land speculators did acquire. Twenty-one individuals on the list of 144 identified speculators acquired 46 of the 163 grants. Fifteen of these grants were made to ten individuals in their own right; the remainder were acquired from others. The names of these individuals are by now familiar to readers.[93] Surprisingly, their acreages were small; the largest holders, who never held more than 800 to 1000 acres, included Jean-Baptiste Baby, Charles Berczy, Horatio Nelson, William McCormick, and Thomas Clark. Yet there are others, unidentified by the procedure adopted here, who are known to have purchased such rights. Among those associated with Essex were Alexander Grant and Matthew Elliott, who respectively purchased 8000 and 700 acres between 1835 and 1837. Other purchasers included Francis Caldwell (2600 acres), William Morris (1400 acres), Allan MacNab (3500 acres), and Malcolm Cameron (1900 acres). All of the last named were, of course, members of the assembly or the executive. Where these acreages were acquired is not clear from the records; obviously it need not have been only in Essex.[94]

SUMMARY AND CONCLUSION

Given that most speculators ultimately aimed to dispose of their land to farmers, they would seem to have chosen well. In some few instances they may have been searching not for farm land per se, but rather primarily for some other resource, such as cedar. This would explain their interest in lots with poor agricultural potential. Yet, overall, they obtained a disproportionally large portion of well-endowed lands, though in some instances the choices were made not by themselves but by previous owners. Burwell could not exercise his knowledge of the area obtained as a surveyor, because he was constrained by having to draw for the land he obtained in recompense for his professional activity. Woods took whatever land he could get. In this he must have been little different from many who took whatever they could, irrespective of quality because the price was right. Yet others may, like Askin, have opted for compactness as a strategy for success and accepted a mixture of land in their "portfolio." There must have been many reasons for the particular patterns of acquisition reflected in patterns of clustering and scatter, but overall few of these speculators stuck to a single township and 77 of the 144 owned land in three or more townships and, of course, in other counties of the province.

Generally, the 144 appear to have behaved rationally with respect to the periods of acquisition and disposal of their land. They acquired land when it was most available, in the early period of the establishment of the colony, and disposed of it in periods of economic and political difficulty. Some of them took longer to do so than others, notably the Loyalist members of group five, who were perhaps the least attuned to notions of market. The net effect of individual astuteness with respect to the behaviour of the market was that most would seem to have made a considerable profit.

Until at least 1835, these people were buying low compared to the market as a whole; it was only after this time that the price paid by the speculators as a group reached market levels. This was especially so in the 1840s as heavy British immigration pushed up demand. Buying low, they made money when they sold, though the full amount is not known because of imprecise data on "carrying charges." The raw data shows that fifty-one of the fifty-eight speculators for whom extant records permit such calculations, actually made a profit. Some cases were spectacular, running as high as 862 per cent; but for the group as a whole, profit averaged 22.4 per cent per annum, far in excess of the usury-law limit of 6 per cent. Though their portfolios contained land on which money had been lost, for most of these people, speculation had produced a more than acceptable return.

Clearly, there were a myriad of approaches used by land speculators to acquire land. Purchase of the privileged grants of the Loyalists, the military, and the militia was one such approach. Yet in Essex this was not as common as one might have expected. Land speculators did use this mechanism in Essex, but perhaps not as much as in newer areas where greater quantities of Loyalist land were located. There was in fact considerable political agitation around the issue of settlement duties on these lands, with politicians who were themselves speculators seeking to secure their removal. They finally did so in a process that began in 1835 and continued with acts of the Upper Canadian assembly in 1837 and 1839 and with the British statute that united the Canadas in 1841.[95]

Other mechanisms used included forcing sales for indebtedness in a number of forms, including tax sales. In particular years, this might mean buying as low as three pence to seven pence per acre; yet even the overall average of 21.17 pence per acre was a fraction of the normal asking price. Paradoxically, the institution of tax sales, which were opposed so vigorously by the powerful here and elsewhere in the province, served in the end the interests of speculators. Twenty-three of the 144 speculators purchased at such sales; at the same time, they deliberately hid land from the taxman, but then so did everyone else. In 1847 it was shown there were 247 individuals owning 423 properties whose land was not included in the assessment roll. Sixty-five of these people, controlling 184 properties, were identified as speculators (Figure 8.23). They were hiding from the tax assessor and, as was demonstrated, had done so on other occasions. Given the minimal penalties involved, and the clause in the legislation permitting redemption, this was a logical strategy employed by almost everyone; indeed, it is likely that the legislation was deliberately written to permit such behaviour.

The disposal of public lands and their acquisition by speculators lay behind many of the grievances that ultimately culminated in rebellion in Upper Canada. Those who administered the system, and their favourites, possessed considerable advantage and there would seem to have been considerable corruption. Even if there was not, the

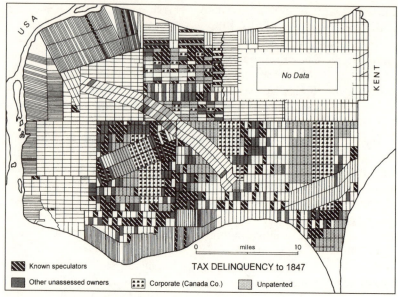

Figure 8.23   Tex delinquency to 1847

Source: AO, F378, HWHM, Schedule of lands not inserted on the assessment rolls; and Abstract Index
to Deeds for Essex County.

cognoscenti knew how to manipulate things to their benefit. It might
seem that the institution of a sales policy for public land in 1825 could
have altered the balance of things, but even then there were those who
knew how to adjust to the new circumstances. Postponing the auction
repeatedly was one mechanism whereby those who could not afford to
wait were disadvantaged. In this way, half-pay officers gained a large
part of the land put up at one auction at Hamilton in the summer of
1833; those who could not afford to wait around returned home the
fifty or sixty miles they had come. This is the exercise of power at the
local level, but it constituted little more than irritation compared to
the larger land system which the St Thomas *Liberal* was quick to
condemn: "The land granting system in this province has ever been a
subject of loud complaint; it is well known to have hitherto been one
of the strongest holds of corruption and to have developed more fully
the operations, extent and objects of government favouritism than
perhaps any other of the very many prolific sources of partial, illiberal
legislation."[96]

The radical Reformers, led by such men as Marshall Spring Bidwell,
Francis Collingwood, and William Lyon Mackenzie, were certain that
they faced entrenched local oligarchies. In every part of Upper

Canada there were collections of individuals, interconnected by marriage, kinship, and economic interest, that effectively determined the shape of local affairs and with whom the individual settler had directly or indirectly to deal. In Essex this would include the Grants, Elliotts, Caldwells, and most especially Askins and Babys. However, the power structure might be composed of single individuals such as Archibald McNab, who in modern-day Renfrew County sought to reconstruct the life of a Scottish laird. Even more powerful was Thomas Talbot,[97] who in Elgin and Middlesex counties built a principality based upon direct government grant and upon compensatory grants given him for his role in supervising settlement, including 68,435 acres in Essex.[98] This idiosyncratic Anglo-Irishman might at his own volition remove the settler's name from the pencilled survey maps which constituted the official record of settlement. So great was his authority that many settlers would forego completing the patenting process if Talbot recognized their right to land. That the state was willing to allow Talbot such a large measure of power, that its records were, at least for a time, his records, testifies to his social position and influence. It was perhaps because of this and his peculiar idiosyncrasies that he appears more visible than either Askin or Baby. The Reformers singled him out for special attention, together with his right-hand man in Middlesex, Mahlon Burwell. It was claimed that these men controlled Middlesex "as absolutely and despotically as is the petty sovereignty of a German despot."[99] They had been able to do this through:

the immense influence their high official stations give them. Magistrates, officers of the excise, surveyors, militia officers, commissioners to carry the appropriateness of public money into effect, all are appointed through the recommendations and influence of these sages of the District – thus forming a host of worthies who are ever at the beck of their Patrons. We assert without fear of contradiction, That the Hon. Thomas Talbot rules with an absolute sway, and his power is infinitely more to be dreaded than that of the King of Great Britain.[100]

Talbot was one of the greatest landowners but in Essex and other counties similar structures existed. Power might be shared by a coterie of owners and speculators. The poor would have little hope of resisting, and indeed, even those better positioned might be helpless. Pell, who lost his land to Clark, knew this:

We are sacrificed one by one. No man of property, and whose fair possessions a legislative councillor or man of political influence may covet (as Ahab did Naboth's vineyard) is safe under the present system, or can tell that his turn may not be next. The law and the courts instead of protecting him join to plunder him, and who can say that he may not be the next victim!!! The choosing of councillors, of judges, of governors, of juries, of sherriffs, of every thing, is a party-job – and as Mr. Randal proved, and I have since found to my cost, the verdict of a jury given, again and again, in the face of the country, is no safeguard ...[101]

How did power operate in Essex? This is considered in the next chapter.

have acquired nearly the whole of the waste lands of the province; they are all-powerful in the chartered banks, and till lately, shared among themselves almost exclusively all offices of trust and profit. The bulk of this party consists, for the most part, of native-born inhabitants of the colony, or of emigrants who have settled in it before the last war with the United States; the principal members of it belong to the Church of England, and the maintenance of the claims of that Church has always been one of its distinguishing characteristics.[2]

FAMILY COMPACT

The term "Family Compact," Graeme Patterson points out, was in its origin the English translation of *pacte de famille*.[3] As such, the phrase simply embodied an agreement in sharing power and patronage. However, the meaning of the term changed in the course of time, beginning perhaps as early as 1830.[5]

W.S. Wallace conceived of the Family Compact as a local oligarchy consisting of individuals of varying talent and intelligence whom "the caprices of a small provincial society ... had pitched into power."[6] Alison Ewart and Julia Jarvis identified it primarily with membership in the executive and legislative councils.[7] Donald Creighton extended its geographical scope to include Lower Canada, seeing it as a small group of merchants, professional men, and bureaucrats whose involvement in business and government was such that the boundaries of the political and commercial state were effectively coterminus.[8] Robert Saunders saw it as an elite of power.[9] Gerald Craig viewed the group as small and tightly knit, consisting of the leading members of the administration who ran the business of government on a day-by-day basis. They were not "all tied together by family connection nor were they the ingrown, selfish, and reactionary group that their opponents wanted the phrase to suggest." Nevertheless, although they often differed among themselves on many matters, they did share a common point of view on certain fundamentals which they held to tenaciously and proudly proclaimed.[10] Others, such as Aileen Dunham[11] and S.F. Wise,[12] have seen the Compact in more abstract terms, as a tendency or a "political epithet" rather than a particular group. Most recently, Graeme Patterson has described the idea of the Compact as arising from "ideas emotively related to particular historical and ideological contexts" and in opposition to "clusters of concepts subsumed by the expression "responsible government.""[13] It is clear from all this that there is no complete agreement as to the nature of the Family Compact or to its degree of cohesion; however, the consensus now seems to favour a loose organization of particular individuals sharing a common interest and operating in particular locales and circumstances at particular times. Even the most abstract conceptions of "family compact" would accept empirical content of this kind; indeed, it is the empirical content that such abstract conceptualizations are designed to "serve."

Whatever the precise definition of the term per se, the Compact's members were linked at various levels of patronage and geographically in a series of regional layers.[14] The layers were held together not only by ties of sentiment but by political position, by family and economic linkage,[15] and perhaps by shared ethnicity and education among the governing elite. The routes to power in Upper Canada included political appointment, military service, commercial ties, and family connection. None of these operated in isolation[16] and power was maximized through overlapping networks of office, commerce, and family. It was perhaps because of the layered, open-ended nature of the system that so many had an interest in its perpetuation. This explains why the Tories held power in all but two of the thirteen elections fought in the province during the first fifty years of its existence.[17] Of course, the number of offices held is of itself no measure of ultimate power, but with distance from the central Family Compact the number and types of office becomes more significant. In a system in which plurality of office was applauded rather than deprecated, a clientage system was established with a few individuals controlling the executive and legislative councils.[18]

Membership in these councils represented the pinnacle of power. Table 9.1 shows that, for the first four legislatures, a small number of individuals, either seven or eight, of whom five were remunerated[19] controlled both councils, effectively stifling any initiative that might come from the House of Assembly. In fact, the Legislative Council was not answerable to the lower house in any case and the governor did not have to pay attention to anything of which he disapproved. As the table shows, overlapping membership of the councils diminished in an almost linear manner as the number of members of the Legislative Council grew, in part because of the need for greater regional representation. Yet, even in the penultimate legislature of Upper Canada (1834–36), those sitting in both councils represented 21.6 per cent of their membership. In itself, this was considerable, but with length of service went prestige and the capacity to influence events and to utilize the systems of which one was a part.

Average service on the Legislative Council was almost twelve years.[21] Eighteen individuals, among them James Baby, Alexander Grant, Dummer Powell, and James Gordon, all of them with Essex connections, exceeded this.[22] On the Executive Council, the average length of service was almost eight years,[20] and three of the four individuals with the longest record of service had associations with the Western Dis-

Table 9.1   Number of positions on the executive and legislative councils of Upper Canada, 1792-1841, and the percentage overlap between the two

Parliament	Session	Executive Council	Legislative Council	Positions held by both[1]	Percentage Overlap
1	1792-1796	10	11	7 (14)	50.00
2	1797-1800	8	11	7 (12)	58.33
3	1801-1804	9	11	8 (12)	75.00
4	1805-1808	9	11	7 (13)	53.85
5	1809-1812	7	11	4 (14)	28.57
6	1812-1816	13	14	6 (21)	28.57
7	1817-1820	6	11	4 (13)	30.77
8	1821-1824	7	13	5 (15)	33.33
9	1825-1828	9	17	5 (16)	31.25
10	1829-1830	6	20	5 (21)	23.81
11	1831-1834	7	32	7 (32)	21.87
12	1835-1836	11	34	8 (37)	21.62
13	1837-1840	11	44	5 (49)	10.20

Source: Compiled from Armstrong, Handbook of Upper Canadian Chronology.

[1] The number in brackets represents the number of individuals.

trict. James Baby served forty-two years, dying in office in 1833; death took Alexander Grant in 1813 after twenty-two years; both were resident in this part of the world. The third councillor was William Dummer Powell, who had early associations with Essex and the wider local area. He might have served even longer than he did had he not embarrassed the governor, who found him out in 1825 after eighteen years on the council. Bishop Strachan's link to the area was, of course, much more tenuous; along with William Allan and John Beverley Robinson, two other key members of the Compact, he had purchased a small acreage in the county. He was the third-longest serving councillor, holding office between 1817 and 1835 as a regular appointee after an initial period of three years as an honorary councillor.

Concomitant with these appointments went the capacity to dispense patronage.[23] In all of this there would seem to be little difference with the British society which the Upper Canadian system mirrored. There, mid-Georgian politics has been portrayed by Sir Louis Namier "as the apogee of oligarchy"[24] in which the few dribbled out offices of state to reward loyalty in friends, family, and clients or to buy off the disaffected. There, too, marriage and personal connections were the mechanisms used to secure the profits and perquisites of the state, which, for many if not all members of the elite, was viewed as a trust operating on their behalf.[25]

Overt Power: The Officeholder

In a seminal paper on the issue of power, Fred Armstrong describes the magistracy as the essential building block of the integrated, hierarchical system which was the Family Compact.[26] Indeed, the ultimate accolade at the local level, in Upper Canada as in England, was appointment as lieutenant for the county.[27] This office, which involved the supervision of the local magistrates and, in the early years, control of the militia, was reserved for the most prestigious local families. Its transfer to Upper Canada was resisted by the Duke of Portland, who had responsibility for the colony. Portland believed that such offices (together with the incorporation of towns and other sorts of jurisdictions) might be used to obstruct the "Measures of Government." Given that the legislative power was to be vested in an assembly, it was only through the executive power vested in the governor that "the sway of this Country can be exercised" and, therefore, "every kind of authority that is not inconsistent with the Constitution" should be concentrated in his hands. County lieutenants would "require to be courted and managed, in order to secure the right direction of the Influence thus unnecessarily given them."[28] Portland argued that "the Power of the Person having the government, is the Power of this country, but such subordinate Powers as are proposed are not ours – We have no connection with them or direct Influence over those who exercise them – They are the means and instruments of independence."[29] Simcoe took the position that, by controlling arbitrary power, such offices might actually foster attachment to government, and he managed to secure the office, at least until his own departure,[30] by horrifying Portland with thoughts of sedition and democratic tendencies. In Essex, the individuals accorded this recognition as de facto members of the aristocracy were Alexander Grant and James and Francis Baby.

Administratively, the magistrates were responsible for the finances of the district, supervising assessment and tax collection, licensing premises, appointing minor officials, conducting marriages,[31] supervising construction, controlling the use of the militia, and hearing civil and criminal cases as well as cases of treason. In its combination of administrative and judicial functions, the Upper Canadian magistracy was similar to its English counterpart, which was based upon ideas of universal obligation and of a "settled, perfect and unchanging order."[32] There appear to have been few differences between the Upper Canadian and English systems,[33] although, interestingly, in the early years Upper Canadian magistrates lacked jurisdiction over property law and this was the basis of much abuse.[34] Still, the influence of the magistracy in Upper Canada was all-pervasive. One presumes that

Table 9.2   Number of transactions made and positions of influence held by sub-groups* for the years 1788–1852

Sub-Group	Number of Transactions			Number of Positions		
	$\bar{x}$	σ	n	$\bar{x}$	σ	n
Non-officeholders	16.77	13.81	93	–	–	93
All officeholders	43.57	53.47	51	4.35	3.66	51
2	55.88	79.59	18	2.50	2.12	18
3	46.88	34.98	18	5.06	2.82	18
4	24.53	20.61	15	5.73	5.06	15

Source: Calculations of the author.
* As defined in the text.

the mixture of administrative and judicial function was purposeful in that it was useful in inculcating notions of authority and instituting measures of control. Armstrong describes the magistrates as "a touch-stone of the ruling class."[35]

As previously mentioned, Appendix 7.3 is a compilation of those who possessed speculative holdings in Essex together with those who, as family members or business partners though not themselves specu-lators, might have offered assistance in accumulating land. It also lists those speculators who held formal power in Essex and the Western District. These data, cross-classified with the acreage held by the spec-ulators for each of two periods, were analysed for the relationship between officeholding and acreage accumulated. Bi-variate regression produced a statistically significant correlation coefficient between these two variables but the plot of the data suggested that there were in fact two populations. Since it was not possible to identify or give meaning to the difference between the two in terms of political power, the results, though statistically significant, were interpreted as being of little substantive value.[36] Table 9.2 was produced instead. It shows the number of transactions made and the number of positions held by subgroups of the power elite.

The table presents the data in terms of officeholding. The first of these are the non-officeholders. The second group includes the JPs, members of the judiciary per se, and the sheriffs. The third group includes members of the House of Assembly and of the respective land boards for the area; the fourth, the most powerful of all, includes the members of the executive and legislative councils. All other appoint-ments, for example, as postmaster, coroner, court clerk, inspector of licences, and customs officials, were regarded simply as just that. These were jobs which in financial terms might or might not be worth having but which in political terms were without real meaning. On the other hand, surveyors were treated as being just as important as other members of the second group and were included in this subclass. In making totals, reappointment to the same office in the same location was counted as one appointment, but if to a second location, it was counted twice. For example, a justice of the peace who received five annual commissions in Essex was counted once, but if he received an additional commission in Welland, then his commission was counted twice. A commission in the militia was not counted in terms of the sub-group of power, although it was undoubtedly a mark of social prestige. Membership in a particular group was determined according to the highest position held. Thus, someone, for example, who was just a magistrate was placed in the second group, but someone who had been a magistrate and was elected to the legislature was placed in the third, more powerful, subclass. Someone who had been a parliamentarian was still counted in this third group, on the ground that he would maintain his influence. This third group included members of the Land Board; thus, John Askin, though never an elected member of the assembly, was placed here.

A series of tests were conducted to see if there were significant differences between the officeholders and those speculators who lacked appointments in the number of transactions conducted, the number of offices held, or the acreage held. Analysis of the number of positions revealed that members of the legislature held a statistically greater number of positions than the JPs[37] but there was no significant difference between the parliamentarians and the members of the executive and legislative councils.[38] With respect to the number of transactions, the JPs and the MHAs proved statistically no different from one another,[39] but the fourth subgroup, the members of the councils, conducted statistically fewer transactions than the others. Perhaps the members of these councils were more concerned with serving or had other sources of compensation, including, if they were one of the five officially recognized appointees, a salary. It is also possible that they had already exhausted their legal entitlement and that, in an age which valued family connection, they saw their role as providing for relatives. Though all would have shared this view, members of the councils would have been best placed to fulfil their intentions. There was a definite difference between the non-officeholders and the officeholders. As Table 9.2 shows, the officeholders as a group conducted many more transactions ($\overline{x}$ = 43.57) than the non-officeholders ($\overline{x}$ = 16.77).[40]

In 1825 and 1852 there was no statistical differences between the various officeholders,[41] although there was a marked difference between those speculators who held office in 1825 and those who were without office.[42] However, by the second period, this distinction had disappeared. The mean acreage for non-officeholders was now 391.39 acres, up somewhat from 325.44 in the earlier period. However, for officeholders it was 707.01 acres, down from 856 acres in the earlier period. In this second period, ending in 1852, there was no statistical difference between the non-officeholders and the office-holders.[43] Moreover, the absolute acreage held had declined dramatically for officeholders in all classes but especially for the MHAS, whose average holdings had fallen from 1264 to 496 acres.

Clearly, something happened between the two time periods, perhaps even greater than the structural change which overtook the system in 1841 as Upper Canada was united with Lower Canada. The union meant the removal of many former officeholders in the House of Assembly and the legislative and executive councils, although they retained their influence as "men of prominence."[44] Many went on to greater eminence. William Morris was one, becoming president of the Executive Council of the United Canadas. Sir Allan Napier MacNab and Sir John A. Macdonald are even more marked cases, the former becoming premier of the province and the latter prime minister of Canada. At the local level, the magistrates would have been little affected by such political developments.

The entrée to official dignity had always been the commission as justice of the peace and from there one might move up in the power structure. Loss of office was rare, most usually occurring because of appointment to some other office with which there was a most obvious conflict, for example, as sheriff. Unless one left "under a cloud," and sometimes when one did, influence and contacts remained. Some never left. Francis Baby had, as Armstrong has shown, the connections to be commissioned from 1796 to the union of the Canadas in 1841.[45] These people continued to serve, as did the more overtly political, but it is clear from Table 9.3 that the association between land and power was greatest in the period before 1825.

How did one obtain appointment as a magistrate? Being literate helped.[46] So did living in remote areas where choice was limited.[47] Once a person was appointed, removal was rare because a magistrate's position in local society usually prevented the worst sort of corruption and "brought out their sense of paternal responsibility,"[48] although, as will be seen below, John Prince would argue otherwise in 1843. Removal could occur if one earned official disapprobation, but this was rare. In 1835, less than two years after his arrival in the Western

Table 9.3   Acreage owned, 1788–1825 and 1826–52, by speculators according to their officeholding status

Sub-Group	Acreage Owned 1788-1825			Acreage Owned 1826-1852		
	$\overline{x}$	σ	n	$\overline{x}$	σ	n
Non-officeholders	325.44	788.67	93	391.39	500.62	93
All officeholders	855.57	1530.75	51	707.01	1546.90	51
2	466.56	818.43	18	332.77	266.48	18
3	1263.16	1777.63	18	496.11	693.00	18
4	833.27	1819.17	15	500.00	891.58	15

Source: Calculations of the author.

* As defined in the text.

District, John Prince, lawyer and gentleman of substance, was appointed to the magistracy. He earned official opprobrium by his summary execution of five Patriot prisoners taken in arms against the Crown in 1838.[49] In fact, many felt that he was executing invaders who had committed murder in Canada and because of this he was able to qualify for a subsequent commission. Prince was confident of his own fitness for the post:

The "materiel" composing the Magistracy of this District is, for the Most part, of an Extraordinary sort, and but ill adapted to vindicate the Laws or to protect the Subject. Such facts have Come to my knowledge within the last Six or Eight Months that would appear incredible, and I forebear to trouble you with their detail. But I have witnessed in men, now in the Commission of the Peace, such ignorance, corruption, and wickedness as is rarely seen elsewhere; and much as it was against my will to do so, (having for the first six years of my life in this District been a *Slave* to the public in my magisterial Capacity) I was prevailed upon a few days since to qualify and again incur the very troublesome duties of the office of a J.P. because I saw justice witheld [sic] from many and tyranny and oppression Exercised over not a few.[50]

An Englishman of such obvious quality and pretence was an obvious candidate; occupationally, being a member of the financially powerful merchant class was also a decided asset, as was having a military position and government connections. Armstrong points to George Meldrum, William Park, and William Hands, among the speculators, as examples of the merchant appointees, and to Iredell, Elliott, Alexander McKee, John Askin, Jr, William Duff, and Thomas Reynolds as examples among the Indian Department and army personnel, but appendix 7.3 reveals many others. In Armstrong's view, perhaps the most important though not the only factor in appointment to the magistracy was family connection: "Once a magistrate's son attained sufficient years he was qualified by heredity to become a magistrate."[51] The local oligarchy had the power to recommend, but ultimately it was the central oligarchy that decided. There were instances where people were imposed from outside. William and Charles Berczy, sons of the speculator and colonizer, William Berczy, are cases in point. Acquiring land in the area, the brothers became magistrates in 1826. William became a district court judge in 1826 and was elected MHA for Kent in 1828. Charles received the lucrative position of postmaster at Amherstburg and, after the Rebellion of 1837, the even more profitable Toronto office.[52]

A commission to the magistracy was the basis of elevation to other offices, including membership in the House of Assembly and, albeit rarely, membership in the executive and legislative councils. As Johnson points out in a study using election to the assembly as a measure of prominence, prior to 1820, 52 per cent of that body's members held other offices. Pluralism was the norm in Upper Canada.[53] Of the fifteen MHAs elected for the counties of Essex and Kent, eleven were magistrates, a somewhat higher proportion than in Upper Canada generally.[54] All but one (Jacques Dupéront Baby, scion of one of the most important families in the district) of those who were appointed from Essex or the entire Western District to the executive and legislative councils were magistrates prior to their elevation.[55] Of the councillors, Francis Bond Head, lieutenant governor in 1837, who was certainly no democrat, who sought to control the affairs of the Land Department himself, and who was not therefore wholly disinterested, could write: "The members naturally are and always have been Land Jobbers. It is their interest and that of the legislative Council that the lands should be divided among the people at a low price not with a view to improving them but to sell them at exorbitant rates to the poor immigrants ... Against this project there is no dissentient voice."[56]

This claim, while undoubtedly exaggerated, had a large measure of truth.[57] The Executive Council was composed of members who were appointed at the pleasure of the government but who were in practice hard to remove, as the case of William Dummer Powell discussed earlier, showed. In this instance, Lieutenant Governor Maitland had great difficulty ridding himself of someone who had become an embarrassment. Even after being pensioned off, Powell continued to agitate. Members of the Executive Council were not necessarily members of the legislature but were sometimes, as we have seen, members of the Legislative Council.[58] In Armstrong's words, "appointments to these councils represented only the peak of the most lucrative road to power: the creative distribution of patronage." That patronage took the form not only of office but also of land.[59]

In the earliest phase, before the power structure had solidified at York, members of the councils were recruited from across the province. Several people in the local Essex oligarchy became part of the establishment at the provincial capital. One of them was Alexander Grant. His position in the navy and in the shipping business gave him great influence and importance from the beginning. He went on to enter the Executive Council and to become administrator of the province in 1805–06. Another executive councillor, James Baby, was chosen for his personal qualities and his ability to represent the French-speaking citizenry in this politically unstable area. By 1815 he was to be inspector general. Others included William Dummer Powell, chief justice of the Court of King's Bench; Prideaux Selby, who acted as receiver general and auditor general of land patents; William Robertson, whose tenure was short-lived. The Legislative Council included Angus McIntosh, chieftain of clan MacKintosh, and the merchant James Gordon. In the earliest years, these people associated with Essex and the Western District were among the most influential people in the whole of Upper Canada.

Interestingly, Table 9.3 shows that the overt benefits of power were not clear, at least in terms of the possession of land; the smallest acreage in both periods was held by the most powerful, the members of the executive and legislative councils who received compensation for their services in land.[60] Powell, who served on the Executive Council for this area for seventeen years, though he came to reside at York, never owned enough land in Essex to be included among the land speculators identified in 1825 or 1852. Yet he received 3000 acres in Hawkesbury in the Eastern District, three town lots in York, and a farm lot in York. His wife, like Powell a Loyalist, and their seven children received 1200 acres each for a family total of 12,800 acres.[61] Grant, who had lived at Grosse Point and had himself administered the province, owned only 580 acres in 1825 (more correctly, his estate owned this land). Yet he is known to have held five separate offices and sixty positions. Councillor Grant was entitled to 6000 acres for himself, and his children, of whom he had twelve, were to receive 1200 acres each for their father's faithful service. This amounted to 20,400 acres, which clearly were held beyond the boundaries of Essex.[62] Prideaux Selby, member of the Executive Council, owned 600 acres in 1825. He also held five offices.[63]

The most powerful in terms of office was James Baby. The longest-serving member of the Executive Council, he held 13 different offices and had 115 positions.[64] Yet he bought only five lots and sold three in Essex during his service.[65] In 1852 his estate owned 641 acres in Essex. Lieutenant Governor Simcoe patented only 1000 acres of Essex land; those stalwarts of the Family Compact, John Strachan, William Allan, and John Beverley Robinson, owned only 305 acres in 1825 and would not have been included in the list of speculators but for the fact that they held a few properties of unknown acreage. By the standards of the time, these are not large amounts of land for members of the ruling elite, although by the standards of the European poor such acreage must have seemed an impossible dream.[66]

Why were the figures so low? Had council members made a realistic assessment of the potential of Essex and decided that the county was not the best endowed? Was it that they purposefully sought to keep their acquisition down in any one county to prevent political embarrassment? Were they simply seeking to spread their investment because there were direct rewards for service? Certainly, Powell held land beyond Essex.

James Baby did so as well. In Yarmouth Township, in modern-day Elgin County, he patented 10,000 acres in his own name and his immediate family patented an additional 8400 acres.[67] In North and South Dorchester he held a further 4600 acres, and in Dunwich Township he owned 1500 acres for a time, though he would surrender these in 1806.[68] At York, Baby built a home on 1500 acres. As a militia colonel, he was entitled to 1200 acres and he sought and likely obtained this in Vespra Township. He speculated in land along Lake St Clair, where, on failing to pay taxes, he stood to lose 9000 acres at one point but was able to redeem them. It is clear that his Essex holdings are not indicative of his capacities in assembling land.[69] In Essex, his maternal relations the Réaumes, also patented 6431 acres in 1801 and 1802; the connection to James and his brother Francis (François) must surely have helped them acquire.[70]

Power and Connection

The Réaumes illustrate the point that the benefits of power in the areas they "represented" might accrue not directly to the officeholder but indirectly to his relations or those who had connection with him. Similarly, the careers of Richard Pollard[71] and William Hands epitomize the potential benefits that could derive from connection and power. These men, who were friends, came to enjoy many positions within the system of local government. Pollard was an English-born merchant who in 1792 became sheriff and in 1794 registrar for the counties of Essex and Kent. At the same time, he became registrar of the Surrogate Court, but he resigned this post to become judge of the same court in 1801. Later, in 1804, he resigned as sheriff to become a priest of the Church of England. His supporters in his pursuit of ordination were no less personages than Chief Justice John Elmsley and Administrator Peter Russell.[72] With the exception of the shrievalty, he held all his offices, which also included membership on the re-established Land Board, until his death in 1824.[73] He was the embodiment of pluralism in officeholding. Armstrong, who sees Pollard as a good example of how the merchant in the right place and time could become important in the power structure of a district, expresses Pollard's occupational pluralism cogently:

Still, there was possibly a brief period in 1802 when he could have arrested a man for murder, incarcerated him, taken him to trial, and led him to the scaffold, all in his capacity as sheriff. He could then have given him the last rites of the church established, as minister or at least theology student, and accepted his will as a judge of surrogate, before finally springing the trap, once again in his capacity as sheriff. It was the Family Compact, not the modern banks, which invented the full service package.[74]

Pollard's career was in some ways very like that of William Hands. Hands never became a cleric though such a possibility had existed at one time.[75] Like Pollard, he was a merchant. When Jay's Treaty was implemented in 1794, he chose the British side and was soon appointed a JP and then treasurer of the Western District. He became postmaster of Sandwich in 1801 and held this until his death in 1836. Having succeeded Pollard first as clerk of the peace, then as sheriff, still later as registrar of the Surrogate Court, he finally succeeded him as judge in 1824. He was appointed sheriff in 1802 and held on to the office until 1833 when he was seventy-three. He became the inspector of licences in 1806, and the collector of customs at Sandwich in 1809. He held both posts until he died. In 1808 he became deputy registrar of Essex and Kent, a post he retained until 1824. In that year the office was split between Essex and Kent counties. Hands's son John received the newly organized post in Essex and Kent went on to become a son-in-law of John C. Askin. Through all this, Hands conducted his own business with some considerable success although he was assisted by deputies. No doubt his advance was also assisted by his acumen in selecting a marriage partner. He had married Mary Abbott. Her father had been involved with Askin in the Miami Company, and her sisters had married into the Babys. Also, Hands was the brother-in-law of

Francis and James (Jacques) Baby, long-serving members of the legislature and the legislative and executive councils respectively.

Connection must, in a general sense, have been extremely important. A measure of this is the fact that, of the fifteen MHAs elected in
the Western District before 1841, two were Babys, one was an Askin
in-law, one was a Hands in-law, and two were Elliotts.[76] Eleven of
them were drawn from the ranks of the JPs. The probability of promotion from JP to assembly member varied with family linkage; of
the 148 magistrates appointed in the district, 48 came from eighteen
families.[77]

The Baby family was actually one of two major social and economic
networks in the county and district. The other was the even more
numerous and probably, in financial terms, more powerful Askins
(Figure 9.1). There were others, such as the Caldwells, who were
linked to the Babys via the marriage of William Caldwell, Sr, to
Suzanne Baby and his son's marriage to Frances Réaume, and the
Grants, although they can also be linked to the Askins. Potentially, the
Askin network was the most important network of interaction in the
area, and it is fortunate that, in this instance, the archival record is so
rich that one can demonstrate actual as opposed to potential interaction. In other cases, one cannot be quite so confident.

The Baby network is presented in Figure 9.2. Within the time-frame
of this book it centred upon James[78] and to a lesser extent Francis,[79]
Jean-Baptiste, and Daniel, who was to become a major-general in the
British army.[80] Competent individuals, they still basked in the reflected
glory of their father, Jacques Dupéront Baby and his brothers who had
fought in the cause of the French king.[81] Though this was very much
an elite of power, the Babys never controlled much land in the area
directly. The network as depicted consists of forty-one people. Twenty-
six were male, and among them one was most likely to find land speculators and indeed landowners at this time. Of the twenty-six, sixteen
are identified in Appendix 7.1 as land speculators. These people controlled at least 4567 acres in 1825 and 7286.5 acres in 1852. In itself,
these are not large figures but one has to remember that for many,
although probably not for James and Francis, land dealing was constant and the actual acreage that passed through their hands was considerably greater. In relative terms, the Baby network "controlled" 13.0
per cent of all identified speculative holdings in 1825 and 19.4 per
cent in 1852.

James was connected to both the Indian Department and the judiciary. His talent was recognized early in his career. He was made a
member of the executive and legislative councils by Lieutenant Governor Simcoe because of his loyalty and the need to represent the

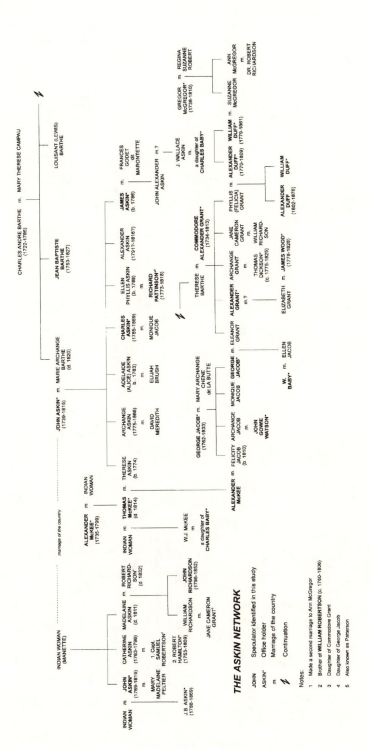

Figure 9.1   The Askin network

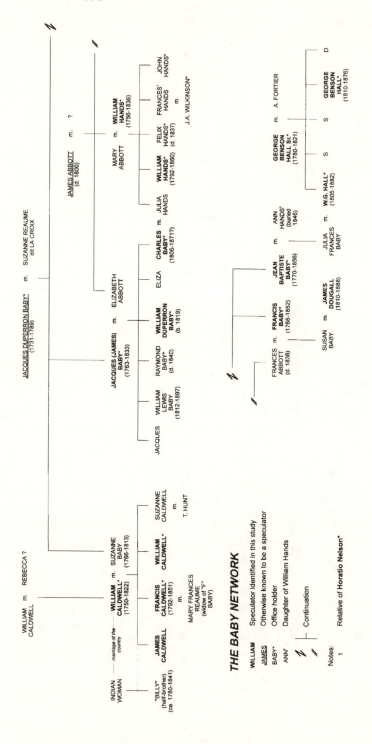

Figure 9.2   The Baby network

French-Canadian community in the area. David William Smith noted the probable influence of James's uncle François[82] with Lord Dorchester in bringing about his appointment to office: "The Interest which brought the Young French Gentleman into the Councils, has prevailed in having him appointed Lord Lieutenant for the County of Kent, & that interest was not only planted previous to the Governments taking place, but seems to have taken exuberant Root in Quebec; where his [James's] Consequence, his Interest, his property & his Loyalty, seem to have been blazoned in lively tropes."[83] In time, James became speaker of the Legislative Council. He also held the title of lieutenant of the county, which marked him as a person of great import. Further, his position as inspector general of public finances (effectively finance minister) – which he held for nineteen years – meant that he controlled the purse strings of the colony.

James Baby elected to join the British and fight under their colours and he paid a price for it – in 1812, when his home was pillaged by American troops. These were impeccable credentials and, together with his personal qualities, led to his becoming an important figure in the Family Compact. James was the epitome of a gentleman. He was tall, good-looking, and well proportioned. According to his grandson, James possessed a "primitive simplicity" and "a moral beauty." He became a friend of Bishop Strachan[84] and of Sir John Beverley Robinson,[85] as well as of two other members of the central Compact, George Herchmer Markland[86] and Thomas Clark.[87] Strachan eulogized him as "a Christian without guile, affable and polished in his manners, courteous in his conversation, dignified in his deportment, warm in his affections, steady in his friendship and unshaken in his principles and the spring of all his actions was of the religious."[88] That said, like others of his time, he built a network of connections which clearly benefitted its members.

James advised his brother Francis to run for parliament. Francis did and was elected for Kent in 1792. He later represented Essex between 1820 and 1830. As lieutenant for Kent County, James made Francis lieutenant-colonel of militia, and in 1794 Francis was appointed a magistrate – a post he would hold for more than forty years. Francis also became lieutenant of Essex county in 1807[89] and in 1819 a member of the reconstituted Land Board of the Western District.[90] Perhaps on the prompting of James, Jean-Baptiste was elected to the fifth parliament and represented Essex between 1808 and 1812. Others bearing the Baby name came to hold important local offices as clerk of the peace, sheriff, and treasurer.

Both James and Francis married into the Abbott family. James Abbott was an important financial player in this part of the country and an associate and friend of another important player, John Askin. James Baby married Elizabeth Abbott and Francis married Frances, or Fanny, Abbott. The third brother, Jean-Baptiste, married Ann Hands. Anne Hands's brother William married a third Abbott sister, Mary. James's son Charles married Julia Hands, the daughter of William and Mary Hands. Jean-Baptiste's daughter married William G. Hall, coroner and revenue collector. A daughter of Charles Baby married the son of Thomas McKee, and another daughter married J. Wallace Askin. Susan, the daughter of Francis Baby married James Dougall, a Scottish-born merchant, financier, and speculator.

The marriages of Baby women with McKee and Askin men allowed the author to link the Babys with the other powerful family of the area, the Askins. Economically, such linkage already existed through the Abbotts. James Abbott, father-in-law of James Baby, was the business partner of the progenitor of the North American branch of the Askins, that is, John Askin, the so-called "Count of Kent." There were 71 persons in the Askin network (Figure 9.1), 72 if A.J. Robertson is accepted as a relation of William Robertson.[91] Of these, 20 were included on the list of 144 speculators and these twenty controlled 16,221 acres in 1825 and 4703.5 in 1852. Yet this was a fragment of what had once been. By 1815, the Askins, father and son, had acquired, together with an associate, John Martin, 18,877 acres in Essex.[92] This was greater than the total of the whole extended network in 1825 and the figure excludes the holdings of John Askin, Sr, in Michigan.[93]

From whom had the Askins, father and son, acquired their land? To 1820, sixty-seven properties had been acquired from the Crown as patent deeds; thirteen came from immediate family, including the Barthes. The remaining seven came from French Canadians, seemingly unrelated. In this period Askin sold land to thirty-three persons. Twenty of the eighty-five parcels that sold went to relatives; sixteen were sold to Isaac Todd and thirty-three to James McGill, no doubt to satisfy his indebtedness. One interpretation of these events is that the function of John Askin (the father and son are indistinguishable) would seem to have been to assemble the land, to have his action sanctioned with the aid of his friends so that it might pass, as it did to patent, and finally to surrender it to Todd and McGill. But this is to misinterpret the relationship with Todd and McGill, which was essentially one of social and economic equality, and to ignore Askin's speculative activities beyond Essex.[94]

John Askin, Sr, died in 1815 and his son in 1819. By 1815, 3679 acres remained in the estate and by 1825 this had been reduced to 2255 acres, as Appendix 7.1 shows.[95] Still, in 1825, 49.9 per cent of all speculator holdings in Essex were controlled by the estates of the

Askins; as late as 1852, the figure was 12.8 per cent. Askin Sr is known to have had formal economic dealings with many individuals, including not only McGill and Todd but also James Abbott, Richard Cartwright, James Gordon, Angus McIntosh, John Martin, George Meldrum, William Park, William Robertson, and Thomas Smith (Appendix 7.3). Many of these men enjoyed office and had in turn their own connections. Of them, Todd, McGill, McIntosh, Smith, and Robertson were identified in the list of speculators included in the cluster analysis presented earlier.

When in 1803 Askin, Sr, sought to secure land in Lower Canada in the name of another, it was to McGill that he turned, writing, "I know your inclinations and that your station as executive councillor furnishes you with the means are my reason for giving you this trouble."[96] Even some of the people included among this network, who were not also included among the identified speculators, were themselves powerful people. John Askin's son-in-law Robert Hamilton, who died in 1809, was one of these and one of the richest men in Upper Canada. Though Askin would not live to see it, Dr Robert Richardson, his daughter Madelaine's husband, would become a member of the Western District Land Board in 1819.[97] Thomas Dickson, his other son-in-law, was also well connected in Niagara; Dickson's cousin William Dickson, who was himself an appointed member of the Legislative Council, acted as Askin's agent. Dickson's cousin Thomas Clark was his business partner in 1803 and would become a member of the Legislative Council in 1815.[98] Askin's brother-in-law, Jean-Baptiste Barthe, was a JP, and his grandson married Sheriff Gregor McGregor's daughter. He himself was the brother-in-law of Alexander Grant, member of the executive Council and administrator of the colony. Though neither William Ancrum nor Arent Schuyler DePeyster were in any way related to him, they were his friends and, as officers commanding at Detroit, could influence things. As noted earlier, Ancrum became his partner in the Moravian purchase in the year in which he (Ancrum) resigned from the army. All of these connections were important both to Askin's success and to the success of others at this time.

John Askin began forging such links early. Born in Augnacloy in the province of Ulster in 1739, Askin[99] emigrated to America in 1758.[100] He must have had some capital because he soon engaged in business as a sutler, provisioning the British army at Albany.[101] After France's capitulation he became a fur trader engaging in a number of partnerships, most notably with James Gordon and Major Robert Rogers. However, as a result of the French and Indian wars and Pontiac's revolt, the firm declared bankruptcy and Askin was not cleared of his debt until 1771,[102] some six to eight years after his move to Michili-mackinac, the furthermost British post on the upper lakes.

Five thousand miles from London, at the junction of lakes Michigan and Huron, Michilimackinac was the strategic centre of a fur-trading operation reaching north of Lake Superior, westward across the Mis-sissippi, and south into the Illinois and Michigan territory. Here, Askin farmed[103] and operated a store from which he traded not only mer-chandise and furs but also black and Indian slaves.[104] He acted as com-missary for the garrison and developed the connections with Isaac Todd, James McGill, and Alexander Henry which were to be so impor-tant to his personal and economic well-being all of his life.[105]

In these earlier years, his relationship with Arent Schuyler DePeyster, the British commandant, was especially important since this man regulated trade with the Indians, could tacitly approve land purchases from the Indians, and controlled the supply of goods upon which so much depended at a time when private shipping was for-bidden on the Great Lakes.[106] Indeed, the good offices of DePeyster may have been important when he ran foul of another authority figure, Lieutenant-Governor Patrick Sinclair of Michilimackinac, a dispute which may ultimately have been instrumental in Askin's removal to Detroit.[107] Presumably, relations with DePeyster's succes-sor, Major William Ancrum, were equally cordial, because in 1805 Askin registered a claim for 24,000 acres on behalf of Ancrum and himself. This was for land in the Michigan territory on both sides of the River aux Hurons and was purchased from the Chippewa. If, as seems most likely, this was the so-called Moravian settlement, Askin enjoyed a special relationship with the commandant at Detroit because, while still in command, Ancrum could legitimize any pur-chase, and indeed he himself acquired the Moravian missionaries' improvements and he and Askin purchased the soil of the improve-ments from the Chippewa.[108]

At Detroit in 1766, Askin manumitted an Indian slave, Manette (Monette), who may well have been the mother of his three oldest chil-dren, Catherine, Madelaine, and John Jr. His first "marriage" to this woman placed him in high regard with the Indians, with whom he engaged in trade and from whom he was to obtain the surrender of large tracts of land. His second marriage was to Marthe-Archange Barthe, who was the daughter of Charles Andrew Barthe, prominent trader of Detroit, and a sister of Jean Baptiste, trading associate of Askin (Figure 9.1).[109] His eldest daughter, Catherine, first married Captain Samuel Robertson, whose younger brother William, himself a partner of Askin, was a major landowner and a member of the executive and legislative councils. On Robertson's death, she married another of her father's partners, Robert Hamilton, a member of the Legislative Council and a most influential man who, according to Owen Chadwick, was probably the richest man in Upper Canada at this time.[110] Hamilton would intervene on Askin's behalf when he had difficulties in land matters. Through a combination of economic and political links, Hamilton was able to assure the future employment and prosperity of his own children, his cousins of the Clark and Dickson families, and the second generation of Askins.[111] Yet even he had trouble keeping up with Askin's incessant requests. In 1803 John Sr sought to secure the position of vendue-master at Amherstburg for his son. John Jr was already collector of customs, a position he had acquired in 1801 through the intervention of Isaac Todd.[112] The father maintained that "the expenses of attending to his duty" were greater than the revenues, a circumstance not unknown in Upper Canada. Moreover, the job had actually damaged his role as merchant. It was not his son's intention to leave the employ of "Mr Park" but to do the task of vendue-master in addition. It is doubtful if Hamilton found anything objectionable in this because such pluralism was common and legal, but he balked because he was ashamed to ask the governor for more favours. So Askin had to turn to another – the Honourable Richard Cartwright.[113] The latter responded: "your son may if he finds it convenient enter upon that Business as soon as it pleases."[114]

Theresa Askin, John's daughter by Marthe-Archange Barthe, married Thomas McKee, the son of Colonel Alexander McKee, who served as deputy superintendent of Indian Affairs for Upper Canada in the six-year period 1794–99. Again, by virtue of his marriage to Barthe, Askin became the brother-in-law to Alexander Grant, Sr, for twenty-two years a member of the legislative and executive councils and for a short time the administrator of Upper Canada.[115] Grant's daughter Archange married Thomas Dickson, Hamilton's cousin, and another married George Jacob, merchant and officeholder (either he or his father was a commissioner of the Clergy Corporation and a member of the Western District Land Board). Marriage, it would seem, was one mechanism whereby Askin ingratiated himself with the Indians from whom he would acquire land and found support with key figures in the political establishment who would sanction his land deals. Like so many of his time, Askin apparently believed that it was never too early to begin making such arrangements. In 1793, for example, he wrote Sampson Fleming, a prominent citizen of Detroit, congratulating him on the birth of a son and suggesting that, since "'he had girls worth looking at,' the newly born might become his son-in-law."[116]

In addition to these marital and blood connections, Askin formed economic links with several important individuals on the western frontier, such as Angus McIntosh, George Meldrum, and the firm of Leith, Shepherd and Duff. His trading activities with Hamilton preceded the marriage of his daughter Catherine to Hamilton in 1785.[117] In 1781 he had signed a co-partnership agreement with Hamilton and Richard Cartwright[118] to tap both the lucrative fur trade and the supply of British garrisons; this lasted until 1784 when it was dissolved with accumulated debts of £9261 due Todd and McGill of Montreal,[119] their principal provisioners. The dissolution was amicable and in the 1790s William Robertson and Isaac Todd lobbied effectively to obtain for Askin, Hamilton, Cartwright, and David Robertson an exclusive contract to supply the British forces in Upper Canada for the years 1793–95.[120] Earlier, Robertson, whose brother Samuel was Askin's son-in-law, had been a partner with Askin for the three-year period 1784–87,[121] as he would be again in 1795. Askin must have possessed some particularly attractive qualities as a person because his friends stood by him through thick and thin. Hamilton provided surety for him in 1796 when he incurred tremendous debts in the fur trade; he helped market his goods and collected his debts; and when it seemed that Askin might not fulfil a grain contract, Hamilton saved the day.[122] None of his friendships was as important as his life-long relationship with Todd and McGill. These men were his main creditors. He vowed to them that "though he could not pay,"[123] they "should not be deceived"[124] and most of his land went to them when his business went into liquidation.[125] These people were important members of an Askin "network" which consisted of at least twenty-one of the fifty-eight capitalists active in the Western District in the years down to 1815 and which acquired no less than 18.3 per cent of all land patented in the three-county area to that time.[126]

Friendships, connections of kin, and economic links were extremely important to Askin's success in land matters, as they were to others of his day.[127] So was his acceptance, because of his first marriage, by the Indians. His son's mixed blood and fluency in the Ottawa and Chippewa languages was a decided asset when he was admitted into partnership with his father in a number of ventures.[128] In 1795 Askin, Sr, dispatched his son to the treaty making taking place between General Anthony Wayne and the Indians at Greenville.[129] Askin, Jr, reported that they had to sit idle at the grand council, not thinking it prudent to bring up the matter of the lands they had already purchased from the Indians, because of Wayne's aversion to having such matters discussed and also because they had not yet met members of the American Congress who might sanction their action.[130] Though young Askin was silent, his intentions must have been known; he was arrested and detained until after the meeting.[131]

This was a costly failure because Askin and his partners had acquired extensive tracts from the Indians. With six other companies, John Askin, Sr, had obtained title to almost one million acres on the Miami (Maumee) River, including the Sandusky peninsula and what is now the city of Toledo. Acting for himself, his son John, William Robertson, Israel Ruland, John Dodemead, Patrick McNiff, and Alexander Henry of Montreal, he bought from the Ottawa and Chippewa a parcel of land commencing at the Cuyahoga River on the south shore of Lake Erie, extending to the entrance of Sandusky Lake, and reaching in depth to the lands ceded to the United States at the crossing place of the Tuscarawas branch of the Muskingum River.[132]

When Congress refused to ratify the Indian deeds which the group held, Alexander Henry proclaimed that "we have lost a fortune of at least one Million of Dollars."[133] In northern Ohio, Askin claimed no less than 5,294,120 acres. In 1795 he obtained a deed for an area of 460,800 acres running westward from Detroit. In the same year, together with William Robertson, Jonathan Schiefflin, and a number of other individuals, Askin took part in an abortive venture to purchase 20,000,000 acres in lower Michigan.[134] In 1786, with the firms of Leith and Shepherd, James Abbott, Angus McIntosh, Meldrum and Park, and Sharp and Wallace, Askin helped form the Miami and Wabash Company to operate in these regions.[135] To strengthen his title, obtained on Indian deeds, he was willing to sell cheaply to "men of interest." He wrote: "They may Almost make their own price for some hundred thousand acres and I think the offer should come from them in which case the affair could be closed soon. [T]hey have no better Deeds than us who purchased, and it must be an Undivided share, for by their securing their own they will secure that of other proprietors which is the reason that I in behalf of myself and them would sell so low."[136]

Speculation on this scale prompts the question of whether the land was obtained in some unsavoury manner. If Askin is to be believed, all was above board. When, in July 1795, he wrote to his son at Greenville, he warned him of subtle forms of bribery that might be employed to subvert him from his prime mission, which was to serve the Indians.[137] Clearly, Askin himself was acquainted with the world he described and he may also have been conscious of creating a permanent record, especially in the light of his son's willingness to treat with Wayne and the Americans. Alternatively, the message may have been absolutely genuine. Not all viewed him as an innocent. Joseph Brant who was acting for the government and had been prevented from meeting with the tribes prior to their meeting with Wayne, laid the blame on Askin and the merchant community for the failure of the negotiations:

I am sorry to find by repeated information during the winter from Detroit that Mr. Askin and some other Merchants have been seducing several Indians to make over the lands to them – last summer they began to set this a going and it was them who prevented our meeting taking place previous to the Indians going to Wayne's treaty. They have now engaged in a company to get from some of the Chippewas all the Wanted and Mingo country from Kaihage upwards ...

It is certainly very hard for poor Indians, that what Wayne left them these fellows with their rum will endeavour to strip them of and Mr. Askin has expressed himself in such a manner, as shows he would make no scruple to endeavour to excite a war among the different nations to answer his selfish purposes.[138]

One might wonder what impact this letter had since its recipient, David W. Smith, was Askin's life-long friend!

Dupéront Baby did not view Askin kindly either, because he believed the land that Askin and Ancrum had acquired from the Moravians and the Chippewa in 1786 was in fact his. He expressed his feelings as follows: "Si le Sr. Askin moteur de cette usurpation est toléré dans cette maneuvre, rien a l'avenir ne l'arretera dans ces pretentions."[139] Again, while there is no evidence that Askin was involved in any impropriety, when, in 1795, he and some others sought to buy the lower peninsula of Michigan, two of his associates, Charles Whitney from Vermont and Robert Randal from Philadelphia, undertook to bribe various members of Congress to get their support.[140]

If selling to men of influence was one mechanism of obtaining sanction for his actions, having powerful friends also helped. The point is well made in the correspondence that flowed between David William Smith and Askin. As explained earlier, Smith was the son of Major John Smith, the commanding officer at Detroit. He became secretary to the Land Board of Hesse and after 1792 was appointed surveyor general of Upper Canada.[141] In both positions he became aware of the needs of settlers and familiar with the inner machinations of government. He also had access to valuable information in terms of survey records, land policy, and the intentions of government and seems to have provided it to a privileged few. Askin acknowledged that he was one of these.[142] Askin had helped secure Smith's election to the House of Assembly in 1792, securing the support of Prideaux Selby who could deliver votes at short notice if Smith's election appeared to falter.[143]

The Smith and Askin correspondence reveals much about the social attitudes of the time. Smith, it is clear, had few scruples about the manner of his election. On 26 July 1792, he wrote to Askin that he would be happy if returned without "an undue election or the appearance of party or bribery." The electorate were to be entertained. "I beg an Ox may be roasted whole on the common and a barrell of Rum be given to the mob, to work down the beef."[144] Further, voters were to be entertained according to their station in life:

The french people can easily walk to the Hustings, but my gentry will require some conveyance, if boats are necessary you can hire them and they must not want beef or Rum ... and I wish that Leith and you should push about the bottle, to the promotion of the Settlements on the Detroit. The more broken heads and bloody noses there is the more election like ... Have proper booths erected for my friends at the Hustings employ Forsyth to make large plumb cake, with plenty of fruit, etc., and be sure let the wine be good and plenty. [L]et the peasants have a fiddle, some beverage and beef.[145]

On 6 August, Smith declared that "I will endeavour to repay you in the House of Assembly; if I succeed."[146] On 13 November 1792, having been elected, Smith confirmed his fealty to Askin, expressing his willingness to resign to his "patron" and declaring that "if ever I have a sliver of Interest or Influence with the Government it shall be exerted to the adoption of your Services, to which I am ever bound, being your debtor from Gratitude and Justice."[147] These sentiments he reaffirmed in his letter of 15 February 1797 – "You will know, my good Sir, that so far as the duty of my public station will admit, you may demand my interference, in anything that may possibly tend to your advantage, without apologizing to me for it. Should any opportunity offer, wherein I foresee the possibility of good to you, you may depend on me ..."[148] Askin expressed his appreciation to Smith, assuring him of reward in the next world where the pursuit of land would be unnecessary.[149] Askin was privileged because Smith would not help everyone, holding that "our House of assembly for the most part have violent leveling principles, which are totally different from the ideas I have been associated with."[150]

Askin was closely associated with the district surveyor, Abraham Iredell, whose advice he sought in selecting land.[151] Like many, he had purchased certificates from original settlers and experienced difficulty in having these recognized. In such circumstances, the cooperation of the surveyor[152] or for that matter the surveyor general[153] might be useful, especially if the deeds were made out to the original purchaser and then transferred. As will be shown later, Iredell would usually cooperate with Askin in the transfer to him of unspecified locations or entitlements. In 1799 he held thirty-one certificates for Askin. Some of these lacked appropriate detail but he wrote, "We can arrange this when I come down."[154]

When, in 1800, Askin was in danger of losing land purchased in this way, Iredell was prepared to provide *post facto* justification. Thirteen magistrates' certificates, he reported, had been presented to him by Askin but not lodged with him because he could not provide land suitable to settle.[155] This was just the sort of support needed but, even so, Askin requested the assistance of Iredell's superior, David William Smith: "I depend on your friendship to settle this matter and if for forms sake the grants must be given in the names of those who got the certificates it's all the same I know they will readily transfer them over to me afterwards I Have their sales of them and Power of Attorney to Receive the Deeds."[156]

In seeking to solve his land problems, Askin also employed the services of the entrepreneur and arch-bureaucrat of the Family Compact, William Allan.[157] Counting on the avarice of officialdom, he advised Allan that "if you find that you can obtain patents in the original proprietors name and that they will be delivered to you paying the fees and producing the peoples power of attorney I shall be very glad indeed. It is a much easier mode than to bring my claims before the Commissioners since they have done it in the case of Chavoir and Vermette pray try if they will do the same in others ..."[158] This was potentially the superior route because court appearances might produce summary solutions, as both Askin and his former partner William Robertson knew. In 1799 Matthew Dolson, Robertson's agent, wrote to him: "Great deal of trouble at the Land Cort. Justice Allcock is lately from the Cort of Chancery and was so hard on me and my son John that he Ordered me out of the Cort House and told Commodore Grant by so many Claims being Signed by Justis Harffy and wrote by my Son that he thought they were false, they only passed 14 claims, Mr. Roe and Mr. Askin will let you know in full."[159]

In a letter of 18 March 1803, Askin informed Allan that Lewis Barthe had appeared at the investigating commission and had acknowledged that Askin had acquired 1200 acres from him. As a result, Askin had acquired the appropriate deed. The "other lots" were given to the Barthes, although "it is a matter of no consequence to me excepting giving me the trouble of giving a power of attorney for as I last mentioned, I would sooner have the deeds made out in the original Proprietors as my own."[160] His requests became so frequent that Allan tired of the task.[161] Askin was willing to pay the fees of the original owners but Allan "need not reveal this."[162]

Askin's claims and those of his former partner, William Robertson, were heard by the Heirs and Devisees Commission in 1803. Askin, who had sent the necessary paperwork to Isaac Todd in Montreal, on hearing of the appointment of William Dummer Powell to the commission, charged with deciding the issue, was "much pleased" and asked for its return.[163] He was not to be disappointed because the legality of the claim was upheld by the commissioners, one of whom was a John Askin![164]

As a merchant, Askin belonged to a class of people about whom Major Robert Mathews, the commanding officer at Detroit, held a low opinion because of their capacity to acquire property through indebtedness after poor people had sweated for years on it. Askin had acquired about eighty lots, it is presumed in this manner, along Lake St Clair, though he claimed that they had been obtained fairly. There is no absolute proof and the properties may simply have been assembled by Lewis Barthe and M. Dequindre for Askin. Hence the sellers may simply have been willing to part with their land and move on. Yet the volume is considerable, and this circumstance together with the fact that the lots were obtained on magistrates' certificates, though not conclusive, is suggestive of a measure of compulsion.[165]

Of course, Askin had to deal with indebtedness frequently. One instance of this reveals the coldness with which he approached the whole business. In 1807 he gave a note of indebtedness for £8NY to Alexander Askin, advising him that "I think you may get something now and give him time for the rest but you would not do right to put him to Gaol, though of necessity you might threaten him."[166] Occasionally, Askin had to resort to law. Thus, in March 1791, by virtue of a writ, he acquired the land of Etiene Laviolet in compensation for his indebtedness.[167]

Askin was also a magistrate and in this capacity could purchase certificates of location from those whose only purpose in acquiring them was to sell them. A number of instances must serve as illustration of Askin's modus operandi and perhaps of a more general process employed by others as well. In one day, 30 March 1795, Dominique Drouillard completed all the steps necessary to acquire and sell 200 acres of land to John Askin, who had sanctioned the acquisition in his capacity as magistrate. On that day, Louvigny Montigny, member of the district Land Board and debtor to Askin, testified that Drouillard had served as a volunteer in the British cause under Captain Henry Bird, acknowledged his loyalty, and recommended him to Askin as a JP.[168] Content that Drouillard was of age (he was thirty years old) and a Christian, Askin administered the oath of loyalty and recommended the man for 200 acres, commending him to the surveyor Abraham Iredell.[169]

The surveyor, as requested by Drouillard, then chose a lot for him and issued him a certificate, for which he signed with his mark.[170] Next Drouillard sold his lot to Askin for £10NY. This transaction was wit-

nessed by Askin's employee, and a future magistrate, Alex
Maisonville.[171] On the reverse of this deed, which the author found in
Askin's records, is the notation:

"personally appeared before me Alexander Grant Esquire, one of his Majesty's
Justices of the Peace for the Western District in Upper Canada and Alex
Maisonville lately clerk to John Askin Senior, who being duly sworn maketh
Oath, that he was present and saw Dominique Drouillard execute the within
Deed of sale to John Askin by making his mark and that he has a perfect
knowledge of said Askin's having paid him for the within mentioned Lot.
Sworn before me at Sandwich this 7th May 1800 signed Alexander Grant JP
and Alex Maisonville.

Grant was a JP, a member of the Land Board, and Askin's brother-in-
law. Here is the process complete: presumably everyone gained, in that
Drouillard received money he would not otherwise have, Askin got the
land at a reasonable price, and perhaps Grant, who must have known
that he was taking part in a doubtful transaction, received reciprocal
treatment on another day. That same day Francis Baby recommended
Simon Le Duc for 200 acres; Askin authorized it and ultimately
received it.[172] The only one who lost in all this was the one they were
all sworn to serve, the King in "right of parliament."
   Dominique was actually the second Drouillard to receive money in
this way but he would not be the last. Five weeks earlier, Jean-Baptiste
Drouillard, also an illiterate, had been authorized to receive land by
Askin, and two days later, on 26 February, Askin paid him £10NY,[173]
witnessed by Maisonville and a Noel Delisle who had drawn the sale.
Subsequent to this event, Drouillard died. Four years later, Alexander
Grant appeared to witness to Drouillard's signature and that of the
witness, confirming the purchase by Askin.[174] A third Drouillard,
Nicholas, had been recommended for land by the surveyor J. Portier
Gignac[175] on 4 January 1796, and Askin had authorized his request.
Nicholas subsequently sold to Askin on 20 June for £10NY. This was
for a lot whose location was unspecified and again Maisonville and
Grant witnessed the business.[176] Gignac also recommended J.B. Le
May Duc, a thirty-year-old labourer, and Askin, as magistrate, accepted
the recommendation.[177] On 26 May 1796 Le May transferred to Askin
the certificate he had been promised for £14.15.11. The price had
gone up and Maisonville and Grant were witnesses to it![178] The final
instance is that of Alexis Dubois, a fifty-three-year-old shoemaker from
Montreal, recommended by William Harffy JP on 17 June 1796.[179] In
short order he acknowledged to Iredell the surveyor that Askin had
paid him for the land.[180] The following day he transferred title to

Askin for £16NY, promising to surrender the certificate when received.[181] Maisonville witnessed this, and four years later Grant was willing to testify that he was there and saw the money transferred in return for the land.[182]

These are only six instances and amount to perhaps 1200 acres, but Askin is known to have acquired 9600 acres in the Western District by purchase of his own and his fellow magistrates' certificates.[183] The correspondence relating to the difficulties he experienced over these lands illustrates the use Askin made of his wide circle of friends. In July 1798 he wrote his brother-in-law, Alexander Grant, his son-in-law Robert Hamilton, and their business partner Richard Cartwright.[184] All three were members of the Legislative Council, which at this point consisted of thirteen individuals of whom two were never sworn or attended and a third had been dropped for non-attendance.[185] Askin, with three votes accounted for, clearly had a fighting chance in the Legislative Council. Additionally, Grant and David William Smith were members of the Executive Council, which had a de facto membership of eight.[186] In fact, Askin's fate would be decided in the Executive Council. He recognized this and the influence that Hamilton, Cartwright, and Grant might have there:

Though I wish to be as little troublesome to my old acquaintances as possible, yet in the present case my interest as well as that of Mssrs Isaac Todd and James McGill is so deeply concerned, that I am obliged to call on all my friends not only to exercise their personal influence on my behalf but also to call to their aid such as are capable from their situations, of giving any, provided you and them think me right after you have heard what I have to say ... and tho you and Mr. Hamilton are not of the Executive Council yet you have influence with those that are.[187]

Cartwright's response was positive. Although he had never thought magistrates' certificates assignable, he would approach the chief justice, since he knew Askin was entitled to "every favour that Government can confer ... I shall most cheerfully exert any little influence that I may possess to get your Claims confirmed and should they not be settled to your Satisfaction before your other Friends and I meet again at York we will try our united efforts in your favor."[188] The chief justice, John Elmsley, whatever he thought of the issue, was aware of the problem. He informed Askin that he knew a house where 500 certificates of a similar nature were awaiting a favourable outcome of the Askin decision before they were in turn brought out.[189] On 2 July 1799 Robert Hamilton wrote Askin from Queenston, informing him that Commodore Alexander Grant, to whom Askin had entrusted the task of securing title, could not find Askin's land certificates. He noted that, if this evidence was not found, increased difficulties would ensue, since there was the prospect of a new governor being appointed and his old friend D.W. Smith might be returning to England.[190] No doubt with this in mind, Askin wrote Smith on 10 July 1799, stating how unfortunate it was that this evidence had been lost since Smith and so many of Askin's friends "were on the spot." He declared that he could furnish affidavits from the magistrates who granted the certificates, as well as from his own clerks, and asked that if the certificates could not be found that he receive an equivalent amount of land – that is, 2800 acres. He had helped secure Smith's election; he now asked the surveyor general to "for God's sake, get me thro' this difficulty. [W]ays and means are better known to you than me. It badly suits my present circumstances to losse 14 lots."[191]

On 15 July, Askin fired off a letter to Isaac Todd, who had a direct interest in the outcome of this affair, informing him of the loss of his certificates and requesting his intervention with Todd's friend Peter Hunter, newly appointed as lieutenant governor of Upper Canada.[192] His letter of 19 July 1799, reiterating his argument that he should be allowed to locate lands gained by magistrates' certificates, exhibits a growing confidence. As a result of Cartwright's intervention, Askin now felt that the chief justice would be sympathetic, as would James Baby.[193] Meanwhile, Grant had recovered the land certificates and informed Hamilton that most of the grantors were now living on the American side, and that several of the certificates had in fact been granted by Askin himself in his capacity as magistrate![194] This did not augur well, and on 3 August 1799 Hamilton wrote Askin as follows: "Should the Commodore [Grant] be unsuccessful in this Council with the Men, I still would maintain the claims. Perseverance I know will do much, when opposed to what they may affect to call the public Good."[195]

The news was as Hamilton suggested. On 13 August 1799 Grant wrote Askin that, because Hamilton, Cartwright, and James Baby had been preoccupied with their own land matters and because Smith had been away, Askin's claim had not been recognized. However, he would try again and would contact Colonel Aeneas Shaw and John McGill that very afternoon.[196] Here is the process continuing, and while the outcome of a particular event may not be known, the reader can be sure that it did not stop because for Askin, as no doubt for others, acquisitiveness was a constant part of life. In this particular case, the issue was resolved in Askin's favour owing to the cooperation of the surveyor general, D. W. Smith, who had directed two of his subordinates to ask the advice of Alexander Grant, Askin's brother-in-law.

These subordinates, William Chewett[197] and Thomas Ridout,[198] who were to become acting surveyor general and surveyor general respectively,[199] reported to Askin that "we find that the 14 Magistrates recommendations you mention will be laid before the Council, the first convenient opportunity ..."[200] When it became clear that there had been surveying difficulties and proper legal descriptions might not be immediately forthcoming, these same individuals were willing to wait: "We shall attend to your wishes respecting the claims allowed you by the Commissioners and not pass the descriptions until they are all in, and then in the manner you direct."[201]

The willingness of so many to act on Askin's behalf undoubtedly contributed to his success in acquiring land. Perhaps it was the sheer daring that attracted and promised success. After all, even at this time, few must have thought it conceivable to acquire 20 million acres. The man certainly had something going for him, for even when he was financially constrained and heavily in debt, he seems to have reached amicable settlements. The classic instance is that of his indebtedness to James McGill, although that may owe more to McGill's personality than to Askin's. In April 1786 Todd and McGill were under pressure from creditors in England and asked Askin to pay his debts in a most delicate language: "The House having wrote you on business, leaves nothing further to say on that head than to conjure you by every tie of friendship to leave no stone unturned in order to make remittances, for this Summer depends our existence as men of Character and Credit."[202] Six years later the bill was still large, totalling £20,217. The firm of Todd and McGill was to be restructured by the addition of Andrew McGill, and in these circumstances the Askin account had to be adjusted. McGill proposed to assume part of the debt interest free so that the dealings with the new firm might be placed on a more secure footing. Two years later, McGill was getting more desperate: "If therefore you have for us that regard and friendship which I never doubted, you will assuredly see the necessity of making every possible exertion to prevent us from being the greatest Sufferers that can probably be instanced in Trade to your part of the world. Unwilling to wound your feelings further I shall not add on this very painful Subject."[203] Askin acknowledged the "tenderness" with which he was treated by Todd and McGill and offered twenty lots, whose value he established, to discharge the debt.[204] The offer was accepted by his debtors, who left him in possession of his home "Strabane," named for the town in the north of Ireland.[205] McGill in his will of 1813 actually left him up to 1600 acres of land in the United States.[206]

Askin also used his influence to direct the system at the local level to his own benefit. In 1801, when Thomas Smith was contemplating resignation as court clerk, Askin, not wishing to take advantage of a friend, hesitated to convey this news to the lieutenant of the county.

Instead, he sought Smith's confirmation because no time could be lost "as the Commodore [Grant acting as administrator of Upper Canada] soon intends to give out some Commissions."[207] Clearly, Askin intended to have some input in the process. Again, when Hands wanted to obtain the office of sheriff soon to be vacated by Richard Pollard, candidate for ordination, Askin was willing to assist by using his friendship and partnership with Isaac Todd to influence the lieutenant governor's decision:

Always troubling you for myself or some others. Mr. Pollard is gone to Quebec in order to obtain Holy orders if he can ... this leaves an opening for the latter place. Mr. Hands of Sandwich who you know well wishes to get that place and the first characters here mean to memorial his excellency the Lieutenant Governor in his behalf as soon as he comes to York there might be an application before that and will you be obliging as to mention Mr. Hands his name and intentions to the Governor in so doing you will serve a poor but worthy man well calculated to fill that office these reasons alone if they were cause to you tho a stranger I'm sure would influence you in his behalf, & I believe you are convinced that for my nearest relative I would not request of you to get an unworthy or unfit person into office (If I thought them such) so as to cause any reflection to your recommendation.[208]

Once again, that sense of opportunism. If Askin did not think of himself as of the "first people," a phrase that the reader will recall also fell from the lips of William Dummer Powell, he was willing to assist them in their objectives; perhaps being seen to be on the side of the winning team was sufficient.

Finally, Askin was willing to seek to change the law in his own interest and that of like-minded people wanting to acquire land. Writing to William Dickson in 1803, he said that when an unpatented property had been sold, the purchaser "is to be considered as the real proprietor, for there is half the people here who sold that never will give any other sale [instrument] than what they made at first which is that they renounced all claim to the lot they sold ..."[209]

William Dickson was Askin's lawyer and agent and himself a land speculator. His cousin, Thomas Dickson, was also a lawyer and a member of the Heirs and Devisees Commission, and his uncle Robert Hamilton, Askin's son-in-law, was one of the biggest speculators in Upper Canada as well as a member of the Heirs and Devisees Commission and of the Legislative Council. Together, these people might influence the outcome of events, creating a property law which their interests required. No doubt Dickson would lend positive reinforcement to views that Askin would express to Hamilton, in his capacity as both his investment associate and his father-in-law. It would take little to convince these people; in August of that same year, Askin had been in the business of selling forty lots, the property of William Robertson, to Dickson and Hamilton.[210]

Though Askin acquired substantial amounts of property from his own endeavours he expected reward for his services to the state. Indeed, like many others, he did not feel that service to the state need limit personal gain. This is revealed in a letter he wrote in 1778 to Sampson Fleming, then working for the Commissariat:

I hear you have an opportunity of making money & I should not be surprized you did not make use of it from a mistaken notion of people in the Service being obliged to live on their pay, don't Injure your famely so much. Your pay and mine together is not able to keep either of our famelies. [T]here is sometimes an oppertunity of making money in the Service without either neglecting a mans duty, or taking one farthing from the Crown, this & this way only I mean or would approve off for instance a merchant furnishes things for Government at a certain Rate, now if I'm in the Service & can furnish them at the same rate & make an advantage to myself is it not as just that I a Servant of the Crown reaps a Bennifitt by government as any merchant whatsoever, & I make no Doubt but your Commanding Officer would indulge you in anything reasonable that was for your advantage.[211]

After Askin himself had served for some twenty-four years and received in his mind insufficient compensation for his efforts, he set out to change his fate by inviting his friends to assist him plead his case. In 1802 he had received 1200 acres for his efforts as a magistrate and member of the Land Board of the District of Hesse. He regarded this as inadequate since he believed 700 to be already his and he had worked two days per week for many years. Indeed, in 1795, he had already asked for a township on the north shore of Lake Erie on his own behalf and that of Alexander Henry but to no avail.[212] He sought Todd's help once more.

... as it is said Members of the Land Board in other Districts helped themselves amply, as they kept no books of records of their transactions, perhaps his Excellency may suppose the case was the same in the western district the contrary may be proved beyond contradiction, by the records now in possession of the Surveyor General of Upper Canada, that the members of that Land Board never received, nor took to themselves, a single foot of lands, as I know you have always possessed the greatest inclination to serve me, I should hope that you could point out to me some means by which I could obtain from the Government, some reward for my service ...[213]

This is interesting, of itself, for what it reveals about perceptions of the land boards as well as for what it says of Askin and no doubt others. Though it may be stretching the truth to claim that Askin did not believe that virtue had its own reward, the mode of acquisition of land by magistrates' certificates suggests more base motives. This had involved at least three magistrates, Louvigny Montigny, Grant, and Askin, all former members of the Land Board of the Western District. Their actions in these instances may have been legal, but they were hardly ethical, and if they had behaved in their own or at least Askin's interest while serving as JPs, they may very well have behaved similarly while members of the Land Board.

Clearly, connection in its many forms was important for everyone, but the Babys and Askins seem to have been particularly adept at forging such links. If they chose to act together they could be a powerful force, because by 1825 the two networks held 63.0 per cent of all speculative holdings and, in 1852, 32.3 per cent. Of course, the acreage on which these percentages are based might of itself be without meaning, although it is interpreted here as a surrogate for power. Indeed, this analysis shows an association between the possession of land and office. Much depends, of course, upon whether the links were actually forged. There is no evidence that all links were connected to any one end. However, there was in the links the potential for common action. Askin's network of interconnections may never have been fully operational, but it possessed the potential. All that was needed for a favourable outcome for a particular event was to identify and connect to the appropriate people.

Commercial networks and land

Were there differences in the amount of land held during the periods ending in 1825 and 1852 that corresponded with commercial and trade activities? The simple answer to this appears to be in the affirmative, especially in the early period when procedures were being established and the merchants, by controlling the credit system, could in fact influence success. There were in fact forty-seven merchants and they amounted to almost a third of all the speculators identified! Inevitably, they became fewer in number as the province developed, and they diversified economically as the staples with which they were primarily associated declined in importance. Askin and McGill epitomize the sequence. Askin first engaged in the Indian and fur trade, then in land, and when that did not deliver what he hoped for, he followed what became a third element in Canadian development – alcohol. Unable to pay the demand notes of Todd and McGill, he paid them in land; in 1803, when neither their nor his own property was selling, he built a distillery![214]

Of course, more merchants acquired land than built distilleries, but over time the size of property holdings of the forty-seven individuals engaged in trade and commerce declined from a mean of 903.49 acres (σ = 1525.01) in 1825 to 574.04 acres (σ = 806.18 acres) in 1852.[215] In both periods the acreage of the non-merchants was less. In 1825 the mean was 272.45 acres and the standard deviation 713.51; in 1852 it was 350.22 with a standard deviation of 414.51. While these might seem different, in fact, statistically the two sets of figures for the non-merchants could have been drawn from the same population.[216] What is especially interesting is that in both periods there was a distinct difference between the acreage of the merchants and that of the other speculators.[217]

An interesting facet of commerce was that over time the nature of the speculators changed with the economy. In the earlier period, many of the land speculators or mortgage investors were directly involved in the fur and Indian trade or at least in supplying the fur trade. Askin and McGill are the most obvious examples, but the list also includes Jean-Baptist Barthe, Edward Ellice, Matthew Elliott, William Caldwell, John and Thomas Forsyth, George Ironside, William Lymbrunner, Alexis Maisonville, Alexander McCormick, Angus McIntosh, William Park, Richard Pattinson, John Richardson, and William Robertson. There were others among the 144 speculators who were recognizably merchants but who had less obvious connections to the fur trade. These included Thomas Clark, James Gordon, Alexander Grant, the George Benson Halls (father and son), George Jacob, Moses David, William McCormick, George Meldrum, William Munger, Charles Askin, and Francis Baby.

Finally, there was a third group of people, those entrepreneurs who became industrialists, who invested in banks and canals, or in breweries and distilleries, or indeed in railways. These people included James Dougall, grain merchant and shipper; Peter Carroll, a surveyor who became a contractor and a director of a bank and of railway and suspension-bridge companies; Peter McGill, the chairman of the St Lawrence and Champlain Railway Company, who became president of the Bank of Montreal in 1834; John Prince, lawyer, entrepreneur, brewer, and mine and railway promoter; John Redpath, industrialist, sugar refiner, director of Telegraph and Fire Assurance Companies; William Allan, who was a director of the Canada Company and of the Welland Canal Company, president of the Bank of Upper Canada, a major shareholder in the British North American Bank, and a governor of the British American Fire and Life Assurance Company; Samuel

Street, younger of the two who carried the name, an investor in railway stock and in the Welland Canal Company; and Thomas Clark (T.C.) Street, president of the Gore Bank and a director of the Canadian Bank of Commerce, the Bank of Upper Canada, and the British American Fire Assurance Company. This third group represented a wholly new dimension, with investments in more intangible resources than fur and land.

Opportunities for investment in non-primary resources or in infrastructure, such as banks, canals, and railway stock, were simply not available to the older speculators. Were there in fact differences that accorded with opportunity? One way to test for this is to examine the three categories and the ages of the speculators who were members of each category. In this way, age becomes a somewhat imperfect surrogate for opportunity. A series of tests for difference in acreage (t-tests) were conducted on samples drawn from the 144 speculators for which the date of birth of the individual was available. The twenty-three persons involved in the fur and Indian trade were born on average in 1760; the eleven without obvious involvement in this business were born on average in 1778; and the nine most obviously commercial-oriented were born on average in 1793.[218] The fur-trade group was statistically different from the second group but the second group was no different from the third. Nonetheless, such investment was an increasingly important feature of the economy and the fur trade per se would seem to have been on the wane. Indeed, based on the available statistics, there would seem to have been an almost thirty-year period between 1775 and 1801 when the people holding land were no longer involved in the fur trade.

Did some interact more than others? Within Table 9.4 is a matrix of interaction for those speculators who had more than ten transactions in the years to 1852. The matrix is arranged from highest to lowest number of transactions along both axes. If some groups whose actions cannot be separated are counted as one, there were twenty-six vendors. Examples include James and William Caldwell and Thain, Richardson and Forsyth. Additionally, there were fifteen others who acquired land. Of the forty-one, the occupations of five are unknown. One (James Baby) was primarily a high officeholder but also a land speculator, one (Macdonald) was a future prime minister who invested in land, two were surveyors (Burwell and Mount), one worked for the commissary at Detroit, two were customs officials (Watson and Hall), and two were lawyers (James Woods and Jonathan Sewell)[219] apparently acting for themselves. The remaining twenty-seven were merchants or businessmen in the wider sense.

Most of the 523 properties that changed hands within this network of exchange lay within the nexus of a few individuals, whose activity is

Table 9.4   Matrix of interaction for larger speculators with ten or more transactions in 1852

	C#	Sell (1788–1852)	A.J. Robertson	Jms. McGill	Jms. Woods	Hon E. Ellice	W. Duff	J.A. MacDonald	R. Pattinson	J.G. Watson	R. Mount	C. Baby	I. Todd	S. Gerard	T. Park Bros.	A. McIntosh	G.D. Hall	J.N. Fulmer	J. Lockhart	J. Sewell	Sam. Street	F.T. Richardson	J. Baby	Hon T. Clark	J. Gordon	E.D. Mathews	T.A. Stayner	Other Acquiring	Total Acquiring
Sell (1788–1852)			88	71	118	36	34	63	85	111	79	5	110	134	82	72	119	45	61	96	104	108	7	22	46	67	100		
J.N. Askin	2	4		40									18															8	80
R. Pattinson	6	85	56		2	4	3																					1	64
M. Burwell	3	17									21																	16	37
F.T. Richardson	1	108				4	12			9					2							2						0	29
Wm Hands Sr, Jr	1	51			2													3				5			4			8	27
W.C. Pickersgill	6	138						24																				0	24
T. McKee	3	74		1	1	4	4																		1			9	22
W. Duff	1	34				10																						9	20
I. Todd	1	110			17																							3	20
W.G. Hall	1	50								1											12							5	18
Wm. McCormick	1	70			1													1				1			4		2	9	17
R.T. Reynolds	1	87													2		4								1			8	16
A. Maisonville	1	135												14		8												0	16
A. McIntosh	5	72								1		1				3												1	16
J. Woods	3	118			1					1																		10	15
J. Brown	1	16				3														12								1	13
J.B. Valade	1	128			2																							13	13
T. Smith	1	97																										10	12
J.W. Caldwell	4	20																	2			3						7	12
A. Harrow	3	132							11																			0	11
S. Gerard	1	134															9											2	11
F. Baby	1	6										1																9	10
F. Caldwell	1	21													3									6				1	10
J.N. Fulmer	1	45				1									2			3										3	10
Jms. McGill	4	71										1																9	10
Other Sellers			1	0	12	4	6	0	1	10	0	15	0	2	6	2	0	5	10	0	0	1	3	0	0	1	9		
Total Sellers			57	41	38	30	25	24	24	22	21	18	18	16	15	13	13	12	12	12	12	12	11	11	11	11	11		

highlighted on the matrix. Interestingly, the Baby Family was not part of this, although Francis Baby did sell nine properties to others who were insufficiently active to be identified. Clearly, the Baby family's role in Essex may have been to serve the state. Of course, like others of their day, they were interested in land for themselves[220] and their relations; however, in Essex at least, they did not operate at a level which would lead to identification here.

This was not so for the Askin network. Askin and Pattinson together sold 144 of the 523 properties acquired. Askin "unloaded" to his friends Todd and McGill and Richard Pattinson to settle outstanding debts. Todd seems to have been more successful than McGill in liquidating these assets. Having acquired eighteen parcels, he sold seventeen to the lawyer James Woods. McGill sold only ten of the forty acquired, one of them to Charles Baby and nine to smaller players in the land market. Pattinson sold fifty-six parcels to A.J. Robertson, who may have been a relative of William Robertson, Askin's former partner. If such a grouping is permitted, this little set may actually have influenced the market and in this Askin was clearly central.

Were land dealings orchestrated in ethnic terms? Table 9.5 reproduces a matrix of interaction for the wider society whose origins are known for the years 1850 and 1851. Land speculators are included.[221] Table 9.6 presents comparable data for the forty-one land speculators discussed above. The tables, while not strictly comparable, are nonetheless useful: their juxtaposition is posited on the notion that this will reveal something of the nature of land speculation and of capital. It is clear from the first of these tables that the majority of sales were made by French Canadians. Of course, this was the single largest group, although the non-French Canadians actually constituted a larger proportion of the population because the census defines this group as the children of all non-French irrespective of origin. Immigration was a dominantly non-French experience and the non-French were significantly younger than the French Canadians.[222] Both groups exhibited characteristics of living among themselves, even with respect to land transfer and speculation. French Canadians conducted 82.9 per cent of their sales and 84.3 per cent of their purchases within their own group. Perhaps understandably, the non-French children of all immigrants did so to a lesser extent. However, the figures were still high (52.5 per cent of sales and 36.1 per cent of purchases). The Scots, constituting only 2 per cent of the population, showed the least ethnocentrism, followed by the demographically older and longer established American population, which sought to sell where it could as it died off or returned to its cultural roots. In contradistinction, the Irish, constituting some 8 per cent of

Table 9.5   Summary matrix of absolute number and percentage of sales and purchases in 1850 and 1851: within known origins

Purchasers	Vendors						
	American	Non-French Canadian	French Canadian	English	Irish	Scot	Total
Americans	8	1	2	1	1	3	16
	S(21.6)	S(1.8)	S(1.1)	S(4.0)	S(3.2)	S(21.4)	S(4.6)
	P(50.0)	P(6.3)	P(12.5)	P(6.3)	P(6.3)	P(18.8)	
Non-French	14	30	22	10	2	5	83
Canadians	S(37.8)	S(52.5)	S(12.1)	S(40.0)	S(6.5)	S(35.7)	S(24.1)
	P(16.9)	P(36.1)	P(26.5)	P(12.0)	P(2.4)	P(6.0)	
French	12	13	150	1	1	1	178
Canadians	S(32.4)	S(22.8)	S(82.9)	S(4.0)	S(3.2)	S(7.1)	S(51.6)
	P(6.7)	P(7.3)	P(84.3)	P(0.6)	P(0.6)	P(0.6)	
English	–	2	3	13	2	1	21
	–	S(3.5)	S(1.7)	S(52.0)	S(6.4)	S(7.1)	S(6.1)
	–	P(9.5)	P(14.3)	P(61.9)	P(9.5)	P(0.5)	
Irish	1	–	4	–	25	1	31
	S(2.7)	–	S(2.2)	–	S(80.6)	S(7.1)	S(9.0)
	P(3.2)	–	P(12.9)	–	S(80.6)	P(3.2)	
Scots	2	11	–	–	–	3	16
	S(5.4)	S(19.3)	–	–	–	S(21.4)	S(4.6)
	P(12.5)	P(78.2)	–	–	–	P(4.9)	
Total	37	57	181	25	31	14	345

Source: AO, Abstract Index to Deeds.

(S) Sales as a percentage; (P) Purchases as a percentage.

the population of the county in 1851, were as self-contained as the French Canadians.

What is immediately clear from examination of Table 9.5 is that there is obviously less symmetry along the diagonal than in the population as a whole, although the statistics for the French Canadians and non-French are little different. It would seem that, for the forty-one largest speculators, the larger dealers in land, there was in fact less ethnic loyalty.[223] This is particularly notable in the case of the Irish and the English though the numbers are small. This was not true of the French Canadians. Among these larger French-Canadian investors, 52.9 per cent of the sales and 81.8 per cent of purchases were con-

Table 9.6   Summary matrix of absolute number and percentage of sales and purchases in 1850 and 1851: within known origins of forty-one land speculators

Purchasers	Vendors						
	American	Non-French Canadian	French Canadian	English	Irish	Scot	Total
Americans	10	18	–	3	2	14	47
	S(11.6)	S(19.7)	–	S(15.0)	S(2.1)	S(21.9)	S(12.6)
	P(21.3)	P(38.3)	–	P(6.4)	P(4.3)	P(29.8)	
Non-French	26	56	–	2	23	29	136
Canadians	S(30.2)	S(61.5)	–	S(10.0)	S(23.9)	S(45.3)	S(36.4)
	P(19.1)	P(41.2)	–	P(2.0)	P(16.9)	P(21.3)	
French	–	1	9	–	–	1	11
Canadians	–	S(1.1)	S(52.9)	–	–	S(1.6)	S(2.9)
	–	P(9.1)	P(81.8)	–	–	P(9.1)	
English	15	7	–	1	–	4	27
	S(17.4)	S(7.7)	–	S(5.0)	–	S(6.3)	S(7.2)
	P(55.5)	P(25.9)	–	P(3.7)	–	P(14.8)	
Irish	4	–	–	–	9	14	27
	S(4.6)	–	–	–	S(9.4)	S(21.9)	S(7.2)
	P(14.8)	–	–	–	S(33.3)	P(51.8)	
Scots	31	9	8	14	62	2	126
	S(36.0)	S(9.9)	S(47.0)	S(79.0)	S(64.6)	S(3.1)	S(33.7)
	P(24.6)	P(7.1)	P(6.3)	P(11.1)	P(49.2)	P(1.6)	
Total	86	91	17	20	96	64	374

Source: AO, Abstract Index to Deeds.

(S) Sales as a percentage; (P) Purchases as a percentage.

ducted within the group. French Canadians, in terms of land dealings, were clearly a society apart!

While the Americans, in Essex as a whole, sold to the non-French and, secondly, to the French Canadians, the speculative group sold primarily to the Scots and the non-French. This may have reflected nothing more than the availability of money and the fact that the Scots were buying, but it may also reflect social and political predisposition. The society of Americans in Upper Canada was one divided ideologically between supporters and opponents of the revolution. The speculative group contained members of the Loyalist elite who feared "the mob" and "democracy" and often looked askance at Americans receiving land from the Crown when they had, in some instances, actually fought against it. Such people might prefer to deal with the Scots![224] The English bought from the Americans and sold to the Scots; 79.0 per cent of sales were with the Scots although again the absolute numbers are low. The Irish sold to the Scots and the Scots sold to everyone but the Scots! Clearly, the Scots were important in the land economy of Essex. However, it has also to be remembered that the most important representatives of the Scots and Irish were McGill and Askin. Most of the sales in Essex conducted by these larger investors took place in the names of McGill, Todd, and Askin, and Askin was in debt to the first named!

What about membership in the armed forces? At least forty-nine of the speculators had been commissioned members of the forces, including in that term the naval service, the commissary, the regular army, and the militia. Since militia service was theoretically required of all adult males sixteen to sixty years of age, only those members who held the King's commission were included here. In 1825 the average of their landholdings was 917.86 acres (σ = 1543.03). In 1852, with some of these individuals dead and others having reduced their estates, the average dropped to 543.77 (σ = 652.57), although statistically these figures appeared little different from one another.[225] Nor was the military and speculator average different from the non-military speculator average in 1851–52 ($\overline{x}$ = 366.21, σ = 523.55 acres), although, in the earlier period, there had been marked differences between non-military speculators, whose mean was found to be 223.96 (σ = 625.18), and those associated with the forces.[226] Of itself, this decline is of little consequence since membership in the forces, like membership in the magistracy, or indeed success as a merchant, might well be the initial recognition of distinction. Indeed, Keith Johnson views a military commission as "a parallel if not more fundamental starting point" to that of magistrate in the search for "prominence," though he sees such a commission as "a measure of power" which assumed rather than bestowed wealth. In particular, a colonelcy was a much sought-after social symbol.[227]

Of course, as Johnson is the first to recognize, there can be no simple single measure of causation. The John Askins, father and son, were magistrates and merchants at one and the same time and one was in the militia as well. James Baby was a colonel of militia and a JP, first appointed to the magistracy in 1788 before his elevation to the cxecutive and legislative councils in 1792. Captain Matthew Elliott commanded in the field, served in the Indian Department, traded with the Indians, rose to be a colonel of militia in 1798, and was elected MHA for Essex in 1800, although he never served as a magistrate. James Gordon was an attorney, had been a partner in trade with Askin at

Albany, and became an ensign of militia in 1807 and a lieutenant-colonel in 1822, the same year he was made a magistrate. He was elected MHA for Kent in 1820 and appointed a member of the Legislative Council in 1828. As these examples show and further examination of appendix 7.3 reveals, possession of land was associated with service in a number of areas. Ultimately, it might be totally independent of all these offices, requiring only a dedicated determination and sufficient cash or credit to accumulate.[228] There can be little doubt, however, that service in a number of offices might ease accumulation because of the social connections thereby acquired, to say nothing of the direct compensation received, for example, for service in the military or indeed as a member of the executive and legislative councils. One such person, compensated as a regular soldier although, as such, he had also served on the Land Board of Hesse, was Major John Smith, the former commandant at Detroit and later (1790–92) at Niagara. He never satisfied any of his claim in Essex; instead, he became the first patentee in Ontario County and received 5000 acres there.[229]

SUMMARY

From the beginning, both in Essex and in Upper Canada generally, there was a relationship between officeholding and access to land, in part because the system was one that rewarded its faithful in this manner. Those who served received land and those with land qualified to serve and so received more. All of this was part of Simcoe's plan to create an aristocracy, which to be independent had to be endowed with the appropriate resources. The entrée to power and to this clientage system was, as Armstrong has noted, the commission as justice of the peace. Perhaps equally important was the military commission, although as Johnson says, this may have been a recognition of wealth rather than a route to it. From such positions, one might hope to rise to the pinnacles of power, membership in the executive and legislative councils.

Interestingly, though there were obvious differences in landholding between officeholders and non-officerholders, the councillors did not control the largest acreage in Essex. Essex was well represented on the executive and legislative councils by Alexander Grant, William Dummer Powell, Prideaux Selby, William Robertson, Angus McIntosh, and the Babys, in particular James. He, like the others mentioned here, held little land in Essex, perhaps out of a sense of delicacy and to avoid the appearance of interest and privilege. Alternatively, all of these people had extensive holdings elsewhere because returns on land were superior to those in Essex.

To be close to these people was to be close to power both because of the assistance that might be needed to acquire land and because of the offices that might be bestowed. This was an age of pluralism, as the careers of Richard Pollard and William Hands epitomize, and a multitude of offices brought salaries and fees. Closeness was attained through connection in business or in marriage to one of the two most interconnected networks of social and economic influence and power, that is, the Askin and Baby groups. Locally, the former may have been financially the most significant, at least before Askin's financial indebtedness to McGill; however, the Baby network reached to the provincial capital through the multitude of offices that James Baby held and through his powerful friends, Bishop Strachan and the chief justice, John Beverley Robinson, and to Quebec through the membership of François Baby, Sr, in that province's Executive Council.

To have access to such networks through family or business was, it would seem, to enjoy privilege in terms both of land and of access to office. However, if the sole goal of one's life was to accumulate property, one of the best routes to this was by being a merchant. The military actually possessed the largest amount of land in 1825 ($\overline{x} =$ 917.86). Its members had been rewarded this land for their service, but by 1852 they owned less ($\overline{x} = 543.77$) because calls on their service had been reduced and the veterans themselves were fewer in number. They were followed by the merchants ($\overline{x} = 903.49$ acres), presumably because of their capacities to perform on an everyday basis in the market and, as was common, to accumulate through indebtedness. Through time, their possession of land was reduced ($\overline{x} = 574.04$ in 1852), but they themselves were no doubt adjusting to the new economic circumstances which were emerging, as Essex and Upper Canada became more industrialized and the nature of commerce and industry changed. In fact, there was no significant difference in acreage among the military, the merchants, and officeholders. However it was accumulated, most of these people held between 850 and 2500 acres in the earlier period when speculation was most marked;[230] even in the second period, from 1825 to 1852, there was no difference among the three groups but the officeholders showed least reduction of acreage. In 1852 they still owned on average 707 acres and 68.26 per cent (one standard deviate) of them owned up to 2253 acres. This was basically unchanged from the equivalent 2386 acres in the earlier timeframe.[231] As always, the politicians survived!

Yet to separate groupings in this way with respect to land, however useful it is as a research device, is to adopt a simplistic approach; it is to look at a part of human activity rather than the whole.[232] Clearly, recognition of individuals turned upon a total image rather than any single attribute. In the earliest times in Essex, there would seem to have been a prejudice against the merchant class, especially on the part of the administration and the British military. Haldimand expressed his desire to exclude "petty traders," and Major Mathews, the officer commanding at Detroit, denigrated their character. Powell could write about the "first people" but, even as he did so, the "first people" were engaging in marked land accumulation and speculation.

Though merchants had been present on the executive and legislative councils from the beginning, they became increasingly significant players. By 1825, having accumulated capital, the merchants were even more essential to the system and were being recognized accordingly by their appointment as magistrates or indeed as colonels of militia. John Askin is a case in point – a former sutler to the army who had through accumulation and networking ingratiated himself with the power structure beyond Essex. With this entreé (appointment as magistrate), such people might aspire to other offices and even to the centres of ultimate patronage, the executive and legislative councils. Askin became a member of the Land Board and a colonel of militia.

If integrity and loyalty were in evidence, the absence of property could soon be remedied from the state's resources in return for service. In short, while land was important, it was not a necessary condition of power. The members of the executive and legislative councils in Essex in this period owned relatively little land in the area, though this may have been a case of their trying to appear to be beyond reproach. In group five, the speculative cluster with the largest property holdings, there were only four members of these councils; in group one, there were eleven former members. The acreage of these groups was very different. Indeed, the acreage of the latter was the lowest of all the officeholders ($\bar{x}$ = 359.2 in 1825 and 284.4 in 1852), little different from the Essex average for all landowners. In 1825 James Baby owned 641 acres and John Askin 2255 acres in Essex. The contrast is marked.

Yet it would also be naive and incorrect to conclude that the possession of land was totally independent of power or vice versa. Clearly this was not so. To be close to these networks of power and influence was clearly important, but if, in addition, one was a merchant and had served in office or in the armed forces, one's prospects of greater advancement and land acquisition increased. This nexus of interconnection was not just how land speculators proceeded, it seems to have been how the very society worked, with networks of influence organized from the local to the larger scale. The Askin records allow one to view this process in terms of his own strategic marriages, his use of marriage as a vehicle of economic and social advancement, his friendship and formal economic links, his service and that of other members of his family in the militia, and his pursuit of politicians. If he sought power he also possessed it; had he not he could not have behaved as he did in, for example, the Drouillard business, nor might he have received the support he got from his fellow magistrates. Though the record is silent on most of the remaining 144 speculators, one presumes that their strategies were little different. Connection in all its forms was important.

What is interesting is that, while links of kin and family were clearly important, and ties of ethnicity in the general population were seen to affect sales, no such effect appeared among the speculators. The wealthy recognized the wealthy. After all, business was business, then as now.

10 The Corporate Sector

INTRODUCTION

To this point the discussion has turned upon the activities of individuals who were indeed the dominant actors throughout the first half of the nineteenth century. In fact, there were two corporate bodies which were active as well and which had come to control most of the former Crown and clergy reserves. These were the Canada Land Company,[1] established in 1826,[2] and the Clergy Corporation, which by 1819 had come to manage the affairs of the clergy reserves subject to the veto of the Executive Council.[3] The removal of both Crown and clergy reserves from state control, more gradual in the latter than in the former case, was a response to political controversy: the campaign against the clergy reserves, as a landed endowment set aside for one portion of the population, was unrelenting from the 1820s on.[4] It also signified recognition of the need for new sources of revenue in the wake of the mother country's refusal after 1817 to continue its support to the colonial government,[5] while at the same time being an effort to stimulate capitalism through the sale of land.[6] Indeed, the institution of higher taxes on land in 1818, the establishment of the Clergy Corporation, the introduction of a sales policy on Crown land, the creation of the Canada Company in 1826, and the inauguration of a sales policy for part of the Clergy Corporation's land in 1827[7] all marked a period of economic adjustment to changed economic circumstances, beginning in the second decade of the century. One of those changed circumstances was disappointment with the revenues generated by renting Crown land in general and Crown and clergy reserves in particular.

REVENUE GENERATION AND CROWN AND CLERGY RESERVES

The first attempts at raising revenue came with the introduction of a system of leasing, which had both revenue-generating and political objectives. Rents were to be set in such a way as to bestow an obvious benefit and for such a duration as to inculcate political gratitude but not sufficiently long as to allow the tenant to forget the hand bestowing the benefit.[8] This was first proposed in 1795[9] and finally introduced in 1802 after two reports by Chief Justice Elmsley in 1798 and 1800.[10] The scheme of 1802, like its earlier counterpart, maintained a staged structure of incremental costs as each stage was reached but at greater costs than in 1798. The first seven years' rents were to be 10 shillings per year for a 200-acre farm. In the second set of seven years it would be 20 shillings and in the third it would be 30 shillings. Unlike the earlier formula applied, new leases were to be limited to twenty-one rather than forty-two years; however, at the government's discretion rents could be paid in grain.[11] At this time it was decided that since the objectives were different, the Crown and clergy reserves should be separated administratively. At the end of the cycle of twenty-one year leases, rents would again rise to 35 shillings, 70 shillings, and 105 shillings for each year of each set of seven years.[12] This pattern continued into the first half of the century.[13]

The leasing policy proved unpopular to many who sought freehold tenure;[14] it also proved unpopular with the authorities who found it difficult to enforce the payment of rents. Collection depended upon the efficiency and integrity of the sheriffs to whom the task was entrusted. Many simply did not fulfil their obligations; "perhaps the worst case was that of Sheriff Hands, who by 1811 had not yet marred his perfect record of no returns from Reserves or glebes in the Western District for over eight years."[15] In his own defence, Hands argued that it was the lack of coercive power that limited his efficiency.[16]

Little interest was shown in leasing the reserves[17] even though the fees involved were a fraction of those paid on freehold property.[18] In part, this may have been because, as John Askin believed, the reserves were intended for the particular friends of government. Most interest came from speculators who, as has been shown, were often engaged in government at some level. These people had little intention of improving the land, simply seeing these lots as sources of valuable timber or as desirable locations from which they hoped to profit as land values rose.[19] Among the leases entered into, in this early period beginning in 1802, were eight lots for which John Askin was the lessee on two and Thomas McCrae, the MHA for Kent, the lessee on the remainder. These lands lay along the Belle, Ruscom, au Pêche, and au Puce rivers in Maidstone and Rochester townships. Some idea of overall costs and the effects of the policy of increments in rent can be illustrated by the case of one of McCrae's lots in Rochester. McCrae rented this 136-acre lot on the Ruscom perhaps as early as 1802[20] and certainly by 1809, when he paid rent of ten shillings per year for it for this and the subsequent years down to 1816. In keeping with overall policy, his rent then increased to one pound per year and this held until 1822, when he paid (22s/6d) for a short time before the rent increased in 1823 to 65 shillings per year and in 1832 to five pounds per year. These were the general rates for a renewed cycle of twenty-one years made under the regulations of 1811. In June 1833, he purchased the whole lot for £64. Effectively, this meant that he had paid 112.9 pence per acre. At a time when land in this area was selling between 311 and 598 pence per acre (Table 8.3), he was paying only about one-third of the going price. Alternatively, he had paid 3.5 pence per acre per year as rent and even less on his other lots, most of which were sold for the same sum of £64 between 1847 and 1850. The Askin estate enjoyed similar pre-emption rights and paid between two and three pence per acre in 1833, 1847, and 1848.[21] With rents like this, it seems difficult to understand why some did not pay them since, theoretically, one could lose all by not doing so. In practice, this was unlikely given the remoteness of some of the land, the desire of the state and the Clergy Corporation for revenue, and the fact that many had simply abandoned the land after stripping the timber. Both McCrae and Askin did pay but others did not.[22] As late as 1843, Thomas Baines[23] of the Clergy Corporation, writing about rents in the whole of Upper Canada, remarked:

... it is proper to mention that a considerable portion is not likely to be collected, as many Clergy Reserves were originally leased either on Speculation or for the purpose of being denuded of their Timber. As regards the aggregate rented a very considerable reduction in the Amt Collectable, must also be expected in as much as these Lots on which the highest rent is charged in the Returns are generally those which were originally leased for the purpose above mentioned.[24]

In fact, arrears on clergy land amounted to £20,949.7s.10d.; of this, the contribution of the Western District, and of Essex within it, was minuscule. Western District arrears amounted to £28.10s.10d., well behind the more central Home District or, in terms of location, the more comparable London District.[25]

Not only were rents in arrears throughout the period but there was relatively little interest in renting itself. By 1826, only 900 clergy leases had been taken out in Upper Canada; by 1827, when most of the Crown reserves were sold to the Canada Company, 883 Crown leases had been made out but of these 220 had expired and had not been renewed. It was perhaps because of this that 200,000 acres of leased Crown reserves were granted to endow King's College, an Anglican establishment and the precursor of the University of Toronto. In the whole Western District in 1802, ten reserves were under lease and no other leases of reserve land were made for another fifteen years. Between then and 1820, one Crown reserve and one clergy reserve were leased. Between 1820 and 1832, when the practice of leasing land in other than the private sector was stopped,[26] eight clergy reserves and one Crown reserve had been leased.[27] By 1828, eleven Crown reserves, totalling 2434 acres, had already been placed in trust for King's College.[28] Yet there were those such as the land agent Joseph Talbot who, while recognizing the abuses of the system, nonetheless advocated continuation of the leasing scheme for those of limited means. This was also to ensure that they would not have to leave for areas where British feeling was "not the most predominant," presumably the United States.[29] In 1835 Thomas Baines, the newly appointed secretary-receiver of the Clergy Corporation, saw revival of leasing as a solution to poverty. He also saw it as the means of maintaining family cohesion as children matured and sought locations near parents. For these reasons, and the fact that the clergy reserves were available in older townships where one need not be exposed to the "hardships and privations of the wilderness," the leasing of these reserves would, he thought, be "most beneficial and popular."[30] This might indeed have been true for some settlers in some areas but overall the leasing policy was simply not viable here or in Upper Canada as a whole since freehold land was what was sought. A dominantly European population looked askance at tenancy since this, in conjunction with natural calamity, had brought it to the New World in the first place. Leasing might be tolerated but only in the short term while capital accumulated in the pursuit of freehold tenure. Because of dissatisfaction with it, because of the need to find monies to compensate for war damages and losses, and because of the controversy surrounding the issue of reserved land itself, a number of individuals argued for a sales policy. The argument became heightened after the British refusal in 1817 to continue its financial support of the colonial government. Given the need to maintain the civil establishment, it was finally decided to sell the reserves.

SALE TO THE CORPORATE SECTOR

To this end a speculative corporation, the Canada Company, had been hastily assembled in the private sector. Government would surrender millions of acres of land to it in return for annual payments which would meet its immediate costs. Though the company was created in 1824, its charter was not issued until 1826 because of a long delay in determining how much of the clergy reserves would be included in the transaction. The issue turned in part upon the valuation of the land included within the agreement since that affected how long payments would be made to the government. Bishop Strachan, alarmed at the value placed upon church land, sought and achieved the withdrawal from the transaction of what he regarded as Church of England property. The Canada Company had to be compensated for the changed terms; instead of the clergy reserves, it received 1.1 million acres of land in what became known as the Huron Tract.[31]

Meanwhile, Strachan agitated in England. Eventually, he returned to Canada with an act of the British parliament that was designed to rescue the church from financial disaster by permitting clergy-reserve sales. The new act limited sales to one-quarter of the resource and no more than 100,000 acres in any one year. Though leasing would continue for another three years, the act, which came into force in January 1829, produced sales of 13,410 acres by November. This was a small acreage, but the act began a process that, together with sales via the Canada Company, would ultimately remove the reserved lands as sources of political agitation though memories of perceived injustice might remain. After 1833, those leasing could purchase; however, this was a privilege and not a right.[32] It was in this way that Askin and McCrae acquired their leased land along the St Clair.

What was the price of Reserve land?

It was argued at the time that the Crown and clergy reserves actually retarded settlement because of their occurrence in blocks or as scattered parcels which created islands of inaccessible land. Was this in fact so? What was the price of these lands and how did this affect their rate of occupation? Were the people who were able to afford such land actual farmers or was it that this land was simply acquired, as tax-delinquent land has been shown to have been, by yet another set of speculators? Since the economic variable is of such importance, it is that which is examined first.

A sample of sales of clergy reserves and Crown land published in the *Upper Canada Gazette*[33] permitted comparison of the price of land for these two categories and for sales that took place between 1830 and 1838 in the case of the former and between 1837 and 1841 in the case of the latter. This sample permitted comparison between "asking price" and what was obtained, although only in the case of the Crown lands. In 1839, 242 parcels of Crown land were advertised for sale in the *Gazette* and in local newspapers. The asking price was commonly eight shillings (96 pence) per acre but the average was higher at 135.6 pence per acre.[34] This compared favourably to the statistics gathered for a sample of twenty-six properties which the *Gazette* reported sold in 1841. The $\bar{x}$ and σ reported for these properties was found to be 126.45 and 55.42 respectively.[35] A test of difference showed none to exist; government was getting what it was asking for, although it is clear that there had been no stampede to buy since only 11.5 per cent of what had been advertised had sold within two years.[36]

The *Gazette* sample of land sold by 1841 provided insufficient detail to permit analysis either through time or indeed between the different parts of the county, but it was possible to compare the relevant statistics for Crown and clergy land when aggregated to the county level. For ninety-nine observations of clergy reserves, a mean price per acre of 128.55 pence was calculated with a σ of 19.63 pence. There would appear to be no difference between the samples and a t test confirmed this.[37] Perhaps this is only to be expected since the two types of land could not be dramatically different in price from one other and still compete.

It seems that, with respect to the amount paid down, there was some difference between the developed and developing parts of the county represented by Malden and Maidstone townships respectively, but the sample sizes were insufficiently large to pursue this for all the constituent areas of the county.[38] However, for the county as a whole, this was quite clear: the average "down payment" on clergy land was 27.8 per cent and on Crown land it was 97.1 per cent.[39] Of the 125 purchases made at this time, eleven were acquired as clergy reserves by six individuals on the list of speculators; another bought the single Crown lot sold by 1841.[40]

The down payment was lower on a sample of sixty-four observations gathered from the Canada Company records. These records included the original price as well as the final price and it was possible to compute the relevant statistics for price, acreage acquired, the terms of the agreement, the actual number of instalments made, and the interest rate paid over the terms of the agreement. With respect to the down payment, both the mode and the median were 20 per cent, generally considered to be the terms under which the company operated.[41] However, in two instances, the company signed for 19.2 per cent and 19.75 per cent. In seventeen cases it received down payments greater than 50 per cent; one was for 99.4 per cent and, in twelve instances, these were outright purchases. In the case of the twelve, or 18.7 per cent of the lots purchased and paid for immediately, this meant that the nine individuals purchasing could pay an average of £103.8s.0d. An F. Chauvin paid £175;[42] a T. Philips bought 300 acres for £225. The rest paid between £50 and £117.7s.5¾d. Perhaps they renegotiated a loan elsewhere because Canada Company interest rates have been thought to have been high, but, taken at face value, this does say something about the capacity to pay in the society of the time. The effect of including these twelve lots in the calculation of down payment is, of course, to raise the average and to skew the distribution above the mode and mean. The mean down payment thus becomes 38.9 per cent and the σ of 31.82 per cent; clearly, the mode with forty-two observations of 20 per cent is the more meaningful statistic.

This is also probably true of the purchase price of Canada Company land for which the mode and median was 120 pence per acre. However, the $\bar{x}$ and σ permit comparison with other statistics. They were 135.09 and 31.05 pence per acre for the period for which data were available.[43] A series of t tests showed that this was statistically no different from the price obtained for clergy reserve or indeed Crown land.[44] These had to be close to one another to compete for clients.[45] Moreover, Essex prices for Canada Company land were seemingly little different from company land as a whole, although the data are not strictly comparable and in the case of Upper Canada there are very few values.[46] For those values that can be obtained for the years before 1833, the Upper Canadian average was 119.3 pence per acre and the Essex average 120.48.[47] For the period 1836 to 1840, the values were higher than in the earlier period but statistically no different between Essex and the province as a whole.[48] However, as Table 8.3 shows, they were different from the general price paid in these years or that paid by speculators in Essex. The comparison is hardly fair since one was the upset price for "raw" land and the others the price of developed farm real estate.

These same data revealed the number of instalments to be close to the idealized model presented by Gates and in the literature on the Canada Company; after the twelve cases in which there were no instalments because the land was purchased immediately are discounted, this was shown to have averaged five payments with a σ of

Table 10.1   Price in pence per acre for Canada Company lands sold
from 1830 to 1873 for which patent dates were available

Year patented	$\bar{x}$	σ	n
1835	297.87	272.94	9
1841	422.13	256.40	9
1846	817.34	792.30	200
Total	735.71	754.5	218*

Source: Calculations by the author.
* 25 properties could not be linked to patent dates.

1.5, based upon a sample of fifty-two observations.[49] However, while
there was close observation of the number of instalments, these were
not made each year. In fact, the number of years to completion averaged 7.4 years with a σ of 6.4 years.[50] Through the use of the original price and the final price, obtained by adding in the annual interest payments, it was possible to obtain the interest rate obtained by
the company. The $\bar{x}$ for the sixty-four observations was found to be
5.2 per cent, with a σ of 7.0; in a few instances, the interest rate was
as high as 35.5 per cent. These figures reveal that Canada Company
rates in Essex were generally less than the interest rate sanctioned by
the usury laws, but the de facto rate was greater when the com-
pounding effect of missing a payment was taken into account. An
effective annual return of 12 per cent was considerable,[51] especially
when it is realized that the Canada Company had actually purchased
these lands for 42 pence per acre in 1824 and been given fifteen
years in which to pay the government.[52] Given that a time-frame of
13.8 years was not unusual in which to complete a purchase from the
company, and given the fact that it operated on at least a 300 percent mark-up on which interest was payable, the absolute returns to
the company were great.

Table 10.1 gives the prices per acre obtained by the company when
land patented in 1835, 1841, and 1846 was *finally* sold. Table 10.2
shows, in addition to the prices paid by speculators and the general
population, the price agreed upon initially by those purchasing from
the Canada Company. Only after every penny due the company had
been paid was the sale acknowledged in the abstract index. This might
take place only many years after patent to the company. Indeed, on
average this took 33.96 years with a σ of 21.39 years (n = 243); in particular years it might take longer, for example, land patented in 1846
took between sixteen and fifty-eight years (n = 202) to reach the stage
where it could be transferred to the purchaser. In Essex, the Canada

Company might have to wait many years to secure its ultimate return. In part, this was because the method of operation did not suit all prospective purchasers. In the earliest years, when the company lacked title, settlers were reluctant to seek land and reluctant to improve land until greater legal protection was available.[53] For its own protection and to avoid taxation, the company operated under a "letter of license" which, together with a location ticket, was granted after promissory notes had been signed by a prospective settler.[54] The settler was now paying taxes on land which was still owned by a corporation and this cannot have been attractive. Whether this was better or worse in Essex than elsewhere awaits further work. It might be that the physical endowment of the county and its relative remoteness discouraged acquisition in this area.

This is not to say that the actual purchase took that long because, as was seen above, this averaged 7.4 years or as much as 13.8 years (1 standard deviate above the mean); however, it could take a longer time to find a suitable purchaser. Though not strictly comparable, tables 10.1 and 10.2 can be used to illustrate the way in which the company made considerable sums of money. Someone acquiring land in 1846 would have paid 168 pence per acre. If this purchase stretched over fourteen years at the upper end of the interest continuum (de facto 12.2 per cent), this same acre would have cost 841.8 pence.[55] This figure exceeds the calculated $\bar{x}$ of 817.34 (Table 10.1) and lies within one σ of the observed values in the abstracts. The statistical parameters are, of themselves, of little interest in this case; rather, the point is that a considerable absolute profit could be made, as all contemporary mortgage holders are only too aware. This is especially noteworthy considering that the land had been purchased for about a twentieth of the price, on credit from the state. The point is all the more poignant when it is recalled that, for many years, the Canada Company had been exempt from taxation until it chose or was pushed to patent[56] and that the tax burden was then transferred to the purchaser who was de facto a tenant until final payment was received.[57] Moreover, in this area, unlike the Huron Tract, the company expended nothing on development, the burden of infrastructure being borne by the state and the taxpayer generally. Since by 1852 the company had succeeded in unloading 239 of the 243 it had patented out of its nominal 299 (79.9 per cent), it had done very well indeed.[58]

The company sold these lots in 508 transactions conducted between 1830 and 1852. The properties averaged 120 acres but purchases, reflecting, one presumes, rising costs, became smaller as time went on until by the middle of the century the average was 98.18

Table 10.2   Land prices on Canada Company properties compared to speculator and general land prices for specified periods (pence per acre)

Date	Canada Company			Speculator	General Population
	$\bar{x}$	σ	n	$\bar{x}$	$\bar{x}$
1831–1835	120.48	8.07	31	184.31	311.60
1836–1840	141.56	19.82	16	509.56	567.40
1841–1845	147.50	20.16	6	520.93	456.80
1846–1852*	169.09	57.10	11	737.44	492.40
Overall	135.09	31.05	64		

Source: AO, Abstract Index to Deeds, Essex County, and Canada Company Registers.

* Canada Company lands were actually for 1850-53 in this sample.

acres.[59] The size, in itself, suggests that the purchasers were small-holders rather than speculators. In fact, examination of all 508 showed that only forty-two individuals purchased more than two parcels and only six of the forty-two exceeded 300 acres. In all, 95 of the 508 concerned transactions involving more than one parcel of land. Moreover, of the forty-two people involved, only six did not acquire contiguous parcels, commensurate with intentions to farm. Only one individual, Robert Anderson, appears on the list of 144 known speculators, although perhaps Daniel Murphy, who acquired 1582.5 acres in Mersea Township in 1846, should be included. In short, the overwhelming majority of these properties were acquired by non-speculators. Presumably, these were poor purchases for speculators. Prices were no better (Table 10.2) than might be paid for other "raw land" and much higher than the going rate at tax sales. The terms of credit were not as good as might be obtained from the Clergy Corporation, whose leases were longer and whose interest rates were lower.[60] Whatever may be thought of the Canada Company's terms, in Essex, speculators stayed out and the company land went to potential farmers.

The Clergy Reserves were clearly different with respect both to who was purchasing and to the price paid. At the nominal level, there were 336 clergy reserve lots in Essex. Examination of the abstracts accounted for 321 patented before 1885. Of these, 174 were sold before 1852. Clearly, the rate of sales was not as great as on Canada Company land, in spite of the fact that after 1834, when the auction system replaced the private sale, the terms were one-tenth down with the balance in nine equal instalments, more generous terms than provided by the company.[61] Moreover, as was seen in the case of McCrae and Askin, lessees were encouraged to purchase. Squatters were permitted to purchase at a valuation based upon the value of unimproved land. Until 1837, actual settlement was not required and rights of pre-emption were granted to individuals who could purchase at prices fixed and agreed upon after inspection.[62] Even so, in Essex, only 54.2 per cent of clergy-reserve land had been disposed of, while almost 80 per cent of Canada Company land had. The figures are not strictly comparable because not all clergy-reserve land had been released to the market. The passage of the imperial Clergy Reserve Act of 1827 permitted the sale of one-quarter of these lands[63] and the act of 1840 limited the amount of existing reserve to be disposed of to 100,000 acres per annum[64] and ended the system of creating reserves.[65] Sales were halted in 1841, and did not resume until 1845, by which time most reserves had been inspected and valued, though the process would continue until 1853.[66] In Essex, the most significant inspections of clergy-reserve land occurred in 1842 and 1844-45.[67] For Crown land, the extant inspection records for 1852 are particularly interesting.[68]

The inspection reports reveal much about the process of settlement. They indicate the distance to mill of each lot; clearly, such access was thought to be important. They also indicate the soil and the timber carried upon it, the latter being, as has been shown, associated with agricultural capacity. Further, they note the amount of cleared land and often the date at which clearance began, so that it is possible to infer something about rates of clearance, at least for some few lots.[69] In particular areas, they put an actual value upon the land, list the names of occupants if there were any, describe the conditions of tenure and the improvements made by those occupying the land, and comment on such matters as might affect the pre-emption rights of squatters or the price they might have to pay for given improvements to the lot.

As noted earlier, the sample of clergy-reserve lands reported in the *Upper Canada Gazette* revealed that until 1841 this land had been selling for an average of 128.6 pence. Compared to this, the "asking price" of 93.9 pence ($\sigma = 25.6$ pence) in 1842 was significantly lower and it would fall again by 1844-45,[70] although, admittedly, the number of lots advertised was small (n=28) and the area from which they were drawn restricted to Tilbury West, Mersea, and Gosfield townships rather than the total county as in 1842. Quite why this was occurring is not absolutely clear, but it would seem to have been a province-wide phenomenon.[71] The requirement of cash payment made during the Sydenham administration of the early 1840s must have served to reduce the price of land. Bishop Strachan believed that those selling for "ready-money" expected a reduction of 50 to 75 per cent; R.B. Sullivan of the Crown Lands Department agreed.[72] This latter logic may also be applicable to Crown land, the price of which dropped markedly between 1839 and 1852[73] although there is evidence to suggest that this may have represented purposeful intervention by the state to secure rapid settlement.[74] Furthermore, the requirement that a lot be evaluated as improved land, with deductions of up to 25 per cent for improvements did not encourage squatters or lessees to acquire land, driving down the price.[75] There must have been general uncertainty about the fate of these lands. There may also have been a "picking over" of lots so that those that remained were of a poorer character.[76]

How fast did the Reserves sell?

The 1842 data on clergy-reserve lands also allow one to comment on differences in the asking price of land throughout the area and on the length of time between advertising and sale. Clergy reserves were at a premium in Malden where there were few for sale. Three lots were advertised in that year for 216 pence per acre. In Rochester, Maidstone, Sandwich, and Tilbury, the respective mean asking prices were 104.8 (σ = 22.4, n of 38), 102.6 (σ = 29.7, n of 35), 98.9 (σ = 9.0, n of 25) and 98.2 (σ = 26.1, n of 47). In a third tier, Mersea and Colchester townships, the $\bar{x}$s were 90.9 (σ = 14.6 and n of 610) and 85.5 (σ = 25.4 and n of 63); and in Gosfield the $\bar{x}$ was 79.0 pence per acre (σ = 7.0 and n of 49).[77] In fact, this fourfold division was quite apparent from the modes and medians, which are probably the better measures. These were 216 pence per acre for Malden, 96 pence for all but Tilbury (90 pence per acre) in the second tier, 90 pence per acre for Colchester and Mersea, and 75 pence per acre in Gosfield. By 1845, five shillings (60 pence) was the common asking price for a reduced territory.

A series of t tests revealed that there were essentially two groupings of townships with respect to the time between advertising and selling clergy-reserve land.[78] The first group was composed of Tilbury and Mersea townships, where the lag was greatest;[79] the second group consisted of the remaining five townships.[80] The overall $\bar{x}$ was found to be 3310.1 days with a σ of 1021.5 based upon 225 observations; the mean and median were 3636 days, that is, nine days short of the time permitted to complete the purchase. The fact that the observed and allocated time come so close to one another lends interpretational meaning to the endorsement as sale, complete with date, that has been subsequently added to the 1842 inspection and valuation reports. This is thought to be the length of time to the completion of the sale rather than the initiation of the sale. If this is correct, clergy-reserve land took substantially longer to sell than Canada Company lots but then the regulations permitted this.[81]

The Conditions of the Reserves, Tenancy, and Government Policy

Only sixteen of the lots inspected in 1842 had names associated with them. Thomas McCrae's name appears six times and John Askin's twice, both of them as original lessees although they or their estates had or would subsequently acquire them.[82] Both the McCrae and Askin properties had tenants on them. John Cotter stated he had permission to occupy lots 2 and 3 in the 1st concession west of the Ruscom River. Two of the Askin properties on the au Pêche River had French-Canadian tenants on part of the property. An Alexander Wallace claimed to have paid £25 for the assignment of the lease on land between the au Pêche and au Puce rivers and had in turn leased land to one Crossan for a five-year term. The Wallace property contained a six-acre holding and a shanty; no information is provided on the Crossan holding but the total improvements were valued at £30 and Wallace and Crossan appear to have been allowed to purchase. Thomas Lawson, identified in the record as a coloured man who had improved four acres, and built a log house, claimed authority to occupy his lot on the au Puce River from the "late Rev. Johnson, Rector of Sandwich." It was offered at eight shillings per acre and sold, presumably to Lawson, in February 1849. In Tilbury Township, Thomas Steers, who carried out the inspection, reported most favourably on the Chauvin brothers. "These four brothers are highly respected and well conducted farmers and Peter has leased the lots and sends rent regularly to the Clergy Corporation." All four properties were converted from leasehold to freehold within four years.[83]

In addition to pointing out the existence of a loghouse or shanty here or there, Steers was at pains to report on the adverse conditions of some lots and the rights of occupants to pre-emption. Lot 1, west of the Belle River, originally leased to T. McCrae, was claimed by W. Markham as the assignee of whoever had made the improvements, which amounted to a log cabin and six acres. He valued the lot at 180 pence per acre and it was sold in November 1848. Steers had reported that he did not believe any of the claimants were entitled to pre-emption and that the land had been plundered of its timber. Markham did not receive the property, nor the lot east of the river, which he also claimed.[84] On lot 14, in the 7th concession west of the Ruscom River in Rochester Township, Steers found Bartholomew Menard with ten acres and a shanty. James Wood had purchased this property from McCrae, who had put James Cahill on it as a tenant. Menard, in turn, leased from Cahill; the person who had made the improvements is unknown but Steers reported that the improvements would not compensate for the plundered timber. The value of these improvements was fixed at £30 but again Steers reported that the lot had been pillaged of its timber resources. This 1842 inspection of Essex clergy reserves reinforces common notions. Most reserves were unoccupied, squatting was more common than formal ownership, cleared acreages were small, and leased land had been stripped of timber.[85]

When clergy-reserve sales did resume, the terms discouraged acquisition: a one-third down payment was required, and interest on land held by squatters was based upon the current rather than the initial value. Clearly, land policy with respect to clergy-reserve land limited sales relative to the former Crown reserves now in corporate hands. The Executive Council was aware of this. In its minutes of 13 October 1840 it recorded that it was unable to "press hard" on clergy reserves, but where only one instalment had been made and more than one was in arrears, the Crown Lands Department, the body managing the resource, should threaten legal proceedings.[86] By November 1845, the Executive Council had decided to amend the rules. Ten years' credit was again offered. Instead of interest on the purchase money, those whose leases had expired were to be charged rent at the rates prevailing when the leasing system was discontinued. Most significantly, land was to be valued at rates which excluded improvements for both lessees and squatters. Squatters could purchase, provided all back rent was paid by 1 January 1847 and a formal application to purchase made. The desire by squatters to take advantage of their pre-emption privileges before this date, together with the accumulated demand that had built up during the years of suspension, meant that the years 1846 and 1847 were years of unusually large demand in Upper Canada and in Essex.[87] Finally, amid continued controversy over the reserves, the decision was made to secularize them. An act of the imperial parliament in 1853 and of the Canadian parliament in 1854, the latter entitled the Clergy Reserve Secularization Act, effectively removed most of the complaints.[88]

Gates argues that clergy-reserve land passed much more rapidly into the hands of people who became independent farmers than did that of the Canada Company. This would not appear to have been so in Essex; the 54.2 per cent reported is based upon the total number of lots and not the numbers released on the market. Although figures are available for Upper Canada with respect to how much clergy-reserve land was released, these are aggregate figures and need not describe particular areas. Hence one can only speculate. Since, of necessity, clergy-reserve land was priced to compete with Canada Company and Crown land – and in fact the terms offered for it were more generous – it should have been quickly grabbed. If it was not, the reason must have been that these lands were part of a larger social issue of great emotional clout that arguably contributed to a rebellion in the province in 1837. Also, because they were still within the control of government, the clergy reserves were subject to constant changes in policy. This may have discouraged investment. Indeed, their possible elimination at any moment to meet the exigencies of politics probably produced an insecurity that dissuaded many from purchasing them. Why this should have affected Essex more than other areas is not certain, although Essex had the added disadvantage of remoteness. Perhaps the willingness to take risks was much less here than in more central areas. Only time and further work will clarify the picture.

How Well Developed were the Reserves?

Were the clergy reserves and the former Crown reserves – since 1826 in the hands of the Canada Company – more or less developed than one another and in comparison to farms in general? Tables 10.3 and 10.4 provide an answer to this question at mid-century. In fact, the Canada Company and clergy reserves were in absolute terms no different from one another or from the non-speculative landholdings with respect to the amount of land held, which is perhaps what is to be expected.[89] This was not so with respect to the amount of land cleared, because while the reserved lands were no different from one another,[90] the clergy reserves, in absolute terms, proved statistically different from other lands.[91] In relative terms, both the clergy-reserve $\bar{x}$ of 21.65 per cent and the Canada Company $\bar{x}$ of 26.38 per cent proved dramatically lower than the overall $\bar{x}$ of 38.24 for non-speculative holdings.[92] In short, the former reserve lands remained, in aggregate, less developed than surrounding territory. There were, however, signs of the beginning of change as a comparison of figures 7.6 and 7.7 show. In the developed west, in the townships of Malden and Sandwich in particular, both Crown and clergy lands had been taken up because of their accessibility to the coast and to the towns of Sandwich and Amherstburg (Figure 10.1). This condition had been described some twenty-two years earlier by John Beverley Robinson: "The truth is while a township is but little settled the reserves are no more a bar to improvement than other unoccupied lands – when that township

Table 10.3   Summary statistics of land held and cleared, clergy reserves, Essex County, 1852

Tnp	Acreage Held		Acreage Cleared		Cleared as % Held		n
	$\bar{x}$	σ	$\bar{x}$	σ	$\bar{x}$	σ	
Col.	52.93	29.88	6.52	3.80	24.12	30.04	25
Gos.	86.69	34.32	18.74	12.60	25.95	21.11	35
Mai.	94.90	12.14	17.40	12.93	18.12	12.62	20
Mal.	82.57	34.80	12.41	9.34	19.12	18.48	28
Mer.	88.13	52.94	7.25	9.74	15.65	17.98	8
Roc.	97.25	47.65	10.00	7.52	10.84	7.46	16
San.	84.82	59.59	17.57	18.14	21.01	21.65	50
Til.W	80.20	68.15	27.80	13.47	58.14	31.01	5
All	85.25	45.95	14.71	13.74	21.65	22.27	187

Source: AO, Assessment Rolls and Abstract Index to Deeds, Essex County

N.B. No data for Anderdon Township.

Col.=Colchester; Gos.=Gosfield; Mai.=Maidstone; Mal.=Malden; Mer.=Mersea; Roc.=Rochester; San.=Sandwich; Til.W=Tilbury West.

Table 10.4   Summary statistics of land held and cleared, Canada Company land, Essex County, 1852

Tnp	Acreage Held		Acreage Cleared		Cleared as % Held		n
	$\bar{x}$	σ	$\bar{x}$	σ	$\bar{x}$	σ	
Col.	150.00	50.00	19.00	16.00	10.25	7.25	2
Gos.	74.42	31.49	18.87	13.93	27.97	17.51	31
Mal.	73.28	27.48	22.53	8.85	35.17	17.37	18
Roc.	97.50	64.18	8.50	8.05	9.17	7.22	4
San.	84.38	38.82	12.33	84.38	24.29	19.48	53
Til.W	51.80	13.00	10.05	51.80	27.43	18.91	5
All	80.06	38.13	12.47	80.06	26.38	18.95	113

Source: AO, Assessment Rolls and Abstract Index to Deeds, Essex County.

N.B. No data for Anderdon, Maidstone, and Malden Townships.

Col.=Colchester; Gos.=Gosfield; Mer.=Mersea; Roc.=Rochester; San.=Sandwich; Til.W=Tilbury West

begins to be tolerably well settled the reserves are eagerly taken up by tenants and are occupied like other lots, and then the grievance ceases. No greater imposition has been practised in this age of humbug, than in the statements which have been made respecting these reserves."[93]

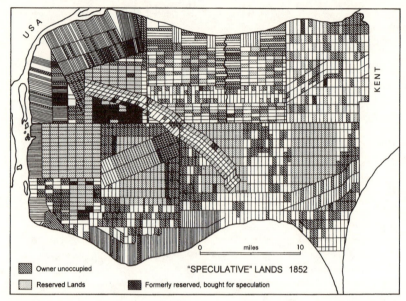

Figure 10.1   Speculative lands, 1852
Source: Compilation of author.

SUMMARY

The second decade of the nineteenth century saw attempts by the British to reduce their colonial expenditures or at least to pass these on to local jurisdictions. Part of the mental attitude of the time was to develop land as a commodity and to create a social and economic climate suitable for the development of capitalism. Beginning in 1825, though there had been earlier attempts to do so, land was to be sold. Within two years a corporate speculative venture, the Canada Land Company, had been chartered by those with an ear to government. And the Clergy Corporation, charged with the management of the clergy reserves, had begun to sell portions of its substantial inventory.

The policy of leasing reserve land, never popular nor in reality revenue-producing, had at the same time been discontinued. The reserves were either sold to those holding pre-emption rights or turned over from the state to produce revenue for King's College, Toronto. Crown lands, Crown reserves, and clergy reserves all sold for around the same price. This was about 120 pence, an equilibrium price produced because of competition for purchasers. Such differences as occurred were in matters relating to down payments, length of lease, or interest rates. On private-sector land, the former Crown reserves surrendered to the Canada Company, the price was no different in Essex than elsewhere in the province. Nor were the terms, which were a down payment of about 20 per cent, lower than that on other categories of land but the length of the lease was theoretically shorter than on clergy-reserve land. In theory, the balance on Canada Company land was paid in five instalments after the initial deposit, but in practice these needed not be annual and most stretched to between seven and fourteen years. During this time, the interest clock still ran and the effect was to produce de facto annual rates of 12 per cent rather than the de jure rate of a maximum 6 per cent recognized by the usury laws.

Given that the company had acquired this land from the state for a small sum, re-payable over fifteen years without interest, it was doing very well indeed. Though it received legal title to these lots in Essex with the acquisition of the patent, the normal requirement of paying taxes thereafter was waived until the company had found a purchaser or in reality a tenant because legal title never passed to the individual until every penny of purchase price and accumulated interest had been paid. Until that final moment, all taxes were paid by the "settler." This was legally justifiable in terms of preserving the company's interest, but the result was that the purchaser's equity would seem to have been minimized. Indeed, some simply walked away from a commitment that proved impossible to bear.

In the interim, the purchaser paid taxes on corporate property. The effect of all this was solid corporate profit. In absolute terms, a property acquired for 42 pence per acre, in a county where the infrastructure had been developed by the state so that company investment here, unlike other areas, was minimal, might be sold for about 168 pence in 1846. If the time taken was "normal," the Essex purchaser of this land would ultimately pay about 816 pence per acre. Of course, the credit system would allow some to purchase and develop land who might not otherwise be able to do so. The system is familiar to anyone who has ever paid a mortgage, but the profits were considerable and the resources on which these profits were based belonged to society as a whole and not just to the business community.

Unlike the Canada Company profits, those of the Clergy Corporation were, in theory at least, designed to permit the established church(es) to continue their ministrations, although this too meant that a select body was to receive state resources. Down payments on clergy reserves were smaller, interest rates were lower, and the length of term was longer than if one purchased from the Canada Company. Yet, in spite of this and because clergy-reserve land, unlike Canada Company land, was still in the hands of the Clergy Corporation and subject to political vicissitudes, the amount of land disposed of was less. In terms of development, the acreage acquired was no different; but in terms of the amount of land cleared, the Clergy Corporation's land was less cleared on average (21.6 per cent) than Canada Company land. Both were less developed than non-speculative holdings, where 26.35 per cent of the lots were cleared. In one sense this substantiates the claims made by many Upper Canadians that clergy and Crown reserves were barriers to settlement. However, the pattern of clearance shown on maps of the time supports what conservatives held, that is, that where the economy demanded it, these lands had been incorporated into local production. If this was true of Essex, it must by extension have been true of more centrally located and populous parts of the commercial and industrializing core, but this still remains to be demonstrated.

11 Context and Conclusion

Patricia Crone has developed a general anatomy of pre-industrial societies to assist in the interpretation of particular ones. Her work, which she describes as "the bluffer's guide" to the behaviour of pre-modern societies, seems applicable to Upper Canada and Essex in the earliest phase of development, from 1788 to about 1850.[1]

Crone's study, which covers several thousand years, uses the terms "pre-industrial"[2] and "agrarian" synonymously but distinguishes between the "primitive" hunting and gathering societies and the more complex, "civilized" societies in terms of their levels of organization and division. The latter societies remained primarily agricultural, manufacturing supplying only part of their wealth and modern industry being completely absent.[3] Clearly, Upper Canada and Essex belonged to this category. Though there is an emerging re-evaluation of the extent to which Upper Canada was a subsistence or a market economy,[4] it was, by any standard, an agricultural one. Timber was an important element in the wealth of the colony and was exported from an early period, but Upper Canada concentrated upon a mixture of grain agriculture (wheat being the dominant crop) and animal husbandry which varied regionally. In Essex, wheat was important, too, though corn was more so. Whatever the "mix," however, the emphasis was clearly agricultural. Moreover, in an age of human and animal muscle, such industry as existed was on a limited scale, complementing the agricultural economy by sawing its lumber, grinding its grain, manufacturing agricultural equipment, and producing the beer and whiskey needed to sustain life on a fast-changing but still difficult frontier.[5]

In surveying such societies, Crone acknowledges that most people were involved directly or indirectly in farm production and that, in the absence of mechanization and, for example, mass-produced fertilizer, productivity was often low. Moreover, in the absence of modern means of communication and transportation, these societies were highly localized and high costs had a marked effect upon peasant trading, which was limited to about four or five miles. Given this and problems of productivity, scarcity was common. Again, transportation problems, together with the fact that producers had to sell soon after harvest, meant that the market was glutted and the prices obtained low. Indebtedness to landlord or merchant was therefore frequent. In all pre-industrial societies, large families were common; birth rates were high because of the need to "adjust" for the effects of war, famine, and high death rates. Depending on the degree of participation in the market economy, such societies might be spoken of "peasant or farm," the difference between the two being that peasants run households whereas farmers run business enterprises.[6] Whether peasants or farmers, such people might constitute as much as 98 per cent of society. Those not directly involved in production, the elite constituting the remaining 2 per cent,[7] might live in cities because of the amenities and excitement offered there. In such societies, lacking the means or inclination towards an elaborate infrastructure of support, self-help was an essential element and it came from the local community, the religious community, and, most especially, the family and the kin group.

The descriptions above cover particular societies in particular circumstances and one cannot expect that all were characteristic of Upper Canada or Essex. Still, many do apply. Most Upper Canadians were involved in agriculture; however, even in the absence of mass fertilization under conditions of initial settlement, North American yields were generally quite high, at least until settlement approached a limit where extensive agriculture could no longer be conducted and repeated cropping led to soil exhaustion and decline in productivity. In Essex, where cultivation had been going on for more than 100 years, yields on wheat in 1852 were 13.3 bushels per acre with a standard deviation of 7.5, and on corn they were 17.4 with a standard deviation of 13.1.[8] Initially, Upper Canadian grain prices were high, but with time, greater production capacity, and increased demand, prices fell to a level where they could bear the costs of freight to the British market and sustain the added effects of a protective British tariff. It would seem that there was never a time when Essex farmers could not afford to eat their own grain, which must testify to the fact that they owned their means of production and lived in "the best poor man's country." That said, the term "peasant" is inappropriate because land was held either in free and common soccage or by those with expectations of such ownership, and also because the word does not recognize the dignity bestowed upon labour in the New World.

While much work still needs to be done on the costs of land acquisition, Essex prices of "farm real estate" were generally low. This must in part explain why indebtedness for land, measured in terms of formal mortgages, was of a low incidence, although if a man's "word was his bond" this might not be the real measure. To date, there are no real measures of "overall" indebtedness. In Essex as elsewhere in Upper Canada, credit was extended to individuals for supplies of all kinds. However, this appears as much a system of record keeping, in a society where barter was common and money was in short supply, as payment for debt.[9]

The literature is replete with notions of the "friction of distance" upon rural life. Crone's estimate of life being led within four to five miles rings true for Upper Canada as a whole and Essex in particular, where ties of kinship were manifest within such limits and proved of greater importance than ethnicity in the building of community.[10]

Families were important as social support and as labour; children, a burden in the Old World, were assets in emerging societies such as Upper Canada where farms were being created from the bush. In Essex, in 1852, the average family size was 5.0.[11] In such societies, self-help was of overriding importance and the influence of the state minimal, although, as in other societies, the role of kinship might diminish as the state assumed increasing control over the lives of individuals.[12]

Crone points out that pre-industrial societies were typically monarchies. The monarch was the ultimate arbiter between the aristocracy and other elites and the potent symbol of the community. If a particular monarch was totally arbitrary and self-serving and ignored the needs of the people, monarchy's legitimacy might be damaged. In this sense, all were constitutional rulers. Where the monarch was the absolute decision maker,[13] those who had access to him or her possessed a huge advantage and such people might be supported "by whole lines of individuals from particular cliques."[14] Given the large distances involved in many states and the slowness of communication, monarchy had to recognize the need for decentralized power since only locals knew exactly what was happening in their region and could decide on an appropriate response.[15] The monarch therefore had an interest in being well represented locally and so sought to create homogeneous and cohesive elites whose role was to develop a common interest in representing and perpetuating the state. Effectively, these elites were connected to power, which might take economic, military, political, or ideological forms.[16]

Monarchy needed land to reward those who served its ends. Land became associated with noble status, authority, and political power.[17] Since it was for such a long time the only real source of wealth, the ownership of land might even be reserved for the servants of the state, "with the result that unconditional ownership of land tended to disappear altogether;"[18] in some late-medieval societies, only nobles might acquire landed estates. Suitably endowed, a nobleman might pursue political or learned ends and "since his honour was vested in the land, he was not likely to treat it as a simple economic asset to be sold off whenever he might need cash to whoever might be able to raise it."[19] The more lavish the endowment the better, since the greater the largesse, the greater the interests of the servants in the survival of the institution itself: "Massive wealth created a gulf between the excluded commoners and the powerful few, giving the latter a common interest, lifestyle and outlook apt to make them stick together as a group, however much they might quarrel among each other."[20] Crone believes that few individuals were simply individuals but rather representatives of larger networks, in this case, elite networks. These elite networks were the focus of local interests who might cater to their needs, thus accessing a hierarchy of interest and connection stretching all the way to the court.[21] However, this was a connection premised upon landed wealth and stood in contradistinction to that controlled by the merchant class. "Mercantile wealth was accumulated outside the ranks of the ruling elite from sources other than land, by means other than political service or mastery of the high culture; hence it posed a threat to the established order."[22] Members of the ruling aristocracy sought to maintain a social distance from the merchants and were given to ostentatious displays and disregard for money; merchants, in this view, had by definition to be calculating and to mix with everyone since profit was their prime concern. Accordingly, they were subversive and had to be kept under control. These views were echoed in Upper Canada.

In such societies, one was unlikely to get far without patronage. Someone recommended the individual as an employee, guaranteed the individual's reliability, and assured the patron that the individual possessed the desired attributes or was of the right social, political, and religious background.[23] Trust was of prime importance in the pre-industrial world, the result being that "such job market as existed was dominated by personal networks."[24] An extended network of relatives, friends, and allies was highly desirable – "there was nothing shameful about patronage as such: it benefitted employer and employee alike. Wherever trust mattered as much as or more than skills, nepotism was a virtue, not a sign of corruption."[25] People might therefore acquire

functions not in response to market forces but rather as a consequence of their ancestry. Yet Crone, who writes in these terms, notes
that even bloodlines need not be necessary; in societies where cash was
short, reciprocal arrangements were important and many individuals
were effectively adopted by others. People came to be of the house and
therefore not independent of mind; the concept of labour, she claims,
as a commodity distinct from the person was weakly developed: "You
could not buy the labour without the man."[26] In such circumstances,
political appointments might be made by private agreement since the
political process shielded those in power from public gaze and rulers
were often thought to be answerable only unto God.

God was important to the ruler. The church might recognize a
ruler's very right to govern. "Religious leaders controlled the definition
of rectitude, frequently including the law and/or access to salvation, a
fact which endowed them with considerable influence over lay behaviour; they invariably possessed some degree of organization, often controlled considerable amounts of land and other wealth acquired
through gifts from the faithful; and they might have a monopoly on lit-
eracy too."[27] Crone notes that, in pre-industrial society, religion might
be the only level of communication above the household level transcending social, cultural, geographical, and political background. She
concludes that "it was overwhelmingly on this channel that broadcasts
were made."[28] Perhaps nowhere was this as clear as in Britain and its
overseas possessions. The Hanoverians swore in their coronation oath
to "maintain the laws of God, the true profession of the gospel and the
protestant reformed religion established by law." They also agreed to
"preserve unto the bishops and clergy of this realm, and to the
churches there committed to their charge, all such rights and privileges
as by law do or shall appertain unto them." The Church of England was
protected against dissenters and Catholics alike. When Englishmen
spoke of the benefits of their constitution, they did so adding "in
church and state."[29] In Upper Canada, the privileges of the Church of
England were maintained and it was endowed with land to allow it to
continue its ministrations. Here too, as in Britain, the church was the
centre of "decency and order" and a prop of good government.[30] The
King used this religious channel to authorise the very form in which
God might be approached on behalf of monarchy.

Britain in the Hanoverian period was a constitutional state but the
elements of that constitution were never totally stated because they
were in the process of being negotiated. Indeed, the main constitutional theme of the reign of King George III[31] was the relationship
between the tripartite elements that composed what was hailed as a
mixed or balanced constitution. This balanced constitution protected

landed property and fostered liberty, the dual foundation of industry, art, and science.[32] Certain negative elements of that constitution were known. Absolute monarchy was proscribed and the King could not rule without parliament, which annually sanctioned money. Beyond this it was unclear what the King could do. There were many private opinions about the respective strengths of monarchy and parliament but they remained formally unstated. Controversies over such issues as the appointment and dismissal of ministries[33] were resolved by experience, convention, and a growing "tradition." Certain residual powers remain to this day in a constitution which, in the British instance though not the Canadian, is still unwritten and is held to have preserved private liberty by preserving "the internal contradictions of the balanced powers."[34]

The "balanced powers" were expressed in a tripartite arrangement most clearly recognizable as King, Lords, and Commons.[35] Men of property in both Britain and North America were terrified that the rabble "would destroy their privileges and their exclusive property rights."[36] Indeed, the defence of property was the prime raison d'être for civil government.[37] The elite viewed democracy as simply mob rule, and to guard against it, sovereignty was to be located in the whole legislature of King, Lords, and Commons. In this way "it was possible to deny the doctrine of popular sovereignty and continue to preach non-resistance and passive obedience"[38] and so preserve privilege.[39]

The heirs of the Glorious Revolution and most especially the "Country Interest" and the "Radical Whigs" believed that the "ancient constitution" had rested upon notions of balance and that this was maintained by civic virtue, independence, and the ownership of land.[40] This idea of a balanced constitution became part of the British political culture of the time and was carried to North America, where in the Thirteen Colonies "radicals," paradoxically citing the "rights of Englishmen," broke with the British parent. Yet even they believed that property and land were clearly the basis of civil society. John Adams made this very point:

Harrington has Shewn that Power always follows Property ... I believe We may advance one Step farther, and affirm that the Ballance of Power in a Society accompanies the Ballance of Property in Land. The only possible Way then of preserving the Ballance of Power on the side of equal Liberty and public Virtue, is to make the Acquisition of Land easy to every Member of Society – to make a Division of Land into Small Quantities, So that the Multitude may be possesssed of landed Estates. If the Multitude is possessed of the Ballance of Power, and in that Case the Multitude will take Care of the Liberty, Virtue and Interest of the Multitude in all Acts of Government.[41]

Though the British and Upper Canadian elites did not subscribe to such largesse, they sufficiently subscribed to the principle underlying it, that they instituted policies which provided land to individuals, reflecting their social status or "quality." Having a stake in the country was thought necessary to preserve the liberty which was the principal objective of the balanced constitution. In Upper Canada, the equivalent trinity to the British King, Lords, and Commons was King, Legislative Council, and House of Assembly.

This "traditional" model of government was celebrated by such worthies as Bishop Strachan and Chief Justice John Beverley Robinson in the manner of a divine gift. In colonial Upper Canada, ultimate responsibility was vested in the Colonial Office and Westminster. However, Britain was distant and effectively government was conducted by the governor and his Executive Council until such times as political rigidity and alienation produced rebellion in this most loyal of provinces in 1837.

Until then, government was operated as in Britain, through local oligarchies; the structure of local government, with its justices of the peace, lord lieutenancies, members of the House of Assembly, and host of minor offices, reflected basically the political order of pre-industrial Britain. However, there were embryonic signs of change. These offices were all highly contested since they were the root of power and prestige as well as money in an age lacking the social support systems of today. They were most frequently bestowed on individuals but success depended upon access to a support mechanism and acceptance by the social and political machinery of the time. In David William Smith's case, this support came from John Askin, whose patronage Smith was quick to acknowledge and for whom he was willing to resign. Askin's support, in turn, rested on connection through "normal" practices of trade, marriage, and kinship to a larger network. This was the now famous or infamous (depending on one's perspective) Family Compact. Hierarchically arranged both socially and geographically, the Compact was the mechanism through which power in all its forms was distributed. It operated on patronage and through the distribution of land, the very basis of life in the eighteenth and nineteenth centuries. In E.P. Thompson's terms, land was the index of influence, "the jumping-off point for power and office and the point to which power and office returned."[42]

Patronage is something that, unless one is the immediate beneficiary, contemporary society tends to sneer at. However, in the eighteenth and nineteenth centuries, people had a different view. There were those who believed it a disgrace to accept public money in any form, though, like the great orator, theorist, and enemy of "placemen," Edmund Burke, they might be content to have a patron provide. In Burke's case, Lord Rockingham provided him with £30,000 per year.[43] On the other hand, there were those such as Henry Dundas, later Lord Melville, who stirred the Commons by asking "if it was not as honourable to be the King's pensioner as Lord Shelburne's."[44]

Richard Pares believes that the difference between eighteenth-century and contemporary attitudes to patronage can be explained in terms of growth in the organized professions[45] and changing attitudes towards various occupations. Historically, schoolteaching and medicine were not acceptable occupations for gentlemen. Life insurance, upon which some rely today, was new and not widespread, and employer-provided pensions were unknown. Moreover, half the professions that "secure our moral superiority" did not then exist,[46] and of those that did exist, the five great ones (the navy, the army, the civil service, the law, the church) were more closely associated with politics than today. Many posts paid insufficiently and brought their holders into debt; for example, the lord lieutenancy of Ireland was thought to cost the incumbent £15,000 per year in 1783.[47] Given that there were no pensions, it was generally accepted that a minister or under-secretary had some right to a "permanency" in the form of a sinecure for himself or his children when he left office. It is easy, Pares concludes, "for us so circumstanced to condemn the men of the eighteenth century, who provided for these things (the survival of the bread-winner) by cadging offices and pensions, for themselves or their children, from the holders of executive power."[48] Even so, in Pares opinion, all was not sordid. "It is a pity that historians should so seldom recognise the fact that men were in politics not only for party and for profit, but most of all for the due exercise of the talents God gave them, and for fun.[49]

Patronage took many forms in Upper Canada; one of the more obvious was appointment to public service which might or might not be revenue producing.[50] Although S.F. Wise has documented the mechanism by which patronage was dispensed in clientage terms,[51] and Keith Johnson has discussed the relationship between social qualities and patronage and shown that, among the 283 MHAS, 112 obtained some revenue-producing appointment,[52] there has as yet been no study of the monies that might have been obtained from a life at the public trough. For example, James Baby was entitled to 6000 acres as an executive councillor but in itself this was hardly compensation for a life of service.[53] Baby may have served because, as a French Canadian, he was flattered by being chosen to serve or because between 1790 and 1839 he was able to obtain, in an age of pluralism, more than 115 appointments or commissions and was terrified to lose the benefit,[54] though there is no guarantee that these would guarantee meaningful income. He may simply have become accustomed to the power and politics, the "fun" that Pares speaks of. He may have been able to gain personally or for his family, through his knowledge of the process of government which perhaps he, more than any other, had. Like many of his time, he acquired land as a speculative venture and his same "access to information" must have stood him in good stead in making such investments. In the same way, Alexander Grant, also of Essex, may have reaped large financial gain not only from his position as administrator of Upper Canada and a host of regional positions but perhaps even more so from his positions as naval superintendent on the Great Lakes and as contractor to government.[55]

The extent of the rewards of office is, in these cases as in so many more, simply not known. Income depended, in some instances, entirely upon fees and this could triple the amount of a salary. Administrator Peter Russell may have gained as much as £30,000 from making his clerks complete more patents per week.[56] William Dummer Powell, who, along with Strachan, was reckoned a master of patronage appointments, stated that Lieutenant Governor Simcoe had created an exorbitant table of fees to repair his own fortune and that council members had knowingly allowed speculators title to land, in the name of settlers, so that they might collect the fees.[57] If it was possible to collect fees for a number of offices, all the better; however, as Johnson points out, it was possible to live on simply one office. Few chose to. In Johnson's study of 112 individuals who held public office, 37 per cent held more than one post and 27 per cent held two or more offices concurrently.[58] In Essex, Hands and Pollard epitomize a pluralism common throughout Upper Canada.

That there was advantage to be had from holding such offices is seen in the number of individuals seeking them. The approach had to be solicitous in case one alienated those in power. As was shown earlier, Askin sought the position of vendue-master for his son, who found the returns of his position of port collector inadequate and his expenditures exceeding his income. The lieutenant governor allowed the appointment since it seems it was anyone's for the asking, presumably because the position was relatively unremunerative.[59] Askin himself was on the lookout, viewing the acreage offered him as inadequate for his service on the Land Board, but he was cautious, worrying that he might ask too much. He wanted to be appointed receiver of the King's reserves in the Western District; in 1803 such an appointment would have consolidated his own position because he was busy trying to augment and consolidate his own acquisition of reserve lands in Rochester and Maidstone townships. He sought Robert Hamilton's advice if this was a sensible request since the land might have been in the hands of the receiver general and his good friend Richard Cartwright. Yet he was anxious to act quickly: "... Delays may be dangerous – everyone is on the look of something and perhaps this involvement may be considerable."[60] Perhaps it was. No further mention is made of the issue; in 1803 the receiver general was none other than the avaricious Peter Russell.[61] Speed was also of the essence in securing Pollard's replacement as sheriff by Hands. Though the "first characters" were going to support this nomination, Askin thought it desirable to head off other strikes by writing to his friend Todd in case "there might be an application before that."[62] In this case, Askin noted that "for my nearest relative I would not request of you to get an unworthy or unfit person into office (if I thought this such) so as to cause any reflection on your recommendation."[63]

Others sought to offer assurance that it was not filthy lucre which moved their application. Thomas Smith, who had been the MHA for Kent, tried to have his nephew appointed registrar of that county in 1828. "The place is of little value in a pecuniary point, perhaps not more than twenty dollars per annum, from the small number of inhabitants ... I would esteem it a mark of His Excellency's Favor, to be pleased to grant me the situation, on giving the surety the law requires. It is not the object of this situation but the gratification of His Excellency's good will towards one devoted to His person and administration."[64] There were powerful opponents who had another person in mind.[65]

All of this suggests that things were as they were in Britain. Some served for the sake of service and the rewards of office both psychological and financial; others served only for the money and the extent of that money cannot as yet be measured or even estimated. This is not to say that there was not corruption. Clearly there was, but it is difficult to lay blame at any one particular door, at least in most cases.

One of the exceptions was noted as early as 1787 by Major Robert Mathews, commanding at Detroit, who reported to General Haldimand that a "set of rascals" had in the absence of the proper administration of justice been able to "take advantages and commit little chicaneries disgraceful to Society, and distressing to Trade and Individuals."[66] Mathews reported on the existence of the "old trade" at Mackinac, where the commanding officer, Captain Robertson,[67] "has made a fortune" in the Indian Department; he also told of the use of bribes and of the boastfulness of one man, who had stated in public that he had not yet met a commanding officer whom he could not "roll in a Beaver Blanket."[68] This was the same post where, a few years earlier, Lieutenant Governor Sinclair had serious clashes with subordinates over discrepancies in the stores, clashes that had resulted in Askin's withdrawal to Detroit.

At Detroit, Mathews reported doubtful conduct on the part of the merchants – "In trade, the lowest of this profession resort to these places, they are without education or sentiment, and many of them without common honesty."[69] Here Mathews seems to exhibit the ancient disdain that members of the elite, in this instance the military elite, felt for the merchant class,[70] a disdain that Pares indicates was common in pre-industrial society: "Mercantile wealth was accumulated outside the ranks of the ruling elite from sources other than land, by means other than political service or mastery of the high culture; hence it posed a threat to the established order."[71] Merchants, it was felt, had to mix with everyone; they were subversive elements who had to be kept under control. This prejudice on the part of the professional soldier was shared by Mathew's commanding officer, Lieutenant-General Frederick Haldimand, whom Mathews described as his "most revered patron" and who warned against permitting little traders from creeping in to the settlement unless they could demonstrate to the "first people" their service and undisputed attachment to government. However, within a short time, the merchants and the officer corps would be doing business together[72] and the merchant class, forerunners in the transition to a full capitalist economy, would become part of the establishment. Askin, who started life as a sutler in the British army, was soon engaged in business with Ancrum and Arent Schuyler DePeyster, who, one presumes, started life as his social superiors. He became a magistrate and ended up a lieutenant-colonel of militia.

Mathews's and Haldimand's sentiments were reflections of the social gradients existing in the larger society, but in fact the officer corps would seem to have had its own problems with corruption. Mathews acknowledged this in his report to Haldimand, pointing out that the "abuses in the Provision and Indian departments were shameful" and that, in spite of Haldimand's express order, the taxes instituted during the earlier French administration (the *lods et ventes*) had been purloined by Lieutenant Governor Jehu Hay and Major Ancrum. Other officers, he concluded, acting from self-interest, financial or otherwise, must have colluded. Ancrum, it will be recalled, had, in conjunction with John Askin, acquired a large acreage of Indian land, though this was expressedly forbidden, soon after he had retired from the army. DePeyster had accepted an Indian gift of land, although this may have been a less doubtful event. This was also the period in which Askin had advised Sampson Fleming that his commanding officer would not frown upon his benefiting personally from government business so long as it cost no more than it would otherwise. In a separate incident, Major Matthew Elliott, suspected of peculation, would be removed as superintendent of Indian affairs for the district of Detroit, in December 1797.

A number of people asserted that corruption was rife in the early administration of Essex. Among them was Patrick McNiff the surveyor. He stated that positions in trade and on the Land Board were incompatible and that actual settlers had been discouraged by powerful individuals who stood to gain by monopolizing land and by obtaining Indian grants which *post facto* they might render legitimate. McNiff, who in the circumstance of the time appears a social misfit and who was himself involved in land speculation in conjunction with John Askin, got short shrift from a land committee in Quebec City dominated by land speculators. His remarks were found to be unjustified and ultimately he was dismissed, ending his days in an American prison.

A second individual who was aware of scurrilous behaviour was Chief Justice William Dummer Powell, against whom a campaign was waged to have him deemed a traitor and who feared for his own life and that of his family. Unlike McNiff (whom he thought instrumental in his being charged) and lesser beings, he survived simply because of his social status and the fact that a royal prince approved of him. He claimed to have been offered a bribe by no less a figure than the attorney general to allow a patent to be issued to the Indians on the Grand River so that the land could be sold.[73] He also claimed that the garrison commander at Detroit, the naval commander, and the superintendent of Indian affairs had all made large fortunes during three years of war.[74] It is impossible to substantiate these and similar charges made against members of the Land Board, although a graphologist may possess insights which I do not (Plate 11.1). At various times, these individuals might have included Alexander Grant, commodore of the lakes and Askin's brother-in-law; Colonel Alexander McKee, superintendent of Indian affairs; Montigny Louvigny, who was Askin's debtor; George Leith, Askin's partner in the Miami Company; William Robertson, Askin's relative by marriage; and John Askin himself. Depending on the date, it might include any one of eight individuals commanding the garrison at Detroit,[75] one of whom (DePeyster) was Askin's friend and one of whom, Ancrum, made off with the *lods et ventes* and became Askin's associate in land speculation upon retirement. One might add here the name of Abraham Iredell, who was himself charged with misconduct as a surveyor, a powerful position in the community. In these circumstances,

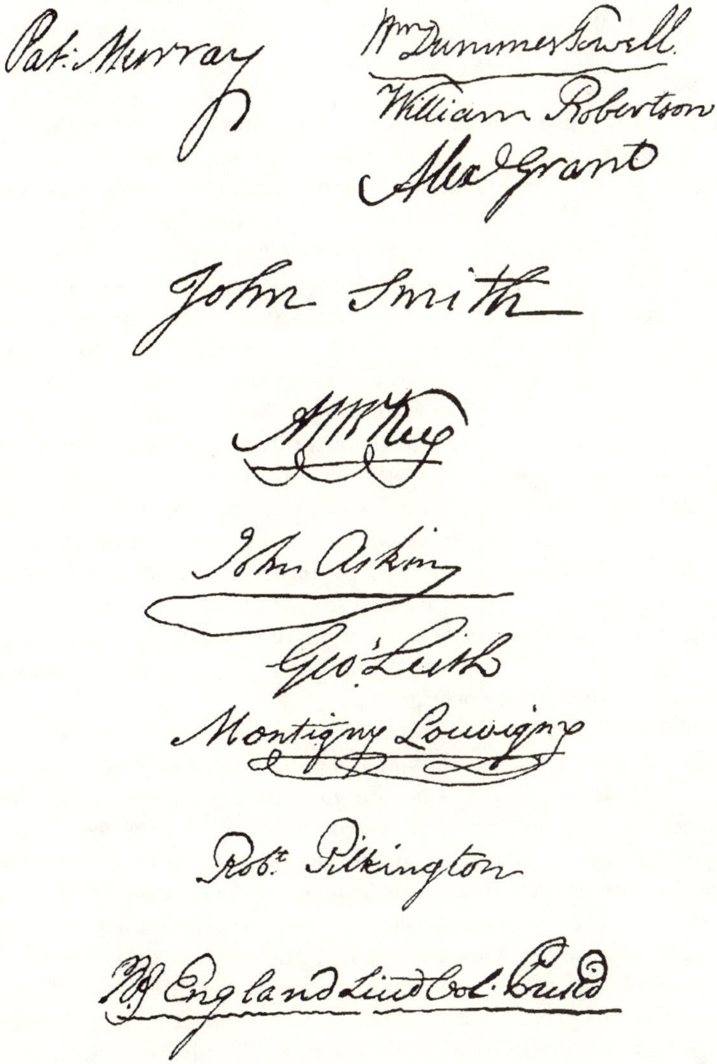

Plate 11.1   Signatures of members of the land board.
Alexander Fraser, *Third Report of the Bureau of Archives for the Province of Ontario*
(Toronto: L.K. Cameron, 1906), cxxxvii.

the reader might feel that the evidence points in a particular direction, that power in a variety of forms might have been used by an individual or individuals to decide or influence the outcome of events, but there is no *absolute proof*. As was shown in Chapter 3, Askin remarked that the people, the country, and the surveyor were all crooked, which may testify to his personal innocence but may also obscure his guilt. There were also other actors such as William Macombe. All this said, however, there was perhaps not one single central figure responsible for the corruption; we may rather be dealing with a pervading climate of graft and acquisition.

There are, however, the documented cases whereby Askin, as magistrate, issued grants to particular individuals. These individuals, sometimes in the space of a single day, obtained an unspecified location from the surveyor (Abraham Iredell), a doubtful act involving one charged with other doubtful acts and an act that did not encourage settlement. They then gave the surveyor the assurance that the appropriate certificates would be surrendered to the purchaser, Askin. The sales were witnessed by Askin's employee (later a magistrate himself) and verified by his fellow magistrate, Alexander Grant. Grant was either part of this deception or was at best naive. Here are clear instances of individuals serving and depriving the state of what it might legitimately expect of public servants, that is, disinterested behaviour aimed at promoting genuine settlement. These individuals were seeking to appropriate the resources of the state to their personal benefit; and, if this was true of the most prominent, one can be certain that such corruption stretched farther down the social continuum.

It would indeed seem that there was a body of people, however constituted, who ensured that benefits accrued to those who counted. Those of little social consequence did not fare as well. These included the articulate and resolute Oneida woman Sally Ainse, whose claim, accepted by Simcoe, was never acted upon. They also included Jacob Schiefflin, who in seeking a strategically positioned grant for himself, claimed only to be emulating his betters but who had a deed negotiated with the Indians set aside at the instigation of the superintendent of Indian affairs. Given the manner in which Schiefflin had proceeded, this was probably the correct outcome but it is clear that the law applied unequally to different people. This became absolutely clear when the Malden land of the Indian officers, obtained on Indian deeds, was sanctioned by the "system": the Indian Affairs officers were socially connected and socially acceptable. Yet, in fairness, this was also a society where Jews received access to the offices of the state in a way that they did not elsewhere.

Given its functional capacity to support life, its evocative power, and the absence of actual monies in Upper Canada land was what was sought by this society and acquisitiveness on a grand scale was possible. This was true not only of individuals but of the state itself, which expanded at the expense of the erosion of Indian sovereignty. Perhaps the Indians never intended the ultimate surrender of their land; rather, they may have seen the situation in terms of granting others permission to use their land and, in return, receiving an acknowledgement of friendship. Yet the state knew what it was about. The sums paid were, by the standards of the time, trivial and the Indians were allowed only to deal with the state's bureaucracy and not "on the open market," though there was little enough of that in the early years. Moreover, it was clear, to some officials at least, that the Indians' view of price would change as they became aware of what the European valued. This is not to say that there were not meaningful relations of respect between individual Europeans and native peoples. Clearly there were. They intermarried, fought, and died together on a frontier with an aggressive American state.

From the beginning, there was a widespread trafficking in land. Whole townships were handed over to individuals (though not in Essex, where Askin was unsuccessful in his attempted acquisition) and there was an extensive traffic in Loyalist and military rights to land. In Essex and the Western District, land speculation appeared early in the form of the accumulation of large Indian grants, either purchased in European terms or received in "love and affection." John Askin, William Robertson, and Richard Pattinson were among those who sought such benefits and did so in a most dramatic manner, training their sights on millions of acres in what became Michigan. Joseph Brant, himself a remarkable man, testified to the involvement of the "first people" and he did not mean his own by this term. Yet, in spite of this and other reports such as Rankin's in 1839, extensive speculation continued. Gates reports that, in 1825, 62 per cent of Upper Canadian land was held in speculation and the figures from Essex support this. By 1825, 63.4 per cent of Essex land had been patented to people who held in excess of 400 acres; and in 1825, 57.43 per cent was owned by people who met this criterion. If the discussion is confined to owner/unoccupied land, the relevant statistics for 1825 and 1852 are 36.2 and 38.4 per cent. This is significant by any stretch of the imagination. Given the withdrawal of such a large proportion of land to the private and corporate sector at this time, the amount locked up as clergy reserves, and the uneven endowment of the county, the "would-be settler" had little choice of land and could not avoid dealing with the speculator. In such circumstances, our image of the opportunities available to "backwoods" settlers has to be redrawn.

That this could occur reflects the fact that this was not a centrally controlled society although it was an ordered one. Part of that order permitted personal acquisition; indeed, acquisitiveness seems to have been as essential to nineteenth-century society as to that of the present day.[76] Then, as now, there was a need to protect society from abuse while at the same time permitting personal gain; the problem was that the legislators were, in some instances, also the speculators and they struggled to protect their own interests, as the debates over taxation exhibited. In the sixfold typology produced of land speculators, the fourth group, which included the most politically powerful, acquired the second-highest acreages. Five of the seven, Edward Ellice, John A. Macdonald, John McGill, William Robertson (all members of the legislative and executive councils or ministers of the Crown), and Samuel Street were not resident in the county; indeed, Robertson and Ellice lived in Britain. All owned land elsewhere in Upper Canada and Ellice owned large portions of the United States. While in 1852 their Essex lands were not poorly developed, a qualification for membership in the Widdis typology as "classical speculators," they were ranked third in terms of acreage cleared. These people acquired their land at sales, especially the most advantageous of all, the sheriff's sale. With the exception of Macdonald, they held their land for the second-longest period of time of any group except the fifth. Like the fifth group, they fit Widdis's description of the "classical speculator" or Shannon's description of the "investor." Group 5 was essentially little different to the fourth except that, with the possible exception of John Jackson, they had enjoyed a long association with the area, most having arrived as Loyalists. Though they cannot have lived on all their lots, not even if these abutted on each other, they all lived (with the possible exception of Jackson) in Essex, or before its surrender, in Detroit. They held land longer than anyone; given this, the extent of their cleared acreage was no better than that of group 1, although in fairness the absolute size of holding was very different. Indeed, by "t" test they were linked with groups 1 and 4. Their rate of return on investment was shown to have been the least of all the groups. In financial terms, they had wasted their talent and that of the state, which had, in part, endowed them.

If time held is a surrogate for profit, then groups 1, 2, and 6 would be the most profitable because these were the "quick-flip" groups. Group 1 was, of course, the largest in terms of speculators and as such contained the greatest variability. Within it were people who made extraordinary profits and some remarkable losses. Presumably, like the sample of fifty-eight as a whole, the members of this group profited markedly. In general, speculators in one area sought to balance off potential loss in one area against profit in another and, as a whole, succeeded in doing so. Group 2 contained a single individual, John Askin.

He was a "quick-flipper" who ultimately lost all on being forced to settle with James McGill. Pattinson and Pickersgill were, in relative terms, "quick-flippers" but both, and most especially Pickersgill, fitted the Widdis category of "land bankers" and assembled land for the quickest "flipper" or speculator of all. John A. Macdonald was essentially in and out of Essex land in a single year! Street, also placed within the fourth group, might belong to the category "land banker" or to Shannon's "land-broker" category. It is not known how much of his land was cleared but he did own land ubiquitously and he did employ agents throughout Ontario. Clearly, the typologies outlined here do not fit each and every circumstance nor can they be expected to, but they do assist in the organization of research. Askin is a case in point. He did not have an agent per se though he did authorize others (William Allan and William Dickson) to act for him in particular dealings, including his son. McGill and he were agents of one another. He controlled an extensive acreage here and in neighbouring Michigan. By these standards, he looks like the land banker or broker *but* he flipped land fast and a lot of it. And so, by this standard, he looks like the speculator or "quick-flipper." In 1852 his properties were also the least developed of all. This is also thought diagnostic of the breed but of course he had been dead thirty-seven years. He does not quite fit. Nonetheless, he was *the* major player in the Essex market.

The analysis of tenure conditions, obtained by comparison of ownership in the abstract index to deeds with occupancy from the assessment rolls or census, permitted the calculation of measures of owner occupancy as well as inferences as to tenancy and the amount of owned but unoccupied land, that is, potential speculative holdings. A high percentage of this land was indeed owned by the 144 individuals whom the cluster analysis put into classes based upon the scale of their operation, the length of time they had held the land, and the number of their transactions. Much of this land was in fact owned by people who were excluded by the algorithm which permitted entry into the analysis when the acreage exceeded 400 acres and the number of transactions was at least three. Unoccupied but owned land obviously existed everywhere but its frequency seemed to increase with distance from the settled area, though there was no absolutely homogeneous, continuous zone. Yet, in these more remote areas, speculators seem to have sought contiguous lots but some chose to scatter, and some such as James Woods simply took what they could get. There were therefore a variety of patterns exhibited, as the nearest neighbour analysis showed. Yet speculative activity was not limited to this outer zone and many of the 144 held land with tenants on it or indeed were to be found among the resident-owner farmers of the longer-established areas along the Lake Erie shore. Clearly, there were a variety of strategies commensurate with personal circumstances and intention, financial capacity, assessment of potential, sense of location, and knowledge of the capacity of the soil to sustain agriculture.

Generally, the speculators acquired relatively more good and imperfectly drained land than there was in the county; the exceptions were Burwell and Woods, who were circumscribed by their method of acquisition. Speculators knew what they were about; for most, this meant the acquisition of well-drained accessible soils capable of supporting wheat. Some chose overall situation over specific location. Askin is one such individual. He chose compactness over specific quality, although his realization that he might obtain leased land at a low price might have assisted the decision. The majority sought to spread their activity over several townships; within townships, some tried to spread their property in such a way as to forestall a number of potential developments or to increase the probability of gain as the neighbourhood improved. Some clustered to gain a particular resource; others had the decision made for them by the prior occupant. For some, the perception of a desirable lot was its cedar rather than its agricultural possibilities; for others, presumably the members of group 1, land anywhere along the Erie shore was the goal.

In terms of development, the 144 speculators were little different from the farm population as a whole in terms of acreage but their properties were actually more cleared than was the norm. Either they had purchased wisely knowing that such developed land commanded a premium, or they had the capital to have it transformed; other possibilities are that they had sought to place tenants on it for a limited time with the deliberate intention of obtaining such a benefit, or that this was a logical response to financial difficulty. Of course, the non-speculators were numerically greater and this group must therefore have possessed greater variability in statistical terms and a much higher percentage of the poor in substantive terms. Given the circumstances of emigration and clearance rates of one to two acres per year, it is perhaps not surprising to find this difference. Still, however explained, these results stand in contrast to the received wisdom and mythology. That said, two groups in particular lagged in their development. Group 3 consisted of Burwell (and heirs) and Woods; the scattered pattern of their lots provided little impetus to development until there was pressure in the immediate neighbourhood. The same may have been true of Askin's property (cluster 2), although it soon became the property of McGill and Todd. All three were soon dead, and without a local representative, it may be that there was simply no one locally to develop their land.

Until 1841, speculators were successful in paying less for land than the general population. After 1841, perhaps because of the optimism following the Union of the Canadas and the greater demand from immigrants escaping events in Europe, they were prepared to pay more. Of the fifty-eight individuals for whom records are available, only seven lost money and the average profit was substantial. Twelve of the fifty-eight showed annual gains of 50 to 200 per cent but returns of 2 to 8 per cent were not unknown. Such investment returns, which admittedly neglect to recognize improvements on the property or actual carrying costs, are impressive. The profit margin was in most cases substantial, certainly outperforming investment in mortgages which were limited by the usury laws to 6 per cent, although, as was seen, these laws were circumvented. For the group as a whole, the return was 22 per cent but this varied through the size continuum.

The returns for the private sector, notably the Canada Company, were equally impressive, averaging 12 per cent on a resource handed to them by the state for a "song" and on extended terms. In this way, as now, the corporations, including within the term the Clergy Corporation, received benefits from the state. Whatever their intentions, they had to compete with one another. They did so more in the terms of business than in terms of the actual price of their respective land. Where demand was highest, these pieces of property were taken up; where demand was less, they remained as undeveloped blocks. This may very well have had a detrimental effect on settlement, but it is clear that the received wisdom on this point is in need of adjustment.

The behaviour of speculators both individual and corporate was, as might be expected, nothing but rational. They reduced their purchases in times of economic difficulty and during the war; they expanded as the economy expanded. The pattern of sales and purchases by individuals was most usually symmetrical, although the pattern of some was by choice or necessity asymmetrical. Presumably, the symmetrical pattern was the most desirable in that, for most, this was a continuous process. Indeed, most were in the market for decades. Given the size of profits, it must have been hard to leave it behind.

With profits of this order, anything that reduced their magnitude must have been anathema to speculators. As indicated, their representatives in the legislature fought tooth and nail to serve their interests and oppose taxation. In this they were not successful, although they were influential enough to blunt the teeth of taxation laws. Paradoxically, the effect of tax legislation was to eliminate the smaller players and to create opportunity for the larger. Local but more especially province-wide players such as Thomas Clark and Samuel Street purchased land which was exposed to the tax collector and whose owners could not redeem it. This was the cheapest of all land – often one-sixtieth of what it would cost in the market. Having purchased, most of these people again sought to hide; given the law, which permitted redemption with little or no penalty, this was only rational. Speculators seem to have been better at hiding than other settlers were. Even so, more than 90 per cent of tax-encumbered land was redeemed.

For many of the speculators, their financial clout and social prestige allowed them to redeem what smaller players could not. For some, the settler and small speculator, the official appearance of the sheriff was something to be feared; for others, he was a government civil servant whose role was to provide necessary information which might be of advantage and for which larger speculators might even be prepared to pay a fee. That the private business life and the official life of the sheriff could be intertwined says something about nineteenth-century ideas of conflict of interest for those who held official positions.

There was in Essex, as elsewhere at this time, a relationship between land acquisition and "connection," whether to officeholders, to the military, or to particular families possessing wealth, position, and prestige. The most powerful of all were those who occupied central positions at the intersection of these three elements. In Essex, this meant the Baby and Askin networks – especially in the early years; one suspects that such connections declined in importance as life became less personal towards mid-century and as land became even more of a commodity controlled by banks and building societies. Until then, personal qualities, including one's character, which was also associated with one's ethnicity, were most significant. The Babys constituted an elite of government officeholders; the Askins, not directly involved in the most overt manifestations of power, nonetheless possessed tentacles that reached out to the executive and legislative councils, where the economic health of so many could in part be decided. These two families controlled 62.3 per cent of the speculative holdings in Essex, and if they had chosen to act together they could have had a remarkable effect on the outcome of events. Even if there was no concerted effort, individual members of these social networks knew whom to see, and how to present the particular case. On a myriad of events, no concerted effort was needed; indeed, if this was perceived to happen, it could lead to social unrest, as in fact did occur in 1837.

Perhaps because of this, and as a stratagem of survival, the politically powerful sought to obtain their land outside the county. However, there were politically significant figures, such as the members of group 4, who controlled sizeable quantities within, including a first minister of Upper Canada and a future prime minister of confederated Canada. Entrée to the corridors of power and ultimately to these councils need not, but generally did come with appointment as a justice of the peace. The distinction in terms of land between the officeholders and the non-officeholders was clear statistically, although not between the JPs and the members of the House of Assembly or indeed between the MHAs and the members of the councils. This is because, while there was no causative link between the three, in substantive terms the probability of reaching the top was not independent of success at either of the other levels. Essex had its representatives at the pinnacle of patronage in Alexander Grant, in William Robertson, perhaps to an extent in William Dummer Powell, and most certainly in James Baby. Their friends, associates, and relatives served at the local level and they were the link to central power. There was an interconnected system of hierarchies, the Family Compact.

Interconnection was in fact how Upper Canada was governed and it was reflected not just in appointments to political institutions but even in family affairs. For example, marriage was used as a social institution by many, to connect families not only to one another but to the political and economic system itself. None illustrates this better than Askin, who pursued marital and political connection purposefully. Such connection was advantageous to the individual but, in an age of extended credit and still emerging legal protection, it was also rational. The stress that was placed on family, on personal qualities, on trust built over time, and on ethnicity was part of the survival strategy of many. These things offered a measure of protection otherwise unavailable.

To the privileged, this was obvious; to those excluded, these elements might place them on the wrong end of a gradient of power and prestige. McNiff and Schiefflin and Ainse are all local examples of the latter. Given such gradients, the only recourse open was an expensive one – recourse to law. Yet, even here, for those few who could afford legal action, there was little prospect of justice when faced with the powerful. Even the relations of the powerful were not immune. Robert Gourlay, author of a statistical survey of conditions in Upper Canada and relative of Robert Hamilton, William Dickson, and Thomas Clark, was charged under the Sedition Act of 1804 by his own kin. Presumably, he seemed an arch-traitor. After an imprisonment of eight months, this broken man was banished from Upper Canada by Chief Justice Powell, at the same assizes at which he threatened the jury if it found for Randal.[77]

Being a merchant was important in the acquisition of land. This might be achieved as a consequence of indebtedness or by active pursuit. Merchants possessed more land than others and were the dominant group in the purchase and sale of land. The term "trader" is included within this designation and might best describe such individuals as Alexander McKee, Thomas McKee, the Caldwells, and Matthew Elliott, men who traded with the Indians and fought alongside them. Within a few years there was a different breed, a more clearly "merchant" class which included such people as William McCormick and the Park brothers. There were others such as Charles Berczy, who established a railroad and was the president of a company supplying gas, light, and water in Toronto; James Dougall, merchant, bank agent, bank director, shipper, contractor, and canal builder; Samuel Street, shipowner, international debt collector, president of a bank and involved with two others as well as with the Life and Fire Assurance Company; Samuel Street, Jr, shareholder in four banks and investor in the Welland Canal; William Morris, distiller, businessman, canal-builder, and politician; and John Prince, brewer and mining entrepreneur. Clearly, times changed and investors in land followed the changes.

For the wider society, those purchasing land tended to do so within the framework of ethnicity, the French Canadian purchasing from his own, the Irish from the Irish, the English from the English. Among the speculators, the French Canadians were the most ethnocentric and the language barrier may have operated here. Generally, however, there was little association across the matrix of interaction for the speculator group. Though the numbers are small in some classes, it would seem that, for the speculators, ethnic origin was less significant than capital availability and willingness to deal. Most appeared to move towards the Scots, who did the least business among themselves and who were in fact numerically few in comparison to others. For these people, the acquisition of land and the associated movement of money would appear to have been freer than it was for their co-nationals who sought a farm to settle.

Overlapping all of this was the military presence, legally required of all in the form of participation in the militia but doubling also with officeholding in the typical manner of pre-industrial societies. Such participation was the ultimate symbol of acceptance of the prevailing political system. Many of the same family served; Askin boasted seventeen family members active during the War of 1812. There were many lieutenant-colonels, including Askin himself. James Baby was one, as was Matthew Elliott, William Berczy the artist and tobacco-grower, Samuel Street, and Thomas C. Street, and so was John Prince, the infamous executioner of American prisoners. Samuel Gerard, shipowner, bank president, and international debt collector, became a major; Charles Askin served under Thomas Clark as a captain, and William

Morris was an ensign. All of these people were merchants or entrepreneurs. If, as a result of their service, they received the privilege of
additional land rights, it was not without reason. They risked all and
two on the list of speculators died most gallantly fighting the Americans: Powell's court clerk, C.A. Smith, was killed at Fallen Timbers,
and Lieutenant-Colonel MacDonnell died at Queenston Heights.
Smith had no actual obligation to be in the field though he felt a
moral obligation to the Indian cause. If these men were part of a patrician banditti, involved in a predatory phase of agrarian and commercial capitalism in which the state was the prey,[78] they paid dearly for it.

Appendices

Appendix 1.1   Essex Soil Quality and Drainage

Class	Symbol	Name	Acreage
1: Light- to Medium-Textured, Well Drained	Ps	Plainfield Sand	1,700
	Bg	Burford Loam	3,700
	Es	Eastport Sand	2,500
	Bg-s	Burford Loam-Shallow/Phase	5,300
	Fsl	Fox Sandy Loam	5,300
	Hl	Harrow Loam	4,000
	Hs	Harrow Sandy Loam	3,500
		Total Acreage Class 1	26,000
2: Light-Textured, Imperfectly and Poorly Drained	Bes	Berrien sand	8,000
	B-s	Brookston Clay Sand Spot/phase	18,000
	Gs	Granby Sand	1,000
	Bel	Berrien Sandy Loam	16,000
	Was	Wauseon Sandy Loam	3,000
	C-s	Caistor Sandy Spot/Phase	1,500
		Total Acreage Class 2	47,500
3: Medium-Textured, Imperfectly and Poorly Drained	Cdl	Colwood Fine Sandy Loam	7,000
	Tfs	Tuscola Fine Sandy Loam	6,000
	Pl	Parkhill Loam	5,000
	P-r	Parkhill Loam Red Sand Spot/Phase	5,000
		Total Acreage Class 3	23,000
4: Heavy-Textured, Imperfectly Drained	Pcl	Perth Clay Loam	8,000
	Cac	Caistor Clay	13,500
	Cacl	Caistor Clay Loam	2,500
	Pc	Perth Clay	9,000
	Fl	Farmington Loam	2,000
		Total Acreage Class 4	35,000
5: Heavy-Textured, Poorly Drained	Bc	Brookston Clay	250,000
	Bcl	Brookston Clay Loam	30,000
	Cc	Clyde Clay	2,500
	Jc	Jeddo Clay	3,500
	Tos	Toledo Silt Loam	1,000
	Toc	Toledo Clay	17,500
		Total Acreage Class 5	304,500

Appendix 1.1   (continued)

Class	Symbol	Name	Acreage
6: Bottom Land,	M	Muck	1,700
Marsh, and Muck	Ma	Marsh	7,000
	B.L.	Bottom Land	7,300
		Total Acreage Class 6	16,000

SUMMARY:

CLASS No.	Acreage	% Total Area Essex
1	26,000	5.75
2	47,500	10.51
3	23,000	5.09
4	35,000	7.74
5	304,500	67.37
6	16,000	3.54
Total Acreage	452,000	100.00

Source: Richards, Caldwell and Morwick, Soil Survey of Essex County.

Appendix 2.1   Survey Documents

The following abbreviations are used: Survey Records (SR); Department of Lands and Forests Ontario (LF); Field Notes (FN); Original Notebook (ONB); Survey Diary (SD); Archives of Ontario (AO)

Township	Surveyor and Date of Survey	Source
Anderdon	P. Carroll in 1835	SR, LF, FN vol. 11, 178–207, and ONB no.21.
	Salter	Park lots, SR, LF, ONB no.22
	McIntosh, 19 Aug.–13 Sept. 1833	SR, LF, Huron reserve
Colchester	A. Iredell, 1 Jan.–15 July 1797	SR, LF, ONB no.129
	T. Smith, 13 Mar.–11 May 1805	SR, LF, ONB no.132
	M. Burwell, 2 July–Nov. 1811	AO, RG1 Series CB–1
	J.A.Wilkinson, 2 Sept.–21 Oct. 1841	SR, LF, SD; AO, RG1 Series CB–1
Gosfield	A. Iredell, 1796	SR, LF, FN vol. 2, 130–42
	T. Smith, 12 May–4 July 1805	SR, LF, SD, 234–65
	M. Burwell, 1821–22	SR, LF, FN vol.11, 67–86, ONB no.416
	M. Burwell, 1823	SR, LF, FN vol. 11, 261–5
	no name, no date but concerned with 2nd con., probably Smith	SR, LF, FN vol. 5, 247
Malden (Bois Blanc)	P. McNiff, no date	SR, LF, FN vol. 1, 279
Malden	A. Iredell, 1795–96	SR, LF, FN vol. 13, 8–12
Malden	A. Iredell, 10 April–11 July 1796	SR, LF, SD 61, FN vol. 11, 155–62 and vol. 2, 136
Malden	A. Iredell, 9 July–31 Dec. 1796	SR, LF, ONB no.513; FN, vol. 11, 158–164 and vol. 2, 136 and 155–8
Malden	A. Iredell, 1795–96	SR, FN vol. 13, 8–12
Malden	A. Iredell	SR, FN vol. 11, 165–6 and vol. 2, 272–3; ONB no.274
Malden and Sandwich	A. Iredell, 1 July–1 Jan. 1797–98	SR, LF, ONB no.604
Malden	P. Carroll, 1831–32	SR, LF, FN vol. 11, 166–77; ONB no.514; AO, SD, shelf 73, box 1
Malden (Amherstburg)	T. Smith, 8 June–3 July 1820 and 2 Dec.–14 Dec. 1820	SR, LF, FN vol. 8, 1–18 and vol. 11, 365–409, ONB no.19
Malden	McIntosh, 19 Aug.–13 Sept. 1833	SR, LF, ONB no.18

Appendix 2.1   (continued)

Township	Surveyor and Date of Survey	Source
Malden (Amherstburg military reserve)	J.A. Wilkinson 1858	SR, LF, FN vol.18, 589–624
Malden (Amherstburg)	J.A. Wilkinson, 13 Sept.–12 Oct. 1858	SR, LF, FN vol 18, 625–30; ONB no.884
Malden	Brodie, 8 Nov.–4 Dec. 1860	SR, LF, ONB no.787, mfm. 794
Mersea, Gosfield, Maidstone, Rochester	A. Iredell, 1796	SR, LF, FN vol. 13, 7–8
Mersea	A. Iredell, 1 July–31 Dec. 1798	SR, LF, SD, and FN, north shore of Lake Erie; FN vol. 3, 100–105
Mersea	T. Smith, 1806	SR, LF, FN vol. 11, 1–16, and 54–67; vol. 5, 242–50; ONB no.133
Mersea	M. Burwell, 1811 and 1816 (Talbot Rd through Mersea)	SR, LF, FN vol. 11, 17–25, vol. 4, 17; ONB no.522
Mersea	M. Burwell, 1836	SR, LF, FN vol. 13, 475–82, ONB no.522
Maidstone (Belle River)	A. Iredell, 1795–96	SR, LF, FN vol. 13, 5–6
Maidstone (Belle River)	A. Iredell, 1796	SR, LF, FN vol. 2, 132
Maidstone (Belle River)	P. McNiff, n.d. but c. 1794	SR, LF, FN vol.1, 274
Maidstone and Rochester	M. Burwell, 1821	SR, LF, FN vol. 11, 220–60
Maidstone and Rochester	A. Iredell, 1796	SR, LF, FN vol. 11, 265
Rochester and Maidstone	M. Burwell, 1824	SR, LF, FN vol. 11, 266–319
Sandwich	A. Iredell, 1 Jan.–15 July 1797	SR, LF, FN vol. 2, 270–2; vol. 11, 213–19, 353–8, and vol. 13, 118–21
Sandwich	A. Iredell, 1 July–13 Oct. 1799	SR, LF, ONB no.765
Sandwich (Town Plot)	A. Iredell, 5 Nov.–17 Dec. 1798	SR, LF, FN vol. 3, 103–5; ONB no.603
Talbot Rd. (Howard, Harwich, Tilbury East and Mersea)	M. Burwell, 1 May–5 Oct. 1816	AO, shelf 73, box 6

Appendix 2.1   (continued)

Township	Surveyor and Date of Survey	Source
Talbot Rd (Romney and Tilbury)	M. Burwell, 1831	SR, LF, FN vol. 13, 451–8
North shore of Lake Erie	A. Iredell, July–31 Dec. 1798	SR, LF, FN vol. 3, 92–6 and 100–111
South shore of Lake Erie	A. Iredell, 1798	SR, LF, FN vol. 3, 99–100
Tilbury and Dover	A. Iredell, 1 Jan.–15 July 1797	AO, shelf 72, box 3; SR, LF, FN vol. 2, 270–2
Tilbury	A. Iredell, 1797	SR, LF, FN vol. 11, 87–90
Tilbury and Raleigh	A. Iredell, 1798	SR, LF, FN vol. 3, 97, 105–8
Tilbury	A. Iredell, 1799	SR, FN vol. 3, 105–8
Tilbury East	M. Burwell, 1822–23	SR, LF, FN vol. 13, 389–420; ONB no.657

Appendix 2.2   Documentary Sources for the Reconstruction of the Crown and Clergy
Reserves

Abbreviations used: Ontario Archives (AO); Crown Land Papers (CLP); Public Record
Office, London (PRO); Colonial Office, London (CO)

Name of Document	Date	Location
1 Assessment Roll for District in 1820	1820	AO, shelf 8, no.5
2 Register of Lands for the Bathurst, Home and Western Districts, Canada Company Papers No. 2	1824–26	AO
3 Schedule of Clergy Reserves	1827	AO, CLP, shelf 46, no.7
4 Schedule of Clergy Reserves in the Western District	1828	AO, CLP, shelf 27, 13 f
5 Schedule of Clergy Reserves in the Undermentioned Townships in the Western District	1828	AO, CLP, shelf 45, no.8 13 g
6 Clergy Reserves in Dawn and Maidstone Townships, Crown Land Papers, Inspection and Valuation Papers	1829	AO, A6–15, vol. 2
7 Clergy Reserves in the Western District, Crown Land Papers	1840–41	AO, A6–15, vol. 4
8 Clergy Reserves in the Western District, Crown Land Papers	1842–43	AO, A6–15, vol. 6
9 Clergy Reserves in the Western District	1844–45	AO, A6–15, vol. 11
10 Certain Lands in Kent, Essex and Lambton Counties	1852	AO, A6–15, vol. 12
11 Certain Lands in Kent and Essex Counties	1859	AO, A6–15, vol. 14
12 A statement of the Clergy Reserves sold and of the amount paid on each lot in the several Districts in that part of this Province, formerly constituting the Province of Upper Canada as they appear from the books of the Land Department of the Province of Canada, 30th June 1841.	1841	AO, Supplement to the *Upper Canada Gazette*

Appendix 2.2   (continued)

Name of Document	Date	Location
13 Abstract Index to Deeds		AO, Genealogical Society of Utah, microfilm
14 Domesday Books		Department of Lands and Forests, Toronto
15 Schedules of Crown Reserves Returned Vacant in Various Districts, Crown Land Papers	1837	AO, shelf 45, no.14
16 A statement of the Crown Reserves sold and of the amount paid on each lot in the several Districts in that part of this Province, formerly constituting the Province of Upper Canada as they appear from the books of the Land Department of the Province of Canada, 30th June 1841.	1841	AO, Supplement to the Upper Canada Gazette
17 Clergy Reserves in Mersea Twp.	PRO, CO401/folio 528	
18 Clergy Reserves in Mersea Twp.	PRO, CO401/folio 529	
19 Clergy Reserves in Gosfield Twp.	PRO, CO401/folio 530	
20 Clergy Reserves in Colchester Twp.	PRO, CO401/folio 533	
21 Clergy Reserves in Malden Twp.	PRO, CO401/folio 534 and 535	
22 Clergy Reserves in Sandwich Twp.	PRO, CO401/	
23 Clergy Reserves in Maidstone Twp.	PRO, CO401/folio 538	
24 Crown Reserves in Maidstone Twp.	PRO, CO401/folio 539	
25 Clergy Reserves in Rochester Twp.	PRO, CO401/folio 540	
26 Crown Reserves in Rochester Twp.	PRO, CO401/folio 541	

N.B. Source items 17–26 are dated 26th April 1825
Source: Clarke, "Documentary and Map Sources," Table 1; items 17–26 from PRO.

Appendix 2.3   Documentary and Map Sources of Patent Data for Essex County,
Ontario

Abbreviations used: Abstract Index to Deeds (AID); Genealogical Society of Utah (GS);
microfilm (mfm.); Ontario Archives (AO)

Township	L. and F. Document	Plan	AO Document
Anderdon	Domesday Book, vol. 76	no.c107	Patent Index, GS885, mfm., AO
Colchester	Domesday Book, vol. 7 Talbot Road, vol. 6	no.53	AID, GS858–66, vols. A and B, mfm., AO
Gosfield	Domesday Book, vol. 7	no.c71, A12 A13, A14, X8, B5	AID, GS894, vols. A and B, mfm., AO
Maidstone	Domesday Book, vol. 7	no.c16	AID, GS926–933, vols. A, mfm., AO
Mersea	Domesday Book, vol. 7	no.c77	AID, GS949–57 vols. A and B, mfm., AO
Rochester	Domesday Book, vol. 7	no.c16, c17	AID, GS963–69 vols. A and B, mfm., AO
Sandwich	Domesday Book, vol. 7	no.c80, c81 c82, c83	AID, GS978–83 vols. A and B, mfm., AO
Tilbury	Domesday Book, vol. 7	no.c28	Patent Index, GS885, mfm., AO
Malden	Domesday Book, vol. 7	no.c6	AID, GS936–940 vol. A, mfm., AO
West Tilbury	Domesday Book, vol. 7		AID, GS1008–1015 vols. A and B, mfm., AO

Source: Clarke, "Documentary and Map Sources," Table 2.

Appendix 2.4   The McKee Treaty of 1790

KNOW ALL MEN BY THESE PRESENTS that we the principal Village and War Chiefs of the Ottawa, Chippewa, Pottowatomy and Huron Indian Nations of Detroit for and in consideration of the sum of Twelve hundred Pounds Currency of the Province of Quebec at Five shillings per Spanish Dollar for valuable Wares and Merchandise to us delivered by the hands of Alexande McKee, Esquire, Deputy Agent of Indian Affairs, the receipt whereof we do hereby acknowledge, have by and with the consent of the whole of our said Nations, given, granted, enfeoffed, alienated and confirmed, and by these presents do give, grant, enfeoff, alien and confirm unto his Majesty George the Third, King of Great Britain, France and Ireland, Defender of the Faith &c. &c. &c. a certain Tract of Land beginning at the mouth of Catfish Creek, commonly called Rivière au Chaudière on the North side of Lake Erie, being the Western extremity of a Tract purchased by his said Majesty from the Messesagey Indians in the year One Thousand seven hundred and eighty Four and from thence running westward along the border of Lake Erie and up the Streight to the mouth of a River known by the name of Channail Ecarté and up the main branch of the said Channel Ecarté to the first fork on the South side, then a due east line until it intersects the Rivière à la Tranche, and up the said Rivière à la Tranche to the North West corner of the said cession granted to his Majesty in the year one Thousand Seven Hundred and Eighty Four, then following the western boundary of said tract being a due South direction until it strikes the mouth of Catfish Creek or otherwise Rivière au Chaudière being the first offset;

RESERVING a Tract beginning at the Indian Officers Land at a small run near the head of the Island of Bois Blanc and running upwards along the border of the Streight to the beginning of the French Settlement above the Head of the Petite Isle au D'inde; then a due East line seven miles, and then South so many miles as will intersect another East line from the mouth of said Run or Gully near the head of said Island of Bois Blanc:

AND another Tract beginning at the mouth of Rivière au Jarvais commonly called Knagg's Creek, running up along the border of the Streight to the Huron Church and one hundred and twenty arpents in depth with all and singular the appurtanences unto the said Tract of land belonging or in any wise appertaining, and the reversion and reversions, remainder and remainders, rents and services of the said premises and all the Estate, right, title, interest, property, cliam or demand whatsoever of us the said Chiefs or any other person or persons whatsover of our said Nations of, in and to the said Tract of Land, or of, in, and to every part and parcel thereof excepting the Reserve aforesaid.

TO HAVE AND TO HOLD the said Lands and premises hereby given and granted, mentioned or intended to be given and granted unto his said Majesty George the Third, His Heirs and Successors for the only proper use and behoof of His said Majesty George the Third, His Heirs and Successors for EVER.

And we the said Chiefs for ourselves and the whole of our said Nations our and their Heirs, Executors and administrators do covenant, promise and grant to and with His said Majesty George the Third, his Heirs and Successors by these presents that His said Majesty, His Heirs and Successors shall and lawfully may from henceforth and for ever after peaceably and quietly, have, hold, occupy, possess and enjoy the said Tract of Land granted, mentioned or intended to be given and granted with all and every of the appurtenances free, clear, and discharged or well and sufficiently saved, kept harmless and indemnified of, from and against all former and other titles, troubles, charges or incumbrances whatever, had, done or suffered or to be had, done or suffered by any of us the said Chiefs, or by any one whatever of the said Nations ours and their Heirs, Executors or administrators; and by these presents do make this our act

Appendix 2.4   (continued)

and Deed irrevocable under any pretence whatever, and have put His said Majesty in full possession and seizin by allowing houses to be built upon the premises.

IN WITNESS wherof, we the said Chiefs, for ourselves and the said Nations have unto these presents made the marks of our different Tribes and affixed our seals at Detroit, District of Hesse in the Province of Quebec, this Nineteenth day of May, in the Thirtieth Year of the Reign of our Sovereign Lord George the Third, King of Great Britain, France and Ireland, Defender of the Faith &c. and in the year of Our Lord one thousand seven hundred and ninety 1790.

Signed, sealed and de-
livered in the present
of us in full Council(Signed)

Patrick Murray, Major
 Commanding Detroit
Richard Porter
 Capt.60 Regt.
Charles Ingram,
 Capt.60 Regt.
John Buller,
 Capt.60 Regt.
J.Hesselbergh
 Lieut.60th Regt.
John Robertson
 Lieut.60th.Regt
David Meredith,
 Lt.R.R.Artillery
E.Cartwright
 Lieut.60 Regt.

Nangie
Chabou quai
Wabandisgais
Mesh qui ga boui

Pottowatomy Nation
(signed)
Skanesque
E.sha ha
Meetego chin

Jo.Jordan
 Lt.60 Regt.
Samuel Gibbs
 Ens.60 Regt.
G.Westphal
 Adjt.60th Regt
Jas Henderson,
 Surgeon
A.Grant,
Alex Harrow,
 Lt.Condr.N.D.P.
P.Frichette, Ptre, Miss
Adhemar St.Matrin,
Gregor McGregor,
 Major Detroit Militia
John Martin,
 Ens. Militia
William Robertson,
T.Smith
 Lieut. Militia

Penash
Shebense
Key way te nan

Huron Nation (signed)
Sastaritsie
Ta hou ne ha wie tie
Skahoumat
Mondoro
Te hatow rence

Thomas Reynolds
 asst.Comss. and
 Storekeeper
Henry Hay, Ensign
Wm. Harffy,
Ottawa Nation (signed)
Egouch-i-ouay
Wawish kuy
Nia ne go
Ki wish e ouan
Atta wa kie
Onagan
Endashin
Maug gich a way

Chippewa Nation (signed)
Wasson
Ti e cami go se
Essebalc
Ouit a nis a

Son din ou
Dou yen tete
Ted y a ta
Tren you maing
She hov na te mon
 Meng da hai
Tsough ka rats y wa
Rou nia hy ra

Recorded by me this 22d day of June 1790, at L'Assomption in the District of Hesse. Register No.C, pp. 374–377
      T.Smith, C.C.P.
      District of Hesse

Source: Lajeunesse, The Windsor Border Region, 171–73.

Appendix 2.5   Survey Systems of Essex County and Dates of Survey

Township	Date	System
Anderdon	1835	Double-Front Special
Colchester North	1832	Double Front
Colchester South	Pt. 1794, 1805	Special
Gosfield North	1823	Double Front
Gosfield South	1796, 1805, 1821–23	Special and Double Front
Malden	1794, 1796, 1831	Single-Front Special
Mersea	1799, 1806, 1860	Single Front
Maidstone	Pt. 1799	Single-Front Special
	Pt. 1821	Double-Front Special
Rochester	1806	Single-Front Special
Sandwich East	1797, 1832	Special and Double Front
Sandwich West	1797	Special
Tilbury North	1824	Double-Front Special
Tilbury West	1824	Double-Front Special

Source: Clarke, "A Geographical Analysis," Appendix 3.1.

Appendix 2.6 Number and type of establishment in each centre

	Sandwich	Amherstburg	Windsor	Kingsville	Colchester	Cedar Creek	Belle River	Albertville	Leamington	Essex Village	Total
Shops	6	14	2	1	2	1	1	1	1	0	29
Taverns	12	10	1	2	1	1	0	0	1	3	31
Tradesmen	17	35	6	0	1	0	0	0	0	0	59
Mills	4	3	0	2	0	0	2	1	0	0	12
Government	13	7	2	1	0	0	0	0	0	0	22
Churches	3	6	0	0	1	0	0	1	1	0	12
Manufactures	5	11	0	0	1	3	0	0	0	0	20
Professionals	14	4	1	0	0	0	0	0	0	0	19
Miscellaneous	2	1	1	0	0	0	0	0	0	0	4
Total	76	91	13	6	6	5	3	3	3	3	208

Source: John Clarke and David L. Brown, "Focii of Human Activity," 57.

Appendix 7.1   List of Speculators with at Least 400 Acres in Essex in One Period or Three Parcels of Unknown Acreage or at Least Three Transactions

Speculator	Time Held (yrs)	Total No. Trans- actions	Acres Owned 1852	Add. Prop.* 1852	Acres Owned 1825	Add. Prop. 1825
C.C. Allen	2.4	35	0.0	0	0.0	0
J. Anderson	0.0	1	417.0	0	0.0	0
R. Anderson	8.0	5	400.0	0	0.0	0
J.B. Arner	16.5	16	689.0	0	369.0	0
John Askin	3.4	188	523.5	3	2255.0	1
James Askin	5.0	34	0.0	0	400.0	0
Charles Baby	0.9	61	1626.0	1	0.0	0
Francis Baby	10.4	30	225.0	5	150.0	3
Hon. James Baby	8.0	15	0.0	0	641.0	2
Jean-Baptiste Baby	13.0	36	1124.0	2	240.0	4
William D. Baby	2.0	11	108.0	2	0.0	0
Jean-Baptiste Barthe	2.0	13	0.0	0	0.0	0
James Bell	4.0	5	400.0	0	0.0	0
William Bell	1.0	7	0.0	0	754.0	1
Charles Berczy	15.0	17	360.0	0	100.0	5
William Berczy	10.5	16	507.0	0	0.0	0
J.B. Bertrand	4.5	12	400.0	0	0.0	0
R. Boyle	7.0	8	354.0	0	0.0	0
J. Brown	6.9	35	200.0	0	1150.0	0
William Buchanan	3.5	16	0.0	0	153.0	0
S. Bullen	3.2	32	0.0	0	0.0	0
H. Burwell	6.3	3	1240.0	0	0.0	0
Mahlon Burwell	2.2	128	2236.0	1	2000.0	0
J. Cahill	15.0	8	570.0	2	0.0	0
Francis Caldwell	8.0	22	626.0	0	300.0	0
J. and W. Caldwell	17.5	44	2303.0	0	2836.0	0
Peter Carroll	1.0	12	0.0	0	0.0	0
Hon. Thomas Clark	0.8	14	1000.0	0	0.0	1
J. Cochrane	20.6	4	200.0	2	0.0	0
J. Cornwall	15.4	27	152.0	0	300.0	1
Mary Cornwall	34.0	4	0.0	0	600.0	0
John Cowan	6.0	4	100.0	0	0.0	0
Caroline Cummings	4.0	5	488.0	0	0.0	0
J. Cunningham	8.5	15	337.5	0	0.0	0
M. David	2.0	6	300.0	0	0.0	4
James Dougall	11.1	40	465.0	2	0.0	0
R. Dowler	17.0	8	474.0	0	374.0	0
W. Drake	16.0	3	600.0	0	0.0	0
Alexander Duff	2.8	34	181.0	0	600.0	0
William Duff	11.5	59	983.0	0	680.0	0
Rev. T. Edwards	7.5	4	0.0	0	634.0	0
Matthew Elliott	16.0	37	0.0	0	4429.0	0
Rev. F.G. Elliott	4.0	9	845.0	0	0.0	0
Sarah Elliott	3.0	11	400.0	0	0.0	0

Appendix 7.1   (continued)

Speculator	Time Held (yrs)	Total No. Trans- actions	Acres Owned 1852	Add. Prop.* 1852	Acres Owned 1825	Add. Prop. 1825
R.H.B. Elliott	34.0	3	1319.0	0	0.0	0
Hon. E. Ellice	23.4	45	3200.0	0	5615.0	0
W. Fleming	11.1	12	0.0	0	400.0	0
L.J. Fluett	2.2	30	100.0	3	0.0	0
G.W. Foot	1.0	7	0.0	0	0.0	0
Ad. Fox	8.0	8	295.0	0	400.0	0
J., J.B. or J.G. Fox	7.3	21	2291.0	0	200.0	0
Forsyth, Thain and Richardson	11.1	40	0.0	0	800.0	0
John Fulmer	7.3	40	480.0	0	300.0	0
S. Gerard	12.6	27	0.0	0	0.0	0
Hon. Prideaux Girty	5.0	31	0.0	0	0.0	0
Hon. James Gordon	10.4	34	506.0	0	790.0	0
Hon. Alexander Grant	13.5	6	0.0	0	580.0	0
W.R. Graham	3.0	3	200.0	0	0.0	0
J. Haggarty	1.0	17	568.0	0	0.0	0
William Gaspé Hall	5.1	41	409.5	13	0.0	0
George Benson Hall	26.3	20	0.0	7	0.0	0
William Hands, Jr and Sr	6.0	5	0.0	0	400.0	0
John Hartley	2.3	19	690.0	0	622.0	0
A. Harrow	1.0	13	0.0	0	0.0	0
George Ironside	21.2	27	200.0	0	800.0	0
George Jacob	4.3	21	420.0	0	0.0	1
John Jackson	30.0	4	400.0	0	0.0	0
F. Janisse	2.0	18	500.0	5	460.0	2
G. Johnson	0.0	8	0.0	0	0.0	0
A. Laferty	18.2	15	208.0	0	747.0	1
Paul Leduc	15.0	6	200.0	0	0.0	3
D. Langlois	6.0	15	160.0	6	0.0	0
Jul. Langlois	17.7	22	116.0	0	720.0	0
E. Larwill	2.0	7	450.0	0	0.0	0
J. Lockhart	11.1	22	618.0	0	50.0	0
A. Maisonville	1.0	28	0.0	0	670.0	3
James Mailloux	15.0	13	160.0	0	1032.0	0
P. Malotte	21.0	10	224.0	0	423.0	0
Joseph Malotte	4.3	16	487.0	0	200.0	0
Edward Matthews	13.0	9	915.0	0	0.0	0
Meldrum and Park	29.0	56	0.0	0	700.0	0
John Maule	37.0	6	1200.0	0	1200.0	0
William Mickle	2.0	7	214.0	1	0.0	1
George Moffatt	5.0	17	0.0	0	0.0	0
Charles Montague	3.0	8	707.0	2	0.0	0
L. Montreille	10.7	32	78.0	0	0.0	0

Appendix 7.1   (continued)

Speculator	Time Held (yrs)	Total No. Trans- actions	Acres Owned 1852	Add. Prop.* 1852	Acres Owned 1825	Add. Prop. 1825
William Morris	19.0	3	400.0	0	0.0	0
Roswell Mount	3.8	32	0.0	0	0.0	0
Joseph Munger	5.0	11	689.0	0	195.0	0
T. Murphy	6.0	10	157.0	1	517.0	0
Matthew McCormick	12.5	18	200.0	0	516.0	0
William McCormick	9.1	44	0.0	0	1918.0	0
Hon. John A. Macdonald	3.7	17	2905.0	0	0.0	0
John MacDonnell	6.0	10	600.0	0	0.0	0
William McGee	9.5	10	200.0	0	0.0	0
Hon A. MacIntosh	20.3	53	0.0	0	589.0	0
Hon. James McGill	30.1	76	2214.0	0	7317.0	0
Rev. McMurray	7.0	8	0.0	0	0.0	0
Alexander McKee	28.7	16	0.0	0	282.0	3
Thomas McKee	3.0	52	984.0	0	1277.0	0
Horatio Nelson	2.8	25	400.0	0	0.0	0
T. Park Brothers	13.0	49	898.0	0	0.0	0
J.R. Park	4.8	28	755.0	0	0.0	0
Daniel Pastorius	10.0	8	0.0	0	401.0	0
Richard Pattinson	11.1	116	0.0	1	2121.0	0
W.C. Pickersgill	6.0	74	0.0	0	0.0	0
Rev. Richard Pollard	3.8	11	0.0	0	0.0	0
John Prince et al.	4.2	40	170.0	0	100.0	0
A. Reid	3.4	10	629.0	0	0.0	0
R.T. Reynolds	6.8	53	500.0	0	860.0	0
Hon. William Robertson	17.0	11	0.0	0	600.0	0
A.J. Robertson	22.0	67	1538.0	8	0.0	0
W. Sanford	15.0	5	400.0	0	0.0	0
L. Scratch	13.0	21	352.0	0	552.0	0
P. Scratch	8.1	21	202.0	0	400.0	0
Hon. Prideaux Selby	13.0	15	0.0	0	600.0	0
S. Sessions	14.7	12	0.0	0	400.0	0
J. Sewell	4.6	20	50.0	0	83.0	2
Thomas Smith	9.8	51	0.0	0	2061.0	7
C.A. Smith	6.1	30	0.0	0	0.0	0
Jn. Snider	14.3	23	104.0	0	414.0	1
Solomon Salmoni	4.3	17	300.0	0	0.0	0
Benjamin Springer	3.0	16	0.0	0	0.0	0
T. Squire et al.	4.2	25	402.0	0	0.0	0
T.A. Stayner	3.4	10	600.0	0	0.0	0
A. Stewart	5.0	12	522.0	0	0.0	0
John Stockwell	20.3	17	270.0	0	469.0	0

Appendix 7.1   (continued)

Speculator	Time Held (yrs)	Total No. Trans- actions	Acres Owned 1852	Add. Prop.* 1852	Acres Owned 1825	Add. Prop. 1825
Hon. John Strachan, Hon. William Allan and Hon. John Beverley Robinson	1.3	24	305.0	0	200.0	0
T.C. Street	2.0	33	557.0	0	0.0	0
Samuel Street	15.0	16	1648.0	0	0.0	0
J. Strong	5.1	34	422.3	1	0.0	0
Charles Stuart	6.8	21	10.0	0	637.0	0
R. Thornton	9.0	16	394.0	0	0.0	0
Isaac Todd	15.0	34	0.0	0	0.0	0
J.B. Valade	15.7	20	0.0	0	0.0	1
J.G. Watson	8.8	63	244.0	3	597.0	2
Hy. Whaley	8.0	6	400.0	0	0.0	0
Asa Wilcox	4.8	19	473.0	0	0.0	0
Elisha Wilcox	n/a	12	0.0	0	590.0	0
H. Wilcox	12.0	10	90.0	0	50.0	0
Isaac Wilcox	9.0	13	300.0	0	600.0	0
John Williams	10.0	14	0.0	0	200.0	0
James Woods	15.1	109	1368.0	1	6604.0	1

Source: Calculations of the author

* "Add Prop." is the number of additional properties with unknown acreage.

Appendix 7.2   Membership in Clusters, based upon Measures of Similarity of Acreage Owned, Total Number of Transactions and Length of Time Held

Cluster 1

C.C. Allen
J. Anderson
R. Anderson
J.B. Arner
James Askin
Charles Baby
Francis Baby
James Baby
Jean-Baptiste Baby
William D. Baby
Jean-Baptiste Barthe
James Bell
William Bell
Charles Berczy
William Berczy
J.B. Bertrand
R. Boyle
J. Brown
William Buchanan
S. Bullen
H. Burwell
J. Cahill
Francis Caldwell
Peter Carroll
Thomas Clark
J. Cochrane
J. Cornwall
John Cowan
Caroline Cummings
J. Cunningham
M. David
James Dougall
R. Dowler
W. Drake
Alexander Duff
William Duff
Rev. T. Edwards
Matthew Elliott
Rev. F.G. Elliott
Sarah Elliott
W. Fleming
L.J. Fluett
G.W. Foot
Ad. Fox

Forsyth, Thain and Richardson
John Fulmer
S. Gerard
Hon. Prideaux Girty
Hon. James Gordon
Hon. Alexander Grant
W.R. Graham
J. Haggarty
William Gaspé Hall
William Hands, Jr and Sr
John Hartley
A. Harrow
George Ironside
George Jacob
F. Janisse
G. Johnson
A. Laferty
Paul Leduc
D. Langlois
Jul. Langlois
E. Larwill
J. Lockhart
A. Maisonville
James Mailloux
P. Malotte
Joseph Malotte
Edward Matthews
William Mickle
George Moffatt
Charles Montague
L. Montreille
William Morris
Roswell Mount
Joseph Munger
T. Murphy
Matthew McCormick
William McCormick
John MacDonnell
William McGee
A. MacIntosh

Rev. McMurray
Thomas McKee
Horatio Nelson
T. Park Brothers
J.R. Park
Daniel Pastorius
John Prince et al.
A. Reid
Rev. Richard Pollard
R.T. Reynolds
William Robertson
W. Sanford
L. Scratch
P. Scratch
Prideaux Selby
S. Sessions
J. Sewell
Thomas Smith
C.A. Smith
John Snider
Salmoni, Solomon
Benjamin Springer
T. Squire et al.
T.A. Stayner
A. Stewart
John Stockwell
John Strachan, William Allan, and John Beverley Robinson
T.C. Street
J. Strong
Charles Stuart
R. Thornton
Isaac Todd
J.B. Valade
J.G. Watson
Hy. Whaley
Asa Wilcox
Elisha Wilcox
H. Wilcox
Isaac Wilcox
John Williams

Cluster 2

John Askin, Sr and Jr

Cluster 3

Mahlon Burwell
James Woods

Cluster 4

J. and W. Caldwell
Edward Ellice
J.B., J., and J.G. Fox
John A. MacDonald
James McGill
A.J. Roberston
Samuel Street

Cluster 5

Mary Cornwall
R.H.B. Elliott
John Jackson
John Maule
Alexander McKee
George Meldrum and William Park
George Benson Hall

Cluster 6

Richard Pattinson
W.C. Pickersgill

Appendix 7.3   Essex Biographical Research

The following table lists biographical information on persons or groups of people related to the participants in the land market in Essex. The names given are those encountered in the land records, and where contractions were encountered it was impossible to identify individuals with complete certainty. Thus, "Jn." might be either John or Jonathan and "Ed." might be Edward or Edwin. It is important to stress the idea of relationship and connection because many important settlers in the area do not appear here because relationship could not be established. The material does not therefore purport to be either exhaustive or complete but a summary of knowledge to date.

Several sources were consulted in the compilation of this appendix. These are given after each entry in square brackets. The notation is cumulative. Material from one source is augmented or corroborated with information from other sources, including the *Dictionary of Canadian Biography* (*DCB*). This most carefully researched and crafted project is now complete to the twentieth century. Rightfully, the *DCB* occupies the last notation in most of the entries which follow.

However, the present work began before the *DCB's* completion and so the reader will find reference to two earlier compilations by the author. One was used as the basis of an earlier article (Clarke, "The Role of Political Position") and is referred to as [1975p]; a second working file was referred to as [Mortp]. Both were subsequently amalgamated into a database designated ESSEXBIO, from which this appendix has been extracted.

The ESSEXBIO database was built from the secondary literature and from the compilations of others. Chadwick's *Ontarian Families* was a starting point. Hamil's *The Valley of the Lower Thames* [Hamil] proved useful, as did the *Atlas of Essex County* published in 1881 [Atlas], Alan Douglas's biography of *John Prince* [Douglas], J.K. Johnson's *Becoming Prominent: Regional leadership in Upper Canada 1791–1841* [JKJ] and E.J. Lajeunesse's *Windsor Border Region* [LAJ]. The last named is a magnificent achievement in all senses of the word, not least for its reference material on the French settlers of the area. It is complemented, in this respect, by the *Genealogy of the French Families of the Detroit River Region, Revision 1701–1936* by Christain Denissen [Denib]. However, the most useful of all in this genre remains the two-volume edition of Milo Quaife's *John Askin Papers*, here designated as JAP.

Among the files and data compilations used were those at the Hiram Walker Historical Museum (now Windsor's Community Museum) and the records from Fort Malden, available from the Mormon Genealogical Society of Salt Lake City on microfilm. As there were no page references in the microfilm, only the microfilm number was used as reference for this material. These numbers run from 0171230 to 0171239.

Various volumes of the *Ontario Register* [Ont. Reg.] yielded data, especially those concerned with Western District marriages. Elliot, Walker, and Stratford Devai's compilation from the militia rolls, *Men of Upper Canada* [MUC] helped supplement the material, as did Wilfrid B. Lauber's *An Index of the Land Claim Certificates of Upper Canada Militiamen Who Served in the War of 1812–14* [Lauber]. However, the most significant published source by a single author was F.H. Armstrong's *Handbook of Upper Canadian Chronology*. In a singular act of generosity and cooperation, Professor Armstrong also made his unpublished compilation of JPS available to this project [Arm].

Appendix 7.3   (continued)

The following abbreviations are used in this table:
General

b.	born
c.	circa
d.	died
m.	married
Capt.	Captain
Col.	Colonel
Comm.	Commission or Commissioner
CCP	Court of Common Pleas
DC	District Court
DCC	District Court Clerk
Dir.	Director
DUE	Daughter of a United Empire Loyalist
D/Sup.	Deputy Superintendent
fl.	flourished
ID	Indian Department
IG	Inspector General
JP	Justice of the Peace
KCB	Knight Commander of the Bath
LA	Legislative Assembly
LC	Legislative Council
L.C.	Lower Canada
Lt.	Lieutenant
Lt. Col.	Lieutenant-Colonel
Lt. Mil.	Militia Lieutenant
Lt. C. Essex	Lieutenant County of Essex
MEC	Member of Executive Council
MHA	Member of House of Assembly
MLBJH	Member of the Land Board, District of Johnstown
MLBHE	Member of the Land Board, District of Hesse
MLBND	Member of the Land Board, Niagara District
MLBWD	Member of the Land Board, Western District
MLC	Member of the Legislative Council
NCO	Non-commisioned Officer
Pres.	President
Regt.	Regiment
R.A.	Royal Artillery
R.N.	Royal Navy
SUE	Son of a UEL
Sup.	Superintendent
U.C.	Upper Canada
UEL	United Empire Loyalist

Geographical Abbreviations

A'burg.	Amherstburg
And.	Anderdon
Colc.	Colchester Township
Gos.	Gosfield Township

Appendix 7.3   (continued)

Mai.	Maidstone Township
Mal.	Malden Township
Mer.	Mersea Township
Roc.	Rochester Township
San.	Sandwich Township
Til.	Tilbury Township
Mtl.	Montreal
WD	Western District
London	London, England
Lond.	London, Upper Canada

To identify how these individuals were involved – if at all – in land speculation and/or mortgaging, the following codes are used:

LS	Land Speculator
Mr	Mortgagor
Me	Mortgagee
MrMe	Mortgagor/Mortgagee
LS/Mr	Land Speculator/Mortgagor
LS/Me	Land Speculator/Mortgagee
LS/MrMe	Land Speculator/Mortgagor/Mortgagee
LS–25	Land Speculator Pre-1825
LS+25	Land Speculator Post-1825
LS±25	Land Speculator Both Periods

This information is found in square brackets under the individual's name.

James Abbott (d.c. 1800)	member of the Miami Company. Father of Frances, Elizabeth, and Mary Abbott, the wives of François Baby, James Baby, and William Hands respectively. A son, James, m. Sarah Whistler, daughter of Capt. John Whistler, U.S.A.; English [0171230].
Sarah (Sally) Ainse (b.c. 1728) (d.c. 1823)	employee of ID. Possibly the wife of Joseph Louise Ainse, interpreter in ID, diplomatic courier [DCB 6].
William Allan (b.c. 1770) (d. 11 July 1853)	merchant, businessman, officeholder, judge, politician, land speculator, and financial adviser to the wealthy and powerful; friend or relation of Edward Ellice, John McGill, Alexander Grant, John Strachan, and Samuel Smith of the Executive Council; lieutenant of Lincoln militia, 1795; major 3rd. Yorks, 1812; JP Home District, 1800; judge of King's Bench, 1818; commissioner for war losses, 1818; militia paymaster, 1818–25; district-treasurer, 1800–21; collector of customs, York, 1800–28; Postmaster, York, 1801; subscriber and president, Bank of U.C., 1821–25 and 1826–35; shareholder in Bank of British North America; MLC, 1825–41; MEC, 1836–41; commissioner of the Canada Company, 1829; director of canal, railroad, and fire-insurance companies, 1825–53; Pres. Toronto Board of Trade, 1834; partner in land speculation with T. Clark and Samuel Street; banker for Forsyth and Richardson [DCB 8].

Appendix 7.3   (continued)

Amherstburg Building Society	McLeod and Menzies [MORTp].
William Ancrum (Ancruam)	major, 34th Foot, 1789; O.C. Detroit, 1784–86; partner with John Askin in the Moravian purchase of 1786 [JAP].
J. Anderson [LS+25]	possibly John Anderson, Scottish emigrant, brother of Robert Anderson [0171230]; trader (NA, Askin Papers).
R. Anderson [LS+25]	possibly Robert Anderson, emigrant from the West Indies. A former plantation owner who came to Mal. when his slaves were liberated [0171230].
Jacob Arner [LS±25]	either the son or father with the same name. The father was a UEL. [0171230]
I. Askew [Mr]	millwright [MORTp]; mason [Douglas].
John Askin Sr (b. 1739) (d. 1815) [LS±25/Mr]	Irish-born son of James Askin and Alice Rea; JP, 1796–1800 and 1806–13 [1975p]; Detroit merchant and speculator, agent of the North-West Co. [MORTp]. Member of Miami Company; Col. of militia; father of three by the Panise woman Manette, and of nine other children with Marthe-Archange Barthe, the daughter of the fur trader Charles Andrew Barthe (b. 22 Feb. 1722) and his wife Mary Therese Campau [DCB 5].
Catherine Askin (b. 1763) (d. 1796)	eldest daughter of John Askin, Sr; m. at fifteen to Capt. Samuel Robertson (d. 1782), brother of William; second wife of Robert Hamilton [JAP].
John Askin, Jr. (b. 1769) (d. 1819) [LS±25/Mr]	Sup/ID, A'burg; Major, 2nd Regt, Essex militia; MLBHE; JP, 1800–10 and 1816–19. customs collector, A'burg 1801; father and son [1975p]. John Jr m. 21 October 1791 Mary Madelaine Peltier [JAP].
Madelaine Askin (d. 10 Jan. 1811)	wife of Dr. Robert Richardson; one of her eight children, William, married Jane Cameron Grant, youngest daughter of Commodore Grant. Another, John, became a well-known author [JAP].
Therese Askin (b. 10 Feb. 1774)	wife of Thomas McKee, son of Alexander McKee of ID; mother of Alexander McKee.
Archange Askin (b. 3 Oct. 1775) (d. 1866)	m. Lt. Col. David Meredith R.A. [JAP].
Adelaide (Alice) Askin (b. 29 May 1783)	daughter of John Askin [1975p]; widow of Elijah Brush, American lawyer.
Charles Askin (b. 18 June 1785) (d. 1869) [Me]	merchant, DCC, 1823–39; JP, 1823–37; Lt. North Essex militia, subsequently Capt. 2nd Lincolns under Col. Thomas Clark. Son-in-law of George Jacob [1975p]; land agent for William and A.J. Robertson as well as Samuel Street.

Appendix 7.3   (continued)

James Askin (b. 9 Nov 1786) [LS±25/Mr]	son of John Askin, Sr; JP, 1816–37 [1975p]; Surrogate Court registrar 1825–51; registrar of Essex, 1831–58; Lt. Col. 2nd. Essex, 1822; husband of Frances Godet *dit* Marentette.
Eleanor (Ellen Phyllis) Askin (b. 17 Apr. 1788)	daughter of John Askin, m. Richard Patterson [1975p].
Alexander Askin (b. 22 Feb. 1791?) (d.c. 1816)	Lt. Mil., youngest son of John Askin [1975p][JAP].
Jean Baptiste Askin (b. 10 Apr. 1788) (d. 14 Nov. 1869)	son of John Askin, Jr, and Indian woman; trader; interpreter; soldier; militia officer; clerk of peace and DCC, 1819–1849, Norfolk; president of Agricultural Society, Middlesex, 1831; Board of Education, London District.
Jacques Dupéront (Duperon, Dupperon) Baby (bapt. 4 Jan 1731) (d. 2 Aug 1789)	soldier of France, trader, land speculator; Capt. ID 1777; acting commissary, 1779; JP, 1784; Lt. Col. Detroit militia; MLBHE; husband of Suzanne Réaume *dit* La Croix [DCB 4]. His brother François (1733–1820) was prominent in Lower Canadian affairs and a close friend of Governor Haldimand [DCB 5].
Hon. James (Jacques) Baby (b. 25 Aug 1763) (d. 19 Feb 1833) [LS–25/Mr]	Detroit-born; Col. of Kent County Militia; D/Sup. ID, 1789; JP, 1788–1837; Surrogate Court judge, 1793; inspector general for U.C., 1815–33; Lt. Col. Essex, 1792–1833; Heirs and Devisees; MEC, 1792–1833; Comm. U.C. and L.C.; Comm. Forfeited Estates; Clergy Comm; MLC, 1792–1833; speaker L.C., 1828. Husband of Elizabeth Abbott, the daughter of James Abbott; friend of John Strachan (his executor), John Beverley Robinson, George Herchmel Markland, and Thomas Clark (one of his executors) [1975p] [DCB 6].
Francis (François) Baby (b. 16 Dec. 1768) (d. 27 Aug. 1852) [LS–25/Me]	Detroit-born; ID officer; JP, 1788–1837; Lt. Col. Essex 1807; MHA Kent, 1792–96; MHA Essex, 1821–30; Col. Mil.; MLBWD, 1819–25. Husband of Frances (Fanny) Abbott, daughter of James Abbott; Susanne Réaume (Rheaume) Baby, mother of James and Francis, also patented sixty-six acres in 1804 [1975p] [DCB 9].
Jean-Baptiste Baby (b. 5 or 10 Jan 1770) (buried Oct 10, 1852) [LS±25/Me]	brother of Francis and James Baby. JP, 1800–10 and 1816–37: MHA Essex, 1808–12; treasurer WD, 1837–49; spirit merchant [Arm]; married Ann Hands; father of W.D. Baby [JAP].
Daniel Baby (b. 28 Dec. 1778) (d. 1858)	brother to James, Francis, and Jean-Baptiste; major-general British army.

Appendix 7.3   (continued)

Charles Baby (b. 21 Dec. 1806) (d. 13 Nov. 1871?) [LS+25]	lawyer; son of James Baby: clerk of the peace, 1836–72. A daughter m. William J. McKee, son of Thomas McKee and Isabella Johnson. Another daughter m. J. Wallace Askin, son of John Alex. Askin [0171230][Arm].
Raymond Baby (d. 1840)	sheriff, 1839–40 [Arm].
S. Baby (b. 24 Nov. 1766?) (d. Feb 1813)	presumably Suzanne Baby, daughter of Jacques Dupéront Baby and Suzanne Réaume; wife of William Caldwell.
William Duperon Baby (b. 16 Apr. 1819) (d.c. 1860) [LS+25]	sheriff and sometime partner of John Prince [Douglas]; child of Ann Hands and Jean-Baptiste Baby [JAP].
William Louis Baby (b. 30 Apr. 1812) (d. 9 Nov. 1897)	son of James Baby and Elizabeth Abbott; author, JP, 1837.
Julia Frances Baby (b. Feb. 1825)	daughter of Jean-Baptist Baby and Ann Hands. Married William G. Hall, son of George B. Hall and Angelica Fortier on 13 June 1838 [DENIB]. See Hall.
Jean-Baptiste Barthe (1753–1827) [LS+25]	brother-in-law of John Askin, Sr. Supplier to the fur trade, associated with John Askin; JP, 1818–26 [1975p].
Lewis (presumably Louison) Barthe	brother-in-law of John Askin [1975p]. Askin purchased 13,000 acres from this man and another called Dequindre.
James Bell (b. 1806) (d. 1891) [LS+25]	possibly James Bell, who was born in Scotland; a school teacher in Colchester [0171232]; or James Bell, JP, 1822–37.
William Bell [LS–25]	probably William Bell, who was born in Scotland; ship's carpenter and "Master Builder" at Fort Malden [0171231].
William Berczy (b.c 1744) (d. 5 Feb. 1813) [LS±25]	Johann Albrecht Ulrich Von Moll Berczy; baptized 10 Dec. 1744; colonizer, author, architect, and painter; petitioner with the German Co. for 1 million acres of Upper Canadian land; associate of Samuel Street [DCB 5]. Father of Charles and William.
C. Berzcy (b. 22 Aug. 1794) (d. 9 Jun. 1858) [LS±25/Mr]	presumably Charles Albert, acting deputy-assistant commissary general, 1814–16; commissariat, 1812; confidential agent of Sir Francis Bond Head 1837; businessman; JP, 1826–33; director Bank of U.C., 1840–43; a founder of the Toronto Simcoe and Lake Huron Railroad; Pres. Consumer's Gas, Toronto, 1848; owner of a company that bought Toronto's Gas, Light and Water Company, 1817. Post office inspector at Toronto, 1835, and postmaster, 1838; friend of T.A. Stayner, the postmaster general [0171231][DCB 8].

Appendix 7.3   (continued)

William Berczy (b. 6 Jan. 1791) (d. 9 Dec. 1873) [LS±25]	William Bent Berczy, painter, tobacco cultivator, merchant; Capt. Canadian Chasseurs 1812; Lt. Col. militia; Lt. Col. (later Col.) 8th militia district, L.C., 1845–63; JP, 1826; MHA Kent, 1828 and 1830; son of Von Moll Berczy [DCB 10].
J.B. Bertrand (b.1802) [LS+25]	farmer, Colchester.
L. Bondy [Me]	possible relation of Joseph Bondy; Lieutenant in Detroit Volunteers; ID.
Bondy references	Mary Jane Bondy, daughter of Laurence Bondy (L. Bondy?), m. Alexis Langlois, son of Alexis Langlois and Louis Bissonnet on 21 Nov. 1814 [DENIB].
	Thomas Bondy m. Julia Bertrand, daughter of Jean-Baptiste Bertrand and Margaret Paré on 6 Oct. 1824 [DENIB].
	Hilary Bondy, daughter of Joseph Bondy m. Susanne Langlois, daughter of Peter Langlois and Harriet Lemay [DENIB].
R. Boyle [LS+25]	perhaps a relation of William (UEL), who arrived in Detroit in 1785.
S. Boyle	possibly Susannah or Susan Boyle, daughter of John Boyle of Ireland [0171231].
J. Brown [LS–25]	perhaps John Brown, husband of Charlotte Malot (m. 18 July 1837)[Ont. Reg.].
W. Buchanan [LS–25/Mr]	perhaps the well-known merchant but more likely the farmer of that name.
H. Burwell [LS+25]	Hercules, Hannibal, or Horatio, sons of Mahlon Burwell [DCB 7].
Mahlon Burwell (b. 18 Feb. 1783) (d. 25 Jan. 1846) [LS±25]	American-born surveyor, businessman, JP, officeholder, Lt. 3rd Regt. Lincoln Militia, 1810; Lt. Col. 1st Regt. Middlesex Militia, 1812; Col. 2nd Middlesex Regt., 1822; JP Lond. District, 1813; commissioner to arrest those suspected of high treason, 1814; registrar Middlesex County 1809; collector of Customs Port Talbot, 1820; commissioner under the Alien Act for the Lond. District, 1822; coroner of Lond. District, 1824; MHA Oxford and Middlesex, 1812–20; MHA Middlesex, 1820 –24; MHA Lond., 1836–41; Port Burwell Harbour Co. entrepreneur; owner of at least 43,284 acres of land in southwestern Ontario plus whatever compensation (possibly cash) he got for eigh- teen township surveys. Loyalist and right hand man of Thomas Talbot [DCB 7].
Joseph Cahill [LS+25]	farmer [Atlas].

Appendix 7.3   (continued)

William Caldwell (b.c. 1750) (d. 20 Feb. 1822) [LS±25]	Northern-Irish, Capt. Butler's Rangers, 1776–84; Caldwell's Rangers 1812–14; JP, 1788–1819; Sup. ID at A'burg, 1814. Husband of Suzanne Baby. Much of the land in this name was granted to either William Caldwell or Capt. William Caldwell. The remainder, therefore, may have been granted to Caldwell's son, William. Caldwell, Sr, was also the father of James, Francis, and Billy, who was a chief of the Pottawatomies. He was a blood relation of Sir John Caldwell (1775–1852), the receiver general of L.C. [1975p].
William Caldwell	son of William Caldwell, Sr; Militia officer; JP, 1788–1837.
James Caldwell [LS±25/Me]	presumably the son of William Caldwell; trading partner of Matthew Elliott. Together, William and James patented 3600 acres in 1798.
Francis X. Caldwell (b. 4 May 1792) (d. 5 Jun. 1851) [LS±25/Mr]	JP, 1833–37; MHA Essex, 1835–40, son of William Caldwell and brother of Billy Caldwell, chief of the Pottawatomi; ensign 1st Essex Militia, 1812; Capt. 1819; collector of customs A'burg, 1831; m. Mary Frances Réaume, widow of Francis Baby; businessman [DCB 8].
Peter Carroll (b. 1806) (d. 18 Sep. 1876) [LS+25]	government surveyor; Crown land agent, contractor; Dir. Gore Bank, Great Eastern Railway and Niagara Suspension Bridge Company.
Richard Cartwright (b. 2 Feb. 1759) (d. 27 Jul. 1815)	Loyalist, Kingston merchant, JP, c. 1785; judge CCP, 1788; Heir and Devisees Midland, 1797; MLBHE Mecklenburg, 1788; militia officer 1793; Lt. County of Frontenac, 1792 [Arm.]; MLC, 1792–1815. A partner with Robert Hamilton, Isaac Todd, James McGill, and John Askin, he left 27,000 acres of Upper Canadian land in 1815. [DCB 5].
J. Cathbertson (J. Cuthbertson) [Mr]	Scottish-born speculator, resident in Sandwich Township [Douglas].
Hon. Thomas Alexander Clark (Clarke) (b.c. 1770) (d. 6 Oct. 1835) [LS+25]	Interpreter ID before 1795 and during 1812 war; merchant of Queenston; Lt. Col. Second Lincolns during 1812 war, Col. 1818. MLC 1815–35. Husband of the grand-daughter of Sir William Johnson and Molly Brant. Scottish-born [1975p]. Cousin of William and Robert Dickson. Land speculator; partner with Askin, Hamilton, and particularly Samuel Street. Had already acquired 1,132.5 acres by 1802 [1975p][DCB 6]. An English millwright in Colchester had the same name in 1788.
John Cornwall [LS±25]	Loyalist, soldier, JP WD, 1797; MHA Essex and Suffolk, 1797–1800. His brother Francis patented 168 acres in 1802. Of the 1534 acres patented by John by 1803, 237 acres were patented by his son, Joshua, and 230 acres were patented by another son, Wheeler [1975p]. Native of Wales, UEL, granted land in Colc [0171233]; contractor with Askin.

Appendix 7.3   (continued)

Mary Cornwall (b. 1792) (d. 1891) [LS–25]	daughter of John Cornwall [1975p]. She married William McCormick, the son of Alexander McCormick [0171236].
Richard Cornwall	presumably a relative of John Cornwall. American-born; Detroit resident master shipbuilder for the Great Lakes.
David Cowan (d. 24 Sep. 1808)	MHA Essex, 1800–08. Ship's Capt.; four years R.N.; patented 1557 acres by 1807. Possibly of Scottish origin; Lt. Provincial Marine. Owner of lots 7 and 8 in Mal., sold by his brother John to Matthew Elliott for £650 [0171233] [1975p].
John Cowan [LS+25]	brother of David, DCC 1842–48, publisher of the Sandwich *Canadian Emigrant.*
C. Cummings (b. 1787) (d. 5 Apr. 1870) [LS+25]	possibly Cuthbert Cummings, Scottish-born Hudson Bay Company trader [DCB 9].
Moses David (b. 1767) (d. 1815) [LS±25]	brother of David David, the fur trader and merchant; son of Lazarus David and Phoebe Samuel; militia volunteer, 1790; merchant in Sandwich; ensign of militia, 1803; Capt. 1807; coroner, 1808; first Jew to hold land; relieved of oath of abjuration in the Christian form and allowed to secure office by bond.
Fontenoy Dequindre [Mr]	Lt. ID during the American revolution [MORTp].
Thomas Dickson (b.c. 1775) (d. 22 Jan. 1825)	Scottish-born, Queenston and Fort Erie merchant, cousin of Robert Hamilton; d/coll. customs at Queenston 1803, Heir and Devisees Commission member; JP, 1800–23, MHA Lincoln, 1812; Lt. Col. militia, 1814; associate judge at treason trials, 1824; husband of Archange Grant [DCB 6].
Robert Dickson (b.1796) (d. 28 Nov. 1846)	nephew of Thomas Dickson; cousin of Thomas Clark; militia officer 1st Lincolns, 1825, lawyer, MHA Niagara Town.
William Dickson (b. 13 Jul. 1769) (d. 19 Feb. 1846)	Scottish-born lawyer, businessman, and speculator; brother of Thomas and cousin of Robert Hamilton and Thomas Clark; speculator in the Mississauga tract and in Indian land in the Grand River; JP; militia soldier; MLC 1815; related by marriage to Catherine Hamilton née Askin; agent for John Askin [DCB 7].
M. Donovan	possibly Matthew Donovan, UEL, father of Sarah and Elizabeth Donovan, wives of Matthew Elliott, Sr, and Jonathan Nelson respectively. Secretary of the Land Board at Kingston, 1789–93.

Appendix 7.3   (continued)

J. Dougall (b. 1810) (d. 1888) [LS±25]/Mr]	presumably James, son of John Dougall; Scottish-born, he married Susan Baby, daughter of Francis Baby. Grain merchant of A'burg: shipper; land speculator; JP, 1837–88; after 1854 municipal councillor and subsequently mayor of Windsor, 1859–61; was a partner with his brother John in the firm of J. and J. Dougall (after 1840 Dougall and Redpath). The two were agents for the Commercial Bank of Kingston; John's father-in-law was John Redpath, the sugar merchant; contractor, canal builder, shipper, and the director of the Bank of Mtl, 1853–69. possibly his elder brother John; merchant, journalist and publisher. [0171233][DCB 11] [Armstrong, 1984]
R. Dowler (b. 1758, d. 1837) [LS±25]	possibly Robert Dowler, UEL of Irish origin. He married Rebecca Davis of the same family as Jefferson Davis, president of the Confederate States. Buried at Christ's Church, Colc.
John Drake	JP, 1796–1810; commanded a vessel engaged in the northwest trade; patented 1261 acres by 1808 [1975p]; Irish-born, Lt. Provincial Marine; former Guinea trader [HAMIL].
Wm. Drake [LS+25]	possibly William Drake (b. 1808) of Kingsville, Gos.; m. Eliza Mailed [0171233].
François Drouillard	speculator in Harwich; Lt. Mil.; patentee of 1200 acres in 1803 [1975p].
J. Drouillard [Mr]	perhaps Joseph, a relative of François Drouillard; a mill operated by a Drouillard existed in Sandwich in 1825 [MORTp].
A. Duff, Sr (b. 1770) (d. Jun. 1809) [LS±25/MrMe]	possibly the father of Alexander Duff; born Scotland; m. Phillis (Phyllis) Grant on 20 Jan. 1801, daughter of Alexander Grant and Theresa Barthe [0171233]; JP, 1803; barrack master at A'burg [mortp].
A. Duff, Jr, (b. 1802, d. 1876)	son of Alexander Duff [0171233]; Lt. 1st Essex, 1826.
William Duff (b. 1779) (d. 12 Jul. 1861) [LS±25/Mr]	barrack master A'burg; adjutant of 1st Essex Militia, 1812; collector of customs Sandwich, 1807; JP, 1813–37; commisioner of customs, 1824; storekeeper; m. 21 Jan. 1810 Susanna McGregor, daughter of Gregor McGregor. First sheriff of Detroit; brother of Alexander Duff [Mortp] [0171233].
C. Durocher	possibly Charles Durocher; merchant at Detroit; Indian trader; m. Geneviève Réaume [0171233].
Edward Ellice (b. 23 Sep. 1783) (d. 17 Sep. 1863) [LS±25]	English entrepreneur and merchant, partner in North-West Co. and in Phyn, Ellice and Inglis; member of the Hudson's Bay Co.; husband of Altheah, younger sister of Earl Gray, and secondly of Lady Leicester, member of the British House of Commons, 1818–26 and 1830–63; secretary to British Treasury, 1830–34 [DCB 9].

Appendix 7.3   (continued)

Charles Elliott	judge DC, 1832–41; resident of San.
Matthew Elliott (b.c. 1739) (d. 7 May 1814) [LS–25/Me]	possibly the elder, Irish-born Matthew Elliott; Capt. ID 1777–84; Col. 1st Essex, 1798–1814; JP, 1788–1813; Sup. ID 1790–94, 1796–97, 1806–14, A'burg; MHA Essex, 1800–12. Partner in the trading firm of Elliott and Caldwell [1975p]. Indian trader, slaveowner, husband of Sarah Donovan [DCB 5].
Captain Matthew Elliott [LS–25/Me]	or the younger Elliott, son of Matthew Elliott and an Indian mother; JP WD, 1832; merchant; this man patented 1220 acres before 1812 [1975p].
Rev. F.G. Elliott [LS+25]	Francis Gore, son of Matthew Elliott, Sr, and Sarah Donovan.
R.H.B. Elliott [LS+25]	Robert Herriott Barclay Elliott, son of Matthew Elliott and Sarah Donovan.
Sarah Elliott [LS+25/MrMe]	the former Sarah Donovan, widow of Matthew Elliott; the daughter of Matthew Donovan, schoolmaster of Detroit [mortp].
William Elliott (b. 1775) (d. July 1860)	lawyer; Capt. 1st Essex Militia; ID; Pension Board WD; MHA Essex, 1830–34; Col. 2nd Regt. of Militia in Patriot raids, 1838 [0171234].
D. Fisher [Me]	perhaps David, a relative of Charles Fisher, blacksmith, or Frederick Fisher, loyalist, spirit merchant, or Daniel, Lt. 1st Essex [MUC].
W. Flemming [LS–25]	Capt. of a vessel in 1795 [JAP].
L.J. Fluett (b. 1800) (d. 13 May 1881) [LS+25]	m. Justine Réaume, daughter of a Petite Côté tavern keeper; lawyer; tutor of Albert Prince, son of Col. John Prince. Town clerk and JP San. [0171234].
George Wade Foot [LS+25]	sheriff, 1840–48 [Arm].
John Forsyth (b. 8 Dec. 1762) (d. 27 Dec. 1837)	merchant, head of Forsyth, Richardson and Co., involved in the X–Y Co; MLC L.C., 1827; ensign Mtl. Militia, 1797; Capt. 1st Battalion Mtl; major 1st Battalion, 1821; Lt. Col. Mtl Calvary, 1828; JP, 1821; husband of Margaret Grant, daughter of the prominent Mtl merchant [DCB 7].
Ad. Fox [LS–25]	perhaps Adelia Fox or more likely Adam Fox, who served as a private in the First Essex Militia.
J.B., J., J.G. Fox [LS±25]	descendants of a loyalist family. A Jeremiah Fox, made a militia land claim.
P. Fox	perhaps Philip (b.1800; d. 19 May 1844), tavern keeper in Romney.

Appendix 7.3   (continued)

James Fraser	Detroit trader c. 1787; sometime attorney at law: speculator in Harwich [1975p].
Jn. Fulmer [LS±25]	possibly John Casper Fulmer, UEL, from Pennsylvania [0171234].
S. Gerard (b. 1767) (d. 24 Mar. 1857) [LS±25]	presumably Samuel Gerrard the Irish-born fur trader, merchant, land speculator, and seigneur; partner with G. Moffatt; partner in Grant, Campion & Co (1795) and in Parker, Gerrard and Ogilvy, suppliers to the XY Company; partner Michilimackinac Company, 1806–32; involved in three interlocking firms in London, Quebec, and Mtl, 1817–21; shipowner; international debt collector; Pres. Bank of Mtl, 1820–26; Dir. Mtl. Savings Bank, 1826; shareholder Bank of Canada; supervisor of Alliance British & Foreign Life & Fire Assurance Co., 1830; agent for Ed. Ellice 1831; militia major, JP, L.C., 1821; seigneur [DCB 8].
P. Girty (b. 1796) (d. 1853) [LS–25/Mr]	presumed to be Prideaux, son of Catherine Malott and Simon (1741–1818), well-known Indian leader against the Americans; school superintendent, Gos. [mortp]. Prideaux Girty ran for the assembly in 1836 against John Prince, Francis Caldwell, and D. Langlois. His sister Sarah m. Joseph Munger of Colc. [0171234]; JP, 1833–36 [Arm].
Hon. James Gordon (b. 26 Aug. 1786) (d. 10 Apr. 1865) [LS±25/Me]	Scottish-born attorney, Albany partner of Askin; executor of Pattinson estate; merchant A'burg; spirit merchant; ensign Essex Militia c. 1807; Lt. Mil., 1809; paymaster WD, 1813; Lt. Col. 1822; MHA Kent, 1820; JP 1822; MLC, 1829–41 [Arm] [JKJ].
Charles Gouin	Lt.Mil. 1778; patented 900 acres in 1802 [1975p]. Presumed relative of Claude JP 1822–37; speculator in Harwich [HAMIL].
W.R. Graham [LS+25]	perhaps the innkeeper in Tilbury East.
Alexander Grant, Sr (b. 20 May 1734) (d. 8 May 1813) includes Alexander Grant, Jr [LS–25]	officer ID; JP Hesse, 1788–94; MLBDH, 1789; MLC, 1792–1813; MEC, 1792–1813; Heir and Devisee Commission, 1798–1812; lieutenant of the county, 1799 and 1807–13; commodore of the upper lakes; administrator of U.C., 1805–06. Husband of Therese Barthe, brother-in-law of John Askin, Sr. Part of his acreage may have included his son's entitlement as a SUE. Alexander Grant, Jr, was an MLC, 1831–41 [Arm.]. Through his ability to allocate cargo-space on Crown vessels before the development of private shipping, Grant was placed at the centre of the commercial network between Detroit and New York [DCB 5].
Grant references	Felicia (Phyllis) Grant, daughter of Alexander Grant, m. Alexander Duff [Denib]. See Duff.
	Eleanor Grant, daughter of Alexander Grant m. George Jacob, Sandwich, son of George Jacob [0171234]. See G. Jacob.

Appendix 7.3   (continued)

	Archange Grant, second wife of Thomas Dickson (bapt. 19 Feb. 1775–22 Jan. 1825). Dickson was a merchant; JP, 1800–1823; member of the Heir and Devisee Commission; MHA Lincoln, 1812–16; Lt. Col. militia, 1814 [DCB 6].
Thérèse Grant (b. 13 Feb. 1776) (d.c. 1801)	m. Thomas Wright, military surgeon, Royal American Regt. [JAP].
Elizabeth Grant	m. 12 June 1804 James Wood, lawyer and speculator (OR).
J. Haggerty (b. 1800, d. 1854) [LS+25]	possibly James Haggerty; of Sandwich and Maidstone; immigrant from Ireland [0171235].
Chs. Hairsine (b. 1775, d. 1857)	possibly Charles Hairsine; immigrant from England [0171235].
George B. Hall (b. Ireland 1780) (d. 9 Jan. 1821) [LS–25]/Mr]	presumably George Benson Hall, Sr; officer R.N. and commodore of the lakes, 1798–1813; sup. dock yard, 1813; naval storekeeper, 1813; major Essex Militia, 1818; merchant and spirit merchant; MHA Essex, 1816–20; JP, 1816–19; patented 800 acres in 1813. [1975p] [DCB 6]. Husband of Angelica Fortier (m. 1 Feb 1806).
George Benson Hall (b. U.C. 1810) (d. L.C. 4 Sep. 1876)	son of the elder of that name; businessman and lumberman [DCB 10]; inspector of licenses [Arm].
W. Gaspé Hall (b. 1805, d. 1882) [LS+25]	possibly William Gaspé Hall; one of the first coroners; collector of inland revenues for the WD; m. [—] Baby [0171235]. Paymaster 3rd. Essex [Douglas].
Joseph Hamilton	JP, 1822 [Arm]; owned three lots not included in the assessment roll of 1847.
Robert Hamilton (b 14 Sep. 1753) (d. 8 Mar. 1809)	Scottish son-in-law of John Askin; fur trader; partner with the Ellice brothers; partner with Richard Cartwright, John Askin, and Todd and McGill; cousin of Thomas Clark and Robert, Thomas, and Warren Dickson of Niagara; retailer and supplier to the fur trade and the British army. Land speculator who "controlled" 130,170 acres. JP Niagara, 1786, MLBND, 1788; Judge DCCP, 1788; MLC, 1792–1809; Lt. County of Lincoln, 1796; member of Heir and Devisees Commission, 1797; second husband of Catherine Askin [DCB 5].
William Hands (b. 10 Aug. 1756) (d. 20 Feb. 1836) [LS±25]	English; JP, 1796–1800; clerk of peace, 1801–02; sheriff, 1802–33; treasurer, postmaster, customs coll. Sandwich, 1809–76, and Registrar of Surrogate Court WD; Surrogate Court judge, 1824–36; inspector of licences; possibly the most extensive collector of offices for himself and his family in Upper Canada. Husband of Mary Abbott, daughter of James Abbott [1975p] [Arm] [JAP]. A trader, he held liquor licences and served in the militia.

William Hands (b. 14 Feb. 1792) (d. 1860)	son of William and Mary Hands.
Hands references	Ann Hands (b. 24 May 1793), child of William Hands and Mary Abbott, who died in 1860. She married Jean-Baptiste Baby on 5 May 1817 [Denib] [Ont. Reg.].
	Frances Hands (b. 18 Apr 1795), daughter of William Hands, m. John Alexander Wilkinson; MHA, Essex; surveyor [0171235].
	John Hands, child of William; ensign 2nd Essex, 1823; registrar of Essex, 1825–30 [MUC].
	Felix Hands (d. 1837), collector of customs and treasurer, 1836–37.
Samuel Harris [Mr]	perhaps Capt. Harris of the *Eagle*.
A. Harrow (b. 1751) (d. Jan. 1811) [LS–25]	Scottish, Lt. naval service, resident of Detroit until c. 1811 [JAP].
Rudolph Huffman	possibly a UEL in Colc.; m. Mrs Stephen Brush, née Jemima [0171235].
Susan Hunt	possibly Susan Caldwell (b. 1786, d. 1880), daughter of Col. Wm. Caldwell and Susan Baby; wife of Theobold "Wolf" Hunt, Lt. 70th Surrey Regt.; Capt. 70th, 1816; nephew of General James Wolfe [0171235].
George Ironside (b.c. 1761) (d. 31 May, 1831) [LS–25/Me]	Scottish-born, Lt. ID, clerk and storekeeper ID, A'burg; Capt. 1st Essex; acting superintendent of ID [1]808; Sup. Amherstburg, 1820; married Voce Massusia, a relative of the native leader "The Prophet"; patented 1,109 acres by 1803 [1975p]. Trader in Maumee [Mortp]; Commission for the Protection of Crown Lands from Injury [LAJ]. Militia [Douglas and DCB 6].
George Ironside (b.c. 1800) (d.14 July 1863)	son of George, clerk ID 1826 and then sup. ID, A'burg 1820–c. 1835; northern sup. Manitowaning; helped negotiate the Manitoulin Treaty in 1862; Capt. 1st Essex, 1838[DCB 9].
George Jacob (b.c. 1762) (d. 24 Dec. 1833) [LS±25]/Me]	English. Husband of Mary Archange Chêne *dit* Labutte; father of Monique and Felicity (b. 1801), respectively the wives of Charles Askin and Alexander McKee, Jr. Archange Jacobs (a third daughter) m. John Gowie Watson, customs inspector [1975p]. JP, 1806–33; Capt. Kent County militia; father-in-law of Alexander McKee.
George Jacob, Jr	spirit and general merchant; JP, 1822–37. m. Eleanor Grant [Mortp]. Someone of this name was a commissioner of the Clergy Corporation in 1819 and patented 1400 acres in Essex in 1808–10. Either George Sr or Jr was the agent for A.J. Robertson and one of them was MLBWD. Capt. 1st Kent militia, 1820 [MUC].

Appendix 7.3   (continued)

John Jackson (b.c. 1764) (d. 1836) [LS+25]	perhaps the St. Kitts-born merchant and pamphleteer; JP, 1836; resident of Georgina Township [DCB 7].
G. Johnson [LS+25]	perhaps Guy Johnson, relation of Sir John.
Daniel Knapp	tavern keeper.
Robert Lacklin	British regular [Douglas]; JP, 1837.
(Lauchlin,Lachan) [Me]	sheriff, 1837–39 [Arm]; soldier.
P.J. LaCroix [Me]	possible kinsman of W. Baby.
A. Langlois	This could be one of a number of people but is probably Antoine (b. 18 July 1774) or Alexis (b. 15 Nov. 1783) [LAJ].
D. Langlois [LS+25]	perhaps Dominique, innkeeper at Petite Côté [Douglas].
E. Larwell (Larwill) [LS+25]	U.S. army officer, school commissioner Raleigh Township; MPP, 1857; registrar Kent County, 1858 [Douglas].
J.P. Leduc [Me]	Owned unassessed land in 1847; a Paul Leduc made a militia claim.
Leith, Sheppard (Shepherd)and Duff [Me]	A'burg merchants; George Leith JP, 1791; MLBHE, 1789–94. The firm of Leith and Shepherd was a partner in the Miami Co. [Mortp]. Shepherd was Thomas Shepherd.
Jn. Little (b. 1730) (d. 1817)	UEL of Irish origin [CARD].
J. Lockhart [LS±25]	perhaps the American-born militia officer.
Jean-Baptiste Testard Louvigny de Montigny (b. 1 Nov. 1750) (d. 24 Feb. 1813)	Quebec-born fur trader and soldier. His second wife was Agathe Hay, daughter of Jehu Hay, lieutenant-governor of Detroit; MLBHE, 1791–92; lieutenant of the counties of Essex and Kent; captain, Royal Canadian Volunteer Regiment, 1795; JP Montreal, 1808 and 1810. In debt to John Askin, he died of battle wounds in the war of 1812 [DCB 5].
William Lymbrunner	His company is described along with Todd & McGill, and Forsyth & Richardson, as one of the principal houses at Quebec City and Mtl. [CARD].
A. Maisonville [Mr]	perhaps Alexis Loranger dit Maisonville, Indian trader, JP, 1788–1813, or his son. In 1825 one Maisonville operated a mill in Sandwich Township; spirit merchant [Mortp]; agent for John Askin [JAP]; clerk to Askin.

Appendix 7.3   (continued)

J. Malotte [LS±25/Mr]	perhaps Joseph Malotte, Lt. Mil. 1st Essex, 1824 [MUC].
P. Malotte [LS±25]	perhaps Peter Malotte, loyalist, New Settlement.
Theo. Mallot	perhaps the T. Mallot, resident of Gos., who married Ann Smith 17 Sept. 1838 [Ont. Reg.]; Lt. Mil. 1st Essex, 1822 [MUC].
George Herchmer Markland (b.c. 1790) (d. 17 May 1862)	ensign Frontenac Militia 1812; MLC 1820–38; MEC, 1822–36; registrar King's College, 1827; secretary-receiver Upper Canada Clergy Corporation, 1828; treasurer for sale of school lands 1831–38; arbitrator of customs revenue between U.C. and L.C., 1828–36; inspector-general of public accounts 1833. He resigned his offices amid sexual and financial scandal. Pupil of Strachan, friend of Robinson and James Baby [DCB 9] [Arm].
John Martin	business partner of John Askin [1975p]; trader.
Thomas Martin (b. 1780?) (d. 26 April 1850) [Me]	perhaps the son of John Martin [Mortp]. m. Charlotte Gignac [JAP].
Ed. Matthews [LS+25]	acquired land from Benjamin Springer.
Lt. John Maule [LS±25]	Loyalist.
A. McCormick (b.1728 or 1743) (d. 1803) [Mr]	possibly Alexander (b. 1728 or 1743, d. 1803), or his son of that name who was brother to William McCormick and a lieutenant of militia in 1826 [MUC], or the elder McCormick's grandson, the child of William McCormick and Mary Cornwall (1811–54). The youngest Alexander married Mary Burwell of Port Talbot in 1845. The grandfather was a native of northern Ireland and an Indian trader [0171236].
Mt. McCormick [LS±25]	possibly Matthew McCormick (b. 1797) of Col., m. Deborah Wright, daughter of Henry Wright; his 1st wife was Deborah Hitchcock [0171236]; Lt. Mil. 1826 [MUC].
William McCormick (b. 30 May 1784) (d. 18 Feb. 1840) [LS±25/MrMe]	American-born child of Alexander McCormick and Elizabeth Turner; JP, 1816; merchant in Colc; MHA Essex, 1812–24 [Mortp]; m. Mary Cornwall, daughter of John Cornwall [0171236]; ensign c. 1807; Capt. 1st Essex, 1812–14; major, 1822; Lt. Col., 1816 [JKJ]; deputy collector at A'burg, 1815; deputy postmaster, 1821; Board Militia Pensions, 1816; lessee Pelée Island 1815; supplier of cedar to the Ohio Railway and Fort Malden [DCB 7].

Appendix 7.3   (continued)

Thomas McCrae (d. 11 Jun. 1814)	MHA Kent, 1800–04; JP, 1806–13 [1975p]; tailor, UEL [HAMIL]; farmer; innkeeper; Capt. Mil., 1804–18 [JKJ].
Sir John A. Macdonald (b. 10 Jan. 1815) (d. 6 Jun. 1891) [LS+25]	lawyer, MHA Kingston, 1844–67 and 1867–74; receiver-general, 1847–48; commissioner of lands, 1847; attorney general of U.C., 1854; premier, province of Canada, 1857; prime minister of Canada, 1867–73 and 1878–91; land speculator; agent for British real estate investors; director of thirteen British and Canadian companies [DCB 11].
McDonnell and Holmes and Company [Mr]	merchants [Mortp]; perhaps William Holmes, partner in North-West Co. and with James Grant; perhaps Ronald McDonnell, soldier, Indian trader, and agent for Leith, Shepherd and Duff [JAP].
John. MacDonnell (b. 19 Apr. 1785) (d. 14 Oct. 1812) [LS+25]	some possibility this is the Scottish lawyer, 1808; MHA Glengarry; acting attorney-general, 1812; negotiator of American capitulation at Detroit; Lt. Col. of militia, killed at Queenston Heights [JAP]. Suitor of Mary Boyle Powell, the daughter of William Dummer Powell. Powell and General Isaac Brock helped secure a number of appointments for him, including that of attorney-general [DCB 5].
J. McDougall [MrMe]	perhaps James (b. 1783?–d. 17 Aug. 1851), fur trader, employee of North-West Co. and the Hudson's Bay Co. [Mortp].
William McGee [LS–25]/Mr]	possibly an Irish emigrant; miller [0171236].
James McGill (b. 6 Oct. 1744) (d. 19 Dec. 1813) [LS±25]	prominent Scottish-born merchant; JP, 1776; land speculator and mortgage holder in Quebec, Kingston, and York and Essex Counties; philanthropist; fur trader; partner with Isaac Todd in the North-West Co., 1779; friend of John Askin, who acted as his agent; relative by marriage of Bishop Strachan; MHA L.C., 1792–96; Montreal West, 1800; and Montreal East, 1804; MEC, 1792; Col. Mil., 1812 [DCB 5].
P. McGill and W. Stephens [Me]	perhaps Peter McGill, who was born Peter McCutcheon but who took his maternal uncle's family name. Scottish-born (August 1789), partner of Samuel Gerrard, he died on 28 September 1860. He was JP, 1827; MLC of U.C., 1832 and of United Canada, 1841–60; speaker of the L.C. assembly, 1847–48; MEC; commissioner of the British American Land Company, 1834; president of the Bank of Mtl, 1834–1860; Chairman of the St Lawrence and Champlain Railway Company, 1834. William Stephens, was a dry-goods merchant of Mtl [Mortp][DCB 8].
Gregor McGregor (b. 1738) (d. 24 Nov. 1810)	trader; sheriff, District of Hesse, 1788; sup. Inland Navigation, 1788; major of militia, 1791; JP, 1800–10 [Arm]. He married (12 Aug. 1776) Regina Suzanne Robert. There were nine children. Of these, Ann became the second wife of Dr Robert Richardson. Suzanne married William Duff.

Appendix 7.3 (continued)

Angus MacKintosh (McIntosh) (b.c. 1755) (d. 25 Jan. 1833) [LS±25/Mr]	father of James McIntosh and son of Duncan, chieftain of Clan McIntosh; JP, 1796–1806 and 1816–19; MLC, 1820. Connected with the North-West Co. and co-partner of the Miami Company [1975p]. Member of reconstituted Land Board, 1822. Merchant, spirit merchant, distiller, shipowner, land speculator [Mortp]. His cousin was Aeneas Shaw of the Executive Council from whom he sought help on land matters.

Ann McIntosh, daughter of Angus McIntosh, m. Henry Jackson Hunt (1811), the second mayor of Detroit [Denib].

Elizabeth McIntosh, daughter of Angus McIntosh, m. Robert Todd Reynolds (R.T. Reynolds?) [DENIB]. |
Alexander McKee, Sr (b.c. 1735) (d. 15 Jan. 1799) [LS–25]	Col.; justice CCP, 1788; Lt. County Essex, 1792–99; JP, 1796; D/Sup. ID of U.C., 1794–99; MLBHE; father of Thomas Mckee. Before coming to Upper Canada he served as d/agent ID, Fort Pitt, Pittsburg, and Detroit. In 1797–98 he patented 2352 acres in the WD [DCB 4].
Thomas McKee (b.c. 1770) (d. 20 Oct. 1814) [LS±25]	son of Alexander McKee; D/I.G.,ID; Sup.ID North West District, 1796–99; Sup. ID WD, 1799; MHA Kent, 1797–1800; MHA Essex, 1800–04 [Mortp]; ensign 4th Battalion 60th Regt, 1791; Lt., 1795; Capt., 1796; major, 3rd Essex Militia, 1812–14. Husband of Therese Askin [DCB 6].
Thomas McLean	perhaps a relation of John McLean, Irish Loyalist.
William McLean [Mr]	perhaps related to John McLean also.
Rev. McMurray	probably the Rev. William McMurray (b. 19 September 1810; d. 19 May 1894). Irish-born cleric of the Church of England and Ireland; pupil of John Strachan and teacher of children of the elite; missionary to the Ojibwa; defender of his church's interest in the clergy reserves [DCB 12].
Sir Allan Napier MacNab (b. 19 Feb. 1798) (d. 8 Aug. 1862)	developer/speculator; purchaser of loyalist rights; regular and militia officer, 1813–38; JP, 1838; registrar Wentworth, 1840; MHA Wentworth and Hamilton, 1830–42; speaker, 1838–41; co-premier, Province of Canada, 1854–56 [DCB 9].
Patrick McNiff (d. May 1803)	Irish-born merchant and surveyor; partner with the Askins and Alexander Henry in the Cuyahoga purchase [JAP]. In 1796 he became surveyor of Wayne County (Michigan) and judge of the CCP [DCB 5].
McTavish, McGillivray and Co. [Me]	merchants and fur traders; members of the North-West Co.; after 1821, when the firm included Thomas Thain, this company was the Mtl agent of the Hudson's Bay Co. [Mortp].
Meldrum and Park [LS–25/Me]	See separate entries for George Meldrum and William Park. Meldrum and Park were members of the Miami Company with John Askin [1975p].

Appendix 7.3   (continued)

George Meldrum (b.c. 1737) (d. 9 Apr. 1817)	Meldrum was trader, coroner; JP, 1796–1800; MLBJH, 1788 [1975p].
Meldrum reference	Mary Ann Meldrum, daughter of George Meldrum; m. 1801 William McDowell Scott, U.S. marshal; justice [0171236].
Antoine Meloche	perhaps a relation of Teresa Meloche, mother-in-law of Claude Thomas Réaume [1975p].
William Mickle [LS+25]	perhaps the man who married (3 March 1852) Mary Arner of Mal. [Ont. Reg.]. Lt. Mil. 1st Essex, 1826 [MUC].
Hon. George Moffat (b. 13 Aug. 1787) (d. 25 Feb. 1865) [LS±25]/Me]	English-born; fur trader and merchant of Mtl.; partner in Gillespie, Moffatt and Co.; land speculator; investor in speculative land companies including the Lower Canada Co.; representative of the British/American Land Company. He was involved in banking, mining, insurance, and railroad companies; president Mtl Board of Trade, MLC, 1831; MEC, 1839; MHA Canada, 1841–47 [Mortp][DCB 9].
William Morris (b. 31 Oct. 1786) (d. 29 Jun. 1858) [LS+25]	Scottish; ensign 1st Leeds, 1812, Lt. Col. 22nd Carletons, 1822; storekeeper, Brockville and Perth; JP, Perth 1818; chief stockholder Tay Navigation Company; MHA Carleton, 1820–24, Lanark, 1824–1828, 1828–30, 1830–34; MLC, 1836–41; warden Johnstown District, 1842; receiver general, 1844; president of Executive Council of United Canada, 1846–47; distiller, businessman, speculator, purchaser of loyalist rights [DCB 8].
David Moses	See entry for Moses David.
S. Mott	merchant, Thames River [0171233].
Roswell Mount (b. 1797) (d. 19 Jan. 1834) [LS+25]	Upper Canada-born surveyor, politician, militia officer, JP, MHA Middlesex, 1830–34; Crown land agent WD, 1832; trained as a surveyor under Mahlon Burwell; SUE; private, 1812–14; Capt. 4th Middlesex Regt., 1823; Lt. Col. 5th Middlesex, 1832 [DCB 6].
Jos. Munger [LS+25]	possibly Joseph Munger (b. 1788); m. Sarah Girty, daughter of Simon Girty (1741–1818). Son of William Munger [0171236].
William Munger (b. 1756, d. 1829) [Mr]	UEL, tavern keeper [Mortp]. Served in Capt. Wm. Caldwell's Co. of Butler's Rangers; his daughter Mary m. Leonard Kratz (Scratch, b. 1756, d. 1829) [0171236].
T. Murphy [LS±25]	possibly Timothy Murphy; ID; patentee of Lot 5 on the south side of the Malden Road, Colc., 1836 [0171236].
Horatio Nelson (Horace) [LS+25]	resident of Gos.; Capt. 3rd Essex; JP, 1837 [Arm].
J. Nelson	If this is Jonathan, he was the sailing master in the marine service. He was married to Elizabeth Donovan and was a brother-in-law of Matthew Elliott [Mortp].

Appendix 7.3   (continued)

J. Nelson and M. Donovan [Mr]	See separate entries.
L. Parent	perhaps Laurent (b. 13 Sep. 1740, d. 1818).
John R. Park (b. 26 Mar. 1801) (d. 2 Oct. 1880) [LS+25/Me]	storekeeper and merchant [Mortp]. John Richardson Park of Colc. and A'burg, originally of Massachusetts; Colc. councillor and treasurer [0171237].
Thomas F. Park (b. 17 May 1799) (d. 1864) [LS+52/Me]	member of A'burg firm of Park and Co.; general merchants, wharfingers, and steamboat owners [Mortp]. American-born.
William Park (buried 4 Oct. 1811)	William Park was the son-in-law of Claude Jean Gouin and the husband of Thérèse Gouin; JP, 1796–1806 [1975p]. He was buried from the home of Richard Pattinson in Sandwich [0171237].
Daniel Pastorius [LS–25/MrMe]	liquor licensee/trader [Mortp].
Mary Ann Patterson (Pattinson)	grand-daughter of John Askin, Sr, and daughter of Ellen Phyllis Askin and Richard Patterson of San. With other persons unidentified, Mary Ann Patterson patented an additional 1000 acres in 1812 [1975p].
Richard Pattinson (Patteson, Patterson) (b. 1773) (d. 1 Jan. 1818) [LS–25/Mr]	Indian trader [JAP]; shipowner; lumberman; m. Judith de Joncaire de Chabert (24 April 1802) and then Eleanor, daughter of John Askin [1975p]; Capt. Essex militia, c. 1807, 1812–24; JP, 1803–16; MHA Essex, 1812–16 [JKJ]. James Gordon and George Jacob were his executors.
T. Paxton [Mr]	non-assessed owner of Essex land in 1847. Possibly this is the man who was reeve of Reach and Scugog, Ontario, in 1852. A naval officer of this name commanding the *Speedy* perished 7–8 October 1804, and a Thomas Paxton, a miller, received 1200 acres from Lieutenant Governor Simcoe c. 1795.
William Dummer Powell (b. 5 Nov. 1755) (d. 6 Sep. 1834)	Loyalist; soldier; judge CCP Detroit, 1789, and U.C., 1791: MLBHE, 1789–92; puisne judge of King's Bench, 1794; Heirs and Devisees, 1797; MEC, 1808–25; treason commissioner, 1814; war losses commissioner, 1815; MLC, and speaker, 1816–25; chief justice U.C., 1816. Major landowner beyond Essex [DCB 6].
Robert Pilkington (b. 7 Nov.1765) (d. 6 July 1834)	English, 2nd Lt. Royal Artillery, 1787; transferred Royal Engineers, 1789; Lt. 1793; captain, 1801; Lt. Col., 1809; Col., 1815; major-general, 1825; inspector of fortifications (U.K.); friend of Elizabeth Simcoe and of John White, attorney general. He acquired 15,000 acres in Pilkington Township and enticed English settlers to his property. He returned to England in 1803. As the engineer at Detroit he was a member of the Land Board [DCB 6].

Appendix 7.3   (continued)

Richard Pollard (b. 1 Jan. 1753) (d. 6 Nov. 1824) [LS–25]	English-born Indian trader, associated with Mackinac Co.; sheriff, Essex and Kent, 1792–24, electoral officer, 1792–1824; registrar Essex and Kent, 1794–1824; registrar of Surrogate Court, 1794–1801; judge of the court, 1801–24; postmaster; JP, 1816–24; MLBWD, 1822; Anglican deacon, 1802; prison chaplain, 1802; priest, 1804; friend of William Hands, who was his executor [DCB 6].
A. Prince [Me]	possibly Arabella or more probably Albert Prince, son of Col. John Prince [Mortp].
John Prince (b. 12 Mar. 1796) (d. 30 Nov. 1870) [LS+25/Me]	English attorney; JP, 1833; Col. 3rd. Essex Militia, 1838; MHA Essex, 1836–54; MLC Western Division, 1856–60; judge of the District of Algoma, judge of the Surrogate Court Sault Ste. Marie, 1860; entrepreneur, brewer, mine and railway promoter [Mortp][DCB 9].
Quetton (Laurent) de St. George (b. 4 Jun. 1771) (d. 8 Jun. 1821)	French royalist refugee, soldier, "Loyalist," merchant, fur trader, shopkeeper at York with branches elsewhere including A'burg; married a Baby; had an estate of 26,000 acres in 1831 [DCB 6].
Jn. Quick	possibly John, the son of Alexander Quick, UEL from Cornwall, England; or his grandson (b. 1813), whose father was Jos. Quick (b.c. 1769, d. 1845); Indian captive; m. 1810 Susannah Munger [0171237].
Charles Reaume (b. 4 Feb. 1743) (d. 20 Feb. 1813)	Capt. ID; recipient of Indian grants, cousin of Claude Thomas Reaume [LAJ].
Charles Reaume reference	Térèsa Réaume, daughter of Charles Réaume (b. 1780); m. Hippolyte Campeau, son of Charles Campeau and Teresa Parent (daughter of Lawrence Parent (b. 1740)) [Denib].
Peter (Pierre) Reaume (b. 6 Oct. 1709)	husband of Susanne Hubert, *dit* Lacroix. Father of Suzanne Réaume, the wife of Jacques Duperron Baby, and of Charlotte, wife of Pierre-Charles Danseau de Muy, son of the commandant of Detroit [1975p].
Claude Thomas Reaume (b. 7 Aug. 1743)	husband of Geneva Janis, son of Pierre and Suzanne Réaume. Brother of Bonadventure. Patentee of 1407 acres in the WD.
Francis Reaume	presumed relative of the Réaumes; patented 1200 acres WD, 1801–02.
Antoine Reaume	presumed relative of the Réaumes; patented 1200 acres WD, 1801; liquor licensee.
Lawrence Reaume	patentee of 1200 acres WD 1801–02; presumed relative of the Réaumes.

Appendix 7.3   (continued)

John Redpath (b. 1796) (d. 5 Mar. 1869) [Me]	perhaps John Redpath, Scottish merchant of Mtl; building contractor Lachine and Rideau canals; dir. Fire Assurance and Telegraph Companies; dir. Bank of Mtl and investor in metals, shipping, and telegraph companies; sugar refiner; industrialist [DCB 9].
Thomas Reynolds and family [LS±25/MrMe]	assistant commissary at Detroit from about 1780 and later at A'burg; JP, 1803–10. Of the 3535 acres patented, by 1808, 1400 acres were patented by Reynold's seven children and 1000 acres were patented in Harwich Township and were never settled [1975p].
Robert Reynolds (b. 1781) (d.c. 1864)	son of Thomas Reynolds [Mortp]; his wife was the widow of McGill's stepson and a beneficiary of his will. He was with the commissary [JAP]; JP, 1818 and 1837 [Arm].
Ebenezer Reynolds	JP, 1813–26; sheriff, 1833–37 [Arm]. Lt. Col. 1st Essex, 1799 (Lauber)
M. Reynolds	Margaret Reynolds (1764–1855), artist [Ont. Reg.].
Hon. J. Richardson (b.c. 1754) (d. 18 May 1831) [LS±25]	probably John Richardson; engaged in uncle's firm of Phyn, Ellice and Company; speculation in bills of exchange; partner in Forsyth, Richardson, Michilimackinac, and the fur companies of the southwest; shareholder in North-West and X-Y companies; distiller; banker; MHA L.C., 1792, 1804, 1811; ensign Mtl Militia 1792; honorary executive councillor, L.C., 1804; judge Court of Appeals; involved in the construction of the Lachine Canal; director of Mtl. Fire Insurance Co. c. 1820; co-founder Bank of Mtl; MLC L.C., 1816; commissioner of import duties, 1793–1828; financier of Mtl. General Hospital; of Scottish origin [DCB 6].
Dr Robert Richardson	of Annandale, Scotland; assistant surgeon, Queen's Rangers; m. Madeline Askin, daughter of John Askin [0171237], and then Ann McGregor [JAP]; MLBWD, 1819.
John Ridsdale [Mr]	storeowner in Colc. [Mortp].
Arthur John Robertson [LS+52/Me]	of Inshes House, Invernesshire, Scotland; chairman, British North American Colonial Committee; possible relation of William Robertson; absentee speculator.
William Robertson (b.c. 1760) (d. 13 Dec. 1806) [LS–25]	justice CCP, 1788; MLBHE, 1789; MEC, 1792; MLC, 1792. Brother of Capt. Samuel Robertson, the son-in-law of John Askin, Sr, by his marriage to Catherine Askin. Clerk to John Askin, 1782 and co-partner with Askin, 1784–87. With Askin and others he engaged in the Cuyahoga purchase in 1795; holder with David Robertson, Richard Cartwright, Robert Hamilton, and John Askin of an exclusive contract to provision Upper Canada's garrisons from 1793 to 1795. A Scottish merchant he moved to England about 1792. Patented 3209 acres by 1813 [1975p][DCB 5].

Appendix 7.3   (continued)

Sir John Beverley
Robinson
(b. 26 July 1791)
(d. 31 Jan. 1863)

lawyer, politican, judge, author; pupil of John Strachan;
Capt. 3rd. Yorks, 1812; Col. 2nd. Regt East York Militia, 1823;
attorney general U.C., 1812–14 and 1818; MHA York,
1820–1830; MEC, 1829–62; MLC, 1830–41; chief justice, 1829–38;
KCB, 1850; baronet of the United Kingdom, 1854; presiding
judge, Court of Errors and Appeals; speculator in land in
Simcoe, York, Ontario and Peel counties [DCB 9]. In Essex he
acted with Strachan and Allan.

Salmon, Salmoni,
Solomon, T.
[LS+25]

possibly Thomas Salmoni; merchant; hotel keeper [0171238].

L. Scratch
[LS–25/MrMe]

private, Butler's Rangers [Mortp].

P. Scratch
(b. 1786, d. 1871)
[LS±25]

possibly Peter Scratch; son of Leonard Scratch and Mary
Munger; m. Mary Wigle (b. 1793, d. 1872) [0171238].

J. Searle
[Mr]

possibly son of William, innkeeper in A'burg [JAP].

Prideaux Selby
(bapt. 21 Dec. 1747)
(d. 9 May 1813)
[LS–25]

Lt. 5th Regt., 1785; ass. secretary of ID, 1792–1809; JP, 1796–1806;
DCC judge, 1800; MEC, 1808–13; auditor general of land
patents, 1809–13; receiver general of public accounts, 1808–13;
English [1975p][DCB 5][Arm].

J. Sewell
(b. 6 Jun. 1766)
(d. 11 Nov. 1839)
[LS–25]

possibly Jonathan Sewell, the American-born son of the
attorney general of Massachusetts; attorney general of Quebec
(pro tem. 1790); solicitor general, 1793; chief justice, 1808–38,
and thereby MEC, 1808; MLC, 1808; speaker L.C., 1809
[DCB 7].

Hon. John Graves
Simcoe
(b. 25 Feb. 1752)
(d. 26 Oct. 1806)

ensign 35 Regt. 1770; Capt. 40th Regt., 1775; major, Queen's
Rangers, 1777; member of the British Parliament, 1790;
first lieutenant governor of Upper Canada. As such he made
large grants but was distrustful of merchants and speculators.
He left on medical leave in 1796 and resigned in 1798. English-
born. [1975p] [DCB 5].

C.A. Smith
[LS+25]/Me]

clerk CCP, 1790–94; adopted chief of the Shawnees, killed at
Fallen Timbers, 1794 [JAP].

Sir David
W.M. Smith
(b. 4 Sep. 1764)
(d. 9 May 1837)

ensign 5th Regt, 1779; Lt., 1792; Capt., 1795; Col. Middlesex
Militia, 1797; Col. York Militia, 1798; JP Nassau, 1792;
lieutenant of the County of York, 1798–1804; master of
Chancery, 1799 [JKJ]. MHA Essex and Suffolk, 1792–96; Lincoln,
1797–1800; Norfolk, Oxford, and Middlesex, 1800–04; speaker
L.A., 1801–02; MEC, 1796–1802; a/surveyor general U.C.,
1792–98; surveyor general, 1798–1804, and during this period
accumulated 20,000 acres in twenty-one townships; commandant
of Detroit. Knight, author, attorney, soldier, and personal friend
of John Askin, who helped secure his election to the legislature.
Born in England, he returned there c. 1804. [1975p][DCB 7].

Appendix 7.3   (continued)

Thomas Smith (b. 1754) (d. 3 Mar. 1833) [LS–25]	Capt. ID, 1776–77; loyalist; Capt. militia; clerk CCP, 1788; JP, 1796; MHA Kent, 1797–1800; d/surveyor, 1799; notary, merchant, and business associate of John Askin [1975p]; received 4455 acres as surveyor [JKJ]. Welsh; m. Angelique Charlotte Crête; by 1804 had patented 1336 acres [1975p][LAJ][JAP].
John Snyder [LS–25]	possibly the UEL; m. Julianna Fox, daughter of Jacob Fox and Madeline Wigle; patented 720 acres by 1808 [0171238].
Benjamin Springer [LS+25]	d/surveyor, trained by Mahlon Burwell. Son of Daniel Springer and Ruth Fairchild [Arm].
T. Squire et al [LS+25]	possibly Thomas Squire (b. 1805, d. 1891); of English origin; blacksmith and farmer [0171238].
T.A. Stayner (b. 16 Dec. 1788) (d. 23 Jun. 1868) [LS+25]	Nova Scotia-born; British regular soldier until 1823; postmaster Quebec, 1824; postmaster general U.C. and L.C., 1827. As postmaster general, he enjoyed a salary comparable to that of the governor general; JP Quebec 1838 and Trois- Rivières, 1839; director, Bank of U.C. [DCB 9].
Jn. Stockwell [LS±25]	possibly the UEL; militia officer or his son of the same name (b. 1795?, d. 13 Aug. 1880); m. Polly Botsford, daughter of Henry Botsford and Nancy (Angelique) McDougall, daughter of Lt. George McDougall and Mary Frances Navarre [0171238].
J. Stokes (d. 1853) [Mr]	butcher; "served the troops of the Rebellion" and later at Fort Malden [0171238].
John Strachan (b. 12 Apr. 1778) (d. 1 Nov. 1867)	Scottish-born; Anglican rector of Cornwall (1803–12) and of York (1812); archdeacon of York, 1827; bishop of Toronto, 1839–67; second husband of Ann McGill (née Wood); speculator in stocks and lands; MEC, 1815–36; MLC, 1820–41. Friend and teacher of the children of the prominent [DCB 9].
Strachan, Allan, and Robinson [LS±25]	See separate entries for John Strachan, William Allan, and Sir John Beverley Robinson.
Samuel Street, Sr (b. 2 Jan. 1753) (d. 3 Feb. 1815) [LS–25]	American-born Loyalist; Indian trader; merchant, land speculator with Oliver Phelps and Nathaniel Gohan in N.Y. Member of Niagara Co.; supplier of Holland Land Co., N.Y.; agent of Wm. Berczy and the German Co.; JP, 1788 and 1796- 1815, District of Nassau; judge Niagara District Court, 1807; D/LT. County of Lincoln; MHA Lincoln, 1797; speaker, 1800, 1808; Capt. 3rd Lincoln Militia, 1809; deputy paymaster militia, 1813–14 [DCB 5].
Samuel Street, Jr (b. 14 Mar. 1775) (d. 24 Aug. 1844) [LS–25]	American-born merchant; nephew of the above; JP, 1796; partner with Thomas Dickson and Thomas Clark, 1798–99, and 1808–35 partner of Thomas Dickson; JP Niagara, 1796; d/registrar Niagara; Capt. 3rd. Lincolns, 1812; Lt. Col., 1822;

Appendix 7.3   (continued)

	Col. 1839; shareholder in four banks, investor in Welland canal, railways, and harbours. Land speculator throughout the province; purchaser of mortgages, tax–delinquent, and loyalist land and land rights; agent for Forsyth and Richardson, lender to the ecclesiastical and political establishments [DCB 7].
Thomas Clark(e) Street (b.c. 1814) (d. 6 Sep. 1872) [LS–25]	son of Samuel; lawyer, director of Niagara Falls Suspension Bridge Co., president Gore Bank, dir. Canadian Bank of Commerce, Bank of U.C., British American Assurance. Land speculator; dealer in mortgages; MHA Welland, 1851 and 1861; JP Welland; Lt. Col. militia. Left an estate of $3–$4 million [DCB 10].
Charles Stuart (b. 1783) (d. 26 May 1865) [LS+25]	Jamaican-born; military service with E. India Co.; JP, 1820–21, abolitionist, and pamphleteer; or a Charles Stewart, also a resident of A'burg, who was MLBWD, 1819–25[DCB 9].
D. Stuart [Me]	perhaps David Stuart (b. 1763, d. 1853), fur trader; cousin of John Stuart of North-West Co.; partner in 1810 in John Jacob's Astor's American Fur Co., co-founder of Astoria [Mortp].
Jms. Stuart	tavern keeper in Dover West.
Hon. Thomas Talbot (b. 19 Jul. 1771) (d. 5 Feb. 1853)	Anglo-Irish aristocrat, regular soldier, friend of Duke of Wellington, private secretary to Simcoe, 1792; Capt. 85th Foot, 1793; major, 1794; Lt. Col. 5th Regt., 1796; O.C 1st Middlesex militia; developer and supervisor of land settlement in twenty-nine townships; MLC, 1809; close friend of William Allan; recipient of 5000 acres as a field officer and acquired 65,000 acres in Dunwich and Aldborough townships in Elgin County [DCB 8].
Thain, Forsyth and Richardson [LS–25]	See John Forsyth, J. Richardson, and Thomas Thain.
Thomas Thain (b. 1761) (d. 1832)	perhaps a relative of Richardson and Forsyth; partner in New North-West Company, 1804–09; later in McTavish and McGillivray (1814); shareholder and director and VP of Bank of Mtl, 1819–25; Lt. militia; MHA Mtl East, 1820–24; shareholder Bank of Canada; commissioner for the Lachine Canal; Scottish origin [DCB 6].
R. Thornton [LS+25]	perhaps Col. Thornton, aide-de-campe; possible relative of Isaac Todd [JAP].
Isaac Todd (b. c. 1742) (d. 22 May 1819) [LS–25]	Irish-born; JP L.C., 1765; fur trader and merchant; partner with the Frobisher brothers and with James McGill, with whom by 1794 he monopolized the Upper Mississippi trade; Mtl agent for Phyn, Ellice and Co., 1774; co-founder of the North-West Co., 1779; with McGill and Askin, a participant in the Miami Co.; Capt. militia, 1787; acquired 44,160 acres in U.C. and L.C., 1802. [DCB 5].

Appendix 7.3   (continued)

John Trudel	possible relative of Abraham Tredell; JP, 1796–1803.
J.G. Watson (John Gowie Watson) [LS±25/Me]	customs inspector [Mortp]; JP, 1826–37 [Arm]; spirit merchant.
J. Wigle	possibly John Wigle (b. 1778); m. 9 Feb 1802, Susannah Scratch [0171239].
L. Wigle [LS+25]	possibly Leonard Wigle of Gos. S. [0171239]; Lt. Mil. 1st Essex [MUC].
Sol. Wigle (b. 1822)	Solomon, farmer and merchant: member Gosfield Council, 1850; future MP [Atlas].
W. Wigle (b. 1781) (d. 1860) [LS±25]	possibly Wendel Wigle, second child of John Wendel Wigle; location in Gos. S. [0171239]; peddler [Douglas].
Asa Wilcox (b, 1802, d. 1892) [LS+25]	Asa, nephew of Asa Wilcox of Colc. [0171239].
Elisha Wilcox [LS−25]	perhaps Eley. Wilcox of Butler's Rangers.
Hezekiah Wilcox (b. 1769) (d. 2 Nov.1851) [LS±25]	son of Elisha (Elijah) or grandson (b. 14 Oct 1822, d. 14 Jan 1897).
Isaac Wilcox (d. 1862) [LS±25]	son of Sarah and Hezekiah.
Wildes, Pickersgill and Company [Mr]	William Conliffe Pickersgill, merchant of New York, and George Wildes, merchant of London [Mortp].
John A. Wilkinson (b. 14 Sept 1789) (d. 17 Sept 1862)	Irish-born; regular and militia soldier, 1814–38; surveyor; judge of Surrogate Court, 1836; MHA Essex, 1824–28 and 1834–36; husband of Frances Hands [Mortp] [Douglas].
Thomas Williams (b. 1768, d.c. 1806)	blacksmith, ID [HAMIL].
	or
Thomas Williams (d. 1785)	Albany-born merchant, justice, and notary who patented 405 acres in 1797 [1975p] [JAP]. Partner of John Casety, husband of Therese Baby.
John Williams [LS−25]	perhaps John R. Williams (b. 1782, d. 1854); mayor of Detroit [JAP] or Lt. Mil. 1st Kent 1825 [MUC].
James Woods (b. 1778, d. 1828) [LS±25/MrMe]	ensign 1804; Capt. of militia, 1812; JP, 1813; attorney, son-in-law of Commodore Alexander Grant [Mortp].

Appendix 7.3   (continued)

W.R. Wood	DCC, 1847–48.
Henry Wright [Mr]	most likely the reeve of Mal., 1850, but possibly an ancestor of the same name who was a UEL [Mortp].
John Wright [Mr]	municipal officer And. 1845; a less probable candidate is a UEL. of that name who acquired land in Gos., 1793–94 [Mortp].

No biographical information was found for the following individuals. They are listed by their land-acquisition activity.

[LS–25] = H. Bruner; F. Gates; Jn. Hartley; Jul. Langlois; Jms. Mailloux; H. McDougall; P. McDougall; E. Phelps; S. Sessions

[LS+25] = S. Bullen; J. Cochrane; Jn. Cunningham; P. Wright; Eliza Wilson; J. Hillair; F. Janisse; J. Marontette; L. Montreille; Chas. Montague; A. Reid; W. Sandford; A., Abel and Alex Stewart; Hy. Whaley; C.L. Wigle

[LS±25] = Rev. Thos. Edwards; A. Laferty; J.B. Ouellette; Mirtle Wigle

[Mr] = S. Hogan; J. House; P. Janette; C. Labadie; J. Laframboise; L.J.F. Laretto; T. McDonell; P. Merhoeff

[Me] = A. Wilcox Jr.; S. Janisse; C. Lamarche; A. Laroque; P.A. Laroque; Margaret McDonald; W.W. Miller; J. Pigot

[MrMe] = Augustin Lagrave

[LS+25/Me] = C.C. Allen

[LS–25/Me] = Joseph Strong

[LS–25/Mr] = J.B. Valade

Appendix 8.1   Sheriff's Deeds in Essex County, 1818-1852

Year	Buyer	Acres	Price (£.s.d)	Pence/Acre	Previous Transaction	Year	Previous Seller	Previous Buyer	Previous Acreage	Price (£.s.d)
Sherrif Sales by Ebenezer Reynolds										
1835	Clarke/Street	45	3.3.3	16.92	Bargain&Sale	1809	P. Godet	Tho. Smith	200	63.4.1
1835	Jn. Fulmer	aol.*	36.5.0		Patent	1806	Crown	Mt.Elliot	aol	
1836	Lachlan	aol	740.0.0		Patent	1819	Crown	Wm.Mccormick	90	
1836	Lachlan	aol	740.0.0	3.53	Patent	1804	Crown	Wm. Wright	162	
1836	Wm. Sanford	100	2.18.9	4.55	Patent	1813	Crown	Simon Girty	all	
1837	Pat Strong	200	3.15.10	4.17	Patent	1826	Crown	M. Burwell	200	64.15.0
1837	Jas. Askin	113	1.19.4	4.70	Bargain&Sale	1826	M. Burwell	R. Mount	aol	85.15.0
1837	J. Morrow	150	2.18.9	4.50	Bargain&Sale	1826	M. Burwell	R. Mount	150	100.0.0
1837	J. Morrow	200	3.15.0	24.75	Bargain&Sale	1826	M. Burwell	R. Mount	200	104.0.0
1838	C. Berczy	40	4.2.6	4.55	Bargain&Sale	1822	Wm. Elliot	M.D. Nelson	aol	
1838	Chs. Berczy	200	3.15.10	15.90	Patent	1826	Crown	M. Burwell	aol	7.10.0
1838	Sam Wise	100	6.12.6	15.90	Indenture	1827	Benj. Mcbean	Benj. Wheet	100	7.10.0
1843	Sam Wise	100	6.12.6		Indenture	1827	Benj. Mcbean	Benj. Wheet	100	
Sherrif Sales by G.W. Foot										
1836	T.C. Street	40	9.5.0	55.50	Bargain&Sale	1803	Jn. Askin	J. Mcgill	aol	
1840	L. Montrail	30	4.3.0	33.20	Bargain&Sale	1807	Jn. Askin	J. Mcgill	200	
1840	T.C. Street	70	4.12.5	15.84	Bargain&Sale	1807	Askin	Jms. Mcgill	200	
1842	J. Prince	aol	175.0.0		Bargain&Sale	1841	Dixie	A. Duff	100	100.0.0
1843	Chs.Woods	45	5.9.4	29.16	Bargain&Sale	1828	M. Burwell	I. Wilcox	aol	50.0.0
1843	Chs.Woods	50	4.12.5	22.18	Bargain&Sale	1807	Jn. Askin	Jms. Mcgill	aol	
1843	Chs.Woods	25	4.12.5	44.36	Bargain&Sale	1803	Askin	Jms. Mcgill	aol	
1843	Chs.Woods	48	4.12.5	23.10	Bargain&Sale	1807	Jn. Askin	Jms. Mcgill	aol	

Appendix 8.1 (continued)

Year	Buyer	Acres	Price (£.s.d)	Pence/ Acre	Previous Transaction	Year	Previous Seller	Previous Buyer	Previous Acreage	Price (£.s.d)
1843	T.C. Street	40	4.17.0	29.10	Bargain&Sale	1803	J. Askin	J. Mcgill	aol.	
1846	J. Mcphartin	50	18.15.0	90.00	Bargain&Sale	1846	F. Tiffany	S. Bullen	aol.	1033.0.0
1847	T.C. Street	47	4.12.5	23.60	Bargain&Sale	1807	Jn. Askin	Jms. Mcgill	aol.	
1847	T.C. Street	45	4.12.5	24.64	Patent	1804	Crown	Jn. Askin	200	
1847	T.C. Street	69	4.12.5	16.07	Bargain&Sale	1831	Wm. Elliot	J. Mcgill	aol.	150.0.0
1847	T.C. Street	40	4.12.0	27.60	Bargain&Sale	1804	Askin	Mcgill	200	
1847	T.C. Street	75	4.12.5	14.79	Bargain&Sale	1807	Jn. Askin	Jms. Mcgill	aol.	
1847	T.C. Street	42	4.12.5	26.40	Bargain&Sale	1807	Jn. Askin	Jms. Mcgill	200	
1847	T.C. Street	75	4.12.5	14.79	Bargain&Sale	1807	Jn. Askin	Jms. Mcgill	aol.	
1847	T.C. Street	aol.	1.10.6		Bargain&Sale	1835	Green	J. Stewart	100	50.0.0
1847	T.C. Street		3.1.5		Bargain&Sale	1826	Mount	I. Wilcox	aol.	150.0.0
1847	T.C. Street	60	315.0.0	1,260	Bargain&Sale	1826	Jane Miller	Jos. Wigle		25.0.0
1848	L.J. Fluette	aol.	47.0.0		Bargain&Sale	1846	J. Reaume	H. Cote	20	7.10.0
1848	T.C. Street	48	4.12.5	23.10	Bargain&Sale	1807	Jn. Askin	Jms. Mcgill	aol.	
1849	Jms. Haggarty	aol.	38.0.0		Indenture	1849	Mcelroy	J. Haggarty	aol.	165.0.0
1849	Jms. Haggarty	aol.	38.0.0		Bargain&Sale	1847	J. Mcelroy	Jms. Cowan	200	150.0.0
1849	Jms. Haggarty	aol.	38.0.0		Indenture	1849	Mcelroy	J. Haggarty	aol.	165.0.0
1849	Jms. Haggarty	aol.	38.0.0		Indenture	1849	Mcelroy	J. Haggarty	aol.	165.0.0

Sherrif Sale by Lachlan

Year	Buyer	Acres	Price (£.s.d)	Pence/ Acre	Previous Transaction	Year	Previous Seller	Previous Buyer	Previous Acreage	Price (£.s.d)
1840	L. Montrail	100	35.0.0	84.00	Bargain&Sale	1837	G. Meldrum	S. Mcknight	aol	2000.0.0

Appendix 8.1 (continued)

Year	Buyer	Acres	Price (£.s.d)	Pence/ Acre	Previous Transaction	Year	Previous Seller	Previous Buyer	Previous Acreage	Price (£.s.d)
Sherrif Sales by Reynolds (E.B?)										
1836	H. Jones	100	52.0.0	124.80	Bargain&Sale	1831	J&D Williams	N. Janette	100	50.0.0
1837	Samuel Street	200	3.7.9	4.06	Bargain&Sale	1826	Mount	I. Wilcox	aol.	200.0.0
1838	L.A Desjarlets	150			Bargain&Sale	1831	L.J. Fluet	P. Chauvin	100	
1838	L.A Desjarlets	200			Bargain&Sale	1831	L.J. Fluet	P. Chauvin	100	
1838	C. Berczy	160	4.2.5	6.18	Bargain&Sale	1828	M. Burwell	I. Wilcox	aol.	50.0.0
Sherrif Sale by S.D. Foot										
1843	Chs. Wood	39	7.3.4	44.10	Bargain&Sale	1835	Brouillet	J. Mcdougall	133	225.0.0
Sherrif Sale by T.C. Street										
1838	C. Berczy	200			Bargain&Sale	1831	Mount	S. Vandeer	100	
1849	C. Cummings	aol.	0.5.0		Bargain&Sale	1835	Green	J. Stewart	100	50.0.0
Other Sherrif Sales										
1818	Jms. Gordon	aol.	355.0.0		Bargain&Sale	1811	Sam. Mckee	Ed Ellice	100	18.15.0
1818	Langlois**	200			Bargain&Sale	1816	S. Cornwall	Langlois**	200*	
1823	J. Richardson	aol.	1600.0.0		Bargain&Sale	1817	R.Reynolds	G.B. Hall	S.1/2	1000.0.0
1823	J. Richardson	aol.	1600.0.0		Bargain&Sale	1817	R.Reynolds	G.B. Hall	S.1/2	1000.0.0
1823	J. Richardson	aol.	1600.0.0		Bargain&Sale	1817	R.Reynolds	G.B. Hall	S.1/2	1000.0.0
1823	Thain***	aol.	1600.0.0		Patent	1813	Crown	G.B. Hall	200	1000.0.0

Appendix 8.1   (continued)

Year	Buyer	Acres	Price (£.s.d)	Pence/Acre	Previous Transaction	Year	Previous Seller	Previous Buyer	Previous Acreage	Price (£.s.d)
1824	J. Gordon	aol.	270.0.0		Bargain&Sale	1823	W. Derenzy	Strachcn,Allan	aol.	0.10.0
1824	Jms. Woods	aol.	29.0.0		Indenture	1822	Wm. Elliot	M.D. Nelson	aol.	104.0.0
1824	Jms. Woods	aol.	29.0.0		Bargain&Sale	1822	Wm. Elliot	M.D. Nelson	aol.	104.0.0
1831	Chs. Askin	187	3.15.0	4.81	Bargain&Sale	1807	Jn. Askin	Jms. Mcgill	aol.	
1831	Ed Butler	2			Bargain&Sale	1802	D.D.	Meldrum/Park	114	
1831	J.B. Cazaran	100			Bargain&Sale	1825	A. Coleman	Jms. Woods	100	
1831	Jn. Early	100	3.13.3	8.79	Patent	1837	Crown	Ann Wilkinson	100	
1831	Jn. Early	100	3.13.3	8.79	Patent	1837	Crown	H.P. Cox	100	
1831	Jn. Fulmer	100	2.0.9	4.89	Patent	1806	Crown	A. Harrow	aol.	
1831	Jn. Fulmer	100	2.0.9	4.89	Patent	1806	Crown	A. Harrow	aol.	
1831	Jn. Hands	66	1.9.7	5.38	Patent	1808	Crown	3 People	200	
1831	O. Bertheler	aol.	3.13.3		Bargain&Sale	1829	Brown	O. Bertheler	aol.	
1831	O. Bertheler	aol.	3.13.3		Patent	1801	Crown	Mt. Elliot	all	
1831	O. Bertheler	aol.	3.13.3		Bargain&Sale	1829	Brown	O. Bertheler	aol.	
1831	O. Bertheler	aol.	3.13.3		Patent	1801	Crown	Mt. Elliot	all	
1831	O. Bertheler	aol.	3.13.3		Bargain&Sale	1829	Brown	O. Bertheler	aol.	
1831	O. Bertheler	aol.	3.13.3		Bargain&Sale	1829	Brown	O. Bertheler	aol.	
1831	O. Bertheler	aol.			Patent	1801	Crown	Mt. Elliot	all	
1831	S. Street	50	1.4.6	5.88	Patent	1857	Crown	T.C. Street	200	
1831	Sam Street	200	3.14.6	4.47	Patent	1810	Crown	G. Dolson	200	
1831	Sam Street	35	1.0.3	6.93	Bargain&Sale	1821	M. Friem	M. Wigle	100	
1831	Sam Street	58	1.11.4	6.48	Bargain&Sale	1810	Ed. Ellice	W. Buchanan	147	50.0.0
1831	Sam Street	100	2.0.10	4.90	Bargain&Sale	1819	M. Roach	Jn. Wigle	aol.	
1831	Sam Street	200	3.13.4	4.40	Bargain&Sale	1809	Jn. Hartley	Wm. Bell	200	20.0.0
1831	Sam Street	all	3.13.4		Patent	1818	Crown	Susan Hunt	200	
1831	Sam Street	200	3.13.4	4.40	Patent	1807	Crown	Susan Leonnay	200	
1831	Sam Street	200	3.13.4	4.40	Bargain&Sale	1829	Jn. Mccormick	Mt. Mccormick	100	62.0.0

Appendix 8.1   (continued)

Year	Buyer	Acres	Price (£.s.d)	Pence/Acre	Previous Transaction	Year	Previous Seller	Previous Buyer	Prev Acre	Price (£.s.d)
1831	Sam. Street	200	3.13.4	4.40	Patent	1805	Crown	J. Kelly	Jos. Bauks	200 0.0
1831	Sam. Street	200	3.13.11	4.44	Bargain&Sale	1817	Mcintosh	J. Baby	200	300.0.0
1831	Sam. Street	213	3.18.0	4.39	Deed Poll	1821	J-B. Baby	A.M. Thompson	aol	
1831	Sam. Street	200	313.0.0	375.72	Patent	1809	Crown	A. Mcintosh	200	
1831	W.G. Hall	80	1.9.6	4.43	Bargain&Sale	1810	J.B. Labadie	W. Berczy	aol	50.0.0
1832	Berczy	50	1.7.0	6.48	Patent	1853	Crown	J-B Tourneaux	200	
1832	Chs. Askin	200	4.10.8	5.44	Patent	1808	Crown	Jms. Crooks	200	
1832	Jms Crooks	200	3.5.5	3.92	Bargain&Sale	1829	J. Dewmore	A. Harrow	200	125.0.0
1832	Jn. Fulmer	200	4.1.7	4.90	Patent	1806	Crown	A. Harrow	all	
1832	Jn. Fulmer	200	4.1.7	4.90	Patent	1806	Crown	Isa. Wright	all	
1832	P. Scratch	200	4.1.8	4.90	Patent	1818	Crown	Mary Seusbaugh	200	
1832	Thos. Clarke	200	4.1.8	4.90	Patent	1811	Crown	F. Brown	200	
1832	Thos. Clarke	200	4.1.7	4.90	Bargain&Sale	1822	Martin	P. Tolman	200	45.0.0
1832	Thos. Clarke	200	4.1.8	4.90	Patent	1811	Crown	R. Phillips	200	
1832	Thos. Clarke	200	4.10.4	5.42	Patent	1816	Crown	Thos. Mitchell	200	
1832	Thos. Clarke	200	4.1.8	4.90	Patent	1818	Crown	Lois Luiss	200	
1832	Wm. Berczy	200	4.1.8	4.90	Bargain&Sale	1816	Geo. Everts	Jms. Draper	200	
1832	Wm. Berczy	200	4.1.8	4.90	Patent	1818	Crown	R. Fitzpatrick	200	
1832	Wm. Berczy	200	4.1.8	4.90	Patent	1811	Crown	E. Tolman	200	
1832	Wm. Berczy	57	2.10.2	10.55	Patent	1808	Crown	Arner/Moss	82	
1832	Wm. Berczy	200	4.1.10	4.91	Patent	1808	Crown	Jn. Stanfield	200	
1833	Wm. Berczy	200	4.1.10	4.91	Patent	1818	Crown	S. Wigle	200	
1832	Wm. Mccormick	200	4.1.8	4.90	Patent	1806	Crown	A. Harrow	all	

Sherrif Sales by unknown sherrif

Year	Buyer	Acres	Price (£.s.d)	Pence/Acre	Previous Transaction	Year	Previous Seller	Previous Buyer	Prev Acre	Price (£.s.d)
1852	W. McCrea	150	33.15.9	54.06	Deed	1849	T. Hirons	Cleary/Hays	200	200.0.0

* aol. among other lands   ** Langlois   ***Thain, Forsyth and Richardson

Notes

CHAPTER ONE

1 Richards, Caldwell, and Morwick report this as the county's total although the classes on the accompanying map total only 452,000 acres. *Soil Survey of Essex County,* 10.

2 Classes 5 and 6 of appendix 1.1 contain 320,500 acres.

3 Morrison, *Garden Gateway to Canada.*

4 Richards, Caldwell, and Morwick, *Soil Survey of Essex County,* 65.

5 Ibid., 74–5.

6 Herniman, "The Development of Artificial Drainage Systems," 13–24; Kelly, "The Artificial Drainage of Land," 279–98.

7 Ibid., Kelly, 292.

8 Clarke and Finnegan, "Colonial Survey Records," 122.

9 Richards, Caldwell, and Morwick, *Soil Survey of Essex County,* 74–5.

10 Clarke, "Social Integration," 390–412.

11 Kelly, "The Changing Attitude of Farmers," 64.

12 Ibid., 67. In relation to the Bartlett print, it is doubtful if such tepees were even seen in the Lake Erie area. While the print conveys the feeling of the immensity of the forest, trees of this magnitude were in fact uncommon. If the person standing in the foreground was five feet tall, then the trees were about eighty-five feet.

13 Ibid., 70–7.

14 The relationship between vegetation cover and the perception of agriculturally viable land is an interesting theme in the historiography of Ontario. It is somewhat paradoxical that, given the wealth of data, the literature is

so thin. See Woods, "Settlement of the Mount Elgin ridges," 23–8; Clarke, "Geographical Analysis of Colonial Settlement in the Western District," 247–57; Brunger, "Analysis of Site Factors," 400–2; Gentilcore, "Changes in Settlement," 418–19; Heidenreich, "A procedure for Mapping the Vegetation," 105–13; Brunger, "A spatial Analysis of Individual Settlement in Southern London District"; Osborne, "Historical Geography: Deciphering the Palimpsest of the Past," 1–9; Chambers, "Images, Acts and Consequences," 197–204.

15 In some instances there were large delays; for example, Mahlon Burwell, who surveyed so much of Essex and southern Ontario as a whole, did not submit his completed field notes on Mersea Township until twelve years after he had completed the survey. Clarke, "Mahlon Burwell," 125–8.

16 Garland and Talman, "Pioneer Drinking Habits," 171–93; Clarke and Brown, "Foci of Human Activity," 31–57; Clark, "The Backwoods Society," 63–80.

17 Talbot, *Five Years Residence in the Canadas*, 59.

18 NA, CO 47, vol. 115, report of Charles Rankin to the Colonial Office, 1826.

19 Field notes (FN) have been widely used for purposes of vegetation reconstruction. For the United States, see Meyer, "The Kankakee Marsh," 366–95; "Circulation and Settlement Patterns," 312–56; Trewartha, "The Vegetal Cover," 109–42; Finley, "The Original Forest Cover"; Lutz, "Original Forest Composition," 1098–1103; and Peters, "No Trees on the Prairies," 19–28. For New Zealand, see Johnston, "Locating the Vegetation of Early Canterbury," 6–15; Forrest, "Locating the Vegetation of Early Coastal Otago" 49–58; and Murton, "Mapping the Immediate Pre-European Vegetation," 262–4. For Canada, see J. David Wood, "The Stage Is Set," 40–50; Leslie J. Wood, "Settlements in the Mount Elgin Ridges," 8–26; Colin J. Wood, "Human Settlement in the Long Point Area," 2–30; Clarke, "Geographical Analysis of Colonial Settlement in the Western District"; Brunger, "Analysis of Site Factors," 400–2; Gentilcore, "Changes in Settlement," 418–19; Heidenreich, "A Procedure for Mapping the Vegetation," 105–13; Weldon, "The Salient Factors", 75–84; Gordanier, "The Settlement of Augusta Township," 49–55; and Skof, "Agriculture in a Forest Setting," 28–32.

20 The six categories were derived by amalgamating classes from this source. Richards, Caldwell, and Morwick, *Soil Survey of Essex County*, 10.

21 Government of Ontario, Department of Lands and Forests (DLF), Burwell's survey of Gosfield Township, SR, FN11, 67–86, and Original Notebook (ONB), 416. Mfm. at Carleton University.

22 Ibid., Burwell's survey of Rochester and Maidstone Townships, Survey Records, FN11, 226–319. Mfm. at Carleton University.

23 Weaver, "Ontario Surveys," 184.

24 Thompson, *Men and Meridians* 1, 218–49; Clarke, "Mahlon Burwell," 125–8.

25 Cartographically, marsh and meadow have had to be combined. In fact, natural meadow was limited to northeastern Tilbury and the western portion of Anderdon Township.

26 At least four references to vegetation type were used before a decision was made for any one lot. At this juncture, the reader is no doubt aware of the avoidance of the term "association." This part of the chapter draws heavily upon the work of the author and Gregory Finnegan, who acknowledge the influence of the botanist P.F. Maycock. See Clarke and Finnegan, "Colonial Survey Records," 119–38, and Maycock, "The Phytosociology of the Deciduous Forests," 379–438. Maycock's paper stresses the role of soil moisture in the ecological tolerance of individual tree species, as well as the continuous character of forest patterns, and denies the usefulness of the distinct-community approach to an understanding of forest ecology. Unlike Maycock, Clarke and Finnegan are not concerned with whether the concept of plant community is botanically viable; they are content to accept, following Maycock's work, the continuous nature of the forest and its relationship to soil-moisture conditions. In fact, this book lends validity to Maycock's views.

27 Maycock, ibid., 398; Fox and Soper, "The Distribution of Some Trees and Shrubs," 12.

28 The reader interested in comparison of Essex with southern Ontario as a whole is referred to Maycock, "The Phytosociology of the Deciduous Forests," 428–36.

29 Kelly, "The Artificial Drainage of Land," 279–97; Herniman, "Development of Artificial Drainage Systems," 13–24.

30 Fox and Soper, "The Distribution of Some Trees and Shrubs," 12.

31 The addition and deletion of particular species in specific locations is a further justification of the classification in Figure 1.5, which seeks to portray the generalized vegetation in the county.

32 Maycock, "The Phytosociology of the Deciduous Forests," 428–36.

33 Blalock, *Social Statistics*, 452. Three classes of land quality, "goodland," "lowland," and "swamp," were used. A chi-square analysis of a three-by-six table produced a value of 122.94, which with 10 degrees of freedom proved significant at the .001 level.

34 The soil texture and drainage classes were again used against three vegetation classes, namely, black ash and elm, elm and basswood, and white oak, maple and beech. The value of chi-square calculated was 100.59.

35 At least four references to vegetation were used before a decision was made.

36 Brunger, "A Spatial Analysis of Individual Settlement," 160–85.

37 Kelly, "Practical Knowledge of Physical Geography," 10–17.

38 Ibid., 11–12; Kelly, "The Evaluation of Land," 57–64.

39 Kelly, "The Artificial Drainage of Land," 179–97; Herniman, "Development of the Artificial Drainage System," 13–24.

40 Maycock, "The Phytosociology of the Deciduous Forests."

41 NA, RG1, Hesse District Records, L4, vol. 1, 186, mfm. C–14026, Patrick McNiff to Lieutenant-Colonel England, 28 December 1792.

42 Kelly, "Practical Knowledge of Physical Geography," 10–12.

43 Reaman, *The Trail of the Black Walnut.*

44 Ontario Research Foundation, map 2225, Ontario Department of Mines and Northern Affairs, 1972.

45 White and Hosie, *The Forests of Ontario,* 46.

46 Wyckoff, *The Developer's Frontier,* 30–41.

47 Peters, "Changing Ideas about the Use of Vegetation," 19.

48 The newspapers examined at the Hiram Walker Historical Museum, Windsor, the Archives of Ontario (hereafter AO), and the NAC were the *Upper Canada Gazette, Western Herald and Farmers Magazine,* the *Amherstburg Courier and Western District Advertiser,* the *Canada Oak,* the *Canadian Emigrant,* the *Western District Advertiser,* and the St Thomas *Liberal.* The Township Papers are in the AO.

49 AO, RG 1, Township Papers, Letters of Colonel John Price, 13 February 1840 and 14–24 April 1854.

50 Wyckoff, *The Developer's Frontier,* 36.

51 Vandall, *Atlas of Essex County,* 17.

52 NA, Major, the Baron de Rottenburg, principal communications in Canada West, 1855. NMC 0012437A–L.

53 NA, RG1, L4, vol. 3, 473–4, report of the proceedings of the Land Board of Hesse from 29 October 1790 to 13 May 1791, by P. McNiff, deputy-surveyor, 9 December 1791.

54 Ibid., 519–23, report of coasting survey pursuant to the order of Patrick Murray, Esq., Commandant of Detroit, by P. McNiff, deputy-surveyor, 16 June 1790.

CHAPTER TWO

1 However see Craig, "The American Impact," 333–52; Patterson, "Whiggery, Nationalism," 29–30; idem., "An Enduring Canadian Myth: Responsible Government," 3–16; Errington and Rawlyk, "The Loyalist-Federalist Alliance," 157–76; Errington, *The Lion, The Eagle, and Upper Canada;* Beer, "Toryism in Transition," 207–25; Taylor, "Reform Challenge," 116–51; Christie, "In These Times of Democratic Rage," 9–47; McNairn, "Publius of the North," 504–37; Noel, "Early Populist Tendencies," 173–87.

2   See also Burroughs, "Loyalist and Lairds," 70–82.

3   DLF, SR, survey plans of McNiff, Burwell, and Ridout (mfm. copies, Carleton University, Ottawa).

4   These included the Rottenburg, Rankin, and Bonnycastle maps. They provided data on the existence of mills, inns, post offices and churches. NA, NMC SV2–400, Rottenburg map 1850, and NMC H1/409; and the Bonnycastle map of 1842, reproduced in Vandall, *Atlas of Essex County*, 33.

5   AO, Surveyor General's Office, township papers of Thomas Parke, C48/C10; Gosfield G12 A/C16; Mersea M40 A/C19; Malden C26; Tilbury C43; Maidstone M17/C26; Sandwich C39, July 1843; NA, NMC G3461G4C3, Atlas of Canada Company maps, vol. 2, 90–102.

6   The Domesday Books were examined in the DLF. The abstract index, normally housed in county registry offices, are included on mfm. in the AO and at Carleton University, courtesy of the Genealogical Society of Utah. These materials are used in chapter 4 to trace the spatial progress of settlement in Essex, and in subsequent chapters to identify ownership. Clarke, "Land and Law" 475–93; Widdis, "Tracing Property Ownership," 83–97; Clarke and Brown, "Focii of Human Activity," 31–57.

7   The Canada Company's register of lands for the Bathurst, Home, and Western districts lists the former Crown reserves purchased by the company in 1827. This document was examined in 1826, two years after the company sought unsuccessfully to obtain half of the clergy reserves. The inclusion of the clergy reserves would seem to indicate that the register was begun in 1824 (see appendix 2.3).

8   These data were of such importance that their existence set the cross-sectional frame of the study itself on the years 1825 and 1850–52.

9   Lajeunesse, *The Windsor Border Region; Gourlay, Statistical Account of Upper Canada; Illustrated Historical Atlas of the Counties of Essex and Kent* (Belden); Smith, *Canada, Past, Present and Future; and Smith's Canadian Gazetteer.*

10 Clarke and Brown, "Focii of Human Activity," 31–57.

11 Eccleshall, *English Conservatism*, 1.

12 Hill, *The World Turned Upside Down.*

13 Hill shows that the changed meaning of "revolution" from astronomy to politics and of "absolute" from "perfect" to "arbitrary" began in the 1640s. See Hill, *A Nation of Change*, 82–101.

14 Eccleshall, *English Conservatism*, 49–53. He points to Robert Saunderson, bishop of Lincoln, as a prime exponent of this view.

15 Some, such as Thomas Hobbes, took the position that in self-interest people were obliged to obey established government but are absolved of obedience when the sovereign can no longer protect them. Oakeshott (ed.), *Leviathan*, 144–5.

16 Roots, "English Politics," 43–5. He points out that to equate Whig with Roundhead and Tory with Cavalier has some plausibility but that old issues were mixed with new and principle and material interest also affected membership in "part" or "faction." Dickinson, in a wonderfully lucid book, points to the shared interest in property held by Tory and Whig alike, the main difference in approach being the route to the protection of it. See Dickinson, *Liberty and Property*, and Gunn, *Beyond Liberty and Property*.

17 See excerpts from Filmer's *Patriarcha or the Natural Power of Kings* quoted in Eccleshall, *English Conservatism*, 53–7.

18 Pares points to the fact that the distinctions of "Whig," "Tory," and "party" changed through the eighteenth century and that in the 1760s a Tory who was not a Jacobite might as well be a Whig. For a discussion of the cement of "party," see Pares, *King George the Third*, 71–92.

19 Locke, writing in 1690, describes the conditions under which it is permissible to defend oneself against the "invasion" of the King and subsequent reversion to a state of nature. Locke, *The Second Treatise of Government*, 112–39. See also Williams, *The Whig Supremacy*, 1–10.

20 Churchill, *A History of the English-Speaking Peoples*, 144. On Burke, see Hearnshaw, "Edmund Burke," 72–99 and Harris, *Burke*, xvi–xxxiii.

21 Watson, *The Reign of George III*, 304.

22 Pares, (*King George the Third*, 119–20) points out that this may have been precipitated by Dunning's famous resolution of April 1780 that the power of the King be diminished. He doubts if the King could have explained the benefits of the "mixed constitution" over that of the simple or the mechanisms by which it as a whole "enlarged the scope of civil liberties." Ibid., 31.

23 Eccleshall, *English Conservatism*, 35–8.

24 Kramnick, "Ideological background," 84–91.

25 Keane, *Tom Paine*, 114–16; see also Sykes, "Thomas Paine," 100–40. Paine's message was well received in Ireland. The Irish patriot Wolfe Tone described the *Rights of Man* as the "Koran" of Belfast. Connolly, "Ulster Presbyterians," 35.

26 The term "Loyalist" implies, in the words of Nelson (*The American Tory*, ix), that attachment to Britain was primary. He would accord the primary motive to the Loyalists' dissent from the views of their fellow Americans. Thus he prefers "Tory" while pointing out that most "Tories" were in English terms "Whigs."

27 On 25 December 1777 William Smith, chief justice of the New York Supreme Court, declared himself "a Whigg of the old Stamp – No Roundhead – one of King William's Whiggs: for Liberty and the Constitution." See Upton, *The Loyal Whig*, frontispiece. He was sworn executive councillor and chief justice of Quebec on 2 November, 1786. Upton, "William Smith," 714–18.

28 Yet anti-Lockean arguments also appeared in the 1820s and 1830s in the statements of Strachan and A.N. Bethune, among others. See Fahey, *In His Name*, 165–68. On Robinson, see Robinson, *Life of Sir John Beverley Robinson*; Saunders, "Sir John Beverley Robinson," 668–78; Brode, *Sir John Beverley Robinson*.

29 In the American colonies, the juridical-rights school was epitomised by Sir William Blackstone, who elaborated upon the common law as the constitutional alternative to despotic rule. According to Brode, Robinson's concern with "the rational effects of justice" during the treason trials of 1814 was "pure whiggism, derived from Blackstone's Commentaries on the laws of England." See Brode, *Sir John Beverley Robinson*, 23. The actual oath taken read: "I A:B due [sic] promise and declare that I will maintain the Authority of the King in His Parliament as the Supreme Legislature of this Province.' See McArthur and Doughty, *Documents Relating*, 22.

30 Romans 13:1–4 and 1 Peter 2: 17. "Honour all *men*. Love the brotherhood. Fear God. Honour the king."

31 Wise, "Upper Canada and the Conservative Tradition," 20–33.

32 Wise, "The Conservative Tradition," 30.

33 Ibid., 31. See also Mills, *The Idea of Loyalty*; Errington, *The Lion, the Eagle and Upper Canada*.

34 Though he fully accepted the revolution, John Adams, the constitutional lawyer and theorist who helped draft the Declaration of Independence and became the country's second president (1796–1800), expressed considerable concern about simple democratic government *in a unicameral assembly*. See C. Bradley Thompson, *John Adams and the Spirit of Liberty*, 175.

35 Boucher, *A View of the Causes and Consequences*, 221. This occurs in a passage on the role of prerogative and influence. Boucher believes that the people approve of the latter. Consequently, there is a need to have the means of obtaining influence. Boucher uses this logic to defend the revenues of the clergy from "public" attack!

36 Quoted in Hamil, "The Reform Movement in Upper Canada," 10; Wise, "The Rise Of Christopher Hagerman," 61–72; Fraser, "Christopher Alexander Hagerman," 365–72.

37 Cruikshank, *Simcoe Papers*, vol. 3, 265. Here Simcoe places emphasis upon functional arguments but there were also organic arguments for the bond between religion, the state, and the superiority of the British constitution. See Fahey, *In His Name*.

38 Taylor, "Reform Challenge in Upper Canada," 124. Noel points out that such meetings were authorized by statute in 1793. He claims that these were "significant innovations which entrenched and expanded the popular element in an otherwise hierarchical political system". Noel, "Early Populist Tendencies," 178.

39 Interestingly, when in 1818 there was deadlock between the House of Assembly and the Legislative Council over the former's right to amend a money bill, the tactic of the assembly was to appeal to the prince regent. This was held to be the constitutionally correct process since it was the duty of the Crown to ensure that such infringements of power did not occur. Noel, "Early Populist Tendencies," 179. Noel also points out that Robert Gourlay, whose views on the government of the day were so unacceptable that he was banished from the colony, wanted the government of Upper Canada overthrown not by the people but by the prince regent! Ibid., 181.

40 Armstrong, *Handbook of Upper Canadian Chronology*, 53. Examples of district representation include William Dummer Powell, Alexander Grant, and James Baby for the Western District; Robert Hamilton and William Dickson for Niagara; and Powell, William Osgoode, John Elmsley, and Thomas Ridout for York.

41 Dunham, *Political Unrest in Upper Canada*, 161.

42 Until the second Rockingham administration of March 1782, cabinet was a body summoned by any minister who needed to discuss any issue with colleagues. After that the right to attend was more closely guarded and Pitt between 1784 and 1793 made it increasingly an executive committee with a collective responsibility. Pitt never bore the title of prime minister but rather that of first lord of the treasury and chancellor of the exchequer. The parallels between the Upper Canadian and British structures, from which the first was derived, are apparent. In Upper Canada, in the absence of the lieutenant-governor, the senior member of the Executive Council bore the title "administrator." Between 1805 and 1806, the administrator was Alexander Grant from Essex. Watson, *The Reign of George III*, 301; Armstrong, *Handbook of Upper Canadian Chronology*, 38.

43 Ewart and Jarvis, "The Personnel of the Family Compact," 209–21; Armstrong, *Handbook of Upper Canadian Chronology*, 38–58.

44 Tully, "The Political Development of the Colonies," 28–38.

45 Watson, *The Reign of George III*, 327.

46 Willey, *The Eighteenth Century Background*, 3–26. Newton saw the laws of gravitation as the manifestation of God's design. See Bronowski, *The Common Sense of Science*, 45.

47 Hume (1711–76) was the author of *Treatise of Human Nature; An Attempt to Introduce the Experimental Method of Reasoning into Moral Subjects*. This was originally published in 1738. His work can, in Willey's terms, be represented as the defence of nature against reason. See Willey, *The Eighteenth Century Background*, 110–35.

48 Ibid., 327.

49 Oliver Goldsmith (1730–74) was the Irish-born author of this volume, published in 1776. Samuel Johnson wrote of him that he was "one who

left scarcely any kind of writing untouched and who touched nothing he did not adorn." *New Encyclopaedia Britannica*, 15th ed., s.v. "Oliver Goldsmith."

50 Watson, *The Reign of George III*, 328.

51 James Boswell (1740–95), friend of Samuel Johnson and author of Johnson's biography (1791).

52 Adam Smith's *An Inquiry into the Nature and Causes of the Wealth of Nations* was originally published in 1776.

53 Tawney, *Religion and the Rise of Capitalism*, 35, quoted in Willey, *The Eighteenth Century Background*, 16.

54 Willey, *The Eighteenth Century*, 17.

55 Watson, *Reign of George III*, 330.

56 Bentham's *Fragment on Government* and *Principles of Morals* were originally published in 1776 and 1780 respectively.

57 In his Vinerian lecture, delivered at Oxford on the 25 October 1758, Blackstone argued that England was perhaps the only country in which political and civil liberty was the purpose of the constitution. "This liberty, rightly understood, consists in the power of doing whatever the laws permit, which is only to be effected by a general conformity of all orders and degrees to those equitable rules of action by which the meanest individual is protected from the insults and oppression of the greatest." Blackstone, *Commentaries on the Laws of England*, vol. 1, 2–3. In the hitherto traditional view, political upheaval crippled law, but in the revolting colonies rebellion was soon justified in terms of a more fundamental law which embodied the ideal of accountability. See Hoffer, *Law and People* 127–53.

58 Watson, *The Reign of George III*, 330.

59 Ibid., 331.

60 Ibid., 331.

61 Romney, "Very Late Loyalist Fantasies," 119–47.

62 Quoted in Eccleshall, *English Conservatism*, 12.

63 O'Brien, *The Great Melody*, 447–8.

64 Or perhaps even an American. For example, John Adams believed that there was in society a natural division into "the one, the few and the many." The difference was that this order was not fixed or permanent but rather "natural" and the virtues required of the "natural aristocracy" could be acquired. The "mixed constitution" which he advocated had been inherited from the Greeks. Its purpose was to prevent the perversion of the three "natural" forms of government into their corrupted counterparts, that is, tyranny, oligarchy, and mob rule. See Thompson, *John Adams*, 171 and 202–28.

65 The royal prerogative, by which council appointments were made, provided, in Robinson's terms, a political role for the "most worthy, intelligent, loyal and opulent." See Fraser, "All the privileges," xxxi.

66 Brode, *Sir John Beverley Robinson*, 220.

67 Ibid., 220.

68 Fraser provides the example of Christopher Hagerman, who, in a debate in the legislature on the selection of grand juries, argued that these people should be "taken from the number of persons of the greatest figure and standing in the country ... such as more likely to be obtained ... from among those persons possessed of the greater amount of property." Fraser, "All the privileges," xxxviii. See also Cross, "The Age of Gentility," 105–17.

69 Saunders, "What Was the Family Compact," 165–78. The term was also known in Pennsylvania. See Nelson, *The American Tory*, 130.

70 Wise,"Sir Francis Bond Head," 342–5.

71 Wise, *A Narrative*, 212–13.

72 Wise, "Liberal Consensus," 12; "Upper Canada and the Conservative Tradition"; "Conservatism and Political Development," 226–43.

73 Howes, "Property, God and Nature," 365–414; UWO, William Robertson Papers, no.25, "Bill of sale of a certain negro man named Cuff to John Laughton," 10 October 1784, and ibid., no.32, "Sale of a negro wench Helene by Jacques Campau," 9 June 1789. In the latter case, three blacks were put up as security that Helene would be handed over to her purchaser, William Groesbeck, in good condition. In January 1787 Thomas Duggan purchased one Josiah Cutten, aged twenty-four, for £124 NY payable in grain; in March 1792 he traded him for a farm on the Thames River. Quaife, *John Askin Papers* 1, 286–7.

74 Baker, "The Reconstruction of Upper Canadian Legal Thought," 219–92; Risk, "The Law and the Economy," 88–131; Brode, *Sir John Beverley Robinson*; Fraser, "All the privileges."

75 Quoted in Brode, *Sir John Beverley Robinson*, 176.

76 Unlike the American jurisdiction where the courts might render acts contrary to the constitution illegal. In 1776 Thomas Paine proclaimed that "in America the law is king." See Tomlins, *Law, Labor and Ideology*, 27.

77 Ibid., 176.

78 Shortt and Doughty, *Documents Relating* vol. 2, 946, Dorchester to Lord Sydney at the Colonial Office, 13 June 1787.

79 Fraser, "Like Eden in Her Summer Dress," 214.

80 Quoted in ibid., 217.

81 Ibid., 233. William Lyon MacKenzie, of course, held to exactly the opposite view. See LeSueur, *William Lyon MacKenzie*, 215.

82 When in 1850 Robinson looked back on his life in Upper Canada he could say, "whatever were the failings of the much abused 'family compact' we had a Government of Gentlemen." Ibid., 222.

83 Pares, *King George III and the Politicians*, 79–80 and 178.

84 In 1805 Sir John Johnson sought the assistance of Edward, Duke of Kent, to become lieutenant governor of Upper Canada. NA, MG11, Q Series, vol. 303, 200–5, Sir John Johnson, 25 August 1805. Edward, a royal duke, was either personally indifferent or more likely constitutionally careful. At any rate he deferred to Lord Castlereagh. Ibid., 198–9, 16 October 1805.

85 Nelson, *The American Tory*, 2.

86 Boucher, *A View of the Causes and Consequences*, 218.

87 Nelson, *The American Tory*, 86.

88 Wise, "Upper Canada and the Conservative Tradition," 26.

89 Ibid., 26.

90 NA, MG23, H I 4, vol. 1, 137–40, W.D. Powell to Adam Gordon, 22 September 1822.

91 Noel, *Patrons, Clients, Brokers*, 61.

92 Ibid., 62.

93 Ibid., 61–78.

94 Wise, *The Conservative Tradition*, 27.

95 Fahey, *In His Name*, 166, quoted from *The Church*, 17 November 1838.

96 Ibid., 168.

97 Ibid., 123.

98 Westfall, *Two Worlds*, 19–49. One cannot but recall Boucher's argument when the Church of Maryland was under financial threat: "this attack on our Church may end, as it did in Cromwell's time with the downfall of the State." See Boucher, *A View of the Causes and Consequences*, 222.

99 Yet, interestingly, in the circumstances of 1837 Bishop Strachan could advise that a deputation be sent to England to warn the government that "if they continue to attend to such persons as Ryerson and Mackenzie & to break down the Constitution the Conservative Party will turn round upon them & first trample on the necks of those miscreants and then govern themselves." Quoted in Fahey, *In His Name*, 79.

100 Westfall, *Two Worlds*, 23.

101 Adamson, "God's Continent Divided," 431 and 437; Westfall, *Two Worlds*, 43.

102 Fraser, "Like Eden in Her Summer Dress," 210. Fahey sees this natural and social order as being rooted in the old Christian perception of the universe as a "Great Chain of Being." See Fahey, *In His Name*, 117.

103 Fraser, "Like Eden in Her Summer Dress," 211.

104 Gates, *Land Policies*, 209.

105 Westfall, "Order and Experience," 5–24.

106 Robinson's charge to the grand jury of the Western District in 1836, quoted in McMahon "Law and Public Authority," 415.

107 Talman ("The Position of the Church of England," 361–75) discusses the provisions in the Constitutional Act for the Church of England. See also Fahey, *In His Name.*

108 Grant, *A Profusion of Spires*, 94; Fahey, *In His Name*, 126.

109 Henderson, *John Strachan*, 110.

110 Grant, *A Profusion of Spires*, 95.

111 Quoted in Landon, *Western Ontario and the American Frontier*, 183. For an analysis of this view and the effect of the rebellion in the London District, see Read, "The Duncombe Rising," 48–69.

112 Grant, *A Profusion of Spires*, 95. Strachan attributed what he regarded as Britain's pre-eminence among nations to the religious establishment. He argued that religious and moral sentiment and feelings towards the state could best be developed through religion. See Henderson, *John Strachan*, 90–5.

113 Wise, *The Conservative Tradition*, 25.

114 Ibid., 25.

115 Wise, "Sermon Literature"; "God's Peculiar People"; Fraser, "Like Eden in Her Summer Dress," 60.

116 Fraser, ibid., 54.

117 Wise, *God's Peculiar People*, 41.

118 Brode, *Sir John Beverley Robinson*, 220.

119 Fraser, *Like Eden in Her Summer Dress*, 213.

120 Westfall, *Two Worlds*, 34.

121 Wise, *The Conservative Tradition*, 23.

122 Craig, "John Rolph," 683–9.

123 Fraser, "William Warren Baldwin," 35–44; Cross and Fraser, "Robert Baldwin," 45–59.

124 Craig, "Marshall Spring Bidwell," 60–4.

125 Wise, *The Conservative Tradition*, 23.

126 Ibid., 24.

127 Ibid., 24–5.

128 Russell, *Attitudes to Social Structure and Mobility.*

129 Noel, *Patrons, Clients, Brokers*, 30.

130 Ibid., 30.

131 Ibid., 30.

132 Taylor, Clarke, and Wightman, "Areal Patterns of Population Change," 27–48; Clarke, Taylor, and Wightman, "Contrasting Land Development Rates," 50–72.

133 The French began their surveys at least as early as 1730, as Commandant de Boishebert's map shows. See Lajeunesse, *The Windsor Border Region*, facing xliv. Twenty-two lots were laid out on the Essex shore by Joseph Gaspard Chaussegros de Lery in 1749. By about 1754, there were some thirty-four property owners on this south shore. See

Chaussegros de Lery, fils, Topographical Map of Detroit (Michigan Public Library, Burton Historical Collection, Detroit). One hundred and fifty six persons were confirmed in possession of land in this area by British deeds issued by the Land Board of Hesse in 1792. Greenwood, *The Seigneurial System*, 35.

134 Gentilcore and Donkin, *Land Surveys of Southern Ontario*, 1–2.

135 Ibid., 2; Gentilcore, "Ontario Emerges from the Trees," 383–91.

136 An earlier concession made in 1783 to a Mr Schiefflin was, on appeal by the Indians, disallowed by the government. NA, RG1, L4, vol.2, 85, 13 October 1783. This is taken by the author as the first meaningful instance of the assertion of British control and intentions in this area, although there were some earlier instances of Indian grants made to individuals and witnessed by the British establishment. The whole issue of Indian grants is discussed in Chapter 3.

137 Fry (Frey) was appointed deputy surveyor by Samuel Holland on 22 December 1784, on the evidence of NA, MG9 D4, Upper Canada Sundries, 1494. Thomson, (*Men and Meridians* vol. 1, 226) gives the date as 19 January 1785.

138 NA, MG11, Q series, vol. 304, no.1, 76–7, copy of a letter from Lieutenant Governor Hay to Philip Fry, deputy surveyor, 25 March 1785; ibid., 78–9, certificate of Philip Fry, deputy surveyor, n.d.

139 "Many of them are very unworthy any indulgence in that way...Several have built upon and improved lands who have no other Pretensions than the Indians consent possession, Captain Bird and Caldwell are of the number ..." See Lajeunesse, *The Windsor Border Region*, 158–9.

140 Ibid., 159–60, Haldimand to Hay, Quebec, 14 August 1784.

141 Ibid., 161, Certificate of Philip Fry, deputy surveyor, n.d. Although Fry does not in this source make any reference to the extension of the survey, Quaife suggests that part of the "New Settlement," a term adopted to distinguish it from the old French settlement at Petite Côté and L'Assomption, was also completed in this year. McNiff argued that the ninety-six lots he found in Colchester Township on 14 July 1794, which he attributed to Fry, had been laid out in 1786. See Quaife, *John Askin Papers* vol. 1, 226, and DLF, Survey Records, Survey Maps, A25, survey map of Patrick McNiff. The "New Settlement," obtained by Colonel Caldwell from the Indians to accommodate the disbanded soldiers of Butler's Rangers which he had commanded, was given to Major Robert Mathews on behalf of government in 1787 and surveyed by T. Smith in 1787. See NA, MG21, B76, 286–92, mfm. H–1441, Major Robert Mathews to General Haldimand, Detroit, 3 August 1787. The *Manual Relating to Surveys and Surveyors* shows Niagara Township as the earliest surveyed, having been laid out in 1787. If this was so, this was later than the Indian

Department officers' grants in Malden and contemporaneous with the survey in what was to become Colchester and Gosfield townships. However, Gentilcore gives the date as 1782. See Gentilcore, "The Beginnings of Settlement," 74.

142 NA, RG10, vol. 1846, IT 25; PRONI T 1473/3. This deed ceding land at the Canard and the island of Bois Blanc was signed on 15 May 1786 and witnessed by seven chiefs of the Ottawa and Chippewa as well as three Europeans. Part of the Canard reserve and the Huron Church reserve was surrendered on 11 September 1800 for £300 in goods received. See *Indian Treaties and Surrenders* I, 30–2.

143 NA, RG 10, vol. 1841, IT 037; NA, RG1, L6B, vol. 25, 1124–32; NA, RG1, L4, vol. 2, 236–40, Dorchester to the Land Board of the District of Hesse, Quebec, 2 September 1789; Detroit Notarial Records, lib. C, 374–7. NA, RG 10, vol. 1840, IT 002 (manuscript original) reel 9938, "Indian Deed of Present Southwestern Ontario to King George III," 19 May 1790. AO, *Report of 1905*, 41, Alexander McKee to the Land Board of the District of Hesse, 21 May 1791; DLF, Survey Records, Survey Letters, vol. 3, 68–70, P. McNiff to Richard England, Detroit, 26 September 1793, regarding the survey of the northern boundary of the Indian purchase of 1790.

144 Robertson had signed ahead in the belief that the reserves were not included. On 7 June 1790 he asked that his name be removed as a witness to the document since it had been altered. Fraser, *Seventeenth Report*, 185. The reader may speculate as to what this might say about the treaty process.

145 AO, *Report of 1905*, 81–2, members of the Land Board for the District of Hesse to His Excellency Lord Dorchester, Detroit, 1 June 1790. In addition to expressing its apprehension at "the evil precedent to the Indians for counteracting their own deeds," the board noted other objections "next from the interruption of the settlement, and its communication, at its very heart, by an extensive waste, through which no roads can be made, and finally, though not the least inconvenience, the neighbourhood of an uncivilised horde." In its report the board acknowledged that McKee believed the restoration of this surrendered land necessary to achieve the greater objective.

146 Edwards, "Patrick McNiff," 551–3.

147 Brock, "Abraham Iredell," 448–9.

148 NA, RG1, L4, vol. 3, P. McNiff to the members of the Land Board for the District of Hesse, 16 June 1790 and 3 July 1790; NA, V30/409, NMC 0044752 (Appendix 2.2).

149 NA, Patrick McNiff, plan of part of the District of Hesse (1815), V30/409, NMC 0044752.

150 DLF, SR, SL, vol. 3, 17, "Letter of Patrick McNiff to the Land Board of Hesse, re the present plan of survey of the New Settlement, east of the

entrance of the Detroit River and of injury to the inhabitants," 12 August 1790.

151 Formal recognition as a township was not accorded the settlement here until the 8 January 1793, when D.W. Smith, now acting surveyor general, so informed the members of the Land Board. AO, *Report of 1905*, 223, D.W. Smith to the members of the Land Board for Kent and Essex, Niagara, 10 January 1793.

152 Ibid., 71, McNiff to the members of the Land Board for the District of Hesse, 30 July 1790. In this he states that, although ordered to do so on 2 July, he had not been able to review the order until 22 July because of pressures of work. On scrutiny, he found the order insufficiently clear and at variance with the established rules of the Crown Lands Department. Clarification was offered him on 30 July 1790 and again on 11 August 1790. Ibid., 23, minute of the Land Board, 11 August 1790.

153 Ibid., 123–6, members of the Land Board of the District of Hesse to Hugh Finlay, chairman of the Land Committee of the Legislative Council, 6 May 1791.

154 Ibid., 63, the Land Board to H. Motz, secretary to Lord Dorchester, October 1790. A simplified version of the original contained in NA, RG1, L4, vol. 4, 81, mfm. C–14026 is to be found in this report but the scheme itself was not simple. The town that was planned would have contained a burial ground; a four-acre parsonage; a four-acre schoolhouse; a four-acre workhouse; townparks for the clergy and the teacher; 144 acres of glebe land to support these worthies; a courthouse; prison; vegetable, meat, and fish markets (each of four acres); five public squares; two squares for hospitals; one-acre residential lots; and eight ninety-six-foot-foot wide principal streets. The scheme, reminiscent of Penn's Philadelphia, never wholly materialized, as the present residents of Colchester village must constantly regret.

155 Ibid., letter to Motz, 63.

156 Ibid., 64, McNiff to the members of the Land Board, 16 November 1790; ibid., 96, circular of D.W. Smith to the members of the Land Board for the District of Hesse, 6 December 1790.

157 Ibid., 96, minutes of the Land Board, 7 December 1790.

158 Presumably in an effort to protect himself from the wrath of the board and whatever pressures it might command, McNiff hastened to finish the drafting of his surveys conducted in 1789 and 1790. On 25th January 1790 he presented D.W. Smith, secretary to the board, "a Plan of part of the District commencing near Point Pele, on the North Shore of Lake Erie and extending from thence, along the waters edge, to the entrance of River Latranche, on the east Shore of Lake St. Clair, and from the entrance of said River, up to the 2nd fork of the same,

deliniated [sic] from actual Surveys, made in the Years 1789 and 1790."
Ibid., 97, D.W. Smith to H. Motz, secretary to the governor, Detroit, 25
January 1791. The original of this can be examined in the NA's
National Map Collection (NMC 0044752).

159 In June 1791 McNiff submitted a report in which he claimed that his
recent survey of the Thames had only confirmed the results which he
had originally submitted to the board on 23 January 1791. NA, RG1, L4,
vol. 4, 147–50, McNiff to the members of the Land Board, 3 June
1791.

160 NA, RG1, L4, vol. 4, 158–9, mfm. C–14026, minutes of the Board, 29
July 1791; ibid., vol. 3, 473–4, 6 August 1791; ibid., 557–9, McNiff to
the Land Board, 28 August 1791 and in DLF, SR, SL, vol. 3, no.28,
McNiff, Register no.2, folio 521.

161 AO, *Report of 1905*, 155, members of the Land Board to Lord Dorchester, 23 September 1791.

162 NA, RG1, L4, vol. 1, 26–8, mfm. C–14026, D.W. Smith, secretary of the
board, to Patrick McNiff, deputy surveyor, District of Hesse, 31 March
1792. McNiff began the work on 5 April and was completing the plans
when he reported to Smith on 20 April. Ibid., 51–2, McNiff to John
Smith, president of the Land Board, n.d.

163 AO, *Report of 1905*, 183–4, minutes of the Land Board for the District of
Hesse, 10 May 1792.

164 NA, RG1, L4, vol. 1, 76–7, mfm. C–14026, letter of instruction to P.
McNiff from D.W. Smith, secretary of the Land Board, 11 May 1792;
ibid., 87–9, McNiff to J. Smith, 31 May 1792.

165 Ibid., 87–9, P. McNiff to John Smith, president of the Land Board of
the District of Hesse, 31 May 1792, 1 June 1792.

166 Ibid., 185–8, and NA, RG1, L4, vol. 3, 636–7, mfm. C–14026. Survey
report of McNiff to Lieutenant-Colonel England, president of the
Land Board of the Counties of Essex and Kent, 28 December 1792,
and DLF, SR, SL, vol. 13, 42–3, register 3, folio 695 (letters received
no.1., 44–6); DLF, SR, SL (letters received no.1, 43) letter of Richard
England to D.W. Smith, December 1792, regarding surveys by McNiff
in the vicinity of Petite Côté and on the Thames River, enclosing copy
of McNiff's report thereon; DLF, Survey Records, Survey Letters, vol. 3,
McNiff no.45–6 (letters received,no.1, 46). Letter of McNiff to D.W.
Smith regarding the survey of the Thames to above Delaware village
and survey in the rear of Petite Côté, 29 December 1792. The order to
survey this part of Petite Côté was issued by D.W. Smith on behalf of
the board on 11 May 1792. See NA, RG1, L4, vol. 1, 76–7, mfm.
C–14026.

167 NA, RG1, L6 B, vol. 3, Departmental Records, Surveyor General, Upper
Canada, no pagination, McNiff to England, 16 January 1793; NA, RG1,

L4, vol. 1, 189–91, McNiff to England, 16 January 1793. See McNiff's map of 1791 [NA, NMC 0016996].

168 Ibid., 189–91, and NA, RG1, L6B, vol. 3, DR–SG, file 1799–1808, 3 pages, McNiff to the members of the Land Board of the Counties of Essex and Kent, 16 January 1793.

169 AO, *Report of 1905*, 218–20, members of the Land Board to Lieutenant Governor Simcoe, 3 February 1793.

170 These recommendations were accepted and McNiff was ordered to carry out the survey in the manner he had recommended. However, in private correspondence with D.W. Smith, secretary of the Land Board, Lieutenant-Colonel England, the last British commandant at Detroit, expressed reservations at both McNiff's competence in this instance and his motives. Throughout these years of self-seeking by many, England would seem to have behaved impeccably, lending some credence to his remarks. Subsequently, John Askin, a member of the board, acquired considerable land in this area. Cruikshank, *The Simcoe Papers* vol. 1, 324–5, R.G. England to D.W. Smith, 1 May 1793; NA, RG1, L4, vol. 1, 218–19, E.J. O'Brien to P. McNiff regarding instructions to survey the Ruscom River, Belle River, Rivière aux Pêches, aux Puce, and la Petite Rivière, 29 March 1793, and ibid., 221–2, McNiff to England, regarding lots on streams flowing into Lake St Clair, 11 April 1793. In this memorandum McNiff reports that he had surveyed a total of fifty-six lots, fourteen on each of the Ruscom, Belle, aux Puce, and aux Pêches rivers. The precise location of these lots is not known.

171 The initial survey was ordered on 5 February 1793. Ibid., 211–12, McNiff to England, 2 March 1793; DLF, SR, SL, vol. 3, 52, McNiff to England, regarding survey from L'Assomption to the Ruscom River, 2 March 1793.

172 NA, RG1, L6 B, vol. 5, no pagination, McNiff to England, 20 May 1793. This source reports that the survey was commissioned on 12 November 1793; DLF, SR, SL, vol. 3, McNiff no.77 (letters received no.2, 360), McNiff to D.W. Smith, "re completion of survey of additional townships as far as the Delaware Village with the loss of two men drowned," 31 January 1794.

173 The terminology is modern. The Thames, still known as the Latranche, flowed through Essex, Suffolk, and Kent counties. A proclamation of 1 January 1800 restricted the boundaries of the county in a manner excluding the townships of the Thames. 38 Geo. III, c. 5.

174 DLF, SR, SL, vol. 3, McNiff no.85, McNiff to England and the members of the Board regarding his survey of Assomption, 20 May 1794; ibid., McNiff no.95 (letters received no.2, 610), McNiff to England re information required as to the settlers on the Thames, at Petite Côté and at

L'Assumption in the New Settlement on Lake Erie, 12 September 1794.

175 Edwards, "Patrick McNiff," 553; DLF, SR, SL, vol. 3, McNiff no.95 (letters received no.2, 160), McNiff to Colonel England, 12 September 1794.

176 Where his biographer points out he acted as a surveyor in Michigan and as a judge of the Court of Common Pleas.

177 In 1795 McNiff had been engaged with John Askin, John Askin, Jr, and Alexander Henry in a massive speculation in Indian lands on the south shore of Lake Erie. The demise of this endeavour, known as the Cuyahoga Purchase, is thought to have cost the partnership at least one million dollars. Edwards, "Patrick McNiff," 553. McNiff was now selling assignments along the Thames River at two dollars each, presumably with the expectation that, if Detroit was now an American post, the future of the Western District was in doubt. NA, MG9, D4, letters received, 1844–45, mfm. 317, A. Iredell to D.W. Smith, 15 October 1796.

178 NA, MG9, D4, no.3, letters received, 959, mfm. M–316. Order-in-Council, 25 June 1795, signed by John Small. Iredell was to "be put upon the establishment and employed instead of Mr.McNiff, and sent to Detroit to execute the Surveys necessary in the Western District."

179 Rorke, "Abraham Iredell," 96–103. Iredell was born in 1751 and fought during the Revolutionary War on the British side in the "Guides and Pioneers." No doubt because of this he was appointed JP in 1796, and commissioner for administering the oath of allegiance in 1800, and returning officer for Kent County in 1800 and 1804. See also Brock, "Abraham Iredell," 448–9.

180 Of course, he himself cast doubt on the behaviour of McNiff. NA, MG9, D4, 1844–45, mfm. 317, 24 January 1799, wherein Iredell charges collusion between Thomas Smith and Ebenezer Allan.

181 Lajeunesse, *The Windsor Border Region*, civ; NA, MG9, D4, letters received, no.4, 1128–9, A. Iredell to D.W. Smith, 7 November 1795; ibid., 1877, A. McKee to A. Iredell, 19 August 1797; DLF, SR, SL, vol. 27, Iredell no.24, letters received no.4, 1335, A. Iredell to D.W. Smith, 18 April 1796; DLF, SR, Survey Notes (hereafter SN), 61; DLF, SR, FN vol. 11, 158–64, survey of Raleigh and Malden, 10 April to 1 July 1796, vol. 2, 136 and 155–62, and ONB, 513, 9 July 9th–31 December 1796.

182 NA, MG9, D4, 1331–2, mfm. M–316, letters received, no.4, 21 July 1795. He notes that he has surveyed but not assigned lots in parts of the townships. He asks for advice in laying out lots "as the French are forming a settlement there."

183 DLF, SR, SN, vol. 13, 5–6, survey notes of Maidstone and Rochester, 1795–96; ibid., vol. 2, 132, and ibid., vol. 11, 265; ibid., vol. 2, 130–42,

survey notes of Gosfield. In Gosfield, Iredell reworked the coast, surveyed earlier by McNiff and even earlier by Frey.

184 By August 1796 he was at lot 103, opposite Hog Island in Sandwich Township. NA, MG9, D4, mfm. M–317, 1843, A. Iredell to D.W. Smith, 21 August 1796.

185 Ibid., letters received no.4, 1227, A. Iredell to D.W. Smith, 26 January 1796.

186 Ibid., 1875, A. Iredell to D.W. Smith, 9 September 1797, shows he had received a plan indicating ten lots in Mersea; ibid., 250, A. Iredell to D.W. Smith, 28 May 1798. The evidence for much of his work in Mersea is cartographic. See DLF, map A27.

187 Ibid., 1848–50, A. Iredell to D.W. Smith, 2 February 1797; ibid., 1859. 9 August 1797; DLF, SR, SN, FN, vol. 2, 270–2, vol. 11, 213–19, 353–8, and vol. 13, 118–21.

188 NA, MG9, D4, 1855, A. Iredell to D.W. Smith, 12 July 1797.

189 Ibid., letters received, no.4, 1227, mfm. M–316, A. Iredell to D.W. Smith, 1796; ibid., letters received, no.6, 1864, P. Selby to A. Iredell, 22 May 1797; ibid., 1869, survey instructions to Iredell, 20 June 1797; DLF, SR, SL, vol. 27, Iredell no.52; DLF, SR, FN, vol. 3, 103–5, Iredell, survey of the Huron reserve for the town of Sandwich, 5–17 December 1798, and ibid., ONB, no.603; ibid., ONB no.604, SD (Survey Diaries) of Malden and Sandwich, 1 July 1797–1 January 1798.

190 DLF, SR, ONB, no.765, Iredell's survey of Sandwich, 1 July–13 October 1799; NA, RG1, L6B, vol. 25, 763–4, A. Iredell to Chewett and Ridout, 15 December 1799.

191 DLF, SR, SL, vol. 27, Iredell no.97 (letters received, no.6, 1875), Iredell to D.W. Smith regarding requests for survey of Gosfield, Colchester, and Mersea, 9 September 1797; DLF, SR, FN, vol. 2, 270–2; vol. 3, 270–2; vol. 11, 87–90, 213–19, 353–8; vol. 13, 118–21, A. Iredell, SD and FN of these townships. See also DLF, SR, SN, ONB, 129, 1 January–15 July 1797 (really a survey of Malden). In Colchester it is possible, on the evidence of DLF map A6, that Iredell surveyed northward for three concessions, although it is also possible that his work was confined to the coast where McNiff had surveyed in 1789–90. Certainly, this area was surveyed by Thomas Smith in 1805.

192 DLF, SR, FN, vol. 3, 97 and 105–8, survey notes of A. Iredell for 1798.

193 DLF, SR, FN, vol. 3, 92–100, survey notes of the Lake Erie shore.

194 DLF, map A27 and A41.

195 NA, MG9, D4, letters received, no.4, Iredell to Smith, 7 November 1795; DLF, SR, FN, vol. 13, 8–12 and SN of Iredell for 1795–96.

196 DLF, SR, ONB, 514, vol. 11, 166–77, FN of P. Carroll; AO, shelf 73, box 1, 24 December 1831–8 April 1832, and DLF, SR, SL, vol. 19, no.8, P. Carroll to William Chewett, 8 April 1832. Carroll received

£27.15s.0d. for surveying the Crown and clergy reserves in Malden. This task took him thirty-seven days. See AO, RG1, A–I–7, 10 April 1832, and Anon., "Peter Carroll," 99–101.

197   DLF, map A27, Iredell, 1798; AO, RG1, A–I–7, subject files, MS 892, reel 12, 12072–6. Smith received 7/6d per day plus expenses for himself and his crew for this work completed between 1 April and 4 July 1806.

198   AO, RG1, A–I–7, subject files, MS 892, reel 12, 12056 and 12060.

199   DLF, map A6, survey plan of Iredell, 1797. As late as 1799 he had not run the second concession of Colchester. See NAC, MG9, D4, 418, Iredell to Smith, 24 January 1799.

200   DLF, map A28, survey plan of Iredell, 1798.

201   See DLF, map A24, Maidstone and Rochester townships.

202   NA, MG9, D4, letters received, no.15, 2091, mfm. M–318, A. Iredell to W. Chewett and T. Ridout, 1 December 1803.

203   Smith was examined by Philip R. Fry in 1787 and authorized to act on Fry's behalf. This action was sanctioned by Ancrum and Matthews, the military commandants. NA, MG18, I 5, Detroit Notarial Records, vol. 4, 63–4, 1790–96, 63–4. I am grateful to Warren Munroe for drawing this to my attention.

204   DLF, SR, ONB 132, survey notes of Colchester by T. Smith, 13 March –11 May 1805; ibid., 234–65, SD of T. Smith for Gosfield, 12 May–4 July 1805, and DLF, SR, FN, L7F, vol. 5, 45; DLF, SR, SL, vol. 31, T. Smith, no.38–9 (letters received, no.15, 2114), T. Smith to Chewett and Ridout, 18 March 1805; ibid., no.47, sketch of a tract of land in Colchester, 15 October 1805; ibid., no.55, 8 January 1806; ibid., sketch of a tract of land in Gosfield, 15 October 1805; ibid., no.54, sketch of Gosfield, 8 January 1806; DLF, SR, SL, vol. 31, T. Smith no.56–7 (letters received, no.15, 2243), T. Smith to C.B. Wyatt regarding conflicting boundaries and the proposed road, Sandwich to Point Pelée, 8 January 1806.

205   DLF, SR, SD of Thomas Smith for 1805, 59 and 61–3.

206   Ibid., 61.

207   Ibid., 65.

208   Smith provides the means of converting on page 61 of his diary, where he states that 39.5 pence Provincial was equal to 60 pence York, yielding a conversion rate of 1.51. At this rate Smith received £14.15s.4d.

209   The material at this point is drawn from Smith's survey diaries.

210   DLF, SR, SD of T. Smith, townships of Colchester and Gosfield, 4 May 1805, 23.

211   Ibid., 47, SD of T. Smith, 28 May 1805.

212   Ibid., 14 June 1806.

213   DLF, SR, SL, T. Smith no.53 (letters received, no.15, 2252), T. Smith to C.B Wyatt, 17 March 1806; ibid., T. Smith no.64–5 (letters received, no.15, 2328), T. Smith to C.B. Wyatt regarding Colchester, Mersea, and

Petite Côté, 9 July 1806. This reports Mersea completed and comments upon disputes over the line in Colchester and Petite Côté.

214   Clarke, "Mahlon Burwell," 125–8; Lewis, "Colonel Mahlon Burwell," 23–8; Blue, "Colonel Mahlon Burwell," 41–56.

215   NA, RG1, L1, Upper Canada Land and State Book (hereafter Land Book) K, vol. 29, 57, mfm. C–103, 24 and 30 March 1819; ibid., 362, 366, and 487, 9 and 24 February 1820; ibid., 188, 13 July 1819; ibid., Land Book L, vol. 30, 19; ibid., 25, 21 February 1821 and ibid., 405, 30 April 1823; ibid., Land Book M, vol. 31, 599 and 604, mfm. C–104, 14th March 1826; ibid., Land Book O, vol. 33, 418, mfm. C–105, 3rd March 1831; ibid., Land Book P, vol. 34, 134, 31 January 1832; ibid., Land Book Q, vol. 35, 321, 27 February 1834; ibid., Land Book R, vol. 36, 149, 28 September 1835; NA, RG1, L3, bundle B13/9, 44, mfm. C–1626, 7 February 1821; ibid., 49, B15/5, mfm. C–1628, 23 March 1827; ibid., B16/98, 52, mfm. C–1629; ibid., bundle 22, part I, and 22/73–73d, 64, mfm. C1634, 19 February and 20 April 1840.

216   Calculation of the author using AO, patent index for Essex County, and NA, RG1 L6B, vol. 4, no pagination, T. Ridout to G. Hellier, secretary to the lieutenant governor, 26 April 1823, and ibid., T. Ridout to G. Hellier, 9 February 1826. The statistics for Rochester Township may include 954 acres in Orford Township.

217   *Manual Relating to Surveys and Surveyors*; Clarke, "Geographical Analysis of Colonial Settlement," appendices 3.1. and 4.3; Gentilcore and Donkin, "Land Surveys"; Gentilcore, "Lines on the Land," 57–73; Blue, "Colonel Mahlon Burwell," 41–55; Thompson, *Men and Meridians*, vol. 1, 236–9; DLF, OFN (Original Field Notes), Letters, Diaries, and Survey Maps. See also AO, RG1, A–I–6, vols. 4–10, 12, 16, 17, 19, and 24, various items, 1809–40; AO, RG1, A–V, vols. 7, 8, 12, and 15, and NA, RG1, E3, vol. 87, Upper Canada State Papers, 48–50, mfm. C–1201.

218   With additional purchases his land holdings amount to at least 43284.8 acres but the discrepancy between sources – the geographically organized patent index and the abstract index to deeds – can be as high as 13.5 per cent. If this is accepted, then his holdings might have been 49,128 acres.

219   Blue, "Colonel Mahlon Burwell," 49; Thompson, *Men and Meridians*, vol. 1, 237.

220   Donald Fraser, *The St. Thomas Journal*, 21 November 1833, quoted in Patterson, "Studies in Elections and Public Opinions," 37–8.

221   AO, RG1, A–I–6, vol. 4, letters of James Green, 13 and 21 February 1805.

222   Sufficient it would seem to train others. See anon., "Peter Carroll," 99–101, and Cameron, "Roswell Mount," 521–2.

223   Thompson, *Men and Meridians* vol. 1, 236–41; NA, RG1, E3, vol. 87, 48–50, instructions to survey; AO, shelf 73, box 6, M. Burwell, west and

north branches of the Talbot Road, 25 July–2 November and 23
August–15 October 1811; Guillet, *Pioneer Travels*, 169.

224 AO, shelf 73, box 6, Burwell survey of 1 May–5 October 1816: DLF, SR,
SL, vol. 113, no.47, M. Burwell to T. Talbot asking how to lay out the
Talbot Road through the swamps, 26 August 1816; ibid., no.48, T.
Talbot to M. Burwell, 30 August 1816, directing Burwell to place the
road where best suited even if through the reserves; DLF, SR, FN vol. 4,
17 and ONB 522.

225 DLF, SR, SL, vol. 2, 26–7, T. Ridout to M. Burwell, April 1821; ibid., vol.
13, no.101 (SL no.1, 44), M. Burwell to T. Ridout, 24 February 1823;
ibid. (SL, no.1, 69), M. Burwell to T. Ridout, 26 March 1823; ibid., vol.
13, no.14, Burwell to Ridout, 5 November, 1824; ibid., vol. 13, no.117,
M. Burwell to T. Ridout, 31 December 1824; ibid., vol. 13, no.127,
Burwell to Ridout, 23 September 1825.

226 DLF, SR, transcribed volumes, vol. 11, 26–7, letter of instruction,
T. Ridout to M. Burwell, 17 April 1821; ibid., vol. 21, 261–5, Ridout to
Burwell, 24 February 1823.

227 DLF, SR, FN, vol. 11, 220–60 and 266–319, survey notes of Burwell for
1821; see Burwell's survey map of Rochester, DLF map 17. Drawn at
forty chains to one inch, the map is signed Port Talbot, 31 December
1824.

228 The survey notes of M. Burwell for 1821–22 can be found in DLF, SR,
FN, vol. 11, 67–86 and 261–5, and ONB 416.

229 DLF, SR, ONB 19, T. Smith for Amherstburg, 8 June 8th–3 July 1820 and
2 December–14 December 1820; DLF, SR, SL, C. Rankin, no.8, vol. 8,
survey of Colchester village lots, C. Rankin to T. Ridout, 20 April 1826;
DLF, SR, field notes of McIntosh in the survey of the Huron reserve, 10
August–13 September 1833; DLF, SR, SL, vol. 131, T. Smith, no.183,
T. Smith to T. Ridout regarding history and disputed boundaries in
Petite Côté, 6 June 1822; DLF, SR, SL, vol. 31, T. Smith, nos. 232–3 and
245–6, T. Smith to T. Ridout regarding the survey of the Cranberry
marsh and the 2nd concession of Petite Côté, 28 November 1825 and
6 July 1828; SD of Wilkinson in Colchester Township, 2 September–21
October 1841; AO, shelf 72, box 3, 72–3.

230 DLF, SR, FN, Peter Carroll, vol. 11, 178–207; ONB 21.

231 DLF, SR, SL, vol. 31, T. Smith no.258–9, T. Smith to W. Chewett regarding the re-survey of Malden, 27 January 1831; ibid., no.8, C. Rankin,
no.11, C. Rankin to T. Ridout regarding irregularities in the survey in
the rear of Colchester and Malden townships, 26 November 1828.

232 NA, RG1, L6B, DR–SG, no pagination, M. Burwell to Thomas Ridout,
Surveyor-General's Office, 17 October 1826, and ibid., vol. 10, file 4,
no pagination, M. Burwell (true copy 27 October 1826), and ibid., no
pagination, 3 April 1828.

233 Executive Council resolution of 24 May 1794, extracted from the minutes of council by John Small and printed in the *Upper Canada Gazette or American Oracle*, vol. 1, no.42, 10 July 1794.

234 AO, 1568 (A–15), Patrick McNiff, "Sketch to show the Extravagant Claims," 1790.

235 NA, MG9, D4, 421–2. A. Iredell to T. Smith, 24 January 1799.

236 Blue, "Colonel Mahlon Burwell," 41.

237 Taylor, "Town and Townships," 88–96; "A Manual Relating to Surveys"; Weaver, *Crown Surveys in Ontario*; Lambert and Pross, *Renewing Nature's Wealth*; Gentilcore, "Lines on the Land," 57–73; "The Making of a Province," 137–55; Gentilcore and Donkin, "Land Surveys of Southern Ontario."

238 NA, MG21, B–124, Haldimand Papers, reprinted in AO, *Report of 1906*, 368–9.

239 Patterson, *Land Settlement*, 26; Gentilcore, "The Making of a Province," 137–55.

240 The Malden Road lots are 100 chains long by, on average, 20 chains wide, conforming to the single-front method.

241 AO, *Report of 1905*, 123, the Land Board to Hugh Finlay, chairman of the Land Committee of the Legislative Council, 6 May 1791.

242 Ibid., 63, the Land Board to H. Motz, end of the month, October 1790.

243 Ibid., 139, minutes of the Land Board, District of Hesse.

244 NA, RG1, L4, vol. 4, 149–50, McNiff to the members of the Land Board, 7 June 1791.

245 Ibid., vol. 3, 557–9, McNiff to the president of the board, 28 August 1791; See also DLF, SR, SL, vol. 3, McNiff no.28, McNiff to Major John Smith, president of the Land Board of Hesse, 28 August 1791.

246 NA, RG1, L4, vol. 3, 473–4, report of the board, 28 August 1791; AO, *Report of 1905*, 64–5, McNiff to the members of the Land Board, 16 November 1790.

247 NA, RG1, L4, vol. 1, 211–15, McNiff to England, 2 March 1793; ibid., 218–19, E.J. O'Brien, secretary to the land Board to McNiff, 29 March 1793.

248 Ibid., vol. 3, 434–47, McNiff to Hugh Finlay, 3 May 1791, and AO, *Report of 1905*, xiii to xclv.

249 Ibid.

250 AO, *Report of 1905*, 123–6, members of the Land Board of the District of Hesse to Hugh Finlay, chairman of the Land Committee of the Legislative Council, 6 May 1791.

251 DLF, SR, SL, vol. 3, 29. Letter of McNiff to the Land Board of Hesse, 8 November 1791.

252 AO, *Report of 1905*, 164, minutes of the Land Board of the District of Hesse, Friday, 30 March 1792.

253 Ibid., 179, members of the board (John Smith, John Askin, George Leith, and Montigny Louvigny), 30 April 1792.

254 Moir, "Church and State in Canada West"; Barkwell, "The Clergy Reserves in Upper Canada"; McDonald, "The Clergy Reserves in Canada"; Jackson, "The Regressive Effects," 258–68; Gates, "The Land Policies"; Richards, "Lands and Policies," 193–209; Wilson, "The Political and Administrative History"; "The Clergy Reserves: Economical Mischiefs," 281–99.

255 Patterson, "Land Settlement in Upper Canada"; Gates, "Land Policies of Upper Canada."

256 Wilson, *The Clergy Reserves of Upper Canada*, 3–280.

257 Patterson, "Land Settlement in Upper Canada," 220.

258 Literally in a dead hand, that is, excluded from the land available to the settler. Wilson, *The Clergy Reserves*, 280.

259 Shortt and Doughty, *Documents Relating* vol. 2, 1044–7.

260 This was included as the second part of Simcoe's proclamation of 1795. See NA, RG1, E3, vol. 87, 1W.

261 Wilson, *The Clergy Reserves*, 3–17.

262 McArthur and Doughty, *Documents Relating*, vol. 2, 21–3 and 61.

263 Ibid., 2, 59n.3; Gates, *Land Policies*, 161.

264 Ibid., 2, 970–87.

265 Regher, "Land Ownership in Upper Canada," 35–48.

266 Cruikshank, *Simcoe Papers* vol. 1, 108–9.

267 Mealing, "Sir David William Smith," 811–13.

268 NA, MG 11 (CO42), Q282 part 1, 110–35, mfm. C–12599, "Report on the Reserved Lands of Upper Canada in Lt. Governor Simcoe's No 34 to His Grace the Duke of Portland," 9 November 1795 (hereafter "Report on the Reserved Lands"); Wilson, *The Clergy Reserves*, 21.

269 AO, Simcoe Papers, envelope 44, Surveyor General's Office, 9 November 1795.

270 NA, MG 11 (CO42) Q282, part 1, 113, "Report on the Reserved Lands."

271 Ibid., 112.

272 In the case of the townships of fourteen concessions and twenty-four lots per concession, the instructions required that ninety-six lots or 28.57 per cent of the lots be reserved. Smith's scheme provided that ninety-eight lots or 29.16 per cent be reserved, but as he pointed out, two lots could easily be disposed of to meet some particular exigency.

273 NA, MG 11 (CO42) Q282, part 1, 128–31, "Report on the Reserved Lands; Proof and Polymetric tables for diagrams A and B," 9 November 1795. I am grateful here for the thoughts of John Nathaniel Clarke.

274 AO, Simcoe Papers, envelope 44, Surveyor General's Office, York, 9 November 1795.

275 NA, MG 11 (CO42) Q282, part 1, 113, "Report on the Reserved Lands."

276 In nominal terms, reserves in Maidstone and Rochester constituted 21 per cent of each township; in Tilbury, the requisite figure was 25.5 per cent. In actual acreage, given the irregular surveys in these townships, the figures may have been closer.

277 Ibid., 115.

278 Ibid., 118.

279 Ibid., 116–17; Wilson, *The Clergy Reserves*, 25.

280 This plan, entitled "Two Sevenths of Certain Old Townships in the Western District Set Apart for the Crown and Clergy," was originally part of the Simcoe report. It was designated Q.S.252. At some point in the past, it and six others were separated from this document and sent to the NMC. The Crown and clergy reserves are marked with Lake and Indian ink respectively.

281 The establishments indicated on these maps were classified under a typology discussed at greater length in Clarke and Brown, "Focii of Human Activity," 31–57.

282 A number of establishments existed at the mouth of Cedar Creek in Gosfield Township. Although never formally recognized as a village, it has been accepted here as a centre of particular importance.

283 NA, MG23, H I 4, vol. 3, 1001, n.d.

284 SR, LF, FN, vol. 11, 178–207, and ONB 21, 1835, and SR, LF, SL (Survey letter), vol. 19, no.27, Carroll to Radenhurst, 9 April 1836.

285 Gates, *Land Policies*, 165.

286 Ibid., 165–7.

287 One of the most vocal opponents of the clergy reserves was Robert Gourlay, who in 1822 published in his *Statistical Account of Upper Canada* the results of a questionnaire circulated in the province. One question asked the recipients to name the cause that most retarded the development of the township. Seventy replies were received. Seventeen named the clergy reserves as one cause of hardship, but none named them as the *sole* cause. Gourlay's analytical ability is seriously questioned by Alan Wilson, who points out that the evidence did not justify Gourlay's singling out the clergy reserves for special consideration. See Wilson, *The Clergy Reserves*, 60–1.

288 This was the initial legislative step. One-quarter of the reserves were to be sold and a maximum of 100,000 could be sold in any one year.

CHAPTER THREE

1 The minutes of the Land Board now appear in four locations: in the AO's third report in 1905; in AO, Jarvis-Powell Papers; in TRL, W.D. Powell Papers; and in NA, RG1, L4, mfm. C–1426.

2   Allen, *His Majesty's Indian Allies*, 34.

3   Quaife, *The Siege of Detroit*; See also Chevrette, "Pontiac," 525–31.

4   Frederickson and Gibb, *The Covenant Chain*; Richter and Merell, *Beyond the Covenant Chain*.

5   Allen, *His Majesty's Indian Allies*, 13.

6   See Brigham, *British Royal Proclamations*, 212–18. Reference is made here and elsewhere in this text to the copy held at the TRL in the Jarvis Papers, B63, "A Proclamation, Johnson Hall, New York, 24th December, 1763." See Stagg, "Anglo-Indians Relations."

7   Sullivan et al., *The Papers of Sir William Johnston*, vol. 2, 434, cited in Thomas, *Sir John Johnson*, 32.

8   Allen, *His Majesty's Indian Allies*, 27; Gwynn, "Sir William Johnson," 394–8.

9   TRL, Jarvis Papers, Royal Proclamation of 1763. Interestingly, Johnson, in informing the Indians that they were subjects of the King, used the accustomed language of the covenant chain and the diplomatic procedures of what White calls the "middle ground." The Indians, Johnson held were now subjects of the King of Great Britain "so far as the same can be consistant with the Indians native rights." Richard White, *The Middle Ground*, 307.

10 Harold Innis describes these relationships in the *Fur Trade in Canada*. The ways in which European and Amerindian societies adjusted to their increasing interrelationship as treated in Ray, *Indians in the Fur Trade* and *Give Us Good Measure*.

11 Peter Wraxall, in McIlwain, *An Abridgement of the Indian Affairs*, ix, and quoted in Allen, *His Majesty's Indian Allies*, 231.

12 "To every person having the rank of a field officer, five thousand. To every captain three thousand acres – To every subaltern or Staff thousand acres – to every noncommissioned officer two hundred, private man, fifty acres " The grants were subject to a quit rent at the end of ten years.

13 General Thomas Gage, the commander-in-chief of British forces in North America from 1764 to 1775, sought to enforce the Royal Proclamation but to little avail. In part this was because he himself did not view the prohibition as an absolute. He allowed for "military tenure" around British posts and held to the view that the French reached the Illinois country before the Illinois fled there and therefore the British held claim to it by right of conquest. White, *The Middle Ground*, 308. See also Wise, "Thomas Gage," 278–81.

14 TRL, Powell Papers, B84, L16, 3–20, "To the King's Most Excellent Majesty: A Report of the Lords of Trade by Sir William Johnson Bart," 7 March 1768.

15 Ibid., 18, "Report of the Lords of Trade to the King's Most Excellent Majesty," 7 March 1768.

16 Ibid., 12. One measure of commercial importance is perhaps the amount of debt in a society. By 1788 Powell estimated that no less than £20,000 was owed to traders in small farms under £100. Ibid., B80, L16, 16–17, W.D. Powell to Henry Motz 7 April 1788.

17 Allen, *His Majesty's Indian Allies*, 36. See also Sosin, "The British Indian Department," 34–50; White, *The Middle Ground*, 362–4.

18 On 17 and 18 September 1765, Pontiac granted two parcels of land to Alex Maisonville and Dr George Anthon. The former was four by eight arpents and the latter four by eighty. Both were strictly illegal. See Lajeunesse, *The Windsor Border Region*, 62, and NA, RG1, L4, vol. 2, 19, Pontiac to George Christian Anthon in the presence of George Croghan, superintendent of Indian affairs. This deed was entered in the register of Detroit on the 26 April 1768, folio 12. See also an Indian deed to Maisonville for an eight-by-eighty-acre parcel on the south side of the Detroit River, made on 2 July 1772 in "natural love and affection," in NA, RG1, L4, vol. 2, 33.

19 Actually François-Marie Picoté de Belestre. See Tousignant and Dionne-Tousignant, "Francois-Marie Picoté de Belestre," 633–5.

20 NA, RG1, L4, vol. 2, 48–52, General T. Gage, to the commanding officer, Detroit, 8 April 1778; see also Lajeunesse, *The Windsor Border Region*, 64–6, where the date is 8 April 1771.

21 Lajeunesse, *The Windsor Border Region*, 131, gift of land of six by forty French acres to Rev. F.X. Huber and the Sisters of the Congregation, 4 March 1782; TRL, Powell Papers, B79, L16, Huron gift (in French) to the son of Bondy, 7 June 1787.

22 Lajeunesse, ibid., 67, Lieutenant Governor Hamilton to General Sir Frederick Haldimand, 9 September 1778.

23 Ibid., 158, Hay to Haldimand, 22 July 1784.

24 *Historical Collections and Research, Michigan Pioneer and Historical Society* (hereafter *Historical Collections*), vol. 14, 16, Alexander Macomb to Captain Henry Bird.

25 Patrick Sinclair (1736–1820) was a Scottish-born soldier. This property was presumably that which he owned at Fort Sinclair (Port Huron, Michigan). It was acquired sometime between 1767 (when the Marines with whom he served were reduced) and 1769 (when he returned to England). The property was sold for debt in 1788. In 1775 he was appointed lieutenant governor and superintendent of Michilimackinac (where Arent DePeyster was the military commander), but because of the revolution he took three years to reach his post. Nonetheless, between 1779 and his departure for Quebec in 1782, he was the most important man on the Upper Great Lakes. Armour, "Patrick Sinclair," 759–60.

26 Armour, "Arent Schuyler DePeyster," 188–90. DePeyster (1736–1822) was the military commandant at Michilimackinac between 1774 and

1779. He was active in diplomacy and secured a truce between the Sioux and Ojibwa and their assistance in defending Michilimackinac where the British had few soldiers. His skills were also used to secure the Indians' assistance in recapturing Montreal in 1776 and in persuading them to join Burgoyne's mission into New York in 1777. From Detroit, where he was appointed in 1779, he directed Indian attacks into Kentucky and he sought to block American attacks on Detroit. He left for England in 1785.

27 AO, F378, Hiram Walker Collection, 20–62, deed of Pontiac to Lieutenant Abbott, September 1766.

28 Much of this would seem to have been a vast timber reserve north of Lake St Clair, given him by the Ojibwa. In 1789 he had 1440 acres of developed land on the American and 720 acres on the British side. Miquelon, "Jacques Dupéront Baby," 38–9. Having fought with France's Indian allies on the Ohio during the Seven Years' War, Baby chose not to return to France as originally intended but to continue in the fur trade at Detroit. Admired by the Indians, with whom he was acquainted since 1753, when as a twenty-two year old he had been Indian agent in Pennsylvania, he served in the Indian Department and acted as commissary. He was made a JP in 1784, became a lieutenant of the Detroit militia in 1787, and was appointed to the Land Board in 1788. He had little opportunity to serve in the last office or enjoy its benefits since he died in August 1789.

29 Farrell, "Settlement along the Detroit Frontier," 95.

30 Ibid., 93–4.

31 Horsman, *Matthew Elliott*, 52–5; ibid., *Expansion and American Indian Policy*, 23. At Vincennes, the treaty signed on 27 September 1792 recognized Indian ownership and the Indian right to sell or not sell. Horsman, *Matthew Elliott*, 94. After Wayne's defeat of the Indians at the battle of Fallen Timbers, things swung in the Americans' favour. Ibid., 101–3.

32 NA, MG23 H1 I, Simcoe Papers (Devon Series), folder 4, file 3, reel A605, Simcoe to Sheaffe, 10 August 1794. Ibid., file 4/6 (n.d.) documents the formal British protest: "Until the existing difference respecting it [The Treaty of Peace] shall be mutually and finally adjusted; the making possession of any part of the Indian territory either for the purpose of war or sovereignty is held to be a direct violation of His Brittanic Majesty's reports as they unquestionably existed before the Treaty." Ibid., file 4/7, dated 16 August 1794, records the receipt of this protest by Thomas Little agent for C. Williams.

33 In part, the British took this position in an attempt to secure justice for the Loyalists and to recover pre-revolutionary debt. American breaches of the treaty of 1783 were acknowledged by no lesser personages than

John Adams and John Jay. At the same time, the British were anxious to keep the fur trade and avoid conflict with the Indians. Creighton, *Dominion of the North*, 184–7, and NA, MG21, B–119, Haldimand Papers, 322–4, Haldimand to DePeyster, n.d. but *c.*1784.

34 Meinig, *The Shaping of America*, 2, 46.

35 See Goltz, "The Indian Revival," 18–32. A significant factor here was the personality of William Henry Harrison, governor of Indiana. His constant demand for Indian land, arguably exceeding American needs, was a significant cause of the revolt of Tecumseth, the pan-Indian resistance leader who helped defend Upper Canada. See Sugden, *Tecumseth*, 186.

36 Wise, "Upper Canada and the Conservative Tradition," 23, and Noel, *Patrons, Clients and Brokers*, 84.

37 Hesse was created by proclamation on 24 July 1788. See Lajeunesse, *The Windsor Border Region*, 105. See also NA, MG9, D4, Upper Canada Sundries, 1469–1472, mfm. C–317, signed George Pownall, secretary and registrar of records, copy of 8 November 1796.

38 Spragge, "The Districts of Upper Canada," 91–100, and Dean, *Economic Atlas of Ontario*, plate 98.

39 Gates, *Land Policies*, 29. The boards were re-established under Maitland in 1815. Ibid., 124.

40 As late as 1793, the boards were anxious to know if they were entitled to refuse land to those of known disloyalty even if they agreed to take the oath. The answer was that it was their "unquestionable duty." See AO, *Report of 1905*, 229, letter of instruction received and read at a Land Board meeting, 8 June 1793.

41 NA, RG1, L1, vol. 18, 73–8, mfm. C–100, rules and regulations for the conduct of the Crown Lands Department, 16 January 1789; read in council chamber, Quebec, 17 February 1789.

42 Not including Sir John Johnson or David William Smith. Johnson, as superintendent of Indian affairs and member of the Land Committee, sat as president of the local board wherever and whenever he was present. He exercised his privilege in the summer of 1790, presiding over important meetings of the Hesse board on 16 July and 11 and 12 August. Lajeunesse, *The Windsor Border Region*, cviii. After 27 October 1792, Smith sat as acting deputy surveyor general. Moorman, "The District Land Boards," 200.

43 Wickwire, "Richard G. England," 306–7.

44 Pilkington (1765–1834) returned to England in 1803: by 1809 he was a lieutenant-general. See Riddell, *La Rochefoucault-Liancourt's Travels in Canada 1795*, 178.

45 It is possible that this appointment was to repay Adhémar St Martin for his loyalty to the British. After 1792 he moved to Michilimackinac where

he served as a JP and notary. Farrell, "Toussaint-Antoine Adhémar dit Saint-Martin," 3–4.

46 Horsman, "Alexander McKee," 499–500.

47 Miquelon, "Jacques Baby dit Duperont," 38–40.

48 Brock, "William Robertson," 718–19.

49 Characterized here as a businessman, he was, in fact, a naval officer on half-pay who had the legal power to put commercial goods on HM ships and therefore exercised considerable influence in the Great lakes area. Later he built his own ships and monopolized all commercial shipping on the Great Lakes. MacDonald, "Commodore Alexander Grant," 167–81; Quaife, "Detroit Biographies," 65–80; Whitfield (in collaboration with), "Alexander Grant." 363–67.

50 Riddell, *The Life of William Dummer Powell*; Mealing, "William Dummer Powell," 605–13.

51 Béland, "Jean-Baptiste-Pierre Testard," 801–3.

52 George Leith was a founding member of the New North-West Company (XY Company), established in 1798 and absorbed by the North-West Company in 1804. See Goldring, "James Leith," 498–9. He was a partner in Leith, Shepherd and Duff. As a merchant he received 1200 acres of land but the source of his appointment was the recommendation of Sir John Johnson. See Cruikshank, *Simcoe Papers*, vol. 1, 192.

53 AO, *Report of 1905*, xcii, cviii, and cxxxvii. See Burton, "Detroit Biographies: John Askin," 1–9; Burton, "Business 'Adventures,'" 49–64; Farrell, "John Askin," 37–9. The officer of engineers who appeared as such on the board was Lieutenant Robert Pilkington.

54 However, as Wickwire points out, he did not neglect his own interest in land, successfully petitioning for 2000 acres on the Thames in 1795. Wickwire, "Richard England," 306–7.

55 Moorman notes that, while serving on the land boards of other jurisdictions, Robert Hamilton owned 83,000 acres, Richard Cartwright 28,632 acres, John Butler 11,300 acres, and David William Smyth some eighty lots on the St Clair. Moorman, "The District Land Boards," 83. In 1792 Askin was in debt to the Montreal firm of Todd and McGill for £20,217. see Quaife, *John Askin Papers* vol. 1, 402–3, "Indebtedness of John Askin," 24 January 1792. See also Wilson, *The Enterprises of Robert Hamilton*.

56 Powell attended fifty-two out of fifty-eight meetings when he resided at Detroit; after his appointment as chief justice, it was inevitable that his appearances would decrease. Moorman has computed the attendance of the members. The following figures indicate the number of meetings attended out of the possible number an individual might have attended: F. Close (0/1); Jacques Baby (0/46); Adhémar St Martin (2/138);

Alexander McKee (9/138); William Robertson (29/138); Alexander Grant (51/138); W. Dummer Powell (52/138); Patrick Murray (13/21); George Leith (37/92); J. Smith (44/50); Richard England (62/67); Montigny de Louvigny (86/92), and John Askin (88/92). Moorman, "The District Land Boards," 199–200.

57 Ibid.

58 NA, MG23, H I 4, William Dummer Powell and Family Papers, vol. 1, 13–16, J. Askin to W.D. Powell, Upper Canada, 25 January 1813.

59 Armstrong, "The Oligarchy of the Western District." See also Watson, *The Reign of George III*, 42–7, on the importance of this system and on the power exercised by magistrates in England.

60 Information provided by F.H. Armstrong, University of Western Ontario.

61 Mealing, "William Dummer Powell," 607, gives the date of his appointment as 2 February 1789. An undated letter of Dorchester's secretary, signed Coffin, seeks permission to advance Powell's name for this judgeship. AO, Jarvis-Powell Papers, 1043, 21. Coffin was Thomas Ashton Coffin, for whom see Caya, "Thomas Ashton Coffin," 192–3.

62 Riddell, *Michigan under the British*, 416.

63 Moorman, "The District Land Boards," 56.

64 Fraser, "George Hillier," 409–10. Hillier had served in the army with Sir Peregrine Maitland and would join him in Jamaica when he was posted there.

65 NA, RG1, E1, State Minute Books for Upper Canada, vol. H, 163–64, mfm. c–98, Earl Bathurst, 30 June 1825, to Lieutenant Governor Maitland. "... and I am to convey to you in reply, my regrets and entire disapprobation of the line of conduct which Mr .Powell had recently adopted ..." Powell was granted an annual pension of £1000 Sterling.

66 Iredell was a surveyor near Philadelphia before the revolution. He worked in New Brunswick as a surveyor before moving to Newark, and then he replaced Patrick McNiff as surveyor in the Western District. In 1796 he was appointed a JP for the Western District. Rourke, "Abraham Iredell," 96–103; Brock, "Abraham Iredell," 448–9.

67 Walter Roe, who arrived in Detroit in 1789, was appointed clerk of the peace for the Western District in 1794, became the deputy-registrar of the district in 1796, and in 1797 was made one of six benchers of the Law Society of Upper Canada. He handled the legal affairs of many, including William Hands JP and Angus McIntosh JP. McIntosh was connected with the North-West Company and a co-partner with Askin in the Miami Company; he was also a member of the Legislative Council. See Farrell, "Walter Roe,", 721–22. Roe, an alcoholic, drowned where there was no water, having fallen off his horse.

68 NA, RG5, A1, Civil Secretary's Correspondence, Upper Canada Sundries, vol. 88, 48630, Thomas Smith to Major George Hillier, 10 April 1828.

69 Ibid., 48,629–32. Independent testimony is afforded by Frederick Arnold, who in 1784 had brought twenty-five families into this area. None had received land and he had been obliged to purchase for £300 a farm that he believed inadequate for his family's needs. The others had become tenants. He reported that many had reproached him and threatened to return to the Unites States, "presuming it is not the intention of Government, to encourage the Population within this District, since so many obstacles are from year to year thrown in the way of establishment." NA, RG1, L4, vol. 3, 452–4, D.W. Smith's report of 23 July 1791.

70 NA, RG5, A1, vol. 88, ibid., 48,630.

71 Ibid., 48,630.

72 Ibid., 48,631.

73 While assistant secretary of Indian affairs, Selby, in the election of 1792, supported Major Smith's son, David William Smith, who was to become surveyor general of Upper Canada. Selby himself would be sworn in as a member of the Executive Council in 1808 and would end his days as receiver general and auditor general of the province. Christie, "Prideaux Selby," 749–50.

74 NA, RG5, A1, vol. 88, 48,720–3, Thomas Smith to Major George Hillier, Petite Côté, 19 April 1828.

75 Interestingly, the governor is said by Smith to have used intermediaries to put the question to him. These were Colonel Matthew Elliott of the Indian Department and Colonel John Askin of the militia. See ibid., 48,722. In fact, his name appears on commissions of July and September 1796. Personal communication with Frederick H. Armstrong.

76 Ibid., 48,721.

77 Ibid., 48,722.

78 A copy of this letter was transmitted to Simcoe by Major John Smith, commanding at Detroit. Smith believed it a forgery. "It is fraught with a good deal of malignity and framed either with intent to do mischief. The diffusion of its contents may be attended with bad consequences, and its author must be a villain of the deepest hue. Mr. Powell has made no certain discovery as yet as to its parent." Smith to Simcoe, Detroit, 30 April 1792. Cruikshank, *Simcoe Papers*, vol. 1, 150.

79 Ibid.

80 NA, RG5, A1, vol. 89, 48,893, Smith to Hillier, 2 May 1828.

81 Smith may have empathized with Powell. He was himself American, and though he had declared his allegiance to Britain in 1788 he may have been aware in the early years that he, too, was not wholly trusted. Upton, "William Smith," 714–18.

82 NA, RG5, A1, vol. 89, 48,892. Smith argued that Todd and McGill had secured Powell's appointment for the consideration of half his salary and

that a quarter was owed to Robertson. Todd and McGill were the principals of the well-known fur-trading company operating out of Montreal. See Momryk, "Isaac Todd," 818–22. Like Askin, Todd was Irish-born and by 1774 the business agent of Phyn, Ellice and Company, to whose London offices William Robertson left in 1790. Askin was the business agent of Todd-McGill in Detroit and when he got into debt with them they accepted land in this area as payment. Cooper, "James McGill," 527–30.

83 NA, RG5, A1, vol. 89, 48,890, Smith to Hillier, 2 May 1828.

84 Ibid., 48,981–6, Smith to Hillier, 13 May 1828.

85 Ibid.

86 Ibid., vol. 90, 49,726–730, mfm. C–6866, Smith to Hillier, 18 August 1828.

87 Ibid., 49,731.

88 This would appear to be James May, who appeared as plaintiff in front of Powell on several occasions. See Riddell, *Michigan Under British Rule*, 170–1, James May v. James Fleet, Court of Common Pleas, L'Assomption, 9 June 1791; ibid., 280–1, James May v. John Williams, 27 August 1792; and ibid., 284–86, May v. Williams, 30 August 1792. Powell found for May against Williams, representative of the King.

89 Ibid.

90 Juries were introduced only in 1792. By 32 George III, C.2, S.I (U.C.), issues of fact were determined by a jury of twelve; issues of law were determined by the court. Powell claimed that, because the law as such was unsatisfactory on the issue of patents, he had decided upon 2000 claims under his own discretion and that there had been no objections! AO, Jarvis-Powell Papers, 1045, 'Notes for Memoir of WDP in Canada,' transcribed version (A df 35, T26), 12.

91 TRL, Powell Papers, B80, L16, 5–6, Dupéront Baby and William Robertson, to Henry Motz, 6 September 1788.

92 NA, MG23, H I 4, vol. 1, 137–40, Powell to Adam Gordon, 22 September 1822. Here Powell expresses the expectation and hope that his son would get the first vacancy in the clerkship of the court over which he presided.

93 In April 1789 Monk was owed money from the balance of Powell's salary and had agreed to pay £150 per annum beginning 1789. He also owed Ellice £136. With this and Smith's statement of Powell's indebtedness to Robertson and Todd and McGill, Powell had little left from his salary of £500 sterling as judge. Mealing, *William Powell*, 607, and NA, MG23, H I 4, Powell Papers, vol. 1, 357–60, J.(I?) Monk to Powell, 16 December 1806.

94 Ibid., vol. 3, 1332, Powell to Duncan Cameron.

95 National Library of Canada, copy of a letter to Major-General Henry Knox, 2 February 1792, reproduced in W.D. Powell, *Story of a Refugee*

(1833), 8–10. The original of this letter was found in the home of Lieutenant Ross Leeven of the 5th Foot. It was discovered on the evening of the 3 April and was forwarded to Powell by Lieutenant Smith, secretary to the commandant at Detroit, on 17 April 1792. TRL, Powell Papers, B79, L16, 87–9. Internal evidence for the authorship of this letter is discussed in ibid. 92–3.

96 This man, who appeared by procuration as attorney in many cases, was officially to replace Thomas Smith as clerk of the Court of Common Pleas in July 1792. In practice he did so after 11 August 1792, when Smith resigned to look after his business as notary public. Riddell, *Michigan under British Rule*, 62 and 428. An adopted chieftain of the Shawnee, he stood with them against the Americans at the Battle of Fallen Timbers. Wounded in the knees, he was quartered by the Americans. The Shawnee exacted revenge on a captured American officer who was literally carved into pound pieces. See Cruikshank, *Simcoe Papers* vol. 3, 29–30.

97 TRL, Powell Papers, B79, L16, 104–5, n.d.

98 According to Mathew Dolson, a prototoype of the forged letter to Knox was seen at his tavern. He argued that it was in McNiff's handwriting and that Walter Roe would confirm this. Roe did not and this alone may have led Powell to the conclusion that Roe was guilty.

99 Kyte Senior, *From Royal Township*, 56.

100 Purportedly the officers sought to institute seigneurial tenure to lord it over the other inhabitants. McNiff was seen as the instigator of division within the Loyalists, "a seditious and dangerous incinderary as well as a common disturber of the peace." Kyte Senior, *From Royal Township*, 62.

101 As the evidence against the officers was whittled away, McNiff collapsed and was unable to continue his testimony. These events took place in 1787 in front of John Collins, deputy surveyor, and William Dummer Powell, one of two members of a board of enquiry. Kyte Senior, *From Royal Township*, 64–6. Although the final report came down hard against the officers, one suspects that Powell would not have appreciated McNiff's attitudes or behaviour.

102 NA, W.D. Powell Papers, vol. 3, 1332, Powell to Duncan Cameron.

103 TRL, Powell Papers, B79, L16, 25 April 1792.

104 Ibid., 98, n.d.

105 Ibid., 110–11, 6 April 1792.

106 Ibid., 99–100, 20 April 1792.

107 Ibid. 101–2, Powell to Lieutenant Selby, and Meldrum and Park, n.d.

108 Ibid., 102, sworn letter of C. Smyth, n.d.

109 Ibid., 102, affidavit of Mathew Dolson sworn in front of John Askin JP, 20 April 1792. McNiff denied that he was there beyond a particular

time; Dolson said the records would show that he was and had consumed two gills of rum. This is the same Dolson whom Thomas Smith declared had falsely accused Ebenezer Allen of bribery.

110 Ibid., 99, n.d.

111 Ibid., B80, L16, 93–6, Hugh Finlay, chairman, Executive Council committee, Quebec, 29 November 1791.

112 AO, *Report of 1905*, 14, 25 June 1790.

113 Ibid., 23–5, Minutes of the Land Board, 11 August 1790.

114 Ibid., 69, McNiff to the board, 26 June 1790.

115 Ibid., 71–2, McNiff to the board, 30 July 1790.

116 Ibid., 95, McNiff to the Board, 3 December 1790.

117 Ibid., 97, D.W. Smith to Henry Motz, secretary to the governor, 25 January 1791. McNiff had requested stationery but the board had declined to supply it, believing this the responsibility of the Surveyor General's Office.

118 Ibid., 220, E.J. O'Brien to McNiff, 5 February 1793.

119 TRL, Powell Papers, B79, L16, 98, memo on forged letter, n.d.

120 McNiff lost little time in transmitting information to Simcoe about the authorship of the treasonable document. See AO, F47, Simcoe Papers, McNiff to Simcoe, 22 May 1792.

121 TRL, Powell Papers, B79, L16, 99–100, n.d.

122 Ibid., 94, evidence of John Cornwall, 10 September 1791.

123 Ibid., 95–6, evidence of Edward Hearle, 10 September 1791.

124 TRL, Powell Papers, B79, 89–91, Powell to Dorchester, n.d.

125 Ibid., 89–91, Powell to Dorchester, n.d.

126 AO, Jarvis-Powell Papers, 1045, 10, notes for Powell memoir, draft text (A df 35).

127 In a letter to Motz, marked "private" and "draft never sent," Powell comments upon the resentments of the Indian Department and the "malignancy of Joseph Brant's Disposition. It is insinuated that I interfere with the department and his Lordship cannot be ignorant of the Jealousy with which such in Department must watch over the Intrusion of Strangers – You know how far I merit their resentment for I beg to be believed that here I hold no Communication with any of the Separate Interests or ever converse with an Indian ..." TRL, Powell Papers, B81, L16, 75–6, n.d. but probably 1787.

128 Ibid., 75–6.

129 AO, Jarvis-Powell Papers, 1045, 10, notes for Powell memoir, draft text (A df 35).

130 As such, he felt free to write to Dorchester privately. "I take the advantage of addressing to you to express myself with a freedom on the Subjects which occur which my Lord Dorchester would not expect in a public letter." In one letter he gave his views of the Huron chief

Doigentete: "… his few adherents … think that he is a conjurer founded upon that universal witchcraft which gives to strong fiends Dominion over the weak." TRL, Powell Papers, B79, L16, 24, n.d. In this same letter he says: "… the Hurons ever incroaching now claim the whole Country and especially that Tract North of the River Canard petitioned for by Captain McKee …"

131 Yet Elinor Kyte Senior points out that McNiff had helped Captain Samuel Anderson escape an American jail during the Revolutionary War, at considerable risk to himself, and that as a wealthy merchant on Staten Island he had lost £6000 to the revolutionaries. Senior, *From Royal Township*, 56.

132 This is an oversimplification of his politics, although he was accused of turning his coat at least twice. He did eventually return to the United states after his problems in Upper Canada and was for a time a judge in Michigan. McNiff had been a partner with John Askin, John Askin, Jr, and Alexander Henry and others in what was known as the Cuyahoga Purchase, a huge tract of Indian land on the south shore of Lake Erie. His biographer describes him as having "flexible ethics." See Edwards," Patrick McNiff," 551–3.

133 Cruikshank, *Simcoe Papers* vol. 3, 129; Armstrong, *Handbook of Upper Canadian Chronology*, 99.

134 AO, *Report of 1905*, 16–7, public notice, 2 July 1790.

135 Ibid., 160, addendum to board proceedings, 1 April 1791.

136 TRL, Powell Papers, B80, L16, 14–15, "Report as to the Carelessness of Secretary Thomas Smyth of the Land Board", September 1790. The substance of this report is that the records in English and most especially French were so poor or non-existent for a full year that legal decisions were prejudiced. On Smith's French, see Riddell, *Michigan under the British*, 428.

137 Riddell, ibid., 428.

138 His Royal Highness had remarked that Powell's "inveterate enemies … had been driven to absurdities which condemned themselves." NA, MG23, H I 4, vol. 4, 135, "Notice of the Progress of William Dummer Powell" (transcribed copy of manuscript originally in the possession of Aemilia Jarvis of Toronto).

139 Mealing, "William Osgoode," 557–60.

140 TRL, Powell Papers, B83, L16, 27, about 21 July 1796 and marked "vindication of letter of 20 July 1796."

141 Mealing, "William Osgoode," 607.

142 Ibid., 608.

143 The testimony is his own. AO, Jarvis-Powell Papers, 1046, transcribed volume, 10, n.d.

144 Mealing, "William Osgoode," 608.

145 Calculation of the author based upon a search of the abstract index to deeds for Essex. Powell is known to have owned one lot in Sandwich in 1795; his lawyer disposed of 12.5 acres for his estate in 1843. Of course, elsewhere in the province, he and his family did acquire land. He received 6900 acres between 1797 and 1823 and his immediate family another 10,000 acres. AO, Jarvis Powell Papers, 1037, statement of lands granted to the Powell family between 1797 and 1823. Myers, hardly an unbiased judge, believes that he and Chief Justice Elmsley may have bought from 20 to 50,000 acres of Loyalist rights. Myers, *History of Canadian Wealth*, 83.

146 NA, MG23, H I 4, vol. 1, 389, Powell to Charles Murray, 27 November, 1824.

147 Romney, "The Spanish Freeholder," 32–47.

148 From Dorsetshire, to which he had retired while Maitland was governor, he sought to maintain his name on both councils by special leave of absence. NA, MG23, H I 4, vol. 1, 182–85, Powell to W. Stanley, Colonial Office.

149 The discussion of the Executive Council, consisting of Powell, James Baby, Samuel Smith, and John Strachan, is to be found in NA, RG1, E1, State Minute Books, 481–8, mfm. C–98, 24–6, January 1825.

150 TRL, Powell Papers, B83, L16, 76–83, n.d., "A memoir on the Subject of Complaint of Sir. P. Maitland against Mr. Powell, the Chief Justice and Correspondence on various issues including the Award of a pension of £1,000"; ibid., letter of Maitland, 24 January 1825; ibid., 84–6, Minutes of the Executive Council, 24 January 1825; and ibid., 89–92, Report of the Executive Council, 26 January 1825. See also NA, RG1, E1, State Minute Books for Upper Canada, Vol. H, 163–4, mfm. C–98, Earl Bathurst, 30 June 1825.

151 NA, RG1, E1, State Minute Books for Upper Canada, vol. H, 163–4, mfm. C–98, Earl Bathurst, 30 June 1825; MG23, H I 4, vol. 4, 1618–21, Charles Murray to Earl Bathurst, and ibid., 1622–3, 20 September 1825, where the award of the pension is acknowledged.

152 NA, MG23, H I 4, vol. 4, 1626–8, memorial of William Dummer Powell, 28 November 1831. Powell claimed that he had opposed the notion that an officer of the Legislative Council might be exempt from arrest for debt, citing 10 Geo. III as his justification. It would seem that Maitland, after accepting legal advice, chose not to pursue the issue.

153 There is a small comment in the Simcoe Papers, the meaning of which is not clear: "P—ll is very quiet as yet; but it is said that he has formed a new party and expects to carry through all the Indian deeds." Cruikshank, *Simcoe Papers* vol. 5, 76, Thomas Smith to Alexander McKee, 6 October 1793.

154 NA, MG21, Add. MSS. 21661–892, Haldimand Papers, mfm. A–670, 327, Major Mathews to Haldimand, 3 August 1787.

155 TRL, Powell Papers, B81, L16, 53–7, Powell to Lord Dorchester, 1 July 1789.

156 TRL, Powell Papers, B84 (Indian Affairs vol.) L16, 1–2, H. Motz to Powell, 17 August 1789.

157 TRL, Powell Papers, B81, L16, the board to Lord Dorchester, 23 August 1789; AO, *Report of 1905*, 3–4, meeting of the board, 28 August 1789; ibid., 28, the board to Lord Dorchester, 28 August 1789.

158 NA, RG1, L4, vol. 2, 230–2, the board to Lord Dorchester, 28 August 1789.

159 Ibid., Dorchester to the Land Board for the District of Hesse, 2 September 1789.

160 Ibid., 249–50, copy of a letter of Motz, 5 October 1789, to Sir John Johnson and in possession of Alexander McKee.

161 AO, *Report of 1905*, 5, meeting of 1 December 1789; ibid., 6, meeting of 7 December 1789.

162 NA, RG1, L4, vol. 2, 255–6, the Board to Lord Dorchester, 17 October 1789. See also AO, *Report of 1905*, 17, minutes of meeting, 16 October 1789.

163 "His confidence in your judgement and Integrity will always incline him to hold you justified in the prudent Exercise of such discretionary Authority, as on Account of the Remoteness of the District, it may be necessary for the Board to assume for a perfect discharge of their trust under unforeseen circumstances, Taking for granted that a religious adherence to the same principles which actuates his Lordship will be maintained by the Board in all such cases. Ibid., 41, Motz to the board, 21 January 1790.

164 Ibid.

165 TRL, Powell Papers, B79, L16, 25–6, Powell to Motz, n.d. but *c.* 1789 or 1790.

166 Lajeunesse, *The Windsor Detroit Region*, 35, circular from Motz to the board, 19 January 1790.

167 AO, *Report of 1905*, 5, 26 October 1789. Some had come forward. See ibid., 7, 10 April 1790.

168 NA, RG1, L4, vol. 2, 272–3; AO, *Report of 1905*, 6, 26 February 1790.

169 This cession, negotiated by Alexander McKee, would later become Anderdon Township. See Lajeunesse, *The Windsor Detroit Region*, 165, "The Chiefs of the Ottawa and Chippewa Nations of Detroit Ceding Land at River Canard and Bois Blanc", 15 May 1786.

170 TRL, Powell Papers, B81, L16, 6, Powell to Motz, 26 December 1789.

171 AO, *Report of 1905*, 9 and 41, 21 May 1790.

172 NA, RG10, vol. 1840, IT 002, Indian deed of southwestern Ontario to George III, 19 May 1790. See also NA, "Appendix to the Sixth Volume of the Journals of the Legislative Assembly of the Province of Canada," no.1, A to T, vol. 6, 1847, map accompanying a "Report on the Affairs of the Indians in Canada, appendix T, 24 June 1847. On this the McKee Treaty territory could be delimited as twenty-four townships; on the basis of township-acreage data generously donated by Dr W.R. Wightman, supplemented by Census of Canada data for 1871 and allowing for the reserves, the acreage of the McKee cession was found to be approximately 1,510,796 acres. Jacobs reports the acreage of the surrender to have been 1,344,000 acres. If so, the price paid was 0.21 pence per acre as opposed to 0.19 using the larger acreage. Jacobs, "Indian land Surrenders," 61–8.

173 TRL, Powell Papers, B81, L16, 58–65, Powell to Motz, n.d. but c. 1790.

174 However, McNiff pointed out that this land at the Canard was very valuable but for the "great resort of Indians to that place during the Summer season, a circumstance ever unfavourable to New settlers in the vicinity of such a place." NA, RG1, L4, vol. 3, 434–37, McNiff to Hugh Finlay, 3 May 1791.

175 Ibid., 58–65, Powell to Motz, n.d. but c. 1790. For other Powell statements on the Huron, see TRL, Powell Papers, B81, L16, 43–8.

176 AO, *Report of 1905*, 9, 22 May 1790, and TRL, Powell Papers, B80, L16, 79, Land Board Minute of same date.

177 Ibid., 106, 25 May 1790.

178 Ibid., 88–91, 28 May 1790.

179 None other than Thomas Smith.

180 Ibid., B81, L16, 58–65, Powell to Motz, n.d.

181 AO, *Report of 1905*, 7, meeting of the Land Board, 16 April 1790.

182 Ibid., 40, McNiff to the board, 14 April 1790.

183 TRL, Powell Papers, B81, L16, 58–65, Powell to Motz, n.d.

184 Lajeunesse, *The Windsor Detroit Region*, 173, Indian speech to Sir John Johnson at the Huron village.

185 NA, RG1, L4, vol. 2, 409, Motz to Hugh Finlay, 20 October 1790.

186 Steele, "Hugh Finlay," 314–19.

187 Hayward, "John Collins," 161–2.

188 TRL, Powell Papers, B80, L16, 97, "Journal of the Proceedings of the Land Committee," 22 October 1790.

189 NA, RG1, L4, vol. 3, 434–7, McNiff to Hugh Finlay, 3 May 1791. Some corroboration of McNiff's position can be found in the Detroit commandant's letter to one Lean Nepeau, in *Historical Collections*, vol. 24, 20; ibid., 75–8, 8 September 1791.

190 Ibid., 411, Sir John Johnson to Hugh Finlay, 29 January 1791, and TRL, Powell Papers, B80, L16, 105, council chambers, Quebec, 4 February 1791.

191 McNiff had asserted that "the Land Board under the directions of the former three ruling members will not in three years if left to themselves place three familys more on the Land than are already there." See *Historical Collections*, vol. 24, 62. The commissioners heard from the District of Hesse on 6 May 1791 and again on 31 October. See AO, *Report of 1905*, 63, letter from the Land Board to Motz, 31 October 1790, and ibid., 123–6, letter from the board to Hugh Finlay, 6 May 1791; TRL, Powell Papers, B80, L16, 93–6, Hugh Finlay, chairman, Executive Council committee, Quebec, 1791, regarding report on the District of Hesse, 29 November 1791. It is not known if it was connected to these events but Robertson held McNiff's power of attorney to land in Cornwall and Charlottenburgh townships and assigned it to Robert Hamilton of Queenston. UWO, William Robertson Papers, item 76, 1 July 1796.

192 Steele, "Hugh Finlay," 318.

193 AO, *Report of 1905*, 12–4, minutes of the Land Board, 18 June 1790.

194 Sir John believed it possible that the Huron might yield enough of the reserve for a town. TRL, Powell Papers, B80, L16, 93–6, findings of the Executive Council on a report on the District of Hesse, Hugh Finlay, chairman, Quebec 29 November 1790.

195 Author's emphasis. On *lods et ventes*, see NA, RG1, L4, vol. 2, 146–8, "Account of lods and Ventes and Quit Rents at Detroit between the 7th April 1775 and the 22 April 1782, by whom collected and to whom paid", signed Henry Hamilton; and ibid., 145–7, "Account of lods and Ventes received during Colonel de Peyster's Command at Detroit, 30 April 1783", signed T. Williams.

196 AO, *Report of 1905*, 123, The Board to Hugh Finlay, Chairman of the Land Committee of the Legislative Council, 6 May 1791.

197 NA, RG1, L6B, vol. 25., Treaty 12, Upper Canada, 1124–32, 10 August 1799, endorsed by Richard Pollard, registrar, on 3 June 1801; See also Lajeunesse, *The Windsor Border Region*, 205–9, Captain Thomas McKee to Captain William Claus, 4 September 1799. This letter is interesting in that McKee agreed that not all the chieftains need be present at the cession since the majority wished to go hunting. Though only two or three might bear the responsibility, all might receive the treaty goods ahead of the official signing. Moreover, when this land was ceded, the rights of European occupants living on it would seem to have been ignored. One of these persons was William Hands, soon to be a person of prominence in Essex but at this time a resident of Detroit. He held 480 acres as an Indian grant. Although his legal title was tenuous, he was permitted to keep this farm because of the expense he had incurred provided his claims did not interfere with those of other proprietors, including his neigh-

bour Pajot. See AO, 20–108 B–3, 159–62, copy of first petition, William Hands to Peter Russell, 20 July 1797, and again 20 January 1807.

198 NA, RG1, L4, vol. 1, 1–21, Major Smith to the board, council chamber, 30 March 1792.

199 Leighton, "Simon Girty," 345–6; Calloway, "Simon Girty: Interpreter and Intermediary" 38–58.

200 Lajeunesse, *The Windsor Border Region*, 155–6, Captain Alexander McKee to Sir John Johnson, Detroit, 11 October 1783.

201 NA, RG1, L4, vol. 2, 85, deed to Jacob Schiefflin, 13 October 1783. This shows a list of seven village and war chiefs in a deed stated by T. Williams to have been registered as pages 283–284 of the register of Detroit; the second part of the document, in which Schiefflin claims that six chiefs of the Chippewa also signed together with two Pottawatomi chiefs, is annotated by Williams as not registered. See also Lajeunesse, *The Windsor Border Region*, 154.

202 Lajeunesse, ibid., 156, Captain Bird to Captain Mathews, 15 October 1783.

203 NA, RG1, L4, vol. 2, 87, Schiefflin to Captain McKee, 15 October 1783.

204 Lajeunesse, *The Windsor Border Region*, 156, Captain Bird to Captain Mathews, 15 October 1783.

205 Alexander McKee, seeking to allay the anger of the Indians, came close to firing Schiefflin. See *Historical Collections*, vol. 10, 203, Captain Alexander McKee to Sir John Johnson, November 1783.

206 Lajeunesse, *The Windsor Border Region*, 157, Haldimand to Sir John Johnson, 15 November 1783.

207 In July 1795 the Ottawa, Ochippouci, and Pottawatomi sold a tract to none other than Schiefflin and his partners Richard Pattinson, Robert Innis, and Jacobus Visgar. Schiefflin is now described as an adopted brother and chief known by the names of Ottason and Ninawenima. This description and the fact that Schiefflin is identified first may have been designed to allay the fears of British officialdom or the American successor state which took control under Jay's Treaty in 1796. The tract ran from the South Raisin River for five leagues (fifteen miles), then northwest for twenty leagues and northeast for twenty leagues until the line struck the head of the River Huron and then turned south to Lake St Clair and the Rouge River below Detroit. This extensive area was sold for £500 sterling. The sale was witnessed by John Askin, John McGregor, Hugh Pattinson, Gregor McGregor, Henry Hay, John Askin, Jr, and John Kerr. The deed, signed by twenty-nine chieftains, was registered on the 17 August 1795 by Walter Roe. All were aware of the official British position on these matters but behaved as if they were not. NA, MG18, I 5, Detroit Notarial Records, tome 4, 98–105.

208 Horsman, "Egushwa," 260–1.

209 NA, RG1, L4, vol. 2, 92–100, council meeting, 18 October 1783. This meeting involved four Ottawa chiefs, seven Chippawa chiefs, and three interpreters. The Huron were absent. McKee attended as deputy agent, DePeyster as commanding officer; there were nine representatives of the Indian Department, including captains Bird, Caldwell, Elliott, La Motte, and Willoe.

210 Ibid., 95.

211 He also warned against the use of rum which one of the chiefs involved in the Schiefflin business had sought. Whether this discussion was innocent or orchestrated is uncertain, but it was pertinent to the argument and the reception of it. See ibid., 98–9, council meeting, 20 October 1783.

212 Ibid., 102–5, 21 October 1783.

213 Ibid., 102–6, 21 October 1783. Emphasis added.

214 Schiefflin was asked to deliver it in the "King's name" and had complied with this request of the commandant. Believing the deed to be title to his property, he had only surrendered it only for safekeeping to DePeyster. DePeyster forwarded it to Haldimand "to be disposed of as you see proper." *Pioneer Collection*, vol. 10, 142–3, DePeyster to Haldimand, 15 July 1783.

215 Thomas McKee, for whom see Clarke, "Thomas McKee," 535–6.

216 NA, RG1, L4, vol. 1, 116–20, Schiefflin to Sir John Johnson, 18 October 1783. The partitioning of this property on 25 August 1784 can be found in *Historical Collections*, vol. 24, 14–15, "Documents relative to Land on Detroit River granted to Lt.Col. H. Bird."

217 Ibid., 119.

218 Author's emphasis.

219 Ibid., 118–19.

220 Ibid., 122–9, Schiefflin to Brigadier-General Sir John Johnson, 24 October 1783.

221 Lajeunesse, *The Windsor Border Region*, 157, Haldimand to Lieutenant Governor Hay, 26 April 1784.

222 Ibid.

223 Ibid.

224 Sutherland, Tousignant, and Dionne-Tousignant, "Sir Francis Haldimand," 887–902.

225 He would be reminded of this service. See *Pioneer Collection*, vol. 10, 239–40, memorial of Matthew Elliot to Haldimand, endorsed 21 July 1784.

226 Lajeunesse, *The Windsor Border Region*, 159; NA, RG1, L4, vol. 2, 178–80, Haldimand to Lieutenant Governor Hay, 14 August 1784.

227 Ibid., 245–6, Major Robert Mathews to Sir John Johnson, 14 August 1784.

228 Lajeunesse, ibid.

229 Ibid., 160–1, Hay to Philip Fry, deputy surveyor, 25 March 1785, and certificate of Fry, 25 March 1785. Lots of six acres in front were surveyed for Caldwell, McKee, and Elliott. Lots of four acres were surveyed for Joncaire Chabert, Thomas McKee, Simon Girty, Anthony St. Martin, Chevalier Chabert, Isidore Chene, and Charles Reaume. The size of frontage was subsequently extended by Major Mathews under the authority of Lord Dorchester.

230 AO, *Report of 1905*, 2–3, 14 August 1789.

231 Ibid., 30–1, Lord Dorchester to the board, 2 September 1789; NA, RG1, L4, vol. 2, 242–6, Dorchester to the Land Board of the District of Hesse, 2 September 1789.

232 AO, *Report of 1905*, xcvi, map of the Indian officer's claims.

233 TRL, Powell Papers, B80, L16, 99, minutes of the Land Committee, 3 December 1790.

234 AO, *Report of 1905*, 222–3, 8 January 1793.

235 NA, MG21, Add. MSS, 21736, mfm. A–670, Mathews to Haldimand, 3 August 1787; NA, RG1, L4, vol. 2, 188–92, Mathews, "List of disbanded Troops and Loyalists to be settled on the North Side of Lake Erie, from a Creek four Miles from the Mouth of the River Detroit, to a small Creek about a Mile and half beyond Cedar River," 1 October 1787; ibid., 182–4, "Return of disbanded Troops and Loyalists Settled in the First Concession on the North Side of Lake Erie, from Marsh Creek four miles from the mouth of the River detroit to Mill Brook about a Mile and a Half beyond Cedar River," T. Smith, New Settlement, 10 January 1789; ibid., vol. 3, 398–406, report A, schedule of locations and index to the schedule, dated 1790 and read in committee, 4 February 1791; ibid., 314–16 and 374–6, "List of the Names of Discharged Rangers, Loyalists and others residing at or near Detroit to whom Provisions are to be granted in Proof to the satisfaction of the Land Board of Hesse that they have actually forgone an Establishment in the lower Districts in order to promote a Settlement at the Mouth of the River detroit, which Provisions are to be continued to them by monthly issues in the same Proportion as were given to the settlers below on further proof that they are actually Improving their lands," 12 January 1791; ibid., vol. 4, 666–71, schedule of two connected townships, no pagination.

236 AO, *Report of 1905*, cxxxi and cxxxii.

237 Officers of field rank would receive 5000 acres, captains 3000, subalterns 2000, NCOs 200 acres, and privates 50 acres. NA, RG1, L4, vol. 2, 203–6, Executive Council meeting, 22 October 1788. This was a marked improvement over the instructions of 1783 whereby majors and above received 1000 acres, captains 700 acres, subalterns 500.

However, it represented a reduction for privates, who were now officially to receive 50 acres although the reality was different in this area.
See also AO, *Report of 1905*, 36, circular from Motz to the board,
19 January 1790.

238 AO, *Report of 1905*, 43–9, 63–4. Pages 271 to 290 of this volume report
on the conditions of grants on 20 December 1793 and include notations such as "sham settler," "no improvement," and "abandoned and
left the country."

239 In May 1790 the board (Powell, Robertson, Grant, and Adhémar St
Martin) petitioned McKee to permit this land to be surveyed, although
it expressed awareness of the problems of Indian title. See *Historical
Collections*, vol. 20, 307–8, the board to Alexander McKee, 14 May
1790.

240 NA, RG1, L4, vol. 1, 170, E.B. Littlehales to the board, 23 October 1792.

241 AO, *Report of 1905*, cxxxii.

242 Goulet, "Phases of the Sally Ainse Dispute," 92–5; Hamil, "Sally Ainse,"
1–26; Clarke, "Sarah Ainse," 7–9.

243 She petitioned Dorchester as such. NA, RG1, L3, vol. 16, mfm.
C–1615, Upper Canada Land Petitions, "A," miscellaneous, no.17,
21 August 1789. Brant accepted her as such, 25 January 1797. Cruikshank and Hunter, *Russell Papers*, vol. 1, 96, and *Historical Collections*,
vol. 12, 173, . Joseph Brant to Butler, 28 June 1795. Yet in 1798 she
claimed to be a Shawnee. NA, RG1, L1, Upper Canada Land Book D,
vol. 22, mfm. C–101, and Cruikshank and Hunter, *Russell Papers*, vol.
2, 137, minutes of the Executive Council, 9 April 1798. There may
not be a conflict here. She may have been Oneida via her husband
Andrew Montour.

244 Quaife, *John Askin Papers*, vol. 1, 193, "Mr. Montague in account current
with Sarah Anis," 23 February 1783.

245 Hamil, *Sally Ainse*, 6.

246 AO, McIntosh Papers, 4 boxes, 1 September 1785 to 22 January 1787.

247 AO, *Report of 1905*, 171, meeting of the Land Board of the District of
Hesse, 13 April 1792; NA, MG18, I 5, Notaires de Detroit, Tome 6,
142–5, 19 July 1789; NA, RG1, L3, vol. 16, Upper Canada Land Petitions, no.17, 21 August 1789; ibid., no.18, 6 May 1791; no.19, 18 May
1792, nos.20 and 21, n.d., no.22, 30 April 1792; no.23, 13 April 1792;
NA, RG3, vol. 3, A4, no.45, C, Testimony of Chiefs, 13 August 1797; NA,
RG1, L4, vol. 1, 32–7, Report K, Land Board District of Hesse, dated
1792 and 1793; AO, RG1, A–1–6, vol. 1, McIntosh Papers, 26 March
1794 and 20 February 1796.

248 NA, RG1, L4, vol. 3, 577, McKee to the board, 30 March 1792.

249 Ibid., 38, deed registered by Monforton for Thames land, 11 October
1783.

250 AO, *Report of 1905*, 171, meeting of the Land Board of the District of Hesse, 13 April 1792.

251 NA, RG1, L4, vol. 1, 21–3, D.W.Smith, to A. McKee; ibid., 29–30, D.W. Smith to A. McKee, 30 March 1792; ibid., 35, report K, Land Board District of Hesse, 13 April 1792.

252 NA, RG1, L4, vol. 1, 254–7, Land Board Minutes and Records, counties of Essex and Kent, 23 August 1793.

253 This route was offered to avoid overruling the board. See AO, *Report of 1905*, 213, Simcoe to England, 14 November 1792.

254 Ibid., 240, Land Board meeting, 6 September 1793.

255 Ibid., 38, E.B. Littlehales to D.W. Smith, 3 November 1793.

256 Although there is no evidence, perhaps this was Joseph Brant for whom she acted as a courier to the tribes.

257 AO, RG1, A–I–6, vol. 1., no.4., Sarah Ainse, 26 March 1794. It is unclear to whom she is addressing this letter. It might be McKee or England (as president of the Land Board) or, as suggested in text, Simcoe himself. It could also be David Smith on the evidence of her letter to him in 1796. AO, *McIntosh Papers*, Letter of Sarah Ainse to D.W. Smith, 20 February 1796. On 15 July 1795 Simcoe informed Dorchester that Mrs Ainse had "been long since directed to be put in the legal possession of her lands." See Cruikshank, *Simcoe Papers* vol. 4, 45, Simcoe to Lord Dorchester, 15 July 1795.

258 *Historical Collections*, vol. 12, 173, Brant to Butler, 28 June 1795, and Cruikshank, *Simcoe Papers*, vol. 2, 251; Cruikshank and Hunter, *Russell Papers*, vol. 3, 12, Sir John Johnson to Peter Russell, 26 May 1799; ibid., 96, speech of Brant, (received from Captain Claus, 25 January 1797), and ibid., vol. 1, 2, Joseph Brant to D.W. Smith, 3 April 1796.

259 AO, McIntosh Papers, Sarah Ainse to D.W. Smith, 20 February 1796.

260 NA, RG1, L3, Upper Canada Land Petitions, vol. 3, mfm. C–1609, A4, no.45, 175, petition of Sarah Ainse, n.d.

261 AO, F47, Simcoe Papers, Sally Ainse to Aguisha, senior Indian chief, 26 January 1795.

262 Indeed, if Tepple is correct, a major motive of the military conquest was to seize the fur trade. Teeple "Land, Labour and Capital," 44–66.

263 Creighton, *Dominion of the North*, 153.

264 Creighton, ibid., 157, makes the point that this was the formal step in the retreat from the Proclamation of 1763 to the old institutions of the French Empire.

265 D.B. Smith points to inadequacies in the translation of even the most basic concepts of British law. See Smith, "The Dispossession of the Mississauga," 67–7.

266 Even then the interpreters misunderstood the geography of the area, Smith, ibid., 75.

267 Fenton, *The Great Law*, 12, 28, 277, 413, and 493. See also Sawaya, *,La Federation des Sept Feux*, 81. Merritt, following Ricouer, argues that in the eighteenth century metaphor was an important part of discourse between Indian and white because it allowed for different meanings within the language used. She points out that, while the Iroquois addressed the French governor in North America as "Father," they thought that he had no power to command "children." The French regarded their role as an extension of patriarchy. Both continued to use the relational metaphor to their own political ends. See Merritt "Metaphor," 74, and White, *The Middle Ground*, 84.

268 Smith, ibid., 74. According to Smith, the Mississauga likely believed that they had a series of profitable rental agreements.

269 This is clearly the Indian view because in 1793 Schiefflin received the governor's approval for 2000 acres and assurances of half-pay as an officer of the Indian Department. Cruikshank, *Simcoe Papers*, vol. 5, 76, Thomas Smith to Alexander McKee, 6 October 1793.

270 In addition to the purchase by Schiefflin, Pattinson, and Visgar, there are a number of Indian purchases described in the Detroit notarial records as late as 1796. These include an area on the west side of Lake St Clair from the Little River to the Salt River, 150 acres in depth, acquired for $500 in 1796 by the merchant firm of Meldrum and Park. NA, MG18, I 5, tome 4, 12–116, 11 June 1796. Another property acquired by this firm from Patrick Sinclair, a tract running from Lake Huron to Lake St.Clair and for four miles in depth, was also acquired about this time. Interestingly, Sinclair had acquired the property in 1788. Meldrum and Parke were sufficiently anxious about the fate of this property to assemble sixteen chieftains to acknowledge their agreement to the transfer. This was presumably a political rather than a legal move but it might also have served legal purposes. NA, MG18, I 5, tome 4, 117–19, 5 June 1795.

271 Thomas McKee accepted the lease of Pelée Island on 1 May 1788. The lease, witnessed by Francis Baby and James Alban, was for 999 years and 3 bushels of Indian corn to be delivered annually. As an employee of the British Indian Department, McKee may have found the lease an acceptable vehicle whereas a "purchase" was not. NA, MG18, I 5, tome 3, 293–4. Similarly A. and J. Caldwell obtained a lease of a thirty-six-square-mile property on 6 May 1788. It, too, was for three bushels of corn to be delivered annually over the ensuing 999 years. NA, MG18, I 5, tome 3, 191–2.

272 TRL, Powell Papers, B79, L16, 95–6, evidence of Edward Hearle, 10 September 1791.

273 AO, *Report of 1905*, 439, P. McNiff to John Collins, 30 September 1791. On this date, seven officers claimed entitlement to 18,000 acres in the district but had only received 1911 acres.

274 Schiefflin seems to have charged that Baby in 1784 had served himself while an officer of the Indian Department. "... je t'adresse la copie de sa lettre au Capt. McKee ... et la copie du compte que je lui ai rendu, de ce dont Chieflin veut me faire un crime." Letter of 28 June 1784 written to his brother and cited in Casgrain, *Mémorial des familles Casgrain*, 91.

275 The minute of the Executive Council which abolished the land boards also set out the terms under which land could henceforth be granted. Being a Christian was one requirement. Perhaps it was for this reason that Schiefflin used an alias. The abstract index to deeds for lot 141/1st Concession of Sandwich record a sale in 1800 to one J. Schiefflin alias Reaume. See also Cruikshank, *Simcoe Papers*, vol. 4, 172–3, minute of the Executive Council, 6 November 1794. Additional circumstantial evidence of his or at least someone of that name's Jewishness is to be found in his employment with the avowedly Jewish Detroit merchant Chapman Abraham (Abram). UWO, William Robertson Papers, item 21, 21 January 1777.

276 Under the Plantation Act of 1740, Jews and dissenters received superior treatment in Britain's overseas colonies than they did in the United Kingdom. As the Godfreys point out, on 18 November 1768, in Quebec, an event unprecedented in the history of Great Britain or its colonies occurred; John Franks took the normal three oaths required to secure public office, swearing the oath of adjuration upon "the faith of a Jew" rather than that of a Christian. In spite of this, in jurisdictions other than Quebec, a period of retrenchment followed: in Upper Canada on 5 January 1798 Mr Justice Elmsley ruled that Jews could not hold land in Upper Canada, although Jews had been acquiring land in British North American colonies since 1661. In reversing this practice, Moses David, a natural-born British subject resident in Essex, played an important part. The change, however, was de facto rather than de jure. In 1803 the Executive Council granted his prayer for relief and he received the patent, in his own right, for land in Sandwich on 20 February 1804. He did so without swearing the oath of adjuration in its Christian form. He seems to have avoided this when he was commissioned a militia officer prior to 1803 although the state oaths were a formal requirement. When appointed coroner of the Western District in 1808, he again escaped taking the oaths by posting a performance bond, an innovative practice designed to meet the requirement of the oath of adjuration. Clearly, Schiefflin was not viewed in the same way. See Godfrey and Godfrey, *Search out the land*; Firth, "John Elmsley," 303–4.

277 AO, HWHC, 20–108–B–3, 161, William Hands to Peter Russell, 20 July 1797.

278 Ibid., 166, signed P.R. and marked "Received 13 July 1798."

279 Ibid., 167, signed Peter Hunter, council chamber, 17 April 1804.

280 Hamil, *Sally Ainse*, 16–7; Cruikshank and Hunter, *Russell Papers*, vol. 1, 2–3, Joseph Brant to D.W. Smith, 3 April 1796.

281 The comparison is not strictly fair because the price paid by the government was for undeveloped land and the statistics of comparison include unknown quantities of developed land and the samples are small. Nonetheless, eight farms in Petite Côté sold between 1788 and 1790 for an average of 436.5 pence per acre. This is 2297.4 times the upset price, which some readers may think unreasonable although *sensu stricto* the figures are not comparable. See Lajeunesse, *The Windsor Border Region*, 330–3. By 1798, land in Essex would be worth 392 pence per acre. See Clarke and Brown, "The Upper Canadian Land Market," 222–34.

282 Cruikshank and Hunter, *Russell Papers*, vol. 2, 300–1, Duke of Portland to Peter Russell, 5 November 1798.

283 Ibid., 1, 277–8, (marked secret and confidential), Duke of Portland to Peter Russell, 11 September 1797,; ibid., 2, 122–23, Peter Russell to the Duke of Portland, York, 21 March 1798.

284 Johnson, "The Mississauga-Lake Ontario Land Surrender," 237–42.

285 A formal sales policy was not instituted until 1825. See Clarke and Buffone, "Manifestations of Imperial Policy" and Johnson, "The Mississauga-Lake Ontario Land Surrender."

286 Cruikshank and Hunter, *Russell Papers*, vol. 1, 277–8, (marked secret and confidential), Duke of Portland to Peter Russell, 11 September 1797.

287 Ibid., 11, 185–6, Peter Russell to Robert Prescott, 15 June 1798; ibid., 233–4, Peter Russell to Joseph Brant, 29 July 1798; ibid., 234–5, J. Givens to Joseph Brant, 30 July 1798, and Joseph Brant to J. Givens, 3 August 1798; ibid., 226–7, Prescott to Russell, 2 August 1798; ibid., vol. 2, 232, Peter Russell to Robert Prescott, no.60, 9 August 1798; ibid., 260–1, Peter Russell to Robert Prescott, 20 September 1798; ibid., 248–9, Robert Prescott to Peter Russell, 23 August 1798; ibid., 278–80, Peter Russell to Robert Prescott, 12 October 1798.

288 Ibid., vol. 3, 195–6, Joseph Brant to Sir John Johnson, 10 May 1799. Brant believed that 15 pence Halifax per acre was a nominal price for a sale of 69,120 acres in this year but it was very different to what had been paid to that point. Indeed, the Executive Council demurred because "it is contrary to past Usages with Indian Nations who have not before (that we have heard of) fettered their cessions of land to the King with any *conditions* whatsoever & because the *price* now demanded is *several times greater* than His Majesty has ever given for Indian land." Ibid., 225–6, Peter Russell to Joseph Brant, 10 June

1799. See also ibid., 205–6, Peter Russell to Duke of Portland, no.61, 26 May 1799.

289 Ibid., 2, 19–22, memoir of William Dummer Powell, 1 November 1797.

290 Ibid., 290–9, minutes of the Executive Council, York, 22 October 1798.

291 AO, RG1, A–VII, vol. 12, Simcoe to Lord Dorchester, 29 February 1798. Simcoe writes: "It cannot admit of a doubt but that every promise made to the Six Nations ought in Equity to be performed and in policy rather enlarged than diminished."

292 NA, MG23, H I 4, vol. 7, 127–8 and 136, "Progress of W.D. Powell," n.d.

293 With Isaac Todd, he had, in London between 1793 and 1795, lobbied to secure subcontracts for himself, his brother David, Richard Cartwright, and John Askin to supply the Upper Canadian garrisons. Brock, "William Robertson," 718–19.

294 The mercantile system flourished on indebtedness or "backward and forward credit." See Haeger, *John Jacob Astor*, 53.

295 NA, MG23, H I 4, vol. 4, 134, "Notes of the Progress of WDP," n.d.

296 Major Richard England became commanding officer at Detroit in June 1792.

297 AO, Jarvis-Powell Papers, 1043, 39, "Notice of the Progress of William Dummer Powell, Chief Justice of the Province of Upper Canada," n.d. This document speaks out against an exorbitant table of fees which, Powell says, Simcoe had devised to repair his personal fortune. This had been overruled by the Duke of Portland, secretary of state. In the same document, Powell also comments upon members of the Executive Council allowing speculators to acquire land in the names of actual settlers in order to obtain fees.

298 NA, MG21, Haldimand Papers, 50, mfm. H–1451, Haldimand to DePeyster, 6 July 1780.

299 Ibid., 71–2, 6 March 1781.

300 Ibid., 74–5, 19 May 1782.

301 Sutherland, "Robert Mathews", 584–5.

302 NA, MG21, Add. MSS., 21661–892, Haldimand Papers, mfm. A–670, 327, Mathews to Haldimand, 3 August 1787. Captain Robertson would appear to be Captain Daniel Robertson, lieutenant governor of Michilimackinac. I am grateful to Charles Whebell for this suggestion. See Armour, "Daniel Robertson," 714–16. There is no evidence of a relationship to William Robertson of the Land Board. See also *Historical Collections*, vol. 20, 286–81, and NA, Haldimand Papers, B76, 286.

303 NA, MG21, B76, 286–92, Mathews to Haldimand, 3 August 1787.

304 There were problems of political allegiance. "There are nevertheless a sad set of Rascals in this Settlement, the majority by far on the side of the old Subjects copying tho' in every degree except disposition, inferior to those of the same description in the lower part of the Province."

It is not absolutely clear if he is speaking of American or French sympathizers though I am inclined to interpret this as the former. Mathews, the soldier, had the solution: "... should matters come to extremities, and they discover the least disposition to be refractory, their Houses stand in awe of two eighteen pounders and four nine Pounders, at the distance of 250 yards." Ibid., 320–1.

305 His biographer, Reginald Horsman, says that "he had been accustomed to working in an atmosphere of crisis, and after that atmosphere evaporated following the signing of Jay's treaty in 1794, he failed to adapt to the more orderly practices of peace-time administration." Horsman, *Matthew Elliott*, 303.

306 UWO, William Robertson Papers, series I, file 3, page 4, item 50, John Askin to William Robertson, letter dated 6 October 1791 but at salutation dated 26 March 1792. The surveyor is, of course, Patrick McNiff.

307 NA, RG1, L4, vol. 2, 65–7, 143, 145–7, "Accounts of Lods et Ventes and quit rents received and still due from 9 November 1775 to 23 April 1782."

308 *Lods et ventes* were a mutation fine of one-twelfth the purchase price. As Greer has shown in his work on Sorel, Saint-Ours, and Saint-Denis, it was common for people to be in arrears. Greer, *Peasant, Lord and Merchant*, 122–9.

309 Armstrong, *Handbook of Upper Canadian Chronology*, 58.

310 Cruikshank, *Simcoe Papers*, vol. 4, 62–5, Edmund Burke to E.B. Littlehales, 14 August 1795.

311 Askin was a partner with Ebenezer Allen and Charles Whitney of Vermont; Robert Randall of Philadelphia and his son John; and Jonathan Schiefflin, William and David Robertson, Robert Innis, and Richard Pattinson, all of Detroit. See Quaife, *John Askin Papers*, vol. 1, 568–72, partnership for purchase of Michigan peninsula.

312 Askin's association with Jonathan Schiefflin, William Robertson, David Robertson, Robert Jones, Richard Pattinson, John Askin, Jr, Ebenezer Allen, Charles Whitney, and Robert Randall was known to Simcoe. Cruikshank, *Simcoe Papers*, vol. 4, 210–11, Simcoe to Phineas Bond, 4 March 1796.

313 Burton, "Business Adventures," 58.

314 Ibid., 58.

315 AO, 1568 (A–15), Patrick McNiff, "Sketch to Show the Extravagant Claims," 1790.

316 NA, RG1, L6B, vol. 25, 972–3, "A Statement from the Auditor's Docket Books of the number of patents for land entered with him to the End of 1799 specifying the Quantity of Acres granted in each District & under each respective Class, according to the distribution of fees

accrued to the Officers under the old regulations, & distinguishing the
No.of grants ... by Government, & in full by the Secretary, & the
number of Grants to that period, which still remain to be accounted for
to the Officers. Read in Council, 13 January 1801." Signed by Peter
Russell.

317 Mealing points out that, though he limited his own reward to 5000
acres, he scattered these around, including 1000 acres in the Western
District. Mealing, *John Graves Simcoe*, 755.

318 Cruikshank states that the Executive Council made awards to about 100
persons by 1796. The following had associations with the Western District and Essex County: W.D. Powell, Prideaux Selby, and D.W. Smith,
provincial officers; Richard Pollard and Walter Roe, district officials;
Francis Drouillard and Charles Morrison, fur traders; John Askin, James
Fraser, William Hands, George Leith, Angus Mackintosh, James Mackintosh, George Meldrum, William Park, George Sharpe, and William
Shepherd, merchants of Detroit. Madam Baby was awarded a grant as
the widow of Dupéront Baby. All of these grants were for 1200 acres.
James Baby received 3000 acres as an executive councillors and Francis
and his younger brothers 1200 acres each. Colonel England received
2000 acres on the Thames for diligently applying himself as president
of the Land Board. This comes to at least 34,000 acres. If this was satisfied in the Western District by 1799, then these individuals alone controlled 15.1 per cent of the land granted. See Cruikshank, *Simcoe
Papers*, vol. 5, 189–92.

CHAPTER FOUR

1 Cruikshank and Hunter, *Russell Papers*, vol. 1, 124, "Minutes of the Executive Council, Council Chamber at Newark," 3 January 1797. This petition was satisfied beyond Essex.

2 Ibid.

3 NA, RG1, L1, vol. 19, Land Book A, mfm. C–101, 299, A21, 12 August
1795. Many of the assumptions about the Loyalists are being reassessed.
See Knowles, *Inventing the Loyalists*.

4 Ibid., vol. 21, Land Book C, 64, 11 April 1797–19 January 1802.

5 Those unlocated were rejected by the Executive Council. Askin was fortunate in that his case was discussed because council had decided not to
examine claims made after June 1799 and he applied in July. Perhaps he
was helped in this consideration by Chief Justice Elmsley, more liberal in
his interpretation of the law than Chief Justice Powell. Elmsley reported
to Askin that he knew a case where there were 500 such claims awaiting
a favourable judgment on Askin's claim. This was presumably old news to
Askin. See Gates, *Land Policies*, 59; NA, RG1 Land Book D, 421 and 437.

6 Gates, *Land Policies*, 28–30.

7 Mezaks, "Crown Grants in the Home District," 126–34; Kennedy, "Records of the Land Settlement," 193–8, and "Records of the Immigration Process," 187–92.

8 See Harring, *White Man's Law*, 41. Harring reports that some of these reports were so contradictory that they often made inconsistent recommendations within the space of a single page. Ibid., 44.

9 Ibid., 50.

10 Ibid., 40.

11 Government claimed to be unable to protect such a large territory, blamed the problem on the Indians, and threatened direct intervention in native affairs. Ibid., 49–53.

12 Gates, *Land Policies*, 305.

13 Gundy argues that this was a recurrent problem but that the Heirs and Devisee Commission held no dogmatic position, resolving each case on its particular merits. For example, one Price Mallory had squatted upon a former clergy reserve in Marysburg Township. This had been granted to a Captain W.C. Rochfort in 1826. Mallory had made considerable improvements and petitioned the lieutenant governor in 1836 for the lot. He was advised to petition the commission and in July 1837 was awarded the lot he had improved. Presumably, Rochfort was compensated elsewhere. In this instance Rochfort was not resident upon the lot but it was not always so. In a second example that Gundy gives, the assignee of the original holder was awarded the land, though a third individual had made considerable improvement. Gundy, "The Family Compact," 141–2. In Westminster Township, in the London District, American squatters were accorded such rights in the early years. See St. Denis, *Byron*.

14 Gates, *Land Policies*, 291.

15 Fraser, "John Macaulay," 513–22.

16 AO, Macaulay Papers, Robinson to Macaulay, 20 July 1852, quoted in Gates, *Land Policies*, 295.

17 Actually he may not have because he made little reference to the Royal Proclamation. For example, he believed that the Grand River valley was not Indian land per se but a political grant to the Six Nations. On the other hand, he held that Walpole Island, as unceded land, was subject to the Royal Proclamation. Harring, who makes these points, also shows that Robinson's Indian law opinions were not consistent. Harring, *White Man's Law*, 65, 69, and 81–90.

18 AO, RG1 A–I–V, Crown Lands and Resources Records, Schedules and Land Rolls, vol. 77, vacant Crown lands, 1861; Gates, *Land Policies*, 294.

19 Ibid., 288.

20 NA, RG1, L6B, vol. 10, Mahlon Burwell to T. Ridout, surveyor general, transmitting table E, "A Statistical Table or Schedule, shewing the names of such persons as have taken possession of the Crown lands along the River St. Clair between the Township of Sombra & the foot of Lake Huron without any Authority, with other matters relating to them, as taken in the Autumn of the Year 1826, and details in the following Columns, 2 April 1828."

21 AO, RG1–C–IV, Crown Land Papers, Township Papers, various items.

22 Ibid., MS658, mfm. 87, 1223–4.

23 Ibid., Township papers, M658, 67, J.B. Lucien to the commissioner of Crown lands, 1 August 1864.

24 However, his neighbour J. Bazial Drouillard was willing to testify that he had been there for fourteen years and that Giniac was the first occupant! Ibid., 69 and 70.

25 Ibid., 70.

26 Gates, *Land Policies*, 289.

27 Ibid., 17.

28 AO, *Report of 1905*, 165, minutes of meetings, Land Board of the District of Hesse, 30 March 1792.

29 Squatting continued late into the century even in older settled areas such as Essex. Government property was not immune and perhaps may have been more vulnerable in that it was thought to be owned by all. A case in point is Point Pelée, where what was sought was not farm land but the cedar, oak, and walnut that it produced. See map by McPhillips, "Plan of the Squatters Holdings, 1889."

30 Gates, *Land Policies*, 174.

31 Ibid., 211.

32 Ibid., 245.

33 Ibid., 246.

34 Ibid., 248–53.

35 AO, RG1–A–I–V, Crown Lands and Resources Records, Crown Land Papers, Instructions and Pamphlets, 28 May 1828. See also Gates, *Land Policies*, 288.

36 Ibid., 290.

37 AO, RG1 A–I–V Crown Lands and Resources Records, Crown Land Papers, Squatters' Circulars, December 1842, 25 January 1844, and 29 January 1851. See also Gates, *Land Policies*, 290–1.

38 Ibid., 291–2.

39 A system of organized fraud was thought to have operated in Huron County whereby speculators had acquired large acreages from squatters enjoying pre-emption rights. William Lyon Mackenzie believed that this would be found to exceed 100,000 acres. Gates, *After the Rebellion*, 282. On Mackenzie, see Armstrong and Stagg, "William Lyon Mackenzie," 496–510.

40 The equation was y (improved acreage) = 5.40 + 2.32(time). With an F of 20.28 this proved significant at p = 0.0002.

41 The equation y = 4.25 + 5.13(miles) was with an F of 10.14 significant at p = 0.005.

42 The equation was y (improved acreage) = 4.92 + 2.76(total family size). The F value was 9.07, significant at 0.007.

43 $\bar{x}$ = 409, σ = 210.2 square feet and "n" of 18.

44 $\bar{x}$ = 907.9, σ = of 456.6.

45 Cruikshank, *Simcoe Papers*, vol. 4, 47–9, "Memorandum Respecting the General State of Landed Property in Upper Canada, Delivered by Mr. Cartwright to E.B. Littlehales and sent in Lt. Governor's no.34 to His Grace the Duke of Portland," 23 July 1795.

46 Gates, *Land Policies*, 35–7; Cruikshank, *Simcoe Papers*, vol. 1, 141, Simcoe to Henry Dundas, 28 April 1792,

47 Gates, "The Heir and Devisees Commission," 21–36; Gundy, "The Family Compact," 129–46 and "Heirs, Devisees and Assigns," 37–51; Mezaks, "Records of the Heir and Devisees Commissions," 199–206. The records of the Heirs and Devisees Commissions are held in NA, RG1, L5, and AO, RG40.

48 Gates, *Land Policies*, 56–7.

49 Ibid., 58.

50 A new Heir and Devisee Act of 1802 allowed claimants to offer a variety of documents other than Land Board certificates (Haldimand's certificates, magistrates' certificates, certificates of the Surveyor General's office, and orders-in-council) as evidence. This more liberal interpretaion of evidence worked to the benefit of speculators but the act of 1805 (45 Geo.III, c.2) again restricted commissioners to hearing the claims of the heirs or devisees of the original nominees. All other liens or encumbrances were to be left to the courts to decide. The members of the second commission were drawn from members of the Executive Council and the Court of King's Bench. This meant that they were, in Gundy's terms, the "Family Compact" at work. However, as Gundy also points out, the record of this second commission was so impressive, its work accomplished without fear or favour, that it was exempted from William Lyon Mackenzie's list of public grievances. Gundy, "The Family Compact," 130.

51 Similarly, Mr Justice Henry Allcock was regarded as too rigid in his interpretation of the Heir and Devisee Act. He found repeatedly that speculators had taken advantage of "the indigent circumstance of the parties & contracted for the purchase of the Lands for considerations outrageously inadequate ..." Gates, *Land Policies*, 58. Askin described him as a "very Impartial good man, but so particular & sticks so close to the law, a very unfitt man to act up to the Spirit of the Act." Askin also noted that he

"did as he pleassed without asking the Sentiments of the othe[r] Commissioners in hardly any case." Armstrong, Allcock's most recent biographer, from whose work these quotations are taken, recognizes that he
was a difficult character and "one of the more unattractive of the many
eccentrics who plagued the Canadas at the opening of the 19th century."
Armstrong, "Henry Allcock," 17–19.

52 Quaife, *John Askin Papers* 2, 260.

53 Gates, *Land Policies*, 60.

54 In Robertson's case, many of his claims dragged on even after his
    death. See "Draft memorandum relating to land in Essex County,
    Upper Canada in the 1820's for which patents have not been obtained
    and which had belonged to the estate of the late William Robertson
    and are now part of the estate of Elizabeth Lucy (Robertson) Ronalds
    and List of lands in western part of Upper Canada belonging to the
    estate of Elizabeth Lucy (Robertson) Ronalds which are not under
    patent, and appearing clear for claim under the commission if claims
    under the original nominees can be proven and the original nominees
    can be shown by proof to be dead or residing outside of Upper
    Canada," UWO, William Robertson Papers, items 15 and 16, no pagina-
    tion. This source relates primarily to his land dealings in neighbouring
    Kent County and his business affairs in Queenston, Montreal, New
    York, and Philadelphia.

55 Gates, *Land Policies*, 60–1 and 322. Gundy does not share the view of
    Gates, pointing to the fact that the records of the second commission
    occupies some fifty linear feet in the AO. See Gundy, "The Family
    Compact," 129.

56 TRL, S.P. Jarvis Papers, B63, Proclamation S125. These lands were subject
    to a quit rent after ten years.

57 Shortt and Doughty, *Documents,* vol. 2, 946, Lord Dorchester to Sydney at
    the Colonial office, 13 June 1787.

58 Patterson, *Land Settlement in Upper Canada,* 40, 53–4, 76, 100–2, 130–1,
    141; Gates, *Land Policies*; Regehr, "Land Ownership in Upper Canada,"
    35–48.

59 Clarke and Buffone, "Manifestations of Imperial Policy," 121–36.

60 NA, RG1, E3, vol. 87, UCSS, "A Proclamation to such as are desirous to
    settle on the lands of the crown in the Province of Upper Canada, by His
    Excellency John Graves Simcoe, Esquire," 7 February 1792. Endorsed by
    Thomas Talbot, this was reprinted at Newark by G. Tiffany in 1795.

61 Cross-sectional analysis of ownership in 1825 and 1852, using the
    abstract index to deeds as a source material, showed that, as might be
    expected, few women owned land in either period. In 1825 there were
    19 out of 516 owners who were women and in 1852 only 10 out of 1604
    women were owners. As a native woman, Ainse, who also used the names

Hands, Montour, Maxwell, and Wilson, may have chosen not to restrict her life by marriage and may therefore have been treated in law as a *femme sole.*

62 Backhouse, "Married Women's Property Law," 212. The roots of this lay in Scripture and, in particular, in Genesis 2:24 and Ephesians 5:22–9, where Paul adjures women to submit to their husbands as head and advises husbands to care for their wives as they would their own bodies. In law, this idea of coverture, whereby both were recognized as one, gave the man control and usually ownership of property. In discussing the acquisition of chattels and goods, Blackstone includes marriage as a means of acquisition. "This depends entirely on the notion of a unity of person between the husband and wife; it being held that they are one person in law, (i) so that the very being and existence of the woman is suspended during the couverture, or entirely merged or incorporated in that of the husband." Blackstone, *Commentaries on the Laws of England,* vol. 1, book 2, 432. See also Chambers, *Married Women,* 53, where she makes the point that, under the common law, the woman's dower right to a one-third interest in her husband's land became operative only after his death, and that Hannah Snider was denied the use of the land for some 30 years. See also Errington, *Wives and Mothers,* 28–52.

63 Backhouse, ibid., 216–c17.

64 TRL, Powell Papers, B79, L16, 57, Catherine de Cou to Peter Russell, n.d.

65 Lieutenant Frederick Dockstader appears on the "Old U.E. List" where he is designated "Indian Department S.G." and his residence is given as the Home District. See United Empire Loyalist Centennial Committee, *The Centennial.*

66 AO, RG8, 1–3, Index to Land Patents, mfm. 1, 112.

67 The Van Emery land was taken out in the Township of Beverley and not in Essex. Catherine seems to have married a Lieutenant John De Cue (or De Pue) who in 1796 acquired 1700 acres in Beverley and Ancaster townships. The "Old U.E. List" includes a John Depew Senior and Junior, both of whom had received provisions at Niagara in 1786. The elder had been in the Indian Department, presumably with Frederic Dockstader. See United Empire Loyalist Committee, *The Centennial,* 164. Presumably these are the same people and Catherine had married John De Cue, De Pue, De Pew. In 1796 both families would seem to have been living in close proximity to one another although perhaps they always had been. Perhaps, too, Catherine's claim was finally recognized. Patents of 6 May and 7 October 1796, *Patent Index,* 24–5.

68 NA, RG1, L1, vol. 31, Land Minute Book M. 420–3, "Letter and Opinion of John Beverley Robinson, Esquire, Attorney General [addressed to R.

Wilmot Horton] on the Prospects of Adopting in Upper Canada, the Rules Established for Granting Lands in New South Wales and Van Diemen's Land," 7 July 1825.

69 This is simply defined by the *Shorter Oxford* (1970) as "a charge upon an estate for some special purpose or a rent usually of a small amount, paid by a freeholder or copyholder in lieu of services."

70 He was appointed lieutenant governor and administrator of Quebec on 7 April 1766. Since Governor James Murray was still officially in charge though he had been recalled to London, Carleton was not commissioned as governor until 12 April 1768. See Browne, "Guy Carleton," 141–54. The dates of appointment and resignation of the various colonial officials are given in Armstrong, *Handbook of Upper Canadian Chronology*.

71 Gates, *Land Prices*, 20.

72 NA, RG1, E3, vol. 87, Simcoe's proclamation of 7 February 1792.

73 Gates, *Land Policies*, 48.

74 Firth, "The Administration of Peter Russell," 163–81; idem., "Peter Russell," 729–32.

75 Ibid., 67.

76 Yet Hunter himself would add to the daily tasks of the clerks of the Surveyor General's Office that of the passing of patents to the Attorney General's Office. Four clerks were involved. Each was to complete the description and necessary parchment of three properties per day, that is, a total of eighteen patents per week per clerk. NA, MG23, H I 4, vol. 4, 50, James Green, secretary to Lieutenant Governor Hunter. "Orders for the Land Granting Department," 6 June 1801. It is possible that Hunter was just a modern manager but he enjoyed a large proportion of the fee. The secretary responsible for overseeing production was also personally responsible for providing the necessary materials. This individual, as Powell (who investigated the office) showed, actually lost money.

77 Gates, *Land Policies*, 65. His most recent biographer does not agree. See Firth, "Peter Russell," 729–83.

78 Anon., "Peter Hunter," 441.

79 Ibid., 439–43.

80 Gates, *Land Policies*, 72.

81 NA, MG23, H I 4, vol. 3, 1052, "First Days in Upper Canada," n.d.

82 These areas were (a) Lake Simcoe/Penetanguishene where the fees were those of 1796; (b) Bay of Quinte; (c) along the Longwoods Road where the fees were those of 1804; and (d) along the road through the rear of Peterborough, Hastings, and Frontenac where the fees were those of 1819.

83 Gates, *Land Policies*, 153.

84   Ibid., 6–7.
85   Ibid., 125.
86   Ibid., 27.
87   Brunger, "A Spatial Analysis of Individual Settlements"; Clarke, "Mapping the Lands Supervised," 8–13.
88   Gates, *Land Policies*, 129.
89   AO, John Askin Papers, F474, MU13. Patent and seal for lot 95 in the 1st concession of Colchester Township, 15 December 1803. Two patents for land in Gosfield provide similar evidence. Antoine Laplante received the patent for 159 acres of lot 22 in the 1st concession on 2 August 1808. This patent was issued under the regulations of 19 July 1796. It was signed by Francis Gore and endorsed by Peter Russell. A house of an acceptable size was to be built and someone was to live on the property for one year but it did not have to be the patentee. White pine was reserved to the state but the lot could be transferred by gift, marriage, descent, or indenture if the seller appeared before a magistrate. AO, F378, HWHM, 20–92 (42). In the same way Jacob Fox received the patent for the rear of lot 24 in the 1st concession on 20 November 1830, showing that such conditions were permitted into later years. The patent endorsed by Sir John Colborne reserved white pine, gold, and silver. Fox was given three years to build but could sell within twelve months if the sale was registered. AO, F378, HWHM, 29–92 (4). In Elgin County, Francis Baby patented lot 19 in the 5th concession of Yarmouth Township on 25 July 1799. Baby enjoyed similar conditions to Askin. He could sell within twelve months after obtaining a certificate from a magistrate. AO, F378, HWHM.
90   AO, *Report of 1921*, 153.
91   Gates, *Land Prices*, 130 and 265.
92   Talbot regarded this as totally inadequate and recommended a five-year residence. See AO, *Report of 1921*, 135; Gates, *Land Policies* 130.
93   Ibid., Gates, 132.
94   Ibid., 133. Gates also points out that, irrespective of residence, Radenhurst, the chief clerk in the Surveyor General's Office, would allow privileged grants to pass to patent if they had been examined by the Heirs and Devisees Commission. Ibid., 135. Radenhurst was accused of partiality towards favourite people but then the whole of the Surveyor General's Office was excoriated: "Nothing is more imperatively called for than a continual and rigid supervision upon the transactions of the department, to prevent a continuance of practices discreditable to the department and prejudicial to the interests of all but a few." AO, *Report of 1921*, 178.
95   Ibid., Gates, 137.
96   Gates to Clarke, 1 June 1971.

97 Only 3280 acres of this was in Essex. Clarke, "Military and United Empire Loyalist," 189.

98 Ermatinger, *The Talbot Regime*, 35. See also Hamil's "Col. Talbot," "Colonel Talbot's Principality," and *Lake Erie Baron*.

99 DLF, Patents Office, Orders in Council, vol. 3, 131–4.

100 Ibid.

101 AO, RG1, C–I–6, Settlement duties.

102 DLF, SR, SL, vol. 34, 5, Benjamin Springer to Hurd, 24 July 1833.

103 Wilson, *The Clergy Reserves*, 57 and 73.

104 NA, RG1, L1, vol. 31, Land Book M, 417, Bathurst to Peregrine Maitland, 28 July 1825.

105 Brode, *Sir John Beverley Robinson*; Saunders, "Sir John Beverley Robinson," 668–78. Robinson was disposed to the needs of capital and capitalists to an extent which Weaver suggests probably affected his judgment as a member of the judiciary. See, for example his "While equity Slumbered," 871–914. See also Cook, "John Beverley Robinson," 338–61.

106 Wilson, *The Clergy Reserves*, 57.

107 Jeans, *An Historical Geography of New South Wales*.

108 NA, RG1, L1, vol. 31, Land Book M, 420, Robinson to R. Wilmot-Horton, 7 July 1825.

109 Ibid., 424–7, 29 October 1825. Those present when the issue was discussed were the chief justice, William Campbell, James Baby, Samuel Smith, and John Strachan. The document is reproduced in Clarke and Buffone, *Colonial Land Policy*, 32–4.

110 Ibid., 426.

111 Ibid.

112 Ibid., 456–8, W. Campbell to Sir Peregrine Maitland, 21 November 1825; ibid., 459–61, "Notice to be published in the Upper Canada Gazette on the new Arrangement for Grants on the waste Lands of the Crown to take Effect 1st January 1826."

113 Patterson, *Land Settlement in Upper Canada*, 145.

114 Sales were envisaged as early as 1798 for Upper Canada. Cruikshank and Hunter, *Russell Papers* vol. 2, 224–5, Russell to Prescott, 29 July 1799, and Patterson, *Land Settlement in Upper Canada*, 143. Russell had proposed a down payment of one eighth the price that Russell believed was necessary to dissuade speculators. See also Riddell, "A Study in the Land Policy," 385–405; Patterson, *Land Settlement in Upper Canada*, 143–5; Wilson, *The Clergy Reserves*, 72–4.

115 NA, RG 1, L1, vol. 31, Land Book M, 425.

116 Ibid., Minutes of Executive Council, 14 March 1826.

117 Talbot argued that the new sales system did not ensure the improvement of land and was not suited to poor settlers. He was able to ensure

that the legislation did not affect the areas he supervised. Gates, *Land Policies*, 171–2.

118 NA, RG1, L1, vol. 31, Land Book M, 457, 21 November 1825.

119 Gourlay (*Statistical Account*, cccxi) argued that, where transportation was poorly developed, land value increased in proportion to population density. See also Goodwin, *Canadian Economic Thought*, 10–20, for elaboration and for discussion of the effect of Gourlay upon Wakefield. See also Clarke and Buffone, *Manifestations of Imperial Policy*, for empirical verification of Gourlay's position.

120 NA, RG1, L1, vol. 31, Land Book M, 426, Campbell to Maitland, 21 November 1825.

121 PRO, CO47, vol. 115 (hereafter CO47). The terms of the schedule by which these data were to be gathered are given in NA, RG1, L1, vol. 31, Land Book M, 501, 16 December 1825.

122 Clarke and Buffone, "Colonial Land Policy," 46.

123 Armstrong, "The Oligarchy of the Western District, 87–102; Clarke, "The Role of Political Position," 18–34; Johnson, "Land Policy, Population Growth,", 41–60; Nelles, "Loyalism and Local Power," 99–114; Noel, *Patrons, Clients, Brokers*; Read, "The London District Oligarchy," 195–209; Richards, "The Joneses of Brockville," 169–84; Saunders, "What Was the Family Compact?," 165–78; Wise, "Upper Canada and the Conservative Tradition," 20–33.

124 Gates, *Land Policies*, 171.

125 Wood, "Human Settlement."

126 Wood, "Settlement of the Mt. Elgin Ridges."

127 Kelly, "The Agricultural Geography."

128 Clarke, "A Geographical Analysis."

129 Brunger, "A Spatial Analysis of Individual Settlement" and "Settler Location in the Talbot Settlement."

130 Johnson, *County of Ontario* and "Land Policy, Population Growth," 41–60.

131 Osborne, "The Settlement of Kingston's Hinterland," 63–79.

132 Widdis, "A Perspective On Land Tenure."

133 Weldon, "The Salient Factors."

134 Akenson, *The Irish in Ontario*, 60–1.

135 Lockwood, *Montague*, 55–7, and *Beckwith*, 2–28.

136 Duncan, "The Prominent Factors."

137 Gordanier, "The Settlement of Augusta Township."

138 Watt, "A Historical Perspective."

139 Hannon, "Land Acquisition and Speculation."

140 Readers needing greater detail on how this was accomplished are referred to my work on Malden Township where the names of owners and of those assessed for each lot are determined. Clarke, "Land and Law," 475–93.

141 Clarke, "Geographical Aspects," 69–112.

142 Clarke, "Land and Law," 475–95.

143 Where a particular instrument provided the link to a prior or subsequent event, a lot could be included in the sample. Where it did not but rather stood out independently, the particular lot was rejected in the calculation. For example, a lot with a particular individual as patentee but without specific connection to a sheriff's sale legitimizing a patent would be rejected. In short, the calculation was performed only where a "logical" series of events could be traced. Clearly, this procedure reduces the variability in the data but that is acceptable; this is purposeful rather than random sampling. The result of testing among 1003 samples in this way was to produce a lag of 4.9 years with a standard deviation of 9.3 years.

144 NA, RG5, B26, Upper Canadian Returns of Population and Assessments, mfm. H–1175, Malden Assessment of 1847.

145 The mode was 6 years, the mean 8.2 years, but in Essex as compared to the Western District it was higher at 12.1 years. Clarke, "A Geographical Analysis," 154–60.

146 Appendix 22 of the JHA/UC cites three documents as the authority by which Colonel Talbot received superintendence over the lands in the Western District. These orders-in-council and orders from the lieutenant governor were dated 15 February 1809, 6 October 1815, and 27 January 1821. A search of the NA and the AO initiated respectively by R.S. Gordon and J. Mezaks, failed to produce the third and last document, Maitland's order of 1821.

147 The Essex figure does not include an unknown acreage assigned to the Middle Road and all vacant land in the document from which the figures are derived: "Statement of Lands in the London and Western Districts which have been placed in the hands of the Honourable Thomas Talbot under Orders in Council and Orders from the Lieutenant Governor of the Province for the time being. Showing the number of lots and number of acres under Patent, the number of lots and number of acres under location and the number of lots and the number of acres which have not as yet been returned by Colonel Talbot." Appendix 22 of the JHA/UC, 1836, 20–3. The parliamentary addresses of 8 February 1836 preceding the appearance of this document may be found in the following: JHA/UC, 1st Sess., 12th Parl., 5 Will., 316; JHA/UC, 2nd Sess., 12th Parl., 5 Will. iv, 1 April 1836; JHA/UC, 2nd Sess., 12th Parl., 6 Will. iv, 5 February 1836, 114.

148 AO, HWHM, Wilkinson Papers, 20–235, 9972.

149 Clarke, "Mapping the Lands Supervised," 8–18.

150 Hamil, *Lake Erie Baron*, 289–90, and AO, letter attached to the front of book E of Talbot's maps.

151 The mean of the data presented by Brunger in his doctoral dissertation was 11.87 years with a σ of 10.83, based upon an "n" of 321. See Brunger, "A Spatial Analysis of Individual Settlement," appendix C. For Essex County, the respective statistics are 20.53, σ of 8.78 and "n" of 461. A difference-of-means test showed the data from Elgin and Middlesex counties to be statistically different from the Essex results. The calculated t was found to be 11.86; that required for significance at the 95 per cent confidence level is 1.645.

152 Gates, *Land Policies*, 171. Gates points out that lost revenues must have amounted to between £35,000 and £40,000.

153 Finnegan, "Cognizance of Land Quality," 103. He also determined the time between patent and first sale to be 5.75 years. Saunders, in his work on Beckwith Township, calculates the lag between entry into Upper Canada and completion of patent in Beckwith. The results are not strictly comparable but nonetheless interesting. His mean for a sample of 36 was found to be 9.61 years with a standard deviation of 8.47 years. Saunders, "The Irish in Beckwith Township."

154 Little was able to differentiate between French-Canadian and Scots patentees. Generally, the Scots patented faster than the French Canadian. This was especially so when the length of time between sales and patent was considered. The modal class for land acquired by sale was found to be fifteen to twenty-nine years among Scots, and for the French Canadians it was greater than fifty years. With respect to "free-grants," 55.4 per cent of French Canadians and 58.2 per cent of Scots occupied the modal class five to nine years. Little, *Crofters and Habitants*, 72.

155 Detailed commentary on the usefulness of patents as source materials in Ontario can be found in Clarke, "A Geographical Analysis of Colonial Settlement," 149–60.

156 This is defined as $P = K/1 + e^{-(a+bt)}$ where P is the accumulated percentage of land acquired, K is the ceiling of land acquisition, "t" is the variable time, "b" is the rate of growth coefficient, and "a" is the constant of integration, positioning the curve on the time scale. The parameters were estimated using the method chosen by Griliches, that is, the transformation of the logistic into an equation linear in "a" and "b." The parameters can be estimated by dividing both sides of the logistic by K/P and taking the logarithm. This yields its linear transform $\log P/(K-P) = a + bt$ and allows the parameters to be estimated by least squares. Griliches, "Hybrid Corn," 501–22. In this instance the value of K was set at 99.9 per cent.

157 Odum, *Ecology*, 123–8.

158 Spiegel, *Schuam's Outline*, 247, gives the following for the comparison of two beta coefficients b_i and b_j.

$$t = \frac{b_i - b_j}{Sy.x/Sx} \cdot \sqrt{N-2}$$

Where t is the desired statistic, b_i and b_j are the respective slopes, $S_{y.x}$ is the standard error of y on x, S_x is the σ and N is the size of sample.

159 Data were taken from the Census of Canada for 1851, 1861, 1871, 1881, and 1891, and from Johnson, "The Settlement of the Western District," 28 and 31. The correlation coefficient between the amount of land patented and the population of Essex, using Johnson's data for the period to 1851, was 0.96. Strictly comparable data are not available for the whole of the nineteenth century, but using the population of Essex and the amount of patenting activity rather than the acreage patented, the correlation coefficient obtained was 0.94.

160 Gates, *Land Policies*, 140.

161 Ibid., 137–40, 170, 186–9, and 265–6.

162 Craig, *Upper Canada*, 25.

163 Clarke, "The Role of Political Position," 18–34.

164 The Canada Company was incorporated in 1826 and acquired 48,441 acres of former Crown reserves in Essex County. AO, Register of Lands for the Bathurst, Home and Western District, Canada Company Papers, no.2, 1824–26, passim; NA, NMC F400, Canada Company Maps, 1826–27.

165 Gates, *Land Policies*, 225.

166 Clarke, "Mapping the Lands Supervised," 8–18.

167 Calculated by the author from AO, Patent Index.

168 Gates, *Land Policies*, 251.

169 Clarke, "A Geographical Analysis," 32–68; Johnson, "The Settlement of the Western District," 30–3.

170 Both the correlation coefficients and the beta coefficients proved significant at the 99.9 per cent confidence level.

171 Clarke, "Geographical Analysis"; "Spatial Variations in Population," 408–11.

172 This was accomplished here by means of the least-square linear-model technique expressed after Krumbein as

$$Z = A_{00} + \sum_{I=1}^{M} \sum_{J=1}^{N} A_N X^I Y^J + e$$

Here, z is an observed mapped variable, x^I and y^J represents successive powers of the co-ordinates x and y, the A's are unknown parameters, and 'e' is an observable random variable with mean zero and variance σ^2. Krumbein, "The General Linear Model," 38–44. See also Chorley and

Haggett, "Trend Surface Mapping," 47–67, and Clarke, "Spatial Variations in Population," 408–11.

173 On methods of survey in Upper Canada, see Weaver, *Crown Surveys in Ontario*; Lambert and Pross, *Reviewing Nature's Wealth*; Gentilcore, "Land Surveys of Southern Ontario," 51–3.

174 AO, *Report of 1905*, xciii–xclv, Letter of Patrick McNiff to Hugh Finlay, 3 May 1791.

175 AO, Simcoe Papers, env. 44, Surveyor General's Office, York, 9 November 1795, and Clarke, "Documentary and Map Sources," 75–83.

176 Clarke, "The Role of Political Position," 28.

177 The category "well drained" included well and imperfectly drained; the category "poorly drained" included poor and very poor drainage conditions.

178 Kelly, "Practical Knowledge," 10–18. However, see also Brunger, "Analysis of Site Factors," 400–2; Gentilcore, "Change in Settlement," 418–19; Widdis, "A Perspective On Land Tenure," 78.

179 Both χ^2 test were conducted using the correction for continuity as suggested by Siegel, *Non-Parametric Statistics*, 107–10.

180 The newspapers examined at the Hiram Walker Historical Museum, the AO and the NA, were the *Upper Canada Gazette*, the *Western Herald and Farmers Magazine*, the *Amherstburg Courier and Western District Advertiser*, the *Canada Oak*, the *Canadian Emigrant and Western District Advertiser*, and the St Thomas *Liberal.*

181 AO, RG1, Township Papers, letters of John Prince, dated 13 February 1840 and 14–24 April 1854.

CHAPTER FIVE

1 This chapter is based largely upon work written in conjunction with D.L. Brown, which appeared in the pages of the *Canadian Geographer* and the *Canadian Historical Review*. The editors of these journals and my co-author are acknowledged for permission to use this work in revised form.

2 Norton, "Rural Land Values."

3 Marr and Paterson, *Canada: An Economic History.*

4 McCalla, "The Wheat Staple," 34–46; "The 'Loyalist' Economy," 279–304; "The Internal Economy," 397–416; and *Planting the Province.*

5 Gagan, *Hopeful Travellers.*

6 Clarke and Brown, "Land Prices in Essex County," 300–17.

7 McCallum, *Unequal Beginnings.*

8 McInnis, "A Reconsideration of the State of Agriculture," 9–49; "The Size Structure of Farming," 313–29; "Marketable Surpluses in Ontario Farming," 395–424.

9 Gray and Prentice, "Exploring the Price of land," 226–39.

10 Ankli and Duncan, "Farm Making Costs," 33–49.

11 Gagan, "The Security of Land," 135–53.

12 McCalla, *Planting the Province*, 29.

13 Before 1847 these deeds are organized at the county level: after 1847 they are organized by township. At the AO they are designated by GS numbers as follows: GS878, vol. A–B, 1797–1809; GS879, vol. C–D, 1809–23; GS880, vol. E–F, 1823–36; GS881, vol. G, 1836–38; GS882, vol. H 1838–42; GS883, vol. I–J, 1842–65. The township identifiers are as follows: Gosfield, GS895, 1847–54; Colchester, GS859, 1847–54; Mersea, GS951, 1847–56; West Tilbury, GS1010, 1847–59; Rochester, GS965 1847–59; Malden, GS937, 1847–55; Maidstone, GS928, 1847–55; Anderdon, GS850, 1847–65; Sandwich GS984, and GS985 for 1847–49 and 1850–53 respectively.

14 An Act Respecting Registrars, Registry Offices, and the Registration of Instruments Relating to Lands in Upper Canada received royal assent on 18 September 1865; *Statutes of the Provinces of Canada*, 29 Vic. C.24. The act applied on and after 1 January 1866 and required all registrations recorded before that date to be included in the abstract index. The abstracts were made from either the original deeds or the registrar's copy books held in the particular county. For example, some of the original copy books can be examined in the archives of the University of Windsor which has had the wisdom and foresight to preserve them from destruction.

15 Clarke, "Land and Law," 475–93; Widdis, "Tracing Property," 83–102.

16 Little makes this point in his work on Winslow Township in Quebec. He points out, that prior to the codification of the civil law in 1866, there was no obligation to register hypotheca and that French Canadians did not allow a hypothec to stand in the way even of further hypotheca on the same property. Little, *Crofters and Habitants*, 172 and 176.

17 *Report from the Select Committee on the Civil Government in Canada*, House of Commons, London, 22 July 1828, 265. See also the comments of Samuel Gale on 13 May 1828, regarding the situation in Lower Canada, ibid., 30–1.

18 Ibid., 256, evidence of W.H. Merritt, 26 June 1828.

19 Ibid., 4 and 40–3. The Canada Tenure Act, an act of the imperial parliament that came into force in 1826, provided for the possibility of mutation from one tenure form to another. The select committee report of 1828 recommended that "in proceedings for the conveyance of land the simplest and least expensive forms of conveyance should be adopted, upon the principles of the law of England, that form which prevails in Upper Canada being probably, under all circumstances, the best which could be selected; that a registration of deeds relating to soccage lands should be established as in Upper Canada." Ibid., 5.

20 In the deeds, only three instances of this could be found before 1836, but the addition of 5/- and in "love and affection" in the abstracts may suggest that inter-family agreements of this kind were much more common. An example is a deed of 1808 by which the Widow Charon conveyed her interest in land to one Antoine Réaume. She insisted upon good lodging, bedding, linen, and woollen wearing apparel, access to the doctor, and a servant when needed and a daily glass of spirituous liquor! She also required burial in the Roman rite, a total of 25 low masses within two years, and the elimination of all debts incurred by herself and her husband. She was to be free to move from Réaume's roof if she so chose and he was to provide suitable alternatives for all her needs. See AO, GS878, vol. B, no.380. For other examples of such arrangements see Gagan, "Indivisibility of Land," 126–41.

21 The abstracts often included multiple transactions as "among other lands." The deeds specify the locations. For example, on the 28 November 1809 William Buchanan, a yeoman of Colchester Township, mortgaged lot 18/2nd Concession (200 acres), the west half of lot 19/2nd concession (100 acres), and 20 acres in the Gore between the 1st and 2nd concession for the sum of £393.5.3. See AO, GS878, entry 126, 155.

22 Ibid. The mortgagees for the transaction involving William Buchanan were Richard Pattinson of Sandwich and William Duff of Amherstburg. The first of these properties included a sawmill whose existence is not recorded in the abstracts. Similarly, the mortgage of the famous Maisonville windmill in Sandwich Township to James Baby is recorded in the deed of 25 May 1802 but was not abstracted in such a way as to show this.

23 For instance, Samuel Harris, yeoman of Gosfield, mortgaged a property to T.F. Park of Amherstburg in June 1848 for £187.10 This property, located on the southern part of the western division of Gosfield, was composed of twenty-three acres but the transaction included a steam engine, boilers, and other apparatus and machinery. See University of Windsor, Land Registry Copy Books, Gosfield Register A, 46, instrument 36.

24 Readers should be aware that this is how the term "mortgage" is used in this study. It represents a credit transaction between people no matter if the instrument used was a mortgage in the strict sense or a "bargain and sale by way of a mortgage."

25 As yet, insufficient work has been done to evaluate the usefulness of this broad source for the whole of Ontario. Weldon, in her research on Hawkesbury, found marked departures from the idealized model of the abstraction process. Gray and Prentice believe in the wisdom of using the deeds over the abstracts. Colin Read, in his study of Norfolk County,

finds the abstracts useful; however, for particular pieces of information he prefers the copy books. Clearly, there may have been regional variation in the manner in which these records were created. See Weldon, "The Salient Factors"; Read, "Assessing Sources for Analyzing Wealth"; and Gray and Prentice, "Exploring the Price of Farmland." In the last named, the authors use my work on Malden Township. Perhaps naturally they assume that what appears in the abstracts is a small proportion of a more complete record available in the original deeds for Essex. As this text points out, the difference was minute.

26 This contrasts with Norfolk County, where Read reports that he deliberately used the copy books for price information because of known deficiencies in the abstracts. Read, "Assessing Sources for Analyzing Wealth," 35.

27 It is possible that the exclusion of these instruments has produced an error in the calculation of the frequency of transfer. If so, the error is small because the frequency of occurrence of these instruments is also small. The reason is that, prior to the passage of the Canada Tenure Act in 1826, these instruments were often used in Quebec to convey. Under such instruments, possession and property were awarded at once. Many lawyers thought that their use was prudent since "bargain and sales" required "tradition or enrolment" and there was no tradition of registration in Lower Canada. See *Report of the Select Committee on Civil Government in the Canadas*, 31 and 197, evidence of Samuel Gale, 13 May 1828 and 26 June 1828; and ibid., 267, evidence of J.C. Grant, 17 June 1828. It is possible that, because lawyers in and near Detroit were acquainted with French tenure, they may have followed French precedent.

28 In Lower Canada, provincial legislation permitted the voluntary sheriff's sale to seek the benefit accorded by a *décret* in French law. Where land was encumbered, everyone received his due from this action and a more secure title was obtained. See ibid., 118, evidence of John Nielsen, 5 June 1828; ibid., 193, evidence of J.C. Grant, 17 June 1828; and ibid., 211, evidence of Robert Gillespie, 1828. In Upper Canada, the registry system, absent in the lower province, protected the interest of lenders more. Sheriffs' deeds were used to secure back taxes by the state or private debts to individuals. The land was disposed of to individuals who sought to gain from the misfortune of others rather than to farm themselves.

29 Widdis, "A Perspective on Land Tenure," 79–85. He shows that land transfers began as early as 1795 but grew in a sustained manner after 1804. Some lots in the fifty-year period were conveyed more than twenty times.

30 The rho value for the relationship between average date of patent in the townships of Essex and the number of transactions was found to be 0.87, significant at 0.05.

31 The respective means and standard deviation for the older townships were found to be: Malden ($\bar{x}$ = 9.7; σ = 12.0), Gosfield (6.4 and 8.9), Sandwich East (5.8 and 11.0), Sandwich West and North (2.8 and 12.0), and Colchester (5.7 and 8.2). For the "newer" townships, the respective statistics were: Maidstone (4.4 and 7.3), Mersea (3.5 and 7.1), Anderdon (3.0 and 4.5), Rochester (2.4 and 4.7), and Tilbury (2.0 and 7.1). Only Malden proved statistically different from the others. When ranked hierarchically, only Malden and Gosfield proved statistically different; t = 2.02, significant at the 95 per cent confidence level. Watt, who has worked on Lennox and Addington counties in the period to 1825, shows that for a sample of thirty-four sales the lag between patent and sale was 9.56 years with a σ of 6.9 years. See Watt, "A Historical Perspective."

32 The respective t values for the boundaries were found to be 2.57, 3.16, and 2.77. With appropriate df, all proved significant at the 95 per cent confidence level.

33 McCalla, *Planting the Province*, 30–4. A t statistic of 1.97 proved statistically significant at the 95 per cent confidence level, the required t being 1.66 at infinity on a one-tailed test.

34 Ibid., 34–42.

35 Mahlon Burwell is one who did. He had received his land here as compensation for his surveying activity. He successfully unloaded eight lots in the five-year period 1821–25 and another twenty-two in 1826–30. The removal of these lands from the calculation changes the respective statistics for both periods. For 1821–25, the new mean and σ, based upon an "n" of 22, would become 4.27 and 4.23 years; that for the period 1826 to 1830 becomes 7.88 and 7.93, based upon an "n" of 17. If this is permitted, it results in a fifth grouping the years 1821–25: t = 1.65, which is only barely significant at the 95 per cent confidence level.

36 Ibid., 193.

37 Ibid., 194.

38 Ibid., 179.

39 McCallum, *Unequal Beginnings*, 14.

40 Gagan, *Hopeful Travellers*.

41 Johnson, "Land policy, Population Growth" and *History of the County of Ontario, 1615–1875*.

42 This is measured at the nominal level and assumes no variation in the acreage patented nor does it say anything about the quality of land. Even in 1851, 33.8 per cent of Essex land remained unpatented.

43 Significant at the 95 per cent confidence level.

44 These data were originally explored in Clarke and Brown, "The Upper Canadian Land Market," 220–34. There is always a hesitation to base a price for any one year on a small number of cases.

45 For these reasons this represents an adjusted price series from that published by the author in 1979; Clarke, "Geographical Aspects of Land Speculation," 69–112.

46 The reader is reminded that, because the sources are silent on this issue, it has not been possible to deflate the price obtained to allow for the value of residences, out-buildings, or livestock. Since these are rarely, if ever, specified in the deeds, one has to presume that they were considered a "constant" or "of a kind." Nonetheless it is because of this that the term "land" has been placed in quotation marks within the subheading.

47 There can be problems with inference when the samples are small as is the case as for the early years. It is for this reason that the discussion in the text usually focuses upon periods of years.

48 Carter-Edwards, "Defending the Straits," 33–43.

49 Surtees, "Indian Participation," 42–8.

50 The 1824 value falls towards the upper end of William McCormick's estimate of good land which he reported as being worth between 240 and 480 pence per acre. Douglas, *A Sketch of the Western District*, 22.

51 After the removal of what seemed duplicate transactions involving the same sellers, dates, and monies from the seigneurial long-lots of Sandwich Township, there were 64 railway transactions made, 32 in each of 1852 and 1853. For 1852, the mean and σ was 12,766.15 and 12,927.32; for 1853, the respective statistics were 20,994.2 and 33,161.88 pence. A t statistic of 1.29 with 39 was not sufficiently high to reject the null hypothesis of insignificant difference. The mean price of non-railway land in 1852 was 419 with a σ of 174 pence per acre.

52 As indicated by their title, Gray and Prentice chose to use the term "farm real estate." For more detail, see Gray and Prentice, *Trends in the Price*.

53 AO, Crown Land Papers, Crown Lands in Upper Canada, Western District, vol. 54, mfm. 12, purchasers of Crown land, 1839–41, advertised in 1839. See also *Upper Canada Gazette*, 15 (1841–42) 46–49, "A Statement of the Crown Lands sold and of the amount paid on each lot in the several Districts in that part of this Province, formerly constituting the Province of Upper Canada as they appear from the books of the Land Department of the Province of Canada," 30 June 1841. Here a skewed sample of 22 observations yielded a mean of 134.7 and a σ of 53.8; the mode and median, the better measures of central tendency in these circumstances, were 96 and 114 pence respectively.

54 AO, RG 1, A–VII, vol. 12, 6 August 1852.

55 In 1861, 15,141 acres of a potential 66,442 acres of vacant land were advertised for sale. See AO, Crown Land Papers, vol. 77, 1861. The modal value obtained was 100 pence and the median was 160 pence, but

the average is quoted in text for comparison with the summary data of Table 5.7.

56   *Upper Canada Gazette* 15 (1841–42), 78–83, "A statement of the Clergy Reserves sold and of the amount paid on each lot in the several Districts in that part of this Province, formerly constituting the Province of Upper Canada as they appear from the books of the Land Department of the Province of Canada," 30 June 1841.

57   The data were skewed, which is why the mean of 136.8 pence and the σ of 24.8 are reported here rather than in text.

58   Gates, *Land Policies*, 148–51.

59   Gagan, *Hopeful Travellers*, 173. Gagan uses a relatively large sample of 1916 for these years; exactly how many observations pertain to the decade 1840–50 is unknown.

60   Gray and Prentice, *Trends In the Price*, 70–81.

61   Watt, "A Historical Perspective."

62   Brunger, "Market-Value of Land." Alan Brunger kindly provided me with these statistics.

63   Ennals, "Land and Society in Hamilton Township," 23.

64   There is always a concern with basing a price upon a small number of possibly extreme values. The number of observations upon which Essex land is estimated here is indeed small before 1807, justifying their grouping into periods, and more generally, the use of generalized trend values in regression. One might also be wary of the numbers with money in any one year. In the Essex sample this was never less than 11 per cent (in 1812) nor more than 70 per cent (in 1835).

65   For example, in the present study an effort was made to ensure that only rural land was included in the analysis, but even in rural areas exceptionally large values were excluded since the reported value might include, for example, machinery or buildings. A variety of acreages may have been used to allow entry to a particular data set. Gray and Prentice permit calculation only when the farm is at least forty-five acres. Gray and Prentice, *Trends In The Price*, 70–81.

66   This may say something about the allometry of land prices and the regionalization of Ontario at this time. Clearly, Essex had a period of stability which contrasted with the soaring development of more central areas such as Peel. The F statistic for the significance of "r" was 5.49, leading to a probability of 0.046.

67   The speaker is the Reverend Bell of Perth, quoted in Lockwood, *Montague*, 102. Lockwood reports that this was true also of Montague, although decline in price was with distance from the Rideau canal.

68   Ennals, "Land and Society in Hamilton Township," 23.

69   This statistic, like the mean and standard deviation, is affected by an unusually high value in 1843 in Peel, where Gagan reports land selling at

$66.19 per acre. On a four-dollar equivalent, this would mean 3971.4 pence per acre. It is no doubt because of this and other outliers that Gagan chose to use a three-year running mean in his regression analysis.

70 $t = 5.3$, significant at the 95 per cent confidence level. These prices would seem to be in line with what Read reports for Colver family sales in Norfolk County. The mean price was 478 pence per acre. See Read, "Assessing Sources for Analyzing Wealth."

71 The t statistic calculated was 9.19 significant at the 95 per cent confidence level.

72 If the three-year running mean calculated by Gagan is used, the mean remains almost unchanged at 1341 pence per acre, although the standard deviation is reduced to 643.1. If the year 1843 is removed from the calculation, the new statistics are 691 and 175.38 respectively for the mean and standard deviation. In this case the price of land is seen to rise between the two periods rather than decline.

73 A series of t tests demonstrated this statistically. For the years 1841 to 1845, Fredericksburg exhibited statistically higher prices than Essex ($t = 4.78$), Essex was significantly different from Duoro ($t=7.08$), and Duoro, Nichol, and Ramsay formed a third set with t statistics of 0.89 and 0.03. In all instances, acceptance or rejection of the null hypothesis was governed by the critical value needed to reject at the 95 per cent confidence level. In the second period, the Essex townships proved insignificantly different from Nichol Township in statistical terms ($t = 0.54$) and dissimilar to Duoro ($t = 6.75$). It is presumed that Essex and Nichol would test different statistically from Peel County. In all of this, it has to be remembered that the Essex values are those of ten townships rather than a single township. Finally, it is worth reporting that, in areas even less favoured in terms of both soil and location, prices would be lower still. In the Johnstown District in 1841, the cost of land was under £1 per acre. See Kennedy, *South Elmsley*, 62. In 1851, in Alfred and Caledonia Townships, the census enumerators reported that land could be had for £1 to £2 per acre. See Gaffield, *Language, Schooling, and Cultural Conflict*, 212.

74 £2½ to £3½ was the figure which was reported by three individuals, Saunders, Moodie, and Grange to a questionnaire sent out by the colonial government in the 1840s. However, A.B. Hawke, the colonial emigration agent, reported £4, the politician Thomas Rolph reported £5 and J.W. Dunber Moodie, sheriff of the Victoria District, believed that up to £7 would be required in the vicinity of towns. These figures are indeed congruent with what has been calculated here. See Ankli and Duncan, "Farm Making Costs," 41.

75 Akenson, *The Irish in Ontario*, 158, reports Crown land in Leeds and Lansdowne selling for eight shillings per acre in the mid-1840s.

76 Ankli and Duncan cite a range of authorities and clearance rates from £2.10.0 to £10 on swampy land. The £4 used here is that of A.B. Hawke, the chief emigration agent for Upper Canada. Twenty-five acres was the average cleared acreage in Essex, based upon the census enumeration returns. See Ankli and Duncan, "Farm Making Costs in Early Ontario," 34–49.

77 Ibid., 48.

78 The number of Crown sales in Upper Canada for the years 1824 to 1851 was obtained from Gates, *Land Policies*, 309.

79 Cowan, *British Emigration in North America*, Table 1.

80 The primary source for the total value of land sales in the United States (1825–1851), the total value of lands sold in Ohio (1814–51), and the total value of lands sold in Michigan (1814–51) was Cole, "Cyclical and Seasonal Variations," 41–53.

81 The primary source of this was the Census of Canada for 1871. This was supplemented by NA, JHA/UC, vol. 6, 1847, appendix no.1, A–T; JHA/UC, vol. 8, 1849, appendix no.1, B and J. Upper Canadian population figures are for the years 1811 and 1824–42. Essex population data are for the years 1805, 1806, 1818–20, 1823–42, 1845, and 1851.

82 Census of Canada 1871, vol. 3, Table XI. Supplemented by NA, JHA/UC, vol. 8, 1849, Appendix no.1, B. Cultivated acreage figures for Essex County were also obtained from various issues of the JHA/UC.

83 This is a derived variable determined from the number of accumulated patents taken out at any one time, and expressed as a percentage of what would ultimately be patented. This quotient is then subtracted from unity.

84 The interest-rate data were obtained from Homer, *A History of Interest Rates*, 208–9 and 1318–20. The British rates were the annual bank rate, which was averaged, and the American rates were the annual averages for commercial paper.

85 Norton, Trist, and Gilbert, "A Century of Land Values." Continuous observations were available for the years 1781 to 1851.

86 Rostow, *British Economy*, 124–5. Data were available for 1781 to 1851.

87 Page, *Commerce and Industry*, 142. Data were restricted to the period 1841–51.

88 Marr and Paterson, *Canada: An Economic History*, 81; NA, JHA/Canada, vol. 3, appendix 7, no.126, 4 October 1843, no.126. Data were for the periods 1752–58 and 1766–1841. These data were slightly different from those reported by Ouellet, Hamelin, and Chabot, "Les prix agricoles," 83–127. A regression of this data set produced a somewhat higher but statistically insignificant correlation of 0.21.

89 The price series used here for central and western Upper Canada were taken from Table C.1 of McCalla, *Planting the Province*, 336–7.

90 Ibid., 336–7.

91 Attempts to lag these data by one to five years provided no improvement in the correlation coefficients, which were also statistically insignificant.

92 Pearson's product-moment correlation coefficient for the relationship of wheat with time was found to be −0.49. The F ratio was 8.08, significant with 1 and 26 df at the 0.008 level. Similarly, the relationship of time and land price in Essex produced an "r" of 0.74 and an "F" of 31.4. This, with 1 and 26 df, proved significant at the 0.00001 level.

93 A *t* ratio of 18.82 proved significant at 0.0001.

94 "Staple theory" owes much to W.A. Mackintosh, H.A. Innis, V.C Fowke, W.T. Easterbrook, and H.G.J. Aitken. See McIntosh, "Economic Factors in Canadian History," 12–25; Innis, "An Introduction to the Economic History," 111–23; and Fowke, *Canadian Agricultural Policy*. The Upper Canadian wheat staple is one of the themes in Aitken and Aitken, *Canadian Economic History*, a perspective preserved in Marr and Paterson, *Canada: An Economic History*. The most recent advocate of this view is McCallum, *Unequal Beginnings*.

95 See Buckley, "The Role of Staple Industries," 439–50; McCalla, "The Wheat Staple," 34–45; McInnis, "Marketable Surpluses in Ontario Farming," 395–424; "The Size Structure of Farming," 312–29; "The Early Ontario Wheat Staple Reconsidered," 17–48; "Ontario Agriculture at Mid-century," 49–83.

96 McCalla, "The Internal Economy of Upper Canada," 397–416, and *Planting the Province*, 67–91.

97 Ibid., 79 and 271.

98 Ibid., 72, 255, and 265. McInnis argues that, given the need for feed and for meat and dairy products for the farm family, 30 per cent of the land under culture was the most that a wheat economy could allocate to its main crop. See McInnis, "Ontario Agriculture at Mid-century," 69.

99 Ibid., 76.

100 Ibid., 88.

101 McInnis, "Ontario Agriculture at Mid-century," 74. See also his earlier "Ontario Wheat Staple Reconsidered" (40), where he maps wheat production by the dot method and in dollar terms. As well, see Wood, "A New Agriculture," Plate 14 of *Historical Atlas of Canada*, vol. 2.

102 McInnis, "Ontario Agriculture at Mid-century," 83.

103 McCalla, "The Wheat Staple," 34–46.

104 See Marr and Paterson, *Canada: An Economic History*, 81; Chalmers, *A History of Currency*, 175–206; and Shortt, "History of Canadian Currency," 116–31.

105 Rohrbough, *The Trans-Appalachian Frontier*, 234.

106 Cole, "Cyclical and Sectional Variations," 41–53.

107 McCalla, *Planting the Province*, 183.

108 Recognition of the first five decades of the nineteenth century as an important stage in the agricultural settlement of Ontario is accorded by a number of scholars. See Jones, *History of Agriculture*, 1–195; Gentilcore, "Change in Settlement," 418–19, and "Settlement," 23–44; Brunger, "A Spatial Analysis"; Johnson, *History of the County of Ontario*; "The Settlement of the Western District," 19–35; Gagan, *Hopeful Travellers*, 143–5; and McCalla, *Planting the Province*. While these authors agree on the overall importance of the first half of the century, they vary in their interpretation of meaningful stages within it. No doubt their individual decisions reflect local conditions. So it is in this work where, for substantive reasons and reasons of data availability, 1825 is recognized as the dividing line.

109 This is largely drawn from Clarke and Brown, "Land Prices in Essex County," 300–17.

110 Clarke and Brown, "Pricing Decisions," 169–76.

111 Siegel, *Non Parametric Statistics*, 202–11.

112 Clarke, "Aspects of Land Acquisition," 98–118.

113 The lots in Essex County that are closer to the town of Chatham in Kent County than to these two centres lie beyond twelve miles and often as much as thirty miles from Chatham. They are few in number relative to those in the western part of Essex. For these reasons, the relationship of land price to distance from Chatham is not portrayed graphically at this juncture.

114 Clarke, "Documentary and map sources," 75–83.

115 Mahlon Burwell began surveying the Talbot Road in 1811 and reached Mersea Township in 1816. Between 1821 and 1825, Burwell completed the Talbot Road through Gosfield and Colchester townships, as well as the Middle Road from Orford Township in Kent County to Maidstone in Essex County.

116 Although Cedar Creek has never formally been recognized as a village, a number of functions were established there, and it is recognized as a centre here.

117 The equations for price and distance to nearest node for the earlier of the two periods and for prices below 1,000 pence was $y = 292.41 - 0.28x$, where y is the price per acre in pence and x the distance to the node. The Pearson product-moment correlation coefficient of -0.21 proved significant at .005 for an "n" of 149. Although statistically the "r's" are not strictly comparable for the second period (n=935), the increased size of the statistic (-0.35) suggests an

increased importance of the developing infrastructure. This second coefficient proved statistically significant at the 0.00001 level.

118 Examination of descriptive statistics and a plot of the data showed they were positively skewed, which confirmed the wisdom of a logarithmic transformation. Experimentation in an earlier paper with an untransformed dependent variable, a logarithmically transformed dependent variable, and logarithmically dependent and independent variables showed the third form to provide the best statistical explanation. Clarke and Brown, "Land Prices in Essex County," 311.

119 All distances were measure in millimetres using the Department of Highways 1:63,360 map of Essex.

120 Clarke and Brown, "Focii of Human Activity," 31–57.

121 The list included those who had more than 400 acres at any one time and whose dealings in land permit the inference that they were speculators. It also includes those identified as land-jobbers in the literature.

122 Some indication for the period 1821–26 can be gained from the descriptive statistics. The mean was 1.39 and the σ 0.8, although the reader should be warned that the data were highly skewed. The plot of the data showed a distinct grouping on the mode which was one. Yet the effect of a few outliers was such that a statistically significant but otherwise spurious relationship of price and number of transactions was found at 0.4.

123 Analysis of the relationship between the signs of the residuals and speculative or non-speculative ownership, using chi-square analysis of a 2x2 contingency table, proved insignificant. The value of chi-square was 0.57, insignificant with one degree of freedom at the 95 per cent confidence level. A similar analysis with soil conditions yielded another insignificant chi value of 2.21.

124 For non-speculators, the average price of land was 1600 pence per acre; the standard deviation was 8138 pence, and the sample size was 968. For speculators, the respective figures were 2160, 10,114, and 103. A difference-of-means test produced a t-value of −0.64, insignificant at the 95 per cent confidence level.

125 Ennals, "Land and Society in Hamilton Township," 23.

126 Johnson, "The State of Agricultural Development," 129.

127 Ibid., 129.

128 There is a remarkable if chance congruence with the results of other work here. Analysis of 1324 property parcels, drawn from the census of 1851 for Essex for purposes of cross-tabulation with ethnic origin, shows that the cropped acreage was actually 18.5 acres on average, which on a grain/fallow basis would be 37 acres. By calculation, the

average yield on wheat was found to be 13.1 bushels per acre. If the farmer received four shillings per bushel, as Johnson suggests, he would have had an annual income of £48.9s.0d. See also Russell, "Wage Labour Rates," 61–80.

129 The terminology and the figures are Russell's. See Russell, "Attitudes to Social Structure," 29. He estimates the income of a "well-to-do" farmer as between £100 and £150.

130 Ibid., 38.

131 Gates, *Land Policies*, 172.

132 Calculation based upon Tables 1 and 3 of Johnson, "The Settlement of Western District," 27 and 29.

133 This is strikingly different from the 92 per cent of farms which, according to McInnis in "Marketable Surpluses," grew some wheat in 1861. It is difficult to assign the components of this either to the regional effect or to differences in the date of reporting.

134 Census of Canada 1851–52, vol. 2, Table 4. Corn covered 5763 acres and oats 5147 acres.

135 McInnis, "Marketable Surpluses," 45. He gives 11.0 acres for 1861.

136 The standard deviation was 7.66 acres based upon a sample of 779.

137 The mean and standard deviations of corn and oats were respectively 4.49 and 3.56 acres (n=856) and 5.56 and 5.46 acres (n=714). The respective t values for the differences between wheat, corn, and oat acreages were 9.3 and 4.5, significant at the 95 per cent confidence level.

138 However, when all land prices were considered, the differences between the two were statistically insignificant. The mean of cleared acreage among the farm community was 16.24 acres, that of the speculators 19.8 acres. The respective standard deviations were 18.24 and 22.19 acres.

CHAPTER SIX

1 McCalla, *Planting the Province*, 29. See also "The Loyalist Economy," 279–304, by the same author.

2 McCalla, *Planting the Province*, 29; *The Upper Canada Trade*, 5.

3 McCalla, *Planting the Province*, 76 and 91.

4 Marr, "Tenant vs Owner," 50–71: Wilson, *A New Lease on Life*.

5 In fact as Mill noted, credit, by increasing purchasing power and demand, increases prices. Mill, *Principles of Political Economy*, vol. 2, 45.

6 As well they might since, on the evidence of John Stuart Mill, the year 1825 was a particularly marked speculative year which resulted in a commercial crisis. See Mill, *Principles of Political Economy*, vol. 2, 45.

7 A commission was established to investigate land prices in Upper Canada in 1825. Among the questions asked was one designed to determine the

credit price of land; another asked the informants what land they knew to have been sold and for what price. The two questions were not linked directly; the answers reported were never specific to a particular property. It is perhaps because of this that in 18 cases out of 163 cash was seen as less desirable than credit. For the remaining 145, the $\bar{x}$ and σ was 26.07 and 14.57 pence respectively; since the data were somewhat skewed, the median may be the better measure of central tendency and it was 23.7 pence. PRO, CO 47, vol. 115. The terms of the schedule by which these data were to be gathered are given in NA, RG1 L1, 501, 16 December 1825. See also Clarke and Buffone, "Colonial Land Policy," 1–46, and "Manifestations of Imperial Policy," 121–36.

8 Shirreff, *A Tour through North America*, 362–5.

9 McCalla, "The Ontario Economy, 97–115. McCall argues that the Ontario economy was linked in this way to the international financial system and so its crises were those of the Western economy. Ibid., 110.

10 McCalla, "Rural Credit," 48. Charles Askin, reporting to William Robertson, Jr, on the disposal of his property in 1804 illustrates this problem of liquidity. He had to accept wheat, rye, wood, flour, and so on. and "had more trouble in turning these afterwards into money than five times as much cash would have given me." NA, MG–19–A–3, Askin Family Papers, vol. 5, 1388, 12 March 1804.

11 Craig, *Upper Canada*, 139–40; Gates, *Land Policies*, 170–5.

12 Trail, *The Backwoods of Canada*, 133.

13 Gagan, "The Security of Land," 135–53.

14 For Upper Canada see An Act Respecting Registrars, Registry Offices, and the Registration of Instruments Relating to Lands in Upper Canada, *Statutes of the Provinces of Canada* 29 Vic. c.24.

15 In Roman law, to which we, in the West, are heir, there were three forms: namely, *fiducia cum creditore*, *pignus*, and *hypotheca*. The first, conducted in front of witnesses, resulted in a transfer of property from the debtor to the creditor. A *pactum fiducaie* executed at the same time bound the creditor to reconvey upon payment of the debt. The second, used mainly for moveable items or chattels, transferred possession to the creditor but ownership was retained with the debtor. The third type restricted the security of the creditor to a lien or charge with the debtor secure in possession and ownership. Variants of these gages appeared in the laws of Germany and, most relevant here, France and England. The possessory gage *hypotheque*, requiring acknowledgement before judge or notary, persists in the law of Quebec. See Hazeltine, "The Gage of Land," 36–50; Turner, *The Equity of Redemption*; *Encyclopedia Britannica*, 12th ed., s.v. "Mortgages."

16 Clarke, "Land and Law," 475–93.

17 Brown, "Equitable Jurisdiction," 276.

18 Ibid., 278; 7 Wm.4 c.2; Banks, "The Evolution of the Ontario Courts," 492–572.

19 Brown, ibid., 279 and 287.

20 Weaver, "While Equity Slumbered," 871–914.

21 The quotation from Thompson, *Whigs and Hunters*, 264, is cited in Weaver, "While Equity Slumbered," 912. Weaver is careful to posit his conclusions in terms of probabilities. To support his argument, he points to the foot-dragging over implementation of a court of chancery and the use of writs of *fieri facias*. By 1809 such writs were used to seize land and eliminate redemption via the office of the sheriff; in England at this time, use of such writs was restricted to seizure of chattels, although, as Riddell shows by 1733 this limitation did not apply in British plantations and colonies. Riddell, "'Fi Fa' Lands," 448–51. See also Romney, "The Ten Thousand Pound Job," 143–99.

22 A celebrated case reported by Romney is that of Robert Randal, who had been involved with John Askin, William Robertson, and others in the attempted purchase of the southern portion of Michigan. As their American agent he had been imprisoned following investigation by the Congress. He subsequently acquired an interest in iron-working at the Chaudière Falls. Two juries upheld his position against Samuel Street, Jr, and Thomas Clark, who had purchased the shares of his former partners. Traditionally, two such verdicts were sufficient to end a matter such as this. However, his property was sold at a sherriff's sale at less than market value, in fulfillment of a judgment brought against him by his own lawyer and creditor Henry John Boulton (son of Mr Justice D'Arcy Boulton), though as a debtor he had not been informed of the impending action. At a fourth hearing in 1817, Randal represented himself. He was opposed by John Beverley Robinson, the pre-eminent lawyer of the time. The judge, William Dummer Powell, threatened the jury with an "attaint" or disciplinary action if they rendered a verdict contradicting the evidence unless they possessed private knowledge that contradicted it. Needless to say, Randal lost. Romney believes that provincial justice was seen to be a "system run by the rich for the rich." Romney, *Mr Attorney*, 65–78. See Lownsbrough, "D'Arcy Boulton," 78–80; Senior, "Henry John Boulton," 69–72.

23 Brode, *Sir John Beverley Robinson*, 149; Weaver, "While Equity Slumbered," 881. Saunders ("Sir John Beverley Robinson," 677) shows that he owned 300 acres in Simcoe County, over 1000 acres in York, some land in Ontario and Peel counties, and 29 parcels elsewhere. Harring makes the point that Robinson was himself a speculator and the brother of Peter, a land speculator, immigration promotor, Crown land commissioner, commissioner of the clergy reserves, and surveyor general of public woods. Robinson had acted for William Dickson in acquiring 94,035 acres of Six

Nations land. He seems to have gone to extraordinary lengths to ensure that the Indian capacity to sell land in the Grand River tract was reduced by law and that the rights of squatters here and on Walpole Island were upheld at least in equity terms. Squatters were, of course, part of the approach used by land speculators to secure their claims by, among other things, frightening off the indigenous population. Moreover, while in matters of common law involving Europeans, Robinson's decisions reflected "polyjuralism," the record is silent on this with respect to native rights. It is possible that he, like many of his time, had simply no consciousness of the legal issues concerning the existence of the native population, but Harring strongly implies that his actions were purposeful. See Harring, *White Man's Law*, 63–90, and Cameron, "Peter Robinson," 752–56.

24 Brown, "Equitable Jurisdiction," 281.

25 Bilak, "The Law of the Land," 183. In this same paper Bilak suggests that mortgages might have been more common but for the paucity of long-term investment capital.

26 Upper Canada, 4 Wm.4, c.1.s.43.

27 Gagan, "The Security of Land," 135–53.

28 Clarke shows that, of the 624 deeds registered and abstracted for Malden Township by 1852, only 88 were mortgages although an additional 16 were recorded as "assignments of mortgages." Bargains and sales numbered 321 and indentures 106. Interestingly, foreclosures numbered zero. See Clarke, "Land and Law," 478.

29 Risk, "The Law and the Economy," 88–131. In this work Risk shows that the courts, while bound to consider English cases, necessarily sought to consider the particular circumstances of Upper Canada, especially the need to see it developed and to this end were willing to review appropriate American precedents. See also Risk, "The Golden Age," 199–239, 307–46, where the vendor/purchaser contract is regarded as the standard form.

30 Bilak, "The Law of the Land," 187.

31 Butler acquired this lot, lot 14 in the 3rd concession of Colchester, by patent on 4 December 1845 and mortgaged it for £1022.2.6 on 12 January 1846. The agreement was for three years and interest was to be paid semi-annually. Butler gave the assurance that he "had good right full dower and lawful and absolute authority" to grant. The deed, which did not specify the interest required, was witnessed by Angus Cameron and James Hamilton of Amherstburg. It involved both land (200 acres) and premises, which would account for the substantial amount involved, and was registered by John A. Askin on 27 April 1847. See University of Windsor, Land Registry Copy Books, Colchester Register A, book 1–56, 7, instrument 6.

32 See appendix 6.1.

33 Burley, "'Good For All He Would Ask,'" 79–99. The same author has shown that in Brantford only 20 per cent of business had mortgages against their holdings in 1851 and that greater indebtedness was associated with declining fortune. In absolute terms, the average mortgage debt was $2253 or approximately £563.5s.0d. Burley, *A Particular Condition in Life*, 120–2.

34 Lemon, "Early Americans."

35 Conant, *Upper Canada Sketches*, 240.

36 Hogan, *Canada, An Essay*, 67.

37 Gagan, "The Prose of Life," 367–81.

38 Noel, *Patrons, Clients, Brokers*.

39 Nehemiah 5:3–5.

40 Woodward, *Canadian Mortgages*.

41 Reid aspired to a career as a painter and needed to be close to "civilization," which he interpreted as Toronto. The threat of foreclosure on his father's property meant that the latter contemplated a move northward to the junction of lakes Huron and Superior, something not welcomed by his younger son. The problem was resolved when George's elder brother, John, took over a neighbouring farm to stave off the threat. Miller, *George Reid*, 21–2.

42 The original of *Mortgaging*, which Reid submitted as a diploma picture for the Royal Canadian Academy, is in the National Gallery of Canada, Ottawa. See also Gagan, "The Indivisibility of Land," 126–41.

43 *Foreclosure of the Mortgage* was destroyed by fire but such was the public reception of his work that Reid was obliged to repaint it from black and white photographic reproductions. See Miller, *George Reid*, 142–3.

44 See University of Windsor, Land Registry Copy Books, Colchester, Register A, book 1–56, 7. The agreement between Butler and Thomas F. Park was witnessed by another Essex merchant, John Richardson Park, described in the agreement as a "Gentleman of the town of Barrie, County of Simcoe." Butler, who was born in the United States, was fifty-seven years of age when he appeared in the Census of Canada for 1851 as entry number 36, Colchester Township.

45 Gagan, "The Security of land," 135–53; Kennedy, "Landowners and Mortgaging."

46 The actual figure based upon an "n" of 39 was $1348.72 converted at $4.00 to the pound. Gagan, "The Security of land," 139 and 152.

47 Kennedy ("Landowners and Mortgaging," 11) based upon an "n" of 16. Little (*Crofters and Habitants*, 172–9) shows considerable differences in mortgaged value between French Canadian and Scottish settlers in Winslow Township, Quebec. The average values of these lands was respectively $123 and $260 for the period 1850–80. As yet, Upper

Canadian historiography has not been able to examine such differences.

48 Gagan, "The Security of Land," 140; Kennedy, "Landowners and Mortgaging," 9.

49 Kennedy, ibid., Table VI, and Gagan, ibid., 145.

50 Ibid., 147.

51 Gagan, "Indivisibility of Land," 126–41.

52 AO, Original Deeds, GS879, no.79, 28 May 1810.

53 AO, Original Deeds, GS879, no.75, 7 April 1810. The phrase used here is one of a very few instances that might support the view that mortgages in Essex *at this time* were to secure an investment rather than acquire land.

54 The payments secured by 182 acres of the north parts of lots 47/1 and 42/2 of Sandwich Township were to be annual. This agreement, entered into on 5 February 1818, was discharged on 11 May 1821. AO, Original Deeds, GS879, no. 40.

55 AO, GS878, no. 128, 158. Augustus L'Husier, yeoman of Sandwich, mortgaged 18/1 Sandwich to William Park for £53.18.0 plus lawful interest. The mortgage was written on 1 January 1802 and discharged on 1 January 1803.

56 Ibid., GS879, 13 March 1819. Under this agreement, the south half of lot 30 in the 3rd concession of Malden was to be mortgaged for £140.

57 For differing interpretations of the importance of wheat, see the work of R.L. Jones, J. McCallum, and, most recently, Douglas McCalla and Marvin McInnis.

58 The usury laws were created under 51 Geo. III (1811) c.9, s.6, in turn derived from the English statute, 13 Eliz. I c.8.

59 Ankli, "Farm Making Costs," 40.

60 George Jervis Goodhue of London, Upper Canada, operated a mortgage-loan business which was thought of as usurious but in fact, as Armstrong has shown, his rates were until 1852 standard, that is, 6 per cent. By 1858 his rates were 18 per cent and by November of that year 24 per cent. Armstrong, "George Jervis Goodhue, Pioneer Merchant," 217–32; "George Jervis Goodhue," 323–4.

61 Conant, *Upper Canada Sketches*, 53.

62 With a calculated F of 6.656 and 48df, this is significant at the 95 per cent confidence level.

63 Clarke and Brown, "The Upper Canadian Land Market," 221–34. This relationship proved significant at the 95 per cent confidence level. An "adjusted" data set, smoothed by five-year running means, produced a correlation coefficient of 0.64 and a t statistic of 5.63 which with 46 df proved significant at the .00001 level.

64 Johnson, "The settlement of Western District," 19–35. Pearson's "r" for the relationship of population and number of sales was 0.88, which with

22 df and an F of 82.79 was significant at the 0.0001 level. Similarly, the relationship of population to number of mortgages proved positive at 0.70. With 22 df and an F of 23.29, this too proved significant at the 0.0001 level.

65 The mortgage rate per thousand was calculated using annual returns of population derived from a variety of sources. The calculated $\bar{x}$ for a sample of 27 was found to be 1.78, the σ was 0.71, and the median was 1.74. Twenty-four of the twenty-seven observations lay within one standard deviation of the mean.

66 The correlation coefficient for the relationship between number of sales and number of mortgages was 0.82, which with 49 df and a calculated F of 102.02 proved significant at greater than .001.

67 The unprededented importation of food from abroad, which Upper Canadian farmers sought to contribute to, together with the high cost of cotton and demands on what Mill called the "circulating currency," produced continued pressure on the loan market in the United Kingdom. However, a major crisis was averted by government intervention. See Mill, *Principle of Political Economy*, vol. 2, 49.

68 Clarke, "Documentary and map sources," 75–83.

69 Clarke, "The role of political position," 18–34; Clarke and Brown, "Pricing Decisions," 169–77. McCalla makes the point that elements of the provincial elite were opposed to curtailing American emigration since such emigrants were the prospective buyers of land in the west, on which many had staked their futures. McCalla, *Planting the Province*, 36.

70 The $\bar{x}$ for the period 1798 to 1825 was 17.61 with a σ of 13.24; the comparable statistics for the period after 1825 were found to be 11.31 and 5.37. A t test showed the means to be significantly different at the 95 per cent confidence level and with 52 df. The t required was 1.67; that obtained was 2.32.

71 But see Silsby, "Frontier Attitudes," 141–61.

72 Gagan, *The Security of Land*, 139; the statistic is based upon an "n" of 39.

73 For the decade ending in 1850, the respective values were Anderdon (55 per cent), Colchester (11.7 per cent), Gosfield (12.4 per cent), Maidstone (3.6 per cent), Malden (14.5 per cent), Mersea (13.3 per cent), Rochester (17.5 per cent), Sandwich (14.4 per cent), Tilbury (0 per cent). The statistic is somewhat different from that of Gagan and Kennedy but this alone cannot account for the difference between the value in Toronto Gore and that in the typical townships of Essex.

74 A parabola fitted to this relationship through time produced an "r" value of 0.95, significant at the 0.001 level.

75 Clarke, "Land and Law," 475–93.

76 Gagan, "The Security of Land," 140.

77 Some individuals did so more than once. For example, W.R. Wood mort-
    gaged lot 68 in the 1st concession of Sandwich on at least four separate
    occasions. See AO, Abstract Index of Deeds, Sandwich Township West "A,"
    162.

78 In Toronto Gore the price of land per acre was approximately 720
    pence; in Essex the comparable figure was 439 pence. See Gagan,
    Hopeful Travellers; Clarke and Brown, "Land Prices," 300–17; Clarke and
    Brown, "The Upper Canadian Land Market," 221–34.

79 In his work on Pebble Township, Bogue reports that 45 per cent of
    homesteads passed to mortgage within the first year and more than half
    within two years. In Linsley, Kansas, he reports 60 per cent within the
    first year and 75 per cent within two years. Bogue, *Money at Interest*, 220
    and 245.

80 A sample of 72, drawn from the copy books, was found to be bi-modal at
    two and five years; the $\bar{x}$ for this sample was 3.27 years with a σ of 2.34
    years.

81 For a number of reasons foreclosure was infrequent. See Curti, *The Making
    of an American Community*, 161; Gates, *Landlords and tenants*, 146–7.

82 Since in Upper Canada writs of *fieri facias* could be used to seize land
    and not just chattels, this figure is low. It would seem that such sales were
    mainly for failure to pay taxes. In seventeen of the thirty-five years for
    which records exist, there were no sheriffs' sales; for the remaining years
    they averaged 7.6. Given the annual number of transactions, this is
    indeed small. Admittedly, court writs and concomitant sheriffs' deeds
    were a most extreme means of resolving issues and would be used only as
    a last resort.

83 In fact the grand mean was found to be £189.13.5.

84 Gagan, "The Security of Land," 139.

85 AO, GS879, no.158, 29 August 1812. This was written to secure a debt
    incurred on 30 November 1810, probably for McIntosh's business prop-
    erty. The mortgagees were W. McGillivray of Hallowell and Roderick
    McKenzie, Angus Shaw, and Archibald Norman McLeod, merchants and
    co-partners in Montreal. The deed for land lying between parts of lots 92
    and 94 Sandwich contains no information on term or interest. It was dis-
    charged in or before 1825.

86 The mortgages for £1113.9.0 Halifax were with Richard and Atkinson
    Pattinson (the firm of Richard Pattinson and Company). Ibid., no.123,
    149. They were to secure four bills of exchange executed between Sep-
    tember 1801 and 1803. See also Clarke, "The Activity," 84–109.

87 This mortgage bore "legal interest," was written in 1803, and was to
    cover the sum of £688.18s.8d. It included all houses, barns, and stables
    and was discharged on 8 May 1809. See Clarke, "Thomas McKee,"
    535–6.

88 Clarke, "The Role of Political Position," 18–34; "Geographical Aspects," 81–129.

89 In some related work it has been shown that the average holding of a group of land speculators was 500 acres. Of the thirteen fur traders and Indian traders identified here, seven held land in the area, averaging 1725 acres.

90 Armstrong, "The Oligarchy."

91 Space precludes a full treatment. Interested readers are directed to the work of Armstrong and Clarke.

92 Armstrong, "Ports of Entry," 137–44. Additionally, William McCormick had been deputy collector, a less lucrative post.

93 Appendix 7.3 records those dealing in land or having connections to those dealing in land. By definition, this and the speculators per se are not the same group of people, though there is considerable overlap. Of the ninety-two people involved in mortgaging in some form, forty-one were exclusively mortgagees and an additional six were both mortgagess and mortgagors, for a total of forty-seven. Of the forty-seven, twenty-two dealt in land as well as mortgages.

94 The Essex figure is 12.4 per cent; the Peel figure 26.92. Gagan, "The Security of Land," 147.

95 Moscovitch, "Les Sociétés de Construction," 514–29.

96 John McLeod is shown in the Copy Books as president and Peter Menzies as treasurer of the society.

97 Douglas, *John Prince.*

98 The $\bar{x}$ price for building societies was 1805.7 pence with a σ of 2844.6. The range was 9447.2 pence. For the private mortgages, the respective values were 406.04, 497.4, and 2117.0 pence. For 18 and 22 df, the calculated t of 2.118 proved significant at the 95 per cent confidence level.

99 Clarke, "Social Integration."

100 Lewis and Urquhart,"Growth and the Standard of Living," 176.

101 Ibid.

102 Elsewhere there are celebrated cases of properties lost to foreclosure or simply indebtedness. Professor Armstrong informs me that Robert Hamilton, Richard Cartwright, and later George Jervis Goodhue all profited greatly in this way (Armstrong to Clarke, personal communication, 15 November 1998). An example is the case of Robert Randal. Thomas Clark secured a judgment which led to the sale of 1200 acres of land in the Niagara peninsula for £40. This failed to satisfy the debt and Clark continued to pursue him for an additional £400. Indebtedness would not be recorded in the land records and so it might well be that such occurrence were more common in Essex than presented here. Romney, *Mr Attorney,* 79.

103 Clarke and Brown, "The Upper Canadian Land Market," 226.
104 Gray and Prentice, *Trends in the Price of Farm Real Estate*, 70.
105 Gagan, *Hopeful Travellers*, 42.
106 McCalla, "An Introduction," 21.
107 NA, Askin Family Papers, vol. 29, 9675–77.

CHAPTER SEVEN

1 Johnson, "Land Policy, Population Growth," 41–60.
2 This affected all levels of society. Bradley notes that the involvement of
   Sir John Johnson, whose services to government entitled him to be the
   first governor of Upper Canada, may have cost him the post. In spite of
   being the confidante of Lord Dorchester, his private interests were considered "too considerable for the detachment of mind necessary to their
   representative in the new province." John Graves Simcoe was appointed
   instead. See Bradley, *The Makers of Canada: Lord Dorchester*, 258.
3 NA, RG1, L1, vol. 3, 434–7, P. McNiff to Hugh Finlay, 3 May 1791.
4 Cruikshank, *Simcoe Papers*, vol. 4, 43–4, R.G. England to Simcoe, 13 July
   1795.
5 Ibid., 44–5, extract of a letter from Matthew Elliott to Colonel McKee,
   13 July 1795.
6 Ibid., 93, E.B. Littlehales to James Green, 17 September 1795.
7 Ibid., 50, Joseph Brant to John Butler, 23 July 1795.
8 Ibid., 217, George Ironside to Prideaux Selby, 16 March 1796.
9 Ibid., 247, Prideaux Selby to Joseph Chew, secretary of Indian Department, 19 April 1796.
10 Simcoe was frustrated in his desire to control speculation by the policy of
   rewarding people for service to the state. For example, Benedict Arnold,
   perhaps Washington's ablest general, had defected to the British side
   and sought compensation of thirty-one square miles of land. Asked his
   opinion, Simcoe had to reply that there was no *legal* objection, but that
   "General Arnold is a character extremely obnoxious to the *original* Loyalists of America." See Scott, *The Makers of Canada: John Graves Simcoe*, 104.
   In fact, Arnold did receive 13,400 acres in the townships of Gwillimbury
   East and North and was made exempt from residency. However, following Simcoe's advice, and to avoid this serving as an example to others,
   the exemption was granted by the Crown and not the colonial authorities. See Fahey, "Benedict Arnold," 28–36. It has to be noted that Simcoe
   himself received 5000 acres as Colonel of the Queen's Rangers.
11 Cruikshank, *Simcoe Papers*, vol. 4, 211, Simcoe to Phineas Bond, 4 March
   1796.
12 His most recent biographer credits him with tightening up the system
   and rescinding township grants where little or no progress had been

made. See Firth, "The Administration of Peter Russell," 163–81; "Peter Russell," 729–32, and Plaunt, "The Honourable Peter Russell," 258–74.

13 General Hunter passed the following judgment on Russell: "Russell is avaricious to the last degree, and would certainly as far as depended upon him have granted land to the Devil and all his Family (as good Loyalists) provided they could have paid the fees." Gates, *Land Policies*, 65.

14 Cruikshank, *Russell Papers*, vol. 3, 278–9, Peter Russell to the Duke of Portland, 18 July 1799.

15 Prescott was appointed governor-in-chief of the Canadas, New Brunswick, and Nova Scotia and commander of the British forces in North America on 15 December 1796. See Burroughs, "Robert Prescott," 690–3.

16 Cruikshank, *Russell Papers*, vol. 2, 224–5, Russell to Prescott, 29 July 1798.

17 Gourlay, *A Statistical Account of Upper Canada*, vol. 1, 280–3. Question 31 of this survey asked: "What in your opinion, retards the improvement of your township in particular, or the province in general; and what would most contribute to the same?" The answers to this question and Gourlay's behaviour caused much agitation in Upper Canada. See Riddell, "Robert (Fleming) Gourlay," 5–133; Craig, *Upper Canada: The Formative Years*, 93–100; Milani, *Robert Gourlay, Gadfly*, 19; Wise, "Robert Fleming Gourlay," 330–6.

18 Moodie, *Roughing It in the Bush*, xvi–xvii.

19 Landon, "The Common Man," 162. The evidence offered is that of "A half pay officer in Canada" writing in the *United Service Journal* of 1839.

20 From "Report on Public Departments," 5th session, 13th Parliament, 1840, 233, cited in Landon, "The Common Man," 170.

21 The quotation is from Shirreff, *A Tour through North America*, 362–5, quoted in Landon "The Common Man," 163.

22 Craig, *Lord Durham's Report*, 119.

23 Patterson, *Land Settlement in Upper Canada*; Gates, *Land Policies*, 342; and Wilson, *The Clergy Reserves*.

24 Gray, "Land Speculation," 64–9.

25 Galbraith, *The Age of Uncertainty*, 16–22; Thompson, "Land Ownership and Economic Growth," 41–66.

26 Hobsbawm, *The Age of Revolution*, 180–201.

27 See Christopher and Connell, "Land and Population," 278–89. In Ireland, absentee landlordism was the cause of political and religious strife which continues to this day, and a contributory factor in the famine of 1847–51, probably the largest human catastrophe in European history to that time. An interesting case of a speculator who operated on both sides of the Atlantic is that of William Scully, the Irish landlord. See also Gates, *Landlords and Tenants*, 266–302.

28 Koebner, "The Concept of Economic Imperialism," 1–29; Hobsbawm, *Age of Revolution*; Gupta, *Agrarian relations*; "Land markets in the North West Provinces," 51–70; Embree, "Landholding in Indian and British Institutions," 33–52; and Neale, "Land Is to Rule," 3–15.

29 Bailyn, *The Peopling*, 66. Not all agree. See Billington, "The Origin of the Land Speculator," 204–12.

30 Hobsbawm, *The Age of Revolution*, 183; Jacobs, "Indian Land Surrenders," 61–8; Lemon, "Early Americans," 115–31.

31 At this point the chapter relies heavily upon Clarke, "Geographical Aspects of Land Speculation," 69–112. Shannon would argue that the use of "speculator" at this juncture is a historiographic concept, rarely found in the literature of the time, which preferred "jobber" or "absentee owner," and that its use obscures the identification of the various classes subsumed under the term. To Shannon, the term is properly limited to those who produce a "quick flip." See Shannon, "Brokers, Land Bankers," 67–99.

32 Jones, *History of Agriculture*, 33–4, 64–5, 68–70, and 202–3; Gates, *Land Policies*; Gourlay, *Statistical Account of Upper Canada*.

33 Gray, "Land Speculation," 68.

34 Boulton, *Sketch of His Majesty's Province*, 8–9.

35 Gagan, "The Security of Land," 135–53. Surprisingly, in Ontario and Canada as a whole, the literature on land speculation is relatively thin compared to that of the United States. Ontario examples include Johnson, "Land policy, Population growth," 41–60; Clarke, "A Geographical Analysis of Colonial Settlement"; "The Role of Political Position," 18–34; "Aspects of Land Acquisition," 98–119; Widdis, "A Perspective on Land Tenure"; "Motivation and Scale," 337–51. In the United States, there is a massive and impressive literature. Outstanding American examples include Ely, "Land Speculation," 121–35; Cole, "Cyclical and Sectional Variations," 229–51; Gates, "The Role of the Land Speculator," 314–33; Billington, "Origin of the Land Speculator," 204–12; Bogue and Bogue, "Profits," 1–24: Swierenga, *Pioneers*; Gates, *Landlords and Tenants*; Mitchell, *Commercialism and Frontier*; Wcykoff, *The Developer's Frontier*; Holtgrieve, "Land Speculation," 53–64; Bailyn, *The Peopling*; Schein, "Unofficial Proprietors," 146–64.

36 Gray, "Land speculation," 68–9.

37 Barlowe, *Land Resources*, 194–5.

38 Gray, "Land Speculation," 64.

39 Gates, "The Role of the Land Speculator," 49; Swierenga, *Pioneers*, 4–6.

40 Barlowe, *Land Resources*, 195.

41 Bogue, "Profits," 23–4; Widdis, "Motivation and Scale," 337–51.

42 AO, Buell Papers, various items, 15 November 1853–9 November 1872: Alexander Cameron to A.N. Buell, 24 November 1853; Cameron to

Buell, 2 December and 5 December 1853; John O'Hare to Buell, 9 December 1853; Buell to Cameron, 12 June 1854; Cameron to Buell, 4 November 1854; Robert Furley to Buell, 10 January 1855; Buell to O'Hare, 5 February 1855; Cameron to Buell, 21 July 1855; J.D. Buell to A.N. Buell, 30 October 1855; Cameron to A.N. Buell, 2 May 1857.

43 Alexander Cameron (1827–93) was an Irish-born lawyer and business-man who married Calcina Medora Buell, daughter of Andrew Norton Buell, on 2 November, 1853. See "Alexander Cameron," 146–7.

44 Andrew Norton Buell (1798–1880), lawyer, businessman, politican, jour-nalist, and officeholder, was born at Brockville, Upper Canada. He helped found the Reform organ the *Brockville Recorder*, which his brother William edited for twenty-eight years. He was rewarded by Robert Baldwin for his efforts: by being appointed registrar of Johnstown in 1842, and clerk of the Court of Common Pleas and registrar of the Court of Chancery in 1849. He was master in Chancery between 1850 and 1870. He became accountant-general in Chancery in 1870. See Johnson, "Andrew Norton Buell," 109–10.

45 AO, Buell Papers, Alexander Cameron to A.N. Buell, 2 December 1853. It was alleged that Cameron had, with ministerial help, purchased a large number of clergy reserves. The action was interpreted by the opposition as proof of the corruption of the government of Francis Hincks. Brode, "Alexander Cameron," 146.

46 Thomas Clark Street (*c.* 1814–72), lawyer, businessman, and politician, was born in Upper Canada. His investment in land and mortgages, in a time before the secret ballot, helped secure his election to the House of Assembly in 1851. In 1860 he entertained the Prince of Wales "on a scale seldom equalled in any colony of England"; when he died he left an estate valued at between $3 and 4 million. See Swainson, "Thomas Clark Street," 668.

47 AO, Buell Papers, Alexander Cameron to A.N. Buell, 24 November 1853. It is worth noting that Cameron is expecting a crude return of about 66.6 per cent per annum. It would seem that this was not to be. Property prices fell and he was left with land he could not sell and mortgages he could not meet. His in-laws helped him until he could get re-estabilised. Later, he would take advantage of government assis-tance to drain farm land in Essex, and in a six-week period in 1872 he sold land to the value of $6000. His biographer, Brodie, notes that he used money on deposit to finance land acquisition and that he and his partner, John Curry, operated under the name of the Essex County Bank. When he died he was reputed to have been worth $1.5 million and was said to be the "richest man in Western Canada." Brodie, "Alexander Cameron," 147.

48 AO, Buell Papers, Alexander Cameron to A.N. Buell, 2 May 1857.

49 The Askin Papers are to be found in a number of depositories – NA in Ottawa, the AO in Toronto, and the Burton Historical Collection in Detroit. An extensive collection has been assembled in two volumes. See Quaife, *The John Askin Papers*, vols. 1 and 2.

50 Clarke, "A Geographical Analysis of Colonial Settlement"; "The Role of Political position," 18–34.

51 Brunger, "A Spatial Analysis," 81.

52 Gagan, "Property and Interest," 63–70.

53 Widdis, "A Perspective on Land Tenure"; "Motivation and Scale."

54 Johnston, *Becoming Prominent*, 56.

55 NA, MG11, Q series 78A, 49–56, Duke of Portland to Prescott, no.18, 8 June 1798; ibid., 80, pt. 1, 37 and 49, letter of Prescott.

56 Widdis, *Motivation*, 341–4; Clarke, "Geographical Aspects of Land Speculation," 71–2.

57 Shannon, "Brokers, Land Bankers," 88.

58 Ibid., 95–6.

59 Ibid.

60 The published census for 1852 reports 2019 occupiers of land in Essex. *Census of Canada 1851/1852*, vol. 2, Table 4.

61 Clarke, "Land and Law," 475–95; Widdis, "Tracing Property Ownership," 83–102.

62 Methodologically, the use of transactions provided the necessary behavioural emphasis; use of this single metric overcame difficulties in measurement when activity was reported in both acreage and number of transactions without an appropriate conversion factor. It also overcame statistical problems of co-linearity. The treatment of residency as a quality also meant that the data set need not contain both nominal and interval levels of measurement.

63 Charles Askin was clearly an important person, as Appendix 7.3 shows. In 1825 he is known to have owned 200 acres and three properties of unknown acreage; in 1852 he had 414 acres and four additional properties. Were it not for the "in-family" limitation he would have appeared in appendices 7.1 and 7.2.

64 For example, one J.B Ouellette conducted seventeen of his forty transactions within the family and was excluded from the list of speculators allowed to enter the cluster analysis.

65 The mean of 422.23 ($\sigma = 575.96$) is based upon 144 observations used in the cluster analysis. It is reported here because of the fact that, though forty-four of these observations were zeroes, these were defining scores in the cluster analysis and the identification of the groups. At least ten of these people for whom biographical information was available were still alive in 1852 and many others were undoubtedly so. Conversely, there were at least thirteen people whose estates were still involved in land and

who were dead in 1852; once again, there may have been more. To have removed either the dead, or those with zero acres from the calculation, would appear to have resulted in error with respect to the group as a whole. Yet, when the forty zeros were removed, the resultant acreage for 100 observations was found to be a mean of 608.01 ($\sigma = 604.2$) This, the acreage for those who actually held land in 1852, was significantly higher than for the entire group ($t = 2.72$, significant at 0.05 for appropriate df). Using the original statistics for cluster 1 (303.7 acres) against the average for the group as a whole, a t of 2.13 was calculated, significant at 0.05.

66 These included James Baby (d. 1833), William Bell (d. 1841), William Berczy (d. 1813), Matthew Elliott (d. 1814), Alexander Grant (d. 1813), William McCormick (d. 1840), Thomas McKee (d. 1814), Angus McIntosh (d. 1833), Roswell Mount (d. 1834), Richard Pollard (d. 1824), William Robertson (d. 1806), Prideaux Selby (d. 1813) and Isaac Todd (d. 1819). Additionally, Thain, Richardson, and Forsyth were all dead by 1832, but they appear here in their corporate persona.

67 I am grateful to Professor Armstrong for this insight.

68 $t = 1.96$, significantly different from the whole at the 95 per cent confidence level.

69 t's of 0.06 and 0.01 respectively were insignificantly strong to reject the null hypothesis.

70 The t for the comparison of the first cluster and the overall average was -0.56, which proved statistically insignificant. This was also so in the comparison of this first cluster and its next ranked cluster, cluster 5. Here the value of t was 1.41, again insignificantly strong to reject the null hypothesis.

71 Excluding Askin and ranking the clusters against one another, the respective t statistics were 0.28, 0.33, 0.22 and 0.02, insufficiently strong for significance at the 95 per cent confidence level.

72 A t value of 0.6 between cluster 1 and the total was insufficient to reject the null hypothesis. This was also true of the relationship with cluster 6 which was most involved with the mortgage market. Here the t value was 1.05.

73 Horsman, *Matthew Elliott* and idem., "Matthew Elliott," 301–3.

74 Farrell, "John Askin," 37–9.

75 This acreage includes 1952 acres which he held jointly with John Martin. As noted in the text, there are difficulties in sorting out Askin's acreage because his son bore the same name. Before 1820, John Askin, Jr, acquired 1100 acres; John Askin, Sr, acquired 5765 acres; and John Askin – whether the father or the son cannot be determined – 12,012 acres in Essex. See Clarke, "The Activity," 84–109.

76 Matthew Elliott and Prideaux Selby, with, respectively, 66.7 per cent of their holdings acquired by patent, exceeded Askin in this category but their absolute number of patents were thirty-seven and fifteen.

77 University of Western Ontario, J120, copy of the will of Mahlon Burwell, 17 January 1846, certified by I. Wallace Askin, 29 January 1875. See also NA, MG24, G46, Lewis to Hercules Burwell, 9 August 1853, 4 pages.

78 Shannon, "Brokers, Land Bankers," 89, based upon a sample of twenty observations for individuals. The mean was shown to be 25.2 with a standard deviation of 9.17. The median was 30.5.

79 This is the same acreage as Gagan reported for the largest absentee speculators in Peel. Gagan, "Property and Interest," 65.

80 Yet all of these groups proved statistically no different from one another, as a series of t tests showed.

81 If, once again, the zeroes are ignored, the statistics for 1825 become 3992.0 as the mean acreage, with a standard deviation of 3130.78 for a sample of four; for 1852, the respective statistics are, then, a mean of 2299.9 with a standard deviation of 604.1 and an "n" of 7. The calculated t of 1.44 proved statistically insignificant for 9 df at the 0.05 significance level.

82 Malcolm Cameron had insufficient acreage to be included in this analysis but owned at least 330 acres in Essex in 1852. Clearly, he would have been placed in cluster 1 along with other members of the legislative and executive councils of Upper and Lower Canada, including James Baby, Thomas Clark, James Gordon, Alexander Grant, George Moffatt, William Morris, John Prince, John Richardson, William Robertson, Prideaux Selby, and John Strachan.

83 The five Babys, Charles, Francis, James, Jean-Baptiste, and William Duperron, acquired on average less than 13 per cent of the holdings by patent. Francis Baby acquired thirty holdings and James Baby fifteen; 83.3 and 73.3 per cent respectively were by purchase in Essex. In 1852 Charles Baby owned 1626 acres and Jean-Baptiste Baby 1124 acres.

84 MacNab, himself a major speculator and an investor in railroads, went so far as to state that all his politics were railroads. See Baskerville, "Sir Allan Napier MacNab," 519–27.

85 Johnson and Waite, "Sir John Alexander Macdonald," 593. The abstracts for Colchester indicate that these parcels were purchased for £680 and sold for £1350.

86 Ibid., 591–612; Johnson, "John A. MacDonald," 141–55.

87 This individual is not mentioned either in Armstrong's *Upper Canadian Chronology* or in the *DCB*. A search of the *DCB*'s files, graciously undertaken by Robert Lochiel Fraser, produced no such name. Nor does it appear in the *Dictionary of National Biography*. Johnson identifies Robertson as a major land speculator involved with the Canada Emigration Association. See Johnson, "Land Policy and the Upper Canadian Elite," 218.

88 NA, MG19–A–3, vol. 31, Askin Family Papers, 10394–6, Arthur J. Robertson to George Jacob, 30 December 1833. I am grateful to J.K. Johnson for this reference.

89 Ibid.

90 Johnson, "Land Policy," 217–33.

91 Johnson, *Becoming Prominent*, 46 and 218. Pattinson is shown here to have been the seventh-largest claimant for war reparations, seeking compensation for the loss of pine, cedar, and oak, ballast stone, a house, two large storehouses, a fowl house, a stable, a slaughterhouse, and a barn.

92 Pattinson, from whom A.J. Robertson obtained land, may simply have been acting for William Robertson's daughter – presumably, the Mary Ann Robertson identified in the abstracts. It is possible that Arthur John Robertson was in fact a relative, perhaps one of two nephews to whom William Robertson (*c.* 1760–1806) left money in his will.

93 This was not always purposely done. It would seem that an additional 1600 acres were allowed to be sold for back taxes. These, too, were acquired by a Mr Robertson, presumably Arthur John. William Draper, on behalf of the Pattinson estate, charged James Gordon with negligence in this affair but Gordon denied it. See AO, HWHC, James Gordon Papers, 20–101, nos.112 and 115, W. Draper to James Gordon, 24 February 1834, and ibid., no.117.

94 Pattinson was not alone. Among the merchant class and traders dealing with Ellice were William Buchanan, Thomas McKee, Duff and Leith, William Park, John Richardson, and the lawyer Joseph Woods.

95 Colthart, "Edward Ellice," 233–9.

96 Cooper, "James McGill," 527–9.

97 Momryk, "Isaac Todd," 818–22.

98 Quaife, *John Askin Papers*, vol. 1, 487–8, James McGill, to John Askin, 10 January 1794.

99 Cooper, "James McGill," 528.

100 Ibid., 528.

101 Charles actually declined compensation for his activity on behalf of Street at tax sales. Instead he asked that the lands which Street had acquired via the activity of Thomas Dickson at similar events, and which had once belonged to William Robertson, be restored to Robertson's heir, a personal friend of Askin. After the sheriff's deeds were obtained, Robertson's daughter would pay the 20 per cent down payment and all other expenses. NA, MG19–A–3, Askin Family Papers, vol. 7, 2291, Charles Askin to Samuel Street, 20 May 1831.

102 Removal of the zeroes from the calculation again changed the statistics but not the magnitude. The mean acreage in 1825 became 674.2 ($\sigma = 333.06$), for an "n" of five, and for 1852 the respective statistics

were 973.0, standard deviation of 499.79, and "n" of three. In neither instance were these shown to be statistically different from one another, the respective t statistics being 1.115 for 11 df and −1.617 for 9 df.

103 Horsman, "Matthew Elliott," 303.

104 For the difference between clusters 4 and 5, the calculated t was 3.07; and for that between cluster 5 and the total, it was found to be 4.6. Both statistics proved significant at the 95 per cent confidence level.

105 There was a statistically insignificant difference between the two at the 95 per cent confidence level; $t = 0.12$.

106 Statistically insignificant from the average of all speculators; $t = 0.25$.

107 $t = 5.91$, significant at the 95 per cent confidence level.

108 Pryke, "William McCormick," 528.

109 Ibid., 527–8. Pryke notes that the Indian title to this island had never been extinguished and that McCormick's lease and subsequent purchase from McKee were of doubtful legality. In 1866 an order-in-council awarded title to the McCormicks. See also AO, HWHC, G.F. Macdonald Papers, 20–135, for McCormick's account of the geography and political circumstance of the Western District in 1824. This was edited and republished by Douglas in 1980.

110 Fraser, "John Mills Jackson," 438–40. Jackson does not appear on the list of JPs provided by Professor Armstrong and has not been counted among Essex JPs though he acted as such in his area of residence.

111 Hoskins, "Angus Mackintosh," 473.

112 Pryke, "George Benson Hall," 308–9. When the Irish-born Hall died at Amherstburg in 1821, he left a farm near the town with a house and barn valued at £2000. Two lots in Amherstburg with a dwelling house, store, shop, and outhouse were valued at £1200, in addition to 800 acres of land valued at £600 and a one-quarter interest in two ships which was worth £40 New York. AO, HWHMC, G.B. Hall Papers, 20–207–1, 17–30, Inventory of the Estate of G.B. Hall, n.d.

113 A measure of the precision obtainable in using this nominal-level data can be obtained from this category. Table 7.5 shows that in 1852 unpatented land amounted to 18.6 per cent of *all* land. Patented land, therefore, equalled 81.4 per cent. However, using counts of the frequency of patents, indicates that it took until 1859 before 75 per cent of Essex was patented. See Figure 4.5.

114 A search of the abstract index to 1852 yielded only twenty-six recorded instances of leases; sixteen were in Sandwich Township, four were in Colchester, three were in Mersea, two were in Gosfield, and one was in Maidstone. Ten were for the period 1800–09, the date of one was unknown, and fifteen covered the period 1833–49. The reason for the dirth between 1809 and 1833 is unknown. Of the twenty-six instruments, fifteen involved people included on the list of speculators:

James Baby, William McCormick, Matthew Elliott, A. Harrow, Richard Pattinson, John Prince, A.J. Robertson, R. McMurray, and P. Scratch. One was described as a life lease between members of the Quick family. Clearly, legal instruments of this kind were used by the more prominent; presumably, most were sharecroppers who conducted their business on the shake of a hand.

115 There are simply not sufficient leases to be found in the land records to support this frequency but tenancy need not be registered. Covenants were often verbal. Wilson points out that rent was often paid by sharecropping or cash. Speculators might try to avoid sharecropping since they had to know something of farming to secure their interest. Sharecropping meant that speculators assumed some of the risk; cash obviated the need for risk taking. In the backwoods, where stock and implements had to be supplied, the rent was usually one-half the crop; in more developed areas it might be one-third the grain and half the hay, that is, where the tenant supplied his own needs. One such agreement that survives is that between John Askin and John Cornwall, made at Detroit in 1786. The purpose was to raise corn. Askin supplied a horse, cow, and plough irons as well as two men. Cornwall received one-third of the crop for his efforts. See Quaife, *John Askin Papers*, vol. 1, 234–5, contract between John Askin and John Cornwall, 11 April 1786.

116 $t = 1.08$, insignificantly different at the 95 per cent confidence level.

117 Gagan, *Hopeful Travellers*, 34.

118 Ibid., 36.

119 Wilson, *A New Lease on Life*, 206. Yet Wilson records much higher rates on Amherst Island. See ibid., 207.

120 Johnson, "The State of Agricultural Development," 113–45.

121 NA, RG5, B26, 6, Upper Canada Return of Population and Assessment, Malden Assessment Roll, 1847.

122 The whole issue of transiency and permanency has received little attention in the Upper Canadian literature. See Widdis, "A Perspective on Land Tenure"; and Norris, "Household and Transiency," 399–413. The statistic that tenants moved almost every two years is based upon my ongoing work on Malden Township.

123 The value of t was calculated as 2.21; at infinity the value required for rejection of the null hypothesis is 1.645 at the 95 per cent confidence level.

124 Ranked hierarchically, the respective t statistics for the subgroups were 0.82, 1.12, 0.1, and 1.15. That for the speculators and non-speculators as a whole was 0.96. These results, with appropriate degrees of freedom, proved insufficient to reject the null hypothesis at the 95 per cent confidence level.

125 The members of the two groups were not identical. The mean for the 1825 group was found to be 1591.8 acres with a standard deviation of 1343.5; for 1852, the respective statistics were 2281.1 and 2051.8.

126 Gagan reports on the holdings of principal absentee proprietors in Peel for the period 1820–40. If the figures for King's College are omitted, the size of the average holding for nineteen individuals is found to be 1606.1 acres with a standard deviation of 1246.2. See Gagan, "Property and Interest," 67. Comparison with the Essex figures for both time periods produced t statistics of 0.042 and -1.121, insufficient to reject the null hypothesis of no difference between Essex and Peel with respect to size.

127 Widdis, "A Perspective On Land Tenure," 60–1. The resulting t statistic for comparison with Essex was 2.33, sufficient to reject the null hypothesis of no difference at the 95 per cent confidence level.

128 Based upon a sample of twenty obtained from Widdis, ibid., 60–1.

129 The mean of a sample of 360 non-speculative owners was found to be 171.69 acres with a standard deviation of 131.14.

130 Strictly comparable data do not exist for Elizabethtown but in 1840 speculative holdings there averaged 596.3 acres with a standard deviation of 355.3 based upon eleven cases. Non-speculative holdings at this time produced a mean of 267.95 with a standard deviation of 39.11 based upon an "n" of 44. Ibid., 66–7.

131 For a sample of 1334 non-speculator owners, the mean acreage was calculated to be 117.8 with a standard deviation of 120.1 acres. The calculated t for difference of means between speculator and non-speculator acreage was found by calculation to be 8.06, significant at the 95 per cent confidence level.

132 The respective statistics for groups four and one and one and five were found to be 0.15 and 0.15 respectively. Those for groups five versus three and three versus two were 1.85 and 3.01.

133 For group five versus one, the t was 0.57; but for groups four, three, and two in sequence, the t statistics were 4.07, 3.4, and 3.4, significant at the 95 per cent confidence level.

134 The t statistic was found to be 5.68, well in excess of the tabulated value needed to reject the null hypothesis at the 95 per cent confidence level. Elsewhere this condition did not hold. For example, using Widdis's data for Elizabethtown, and cross-classifying his data on large landholders with known speculators and their cleared acreage, the following statistics were obtained. For the speculators, the cleared acreage was 20.52 perent of lots with a standard deviation of 8.02 per cent; for the non-speculators, the relevant statistics were 20.55 and 10.36. The t statistic of -0.0117 proved with 47 df to be insufficient to reject the null at the 95 per cent confidence level. By 1840, in Elizabethtown

Township, the cleared acreage on speculative holdings and non-speculative holdings proved significantly different, but in the "normal" direction of non-speculative holdings. The statistics for the latter were found to be 24.45, 11.41 with an "n" of 44; for the former, the respective statistics were 22.14, 16.3 with an "n" of 11. Student's t was calculated at 2.31, significant with 53 df at the 95 per cent confidence level. Ibid., 60-1.

135 Calculation from patent index for Essex. See Clarke, "Geographical Aspects of Land Speculation," 83.

136 Johnson, in his work on the Home District, which included the modern city of Toronto, writes about speculation. He recognizes absentee "official grantees" using a scale of 500 acres but does not equate this figure with the label "speculator," though he notes a number of "likely speculators." He observes that such "official grantees" received 66 per cent of all grants in the year 1796 and that, for the first five years, 55.4 per cent of the lands patented went to recipients of more than 500 acres. Johnson, "Land Policy, Population Growth," 45.

137 Gates, *Land Policies*, 342.

138 Calculation from abstract index for Essex. The difference between the patented land and the calculated acreage in 1825 is 0.8 per cent. The absolute acreage did not include 244 parcels for which no acreage was available in the abstracts. If this "explains" the absolute difference of 1146 acres, these parcels were small (4.7 acres) and the level of error minimal.

139 Calculated from the abstract index. This contrasts with the 157,966 acres reported "held" by the *Census of Canada 1851/52*, vol. 2, Table 4.

140 Johnson, *Land Policy*, 52. Names familiar in Essex include Major John Smith, Alexander Grant, William Allan, John Graves Simcoe, and John McGill.

141 Gagan, "Property and Interest," 65-6.

142 To the east, in Elizabethtown Township, which includes the modern city of Brockville, Widdis's figures suggest that in 1825 speculators controlled 17.3 per cent of the area. See Widdis, "A Perspective On Land Tenure," 60-1.

143 Clusters 2 and 6 had to be omitted. The respective t statistics for the comparison between the two periods were for clusters 1, 3, 4, and 5: 0.36, -0.95, 0.015, and -0.22. These results were not sufficient to reject the null hypothesis at the 95 per cent confidence level.

144 Clarke, "Geographical Aspects of land Speculation," 91. Gagan shows that in Peel County 2 per cent of the proprietors controlled almost 18 per cent of the patented acreage. See Gagan, "Security of Land," 65. In Elizabethtown Township the top ten owners controlled 10.4 per cent. Widdis, "Motivation and Scale," 341.

145 This inference is based upon the 1238 landowners identified in the abstracts and not the 2019 *occupiers* reported in the *Census of Canada 1851/52*, vol. 2, Table 4. The difference is presumably one of definition. Otherwise this group becomes even more a minority, at 4.36 per cent of the total.

CHAPTER EIGHT

1 Clark and Evans, "Distance to Nearest Neighbour," 445–53.
2 All proved statistically significant at the 99.9 per cent confidence level. King, *Statistical Analysis in Geography*, 100.
3 See Clarke and Brown, "Focii of Human Activity," 31–57, and AO, Abstract Index to Deeds, Sandwich Township.
4 Hoskins, "Angus Mackintosh," 153–4.
5 Macdonald seems to have acquired no less than fifty-eight from Wilde, Pickersgill and Company, including land formerly owned by James Holmes and sold at auction to meet his bankruptcy. See Johnson, *The Letters of Sir John A. Macdonald*, vol. 1, 196, John A. Macdonald to John Rose, 3 August 1853.
6 Ibid., 193, John A. Macdonald to Malcolm Cameron, 8 March 1853.
7 Ewart was also an architect, builder, and businessman and a founding director, with William Allan and others, of the Toronto and Lake Huron Rail Road Company. See MacRae, "John Ewart," 280–2.
8 Johnson, *Letters of Sir John A. Macdonald*, vol. 2, 194, John A. Macdonald, Toronto to John Rose, 9 July 1853. John Rose might well be the man who married Ellen Phylis Pattinson, the daughter of John Askin and widow of Richard Pattinson. She remarried at Inches House, Invernesshire, the home of A.J. Robertson, on 26 February 1833. I am grateful to F.H. Armstrong and J.K. Johnson for the information which permits this inference of connection.
9 Ibid., 195.
10 Even earlier he expressed apprehensions about land investments in the light of political uncertainties and thereby insecurity of tenure. "Houses and lands can never produce much benefit to Merchants," he wrote in 1786. Quaife, *John Askin Papers*, vol. 1, 235–7, James McGill to John Askin, 12 April 1786.
11 A simple regression of speculator prices and general land prices produced a Pearson's "r" of 0.47, which, with 47 df and an F of 13.60, proved significant at 0.0001. The equation describing this relationship was $y = 290.02 + 0.273x$ where Y was the dependent variable (general price) and x the independent (speculator price). If the analysis is restricted to prices below 720 pence, considered elsewhere to be the boundary of the farm community, "r" increases to 0.57, which, with 47 df

and an F of 22.45, is significant at the 99.9 per cent confidence level. The resultant equation was $y = 271.38 + 0.294x$. See Clarke and Brown, "Pricing Decisions," 169–77.

12 Based upon the work of Shannon. See Shannon, "Brokers, Land Bankers," 100.

13 AO, Abstract Index to Deeds, Colchester Township, lot 9 in the 3rd concession.

14 Ibid., lot 12 in the 12th concession. It was purchased in 1837.

15 For an "n" of 120 properties and a standard deviation of 101.2 per cent.

16 For eighty-three properties for which profit was available, the mean was 22.4 per cent with a standard deviation of 88.8 per cent. The calculation included both profits and losses and was averaged for each of the fifty-eight portfolios. D'Arcy Boulton, writing in 1805, noted that "in truth, any person capable of advancing money may purchase very low, and sell at an advance of one, or even two hundred percent profit, payable by installments." See Akenson, *The Irish in Ontario*, 107.

17 A logarithmically transformed dependent variable yielded a simple "r" of 0.45. With an F of 30.33 and 73 df, this proved significant at .0001. The form of the equation was $\log y = 1.51 + -0.043x$.

18 One individual, John McDonnell, was removed from the third class. He had gained a 400 per cent return in one year. His inclusion within this third class would have distorted the expected results; the average and standard deviation would have been 31.87 and 103.3 respectively.

19 Senior, "Henry John Boulton," 69–72.

20 Lownsbrough, "D'Arcy Boulton, 78–80.

21 Robinson's brother, Peter, was the son-in-law of D'Arcy Boulton, Jr. Cameron, "Peter Robinson," 753.

22 Much of this is drawn from Romney, *Mr. Attorney*, 65–82.

23 Ibid., 73.

24 Mills, *The Colonization of Australia*, 63; Johnson, "Land Policy," 53–8. Gibbon Wakefield (with R.D. Hanson) was the author of "On the Disposal of Waste Land in the Colonies (appendix B of the famous Durham Report). See Goodwin, *Canadian Economic Thought*, 20–32.

25 Gates, *Land Policies*, 143.

26 Ibid., 145.

27 The rate of taxation was one penny to the pound. Cultivated acreage would therefore face one penny per acre and wild land one fifth of this. Ibid., 233.

28 Ibid., 147.

29 Dickson would seem to have bought forty lots, the property of William Robertson, from John Askin. See NA, M–19–A–3, vol. 2, 191, 11 August 1803.

30 Gates, *Land Policies*, 147.

31 Ibid., 149.

32 AO, HWHM, 20–248, "Certificates of Sales of lands in the Western District for taxes due thereon ending 16th July 1820 and sold in 1831 and Certificates for the tax period 1824–1832" (hereafter cited as Certificate of Sales).

33 Gates, *Land Policies*, 150.

34 Askin may have been acting here as the agent of Samuel Street. In a letter to Street he declined payment for his services but asked instead for a favour. One of Street's agents, Thomas Dickson, had secured land once owned by William Robertson but given to others because the title was not totally clear. Askin wished to restore this to Robertson's heir, a female friend, and offered the 20 per cent required to secure the sheriff's sale together with all other expenses. NA, M–19–A–3, vol. 7, 2291, Charles Askin to Samuel Street, 20 May 1831.

35 AO, HWHM, Certificates of Sales.

36 Ibid.

37 Quotation from the Quebec *Mercury*, cited in Gates, *Land Policies*, 150.

38 AO, HWHM, 20–248, lands to be put up for sale for back taxes, April 1840.

39 This statement is based upon examination of the abstract index to deeds. In the determination of the fate of each property, redemption was inferred when the family name was the same as the name of those in arrears.

40 The remaining individuals include Charles Berczy, R. Boyle, Joseph Cahill, Francis and James Caldwell, J. (and H.) Cornwall, Moses David, Alexander Duff, S. Dowlar (heir of R. Dowler), Edward Ellice, S. Gerard, Prideaux Girty, James Gordon, J. Haggarty, W.G. Hall, J. Jackson, A. Lafferty, D. Langlois, J. Langlois, William McCormick, Angus McIntosh, L. Montreille, T. Murphy, H. Nelson, Daniel Pastorius, C.A. Smith, A. Stewart, J. Strong, J.G. Watson, E. Wilcox, J. Williams, and James Wood.

41 AO, HWHM, Certificates of Sales.

42 These included John and Charles Askin, William and Charles Berczy, Thomas Clark, C. Cummings, L.J. Fluette, J. Fulmer, James Gordon, James Haggarty, William G. Hall, John Hands, William McCormick, D. Langlois, L. Montrail (Montreille), John Prince, John Richardson, Thain, Forsyth and Richardson, W. Sandford, Samuel Street, T.C. Street, and C. and James Woods.

43 There were in fact at least another seven in Essex and one in Kent. John Hands, son of William Hands, sheriff of the district, purchased 1054 acres in Essex and additional land in Kent at the sales for assessment in 1830. These purchases would seem not to have been registered. He paid

4.76 pence per acre and presumably learned of the opportunity from his father.

44 Elsewhere, speculators let large amounts of land go to the sheriff's sale, tacit acknowledgment that the profits expected were less than the combined total of all carrying charges. In Leeds and Lansdowne Township this amounted to 22 per cent of speculative holdings. Akenson, *The Irish in Ontario*, 163.

45 However, these were statistically insignificant at the 95 per cent confidence level on a series *t* tests.

46 The twenty-three included John and Charles Askin, Charles and William Berczy, Thomas Clark, C. Cummings, L.J. Fluette, John Fulmer, Forsyth and Richardson, James Gordon, W.G. Hall, James Haggarty, John Hands, D. Langlois, L. Montreille, W. McCormick, John Prince, John Richardson (Forsyth and Richardson), W. Sandford, Samuel Street, T.C. Street, C. Woods and James Woods.

47 NA, M–19–A–3, vol. 5, 1352, Charles Askin to William Robertson, 24 July 1804.

48 NA, MG24, G46, Burwell Papers, Leonidas to H. Burwell, 9 August 1853.

49 AO, HWHM, James Gordon Papers, nos.20–101, 112, and 115, W. Draper to James Gordon, 24 February 1834; and nos.117, 121–4, G. Moffatt to J. Gordon, 22 March 1834. See also AO, HWHM, Woods Family Papers, no.5.

50 AO, HWHM, Hands Papers, 20–108–A–3, no.103, reveals that 3170 acres belonging to the estate of John Hands was in this condition for the tax years 1830, 1831, and 1832.

51 Hands was not only the sheriff but had been appointed deputy registrar of Kent and Suffolk in 1808 and judge of the Surrogate Court in 1824; as well, in 1828, he was appointed postmaster by another of our speculators, T.A. Stayner. From these and other offices he derived considerable revenues and fees. Ibid., 20–108–B–3, 148–50.

52 Ibid., 20–108–E–3, 2191. James Gordon, Stamford, 27 January 1835.

53 Ibid., 20–108–E–2, no.1868, M. Meredith to William Hands, 28 September 1833.

54 Ibid., 20–108–E–2, no.1761, T. Clark to William Hands, 2 February 1833.

55 Ibid., 20–108–D–1. Angus MacIntosh to William Hands, 11 August 1827.

56 Ibid., 20–108–E–2, no.1992, M. Burwell to W. Hands, 26 May 1834.

57 Ibid., 20–108–E–2, no.2115, 14 October 1834.

58 Robert Grant was also the executor of the estate of another powerful magnate, Thomas Dickson of Queenston. Dickson owned 800 acres in Harwich and Mersea townships on which taxes were due in 1832 and 1834.

59 Ibid., 20–108–E–2, no.2113, Robert Grant to William Hands.

60 Ibid., 20–108–D–1, no.988, Forsyth and Richardson to the treasurer of the Western District, 14 May 1825, and their letter of 3 October 1827.

61 Ibid., 20–108, no.880, Forsyth and Richardson to William Hands, 20 April 1824.

62 Ibid., 20–108–C–4, no.901, Forsyth and Richardson to W. Hands, 18 June 1824.

63 Ibid., 20–108–D–1, C. Richardson to William Hands, 13 May 1828.

64 Ibid., 20–108–E–2, no.1903, letter of C. Duncombe, 8 December 1833; ibid., 20–108–E–2, no.1978, 1 May 1834.

65 Ibid., 20–108–E–3, no.2231, Clark and Street to W. Hands, 14 February 1835.

66 Ibid., 20–108–E–3, no.2324, 14 April 1835.

67 Romney, *Mr Attorney*, 78.

68 Gates, *Land Policies*, 151.

69 Ibid.

70 Earlier work using a simple definition of speculation (acreages greater than 400) showed that in 1825 only 44 per cent of speculative holdings were assessed, compared to 74.9 of non-speculative holdings. Clarke, "Geographical Aspects of Land Speculation," 91.

71 John Askin, Charles and John Askin, C.C. Allen, Jean-Baptiste Baby, Charles Berczy, William Berczy, R. Boyle, Mahlon Burwell and his heirs, Francis Caldwell, Thomas Clark, J. Cochrane, John Cornwall, C. Cummings, William Drake, Alexander Duff, James Dougall, F. Elliott, Sarah Elliott, James Cowan, T. Edwards, Moses David, J. and J.G. Fox, James Gordon, John Forsyth, J. Haggerty, John Jackson, G. Ironside, J. Lockhart, P. Leduc, J. Maule, Edward Matthews, William Morris, T. Murphy, John A. Macdonald, James McGill, the Reverend McMurray, Thomas Mckee, Horatio Nelson, Alexander McKee, Richard Pattinson, T. Park, T.F. Park, the Park Brothers, J.R. Park, W.C. Pickersgill, A.J. Robertson, J. Richardson et al., A. Robertson, P. Scratch, L. Scratch, T. Smith, A. Stewart, Samuel Street, Street and Clark, T.C. Street, T.A. Stayner, R. Thornton, J.G. Watson, and J. Woods. The Reverend McMurray may have been William McMurray, the Irish-born cleric of the Church of England. See the biography of him by Richard Ruggle in *DCB*, vol. 12, 681–2.

72 The analysis was structured as a two-by-two contingency problem, the respective cells being speculator and non-speculator and the number of properties under and over three. The cells, from a to d, were 46, 175, 19, and 7. The value of chi calculated was 33.1, significant at 0.001 and beyond.

73 For "speculators," the size of sample was 167 and for the "remainder" it was 185. The t statistic required at infinity for significance at 0.05 is 1.645 and that obtained by calculation was 4.89.

74 AO, HWHM, Fox Family Papers, 20–92–2, no.849.

75 Gates, upon whose work these estimates are based, reports that there are
    gaps which have so far been impossible to fill. If only warrants and fiats
    to privileged grantees are considered, the total acreage granted to 1835
    was 985,300 acres, of which 955,100 or 96.9 per cent had been issued by
    1818. After 1818, "Orders in Council to serve as warrants" continued to
    be issued to those prepared to await the repeal of settlement duties while
    securing their entitlement. If these are added, the figure becomes
    1,215,100. By this standard, the relevant statistic is 78.6 per cent issued
    by 1818. Yet, in Table II,Gates cites a figure of 3,020,685 acres. If this is
    the appropriate base, warrants and fiats plus orders-in-council for Loyal-
    ists, military, and militia grants (84,600 acres) constituted as a percent-
    age of total privileged claimants (ever issued and however defined), 28
    per cent of total. See Gates, *Land Policies*, 139.

76 These are based upon Stratford-Devai and Elliott, "Upper Canada Land
    Settlement Records," and Clarke, "Military, Loyalist." Of the 163, 64 were
    militia grants, 20 were to the military, 14 were to Loyalists, 40 were to
    the sons of Loyalists, and 24 were to the daughters of Loyalists.

77 Gates, *Land Policies*, 132.

78 Ibid., 133. In the discussion in the House of Assembly in 1835, Gates
    points out that Reform members were equally divided among supporters
    and opponents of the suggestion that settlement duties be abolished. She
    names five – all of them small speculators. Ibid., 137.

79 Ibid., 134.

80 $t = 2.19$ with 37 df, significant at 0.05. Ibid., 333–4.

81 Sir Richard Bonnycastle held that, if it had been known how much land
    was held by officers of the Crown Lands Department, "wonders at the dif-
    ficulties and disgusts of expectant settlers would vanish ..." Quoted in
    ibid., 136.

82 Interestingly, this was in the new townships of Lambton County where
    the new immigrants were settling and not in Essex.

83 Gates to Clarke, personal communication, 1 January 1971, cites CO42, Col-
    borne to Stanley, 8 April 1834, no.23, as the source of this information.

84 John Radenhurst was appointed first clerk in the Surveyor General's
    Office on 9 February 1829 and held the appointment until 1840. Arm-
    strong, *Handbook of Upper Canadian Chronology*, 47. He is considered unre-
    liable by Gates and would seem to have misinformed Wakefield, leading
    to errors in Lord Durham's report. Gates, *Land Policies*, 230.

85 Gates, *Land Policies*, 135–6.

86 Gates lists thirteen members of the legislature who located such rights.
    Among them were five with associations in the Western District and
    Essex: Francis Caldwell, A. McLean, William Morris, Allan Napier
    MacNab, and Malcolm Cameron. Ibid., 334.

87 Ibid., 135.

88 Craig, *Upper Canada: The Formative Years*, 226.

89 Gates, *Land Policies*, 137.

90 Ibid., 137.

91 Ibid., 138.

92 Gates gives 3,937,698 as the total acreage issued between 1791 to 1838. Ibid., 139.

93 Jacob Arner (2), John Askin (2), Jean-Baptiste Baby (5), William Duff (2), Charles Berczy (5), William Berczy (1), Francis Caldwell (1), William Hands (2), William McCormick (4), A. Stockwell (1), William Duperon Baby (1), T.C. Street (1), Robert Richardson (1), James Dougall (1), Horatio Nelson (5), John Hands (2), C.C. Allen (2), A. Stayner (2), Thomas Clark (4), Charles Stewart (1), Samuel Street (1).

94 There was also an A. Mclean who purchased 1600 acres. This was a name known in Essex but there may simply be confusion here with the Allan McLean who, with T. McLean, purchased 36,100 acres of Loyalist rights in the province before 1818. This man was the member for Frontenac between 1804 and 1824. See Armstrong, *Handbook of Upper Canadian Chronology*, 67. There was also a registrar of Frontenac County who bore the name and who held office from 1796 to at least 1839, ibid., 155. An A. McLean, whom Gates identifies as a member of the legislature, acquired 1600 acres of Loyalist entitlement in 1839–40. Gates, *Land Policies*, 333. This might have been the Allan McLean discussed above or Archibald McLean (1791–1865). Archibald was a pupil of John Strachan. He was wounded at Queenston Heights in 1812. He served in the House of Assembly for Stormont, 1820–34, and as the member for Cornwall until 1836, when, again elected for Stormont, he became the speaker of the assembly. A lieutenant-colonel of militia, he was successively judge of the Court of King's Bench for the Western Circuit (1837), judge of the Court of Common Pleas (1850,) and chief justice of the Court of Queen's Bench (1862). It is tempting to include him among the Essex speculators but the evidence is too tenuous. See Hodgins, "Archibald McLean," 512–13.

95 Gates, *Land Policies*, 141.

96 Quoted in St Thomas *Liberal*, 25 July 1833, cited in Landon, "The Common Man," 164.

97 There was also Peter Robinson, John Beverley's brother, who acted as an agent of emigration and colonization, exercising power over many in the Peterborough area and the Ottawa valley. He became a member of the executive and legislative councils, surveyor of the woods, and a commissioner for the clergy reserves. Some might argue that Talbot and McNab, both of whom received land for their roles as colonizers, were in fact speculators. While it is certain that these people did not act

without compensation and were undoubtedly desirous of whatever increment the land could yield, they are not considered speculators *sensu stricto* in this volume. Brunger, "Thomas Talbot," 857–62; Read, "The London District Oligarchy," 195–209. See Cameron and Gwyn, "Archibald McNab," 584–8; Cameron, "Peter Robinson," 752–6.

98 Clarke, "Mapping the Lands," 8–13.
99 Landon, "The Common Man," 164.
100 Landon, "The Common Man," 164–5.
101 Romney, *Mr Attorney*, 74.

CHAPTER NINE

1 Earl Durham's Report, 4th Sess. 13th Parliament, 2. Vic., 1839.
2 *Report on the Affairs of British North America*, 147–8, cited in Dunham, *Political Unrest*, 32–3.
3 Patterson, *History and Communications*, 146.
4 However, there are those who would argue that to discuss this in such terms is to lend too much philosophical attention to what was essentially a coterie of backwoodsmen.
5 Patterson, *History and Communications*, 146.
6 Wallace, *The Family Compact*, 28–9.
7 Ewart and Jarvis, "The Personnel of the Family Compact," 209–19.
8 Aitken could distinguish the two elements. See Aitken, "The Family Compact," 63–76.
9 Saunders, "What Was the Family Compact?" 165–70; see also Earl, *The Family Compact: Aristocracy or Oligarchy?*
10 Craig, *Upper Canada*, 107.
11 Dunham, *Political Unrest*, 44.
12 Wise, "Upper Canada and the Conservative Tradition," 20–33.
13 Patterson, *History and Communications*, 140.
14 Landon, "The Common Man," 154–70. See also Wise, "Upper Canada and the Conservative tradition," 20–33.
15 Clarke, "The Role of Political Position," 18–34. See also Gagan "Property and Interest," 63–70, and Katherine McKenna, "The Role of Women."
16 Armstrong, "John Strachan, Schoolmaster," 162–3.
17 Armstrong "The Oligarchy," 87.
18 Dunham, *Political Unrest*, 17–36.
19 Ibid., 19. These five received £100 per year.
20 The mean for a "n" of 37 was found by calculation to be 7.86 years with a standard deviation of 7.96. The data were drawn from Armstrong, *Handbook of Upper Canadian Chronology*, 39–41.
21 Mean of 11.86 and standard deviation of 8.94 years based upon an "n" of 69. The data were again drawn from Armstrong, ibid., 55–8.

22 Thomas Talbot and Bishop Jacob Mountain never attended at all. Baby was again the longest-serving member of the sixty-nine members of this council.

23 Armstrong, "John Strachan, Schoolmaster," 163.

24 Namier, *The Structure of Politics*; Plumb, *The Growth of Political Stability*.

25 Porter, *English Society*, 76 and 113.

26 Armstrong,"The Oligarchy," 87–102.

27 Simcoe conferred this office upon those "Persons who seem most respectable to His Majesty's Government for their property, Loyalty, Abilities, and Discretion in their several Counties, and who from a Combination of such Possessions and Qualities acquire that weight, respect, and public confidence which renders them the natural support of Constitutional Authority." In doing so, Simcoe believed that he supported the British constitution, which "approves making a due provision for that legal Aristocracy which the Experience of Ages has proved necessary to the Ballance and Permanency of her inestimable form of Government." Cruikshank, *Simcoe Papers*, vol. 1, 245.

28 Ibid. 4, 12, Duke of Portland to Simcoe, 20 May 1795.

29 Ibid.

30 Scott, *The Makers of Canada*, 198; Cruikshank, *Simcoe Papers*, vol. 1, 206, the Duke of Portland to Simcoe, 3 March 1796; ibid., 309–11, Simcoe to the Duke of Portland, 20 June 1796.

31 In the absence of appropriate clergy, marriages were often recognized after the event by declaration in front of a magistrate. John Askin, Jr, married Madelaine Peltier in this manner on 21 October 1791; Prideaux Selby, acting as magistrate, married Thomas McKee and Therese Askin on 17 April 1797; and Richard Pattinson and Julia Chabert on 24 April 1802. There are many more instances. See Wilson, "Marriages of the Western District," 48–85.

32 Watson, *The Reign of George III*, 45.

33 Dunham, *Political Unrest*, 23.

34 NA, MG21, Add. MSS. 21661–892, 327, Mathews to Haldimand, 3 August 1787.

35 Armstrong, *Handbook of Upper Canadian Chronology*, 93.

36 The Pearson correlation co-efficient for a sample of 144 was 0.26, significant at the 95 per cent confidence level.

37 $t = 3.01$ with appropriate degrees of freedom significant at 0.05.

38 $t = 0.222$, insignificant to reject the null at 0.05.

39 $t = 0.41$, insignificant at the 95 per cent confidence level.

40 $t = 3.48$, significant at the 95 per cent confidence level.

41 The respective t's for 1825 were 1.67 for differences between the JPs and those who were also members of the House of Assembly and 0.66 for the assembly members versus the members of the executive and leg-

islative councils. For 1852, the same statistics were 0.91 and 0.01, again insignificant.

42 A t = 2.28 significant beyond the 95 per cent confidence level. Johnson provides some figures for MHAs and the size of their land grants which show that, after 1820, the average grant was 612.1 acres, down from the earlier period when the grants averaged 1594.2 acres. Within the limits identified here – our interest is those speculators who were MHAs and our results are for 1825 rather than 1820 – Essex grants would appear somewhat larger than those in Upper Canada as a whole. See Johnson, *Becoming Prominent*, 53.

43 A t = 1.40, insufficient to reject the null hypothesis at the 95 per cent confidence level.

44 Yet, in one case involving a prominent member of the Baby family, the "influence" would seem to have died with the union of Upper and Lower Canada. James Baby, great-nephew of François Baby of the Executive Council of Lower Canada and nephew of James Baby, leading figure of the Upper Canadian Compact, sought compensation in 1836 for activity during the War of 1812. His uncle James had died in 1833 but his father, who had been lieutenant for the county of Essex, lived on until 1852. James was told that he ought to have applied earlier and that his wartime services should have been free. NA, RG1, L3, vol. 61, B20/163, Upper Canada Land Petitions, mfm. C–1633, 8 June 1837.

45 Armstrong, "The Oligarchy," 95.

46 William Robertson informed the Executive Council that Matthew Elliott and A. Maisonville signed in a mechanical manner, that neither could read or write, and that Captain Caldwell did not have a good education. If more magistrates were needed, he recommended Askin and Leith. See Riddell, *Michigan under the British*, 416.

47 François-Alexandre-Frédéric La Rochefoucauld, hardly a friend of Upper Canada or the British, reported in 1795 that "the justices of the peace are elected from among those persons, who are best qualified for such an office; but, in a country so recently settled men worthy of the trust cannot be numerous." Riddell, *La Rochefoucault-Liancourt's Travels*, 40.

48 Watson, *The Reign of George III*, 47. In Britain, Sir John Fielding (1721–80), a police magistrate and co-founder of the Bow Street runners, reported that one of his predecessors sought to take £1000 per year from his office. On the evidence of John Townsend, a Bow Street officer who testified before a parliamentary committee of 1816, justice was all a trading business. Issues were decided upon the relative contents of the basket of goods offered by the plaintiffs. Moreover, women were systematically rounded up for prostitution but never sentenced because the benefits to the magistrate came from bailing them. Additionally,

innocent parties were charged and indeed sentenced so that magistrates could profit from the fees allowed informers. See anon., *The Social Horizon*, 90, where the author proclaims that the government and the upper classes acquiesced in this system because it created obsequious magistrates who would do the bidding of those in authority.

49 Douglas, "John Prince," 643–7.

50 Ibid., 55, John Prince to Robert Baldwin, 24 March 1843.

51 Armstrong, "The Oligarchy," 97.

52 Ibid., 98.

53 Johnson, *Becoming Prominent*, 20.

54 Ibid., 66–7. Here Johnson reports that, of the 283 MHAs he studied, 65 per cent were magistrates, although, if only the pre-1820 period is considered, 74 per cent were. Of the magistrate-MHAs, 64 per cent had been magistrates before their election.

55 Armstrong, "The Oligarchy," 94; *Handbook of Upper Canadian Chronology* 53–5.

56 Head to the Baron Glenelg, Colonial Secretary, 30 December 1836, cited in Gates, *Land Policies*, 191. Gates concludes that in fact it was the small group of Reformers, supposedly hostile to British immigration, who consistently supported free-grant proposals, regulated by law. See ibid., 194.

57 Gates notes that W. Spragge, while clerk in the Surveyor General's office, located 52,600 acres of Loyalist land between 1835 and 1837 on behalf of himself and others. Thirteen MHAs are named, four of whom were active in Essex: Francis Caldwell, Matthew Elliott, William Morris, and Allan Napier MacNab. Others active in the larger Western District were Malcolm Cameron and Alexander Grant of the executive and legislative councils, in addition to John Elmsley, Jr. Ibid., 133 and 334.

58 Armstrong, *Handbook of Upper Canadian Chronology*, 38–58; Ewart and Jarvis, "The Personnel of the Family Compact," 209–21.

59 Armstrong, "John Strachan, Schoolmaster," 163.

60 NA, RG1, L31, Lower Canada Land Papers, 18148–9, mfm. C–2506, François Baby to Sir Gordon Drummond, 1 May 1816. Here Baby seeks compensation for his service as executive councillor, in keeping with the Duke of Portland's despatch of 6 June 1801 authorizing 12,000 acres for each executive councillor.

61 Patterson, *Land Settlement*, 63.

62 Ibid., 63; Whitfield, "Alexander Grant," 363–7.

63 Christie, "Prideaux Selby," 749–50.

64 He became increasingly dependent on the emoluments from office and this may have compromised him politically. See Clarke, "James Baby," 22.

65 He bought two lots from his brother Jean–Batiste Baby, one from W.F and J. Monforton, and two from A. Maisonville. He sold to C. Pagot, to the Monfortons, and to J.B. Tourneaux.

66 Johnson documents this process whereby official grantees received compensation in the Home District. Such was the extent of the "rush" that genuine settlers found themselves land-locked by absentee holders. Johnson, "Land Policy," 42–3; *History of the County of Ontario*, 39; Gagan "Property and Interest," 63–70.

67 AO, Patent Index for Essex. The seven members of the Baby family included Mrs Susan Baby, Jean-Baptiste, Francis, Lewis, Anthony, Daniel, and Peter Baby, who each received 1200 acres. Clarke, "The Role of Political Position," 32.

68 Clarke, "James Baby," 21–2.

69 NA, RG1, L1, vol. 24, Upper Canada Land Book F, 279–81, 12 March 1805, provides authorization for acquisition of some of his land in Yarmouth, Malden, and Sandwich townships. This document, signed by Peter Russell as presiding councillor, contains the notation that Baby was entitled to 6000 acres as an executive councillor but because of imprecise description should be allowed only 5300 acres as of 12 March 1805.

70 Clarke, "The Role of Political Position, 24–5. Francis, who was the MHA for both Kent and Essex counties, was more active in Essex than James. The abstract index reveals that he and his estate sold sixteen properties and acquired seven in Essex.

71 In spite of a multitude of offices, this "charitable, kind and humane" man died with little funds or property. See Headon, "The Discreet and Good," 160–7; Young, "The Revd. Richard Pollard," 3–28, and Millman, "Pioneer Clergy," 10.

72 His biographer, Headon, points out that while he exhibited a degree of piety, his main qualifications were that he would support law and order and "would not rock the boat as far as his friends were concerned by holding up their activities to an over-zealous scrutiny. He would not denounce them from the pulpit." Headon, "The Discreet and Good," 162.

73 AO, RG1, C IV, Township Papers, mfm. MS658, 2 October 1822. The other members were Angus McIntosh and George Jacob. It would appear that Francis Baby, Charles Stewart, and Robert Richardson were also members of the board at this time. Stratford-Devai and Elliott, "Upper Canada Land Settlement Records," 132–47.

74 Armstrong, "The Oligarchy," 99.

75 Headon, "The Discreet and Good," 162.

76 At 40 per cent, this is higher than the 29 per cent of MHAs who were directly related by family connection. Johnson, *Becoming Prominent*, 159.

77 The eighteen families included two members from each of the Berczy, Caldwell, Duff, Elliott, Gordon, Jacob, Mirchell, Talfourd, and Watson families, three McCraes, McGregors, McIntoshes, and Smiths, and four

Askins, Babys, Joneses, and Reynolds. See Armstrong, "The Oligarchy," 97.

78 Clarke, "James Baby," 21–2.

79 Clarke, "François Baby," 33–5.

80 Casgrain states that Jean-Baptiste was born 20 January 1770 and died at Sandwich "vers 1854"; Daniel was born on 28 December 1778 and died in London in 1858. Casgrain, *Mémorial des Familles Casgrain*, 100.

81 Miquelon, "Jacques Baby dit Duperron," 38–40. Dupéront was the father of James Baby. He and his brothers Louis and Antoine fought in the Ohio valley with France's Indian allies. François Baby, uncle of Francis Baby (1768–1852), was their business partner in Montreal. See Clarke, "François Baby," 41–5.

82 Clarke, ibid., 41–6.

83 Clarke, "James Baby," 21.

84 Yet, in the early part in their association, Strachan thought him "slow of apprehension" and capable of being manipulated so long as he was given his "place." Later they became close friends. AO, Macaulay Papers, Strachan to John Macaulay, 12 December 1822.

85 Saunders, "Sir John Beverley Robinson," 668–78.

86 Burns, "George Herchmer Markland," 534–6.

87 Parker and Wilson, "Thomas Clark," 147–9.

88 Clarke, "James Baby," 22.

89 Clarke, "Francis Baby," 33–5.

90 Stratford-Devai and Elliott, "Upper Canada Land Settlement Records," 132–37.

91 Charles Askin acted as A.J. Robertson's agent.

92 Clarke, "The Activity," 93–4.

93 In 1802, with William Robertson he owned 6545 acres on the American shore. See Detroit Public Library, Burton Historical Collection (hereafter BHC) LMS., *John Askin Papers*, J. Askin, 20 July 1802.

94 Indeed, Askin acted for McGill, who was not always comfortable in dealing in land, and Askin's indebtedness was in areas other than land dealing. Quaife, *John Askin Papers*, vol. 2, 236, James McGill to John Askin, Montreal, 12 April 1786; ibid., 487–8, McGill to Askin, 10 January 1794; BHC, LMS, Askin to Robert Hamilton, 30 July 1801; ibid., power of attorney from Todd and McGill to Askin, 19 April 1805; and ibid., sales agreement, 20 March 1808.

95 Calculation of the author. See also AO, *Askin Papers*, "Memorandum of Land Belonging to the Estate of the late John Askin and Archange Askin." This document is undated but a notation compares taxes in the Western District with those in 1836 in Wayne County, Michigan, where the Askin estate was administering an acreage of 2804 acres. Some of this would seem to have come from the sale in 1833 and 1847 and

1848 of clergy reserves originally leased by Askin on the Pike River. The effective price of this land including rent and final purchase, was £57 for 150 acres and £64 for 200 acres, but considering that these figures included rent for upwards of thirty-one years, the cost was between 2.3 and 3.04 pence per acre per year!

96   NA, MG–19–A–3, vol. 2, 401, John Askin to James McGill, 24 May 1803.
97   Stratford-Devai and Elliott, "Upper Canada Land Settlement Records," 135.
98   Parker and Wilson, "Thomas Clark," 148.
99   John was the eldest of the five children of Alice Rea and James Askin (Erskine). See Burton, "Detroit Biographies," 49–64; Quaife, *John Askin Papers*, vol. 1, 477–8, John Askin to John Erskine, 1 July 1793. Erskine replied to this letter of inquiry, noting that his family had fled Scotland in 1715 after the Jacobite rebellion and settled in Muff and Killybegs in Donegal. A resident of Ireland, he wrote to Askin from Maryland, apologizing for the delay in his response; he had been in Philadelphia viewing land he had acquired! It would seem that acquisitiveness ran in the family. See NA, MG–19–A–3, vol. 16, 5471, John Erskine to John Askin, 7 January 1794.
100 Ibid., vol. 1, 34, John Askin to Simcoe, 29 May 1795.
101 Burton, "Detroit Biographies," 50.
102 Quaife, *John Askin Papers*, vol. 1, 43–5, discharge from the creditors of John Askin, 1771. See also Farrell, "Detroit, 1783–1796"; "John Askin," 37–9.
103 He did so on a contractual basis with John Cornwall. NA, MG–19–A–3, vol. 14, 4948, 13 October 1786.
104 Armour and Widder, *At the Crossroads*, 80. NA, MG–19–A–3 yields an inventory of Askin's estate in 1776 and reveals that he possessed six slaves, that is, two black men valued at £100 NY each, two Indian boys, each worth £50 NY, and two Panisse "wenches" worth £50 and £40 respectively.
105 The relationship among Isaac Todd, James McGill, and Askin was one not just of mutual gain but of genuine friendship and trust. As a friend, McGill carried Askin's debts, which eventually amounted to £20,217. See Quaife, *John Askin Papers*, vol. 1, 402, McGill to Askin, 24 January 1792. He left him in possession of "Strabane," called after his north Irish home; see ibid., 2, 347–8, gift of Strabane, 24 June 1801. He remembered him in his will by a gift of 1600 acres of land in Michigan. See Burton, "Business Adventures," 62; NA, MG–19–A–3, vol. 24, 8150–69, will of James McGill, 30 December 1813.
106 Farrell, "John Askin," 38.
107 Ibid., 38; Armour and Widder, *At the Crossroads*, 135–6, 141 and 153. Sinclair had relieved Askin of his position in the commissary, seized

vessels belonging to Askin and his partner and relation Barthe, and arrested Askin's son-in-law, Samuel Robertson. NA, MG21, British Museum, ADD21757, 461–2, A. DePeyster to Mason Bolton, 13 August 1780, describes the nature of the intervention on Askin's behalf.

108 The Moravian missionaries were at pains to point out that the land belonged to the Chippewa. What the missionaries sought was Ancrum's sanction that they deserved compensation. See Quaife, *John Askin Papers*, vol. 1, 218–22, David Zeisberger, John Heckenwelder, William Edwards, George Youngman. and on behalf of Gottlob Senseman and Michael Young, to William Ancrum, 26 February 1786; and ibid., Heckenwelder to Askin, 222–4. In this second letter Heckenwelder refers to the fact that, if the sale of improvements was seen to be with permission of the commandant, it would encourage buyers. Ancrum had offered to buy these improvements himself and to present the case to the commander-in-chief, since, one presumes, all knew this act to be at variance with official British policy. See ibid., 224, John Askin to Heckenwelder, Edwards, and their "Brethern," 1 March 1786. He and Ancrum, who was soon to resign his command, had purchased these improvements for $400, together with the soil of this and adjoining land from eleven chieftains for an undisclosed price. See ibid., 227–30. Quaife claims that this document was prepared to substantiate James McGill and Isaac Todd's claim to these lands and that it is substantially the same as one prepared on 10 November 1810; see ibid., 227. This land would appear to be the same as the 24,000 acres referred to above, part of which Askin sold in 1796. Thereafter he acted as Ancrum's agent in settling the claim. NA, MG–19–A–3, vol. 4, 606–9, John Askin to the recorder of the land office of Detroit, Michigan Territory, 28 October 1805.

109 Armour and Widder, *At the Crossroads*, 35.

110 Robert Hamilton (d. 1811) was the founder of Queenston, the lieutenant of the County of Lincoln in 1804, and a member of the Legislative Council from 1792 to 1811. See Chadwick, *Ontarian Families*, 143; Armstrong, *Handbook of Upper Canadian Chronology*, 33; Quaife, *John Askin Papers*, vol. 1, 14; and Wilson, *The Enterprises of Robert Hamilton*.

111 Wilson, "Robert Hamilton," 404–5.

112 Quaife, *John Askin Papers*, vol. 2, 347–8, John Askin, Sr, to Isaac Todd, 24 June 1801.

113 NA, MG–19–A–3, vol. 2, 323, John Askin to Richard Cartwright, 8 January 1803.

114 Ibid., vol. 14, 4704, Richard Cartwright to John Askin, 7 February 1803.

115 Armstrong, *Handbook of Upper Canadian Chronology*, 13 and 33. In this role he authorized grants to two of Askin's children. See AO, John Askin Papers, 27 February 1806 and 14 August 1806.

116 Quaife, *John Askin Papers*, vol. 1, 78, Askin to Sampson Fleming, 28 April 1793.

117 Wilson states that this took place in 1785. See Wilson, *The Enterprises of Robert Hamilton*, 59.

118 Rawlyk and Potter, "Richard Cartwright," 167–72.

119 Farrell, "John Askin," 38.

120 Rawlyk and Potter, "Richard Cartwright," 168.

121 Brock, "William Robertson," 718–19.

122 Wilson, *The Enterprises of Robert Hamilton*, 64.

123 NA, MG–19–A–3, vol. 2, 330, John Askin to Isaac Todd and James McGill, 7 February 1803.

124 Ibid., 327–9, John Askin to James and Andrew McGill, 3 February 1803.

125 Quaife, *John Askin Papers*, vol. 1, 235–7, James McGill to John Askin, 12 April 1786; ibid., 402–4, McGill to Askin; ibid., 487–8, McGill to Askin, 10 January 1794; NA, MG–19–A–3, vol. 24, 8111–14, lands sold to Todd and McGill but divided as of November 1803. This last transaction records the transfer of twenty-one parcels totalling 9337 acres and valued at £11,784.

126 Clarke, "A Geographical Analysis" and "The Role of Political Position," 18–34.

127 Wilson, *The Enterprises of Robert Hamilton*, 58–67.

128 John Askin to Isaac Todd, 9 July 1793, cited in Burton, "Business Adventure of Bateau Days," 8–9.

129 Cayton, "Noble Actors," 235–69.

130 NA, MG–19–A–3, vol. 5, 1273, 8 August 1795.

131 Quaife, *John Askin Papers*, vol. 1, 550–2, John Askin, Sr, to John Askin, Jr, 5 July 1795; Burton, "Detroit Biographies," 59.

132 Burton, ibid., 57–8.

133 Armour, "Alexander Henry," 316–18. Askin had Henry's power of attorney to act as he might on his behalf, NA, MG–19–A–3, vol. 7, 6754, 19 April 1805.

134 Burton, "Detroit Biographies," 2; Quaife, *John Askin Papers*, vol. 1, 568–72, partnership agreement. See also BHC, *Askin Papers* L2, memorandum of John Askin, n.d.

135 Quaife, *John Askin Papers*, vol. 1, 275.

136 Ibid., vol. 2, 176, John Askin, to Solomon Sibley, 22 January 1799.

137 Ibid., vol. 1, 550–2, John Askin, Sr, to John Askin, Jr, 5 July 1793, concerning Askin Jr's behaviour at the Grand Council; see MG–19–A–13, vol. 5, 1273, John Askin, Jr, to John Askin, Sr, 8 August 1795.

138 Cruikshank, *Russell Correspondence* vol. 1, 2, Joseph Brant to D.W. Smith, 3 April 1796. The Kaihage spoken of is presumably Cahiagué, the main Huron settlement in modern Simcoe County, Ontario.

139 Quaife, *John Askin Papers*, vol. 1, 220 and 228; Archives du Seminaire de Quebec, Fonds Casgrain 0423, 348–53, Dupéront Baby to François. Baby, 8 May 1786.

140 Burton, "Detroit Biographies," 58.

141 Armstrong, *Handbook of Upper Canada Chronology*, 47.

142 NA, MG–19–A–3, vol. 1, 221–4, John Askin to D.W. Smith, 17 January 1802.

143 Selby, at the time, was the auditor general of land patents, which were, the reader will recall, the key to enfranchisement. Quaife, *John Askin Papers* 1, 429, P. Selby to John Askin, 17 August 1792.

144 Ibid., 1, 416, D.W. Smith to John Askin, 26 July 1792.

145 Quaife, *John Askin Papers*, vol. 1, 427–8, D.W. Smith to John Askin, 14 August 1792.

146 Ibid., 420, D.W. Smith, 6 August 1792.

147 Ibid., 447, D.W. Smith to John Askin, 13 November 1792.

148 Ibid., 2, 90–1, D.W. Smith to John Askin, 15 February 1797.

149 BHC, LMS, John Askin to D.W. Smith, 12 May 1801.

150 Quaife, *John Askin Papers*, vol. 1, 436–7, D.W. Smith to John Askin, 2 October 1792.

151 Ibid., 2, 100–1, J. Askin to Abraham Iredell, 2 January 1799.

152 Askin's views of the importance of surveyors reach us through the thoughts of his son Charles. Writing to William Robertson, Jr, as his agent in 1804, Charles speaks of the importance of cultivating the surveyor and of paying taxes since "my father thinks it is right I should pay for it's not for your interest to be on a bad footing with the surveyor and paying taxes gives you a better title." NA, MG–19–A–3, vol. 5, 1352–4, Charles Askin to William Robertson, 24 July 1804.

153 Ibid., 1, 48–50, John Askin to D.W. Smith, 12 March 1798. Here Askin acknowledges having received 13,000 acres on magistrate's certificates from Louis Barthe and an M. Dequindre. For recognition of the power of the surveyor general, see Burke, "'I was everything...'"

154 NA, MG–19–A–3, vol. 21, 6922, A. Iredell to John Askin, 1 August 1799.

155 Ibid., 6927, A. Iredell to John Askin, 31 May 1800. He would also provide Askin with a surveyor's certificate. This stated that, while he ought to have been able to provide land, actual survey had been stopped by an order-in-council. Ibid., 6930, A. Iredell certificate, 31 May 1800.

156 This claim was for eighty lots mainly along the Ruscom, Belle, Puce, and Pêche rivers. Quaife, *John Askin Papers*, vol. 2, 100–2, J. Askin to D.W. Smith, 3 April 1797.

157 Magill, "William Allan," 101–13. His *DCB* biographers describe him as the unquestioned doyen of Upper Canadian business. See anon., "William Allan," 10.

158 NA, MG–19–A–3, vol. 2, 354, John Askin to William Allan, 18 March 1803.

159 Ibid., vol. 15, 5212, Matthew Dolson to W.R. Robertson, 30 October 1799.

160 Ibid., vol. 2, 354, John Askin to William Allan, 18 March 1803.

161 Ibid., vol. 11, 4072–3, William Allan to John Askin, 13 April 1803.

162 Ibid., vol. 2, 38, John Askin to William Allan, 12 March 1803.

163 Ibid., vol. 1, 267, John Askin to Isaac Todd, 13 July 1802.

164 NA, RG1, L5, Heir and Devisees Commission, vols. 43–6, and BHC, LMS, John Askin Papers, John Askin to J. Robertson, 30 June 1803.

165 Lajeunesse, *Windsor Border Region*, 186, John Askin to D.W. Smith, 3 April 1797. This involved 13,000 acres. NA, MG–19–A–3, vol. 1, 48–50, John Askin to D.W. Smith, 12 March 1798.

166 AO, John Askin Papers, John Askin to Alexander Askin, 11 June 1807. See also ibid., agreement of bargain and sale, John Hembrow to John Askin, 4 November 1806.

167 Laviolet's land lay not in Essex but on the Raisin River in what became Michigan. See Quaife, *John Askin Papers*, vol. 1, 370–2, indenture between Gregor McGregor, sheriff for the District of Hesse, and Askin. He did not always initiate legal proceedings but like many benefited from them. See ibid., vol. 1, 368–9, indenture for the sale of Joseph Cadet's farm, and BHC, LMS, John Askin Papers, 19 July 1806.

168 NA, MG–19–a–3, vol. 15, 5310, 30 March 1796.

169 Ibid., 5313, 30 March 1796.

170 Ibid., 5308, 30 March 1796.

171 Ibid., 5311, 30 March 1796.

172 Ibid., vol. 23, 7886, 30 March 1796.

173 Ibid., vol. 15, 5315 and 5316. Here Drouillard acknowledged receipt of £10.

174 Ibid. Alexander Grant witnessed to the authenticity of the signatures on 7 May 1800.

175 NA, MG–19–A–3, vol. 15, 5321, 4 January 1796.

176 Ibid., vol. 15, 5321–3, 7 May 1800.

177 Ibid., vol. 23, 7904.

178 Ibid., 7902, 26 May 1796.

179 Ibid., vol. 15, 5331, 17 June 1796.

180 Ibid., 5333.

181 Ibid., 5336, 18 June 1795.

182 Ibid., 5335, 7 May 1800.

183 Gates, *Land Policies*, 43; BHC, LMS, John Askin Papers, Askin to Grant, 13 June 1799.

184 Rawlyk and Potter, "Richard Cartwright," 167–72.

185 Armstrong, *Handbook of Upper Canadian Chronology*, 55.

186 Ibid., 39–40.

187 Quaife, *John Askin Papers*, vol. 2, 144–7, John Askin to Richard Cartwright, Detroit, 12 July 1798.

188 NA, MG–19–A–3, vol. 14, 4701, Richard Cartwright to John Askin, 20 August 1790; Cruikshank, *Russell Correspondence*, vol. 2, 246, Richard Cartwright to John Askin, 20 August 1798.

189 Quaife, *John Askin Papers*, vol. 2, 300–1.

190 Ibid., 223–4, Robert Hamilton to John Askin, 2 July 1799.

191 Ibid., 228–9, John Askin to D.W. Smith, 10 July 1799.

192 Ibid., 231, John Askin to Isaac Todd, 15 July 1799. In 1799 Hunter was a colonel in the army but held the local rank of lieutenant-general. In April 1802 he became a full lieutenant-general. Anon., "Peter Hunter," 439.

193 Quaife, ibid., vol. 2, 232–3, J. Askin to Alexander Grant, 19 July 1799.

194 Ibid, 236–7, Alexander Grant to Robert Hamilton, July 1799.

195 Ibid., 238–9, Robert Hamilton to John Askin, 3 August 1799.

196 Ibid., 241–2, Alexander Grant to John Askin, 13 August 1799. Aeneas Shaw and John McGill were both members of the executive and legislative councils. Shaw attended regularly and McGill seems to have been the workhorse of the Executive Council, which is presumably why Grant would "target" them. See Armstrong, *Handbook of Upper Canadian Chronology*, 39 and 53–5; Mealing, "Aeneas Shaw," 752–3, and idem., "John McGill," 451–3.

197 Simpson, "William Chewett," 174–6.

198 Burns, "Thomas Ridout," 647–8.

199 Armstrong, *Handbook of Upper Canadian Chronology*, 47.

200 NA, MG–19–A–3, vol. 14, 4726, Chewett and Ridout to John Askin, 16 August 1799.

201 Ibid., 4728, Chewett and Ridout, 5 November 1799.

202 Quaife, *John Askin Papers*, vol. 1, 235, James McGill to John Askin, 12 April 1786.

203 McGill to Askin, Montreal, 10 January 1794, quoted in Frost, *James McGill of Montreal*, 119.

204 Quaife, *John Askin Papers*, vol. 2, 513–15, John Askin to James McGill, 23 April 1806.

205 Ibid., 704–6, John Askin to Isaac Todd, 14 April 1812.

206 NA, MG–19–A–3, vol. 24, 8150–69, will of James McGill, 30 December 1813.

207 Ibid., vol. 2, 539, John Askin to Thomas Smith, 24 March 1801.

208 Ibid., vol. 1, 240–1, John Askin to Isaac Todd, 13 February 1803.

209 Ibid., vol. 2, 515, John Askin to William Dixon, 26 November 1803.

210 Ibid., 191, John Askin to William Dickson, 11 August 1803.

211 Quaife, *John Askin Papers*, vol. 1, 86–7, John Askin to Sampson Fleming, 10 May 1778.

212 NA, MG–19–A–3, vol. 1, 34, John Askin to Simcoe, 29 May 1795. While making his claim for service, Askin noted the loss of property at Lachine and Montreal to the value of £1700 and in Essex to the value of £200; the latter property had been destroyed by Colonel Caldwell to deny it to the American enemy.

213 Ibid., vol. 1, 269–71, John Askin to Isaac Todd and James McGill, 24 July 1802.

214 Ibid., vol. 2, 330, John Askin to Isaac Todd and James McGill, 7 February 1803.

215 $t = 1.67$ which with 46 df proved significant at 0.05.

216 $t = 1.01$, insufficient to reject the null hypothesis at the 95 per cent confidence level.

217 For 1825, the calculated t was found to be 2.67 with 142 df, significant at 0.05; and for 1852 it was calculated at 1.77, sufficient to reject the null on a one-tailed test at the 95 per cent confidence level.

218 The actual means and standard deviations were 1760.08 and 14.76 for the first group, 1778.09 and 23.15 for the second, and 1793.56 and 15.13 for the third.

219 Greenwood and Lambert, "Jonathon Sewell," 782–3.

220 A celebrated case of a land speculation by a Baby is that chronicled in *Regina* v. *Baby*. It is not clear which of the Babys was involved but the land in question included the site of Baby's mill near the town of Sandwich. The mill had belonged to James Baby, but since he was dead when the case was heard in 1854, the defendant must have been one of his children. While the land had been acquired from the Indians, Baby had claimed title to a larger area than the Indians had sold. He also claimed to represent the native interest. The Indians, realizing this betrayal, rescinded the agreement to sell and agreed to testify for the Crown. Baby was convicted of violating the Indian Act of 1839. The judge in the case was John Beverley Robinson, who argued that Baby "knew that the Indians had not the legal title which was vested in the Crown ..." Harring, *White Man's Law*, 79.

221 See Clarke, "Social Integration," 406. The data in this article have been adjusted to eliminate sales and purchases to corporations.

222 Clarke and Skof, "Social Dimensions," 107–36.

223 This was also true of marriage. There are in fact many instances of intermarriage among the elite, across linguistic and religious barriers. For example, Askin, Grant, and Caldwell married francophones and some of the Baby children married anglophones.

224 To this day there are Loyalist descendants who will not enter the United States because of the harassment of family members in the distant past.

225 $t = 1.54$ for the difference between the two periods, insignificant at 0.05.

226 Significant difference was found at the 95 per cent confidence level with a t of 2.99.

227 Johnson, *Becoming Prominent*, 75–8. Here the rate of participation in the military is shown to have gone up over time. The average age at first militia commission is shown to have been 30.9 years, rather than the 35.5 years for first civil appointment. Ninety per cent of MHAs had done some military service prior to their election. The reader is reminded that the focus of the two studies is different.

228 A measure of the overlap can be seen in the case of the military and the merchants. Of the forty-seven merchants, twenty were associated with the military and twenty-seven were not. Ninety-seven of the 144 were not merchants, and of these seventy were not associated with the military. A chi-square test of the relationship between status (as merchant or member of the military) and the possession of land produced a chi-square value of 3.15. This was insufficient to reject the null hypothesis at the ninety-five per cent confidence level; statistically, there was no difference between the military and the merchants..

229 Johnson, "Land Policy," 44.

230 For 1825, the respective t values were, in order of ascending acreage, 0.15 and 0.04. In 1852 the values for difference between the military and the merchants were found to be 0.015, and those for the difference between the merchants and the officeholders were 0.53. All proved insufficient to reject the null hypothesis of no difference.

231 $t = 0.53$, insufficient at appropriate degrees to reject at the 95 per cent confidence level; in fact, the other relationships produced similar statistical results.

232 This is immediately apparent when the same acreage is operationally counted twice under two or more categories.

CHAPTER TEN

1 In spite of the importance of this company, it has been much neglected in Upper Canadian and imperial history. The earliest work is that of Lizars; more recent is that of Karr, Lee, and, the most definitive, Hall. See Karr, "The Foundation"; Lee, "The Canada Company 1826–1853"; and Hall, "The Canada Company 1826–1843."

2 There is a tendency for Canadianists to think of the Canada Land Company as the only company of significance established at this time or

at least the most important. In fact, there were more than 600 such companies established in 1826 in the United Kingdom. Hall quotes the *Times* of 20 April 1826 reporting that joint-stock companies "spouted in shoals like herring from the Polar Seas." Hall, "The Canada Company 1826–1843", 104.

3 Wilson gives 30 April 1819 as the date for the establishment of the commission in Upper Canada. See Wilson, *The Clergy Reserves*, 65. AO, RG1, A–VII, Crown Lands, Orders and Regulations, vol. 2, 36–55, shows that the date of registration in Liber F, folio 352, was 4 May 1819. The initial members were Jacques Baby, Thomas Ridout, George Jacob, and Bishop Jacob Mountain of Quebec.

4 One of the most vocal opponents of the clergy reserves was Robert Gourlay, who in 1822 published in his *Statistical Account of Upper Canada* the results of a questionnaire circulated throughout Upper Canada. One question asked the recipients to name the cause that most retarded development in their township. Seventy replies were received, seventeen named the clergy reserves as one cause of hardship, none named them as the *sole* cause. Gourlay's analytical ability is questioned by Professor Wilson, who argues that there is not the evidence to justify singling out the clergy reserves for special consideration. Wilson, *The Clergy Reserves*, 60–1.

5 Gates, *Land Policies*, 165–7.

6 Clarke and Buffone, "Manifestations of Imperial policy," 121–36.

7 Gates, *Land Policies*, 207.

8 Wilson, *The Clergy Reserves*, 32.

9 Gates, *Land Policies*, 163.

10 Wilson, *The Clergy Reserves*, 33.

11 This was not unreasonable given that this was still not a monetary economy. Two instances involving the "well-off" illustrate the point. Askin, writing to Baby in 1803, expresses his willingness to receive immediate payment for a debt in goods but to wait a year for payment in cash. NA, MG–19–A–3, vol. 2, 397, John Askin to James Baby, 19 May 1803. In that same year William Allan acknowledged to Askin that, though he had reported all payments to Askin in cash, he had received wheat, rye, wood, and flour and had difficulty converting these things into actual money. Ibid., vol. 11, 4072–3, Allan to John Askin, 13 April 1803.

12 Wilson, *The Clergy Reserves*, 44, and Gates, *Land Policies*, 165. They seem to differ by ten shillings in the rent appropriate to the third stage or cycle set in 1819.

13 In 1823 the Clergy Corporation set 65s., 100s., and 135s. as the rents payable for the next three seven-year periods and for leases entered into prior to 1811; rents on renewals made under the regulations of 1811 were to be 80s., 115s., and 150s. See Gates, *Land Policies*, 199.

14 By 22 September 1803, 140 Crown reserves and 173 clergy reserves had been leased in Upper Canada; of these, ten and nine respectively were in the Western District. Wilson, *The Clergy Reserves*, 36.

15 Gates, *Land Policies*, 165.

16 Wilson, *The Clergy Reserves*, 41.

17 Gates reports that in 1827 less than 15 per cent of Upper Canadian Crown reserves had been leased – in absolute terms, 1232 lots. See Gates, *Land Policies*, 165. This compares to the approximately 900 lots that Bishop Strachan estimated had been leased in Upper Canada by 1826. Strachan's estimate was qualified by the fact that only about 100 lessees paid regular rents. Wilson, *The Clergy Reserves*, 37.

18 Gates reports that in 1802 the patent fee on leases was 32s/6d but only 2s/6d was payable by the lessee. Gates, *Land Policies*, 164.

19 Ibid., 165.

20 AO, RG1, A–IV, vol. 38, signed Thomas Ridout, Surveyor General's Office, 22 October 1827, shows seven lots totalling 1064 acres rented by McCrae on 9 June 1802 and 400 acres rented by John Askin on 2 March 1802 and 15 July 1802.

21 AO, RG1, B–II, vol. 7, Crown Lands and Clergy Reserve Accounts, series B, London and Western Districts, 1802–36.

22 In 1835, two years after leasing had been formally ended on clergy land, Baines submitted a report on the prospects of recovery of finances. He considered only 4.5 per cent of those holding leases reliable and viewed 12 per cent as permanent defaulters. Those in default for one year amounted to 47.7 per cent and 35.7 per cent might pay up. Total arrears were £31,492. Wilson, *The Clergy Reserves*, 102.

23 Both forms are found in the documentary evidence; Wilson offers a third by adding an "s." Ibid., 102.

24 AO, RG1, B–III, vol. 29, 17 February 1843 but signed by T. Bain, 7 July 1843.

25 Arrears in the Home District amounted to £7747.13.3, followed in rank order by the Newcastle, Midland, and Prince Edward districts. London ranked fourth with arrears of £2403.4s.9d. AO, RG 1, B–III, vol. 29, T. Bain, 7 February 1843. The whole issue of revenues is complicated by the fact that Baines was exposed in 1855 as a master embezzler, but it is thought that before 1845 the accounts of receipts from clergy lands are probably genuine. Wilson, *The Clergy Reserves*, 101.

26 Ibid., 100.

27 Clarke, "Documentary and Map Sources," 75–83.

28 Calculations from the abstract index to deeds for Essex. This was a common mechanism of British policy in both India and Ireland and perhaps elsewhere in British possessions. In Ireland, Trinity College enjoyed a similar bounty as King's College did in Upper Canada.

29 NA, RG5, A1, vol. 151, 82521–3108, Joseph Talbot, 30 March 1835.

30 NA, RG1, L3, Upper Canada Land Petitions B, bundle 20, part 1, vol. 60, 7, 7a and 7b.

31 Gates, *Land Policies*, 72–87.

32 Wilson, *The Clergy Reserves*, 102 and 107.

33 NA, Supplement to the *Upper Canada Gazette* for 1841, 46–50 and 78–84.

34 The newspapers included the Sandwich *Emigrant*, the *Western Herald*, and the *Upper Canada Gazette*. The mode and median for these data were both 96 pence but the $\bar{x}$ was found by calculation to be 135.69 with a σ of 76.3 pence per acre. The overall $\bar{x}$ was raised by the inclusion of lands in Anderdon for which the $\bar{x}$ of a sample of 61 was found to be 243.52 with a σ of 84.8. Both sets of data but most especially the Anderdon subset were skewed (Pearson's skew was 2.25) and the mode and median were at 180 pence per acre, perhaps the better measures of central tendency.

35 These statistics are based upon *Upper Canada Gazette* figures. Some data have survived for Crown land in Tilbury Township for the years 1840 to 1850 which suggest a lower price of 96 pence per acre in 1841, holding until 1850. Tilbury was among the most remote and poorly endowed of the townships. AO, RG1, B-III, vol. 28, Crown Reserves in the Western District, 1841.

36 The *t* statistic was found to be 0.88, insufficiently large given the requisite degrees of freedom for significance at the 95 per cent confidence level.

37 The calculated value of *t* was 0.18, insignificant at the 95 per cent confidence level.

38 For Maidstone the $\bar{x}$ and σ based upon an "n" of 20 was 22.0 and 23.58; for Malden the $\bar{x}$ was found to be 70.0 with a σ of 35.59 based upon a sample of 15. The calculated *t* was found to be 4.38, significant beyond the 0.05 level. These results were obtained for the Gazette sample of 1841. However, in a similar vein, it is interesting to record the difference in asking price demanded in 1839. In Anderdon Township, which until only four years earlier had been an Indian reserve, the price asked was 241.52 pence per acre with a F of 83.5 based upon a sample of 63. In the rest of Essex the requisite statistics were found to be 97.71 and 6.61 pence per acre. A *t* of 13.32 confirmed that these were statistically different results. Anderdon was from a locational perspective prime real state. It is not known what prices were obtained in the end but interestingly the advertisement for these lands appeared in a single local paper, the *Western Herald*.

39 The respective σ's were 30.54 and 14.42; *t* was highly significant at 16.43. The reader should be aware of the fact that this is Crown land

and not former Crown reserve, which had passed to the Canada
Company. That the down deposit was so high most likely reflects the
passage in 1837 of the Public Land Disposal Act, which abolished earlier
provisions for credit and which, after 15 June 1837, required full
payment within fourteen days. Gates, *Land Policies*, 192.

40 George Jacob bought three clergy lots, James Dougall three, Charles
Askin two, Alexander Duff one, J. Strong one, and L.J. Fluett one.
Prideaux Girty purchased the Crown land.

41 The balance was due in five annual instalments at 6 per cent. Gates,
Land Policies, 169.

42 This is undoubtedly François Chauvin, proprietor of the Goose Tavern,
west of Stoney Point. Morrison, *Garden Gateway*, 18. Chauvin was also a
purchaser of clergy land. AO, RG1, A–VI–15, vol. 6, Clergy Reserves in the
Western District, 1842–43.

43 The price appears to rise through the third and fourth decades. For
1830–34 the $\bar{x}$ and σ were 120.48 and 8.07 with an "n" of 31; for
1836–40 the same statistics were 141.56, 19.8,16; for 1841–45, 147.5,
20.16, and 6; for 1846–52, 160.09, 57.1, and 11. However, Student's t
showed the last three to be no different from one another statistically,
with values of 0.57 and 0.62; the first two, 1831–35 versus 1836–40, were
different since the t statistic was 3.96.

44 The t statistic for the upset price of clergy land versus Canada Company
land was 1.49, insufficiently large at the 0.05 confidence level; that for
Crown land versus Canada Company land was t equal to 0.75, again statistically insignificant.

45 Indeed this competition led after 1834 to a greater concentration by the
company on its Huron Tract and to the desire on the part of the
company to manage the clergy lands on a percentage basis. See Hall,
"The Canada Company 1826–1843," 287; Gates, *Land Policies*, 250.

46 The Upper Canadian values were gleaned from the pages of Hall and
Gates. They refer to yearly averages and are based upon gross sales and
acreage figures. The relevant statistics of $\bar{x}$ and σ are nominally the
same as those for Essex but the Essex statistics are based upon *individual* sales.

47 The Upper Canadian values are for the years 1829 to 1833; the Essex
figures for 1830 to 1833. The respective means were found to be 9.13
(n=4) and 8.07 (n=30). In substantive terms different, it is doubtful if t
adds much here but it was found to be 0.27. This proved insignificant at
the 95 per cent confidence level.

48 As shown earlier, the Essex mean was found to be 141.56; for Upper
Canada, the Canada Company lands were selling for 146.67 pence per
acre with a standard deviation of 4.99 based upon observations over a
four-year period. At 0.87, t was insufficient to reject the null hypothesis.

49 Theoretically, the land was purchased in five years. Patrick Shirreff, in his *Tour through North America* published in 1835, noted that the costs of establishment were so great as to retard the rate of repayment and that the interest rate on the unpaid instalments was "more than the cleared part of the farm will yield of profit at the end of five or six years." Sheriff, quoted in Hall, "The Canada Company, 1826–43," 328.

50 Such figures are only now coming available and studies of other areas are needed. In 1842, the company published a pamphlet arguing its own success in that 503 of the 724 settlers who had acquired company land in thirty-eight townships had completed the purchase. Hall suggests that this cannot have been achieved in the requisite five years since most of these people had only taken up land in the period 1827–35. If, in fact, completion was as in Essex, then Hall's inference is statistically substantiated. Hall, "The Canada Company 1826–1843," 411.

51 In fairness to the company, in 1837 it had to borrow in London at 12.5 per cent. Ibid., 345.

52 Gates, *Land Policies*, 169. An 1836 Canada Company memorandum printed in Lizars' *In the Days*, 134–5, claims that a circular sent to the magistrates found that the mean value of land in Upper Canada was 40.5 pence, less than the 42 pence paid by the company. Interestingly, it also cited a sheriff's sale in the Western District, whereby 3000 acres had reached 4.5 pence per acre, as further proof of the excessive price the company had paid.

53 Hall, "The Canada Company 1826–1843," 247.

54 Ibid., 282.

55 Henry Ransford, treasurer of the Huron Council, which was in dispute with the company over the taxation of waste lands, pointed to the "poor and ignorant settler" who, attracted by the notion of no down payment, signed up for a twelve-year lease on a lot five or six concessions from a road "for which in the end he will pay up over forty dollars an acre." Converted to sterling, this would amount to about 2400 pence per acre. Lizars, *In the Days*, 142–4.

56 In 1835 a select committee of the House of Assembly reported in favour of abolishing the company's charter or of taxing all the land at its disposal so as to force sale. This had the desired effect. Gates reports that by 1838 there was no validity to the charge of tax evasion. Gates, *Land Policies*, 225.

57 Gates points out that, by 1838, 49.3 per cent of all its Upper Canadian holdings were in possession of settlers paying taxes and that the company paid taxes on the remainder of its holdings. Ibid., 225.

58 There were 299 lots; four of these were patented between 1846 and 1873. This leaves fifty-six lots unaccounted for. These were either never officially acquired, though they might appear in the cartographic evi-

dence as Crown reserves, or leased and sold before the company assumed responsibility. Another possibility is that, as leased land, they were handed over to King's College, Toronto, in 1827.

59 For the sample of 64, the $\bar{x}$ was actually 120.34 with a σ of 69.63 pence. For the period 1830 to 1835 and a sample of 31, the respective statistics were 139.87 and 94.52, for the period 1836 to 1840 the $\bar{x}$ and σ was 106.25 (n=16), for 1841 to 1845 it was 97.69 and 3.73 (n=6), and for 1846 to 1852 it was 98.18 and 5.75 (n=11). In fact the only statistical difference in these figures was found between the first and second time periods; the t calculated was 1.83, significant at the 95 per cent confidence level.

60 This changed in 1852 when Crown land west of Durham and Victoria counties was offered at 7s/6d per acre (90 pence). This was payable in ten instalments with interest, one tenth down at the time of sale. AO, RG1, A–VII, vol. 12, 6 August 1852.

61 Gates, *Land Policies*, 211; Wilson, *The Clergy Reserves*, 106. Twenty lots in the Western District were put up at these rates to be sold on 7 June 1836 and on the first Tuesday in July, August, September, and October. See NA, RG1, L3, vol. 60, mfm. C–1632, Sale of Clergy Reserves in the Western District.

62 NA, RG1, A–VII, vol. 13, 64–5, 19 March 1842. Where clergy land had been leased it could be purchased five years before the sale, and if occupation was required, and had been interrupted, interest at 6 per cent from the date of expiry of the lease would suffice. The purchase agreement could be ended at any time.

63 Gates, *Land Policies*, 208.

64 Ibid., 242–3.

65 Wilson, *The Clergy Reserves*, 159.

66 Gates, *Land Policies*, 247–8.

67 AO, RG1, A–VI–15, Inspection and Valuation Reports of lands in the Western District, 1794–1909. Of the eighteen volumes in this series volume six pertains to clergy reserve inspections in Essex in 1842–43 and volume eleven covers 1844 to 1845.

68 Ibid., vol. 12, Certain Lands in Kent, Essex and Lambton Counties 1852, contains the results of inspections of all lands in Tilbury, Mersea, and Maidstone townships. It describes Crown land in all its forms and some clergy lots in Tilbury, then administered by the Crown Lands Department.

69 They have been used to measure "development" by Gentilcore, "Change in Settlement," 418–19.

70 The 1844–45 data were skewed (Pearson's skew was 2.47); arguably the mode and median at 60 pence are the better measures of central tendency. By way of comparison, the equivalent statistic for the lots adver-

tised in 1842 was 90 pence per acre. Clearly there is a difference. Between the 1841 sample of 99 observations of actual sales and the advertised price of 321 observations in the Inspection Reports of 1842, a significant negative t of -14.2 was reported. Between the advertised prices of 1842 and those of twenty-eight observations of such prices for 1844–45, a negative relationship, equally significant at the 95 per cent confidence level, was inferred from a t statistic of -2.66.

71 Wilson shows the average price of clergy land to have been 161 pence between January 1829 and December 1832. Wilson, *The Clergy Reserves*, 104. Gates states that, from 1845 to 1854, clergy reserves sold for an average of 140 pence per acre. Gates, *Land Policies*, 253.

72 Wilson, *The Clergy Reserves*, 162.

73 Gates describes this decline in Crown reserve sales for the years 1838 to 1842 and the institution of a leasing system in 1842. Gates, *Land Policies*, 170. By 1852, the $\bar{x}$ price asked for Crown as opposed to reserve land was 49.33 with a σ of 17.15 pence. The mode and median were now exactly half of their equivalents in 1839, that is, 48 pence per acre. AO, RG1, A–VI–15.

74 Wilson, *The Clergy Reserves*, 164.

75 Ibid., 162.

76 In Tilbury Township, in 1852, six lots advertised in 1845 at 90 pence per acre were offered in 1852 at "fire prices" of 42, 48, and 60 pence per acre. AO, RG1, A–VI–15, vols. 11 and 12.

77 For consistency in the use of statistics, t tests are reported at this point. A series of t tests supported this fourfold division, the critical statistics being 1.7 for the difference between Tilbury and Mersea and 1.91 for the difference between Colchester and Gosfield. These proved significant at the 95 per cent confidence level.

78 The t value for the difference of the two was 1.83, significantly different at the 95 per cent confidence level.

79 In Tilbury the lag was 3753.2 days with a σ of 879.3 days and an "n" of 47; in Mersea it was 3658.3 days with a σ of 792.7 and an "n" of 50.

80 The Sandwich $\bar{x}$ was 3173.3, with a σ of 1178.9 based upon an "n" of 25; the requisite values for Rochester were 3171.8, 656.2, and 34; for Colchester they were 2929.9, 898.9, and 42; and in Maidstone they were 2792.1, 1495.84, and 29. In Gosfield Township, the mean, mode, and median were all 768 days but based only upon three observations.

81 For clergy land the $\bar{x}$ and σ were found to be 9.06 years and 2.79 respectively based upon a sample of 225; for the Canada Company, as reported earlier, it was 7.4 and 6.4 years based upon a sample of 64. The calculated value of t was 2.01 years, significant at the 95 per cent confidence level.

82 The 1842 inspection records that lot 3 east of the Puce, leased by McCrae on 9 July 1842, was sold presumably by the corporation in 1842

to one Young, heir-at-law of McCrae. It contained a log house, barn, and forty acres and was valued at eight shillings per acre.

83 Though the value of improvements was different one to another, all four were valued at fifteen shillings (180 pence). The properties were all on lot 2 in the broken front of Tilbury. Peter had a house and a barn and improvements valued at £110. François, as suggested earlier, had a tavern in addition to a barn and a stable and improvements valued at £150. Lombard had a house and eight acres valued at £55. The fourth brother, whose initial alone is known, owned a house and five acres valued at £35. AO, Clergy Reserves, 1842.

84 AO, Abstract Index to Deeds, Essex County.

85 This was also true of Crown land. Of the 123 properties administered by the Crown Lands Department in 1852, 38 lots had seen some hitherto unrecorded action. Most commonly this was the chopping of a few acres and perhaps the building of a house. However, William McClary, who performed the formal inspection, recorded such items as "slashed three acres in front ... neither could be found" or "never lived there except when chopping," or "left immediately." Most could no longer be found although that might not end their claim; in fact, in only four instances could anything approximating formal ownership be determined. Jonathan Wigfield was described as the occupant of lot 228 south of the Talbot Road in Mersea and claimed title by virtue of a bond. Matthew Jeffrey held land as a tenant under one Thomas Whittle. Whittle had been located by Thomas Talbot about 1830, had eighteen to twenty cleared acres, and received the patent to part of lot 1 in the 6th concession of Mersea in 1852. The north part of this lot had been located in 1839 by Daniel Bis, who had died in 1842, and his daughter, a Mrs Ryall, claimed it. James Pearson was the occupant of lot 3 in the 9th concession of Mersea. In 1844 he had built a log house and slashed 100 feet of frontage and the road to a depth of two rods. He had 2.5 acres cleared when the inspection was carried out. He sold this land in 1857 and a patent was issued in 1864. The inspector reported that the settlement duties seemed to have been completed on lot 22 in the 10th concession of Mersea in the same manner, although six acres had been cleared by its occupant, an M. Ameson. In fact, the patent was subsequently issued to him in 1852. Many lots seem to have been stripped. In Tilbury, W. Brush had removed much of the oak from lot seven in the 4th concession, though good timber remained. On lot 12 in the 6th concession of Maidstone Township, "one Liberty has cut down all the oak trees and made them into square timber which is now lying on the lot." AO, Inspection Reports, vol. 12, 1852.

86 AO, RG1, A–VII, vol. 13, 1–3, Executive Council meeting, 13 October 1840, endorsed by W. Allan.

87 Gates reports 569 acres of clergy reserves sold in 1844, 40,602 in 1845, 179,271 in 1846, and 196,568 in 1847. See Gates, *Land Policies*, 253.
88 Ibid., 252.
89 The *t* calculated for the difference of mean between the former Crown and clergy reserves was 1.05, insufficient to reject the null hypothesis. For the second set, the difference between the clergy and Canada Company lands was found by calculation to be 1.03 and 0.19 respectively.
90 *t* was 0.29, insignificant at the 95 per cent confidence level.
82 *t* was found to be 3.84 for this relationship and to be 1.15 for the relationship between Canada Company land and society as a whole. The former proved significant at the 95 per cent confidence level; the latter did not.
92 Comparison of the respective statistics for the Canada Company and Clergy lots with the overall mean produced ± statistics of −6.02 and −9.02 respectively. These proved significant at the 95 per cent confidence level. A similar comparison of clergy and Canada Company land produced a value of 1.95, indicating a significantly higher level of achievement on Canada Company lots.
93 Gates, *Land Policies*, 210.

CHAPTER ELEVEN

1 Crone, *Pre-Industrial Societies.*
2 E.P. Thompson would argue that this term, like some others (traditional, paternalism, and modernization), leads people to view society in terms of a self-regulating sociological order. It appears timeless and value-free. The author agrees with these comments but employs the term precisely for the reason Thompson criticizes it, that it is "a tent within whose spacious folds there sit beside each other West of England clothiers, persian silversmiths, Guatemalan shepherds, and Corsican bandits." Thompson, *Customs in Common,* 18–19.
3 Crone. *Pre-Industrial Societies,* 4.
4 McCalla, *Planting the Province.*
5 Gilmour, *Spatial Evolution of Manufacturing.*
6 Crone, *Pre-Industrial Societies,* 4.
7 Ibid., 15.
8 Calculation of the author using the census-enumeration returns of the Census of Canada 1851–52. At the county level, Essex stood twenty-sixth in wheat acreage as a percentage of cultivated acreage in 1851. At the county level, the requisite statistics on wheat yields for the forty counties were a mean of 14.86 bushels per acre with a standard deviation of 3.42. Though these results are not strictly comparable to those obtained for the 769 properties which carried wheat, a difference-of-means test sug-

gested no significant difference at the 95 per cent confidence level; t was 1.52. With respect to corn, the Upper Canadian yields were higher than those of Essex (21.7 with σ of 6.26; t at -3.94 was statistically significant at the 95 per cent confidence level, but, of course, Essex was pre-eminent in corn production, ahead of neighbouring Kent in terms of corn acreage as a percentage of cultivated land.

9 Yet William Dummer Powell could record of the Detroit settlement in 1788: "... The difficulty of compelling payment has produced generally, in the Settlement, a species of depravity, which in other Societies is limited to a few, and those only the most worth of it, I mean the public avowal of Debt and Means to pay while payment is withheld for compulsory Process, and this Infamy is become so common as scarcely to be thought wicked or disgraceful." TRL, B80 L16, 16–17, Powell to H. Motz, 7 April 1788.

10 Gentilcore, "Settlement," and Clarke, "Social Integration." Clarke ("Geographical Aspects of Land Speculation," 93) shows a significant difference between speculator and non-speculator at two miles but notes that in 1825 all lots were within six miles of road or coast.

11 Clarke and Skof, "Social Dimensions," 121.

12 Crone, *Pre-Industrial Societies*, 6.

13 Vincent believes that absolutism was a relatively late addition to the European political vocabulary and that, while Jean Bodin's work influenced its theories and practices in the sixteenth century, absolutism was a retrospective judgment from the early eighteenth century. Vincent, *Theories of the State*, 45–76.

14 Crone, *Pre-Industrial Societies*, 60.

15 Ibid., 45.

16 Pareto traces the first use of the term "elite" to 1823 and distinguishes among a "governing elite," a "non-governing elite," and a "non-elite." Under European feudalism, a warrior caste that concentrated land, military force, political authority, and the ideological support of the church was a "governing elite" which came close to what Marx would call a "ruling class." See Pareto, *A Treatise on General Sociology*, and Bottomore, *Elites and Society*, 1–2, 19. As used here, "governing elite" and "power elite" are interchangeable.

17 According to Vincent, increasing recognition of patrimonial property admitted the King's right to rule and territory. Vincent, *Theories of the State*, 63.

18 Crone, *Pre-Industrial Societies*, 25.

19 Ibid., 26.

20 Ibid., 66.

21 Ibid., 69.

22 Ibid., 70.

23 Ibid., 32.

24 Ibid., 32.

25 Ibid., 33.

26 Ibid., 31.

27 Ibid., 65.

28 Ibid., 80.

29 Speck, *Stability and Strife*, 11–12.

30 AO, F47, Cortland to Lord Dorchester, 7 May 1795. I am grateful to Sandra Guillaume for locating this document.

31 Pares, *George III*, 35.

32 Speck, *Stability and Strife*, 2.

33 Pares, *George III*, 93–142.

34 Ibid., 32.

35 Ibid., 33, points out that Locke spoke of executive, legislative, and federative powers; Montesquieu of legislative, executive, and judicial.

36 Dickinson, *Liberty and Property*, 17.

37 "Civil Government so far as it is instituted for the security of property, is in reality instituted for the defence of the rich against the poor, of those who had some property against those who have none at all." Smith, *An Inquiry into the Nature*, vol. 2, 715.

38 Dickinson, *Liberty and Property*, 43–7.

39 Yet there were fears that Crown privilege would replace the Royal prerogative as the greatest threat to the independence of parliament and the liberties of the individual: "It is to be feared that, of late years, by making the highest stations of the kingdom the rewards of treachery and base compliance, by bribing members of parliament with pensions and places, and by the immense gains which a neglegient and corrupt ministry has suffered private men to make out of the kingdom's treasure, almost all ranks of men are come to be deprived in their principles; and to own a sad truth, none are ashamed of having notoriously robbed the nation ... The little publick spirit that remained among us, is in a manner quite extinguished. Every one is upon the scrape for himself, without any regard to his country; each cheating, raking and plundering what he can, and in a more profligate degree than ever yet was known. In short, this self-interest runs through all our actions, and mixes in all our councils; and, if truly examined, is the very rise and spring of all our present mischiefs." Algernon Sidney, *Discourses concerning Government* (1698), cited in Dickinson, *Life and Property*, 110.

40 Dickinson, *Liberty and Property*, 103–4.

41 John Adams, quoted in Thompson, *John Adams*, 210.

42 Thompson, *Customs in Common*, 16 and 26.

43 Pares, *George III*, 6.

44 Ibid. Shelburne and Rockingham were thought to be the largest absentee landlords in Ireland.

45 Ibid., 16.

46 Ibid., 17.

47 Ibid., 27.

48 Ibid., 17.

49 Ibid., 30.

50 This was an ancient practice. Paul Veyne points out that in the Roman world public offices were treated as "though they were private dignities, access to which depended on private contacts" and that public officials simply paid themselves. Veyne, "Where Public Life Was Private," 95–115.

51 Wise, "Upper Canada and the Conservative Tradition."

52 Johnson, *Becoming Prominent*, 17.

53 If Baby disposed of this acreage all at once, he might have obtained £30,000 for forty-one years of service to the state. Of course, he would have enjoyed fees from some offices as well. He would have averaged $3658 per year. Some might say that was hardly out of place for one so eminent, considering that large farmers might receive $1500 per year. However, the latter figure would not seem to include costs. The public salary of the attorney general and of the president of King's College was $1200. By this standard, Baby did well indeed. See Russell, "Attitudes to Social Structure," 72.

54 Clarke, "James Baby," 22.

55 Whitfield, "Alexander Grant," 363–7.

56 NA, MG23, H I 4, vol. 4, 137, Narrative of William Dummer Powell.

57 AO, Jarvis Powell Papers, 1043, 39, "Notice of the Progress of William Dummer Powell," 39.

58 Johnson, *Becoming Prominent*, 18.

59 NA, MG–19–A–3, vol. 2, 323, John Askin to Richard Cartwright, 8 January 1803; ibid., vol. 14, 4704, Richard Cartwright to John Askin, 7 February 1803.

60 NA, MG–19–A–3, vol. 1, 321–2.

61 Armstrong, *Handbook of Upper Canadian Chronology*, 46.

62 NA, MG–19–A–3, vol. 1, 240–1, John Askin to Isaac Todd, 13 February 1803.

63 Ibid.

64 NA, RG5, A1, 499737, Thomas Smith to George Hillier, private secretary to the lieutenant governor, 20 August 1828.

65 Ibid., 49765, Petition of William Duff, Charles Elliott, Charles Berczy, B. Macon, William McCormick, and George Jacob, 23 August 1828.

66 NA, MG23, vol. 5, catalogue 21736, 328, Robert Matthews to Haldimand.

67 This would appear to be Daniel Robertson, for whose career see Armour, "Daniel Robertson," 714–16. I am grateful to Charles Whebell for the identification of this individual.

68 Ibid., 322.

69 Ibid., 321.

70 Wilson, "The Struggle for Wealth," 137–54. Wilson points out that many of the traders on the Niagara frontier were themselves ex-military men and that contracts were awarded largely on the basis of favouritism. The cost of provisioning the Indians at Detroit, Niagara, and Michilimackinac is thought to have exceeded the cost of the whole military establishment in Canada, not including provisions. Peculation was common; the firm of Taylor and Forsyth, with connections to Guy Johnson, superintendent of the Six Nations, was found to have been padding its books and the scandal irreparably damaged Johnson's reputation. The full extent of the problem, which was sufficient to ensure Johnson's replacement, is not known because the records are scattered between three archives and a number of series. I am grateful to Patricia Kennedy of the NA for bringing this problem to my attention.

71 Pares, *George III*, 70. Veyne points out that a clear distinction was made in the ancient world between the merchant and the landowner who engaged in commerce to become wealthy; the important thing was not to begin in trade. Veyne, "'Work' and Leisure," in Ariès and Duby, *A History of Private Life*, 124.

72 This is the traditional description, which in Marxist parlance would be summarized as the process whereby an emergent "progressive bourgeoisie" engaged a backward "ancien regime." However, Wallerstein takes the view that historical capitalism was constructed by a landed aristocracy that, aware of the demise of the old system, transformed itself into a bourgeoisie. Wallerstein, *Historical Capitalism*, 105.

73 NA, MG23, H I 4, vol. 3, 1335, n.d. Here Powell reports the attorney general stating "In bribing my opinion if a patent should be granted for the Grand River Tract and the tribes should sell to Congress, it would not raise an 'Imperium in Imperio.'"

74 AO, Jarvis-Powell Papers, 29, "Notice of the Progress of William Dummer Powell."

75 The eight officers commanding at Detroit between 1779 and 1792 were Major Arent DePeyster (1779), Major William Ancrum (1784), Captain Thomas Bennett (1786), Major Robert Mathews (1787), Major F. Close (1788), Major Patrick Murray (1789), Major John Smith (1790), and Colonel R.G. England (1792). Lajeunesse, *The Windsor Border Region*, appendix VII, 356. Mathews accused Ancrum and Lieutenant Governor Hay of peculation and reported that Lieutenant Governor Hamilton owed money for *lods et ventes* and might therefore have "turned a blind

eye." Major Murray would not, according to the testimony of Thomas Smith, sit on the Board because of its attitude to the Huron, nor would Colonel McKee.

76 Lemon, "Early Americans," 118–22.
77 Romney, *Mr Attorney*, 86–7.
78 Thompson, *Customs in Common*, 26–7.

Bibliography

CARTOGRAPHIC SOURCES

National Map Collection, National Archives of Canada: General

Anonymous, "Part of the River Thames in Upper Canada," *c.* 1793. H1/400, NMC 14905.

Anonymous, "Part of the Detroit River." A French survey of 1750, used by Collot, Detroit 1796. H3/410, NMC 116581. Shows villages of the Huron and Ottawa and surveyed lots on both sides.

Ford, Hy., and Patrick McNiff, "A survey of the south shore of Lake Erie taken in 1789," 3 sections. R/410, NMC 53796.

Abraham Iredell, "A Sketch of part of the Western District," no.15, Surveyor General's Office, Newark, 2 August 1795. NMC H3/409. Signed D.W. Smith, assistant surveyor general.

Abraham Iredell, "Malden," *c.* 1796. An Iredell base used to show ownership including that of the Canada Company.

Abraham Iredell, "Plan shewing the site ... of Amherstburg, and the land ... for Government," 1797 (1806), H3/440.

Abraham Iredell, "Sandwich," 1803, H3/430, NMC 022197. Shows lots 63–128 and 3rd. con. and 4 lots of P. Selby.

Baron de Rottenburg, "Map of the Principal Communications in Canada West compiled ... by Major Baron de Rottenburg." 1850, H1/400, NMC 0012437.

Patrick McNiff, "A plan of part of the New Settlements of the north bank of the southwest branch of the St. Lawrence River ... 1786," 5 sections. H2/400, NMC 0021346. The so-called Loyalist Map.

Patrick McNiff et al., "Plan of part of His Majesty's province of Quebec from Montreal westward: part of the Ottawa River, the river Iroquois, as far as Kingston, the w(?) south shore and part of the north shore of Lake Erie, Detroit River and part of Lake St. Clair, delineated from my own surveys, made in the Years, 1784, 1785, 1786, 1787, 1789." 1: 950400. 16 March 1790. NMC 117660.

Patrick McNiff, "A Plan of part of the east shore of Lake Erie in the District of Hope [sic] from Point Pelee," 1790. H3/409, NMC 0003029.

Patrick McNiff, "Map of Part of the Province of Quebec, comprehending also Nova Scotia, New Brunswick, the Island of ...," 5 sections, 1791. V3/1000, NMC 17923.

Patrick McNiff, "A plan of Lake Erie, Detroit River, part of Lake St. Clair & River La Tranche from actual surveys in the years 1789, 1790 & 1791," 1791. H1/400, NMC 0016996. Map shows the Caldwell grant (1788) in Malden and lots 97 to 75 in Colchester.

Patrick McNiff, "Colchester", 1794. M/430.

Patrick McNiff, "Plan of the settlement of Detroit," 1796, NMC Atlas Case F–176.

Patrick McNiff, "A Plan of part of the district commencing near Point Pele, on the north shore of Lake Erie and extending from thence, along the waters edge, to the entrance of River Latranche, on the east Shore of Lake St.Clair, and from the entrance of said river, up to the 2nd fork of the same, delineated from actual surveys, made in the Years 1789 and 1790." (1815) V30/409, NMC 0044752.

William Parke, "Map of Sandwich with the position and situation of the lands of William Park & Meldrum & Park together with notes & references, transcribed by William Park," 40 chains, 30 December 1800. NMC 0003600.

National Map Collection, National Archives of Canada: Reserve Lands

Surveyor-General's Office (SGO), "Two sevenths of certain old townships in the Western District set apart for the Crown and Clergy, as specified on this plan, in the diagram washed with Lake and Indian ink," c. 1795. F/400, NMC 1212171.

SGO, "Diagram A, The chequered plan," 1789–1929. H3/400, NMC 000282 (old QS246, folio 121). Designed to determine the reserved lots, designated R.

SGO, "Diagram B, on the principle of the chequered plan," 1789–1929. H3/400, NMC 000284 (old QS248, folio 123). The reserved lots, are distinguished by the letter R; no colour.

SGO, "The chequered plan discriminating the reserves of the Crown from that of the clergy, 1789–1829." H3/400, NMC 000283 (old QS247, folio 122). The Crown lots are washed with lake and clergy lots with Indian ink.

SGO, "Diagram B, on the principle of the chequered plan and discriminating the reserves of the Crown from those of the clergy, 1789–1829." H3/400, NMC 000285 (old QS249, folio 124). Crown lots are in lake and the clergy lots in Indian ink.

SGO, "A Diagram on the principle of the chequered plan discriminating the reserves of the Crown from those of the Clergy, 1789–1829". NMC 000287 (old QS260). Crown lots are washed in lake and the clergy lots in Indian ink.

SGO, "Suppose the township of Newtown," NMC 000288 (old QS255).

SGO, "Township No.1", NMC 000291 (old QS285).

SGO, "Township No.2", NMC 000292 (old QS286).

SGO, "Township No.3", NMC 000293 (old QS287).

SGO, "Township No.4", NMC 000294 (old QS288).

Archives of Ontario

Anonymous, "Malden Township with a part of the Huron reserve," *c.* 1791, AO C26 (old Q68). Shows Indian officers grants and the Huron cornfields. The Caldwell grant is shown to be 3050 statute acres and three square chains. The boundary of the Indian reserve (Anderdon) is marked 13 and 14 August 1790, by order of Sir John Johnson.

Anonymous (Smith 1798?), copy by W. Chewett of "Sandwich," n.d, marked S73, AO (S73).

Anonymous, a copy by Chewett of a "Plan of Malden Township and the Huron reserve" (M19B), forty chains to an inch, *c.* 1821. AO, C.26.

Mahlon Burwell, "Maidstone and Rochester", forty chains, 1824. W. Chewett's copy of Burwell's plan. AO 613.7 M28.

Patrick McNiff, "Sketch of Lake Erie, Detroit River, Lake St. Clair and part of Lakes Huron and Ontario intended to show the extravagant claims to lands in the District of Hesse." Approximate scale of fifteen miles to an inch; dated to approximately 1790. AO, 1568 (A–15). Copied from an original by Lieutenant John Frederick Holland.

Patrick McNiff, "Plan of part of the east (north) shore of Lake Erie and part of the east shore of the Detroit in the District of Hesse from Point Pele to the Detroit River with the names of the proprietors inserted in the lots including likewise a tract reserved for the Huron Indians," 1790. Scale of forty chains to the inch. AO, 3019 (A–13) Negative. Shows the Malden properties of captains Caldwell, Ford, La Motte, McKee, Bird, and Elliott.

Patrick McNiff, "A plan of part of the District of Hesse commencing near Point Pele in the north shore of Lake Erie and extending from thence along the water's edge to the entrance of River La Tranche on the east shore of lake St. Clair and from the entrance of the said river up to the 2d fork of the same delineated from actual survey made in the years 1789 and 1790." No scale given. Endorsed January 1791; AO, Simcoe Collection 446892–5, (F–47–5–1–0–5).

Patrick McNiff, "A plan of Lake Erie, Detroit River, a part of Lake St. Clair and River La Tranche from actual surveys made in the years 1789, 1790 and 1791," Detroit, May 1791, scale 1" to 4.5 miles. AO, Simce Papers 446890. A compilation resulting from the work of Ford and McNiff with input from the Indians.

Patrick McNiff, "A plan of part of the District of Hesse in two separate parts commencing near Point Pele on the north shore of Lake Erie and extending fron thence along the waters edge to the entrance of River La Tranche on the east shore of lake St. Clair and from the entrance of the said river up to the second fork of the same." Scale one inch to forty chains. Possibly finished 19 March 1791. AO, 3083. Delineated from actual surveys in the years 1789 and 1790.

Patrick McNiff and Abraham Iredell?, "A rough sketch of Lake St. Clair and part of the Detroit River and River St. Clair with the adjacent country from actual surveys," 360 chains to the inch, Detroit, February 1797. AO, B–67. A Copy of the original in the Winthrop Sargent Papers, Ohio. Sandwich, c. 1797.

Patrick McNiff and Abraham Iredell, Chewett's copy of "Sandwich," c. 1797. AO, C18. Shows southern extension of the Huron reserve.

Thomas Parke, "Malden," 1843. AO, C–277–1–267–0–2.

Thomas Parke, "Survey grid of Sandwich showing the reserves," July 1843, C 277–1–368–0–5.

Thomas Ridout (signed), "Plan of Sandwich Township (C17), York, 17 April 1821. The 2nd. concession is marked "erroneous" and "see Burwell's own plan" no.28. Scale of forty chains to the inch. AO, C39 negative.

Thomas Smith, "Sandwich," 28 May 1798 and Survey of Fere's land in rear of lots 37 to 47 conforming to the original survey of P. McNiff, 16 May 1794. AO Case C.

Thomas Smith, "Sandwich," c. 1798. AO, Case C D.39.

Talbot Maps, Book C, "Romney and Tilbury," signed T. Ridout, 8 June 1811. AO, F501–1–0–0–30.

Talbot Maps, Book E, map 5, "Mersea Township," Mahlon Burwell, copy by JGC and signed by Thomas Ridout. AO, F501–1–0–0–22.

Talbot Maps, Book E, map 7, "Mersea Township," Mahlon Burwell, 30 November 1816. AO, F501–1–0–0–21.

Talbot Maps, Book E, map 10, "Maidstone and parts of Rochester and Sandwich," Mahlon Burwell, 29 November 1824. AO, F501–1–0–0–18.

Talbot Maps, Book E, "Talbot Road through Sandwich, Maidstone and Rochester," Mahlon Burwell, 1824. AO, F–501–1–0–0–18.

Talbot Maps, Book C, "Sandwich", signed T. Ridout, 15 February 1826. Scale of forty chains to the inch. AO, F501–1–0–0–32. Shows vacant land on Talbot Road.

Talbot Maps, Book C, map 3, "Tilbury West," copy by James Grant Chewett (JGC), 15 February 1826, signed by Thomas Ridout. AO, F501–1–00–36.

Talbot Maps, Book C, "Tilbury East," 1826, signed by T. Ridout, AO, C277–1–406–0–1.

Talbot Maps, Book C, map 16, "Maidstone," copy by JGC, signed by T. Ridout, 15 February 1826. AO, F501–1–0–0–19.

Talbot Maps, Book E, map 3, "Sandwich," copy by JGC, 15 February 1826, signed by Thomas Ridout. AO, F501–1–0–0–32.

Department of Lands and Forests
(Government of Ontario)

Anonymous, "Colchester & Gosfield," n.d, DLF–X9.

Anonymous, "Malden," 1846, DLF 1557. Possibly Parke.

Mahlon Burwell, "Talbot Road through Mersea," n.d., forty chains, DLF 19.

Mahlon Burwell, "Tilbury West," forty chains, 31 December 1824. Ordered 17 April 1821, DLF–#31. It shows Talbot lands, Crown and clergy reserves, and Canada Company lands.

Mahlon Burwell, "Colchester," 17 Apr 1821, forty chains. Survey ordered 1821 but entered 10 February 1832, DLF–#3.

Mahlon Burwell, "Gosfield," 27 April 1821 but endorsed York, 26 March 1823, 40 chains, DLF–B5.

Peter Carroll, "Malden," forty chains to an inch, 23 December 1831. DLF–AB16. Shows reserves and gives their acreage.

Abraham Iredell (?), A copy of "Gosfield East," n.d but c. 1796, DLF–X8. Copy certified by Samuel Holland.

Abraham Iredell, "Malden," c. 1796. Iredell base used to show owners including Canada Company. DLF–A25.

Abraham Iredell, "Malden," scale of forty chains to the inch, April 1796, DLF–A15 and 1555. Shows land of the Indian officers and other notables as well as the Canada Company lands.

Abraham Iredell, "Colchester," lots 97 to 33, possibly 1797, DLF–A6.

Abraham Iredell?, "Sandwich and Petite Cote," forty chains, 39 January 1797, DLF–A41. Shows names of landowners.

Abraham Iredell, "Sandwich," 20 January 1797, DLF–A36. Shows lots 1–57 Petite Côté. 1st con. and lots 1–12 and 30–45/2nd.

Abraham Iredell, "Sandwich," 10 July 1797, DLF–B16. A plan of the 1st. con. correcting errors on A36.

Abraham Iredell, "Sandwich," twenty chains, 31 December 1797, DLF–A34; a memo of L.V. Rorke, Surveyor/General (16 Mar 1929), designates this "the authentic Plan."

Abraham Iredell, "Mersea," 22 January 1799, DLF–A27. It seems that he did lots 1–13 along the coast and cons. 1 and 2, lots 1–6; perhaps four concessions.

Abraham Iredell(?), "Tilbury West," forty chains, 24 Jun 1799, DL–A24.

Abraham Iredell, "Gosfield," forty chains to one inch, DLF–A13. Endorsed by Iredell 9 July 1800; lots 1–32.

Abraham Iredell, Sandwich, 3 July 1803; DLF–A35. Lots 63–128, 3rd con. Surveyed at request of Hon. James Baby.

Patrick McNiff, "Colchester," water lots, 14 July 1790. DLF–49. Acknowledges prior survey in 1786, presumably by T. Smith in 1788.

Patrick McNiff, "Malden," 6 and 7 July 1790; certified July 1794. It shows the Indian officers' and Caldwell grants as well as a proposed fort. DLF–A25.

Patrick McNiff, "Sandwich," 1793, DLF–A37; lots 63–154 L'Assomption; originally with DLF map A42.

Patrick McNiff(?), "A copy of Sandwich and Petite Côte," endorsed by William Chewett and Thomas Ridout, 1802, DLF–A38. Shows 2nd concession.

Patrick McNiff," Gosfield," n.d. DLF–A12. Shows lots 33 to 1 in the front and 1–13/2nd 10–13/3rd concessions.

G. McPhillips, "Plan of the squatters holdings on the naval reserve at Point Pelee in the Township of Mersea," Windsor, July 30 1889. DLF–1662, "M" drawer, surveys vault.

Signature obscure, "Gosfield," n.d, forty chains. DLF–A14 (copy).

Thomas Smith, "Colchester Concessions 1–4," possibly 1805–06, DLF–#4.

Thomas Smith, "Mersea," 16 March 1806, forty chains, DLF–A26.

Thomas Smith, "Sandwich and L'Assomption," 23 January 1807, DLF–A39. Delimits P. Selby's land in 4th, 5th, and 6th concessions.

Thomas Smith(?), "Gosfield," n.d. DLF–A15. Survey limited to con. 4, 1–6, and con. 6 on east. Pre-Burwell (no Talbot Rd.). Shows reserves.

Carleton University Map Library

National Topographic Series, Essex 1:63360, Survey and Mapping Branch, 1950.

[*Canada 1:50 000*] Army Survey Establishment, 1:50 000, Ottawa: Army Survey Establishment, R.C.E. 1908, recompiled, drawn, and printed 1955–57, 40J/2.3.6.7. Ed. 3 ASE.

PRIMARY SOURCES

Note: the citations used are in some cases rather old and have been updated by the institutions holding the originals. In some cases this has happened more than once and indeed at the time of writing this process still continues. It is hoped that in all cases sufficient information is included to trace the originals.

National Archives (NA)

RG1, E1, State Minute Books for Upper Canada
RG1, E3, Upper Canada State Papers
RG1, L1, Executive Council Records, Upper Canada, 1792–1841
RG1, L3, Executive Council Records, Upper Canada Land Petitions
RG1, L4, Upper Canada Land Boards Records, Reports of the District of Hesse
RG1, L5, Records of the Heir and Devisees Commission, Western District, 1798–1804
RG1, L6, Departmental Records:
    A. Attorney-General, Upper Canada
    B. Surveyor-General, 1784–1856
    C. Receiver-General
    D. Inspector-General
RG5, A1, Civil Secretary's Correspondence, Upper Canada Sundries
RG5, B26, Upper Canada: Returns of Population and Assessment
RG7, Miscellaneous Records, Upper Canada, Canada Company Records
RG10, Indian Treaties
RG68, Records of the Registrar-General, Key to General Index, 1651–1947
MG9, D4, Upper Canada Sundries, 1845–50
MG11 Q Series
MG18, I 5, vols, 1–7, Detroit Notarial Register
MG–19–A–3, Askin Family Papers
MG21, Frederick Haldimand Papers
MG23, William Dummer Powell Papers
MG24, B9, John Beverley Robinson Papers
MG24, G46, Mahlon Burwell and Family Papers
MG24, L3, Transcripts of Baby Papers
MG30, D1, F.J Audet Biographical Notes

National Library of Canada (NLC)

Arent dePeyster, *Miscellanies of an Officer* (Dumfries, Scotland, 1813)

Archives of Ontario (AO)

Abstract Index to Deeds, Essex County (Genealogical Society of Utah)
Patent Index, Essex County (Genealogical Society of Utah)
F31, Samuel Peter Jarvis and William Dummer Powell Collection (Jarvis/Powell Papers)
F27, John Elmsley Macaulay and John Simcoe Macaulay Collection (Macaulay Papers)
F47, Simcoe Family Fonds (Simcoe Papers)

F62, A.N. Buell Family Fonds (Buell Papers)

F129, Canada Company Papers, Register of Lands for the Bathurst, Home and Western Districts, No.2., 1824–26

F474, John Askin Papers, MU13

F501, Thomas Talbot Papers

F602 and 603, Land Records Collection

F2128, Jacques Duperon Baby Family Fonds, MU18 (Baby Papers)

RG1, Crown Land Papers

RG1–366, Survey Instruction Books

RG1, A–I–1, Letters Received by the Surveyor-General, 1766–1913

RG1, A–I–2, Surveyor-General's Letter Books, 1792–1908

RG1, A-I-3, Surveyor–General's Registers, 1833-1859

RG1, A–I–6, Original letters, Surveyor General and Commissioner of Crown lands, 1797–1805

RG1, A–I–7, Subject Files, Crown and Clergy Reserves, 1790–1890

RG1, A–II–1, Surveyor-General's Reports, 1788–1857

RG1, A–II–4, Heir and Devisees Certificates of Search, 1830–1872

RG1, A–II–5, Heir and Devisees Commission Reports, 1791–1886

RG1, A–II–6, Statements, 1811–1922

RG1, A–III, Registers, 1797–1896

RG1, A–IV, Schedules and Land Rolls, 1784–1822

RG1, A–VI–15, Western District Inspection and Evaluation Reports, Western District, 1794–1909

RG1, A–VII, Miscellaneous Records, Orders and Regulations, 1788–1914

RG1–B–II, Account Books, Clergy Reserve Rent Books, London and Western Districts, 1802–36; Western District Clergy Reserve Leases; Clergy reserves Rent Accounts, B Series, vol. 7–13, London and Western, Newcastle, Johnston, Ottawa and Eastern Districts, 1802–59; C Series, Home, Gore, London, Western, Midland and Newcastle, 1802–59

RG1–B–III, Statements, Clergy Reserve Leases; Clergy Reserves Sold and Cash Received, 1829–35, vol. 14; Clergy Reserves Sold in Western District, 1841, vol. 27; Amounts Due on Clergy Reserves Leases, 1842, vol. 29; Lands Leased and Sold up to 1853, vol. 35;

RG1, CB–1, Survey Diaries and Field Notes, 1790–1928

RG1, C–I–1, Petitions and Applications, 1827–65, Commissioner of Crown Lands

RG1, C–I–2, Orders in Council, 1792–1864

RG1, C–I–3, Fiats and Warrants, 1796–1885

RG1, C–I–6, Settlement Duties, 1800–30

RG1, C–I–7, Descriptions, 1794–1982, Western and London District, 1795–1810 (Docket Books)

RG1, C–I–8, Patents, 1793–1896

RG1, C–I–11, Domesday Books 1801–1967

RG1, C–II–1, Leases, 1801–40 (Crown Land)

RG1, C–II–2, Leases, 1801–30

RG1, C–II–3, Miscellaneous Records, Crown and Clergy Reserve Schedules, 1802–47

RG1, C–III–2, Applications, Crown and Clergy Reserve Purchases

RG1, C–III–3, Sale of Clergy Reserves, 1829–1924, vol. 10, Western and Midland District, 1835

RG1, C–III–4 Sales of Crown Lands, 1820–71

RG1, C–III–5, Sale of Crown and Clergy Lands, 1832–1905, vol. 8., Western and Home District, 1835–36

RG1, C–I–V, Township Papers, 1783–c. 1880

RG8, I–3, Index to Land Patents, 1790–1912

RG21 Municipal Records

RG40, Heirs and Devisees Commission Reports

Supplement to the Upper Canada Gazette, A Statement of the Clergy Reserves Sold, 30 June 1841

Supplement to the Upper Canada Gazette, A Statement of the Crown Lands sold, 30 June 1841

Appendix no.22 of the *Journal* of the House of Assembly of Upper Canada, 1836, 20–3, "Statement of lands in the London and Western districts which have been placed in the hands of the Honourable Thomas Talbot."

Archives of Ontario, Hiram Walker Historical Collection (F378)

HWHC, 20–10, John Askin Papers

HWHC, 20–11, Baby Family Papers

HWHC, 20–18, Baptiste Berthier Papers

HWHC, 20–20, Jean Baptiste Beaubien Papers

HWHC, 20–52, Cornwall Family Papers

HWHC, 20–62, Labadie Family Papers

HWHC, 20–76, Matthew Elliott Papers

HWHC, 20–92, Fox Family Land Papers, 1797–1860

HWHC, 20–96, John Giles and David Elston Papers

HWHC, 20–101, Hon. James Gordon Papers, 1813–36

HWHC, 20–104, Grant Family Papers

HWHC, 20–107, Hall Family Papers

HWHC, 20–108, Hands Family and William Hands Business Papers, 1785–1835

HWHC, 20–135, G.F. MacDonald Papers

HWHC, 20–137, McIntosh Family

HWHC, 20–140, Alexander and William Macomb

HWHC, 20–141, Maisonville Family

HWHC, 20–148, McCormick Family
HWHC, 20–153, McKee Family Papers
HWHC, 20–160, McDonnell Family
HWHC, 20–176, Ouellette Family
HWHC, 20–178, Parke and Company
HWHC, 20–180, Richard Pattinson Papers
HWHC, 20–193, Reaume Family
HWHC, 20–216, Thomas Smith Papers
HWHC, 20–235, Wilkinson Family Papers
HWHC, 20–242, Woods Family Papers

Department of Lands and Forests, Government of Ontario (DLF)

Patents Office, Copies of the Orders-in-Council, vol. 3, "Committee Report to His Excellency Francis Gore Esquire, Lieutenant Governor of the Province of Upper Canada, 15th February 1809."
Survey Records
Original NoteBooks
Field NoteBooks
Surveyor's Letters
Domesday Books, vols. 6, 7, and 76

Hiram Walker Historical Museum, Windsor

Schedules of lands not inserted in the Assessment Rolls for various townships in the Western District and for the years 1846 and 1847

Toronto Reference Library (TRL)

Powell Papers, B80, B81, B84
Robert Baldwin Papers
W.W. Baldwin Papers
Jarvis Papers

Burton Historical Collection, Detroit Public Library, Michigan

Askin Papers
Baby Family Collection

University of Western Ontario (UWO)

William Robertson Papers

University of Windsor (UW)

Anderdon Township, Land Registry Copy Books, Register A, Book nos.1–25, instruments 45–342, 26 Jan. 1852 to 7 Jan. 1865

Colchester Township, Land Registry Copy Books, Register A, Book nos.1–56, instruments 13–341, 4 Aug. 1847 to 4 May 1854

Gosfield Township, Land Registry Copy Books, Register A, Book nos.1–161, instruments 1–353, 8 April 1847 to 7 Oct. 1854

Mersea Township, Land Registry Copy Books, Register A, Book nos.1–351, instruments 1–364, 19 April 1847 to 4 Oct. 1856

Tilbury West Township, Memorials, Book nos.1–726, instruments 1–69, 14 Aug. 1809 to 21 Nov. 1851

Tilbury West Township, Land Registry Copy Books, Register A, Book nos.1–727, instruments 1–333, 22 May 1847 to 21 March 1859

Maidstone Township, Land Registry Copy Books, Register A, Book nos.1–292, instruments 1–360, 8 April 1847 to 3 Nov. 1847

Rochester Township, Land Registry Copy Books, Register A, Book nos.1–453, instruments 1–354, 8 April 1847 to 6 Aug. 1859

Malden Township, Land Registry Copy Books, Register A, Book nos.1–330, instruments 1–319, 7 April 1847 to 6 Sept. 1853

Old Sandwich Township, Land Registry Copy Books, Register A, Book nos.1–485, instruments 1–294, 26 March 1847 to 29 Dec. 1849

British Museum/British Library (BM/BL)

Gladstone Papers, Add. MS.44609, vol. 524, 13 and 18, "Provisions for Division of Clergy Corporation assets under the Act of 1840"; Add. MS.44571, vol. 495, 136, A Bill to Authorise the Upper Canadian Government to Make Provision concerning the Clergy Reserves, 17 Feb. 1853; Add. MS44567, vol. 482, 38 and 39, 101–17, "Petitions and Letters concerning the Clergy Reserves"

Public Record Office (PRO)

CO42/317
CO47
CO401, Crown and Clergy Reserves
CO537/142

University of Cambridge

"Report from the Select Committee on the Civil Government of Canada, House of Commons, London, 22nd July 1828"

Public Record Office of Northern Ireland (PRONI)

T1473/3, Ottawa and Chippewa Treaty, 15 May 1786

SECONDARY SOURCES

Acheson, T. William. "The Nature and Structure of York Commerce in the 1820s." In *Historical Essays on Upper Canada*, edited by J.K. Johnson and B.G. Wilson, 171–93. Ottawa: Carleton Library University Press 1989.

Adamson, Christopher. "God's Continent Divided: Politics and Religion in Upper Canada and the Northern and Western United States, 1775 to 1841." *Comparative Studies in Society and History* 36, no.3 (1994): 417–46.

Ahmad, N. *Muslim Separation in British India: A Retrospective Study*. Lahore: Ferozsons 1991.

Aitken, Hugh G. "The Family Compact and the Welland Canal Company." *Canadian Journal of Economics and Political Science* 18, no.1 (1952): 63–76.

Aitken, William Thomas and Hugh G.J. Aitken. *Canadian Economic History*. Toronto: Macmillan 1956.

Akenson, Donald H. *The Irish in Ontario: A Study in Rural History*. Kingston and Montreal: McGill-Queen's University Press 1984.

Allaire, Gratien. "Thomas Thain." In *Dictionary of Canadian Biography*. Vol. 6. Toronto: University of Toronto (1987): 764–6.

Allen, J.W. "Jeremy Bentham." In *The Social and Political Ideas of Some Representative Thinkers of the Revolutionary Era*, edited by F.J.C. Hearnshaw, 181–200. New York: Barnes and Noble 1967.

Allen, Robert S. "The British Indian Department and the Frontier in North America, 1755–1830." *Occasional Papers in Archaeology and History* 14 (1975): 5–125.

– "Robert Dickson." In *Dictionary of Canadian Biography*. Vol. 6. Toronto: University of Toronto (1987): 209–11.

– "His Majesty's Indian Allies: Native Peoples, the British Crown, and the War of 1812." *Michigan Historical Review* 14, no. 2 (1988): 1–24.

– *His Majesty's Indian Allies: British Indian Policy in the Defence of Canada, 1774–1815*. Toronto: Dundurn Press 1993.

Allodi, Mary M., Peter N. Moogk, and Beate Stock. *Berczy*. Ottawa: National Gallery Of Canada 1991.

Anderson, Michael. *Family Structure in Nineteenth-Century Lancashire*. Cambridge, U.K.: Cambridge University Press 1971.

Andre, John and J. Russell Harper. "William Bent Berczy." In *Dictionary of Canadian Biography*. Vol. 10. Toronto: University of Toronto (1972): 50–1.

Ankli, R.E. and Duncan, K.J. "Farm Making Costs in Early Ontario." In *Canadian Papers in Rural History*, vol. 4, edited by D.H. Akenson, 33–49. Gananoque, Ont.: Langdale Press 1984.

Anonymous. *The Social Horizon.* 2nd ed. London: Swan Sonnenschein 1893.

– "Peter Carroll." *Annual Report of the Association of Ontario Land Surveyors,* 99–101. Toronto: Association of Ontario Land Surveyors 1920

– (with assistance from L.V. Rorke). "Abraham Iredell." *Annual Report of the Association of Ontario Land Surveyors,* 96–103. Toronto: Association of Ontario Land Surveyors 1935.

Armour, David A. "Patrick Sinclair." In *Dictionary of Canadian Biography.* Vol. 5. Toronto: University of Toronto Press (1983): 759–61.

– "Alexander Henry." In *Dictionary of Canadian Biography.* Vol. 6. Toronto: University of Toronto Press (1987): 316–18.

– "Arent Schuyler DePeyster." In *Dictionary of Canadian Biography.* Vol. 6. Toronto: University of Toronto Press (1987): 188–91.

Armour, David A. and Keith R. Widder. *At the Crossroads: Michilimackinac during the American Revolution.* Midland, Mich.: Mackinac Island State Park Commission, 1986.

Armstrong, Frederick H. "Ports of Entry and Collectors of Customs in Upper Canada, 1797–1841." *Inland Seas* (summer 1970): 137–44.

– "George Jervis Goodhue: Pioneer Merchant of London, Upper Canada." *Ontario History* 63, no.4 (1971): 217–32.

– "The Scottish Immigrant and the Family Compact: Assimilation vs Opposition." Paper presented at the Sixth Colloquium on Scottish Studies, Guelph, 1974, 11–18.

– "George Jervis Goodhue." In *Dictionary of Canadian Biography.* Vol. 9. Toronto: University of Toronto Press (1976): 323–4.

– "The Oligarchy of the Western District of Upper Canada, 1788–1841." *Canadian Historical Association Historical Papers* (1977): 87–102.

– "Henry Allcock." In *Dictionary of Canadian Biography.* Vol. 5. Toronto: University of Toronto Press (1983): 17–19.

– "James Dougall and the Founding of Windsor, Ontario." *Ontario History* 76, no. 1 (1984): 3–31.

– "John Strachan, Schoolmaster, and the Evolution of the Elite in Upper Canadian Ontario." In *An Imperfect Past: Education and Society in Canada's History,* edited by J.D Wilson, 154–69. Vancouver, Canadian History of Education Association: University of British Columbia 1984.

– *Handbook of Upper Canadian Chronology.* Toronto: Dundurn Press 1985.

Armstrong, Frederick H. and Ronald J. Stagg. "William Lyon Mackenzie." In *Dictionary of Canadian Biography.* Vol. 9. Toronto: University of Toronto Press (1976): 496–510.

Arthur, Elizabeth. "Henry Hamilton." In *Dictionary of Canadian Biography.* Vol. 4. Toronto: University of Toronto Press (1979): 321–4.

Atack, Jeremy. "Tenants and Yeomen in the Nineteenth Century." *Agricultural History* 62, no.3 (1988): 6–32.

– "The Agricultural Ladder Revisited: A New Look at an Old Question with Some Data for 1860." *Agricultural History* 63, no.1 (1989): 1–25.

Ayling, Stanley. *George the Third.* London: Collins 1972.

Backhouse, Constance B. "Pure Patriarchy: Nineteenth-Century Canadian Marriage." *McGill Law Journal* 31, no.2 (1986): 264–312.

– "Married Women's Property Law in Nineteenth-Century Canada." *Law and History Review* 6, no.2 (1988): 211–57.

– *Petticoats and Prejudice: Women and Law in Nineteenth-Century Canada.* Toronto: Women's Press 1991.

Bailyn, Bernard. *The Peopling of British North America; An Introduction.* New York: Alfred Knopf 1986.

Baker, George B. "The Reconstitution of Upper Canadian Legal Thought in the Late-Victorian Empire." *Law and History Review* 3 (1985): 219–92.

– "So Elegant a Web: Providential Order and the Rule of Secular Law in Early Nineteenth Century Upper Canada." *University of Toronto Law Journal* 38, no.2 (1988): 184–205.

Banks, Margaret A. "The Evolution of the Ontario Courts 1788–1981." In *Essays in the History of Canadian Law* vol. 2, edited by D.H. Flaherty, 492–572. Toronto: University of Toronto Press 1983.

Barkwell, Gordon. "The Clergy Reserves in Upper Canada: A Study in the Separation of Church and State, 1791–1854." PHD thesis, University of Chicago, 1953.

Barlowe, Raleigh. *Land Resources: The Economics of Real Property.* 2nd ed. Englewood Cliffs, N.J.: Prentice Hall 1972.

Baskerville, Peter A. "Sir Allan Napier MacNab." In *Dictionary of Canadian Biography.* Vol. 9. Toronto: University of Toronto Press (1976): 519–27.

Bayly, C.A. *Indian Society and the Making of the British Empire.* Cambridge, U.K.: Cambridge University Press 1988.

Beer, Donald R. "Toryism in Transition: Upper Canadian Conservative Leaders, 1836–1854." *Ontario History* 80, no.3 (1988) 207–25.

Béland, François. "Jean-Baptiste-Pierre Testard Louvigny de Montigny." In *Dictionary of Canadian Biography.* Vol. 5. Toronto: University of Toronto Press (1983): 801–3.

Belden, H. and Company. *Illustrated Historical Atlas of the Counties of Essex and Kent, 1881.* Repr., Owen Sound, Ont.: Richard, Bond and Wright 1973.

Bentham, Jeremy. *A Fragment on Government and an Introduction to the Principles of Morals and Legislation.* Oxford, U.K.: Blackwell 1948.

Berkner, L.K. "Rural Family Organization in Europe: A Problem in Comparative History." *Peasant Studies Newsletter* 1 (1972): 145–55.

Bidwell, R.L. *Currency Conversion Tables: A Hundred Years of Change.* London: Rex Collings 1970.

Bilak, Daniel A. "The Law of the Land: Rural Debt and Private Land Transfer in Upper Canada, 1841–1867." *Histoire Sociale/Social History* 20 (1987): 177–88.

Billington, Raymond A. "The Origin of the Land Speculator as a Frontier Type." *Agricultural History* 19, no.4 (1945): 204–12.

Blackstone, Sir William. *Commentaries on the Laws of England in Four Books.* 2 vols. Edited by George Sharwood. Philadelpia: J.B. Lippincott 1878.

Blalock, Hubert M. *Social Statistics.* Toronto: McGraw Hill 1960.

Bloomberg, Susan E. et al. "A Census Probe into Nineteenth-Century Family History: Southern Michigan, 1850–1880." *Journal of Social History* 5 (1971): 26–45.

Blue, Archibald. "Colonel Mahlon Burwell, Land Surveyor." *Proceedings of the Royal Canadian Institute.* Toronto: Murray Printing 1899, 41–56.

Bogue, Allan G. *Money at Interest: The Farm Mortgage on the Middle Border.* Lincoln: University of Nebraska Press 1955.

– *From Prairie to Corn Belt: Farming on the Illinois and Iowa Prairies in the Nineteenth Century.* Chicago: University of Chicago Press 1963.

Bogue, Allan G. and Margaret B. Bogue. "Profits and the Frontier Land Speculator." *Journal of Economic History* 17, no.1 (1957): 1–24.

Bogue, Margaret B. *Patterns from the Sod: Land Use and Tenure in the Grand Prairie, 1850–1900.* Springfield: Illinois State Historical Library 1959.

Bottomore, Tom. *Elites and Society.* New York: Routledge 1993.

Boucher, Jonathan, ed. *Reminiscenes of an American Loyalist, 1738–1789: Being the Autobiography of the Reverend Jonathan Boucher, Rector of Annapolis in Maryland and afterwards Vicar of Epsom, Surrey, England.* Repr., Port Washington, N.Y.: New York Kennikat Press 1967.

– *A View Of the Causes and Consequences of the American Revolution in Thirteen Discourses Preached in North America between the Years 1765 and 1775.* New York: Russell and Russell 1967.

Boulton, D'Arcy. *Sketch of His Majesty's Province of Upper Canada.* London: C. Rickaby 1805. National Library of Canada, Ottawa. Microfiche.

Bradley, Arthur Granville. *The Makers of Canada: Lord Dorchester.* Canadian Club Edition. Toronto: Morang and Company 1910.

Brannigan, Colm J. "'A Pamphlet of a Very Scurrilous Nature': A Libel Case from Upper Canada of the 1840s." In *Canadian Papers in Rural History*, vol. 4, edited by D.H. Akenson, 179–99. Gananoque, Ont.: Langdale Press 1984.

Bridgman, H.J. "William Morris." In *Dictionary of Canadian Biography.* Vol. 8. Toronto: University of Toronto Press (1985): 638–42.

Brigham, Clarence S. *British Royal Proclamations to America, 1603–1783.* Repr. New York: Ben Franklin Society 1968.

Brock, D.J. "Abraham Iredell." In *Dictionary of Canadian Biography.* Vol. 5. Toronto: University of Toronto Press (1983): 448–9.

– "William Robertson." In *Dictionary of Canadian Biography.* Vol. 5. Toronto: University of Toronto Press (1983): 718–9.

Brode, Patrick. *Sir John Beverley Robinson: Bone and Sinew of the Compact.* Toronto: University of Toronto Press 1984.

- "Alexander Cameron." In *Dictionary of Canadian Biography*. Vol. 12. Toronto: University of Toronto Press (1990): 146–7.

Bronowski, Jacob. *The Common Sense of Science*. Cambridge, Mass.: Harvard University Press 1978.

Brooke, John. *King George III*. London: Anchor Press 1972.

Brown, David L. "Census Records of Upper Canada 1791–1891." *Proceedings: Ontario Genealogical Society Seminar '88*. Toronto: Ontario Genealogical Society 1988, Q1–Q21.

Brown, Elizabeth. "Equitable Jurisdiction and the Court of Chancery in Upper Canada." *Osgoode Hall Law Journal* 21, no.2 (1983): 275–314.

Brown, Wallace and Hereward Senior. *Victorious in Defeat: The Loyalists of the American Revolution in Exile*. Toronto: Methuen 1984.

Browne, G.P. "Guy Carleton, 1st Baron Dorchester." In *Dictionary of Canadian Biography*. Vol. 5. Toronto: University of Toronto Press (1983): 141–54.

Brunger, Alan G. "Analysis of Site Factors in Nineteenth Century Ontario Settlement." In *International Geography* vol. 1, edited by W.P. Adams and F. Helleiner, 400–2. Toronto: University of Toronto Press 1972.

- "A Spatial Analysis of Individual Settlement in Southern London District, Upper Canada, 1800–1836." PHD thesis, University of Western Ontario 1973.

- "Geographic Patterns of Early Settlement: Social Institutions on the Frontier of Upper Canada." *Bamberger Geographische Schriften* 4 (1982): 267–84.

- "Geographical Propinquity among Pre-famine Catholic Irish Settlers in Upper Canada." *Journal of Historical Geography* 8, no.3 (1982): 265–82.

- "Thomas Talbot." In *Dictionary of Canadian Biography*. Vol. 8. Toronto: University of Toronto Press (1985): 857–62.

- "Market-Value of Land in Early Ontario: Geographical Pattern and Process." Paper presented at the Eastern Historical Geography Association, Williamsburg, Va., 1988.

Buckley, Kevin A.H. "The Role of Staple Industries in Canada's Economic Development." *Journal of Economic History* 18, no.4 (1958): 439–50.

Burghardt, Andrew F. "The Origin and Development of the Road Network of the Niagara Peninsula, Ontario, 1770–1851." *Annals of the American Association of Geographers* 59, no.3 (1969): 417–40.

Burke, Kathleen. "'I was everything when with you, but here nobody ...': Upper Canada's First Surveyor General Returns to Britain." *Ontario History* 91, 1 (1999): 1–18.

Burley, David G. "'Good for All He Would Ask': Credit and Debt in the Transition to Industrial Capitalism – The Case of Mid-nineteenth Century Brantford, Ontario." *Histoire Sociale/Social History* 39 (1987): 79–99.

- *A Particular Condition in Life: Self Employment and Social Mobility in Mid-Victorian Brantford, Ontario*. Kingston and Montreal: McGill-Queen's University Press 1994.

Burns, Robert J. "George Herchmer Markland." In *Dictionary of Canadian Biography*. Vol. 9. Toronto: University of Toronto Press (1976): 534–6.
– "Thomas Ridout." In *Dictionary of Canadian Biography*. Vol. 6. Toronto: University of Toronto Press (1987): 647–8.
Burroughs, Peter. "Robert Prescott." In *Dictionary of Canadian Biography*. Vol. 5. Toronto: University of Toronto Press (1983): 690–3.
– "Loyalists and Lairds: The Politics and Society of Upper Canada Reconsidered." *Journal of Imperial and Commonwealth History* 19, no.1 (1991): 70–82.
Burton, Clarence Monroe. "Business 'Adventures' of Bateau Days." *Burton Historical Collection Leaflet* 3, nos.1–2 (1923): 49–64.
– "Detroit Biographies: John Askin." *Burton Historical Collection Leaflet* 3, no.4 (1925): 1–9.
– "Detroit Biographies: John Askin." *Burton Historical Collection Leaflet* 3, no.4 (1925) 49–64.
Calloway, Colin G. "Simon Girty: Interpreter and Intermediary." In *Being and Becoming Indian: Biographical Studies of North American Frontiers*, edited by James A. Clifton, 38–58. Chicago: The Dorsey Press 1989.
Cameron, Alan and Julian Gwyn. "Archibald McNab." In *Dictionary of Canadian Biography*. Vol. 8. Toronto: University of Toronto Press (1985): 584–8.
Cameron, James M.S. "The Canada Company and Land Settlement as Resource Development in the Guelph Block." In *Perspectives on Landscape and Settlement in Nineteenth Century Ontario*, edited by J.D. Wood, 141–59. Toronto: McClelland and Stewart 1975.
– "The Place, the Office, the Times and the Men." In *The Pre-Confederation Premiers: Ontario Government Leaders, 1841–1867*, edited by J.M.S. Careless, 3–31. Toronto: University of Toronto Press 1980.
Cameron, Wendy. "Roswell Mount." In *Dictionary of Canadian Biography*. Vol. 6. Toronto: University of Toronto Press (1987): 521–23.
– "Peter Robinson." In *Dictionary of Canadian Biography*. Vol. 7. Toronto: University of Toronto Press (1988): 752–6.
Carswell, John. *From Revolution to Revolution: England 1688–1776*. London: Routledge and Kegan Paul 1973.
Carter-Edwards, Dennis. "Defending the Straits: The Military Base at Amherstburg." In *The Western District*, edited by K. Pryke and L. Kulisek, 33–41. Windsor: University of Windsor Press 1983.
– "George Ironside." In *Dictionary of Canadian Biography*. Vol. 6. Toronto: University of Toronto 1987.
– "The War of 1812 along the Detroit Frontier: A Canadian Perspective." *Michigan Historical Review* 13, no.2 (1987): 25–50.
Casgrain, Charles-Eusebe. *Mémoires de famille*. Quebec: Rivière Ouelle 1891. National Library of Canada, Ottawa. Microfiche.
Casgrain, Philippe-Baby. *Mémorial des Familles Casgrain, Baby et Perrault du Canada*. Quebec: Darveau 1898. National Library of Canada, Ottawa. Microfiche.

Caya, Marcel. "Thomas Ashton Coffin." In *Dictionary of Canadian Biography*. Vol. 5. Toronto: University of Toronto Press (1983): 192–3.

Cayton, Andrew R.L. "Noble Actors upon the Theatre of Honour: Power and Civility in the Treaty of Greenville." In *Contact Points: American Frontiers from the Mohawk Valley to the Mississippi, 1750–1830*, edited by Andrew R.L. Cayton and Frederika J. Teute, 235–69. Chapel Hill: University of North Carolina Press 1998.

Chadwick, Edward Marion. *Ontarian Families: Genealogies of United Empire Loyalist and Other Pioneer Families of Upper Canada.* 2 vols. Toronto: Rolph, Smith and Company 1895 and 1898.

Chadwick, Owen. *The Secularization of the European Mind in the 19th Century.* Cambridge, U.K.: Canto 1990.

Chalmers, Robert. *A History of Currency in the British Colonies.* London: Eyre 1893.

Chambers, Anne Lorene. "Married Women and the Law of Property in Nineteenth-Century Ontario." PHD thesis, University of Toronto, 1994.

– *Married Women and Property Law in Victorian Ontario.* Toronto: Osgoode Society for Canadian Legal History 1997.

Chambers, Robert W. "Images, Acts and Consequences: A Critical review of Historical Geography." In *Period and Place: Research Methods in Historical Geography*, edited by A.R.H. Baker and M. Billing, 197–204. Cambridge, U.K.: Cambridge University Press 1982.

Chapman, L.J. and Donald F. Putnam. "Climates of Southern Ontario." *Scientific Agriculture* 18 (1938): 401–46.

– *The Physiography of Southern Ontario.* Toronto: University of Toronto Press 1966.

Chevrette, Louis. "Pontiac." In *Dictionary of Canadian Biography*. Vol. 3. Toronto: University of Toronto Press (1974): 525–31.

Chorley, Richard J. and Peter Haggett. "Trend Surface Mapping in Geographical Research." *Transactions and Papers, Institute of British Geographers* 37 (1965): 47–67.

Christie, Carl. "Prideaux Selby." In *Dictionary of Canadian Biography*. Vol. 5. Toronto: University of Toronto Press (1983): 749–50.

– "Robert Pilkington." In *Dictionary of Canadian Biography*. Vol. 6. Toronto: University of Toronto Press (1987): 582–3.

Christie, Nancy. "In These Times of Democratic Rage and Delusion": Popular Religion and the Challenge to the Established Order, 1760–1815." In *The Canadian Protestant Experience, 1760–1990*, edited by G. Rawlyk, 9–47. Kingston and Montreal: McGill-Queen's University Press 1990.

Churchill, Winston. *A History of the English-Speaking Peoples.* 4 vols. London: Cassell 1958.

Clark, Colin. *Population Growth and Land Use.* New York: St Martin's Press 1967.

Clark, Philip J. and Francis C. Evans. "Distance to Nearest Neighbour as a Measure of Spatial Relationships in Populations." *Ecology* 35, no.4 (1954): 445–53.

Clark, Samuel Delbert. *Church and Sect in Canada.* Toronto: University of Toronto Press 1948.

- "The Backwoods Society of Upper Canada." Ch. 4 in *The Developing Canadian Community.* Toronto: University of Toronto Press 1962.

Clarke, John. "A Geographical Analysis of Colonial Settlement in the Western District of Upper Canada." PHD thesis, University of Western Ontario 1970.

- "Documentary and Map Sources for Reconstructing the History of the Reserved Lands in the Western District of Upper Canada." *Canadian Cartographer* 8, no. 2 (1971): 75–83.

- "Mapping the Lands Supervised by Colonel the Honourable Thomas Talbot in the Western District of Upper Canada, 1811–1849." *Canadian Cartographer* 8, no.1 (1971): 8–18.

- "Military, Loyalist, and Other Land Grants in the Western District, 1836." *Ontario Register* 4, no.3 (1971): 129–44.

- "Spatial Variations in Population Density, Southwestern Ontario in 1851." In *International Geography* vol. 1, edited by W.P. Adams and F. Helleiner, 408–11. Toronto: University of Toronto Press 1972.

- "Military and United Empire Loyalists in the Western District of Upper Canada in 1836." *Canadian Cartographer* 11, no.2 (1974): 186–90.

- "Land Acquisition in Essex County 1788–1900." In *The Settlement of Canada: Origins and Transfer,* edited by B.S. Osborne, 214–16. Kingston: Proceedings, British Canadian Symposium in Historical Geography, Queen's University 1975.

- "The Role of Political Position and Family and Economic Linkage in Land Speculation in the Western District of Upper Canada, 1788–1815." *Canadian Geographer* 19, no.1 (1975): 18–34.

- "Nineteenth Century Land Acquisition Slopes, Essex County, Ontario." *International Geographical '76, Historical Geography,* 43–6. Moscow: Twenty-third International Geographical Union 1976.

- "Aspects of Land Acquisition in Essex County, Ontario, 1790–1900." *Histoire Sociale/Social History* 11 (1978): 98–119.

- "Land and Law in Essex County: Malden Township and the Abstract Index of Deeds." *Histoire Sociale/Social History* 11 (1978): 475–93.

- "The Activity of an Early Canadian Land Speculator in Essex County, Ontario: Would the Real John Askin Please Stand Up?" In *Canadian Papers in Rural History* vol. 3, edited by D.H. Akenson, 84–109. Gananoque, Ont.: Langdale Press 1982.

- "François Baby (1733–1820)." In *Dictionary of Canadian Biography.* Vol. 5. Toronto: University of Toronto Press (1983): 41–6.

- "Geographical Aspects of Land Speculation in Essex County in 1825: The Strategy of Particular Individuals." In *The Western District,* edited by K. Pryke and L. Kulisek, 69–112. Windsor: University of Windsor Press 1983.

- "Thomas McKee." In *Dictionary of Canadian Biography*. Vol. 5. Toronto: University of Toronto Press (1983): 535–6.
- "François Baby (1768–1852)." In *Dictionary of Canadian Biography*. Vol. 8. Toronto: University of Toronto Press (1985): 33–5.
- "James Baby." In *Dictionary of Canadian Biography*. Vol. 6. Toronto: University of Toronto Press (1987): 21–2.
- "Sarah Ainse." In *Dictionary of Canadian Biography*. Vol. 6. Toronto: University of Toronto (1987): 7–9.
- "Mahlon Burwell." In *Dictionary of Canadian Biography*. Vol. 7. Toronto: University of Toronto Press (1988): 125–8.
- "Social Integration on the Upper Canadian Frontier: Elements of Community in Essex County, 1790–1850." *Journal of Historical Geography* 17, no. 4 (1991): 390–412.
- Clarke, John and David L. Brown. "Focii of Human Activity, Essex County, Ontario, 1825–52: Archival Sources and Research Strategies." *Archivaria* 12 (1981): 31–57.
- "Land Prices in Essex County, Ontario, 1798 to 1852." *Canadian Geographer* 26, no.4 (1982): 300–17.
- "Pricing Decisions for Ontario Land: The Farm Community and the Speculator in Essex County during the First Half of the Nineteenth Century." *Canadian Geographer* 31, no.2 (1987): 169–76.
- "The Upper Canadian Land Market: Insights from Essex County." *Canadian Historical Review* 69, no.2 (1988): 221–34.
- Clarke, John and Gregory F. Finnegan. "Colonial Survey Records and the Vegetation of Essex County, Ontario." *Journal of Historical Geography* 10, no.2 (1984): 119–38.
- Clarke, John and John Buffone. "Colonial Land Policy: The 'New System' in Upper Canada in 1825." Discussion Paper 12, Department of Geography: Carleton University 1994.
- "Social Regions in Mid-Nineteenth Century Ontario." *Histoire Sociale/Social History* 28 (1995): 193–217.
- "Manifestations of Imperial Policy: The New South Wales System and Land Prices in Upper Canada in 1825." *Canadian Geographer*, 40, no.2 (1996): 121–36.
- Clarke, John and Karl Skof. "Social Dimensions of an Ontario County 1851–52." In *Our Geographical Mosaic: Research Essays in Honour of G.C. Merrill*, edited by D.B. Knight, 107–36. Ottawa: Carleton University Press 1985.
- Clarke, John and Peter K. McLeod. "Concentrations of Scots in Rural Ontario, 1851–1901." *Canadian Cartographer* 11, no.2 (1975): 107–13.
- Clarke, John, Harry W. Taylor, and W. Robert Wightman. "Areal Patterns of Population Change in Southern Ontario 1831–1891: Core, Frontier and Intervening Space." *Ontario Geography* 12 (1978): 27–48.

Clifton, James. "Merchant, Soldier, Broker: A Corrected Obituary of Captain Billy Caldwell." *Journal of the Illinois State Historical Society* 71 (1978): 185–210.

– "Personal and Ethnic Identity on the Great Lakes Frontier: The Case of Billy Caldwell, Anglo–Canadian." *Ethnohistory* 78 (1978): 69–94.

– "The Re-emergent Wyandot: A Study in Ethnogenesis on the Detroit River Borderland, 1747." In *The Western District*, edited by K. Pryke and L. Kulisek, 1–17. Windsor: University of Windsor Press 1983.

– "Billy Caldwell." In *Dictionary of Canadian Biography*. Vol. 7. Toronto: University of Toronto Press (1988): 132–3.

Cogswell, S. "Tenure, Nativity and Age as Factors in Iowa Agriculture, 1850–1880." PHD thesis, University of Iowa 1972.

Cohen, Marjorie G. *Women's Work: Markets and Economic Development in Nineteenth-Century Ontario.* Toronto: University of Toronto 1988.

Cole, Arthur H. "Cyclical and Sectional Variations in the Sale of Public Lands, 1816–1860." *Review of Economics and Statistics* 9 (1927): 41–53.

Colthart, J.M. "Edward Ellice." In *Dictionary of Canadian Biography*. Vol. 9. Toronto: University of Toronto Press (1976): 233–9.

Conant, Thomas. *Upper Canada Sketches.* Toronto: B. Dawson 1898. National Library of Canada, Ottawa. Microfiche.

Connell, K.H. "Land and Population in Ireland." *Economic History Review* 2nd series, 2, no.3 (1950): 278–89.

Connolly, S.J. "Ulster Presbyterians: Religion, Culture, and Politics, 1660–1850." In *Ulster and North America: Transatlantic Perspectives on the Scotch-Irish*, edited by H.T. Bletchen and K.W. Woods, Jr, 24–60. Tuscaloosa and London: University of Alabama Press 1997.

Cook, Terry. "John Beverley Robinson and the Conservative Blueprint for the Upper Canadian Community." *Ontario History* 64, no.2 (1972): 79–94.

– "The Canadian Conservative Tradition: An Historical Perspective." *Journal of Canadian Studies* 8, no.4 (1973): 31–9.

Cooper, J.I. "James McGill." In *Dictionary of Canadian Biography*. Vol. 5. Toronto: University of Toronto Press (1983): 527–30.

Cowan, Helen. *British Emigration to North America: The First Hundred Years.* Toronto: University of Toronto Press 1961.

Cowan, Hugh. *Detroit River District.* Toronto: Algonquin Historical Society of Canada 1929.

Craig, Gerald M. "The American Impact on the Upper Canadian Reform Movement before 1837." *Canadian Historical Review*, 29, no.4 (1948): 333–52.

– *Lord Durham's Report: An Abridgement.* Ottawa. Carleton University Press 1982.

– *Upper Canada: The Formative Years, 1784–1841.* Toronto: McClelland and Stewart 1963.

– ed. *Lord Durham's Report: An Abridgement of Report on the Affairs of British North America.* Repr., Toronto: Carleton Library Series and McClelland and Stewart 1966.

– "Marshall Spring Bidwell." In *Dictionary of Canadian Biography.* Vol. 10. Toronto: University of Toronto Press (1972): 60–4.

– "John Rolph." In *Dictionary of Canadian Biography.* Vol. 9. Toronto: University of Toronto Press (1976): 683–90.

– "John Strachan." In *Dictionary of Canadian Biography.* Vol. 9. Toronto: University of Toronto Press (1976): 751–66.

Creighton, Donald. *The Empire of the St. Lawrence.* Boston: Mifflin 1956.

– *Dominion of the North: A History of Canada.* Toronto: MacMillan 1962.

– *John A. MacDonald.* 2 vols. Toronto: Macmillan 1965.

Crone, Patricia. *Pre-Industrial Societies.* Oxford, U.K.: Blackwell 1989.

Cross, Michael S. "The Age of Gentility: The Formation of an Aristocracy in the Ottawa Valley." *Annual Report of the Canadian Historical Association* (1967): 105–17.

Cross, Michael S. and Robert L. Fraser. "Robert Baldwin." In *Dictionary of Canadian Biography.* Vol. 8. Toronto: University of Toronto Press (1985): 45–59.

Cruikshank, Ernest Alexander. *The Correspondence of Lieut. Governor John Graves Simcoe.* 5 vols. Toronto: Ontario Historical Society 1923–31.

Cruikshank, E.A. and A.F. Hunter. *The Correspondence of the Honourable Peter Russell.* 3 vols. Toronto: Ontario Historical Society 1932–36.

Curti, Merle Eugene. *The Making of an American Community: A Case Study of Democracy in a Frontier County.* Stanford, Calif.; Stanford University Press 1959.

Daniels, Bruce C. "Diversity and Democracy: Officeholding Patterns among Selectmen in Eighteenth-Century Connecticut." In *Power and Status: Office Holding in Colonial America,* edited by B.C. Daniels, 36–52. Middleton, Conn.: Wesleyan University Press 1986.

Darroch, Gordon. "Migrants in the Nineteenth-Century: Fugitives or Families in Motion?" *Journal of Family History* 6 (1981): 257–77.

– "Occupational Structure, Assessed Wealth, and Homeowning during Toronto's Early Industrialization, 1861–1899." *Labour/Le Travailleur* 11 (spring 1983): 31–61.

– "Half Empty or Half Full: Images or Interpretations in the Historical Analysis of the Catholic Irish in Nineteenth-Century Canada." *Canadian Ethnic Studies* 25, no. 1 (1993): 1–8.

Darroch, Gordon and Michael Ornstein. "Ethnicity and Occupational Structures in Canada in 1871: The Vertical Mosaic in Historical Perspective," *Canadian Historical Review* 61, no.3 (1980): 305–33.

– "Ethnicity and Class, Transitions over a Decade: Ontario, 1861–1871." *Canadian Historical Association, Historical Papers* (1984): 111–37.

Darroch, Gordon and Leo Soltow. *Property and Inequality in Victorian Toronto: Structural Patterns and Cultural Communities in the 1871 Census.* Toronto: University of Toronto Press 1994.

Davis, Lance E. and Robert A. Huttenback. *Mammon and the Pursuit of Empire: the Political Economy of British Imperialism 1860–1912.* Cambridge, U.K.: Cambridge University Press 1986.

Davis, Ralph. *The Rise of the Atlantic Economies.* Ithaca, N.Y.: Cornell University Press 1973.

Dean, Wiiliam J., ed. *Economic Atlas of Ontario.* Toronto: University of Toronto Press 1969.

Deane, Phyllis and William A. Cole. *British Economic Growth 1688–1959: Trends and Structure.* Cambridge, U.K.: Cambridge University Press 1969.

Demos, John. *A Little Commonwealth: Family Life in Plymouth Colony.* New York: Oxford University Press 1970.

Denissen, Christian. *Genealogy of the French Families of the Detroit River Region, 1701–1911.* 2 vols. Edited by H.F. Powell. Detroit: Society for Genealogical Research 1976.

DePeyster, Arent Schuyler. *Miscellanies by an Officer* ... Dumfries, Scotland: Munro 1813. National Library of Canada. Microfiche.

Désilets Andrée. "George Benson Hall." In *Dictionary of Canadian Biography.* Vol. 10. Toronto: University of Toronto Press (1972): 329–30.

Deslauriers, Peter. "Samuel Gerrard." In *Dictionary of Canadian Biography.* Vol. 8. Toronto: University of Toronto Press (1985): 320–2.

Di Matteo, Livio and Peter George. "Canadian Wealth Inequality in the Late Nineteenth Century: A Study of Wentworth County, 1872–1902," *Canadian Historical Review* 73, no.4 (1992): 453–83.

Dickason, Olive Patricia. *Canada's First Nations: A History of Founding Peoples from Earliest Times.* Toronto: McClelland and Stewart 1992.

Dickinson, Harry T. *Liberty and Property: Political Ideology in Eighteenth-Century Britain.* London: Weidenfeld and Nicolson 1977.

Dictionary of Canadian Biography (in collaboration). "Peter Hunter." Vol. 5. Toronto: University of Toronto Press (1983): 439–43.

– "William Allen." Vol. 8. Toronto: University of Toronto Press (1985): 4–12.

Dogan, Mattei and Stein Rokkan, eds. *Quantitative Ecological Analysis in the Social Sciences.* Cambridge, Mass.: MIT Press 1969.

Douglas, R. Alan. "John Prince." In *Dictionary of Canadian Biography.* Vol. 9. Toronto: University of Toronto Press (1976): 643–7.

– ed. *John Prince 1796–1870: A Collection of Documents.* Toronto: University of Toronto Press 1980.

– ed. *A Sketch of the Western District of Upper Canada being the Southern Extremity of that Interesting Province by William McCormick.* Windsor: Essex County Historical Association and University of Windsor Press 1980.

– "Charles Reaume." In *Dictionary of Canadian Biography*. Vol. 5. Toronto: University of Toronto Press (1983): 710–11.

Duffy, Dennis. *Gardens, Covenants, Exiles: Loyalism in the Literature of Upper Canada*. Toronto: University of Toronto Press 1982.

Duncan, John Lindsay. "The Prominent Factors Contributing To Original Settlement of Drummond Township, Ontario." Geography BA thesis, Carleton University 1987.

Dunham, Aileen. *Political Unrest in Upper Canada, 1815–1836*. Toronto: McClelland and Stewart Ltd 1963.

Earl, David W.L., ed. *The Family Compact: Aristocracy or Oligarchy?*. Toronto: Copp Clark Publishing 1967.

Easterlin, Richard A. "The American Population." In *American Economic Growth: An Economist's History of the United States*, edited by L.E. Davis, 121–83. New York: Harper and Row 1972.

Eccleshall, Robert. *English Conservatism since the Restoration: An Introduction and Anthology*. London: Unwin 1990.

Edwards, Ron. "Patrick McNiff." In *Dictionary of Canadian Biography*. Vol. 5. Toronto: University of Toronto Press (1983): 551–3.

Elliott, Bruce S. *Irish Migrants in the Canadas: A New Approach*. Kingston and Montreal: McGill-Queen's University Press 1988.

Elliott, Bruce S., Dan Walker, and Fawne Stratford-Devai. *Men of Upper Canada – Militia Nominal Rolls 1828–29*. Toronto: Ontario Genealogical Society 1995.

Ely, R.T. "Land Speculation." *Journal of Farm Economics* 2, no.3 (1920): 121–35.

Embree, Ainslee T. "Landholding in Indian and British Institutions." In *Land Control and Social Structure in Indian History*, edited by R.E. Frykenberg, 33–52. Madison: University of Wisconsin Press 1969.

Ennals, Peter. "Land and Society in Hamilton Township 1797–1861." Ph.D. diss., University of Toronto, 1978.

Ermatinger, Charles Oakes. *The Talbot Regime*. St Thomas, Ont.: *Municipal World* 1904.

Errington, Jane. *The Lion, the Eagle, and Upper Canada: A Developing Colonial Ideology*. Kingston and Montreal: McGill-Queen's University Press 1987.

– "Thomas Markland." In *Dictionary of Canadian Biography*. Vol. 7. Toronto: University of Toronto Press (1988): 583–5.

– *Wives and Mothers, School Mistresses and Scullery Maids: Working Women in Upper Canada 1790–1840*. Kingston and Montreal: McGill-Queen's University Press 1995.

Errington, Jane and George Rawlyk. "The Loyalist-Federalist Alliance of Upper Canada." *American Review of Canadian Studies* 14, no.2 (1984): 157–76.

Ewart, Alison and Julia Jarvis. "Personnel of the Family Compact." *Canadian Historical Review* 7 (1926): 209–21.

Fahey, Curtis. "Benedict Arnold." In *Dictionary of Canadian Biography*. Vol. 5. Toronto: University of Toronto Press (1983): 28–36.

– *In His Name: The Anglican Experience in Upper Canada, 1791–1854*. Ottawa: Carleton University Press 1991.

Farrell, Betty G. *Elite Families: Class and Power in Nineteenth Century Boston*. Albany: State University of New York Press 1993.

Farrell, David R. "Detroit, 1783–1796: the Last Stages of the British Fur trade in the Old Northwest." PHD thesis, University of Western Ontario, 1968.

– "Settlement along the Detroit Frontier, 1760–1796." *Michigan History* 52 (1968): 91–106.

– "John Askin." In *Dictionary of Canadian Biography*. Vol. 5. Toronto: University of Toronto Press (1983): 37–9.

– "Walter Roe." In *Dictionary of Canadian Biography*. Vol. 5. Toronto: University of Toronto Press (1983): 721–2.

Fenton, William Nelson. *The Great Law and the Longhouse: A Political History of the Iroquois Confederacy*. Norman: University of Oklahoma Press 1998.

Finley, Robert W. "The Original Forest Cover of Wisconsin." PHD thesis, University of Wisconsin 1951.

Finnegan, Gregory. "Cognizance of Land Quality: Surveyor, Speculator and Settler in Fitzroy Township, Ontario 1822–1861." MA thesis, Carleton University, 1984.

Firth, Edith G. "The Administration of Peter Russell, 1796–1799." *Ontario History* 48, no.4 (1956) 163–81.

– "Peter Russell." In *Dictionary of Canadian Biography*. Vol. 5. Toronto: University of Toronto Press (1983): 729–32.

– "John Elmsley." In *Dictionary of Canadian Biography*. Vol. 5. Toronto: University of Toronto Press (1983): 303–4.

Fisk, John. *The American Revolution*. 2 vols. New York: Houghton, Mifflin 1891.

Forrest, J. "Locating the Vegetation of Early Coastal Otago: A Map and its Sources." *Transactions of the Royal Society of New Zealand* 2 (1963): 49–58.

Forster, B. "Finding the Right Size: Markets and Competition in Mid- and Late Nineteenth-Century Ontario." In *Patterns of the Past: Interpreting Ontario's History*, edited by R. Hall, W. Westfall, and L.S. MacDowell, 150–73. Toronto: Dundurn Press 1988.

Fowke, Vernon Clifford. *Canadian Agricultural Policy*. Toronto: University of Toronto Press 1946.

Fox, W.S. and J.H. Soper. "The Distribution of Some Trees and Shrubs of the Carolinian Zone of Southern Ontario." Part 1 in *Transactions of the Royal Canadian Institute* 29 (1952): 65–84.

– "The Distribution of Some Trees and Shrubs of the Carolinian Zone of Southern Ontario." Part 2 in *Transactions of the Royal Canadian Institute* 30 (1953): 3–32.

- "The Distribution of Some Trees and Shrubs of the Carolinian Zone of Southern Ontario." Part 3 in *Transactions of the Royal Canadian Institute* 30 (1953): 99–128.

Fraser, Alexander, ed. *Seventeenth Report of the Department of Public Records and Archives of Ontario 1928.* Toronto: King's Printer 1929.

Fraser, Robert L. "Like Eden in Her Summer Dress: Gentry, Economy and Society: Upper Canada 1812–1840." PHD thesis, University of Toronto 1979.

- "John Macaulay." In *Dictionary of Canadian Biography.* Vol. 8. Toronto: University of Toronto Press (1985): 513–22.
- "Christopher Alexander Hagerman." In *Dictionary of Canadian Biography.* Vol. 7. Toronto: University of Toronto Press (1988): 365–72.
- "George Hillier." In *Dictionary of Canadian Biography.* Vol. 7. Toronto: University of Toronto (1988): 409–11.
- "John Mills Jackson." In *Dictionary of Canadian Biography.* Vol. 7. Toronto: University of Toronto Press (1988): 438–40.
- "William Warren Baldwin." In *Dictionary of Canadian Biography.* Vol. 7. Toronto: University of Toronto Press (1988): 35–44.
- "'All the Privileges which Englishmen Possess': Order, Rights, and Constitutionalism in Upper Canada." Ch. 1 of *Provincial Justice.* Toronto: University of Toronto Press 1992.

French, Goldwin S. *Parsons and Politics: The Role of Wesleyan Methodists in Upper Canada and the Maritimes from 1780 to 1855.* Toronto: Ryerson Press 1962.

Frost, Stanley B. *James McGill of Montreal.* Kingston and Montreal: McGill-Queen's University Press 1995.

Gaffield, Chad. *Language, Schooling and Cultural Conflict: The Origins of the French-Language Controversy in Ontario.* Kingston and Montreal: McGill-Queen's University Press 1987.

- "Children, Schooling, and Family Reproduction in Nineteenth Century Ontario." *Canadian Historical Review* 72, no.2 (1991): 157–91.

Gagan, David. "Enumerator's Instructions for the Census of Canada 1852 and 1861." *Histoire Sociale/Social History* 7 (1974): 355–65.

- "The Security of Land: Mortgaging in Toronto Gore Township 1835–95." In *Aspects of Nineteenth Century Ontario,* edited by F.H. Armstrong, H.A. Stevenson, and J.D. Wilson, 135–53. Toronto: University of Toronto Press 1974.
- "Geographical and Social Mobility in Nineteenth-Century Ontario: A Microstudy." *Canadian Review of Sociology and Anthropology* 13, no.2 (1976): 152–64.
- "The Indivisibility of Land: A Microanalysis of the System of Inheritance in Nineteenth-Century Ontario." *Journal of Economic History,* 36, no.1 (1976): 126–41.
- "'The Prose of Life': Literary Reflections of the Family, Individual Experience and Social Structure in Nineteenth-Century Canada." *Journal of Social History* 9, no.3 (1976): 367–81.

- "Land, Population and Social Change: The 'Critical Years' in Rural Canada West." *Canadian Historical Review,* 59, no.3 (1978): 293–318.
- "Property and Interest: Some Preliminary Evidence of Land Speculation by the Family Compact in Upper Canada 1820–1840." *Ontario History* 70, no.1 (1978): 63–70.
- *Hopeful Travellers: Families, Land and Social Change in Mid-Victorian Peel County, Canada West.* Toronto: University of Toronto Press 1981.
- "Class and Society in Victorian English Canada: An Historiographical Reassessment." *British Journal of Canadian Studies* 4, no.1 (1989): 74–87.
Gagan, David and Herbert Mays, "Historical Demography and Canadian Social History: Families and Land in Peel County, Ontario." *Canadian Historical Review* 54, no.1 (1973): 27–47.
Gagan, David and H.E. Turner. "Social History in Canada: A Report on the 'State of the Art.'" *Archivaria* 14 (summer 1982): 27–52.
Galbraith, John K. *The Age of Uncertainty.* Boston: Houghton 1977.
Garland, M.A. and J.J. Talman. "Pioneer Drinking Habits and the Rise of the Temperance Agitation in Upper Canada prior to 1840." In *Aspects of Nineteenth-Century Ontario,* edited by F.H. Armstrong, H.A. Stevenson, and J.D. Wilson, 171–93. Toronto: University of Toronto Press 1974.
Gates, Lillian F. "The Heir and Devisee Commission of Upper Canada, 1797–1805." *Canadian Historical Review* 38 (1957): 21–36.
- *Land Policies of Upper Canada.* Toronto: University of Toronto Press 1968.
- *After the Rebellion: The later Years of William Lyon Mackenzie.* Toronto: Dundurn Press 1988.
Gates, Paul W. "The Role of the Land Speculator in Western Development." *Pennsylvania Magazine of History and Biography* 66 (1942): 314–33.
- *Landlords and Tenants on the Prairie Frontier: Studies in American Land Policy.* Ithaca, N.Y.: Cornell University Press 1973.
Gentilcore, R. Louis. "The Beginnings of Settlement in the Niagara Peninsula, 1782–1792." *The Canadian Geographer* 7, no.1 (1963): 72–82.
- "Lines on the Land: Crown Surveys and Settlement in Upper Canada." *Ontario History* 61, no.2 (1969): 57–73.
- "Change in Settlement in Ontario 1800–1850: a Correlation Analysis of Historical Source Materials." In *International Geography* vol. 1, edited by W.P. Adams and F. Helleiner, 418–19. Toronto: University of Toronto Press 1972.
- "Settlement." In *Ontario: Studies in Canadian Geography,* edited by R.L. Gentilcore, 23–44. Toronto: University of Toronto Press 1972.
- "Ontario Emerges from The Trees." *The Geographical Magazine* 45, no. 5 (1973): 383–91.
- "The Making of a Province: Ontario to 1850." *American Review of Canadian Studies* 14, no.2 (1984): 137–55.
- *Historical Atlas of Canada: The Land Transformed.* Toronto: University of Toronto Press 1993.

Gentilcore, R. Louis and J. David Wood. "A Military Colony in The Wilderness." In *Perspectives on Landscape and Settlement in Nineteenth Century Ontario*, edited by J.D. Wood, 32–50. Toronto: University of Toronto Press 1975.

Gentilcore, R. Louis and M. Kate Donkin. *Land Surveys of Southern Ontario: An Introduction and Index to the Field Notebooks of the Ontario Land Surveyors, 1784–1859*. Toronto: Cartographica Monograph, 8 1973.

Gilmour, James. *Spatial Evolution of Manufacturing: Southern Ontario, 1851–1891*. Toronto: University of Toronto 1972.

Glazebrook, George Parkin de Twenebroker. *A History of Transportation in Canada*. Toronto: Ryerson Press 1938.

Godfrey, Sheldon J. and Judy C Godfrey. *Search Out the Land; The Jews and the Growth of Equality in British Colonial America 1740–1867*. Kingston and Montreal: McGill-Queen's University Press 1995.

Goheen, Peter. *Victorian Toronto, 1850–1900*. Chicago: University of Chicago Press 1970.

Goldring, Philip. "James Leith." In *Dictionary of Canadian Biography*. Vol. 7. Toronto: University of Toronto Press (1988): 498–9.

Goltz Jr, H.C.W. "The Indian Revival: Religion and the Western District." In *The Western District*, edited by K. Pryke and L. Kulisek, 18–41. Windsor: University of Windsor Press 1983.

Goode, William Josiah. *World Revolution and Family Patterns*. New York: Free Press of Glencoe 1963.

Goodwin, Craufurd D.W. *Canadian Economic Thought: The Political Economy of a Developing Nation 1814–1914*. Durham, N.C.: Duke University Press 1961.

Gordanier, Deborah Ann. "The Settlement of Augusta Township, Upper Canada." MA thesis, Carleton University 1982.

Gorrie, Peter. "The Enchanted Woodland." *Canadian Geographic* 114, no.2 (1994): 32–42.

Goulet, Louis. "Phases of the Sally Ainse Dispute." *Kent Historical Society, Papers and Addresses* 5 (1921): 92–5.

Gourlay, Robert. *A Statistical Account of Upper Canada*. 2 vols. London: Simpkin and Marshall 1822. National Library of Canada, Ottawa. Microfiche.

Government of Canada. *Indian Treaties and Surrenders from 1680 to 1890*. 3 vols. Ottawa: Queen's Printer 1891–1912. Repr., Toronto: Coles 1971.

Grant, John Webster. *A Profusion of Spires: Religion in Nineteenth-Century Ontario*. Toronto: University of Toronto Press 1988.

Greven, Philip J. *Four Generations: Population, Land, and Family in Colonial Andover, Massachusetts*. Ithaca, N.Y.: Cornell University Press 1970.

Gray, Edward C. and Barry E. Prentice, "Trends in the Price of Farm Real Estate in Central Wellington County (Ontario) since 1836," School of Agricultural Economics and Extension Division, University of Guelph, AEE/82/1, January 1982.

- "Factors Affecting Farm Real Estate Prices in Central Wellington County (Ontario)," School of Agricultural Economics and Extension Education, University of Guelph, AEEE/82/6, May 1982, 1–56.
- "Exploring the Price of Farmland in Two Ontario Localities since Letters Patenting." In *Canadian Papers in Rural History*, vol. 4, edited by D.H. Akenson, 226–39. Gananoque, Ont.: Langdale Press 1984.
- Gray, Lewis C. "Land Speculation." In *Encyclopaedia of the Social Sciences*, edited by E.R.A. Seligman and A.S. Saunders, vol. 9, 64–69. 12th ed. New York: Macmillan 1957.
- Greenwood, Charles T. *The Seigneurial System in Early French Canada and the Detroit River Region*. Windsor, Ont.: The Essex-Kent Regional Tourist Council 1963.
- Greenwood, F. Murray. *Legacies of Fear: Law and Politics in Quebec in the Era of the French Revolution*. Toronto: University of Toronto Press 1993.
- Greenwood, F. Murray and James H. Lambert. "Jonathan Sewell." In *Dictionary of Canadian Biography*. Vol. 7. Toronto: University of Toronto Press (1988): 782–92.
- Greer, Allan. *Peasant, Lord, and Merchant: Rural Society in Three Quebec Parishes 1740–1840*. Toronto: University of Toronto Press 1985.
- Griliches, Z. "Hybrid Corn: An Exploration in the Economics of Technological Change." *Econometrica* 25, no.4 (1957): 501–22.
- Guillet, Edwin C. *Pioneer Travels in Upper Canada*. Toronto: University of Toronto Press 1966.
- Gundy, H. Pearson. "The Family Compact at Work: The Second Heir and Devisee Commission of Upper Canada, 1805–1841." *Ontario History* 66, no. 3 (1974): 129–146.
- Gunn, John A.W. *Beyond Liberty and Property: The Process of Self-Recognition in Eighteenth-Century Political Thought*. Kingston and Montreal: McGill-Queen's University Press 1983.
- Gupta, Shiv Dayal. "Land Markets in the North West Provinces in the First Half of the Nineteenth Century." *Indian Economic Review* 4, no. 2 (1958): 51–70.
- Agrarian Relations and Early British Rule in India. New York: Asia Publishing House 1963.
- Gwyn, Julian. "Sir William Johnson." In *Dictionary of Canadian Biography*. Vol. 4. Toronto: University of Toronto Press (1979): 394–8.
- Habakkuk, H. John. "Family Structure and Economic Change in Nineteenth-Century Europe." *Journal of Economic History* 15 (1955): 1–12.
- Haeger, John D. *John Jacob Astor, Business and Finance in the Early Republic*. Detroit: Wayne State University Press 1991.
- Hall, Roger D. "The Canada Company, 1826–1843." PHD thesis, Cambridge University 1973.
- Hamil, F. Coyne. "Sally Ainse, Fur Trader." *Algonquin Club, Historical Bulletin* 3 (1939): 1–26.

- Early Shipping and Land Transportation on the Lower Thames." *Ontario History* 34 (1942): 46–62.
- "The Detroit River French." *Western Ontario Historical Notes* 3, no.2 (1945): 27–30.
- "Col. Talbot and Early History of London." *Ontario History* 43, no.4 (1951): 159–75.
- *The Valley of the Lower Thames, 1640–1850*. Toronto: University of Toronto 1951.
- "Colonel Talbot's Principality." *Ontario History* 44, no.4 (1952): 183–93.
- *Lake Erie Baron*. Toronto: Macmillan 1955.
- "The Reform Movement in Upper Canada." In *Profiles of a Province: Studies in the History of Ontario*, edited by G. Firth, 9–19. Toronto: Ontario Historical Society 1967.

Hannon, Sally. "Land Acquisition and Speculation." Unpublished paper, Department of Geography: Carleton University 1974.

Harring, Sidney L. *White Man's Law: Native People in Nineteenth-Century Canadian Jurisprudence*. Toronto: University of Toronto Press 1998.

Harris, Ian, ed. *Burke: Pre-Revolutionary Writings*. Cambridge, U.K.: Cambridge University Press 1993.

Harris, R. Cole. "The Simplification of Europe Overseas." *Annals of the Association of American Geographers* 67, no.4 (1977): 469–83.

- "Power, Modernity and Historical Geography." *Annals of the Association of American Geographers* 81, no.4 (1991): 671–83.

Hartz, Louis. *The Founding of New Societies: Studies in the History of the United States, Latin America, South Africa, Canada and Australia*. New York: Harcourt 1964.

Harwood, F.N., ed. *The Township of Sandwich: Past and Present*. Repr., Windsor, Ont.: Essex County Historical Association and the Windsor Public Library Board 1979.

Hayward, Robert J. "John Collins." In *Dictionary of Canadian Biography*. Vol. 4. Toronto: University of Toronto Press (1979): 161–2.

Hazeltine, Harold Dexter. "The Gage of Land in Medieval England." *Harvard Law Review* 18, no.1 (1904): 36–50.

Headon, Charles. "The Discreet and Good Richard Pollard: The Problems of a Clergyman and Office-Holder." In *The Western District*, edited by K. Pryke and L. Kulisek, 160–7. Windsor, Ont.: University of Windsor Press 1983.

- "Richard Pollard." In *Dictionary of Canadian Biography*. Vol. 6. Toronto: University of Toronto Press (1987): 599–602.

Hearnshaw, Fossey John Cobb. "Edmund Burke." In *The Social and Political Ideas of Some Representative Thinkers of the Revolutionary Era*, edited by F.J.C. Hearnshaw, 72–99. New York: Barnes and Noble 1967.

- *The Social and Political Ideas of Some Representative Thinkers of the Revolutionary Era*. New York: Barnes and Noble 1931.

Heidenreich, Conrad E. "A Procedure for Mapping the Vegetation of Northern Simcoe County from the Ontario Land Survey." Appendix, *Land Surveys of Southern Ontario: An Introduction and Index to the Field Notebooks of the Ontario Land Surveyors, 1784–1859*, 103–13. Toronto: Cartographica Monograph 8, 1973.

Henderson, John L.H, ed. *John Strachan: Documents and Opinions: A Selection.* Toronto: McClelland and Stewart 1969.

Herniman, Charles. "The Development of Artificial Drainage Systems in Kent and Essex Counties, Ontario" *Ontario Geography* 2 (1968): 13–24.

Héroux, André. "Sir John Caldwell." In *Dictionary of Canadian Biography.* Vol. 7. Toronto: University of Toronto Press (1988): 133–6.

Hill, Christopher. *The World Turned Upside Down: Radical Ideas during the English Revolution.* London: Penguin 1975.

– *A Nation of Change and Novelty: Radical Politics, Religion and Literature in Seventeenth-Century England.* London: Routledge 1990.

Historical Collections and Researches Made by the Pioneer and Historical Society of the State of Michigan. Vol. 12. (Lansing, Mich.: Thorp and Godfrey 1888); vol. 14 (Lansing, Mich.: Darius and Thorp 1890); vol. 20 (Lansing, Mich.: Robert Smith 1892); vol. 24 (Lansing, Mich.: Robert Smith 1895).

Hoberg, Walter R. "Early History of Colonel Alexander McKee." *Pennsylvania Magazine of History and Biography* 58 (1934): 26–36.

– "A Tory in the NorthWest." *Pennsylvania Magazine of History and Biography* 59 (1935): 32–41.

Hobsbawm, Eric J. *The Age of Revolution, 1789–1848.* Cleveland: World Publishing 1962.

– *The Age of Capital, 1848–1875.* London: Sphere 1975.

Hodgins, Bruce W. "Archibald McLean." In *Dictionary of Canadian Biography.* Vol. 9. Toronto: University of Toronto Press (1976): 512–13.

Hoffer, P.F. *Law and People in Colonial America.* Baltimore and London: Johns Hopkins Press 1998.

Hofstra, W.R. "Land, Ethnicity, and Community at the Opequon Settlement, Virginia, 1730–1800." In *Ulster and North America: Transatlantic Perspectives on the Scotch-Irish,* edited by H.T. Bletchen and K.W. Woods, Jr, 167–88. Tuscaloosa and London: University of Alabama Press 1997.

Hogan, J. Sheridan. *Canada: An Essay.* Montreal: Briggs 1855. National Library of Canada, Ottawa. Microfiche.

Holtgrieve, Donald G. "Land Speculation and Other Processes in American Historical Geography." *Journal of Geography* 75, no.1 (1976): 53–64.

Homer, Sidney. *A History of Interest Rates.* 2nd. ed. New Brunswick, N.J.: Rutgers University Press 1963.

Horowitz, Gad. "Conservatism, Liberalism and Socialism in Canada: An Interpretation." *Canadian Journal of Economics and Political Science* 32 (1966): 143–71.

Horsman, Reginald. "British Indian Policy in the Northwest, 1807–1812." *Mississippi Valley Historical Review* 45, no. 1 (1958): 51–66.

- "American Indian Policy in the Old Northwest, 1785–1812." *William and Mary Quarterly* 18 (1961) 35–53.
- "The British Indian Department and the Abortive Treaty of Lower Sandusky, 1793." *Ohio Historical Quarterly* 70, no.3 (1961): 189–213.
- "The British Indian Department and the Resistance to General Anthony Wayne, 1793–1795." *Mississippi Valley Historical Review* 49, no.2 (1962): 269–90.
- *Matthew Elliott, British Indian Agent.* Detroit: Wayne State University 1964.
- *Expansion and American Indian Policy, 1783–1812.* Norman: State University of Oklahoma Press 1967.
- *The Frontier in the Formative Years, 1783–1815.* New York: Holt, Rinehardt and Winston 1970.
- "Alexander McKee." In *Dictionary of Canadian Biography.* Vol. 4. Toronto: University of Toronto Press (1979): 301–3.
- "Egushwa." In *Dictionary of Canadian Biography.* Vol. 4. Toronto: University of Toronto Press (1979): 260–1.
- "Matthew Elliott." In *Dictionary of Canadian Biography.* Vol. 5. Toronto: University of Toronto Press (1983): 499–500.
Hoskins, R.G. "Angus Mackintosh, the Baron of Moy Hall." In *The Western District*, edited by K. Pryke and L. Kulisek, 146–59. Windsor, Ont.: University of Windsor Press 1983.
- "Angus Mackintosh of Mackintosh." In *Dictionary of Canadian Biography.* Vol. 6. Toronto: University of Toronto Press (1987): 473.
Houston, Susan E. and Alison Prentice. *Schooling and Scholars in Nineteenth-Century Ontario.* Toronto: University of Toronto Press 1988.
Howes, David. "Property, God and Nature in the Thought of Sir John Beverley Robinson." *McGill Law Journal* 30 (1985): 365–414.
Hume, David. *Treatise of Human Nature: An Attempt to Introduce the Experimental Method of Reasoning into Moral Subjects,* 2 vols. London: Longmans 1874.
Innis, Harold A. "An Introduction to the Economic History of Ontario from Outpost to Empire." *Papers and Records of the Ontario Historical Society* 30 (1934): 111–23.
- *The Fur Trade in Canada: An Introduction to Canadian Economic History.* Toronto: University of Toronto Press 1970.
Jacobs, Dean. "Indian Land Surrenders." In *The Western District*, edited by K. Pryke and L. Kulisek, 61–8. Windsor, Ont.: University of Windsor Press 1983.
Jackson, W.A. Douglas. "The Regressive Effect of Late Eighteenth Century British Colonial Policy on Land Development along the Upper St. Lawrence River." *Annals of the Association of American Geographers* 45, no.3 (1955): 258–68.
Jeans, Dennis N. *An Historical Geography of New South Wales to 1901.* Sydney: Reed Education 1972.

Jennings, Francis. *Empire of Fortune: Crowns, Colonies and Tribes in the Seven's Year War in America.* New York: Norton 1988.

Johnson, Hildegard Binder. *Order upon the Land: The US Rectangular Land Survey and the Upper Mississippi Country.* Toronto: Oxford University Press 1976 .

Johnson, J. Keith, ed. *Letters of Sir John A. Macdonald.* 2 vols. Ottawa: Public Archives of Canada 1968 and 1969.

– "John A. MacDonald and the Kingston Business Community." In *To Preserve and Defend: Essays on Kingston in the Nineteenth Century*, edited by G. Tulchinsky, 141–55. Kingston and Montreal: McGill-Queen's University Press 1976.

– *Becoming Prominent: Regional Leadership in Upper Canada, 1798–1841.* Kingston and Montreal: McGill-Queen's University Press 1989.

– "Land Policy and the Upper Canadian Elite Reconsidered: The Canada Emigration Association, 1840–1841." In *Old Ontario: Essays in Honour of J.M.S. Careless*, edited by D. Keane, C. Read, and F.H. Armstrong, 217–32. Toronto: Dundurn Press 1990.

Johnson, J. Keith and Peter B. Waite. "Sir John Alexander MacDonald." In *Dictionary of Canadian Biography*. Vol. 12. Toronto: University of Toronto Press (1990): 591–613.

Johnson, Leo A. "Land Policy, Population Growth, and Social Structure in the Home District, 1793–1851." *Ontario History* 63, no.1 (1971): 41–60.

– "Andrew Norton Buell." In *Dictionary of Canadian Biography*. Vol. 10. Toronto: University of Toronto Press (1972): 109–10.

– *History of the County of Ontario, 1615–1875.* Whitby: Ontario County Council 1973.

– "The Settlement of Western District." In *Aspects of Nineteenth Century Ontario*, edited by F.H. Armstrong, H.A. Stevenson and J.D. Wilson, 19–35. Toronto: University of Toronto Press 1974.

– "The State of Agricultural Development in the Western District to 1851." In *The Western District*, edited by K. Pryke and L. Kulisek, 113–45. Windsor, Ont.: University of Windsor Press 1983.

– "The Mississauga-Lake Ontario Land Surrender of 1805" *Ontario History* 83, no.3 (1990): 233–53.

Johnston, W.B. "Locating the Vegetation of Early Canterbury: A Map and the Sources." *Transactions of the Royal Society of New Zealand* 2 (1961): 6–15.

Jones, Elwood H. "Charles Burton Wyatt." In *Dictionary of Canadian Biography*. Vol. 7. University of Toronto Press (1988): 929–30.

Jones, Robert L. *History of Agriculture in Ontario, 1613–1880.* Toronto: University of Toronto Press 1946.

Karr, Clarence. "The Foundation of the Canada Company 1823–1843." MA thesis, University of Western Ontario 1966.

– *Canada Land Company: The Early Years.* Toronto: Ontario Historical Society 1974.

Katz, Michael B. *The People of Hamilton, Canada West: Family and Class in a Mid-Nineteenth-Century City.* Cambridge, Mass.: Harvard University Press 1975.

Kealey, Gregory S. "Labour and Working Class History in Canada: Prospects for the 1980s." *Labour/Le Travailleur* 7 (spring 1981): 67–94.

Keane, John. *Tom Paine: A Political Life.* Toronto: Little, Brown 1995.

Kelly, Kenneth. "The Agricultural Geography of Simcoe County, 1820–1880." PHD thesis, University of Toronto 1968.

– "The Evaluation of Land for Wheat Cultivation in Early Nineteenth Century Ontario." *Ontario History* 62, no.1 (1970): 57–64.

– "The Changing Attitude of Farmers to Forest in Nineteenth Century Ontario." *Ontario Geography* 8 (1974): 64–77.

– "Practical Knowledge of Physical Geography in Southern Ontario during the Nineteenth Century." In *Physical Geography: The Canadian Context*, edited by A. Falconer, B.A. Fahey, and R.D. Thompson, 10–17. Toronto: McGraw-Hill Ryerson 1974.

– "The Artificial Drainage of Land in Nineteenth Century Southern Ontario." *Canadian Geographer* 19 (1975): 279–98.

Kelsay, Isabella Thompson. *Joseph Brant 1743–1803: Man of Two Worlds.* Syracuse, N.Y.: Syracuse University Press 1984.

Kennedy, James R. "Landowners and Mortgaging in Marlborough Township, 1841–1880." Unpublished paper, Department of History: Carleton University 1981.

– *South Elmsley in the Making 1783–1983.* Lombardy, Ont.: Corporation of the Township of South Elmsley 1984.

Kennedy, Patricia. "Records of the Immigration Process in the Pre-Confederation Era." *Families* 16, no.4, (1977): 187–92.

– "Records of the Land Settlement Process in the Pre-Confederation Era." *Families*, 16, no.4 (1977): 193–8.

Kimball, Leroy Elwood. "The Smiths of Haverstraw: Some Notes on a Highland Family." *New York History* no.17, 4 (1935): 392–404.

King, Leslie J. *Statistical Analysis in Geography.* Englewood Cliffs, N.J.: Prentice Hall 1969.

Knowles, Norman. *Inventing the Loyalists: The Ontario Loyalist Tradition and the Creation of Usable Pasts.* Toronto: University of Toronto Press 1997.

Koebner, Richard. "The Concept of Economic Imperialism." *Economic History Review* 2nd series, 1, no.1 (1949): 1–29.

Kramnick, Isaac. "Ideological Background." In *The Blackwell Encycopedia of the American Revolution*, edited by J.P. Greene and J.R. Pole, 84–91. Oxford, U.K.: Blackwell 1991.

Krumbein, William Christian. "The General Linear Model in Map Preparation and Analysis, Computer Contribution no. 12." *Kansas State Geological Survey*, Lawrence, Kansas (1967): 38–44.

Krumbein, William Christian and Franklin A. Graybill. *An Introduction to Statistical Models in Geology*, New York: McGraw-Hill 1965.

Kulisek, Larry. "Francis Xavier Caldwell." In *Dictionary of Canadian Biography*. Vol. 8. Toronto: University of Toronto Press (1985): 119–21.

– "William Caldwell." In *Dictionary of Canadian Biography*. Vol. 6. Toronto: University of Toronto Press (1987): 101–4.

Kyte Sr, Elinor. *From Royal Township to Industrial City: Cornwall 1784–1984*. Belleville, Ont.: Mika Publishing 1983.

Ladell, John L. *They Left Their Mark: Surveyors and Their Role in the Settlement of Ontario*. Toronto: Dundurn Press 1983.

Lajeunesse, Ernest J. *The Windsor Border Region: Canada's Southernmost Frontier*. Toronto: University of Toronto Press 1960.

Lambert, Richard Stanton and A. Paul Pross. *Renewing Nature's Wealth*. Toronto: Department of Lands and Forests 1967.

Landon, Frederick. "The Talbot Settlement." Ch. 4 of *The Province of Ontario, A History, 1615–1927*, 1. Toronto: Dominion 1927.

– *Western Ontario and the American Frontier*. Toronto: Ryerson Press 1941.

– "The Common Man in the Era of the Rebellion in Upper Canada." In *Aspects of Nineteenth Century Ontario*, edited by F.H. Armstrong, H.A. Stevenson, and J.D. Wilson, 154–70. Toronto: University of Toronto Press 1974.

Laslett, Peter. *The World We Have Lost*. London: Methuen 1965.

Lauber, Wilfred R. *An Index of the Land Claim Certificates of Upper Canada Militiamen Who Served in the War of 1812–1814*. Toronto: Ontario Genealogical Society 1995.

Lauriston, Victor E. *Romantic Kent: More Than Three Centuries of History, 1626–1952*. Chatham: Shepherd Printing 1952.

Lebergott, Stanley. *Manpower in Economic Growth: The American Record since 1800*. New York: McGraw-Hill 1964.

Lee, R.C. "The Canada Company, 1826–1853; A Study in Direction." MA thesis, University of Guelph 1967.

Leighton, Douglas. "George Ironside (*c.* 1800–1863)." In *Dictionary of Canadian Biography*. Vol. 9. Toronto: University of Toronto Press (1976): 408–9.

– "Simon Girty." In *Dictionary of Canadian Biography*. Vol. 5. Toronto: University of Toronto Press (1983): 345–6.

Lemon, James T. "Early Americans and Their Social Environment." *Journal of Historical Geography* 6, no.2 (1980): 115–31.

LeSueur, William Dawson. *William Lyon MacKenzie: A Reinterpretation*, edited by A.B. McKillop. Toronto: Macmillan 1979.

Lewis, Ella N. "Colonel Mahlon Burwell." In *Sidelights on the Talbot Settlement*, 23–8. St Thomas, Ont.: Sutherland Press 1938.

Lewis, Frank D. and M.C. Urquhart. "Growth and the Standard of Living in a Pioneer Economy: Upper Canada, 1826 to 1851." *William and Mary Quarterly* 3rd series, 56, no.1, (1999): 151–81.

Little, John I. *Nationalism, Capitalism and Colonization in Nineteenth-Century Quebec: The Upper St. Francis District.* Kingston and Montreal: McGill-Queen's University Press 1989.

– *Crofters and Habitants: Settler Society, Economy, and Culture in a Quebec Township, 1848–1881.* Kingston and Montreal: McGill-Queen's University Press 1991.

Lizars, Robina and Kathleen M. Lizars. *In the Days of the Canada Company: The Story of the Settlement of the Huron Tract and a View of the Social Life of the Period, 1825–1850.* Toronto: William Briggs 1896.

Locke, John. *The Second Treatise of Government.* Edited by Thomas P. Peardon. New York: Macmillan 1989.

Lockridge, Kenneth A. "Land, Population and the Evolution of New England Society, 1630–1790." *Past and Present* 39 (1968): 62–80.

Lockwood, Glenn J. *Montague: A Social History of an Irish Ontario Township, 1783–1980.* Smith Falls, Ont.: Corporation of the Township of Montague 1980.

– "Irish Immigrants and the 'Critical Years' in Eastern Ontario: The case of Montague Township, 1821–1881." *Canadian Papers in Rural History* vol. 4, edited by D.H. Akenson, 153–78. Gananoque, Ont.: Langdale Press 1984.

– *Beckwith: Irish and Scottish Identities in a Canadian Community 1816–1991.* Carleton Place, Ont.: Township of Beckwith 1991.

Longley, Ronald Stewart. "Emigration and the Crisis of 1837 in Upper Canada." *Canadian Historical Review* 17 (1936): 29–40.

Lower, Arthur R.M. "Immigration and Settlement in Canada, 1812–1820." *Canadian Historical Review* 3, no.11 (1922): 37–47.

– "The Assault on the Laurentian Barrier, 1850–1870." *Canadian Historical Review* 10 (1929): 294–307.

– *Settlement and the Forest Frontier in Eastern Canada.* Toronto: Macmillan 1936.

– *The North American Assault on the Canadian Forest.* Toronto: Ryerson Press 1938.

Lownsbrough, John. "D'Arcy Boulton." In *Dictionary of Canadian Biography.* Vol. 6. Toronto: University of Toronto Press (1987): 78–80.

Lutz, H. "Original Forest Composition in North-West Pennsylvania." *Journal of Forestry* 38 (1930): 1098–1103.

McArthur, Duncan A. and Arthur G. Doughty, eds. *Documents Relating to the Constitutional History of Canada, 1791–1818* Ottawa: King's Printer 1914.

McCalla, Douglas. "The Wheat Staple and Upper Canadian Development." Canadian Historical Association *Historical Papers* (1978): 34–46.

– *The Upper Canada Trade, 1834–1872: A Study of the Buchanans' Business.* Toronto: University of Toronto Press 1979.

– "The 'Loyalist' Economy of Upper Canada, 1784–1806." *Histoire Sociale/Social History* 16 (1983): 279–304.

- "An Introduction to the Nineteenth-Century Business World." In *Essays in Canadian Business History*, edited by T. Traves, 13–23. Toronto: McClelland and Stewart 1984.
- "The Internal Economy of Upper Canada: New Evidence on Agricultural Marketing before 1850." *Agricultural History* 59, no.3 (1985): 397–416.
- "Forest Products and Upper Canadian Development, 1815–46." *Canadian Historical Review* 68, no.2 (1987): 159–98.
- "Rural Credit and Rural Development in Upper Canada, 1790–1850." In *Patterns in the Past: Interpreting Ontario's History*, edited by R. Hall et al., 37–54. Toronto: Ontario Historical Society 1988.
- *Planting the Province: The Economic History of Upper Canada.* Toronto: University of Toronto Press 1993.
- "The Ontario Economy in the Long Run." *Ontario History* 90, no.2 (1998): 94–115.

McCalla, Douglas and Peter George. "Measurement, Myth, and Reality: Reflections on the Economic History of Nineteenth-Century Ontario." *Journal of Canadian Studies* 21, no.3 (1986): 71–86.

McCallum, John. *Unequal Beginnings: Agriculture and Economic Development in Quebec and Ontario until 1870.* Toronto: University of Toronto Press 1980.

McCrone, David and Brian Elliott. *Property and Power in a City: The Sociological Significance of Landlordism.* London: Macmillan 1989.

McDonald, A.H.G. "The Clergy Reserves in Canada to 1828." MA thesis, University of Toronto, 1925.

MacDonald, G.F. "Commodore Alexander Grant." *Ontario Historical Society Papers and Records* 22 (1925): 167–81.

McDonald, John Fasken. "An Analysis of the Location of Selected Occupations in Ottawa: 1870, 1902, 1945." BA thesis, Carleton University 1976.

Macdonald, Norman. *Canada, 1763–1841: Immigration and Settlement; the Administration of the Imperial Land Regulations.* London: Longmans 1939.

McEvoy, John Millar. "The Ontario Township." In *Toronto University Studies in Political Science*, 1, edited by W.J. Ashley. Toronto: Warwick and Sons 1889. National Library of Canada, Ottawa. Microfiche.

McGlinn, Lawrence. "Power Networks and Early Chinese immigrants in Pennsylvania." *Journal of Historical Geography* 21, no.4 (1995): 430–43.

McIlwraith, Thomas F. "The Adequacy of Rural Roads in the Era before Railways: An Illustration from Upper Canada." *Canadian Geographer* 14, no.4 (1970): 344–60.

- "Transportation in the Landscape of Early Upper Canada." In *Perspectives on Landscape and Settlement in Nineteenth Century Ontario*, edited by J.D. Wood, 51–63. Toronto: McClelland and Stewart 1975.

McInnis, R. Marvin. "Farm Households, Family Size and Economic Circumstances in Mid-Nineteenth Century Ontario." Paper presented for the Cliometrics Conference, Madison, Wis., April 1974.

– "A Reconsideration of the State of Agriculture in Lower Canada in the First half of the Nineteenth Century." In *Canadian Papers in Rural History* vol. 3, edited by D.H. Akenson, 9–49. Gananoque: Langdale Press 1982.

– "Marketable Surpluses in Ontario Farming 1860." *Social Science History* 8 (1984) 395–424.

– "The Size and Structure of Farming, Canada West, 1861." *Research in Economic History Supplement* 5 (1989): 313–29.

– "The early Ontario wheat staple reconsidered." In *Canadian Papers in Rural History*, vol. 8, edited by D.H. Akenson, 17–48. Gananoque: Langdale Press 1992.

– "Ontario Agriculture at Mid-Century." In *Canadian Papers in Rural History* vol. 8, edited by D.H. Akenson, 49–83. Gananoque, Ont.: Langdale Press 1992.

McIntosh, W.A. "Economic Factors in Canadian History." *Canadian Historical Review* 4, no.1 (1923): 12–25.

McKee, Raymond W. *The Book of McKee*. Dublin: Hodges Figgis 1959.

Mckenna, Katherine. "The Role of Women in the Establishment of Social Status in Early Upper Canada." *Ontario History* 83 (1990): 179–206.

McMahon, Donald J. "Law and Public Authority: Sir John Beverley Robinson and the Purposes of the Criminal Law." *University of Toronto Faculty of Law Review* 46, no.2 (1988): 390–423.

McNairn, Jeffrey L. "Publius of the North: Tory Republicanism and the American Constitution in Upper Canada, 1845–54." *Canadian Historical Review* 77, no.4 (1996): 504–37.

MacPherson, C.B, ed. *Property: Mainstream and Critical Positions*. Toronto: University of Toronto Press 1981.

MacRae, Marion Bell. "John Ewart." In *Dictionary of Canadian Biography*. Vol. 8. Toronto: University of Toronto Press (1985): 280–2.

Marr, William L. "Tenant versus Owner Occupied Farms in York County, Ontario, 1871." In *Canadian Papers in Rural History*, vol. 4, edited by D.H. Akenson, 50–71. Gananoque, Ont.: Langdale Press 1984.

– "The Distribution of Tenant Agriculture in Ontario, Canada, 1871." *Social Science History* 11 (summer 1987): 169–86.

Marr, William L. and Donald G. Paterson. *Canada: An Economic History*. Toronto: Gage 1980.

Marshall, Peter. "The West and the Indians, 1756–1776." In *The Blackwell Encyclopedia of the American Revolution*, edited by J.P. Greene and J.R. Pole, 153–60. Oxford, U.K.: Blackwell 1991.

Marshall, P.J. *Bengal: The British Bridgehead, 1740–1828*. Cambridge, U.K.: Cambridge University Press 1990.

Martin, Larry Roland Gibbs. *Land Use Dynamics on the Toronto Urban Fringe.* Ottawa: Information Canada 1975.

Martineau, André. "Thomas Allen Stayner." In *Dictionary of Canadian Biography.* Vol. 9. Toronto: University of Toronto Press (1976): 742–3.

Matthews, B.C. "Soil Resources and Land-Use Hazards in Southern Ontario." *Canadian Geographer* 8 (1956): 55–62.

Maycock, Paul F. "The Phytosociology of the Deciduous Forests of Extreme Southern Ontario." *Canadian Journal of Botany* 41, no.3 (1963): 379–438.

Mays, Herbert J. "A Place to Stand: Families, Land and Permanence in Toronto Gore Township, 1820–1890." Canadian Historical Association, *Historical Papers* (Montreal 1980): 185–211.

Magill, M.L. "William Allan: A Pioneer Business Executive." In *Aspects of Nineteenth Century Ontario,* edited by F.H. Armstrong, H.A. Stevenson, and J.D. Wilson, 101–13. Toronto: University of Toronto Press 1974.

Manual Relating to Surveys and Surveyors, 1st ed. Toronto: Association of Land Surveyors 1959.

Mealing, Stanley R. "Aeneas Shaw." In *Dictionary of Canadian Biography.* Vol. 5. Toronto: University of Toronto Press (1983): 752–4.

– "John Graves Simcoe." In *Dictionary of Canadian Biography.* Vol. 5. Toronto: University of Toronto Press (1983): 754–9.

– "John McGill." In *Dictionary of Canadian Biography.* Vol. 6. Toronto: University of Toronto Press (1987): 451–4.

– "William Dummer Powell." In *Dictionary of Canadian Biography.* Vol. 6. Toronto: University of Toronto (1987): 605–13.

– "William Osgoode." In *Dictionary of Canadian Biography.* Vol. 6. Toronto: University of Toronto Press (1987): 557–60.

– "Sir David William Smith." In *Dictionary of Canadian Biography.* Vol. 7. Toronto: University of Toronto Press (1988): 811–14.

– "The Enthusiasms of John Graves Simcoe." In *Historical Essays on Upper Canada,* edited by J.K. Johnson and B.G. Wilson, 302–17. Ottawa: Carleton Library University Press 1989.

Meinig, Donald W. *The Shaping of America: A Geographical Perspective on 500 years of History: Continental America, 1800–1867.* New Haven: Yale University Press 1993.

Merritt, Jane T. "Metaphor, Meaning, and Misunderstanding: Language and Power on the Pennsylvania Frontier." In *Contact Points: American Frontiers from the Mohawk Valley to the Mississippi, 1750–1830,* edited by Andrew R.L. Cayton and Frederika J. Teute, 60–87. Chapel Hill: University of North Carolina Press 1998.

Meyer, A. "The Kankakee marsh of Northern Indiana and Illinois." *Michigan Academy of Science, Arts and Letters* 21 (1935): 359–96.

– "Circulation and Settlement Patterns of the Calumet region of North-West Indiana and Illinois." *Annals of the American Association of Geographers* 46, no.3 (1956): 312–56.

Mezaks, John. "Crown Grants in the Home District: System and Records." *Families* 14, no.4 (1975): 126–34.

– "Records of the Heirs and Devisees Commission." *Families* 16, no. 4 (1977): 199–206.

Milani, Lois D. *Robert Gourlay Gadfly: Forerunner of the Rebellion in Upper Canada 1837.* Thornhill, Ont.: Ampersand Press 1971.

Milibrand, Ralph. *The State in Capitalist Society.* New York: Basic Books 1969.

Mill, John Stuart. *Principles of Political Economy with Some of Their Applications to Social Philosophy.* 2 vols. Introduction by Arthur T. Hadley. Rev. ed. New York: P.F. Collier 1900.

– *Utilitarianism, Liberty, Representative Government.* Edited by Harry Burrows Acton. London: J.M. Dent 1972.

Miller, Muriel. *George Reid: A Biography.* Toronto: Summerhill 1987.

Millman, Thomas R. "Pioneer Clergy of the diocese of Huron: Richard Pollard." *Huron Church News.* Sunday, 1 March 1953, 10.

Mills, David. "The Concept of Loyalty in Upper Canada, 1815–1850." PHD thesis, Carleton University, 1981.

– *The Idea of Loyalty in Upper Canada, 1784–1850.* Kingston and Montreal: McGill-Queen's University Press 1988.

Mills, Richard Charles. *The Colonization of Australia, 1829–42: The Wakefield Experiment in Empire Building.* Repr. London: Dawsons of Pall Mall 1968.

Miquelon, Dale. "Jacques Baby dit Dupéront." In *Dictionary of Canadian Biography*, Vol. 9. Toronto: University of Toronto Press (1979): 38–40.

Mitchell, Robert D. *Commercialism and Frontier: Perspectives on the Early Shenandoah Valley.* Charlottesville: University of Virginia Press 1977.

Modell, John. "Family and Fertility on the Indiana Frontier 1820." *American Quarterly* 23 (1971): 615–34.

Modell, J. and H.K. Tamara. "Urbanization and the Malleable Household: Boarding and Lodging in Nineteenth-Century Families." *Journal of Marriage and the Family* 35 (August 1973): 467–79.

Moir, John S. "The Settlement of the Clergy Reserves." *Canadian Historical Review* 37, no.1 (1956): 46–62.

– *Church and State in Canada West: Three Studies in the Relation of Denominationalism, 1841–67.* Toronto: University of Toronto Press 1959.

Momryk, Myron. "Isaac Todd." In *Dictionary of Canadian Biography.* Vol. 5. Toronto: University of Toronto Press (1983): 818–22.

Moodie, Susannah. *Roughing It in the Bush; or, Forest Life in Canada.* Toronto: McClelland and Stewart 1962.

Moore, D.S. and G.P. McCabe. *Introduction to the Practice of Statistics.* New York: W.H. Freeman 1989.

Moorman, David. "The District Land Boards: A Study of Early Land Administration in Upper Canada, 1788–94." MA thesis, Carleton University 1992.

Morrison, Hugh MacKenzie. "The Crown Land Policies of the Canadian Government, 1838–72." PHD thesis, Clark University, 1933.
– "The Principle of Free Grants in the Land Act of 1841." *Canadian Historical Review* 14 (1933): 392–407.
Morrison, Neil F. *Garden Gateway to Canada: One Hundred Years of Windsor and Essex County, 1854–1954.* Toronto: Ryerson Press 1954.
Morwick, F.F. "Soils of Southern Ontario." *Scientific Agriculture* 13 (1933): 449–54.
Moscovitch, Alan. "Les Sociétés de Construction au Canada avant 1867: Preliminaires a une Analyse." *L'Actualité économique: revue d'analyse économique* 59, no.3 (1983): 514–29.
Murrin, John M. "Review Essay." *History and Theory* 11, no.2 (1972): 226–75.
Murton, Brian J. "Mapping the Immediate pre-European Vegetation on the Coast of the North Island of New Zealand." *Professional Geographer* 20, no.4 (1968): 262–4.
Myers, Gustavus. *History of Canadian Wealth.* New York: Argosy-Antiquarian 1968.
Namier, Lewis. *The Structure of Politics at the Accession of George III.* 2nd ed. London: St Martin's Press 1957.
Neale, Walter E. "Land Is to Rule." In *Land Control and Social Structure in Indian history*, edited by R.E. Frykenberg, 3–15. Madison: University of Wisconsin Press 1969.
Neatby, Hilda. "Chief Justice William Smith: An Eighteenth Century Whig Imperialist." *Canadian Historical Review* 28, no.1 (1947): 44–67.
Nelles, H. Victor. "Loyalism and Local Power: The District of Niagara: 1792–1837." *Ontario History* 58 (1966): 99–114.
Nelson, William H. *The American Tory.* Boston: Northeastern University Press 1992.
Noel, Sidney J.R. *Patrons, Clients, Brokers: Ontario Society and Politics, 1791–1896.* Toronto: University of Toronto Press 1990.
– "Early Populist Tendencies, in the Ontario Political Culture." *Ontario History* 90, no. 2 (1998): 173–187.
Norris, Darrell A. "Household and Transiency in a Loyalist Township: The People of Adolphustown, 1784–1822." *Histoire Sociale/Social History* 13 (1980): 399–413.
– "Migration, Pioneer Settlement, and the Life Course: The First Families of an Ontario Township." In *Canadian Papers in Rural History* vol. 4, edited by D.H. Akenson, 130–52. Gananoque, Ont.: Langdale Press 1984.
Norton, Trist and Gilbert. "A Century of Land Values." *The Times* (London). Saturday, 20 April 1889, 11.
Norton, William A. "Rural Land Values and Land Use Patterns in Mid-Nineteenth Century Southern Ontario." MA thesis, Queen's University 1969.

Oakeshott, Michael (ed.). [Thomas Hobbes], *Leviathan or the Matter, Form, and Power of a Commonwealth, Ecclesiastical, and Civil.* New York: Macmillan 1947.

O'Brien, Conor Cruise. *The Great Melody: A Thematic Biography and Commented Anthology of Edmund Burke.* London: Minerva 1992.

Odum, Eugene Pleasants. *Ecology.* New York: Holt 1963.

Osborne, Brian S. "Historical Geography: Deciphering the Palimpsest of the Past." *Queen's Geographer,* Queen's University, Kingston (1974): 1–9.

– "The Settlement of Kingston's Hinterland." In *To Preserve and Defend: Essays on Kingston in the Nineteenth Century,* edited by G. J. Tulchinsky, 63–79. Kingston and Montreal: McGill-Queens University Press 1976.

Ouellet, Fernard, Jean Hamelin, and Richard Chabot. "Les Prix Agricoles dans les Villages et les Compagnes du Quebec d'avant 1850: Aperçus Quantitatifs." *Histoire Sociale/Social History* 15 (1982): 83–127.

Packer, Robert W. "The Geographical Basis of the Regions of Southwestern Ontario." *Canadian Historical Association Reports* (1953): 45–52.

– "The Physical Geography of the Fifteen Counties of Southwestern Ontario." *Western Ontario Historical Notes* 12, no.3 (1954): 53–62.

Page, William. *Commerce and Industry.* New York: Kelley 1968.

Pares, Richard. *King George the Third and the Politicians.* London: Oxford University Press 1967.

Pareto, Vilfredo. *A Treatise on General Sociology.* New York: Dover 1963.

Parker, Bruce A. (in collaboration with DCB). "Samuel Street." In *Dictionary of Canadian Biography.* Vol. 5. Toronto: University of Toronto Press (1983): 781–83.

Parker, Bruce A. and Bruce Wilson. "Thomas Clark." In *Dictionary of Canadian Biography.* Vol. 6., Toronto: University of Toronto Press (1987): 147–50.

Parkins, Almon Ernest. *The Historical Geography of Detroit* (Port Washington, N.Y.: Kennikat Press 1970.

Patterson, G.C. *Land Settlement in Upper Canada, 1783–1840.* Sixteenth Report of the Department of Archives for the Province of Ontario, edited by Alexander Fraser. Toronto: Clarkson W. James 1921.

Patterson, Graeme H. "Studies in Elections and Public Opinions in Upper Canada." PHD thesis, University of Toronto 1969.

– "Whiggery, Nationality and the Upper Canadian Reform tradition." *Canadian Historical Review* 56, no.1 (1975): 25–44.

– "An Enduring Canadian Myth: Responsible Government and the Family Compact." *Journal of Canadian Studies* 12, no.2 (1977): 3–16.

– "Early Compact Groups in the Politics of York." In *Old Ontario: Essays in Honour of J.M.S.Careless,* edited by D. Keane, C. Read and F.H. Armstrong, 174–91. Toronto: Dundurn Press 1990.

– *History and Communications: Harold Innis, Marshall McLuhan, and the Interpretation of History.* Toronto: University of Toronto Press 1990.

Peardon, Thomas P. (ed.) [John Locke], *The Second Treatise of Government*. New York: Macmillan 1989.

Pentland, Harry Clare. "The Development of the Capitalistic Labour Market in Canada." *Canadian Journal of Economics and Political Science* 25 (1959): 450–61.

Peters, Bernard C. "No Trees on the Prairies: Persistence of Error in Landscape Terminology." *Michigan History* 54, no.1 (1970): 19–28.

– "Changing Ideas about the Use of Vegetation as an Indicator of Soil Quality: Examples of New York and Michigan." *Journal of Geography* 72, no.2 (1973): 18–28.

Pigot, F.L. "James Robertson." In *Dictionary of Canadian Biography*. Vol. 5. Toronto: University of Toronto Press (1983): 716–17.

Pioneer Collection, Report of the Pioneer and Historical Society of the State of Michigan. Vol. 10. Lansing, Mich.: Thorp and Godfrey 1886.

Piquette Bibeau, Claudette et al. *Mariages: St-Jean-Baptiste d'Amherstburg, 1802–1985*. Ottawa: Société Franco-Ontarienne d'Histoire et de Généalogie 1987.

Plaunt, Dorothy Reynolds. "The Honourable Peter Russell: Administrator of Upper Canada, 1796–1799." *Canadian Historical Review*. 20, no.3 (1939): 258–74.

Plumb, John Harold. *England in the Eighteenth Century*. Harmondsworth: Penguin 1950.

– *The Growth of Political Stability in England: 1675–1725*. London: Macmillan 1967.

– *The First Four Georges*. London: John Wiley and Sons 1974.

Porter, Roy. *English Society in the Eighteenth Century*. London: Penguin Books Ltd 1982.

Powell, William Dummer. *Story of a Refuge*. Toronto: The *Patriot* Office 1833. National Library of Canada, Ottawa. Microfiche.

Primack, Martin L. "Farm Formed Capital in American Agriculture, 1850–1910." PHD thesis, University of North Carolina 1963.

– "Farm Construction as a Use of Farm Labor in the United States, 1850–1910." *Journal of Economic History* 25 (1965): 114–25.

– "Farm Fencing in the Nineteenth Century." *Journal of Economic History* 29 (1969): 287–9.

Pryke, Kenneth G. "George Benson Hall." In *Dictionary of Canadian Biography*. Vol. 6. Toronto: University of Toronto Press (1987): 308–10.

– "William McCormick." In *Dictionary of Canadian Biography*. Vol. 7. Toronto: University of Toronto Press (1988): 527–9.

Quaife, Milo M. "Detroit Biographies: Commodore Alexander Grant." *Burton Historical Collection Leaflet* 6, no. 5 (1928): 66–80.

– *The John Askin Papers*. 2 vols. Detroit: Detroit Library Commission 1928–31.

– *The Siege of Detroit in 1763*. Chicago: Donnelly 1958.

Ramirez, Bruno. *On the Move: French-Canadian and Italian Migrants in the North-Atlantic Economy, 1860–1914.* Toronto: McClelland and Stewart 1991.

Rawlyk, George A., ed. *The Canadian Protestant Experience, 1760 to 1990.* Kingston and Montreal: McGill-Queen's University Press 1990.

Rawlyk, George A. and Janice Potter. "Richard Cartwright." In *Dictionary of Canadian Biography.* Vol. 5. Toronto: University of Toronto Press (1983): 167–72.

Ray, Arthur J. *Indians in the Fur Trade: Their Role as Trappers, Hunters and Middlemen in the Lands Southwest of Hudson Bay, 1660–1870.* Toronto: University of Toronto Press 1974.

– *"Give Us Good Measure": An Economic Analysis of Relations Between the Indians and the Hudson's Bay Company before 1763.* Toronto: University of Toronto Press 1978.

– "William Holmes." In *Dictionary of Canadian Biography.* Vol. 4. Toronto: University of Toronto Press (1979): 365–6.

Read, Colin. "The Duncombe Rising, Its Aftermath, Anti-Americanism, and Sectarianism." *Histoire Sociale/Social History* 9 (1976): 47–69.

– "The London District Oligarchy in the Rebellion Era." *Ontario History* 72, no.4 (1980): 195–209.

– "Canadian Loyalism: The Tangled Roots of a Nation's Past." *Area Studies Tsukuba* 5 (1987): 83–94.

– "Assessing Sources for Analyzing Wealth, Income, and Identity: Ontario Land Records, 1792–1851." Paper presented at the annual meeting of the Social Science History Association, Atlanta, Ga, October 1994.

– "The Land Records of Old Ontario." *Histoire Sociale/Social History* 30 (1997): 127–41.

Read, Colin and Ronald J. Stagg. *The Rebellion of 1837 in Upper Canada.* Don Mills, Ont.: The Champlain Society and Carleton University Press 1985.

Read, David B. "Chief Justice William Dummer Powell." Ch. 2 in *The Lives of the Judges of Upper Canada and Ontario from 1790 to the Present Time.* Toronto: Rosewell 1888.

– "The Backwoods Society of Upper Canada." Ch. 4 in *The Developing Canadian Community.* Toronto: University of Toronto Press 1962.

Reaman, George E. *The Trail of the Black Walnut.* Toronto: McClelland and Stewart 1957.

– *A History of Agriculture in Ontario.* Toronto: Saunders 1970.

Regehr, Theodore D. "Land Ownership in Upper Canada, 1783–1796: A Background to the First Table of Fees." *Ontario History* 55, no.1 (1963): 34–8.

Richards, Elva M. "The Joneses of Brockville and the Family Compact." *Ontario History* 60, no.4 (1968): 169–84.

Richards, J. Howard. "Lands and Policies: Attitudes and Controls in the Alienation of Lands in Ontario during the First Century of Settlement." *Ontario History* 50 (1958): 193–209.

Richards, N.R., A.G. Caldwell, and F.F. Morwick. *Soil Survey of Essex County*, 11. Guelph, Ont.: Ontario Soil Survey 1949.

Riddell, R.G. "A Study of the Land Policy of the Colonial Office, 1763–1865." *Canadian Historical Review* 18 (1937): 385–405.

Riddell, William Renwick. "Robert (Fleming) Gourlay." *Ontario History* 14 (1916): 5–133.

– ed. *La Rochefoucault-Liancourt's Travels in Canada: 1795, with Annotations and Structures by Sir David William Smith and Notes by William Renwick Riddell.* Thirteenth Report of the Bureau of Archives for the Province of Ontario 1916. Toronto: A.T. Wilgress 1917.

– *The Life of William Dummer Powell, First Judge at Detroit and Fifth Chief Justice of Upper Canada.* Lansing: Michigan Historical Commission 1924.

– *Michigan under British Rule: Law and Law Courts, 1760–1796.* Lansing: Michigan Historical Commission 1926.

– "'Fi. Fa. Lands' in Upper Canada" *Canadian Bar Review* 7 (1929): 448–51.

Riddy, John. "Some Official British Attitudes Towards European Settlement and Colonization in India up to 1865." In *Essays in Indian History*, edited by D. Williams and E.D. Watts, 17–41. India: Asia Publishing House 1973.

Risk, R.C. "The Golden Age: The Law about the Market in Nineteenth Century Ontario." *University of Toronto Law Journal* 26, no.3 (1976): 307–46.

– "The Last Golden Age: Property and the Allocation of losses in Ontario in the Nineteenth Century." *University of Toronto Law Journal* 27, no.2 (1977): 199–239.

– "The Law and the Economy in Mid-Nineteenth Century Ontario: A Perspective." In *Essays in the History of Canadian Law*, vol. 1, edited by D.H. Flaherty, 83–131. Toronto: University of Toronto Press 1981.

Robertson, J. Ross. *The Diary of Mrs. John Graves Simcoe, Wife of the First Lieutenant-Governor of the Province of Upper Canada, 1792–6, with Notes and a Biography.* Toronto: William Briggs 1911.

Robinson, C.W. *Life of Sir John Beverley Robinson.* Toronto: Morang 1904.

Robinson, Warren C. "Urban Rural Differences in Indian Fertility." *Population Studies* 14 (1961): 218–34.

Rogers, Edward. S. and Donald B. Smith, eds. *Aboriginal Ontario: Historical Perspectives On the First Nations.* Toronto: Dundurn Press 1994.

Rohrbough, Malcolm J. *The Trans-Appalachian Frontier: Societies and Institutions, 1775–1850.* New York: Oxford University Press 1978.

Romney, Paul. "'The Ten Thousand Pound Job': Political Corruption, Equitable Jurisdiction, and the Public Interest in Upper Canada, 1852–6." In *Essays In the History of Canadian Law*, vol. 2, edited by D.H. Flaherty, 143–99. Toronto: University of Toronto Press 1983.

– "The Spanish Freeholder Imbroglio of 1824: Inter-Elite and Intra-Elite Rivalry in Upper Canada." *Ontario History* 76, no.1 (1984): 32–47.

- *Mr. Attorney: The Attorney General for Ontario in Court, Cabinet, and Legislature, 1791–1899.* Toronto: University of Toronto Press 1986.
- "From the Types Riot to the Rebellion: Elite Ideology, Anti-Legal Sentiment, Political Violence, and the Rule of Law in Upper Canada." *Ontario History* 79, no.2 (1987): 113–44.
- "Re-inventing Upper Canada: American Immigrants, Upper Canadian History, English Law, and the Alien Question." In *Patterns in the Past: Interpreting Ontario's History,* edited by R. Hall et al., 78–107. Toronto: Ontario Historical Society 1988.
- "Very Late Loyalist Fantasies: Nostalgic Tory History and the Rule of Law In Upper Canada." In *Canadian Perspectives on Law and Society: Issues in Legal History,* edited by W.W. Pue and B. Wright, 119–47. Ottawa: Carleton University Press 1988.
Roots, Ivan. "English Politics, 1625–1700." In *Into Another Mould: Change and Continuity in English Culture, 1625–1700,* edited by T.G.S Cain and K. Robinson, 18–51. London: Routledge Press 1992.
Rorke, L.V. "Abraham Iredell." *Annual Report, Association of Ontario Land Surveyors* (1935): 96–103.
Rostow, Walt Whitman. *The British Economy of the Nineteenth Century: Essays.* Oxford, U.K.: Clarendon Press 1949.
Rousseau, Jean-Jacques. *The Social Contract and Discourses.* Edited by George Douglas Howard Cole. London: J.M. Dent 1993.
Ruggles, Richard E. "William McMurray." In *Dictionary of Canadian Biography.* Vol. 12. Toronto: (University of Toronto Press 1990): 681–2.
Russell, Peter A. "Attitudes to Social Structure and Social Mobility in Upper Canada." PHD thesis, Carleton University 1981.
- "Upper Canada: A Poor Man's Country? Some Statistical Evidence." In *Canadian Papers in Rural History,* vol. 3, edited by D.H. Akenson, 129–47. Gananoque, Ont.: Langdale Press 1982.
- "Wage Labour Rates in Upper Canada, 1818–1840." *Histoire Sociale/Social History* 16 (1983): 61–80.
- "Church of Scotland Clergy in Upper Canada: Culture Shock and Conservatism on the Frontier." *Ontario History* 73, no.2 (1987): 88–111.
- *Attitudes to Social Structure and Mobility in Upper Canada 1815–1840: 'Here We Are Laird Ourselves'.* Lewiston, N.Y. and Queenston, Ont.: Edwin Mellen Press 1990.
Sainsbury, John. *Disaffected Patriots: London Supporters of Revolutionary America, 1769–1782.* Kingston and Montreal: McGill-Queens University Press 1987.
St Denis, Guy. *Byron: Pioneer Days in Westminster Township.* Lambeth, Ont.: Crinklaw Press 1985.
Saunders, Robert E. "What Was the Family Compact?" *Ontario History* 49 (1957): 165–70.
- "Sir John Beverley Robinson." In *Dictionary of Canadian Biography.* Vol. 9. Toronto: University of Toronto Press (1976): 668–79.

Sawaya, Jean-Pierre. *La Fédération des Sept Feux de la Vallée du Saint-Laurent: XVIIe au XIXe siècle.* Sillery, Que.: Septentrion 1998.

Schein, R.H. "Unofficial Proprietors in Post-Revolutionary Central New York." *Journal of Historical Geography* 17, no.2 (1991): 146–64.

Scott, Duncan Campbell. *The Makers of Canada: John Graves Simcoe.* Canadian Club Edition. Toronto: Morang 1910.

Scott, John. *The Upper Classes: Property and Privilege in Britain.* London: Macmillan 1982.

Semple, Neil. "The Quest for the Kingdom: Aspects of Protestant Revivalism in Nineteenth Century Ontario." In *Old Ontario: Essays in Honour of J.M.S. Careless,* edited by D. Keane, and C. Read, and F.H. Armstrong, 95–117. Toronto: Dundurn Press 1990.

Senior, Hereward and Elinor Senior. "Henry John Boulton." In *Dictionary of Canadian Biography.* Vol. 9. Toronto: University of Toronto Press (1976): 68.

Shannon, Bill. "Brokers, Land Bankers, and 'Birds of Evil Omen': The Effect of Land Policies on Settlement in Upper Canada's Collingwood Township 1834–1860." MA thesis, University of Ottawa 1989.

Shirreff, Patrick. *A Tour through North America, Together with a Comprehensive View of the Canadas and the United States as Adapted for Agricultural Emigration.* Edinburgh: Oliver and Boyd 1835. National Library of Canada, Ottawa. Microfiche.

Shortt, Adam. "History of Canadian Currency." In *Money and Banking in Canada: Historical Documents and Commentary,* edited by E.P. Neufeld, 116-31. Toronto: McClelland and Stewart 1967.

Shortt, Adam and Arthur G. Doughty, eds. *Documents Relating to the Constitutional History of Canada, 1759–1791.* 2nd ed. 2 vols. Ottawa: King's Printer 1918.

– "Founders of Canadian Banking: The Hon. Wm. Allan, Merchant and Banker." In *Adam Shortt's History of Canadian Currency and Banking, 1600–1880,* 790–802. Toronto: Canadian Bankers' Association 1986.

Siegel, S. *Non-Parametric Statistics for the Behavioral Sciences.* New York: Hill 1956.

Silsby, Robert S. "Frontier Attitudes and Debt Collection in Western New York." In *The Frontier in American Development: Essays in Honor of Paul W. Gates,* edited by D.M. Ellis, 141–61. London: Cornell University Press 1969.

Simpson, Donald G. "Charles Stuart." In *Dictionary of Canadian Biography.* Vol. 9. Toronto: University of Toronto Press (1976): 769–70.

Simpson, Richard J. "William Chewett." In *Dictionary of Canadian Biography.* Vol. 7. Toronto: University of Toronto Press (1988): 174–6.

Sims, W.A. "James Grant Chewett." *Annual Report of the Association of Ontario Land Surveyors,* 112–17. Toronto: Association of Ontario Land Surveyors 1921.

Skof, Karl. "Agriculture in a Forest Setting: Lanark County." MA thesis, Carleton University 1988.

Smith, Adam. *An Inquiry into the Nature and Causes of the Wealth of Nations (1776).* 2 vols. Edited by R.H. Campbell and A.S. Skinner. Oxford, U.K.: Clarendon Press 1976.

Smith, Allan. "The Myth of the Self-made Man in English Canada, 1850–1914." *Canadian Historical Review* 59 (1978): 189–219.

Smith, Donald B. "The Dispossession of the Mississauga Indians: A Missing Chapter in the Early History of Upper Canada." *Ontario History* 73, no.2 (1981): 67–87.

Smith, George and Leslie K. Smith. "Reminiscences of the First Sarnia Survey." *Ontario History* 59, no.2 (1967): 79–88.

Smith, William Henry. *Smith's Canadian Gazetteer.* Toronto: H. and W. Rowsell 1846. National Library of Canada, Ottawa. Microfiche.

– *Canada: Past, Present and Future.* 2 vols. Toronto: T. Maclear 1851. National Library of Canada, Ottawa. Microfiche.

Snell, Ronald K. "'Ambitious of Honor and Places': The Magistracy of Hampshire County, Massachusetts, 1692–1760." In *Power and Status: Office Holding in Colonial America,* edited by B.C. Daniels, 17–35. Middleton, Conn.: Wesleyan University Press 1986.

Sosin, Jack M. "The British Indian Department and Dunmore's War." *The Virginian Magazine of History and Biography* 74 (1966): 34–50.

Speck, William Arthur. *Stability and Strife: England, 1714–1760.* Cambridge, U.K.: Edward Arnold 1977.

– "The Structure of British Politics in the Mid-Eighteenth Century." In *The Blackwell Encyclopaedia of the American Revolution,* edited by J.P. Green and J.R. Pole, 1–8. Oxford, U.K.: Blackwell 1991.

Spelt, Jacob. *Urban Development in South-Central Ontario.* Toronto: McClelland and Stewart 1972.

Spiegel, Murray R. *Schuam's Outline of Theory and Problems of Statistics.* New York: McGraw-Hill 1961.

Spragge, C. "The History of the Land Record Copy Books." In *Land Records in Ontario Registry Offices,* A.D. McFall and J. McFall, eds., 11–13. Toronto: Ontario Genealogical Society 1984.

– "Organizing the Wilderness: A Study of a Loyalist Settlement, Augusta Township, Grenville County, 1784–1820." PHD thesis, Queen's University 1986.

Spragge, George W. "The Districts of Upper Canada, 1788–1849." *Ontario Historical Society Papers and Records* 39 (1947): 91–100.

– "Colonization Roads in Canada West, 1850–1867." *Ontario History* 49 (1957): 1–18.

Stanley, George F.G. "The First Indian 'Reserves' in Canada." *Revue d'histoire de l'Amérique Française* 4 (1950): 178–209.

Steele, I.K. "Hugh Finlay." In *Dictionary of Canadian Biography.* Vol. 5. Toronto: University of Toronto Press (1983): 314–19.

Stratford-Devai, Fawne and Bruce S. Elliott. "Upper Canada Land Settlement Records: The Second District Land Boards, 1819–1825." *Families* 34, no.3. (1995): 132–47.

Sugden, John. *Tecumseth: A Life*. New York: Henry Holt 1998.

Surtees, Robert J. "The Development of an Indian Reserve Policy in Canada." *Ontario History* 61 (1969): 87–98.

– "Indian Land Cessions in Ontario, 1763–1862: The Evolution of a System." PHD thesis, Carleton University 1982.

– "Indian Participation in the War of 1812: A Cartographic Approach." In *The Western District*, edited by K. Pryke and L. Kulisek, 42–8. Windsor, Ont.: University of Windsor Press 1983.

– "Land Cessions, 1763–1830." In *Aboriginal Ontario: Historical Perspectives on the First Nations*, edited by E.S. Rogers and D.B. Smith, 92–131. Toronto: Dundurn Press 1994.

Sutherland, Stuart R.J. "Robert Mathews." In *Dictionary of Canadian Biography*. Vol. 5. Toronto: University of Toronto Press (1983): 584–5.

Sutherland, Stuart R.J., Pierre Tousignant, and Madeleine Dionne-Tousignant. "Sir Frederick Haldimand." In *Dictionary of Canadian Biography*. Vol. 5. Toronto: University of Toronto Press (1983): 887–904.

Swainson, Donald. "Thomas Clark Street." In *Dictionary of Canadian Biography*. Vol. 10. Toronto: University of Toronto Press (1972): 668–9.

Sweeny, Robert. "Peter McGill." In *Dictionary of Canadian Biography*. Vol. 8. Toronto: University of Toronto Press (1985): 540–44.

Swierenga, Robert P. *Pioneers and Profits: Land Speculation on the Iowa Frontier*. Ames: Iowa State University Press 1968.

Sykes, N. "Thomas Paine." In *The Social and Political Ideas of Some Representative Thinkers of the Revolutionary Era*, edited by F.J.C. Hearnshaw, 100–40. New York: Barnes and Noble 1967.

Talbot, Edward Allen. *Five Years Residence in the Canadas: Including a Tour through Part of the United States of America*, vol. 1. London: 1824. National Library of Canada, Ottawa. Microfiche.

Talman, James J. "Travel in Ontario before the Coming of the Railway." Ontario Historical Society, *Papers and Records* 29 (1933): 85–102.

– "The Position of the Church of England in Upper Canada, 1791–1854." *Canadian Historical Review* 15 (1934): 361–75.

– "Early Ontario Land Records as a Source of Local History." *Western Ontario Historical Notes* 8, no.4 (1950): 130–4.

– "The Development of the Railway Network of Southern Ontario to 1876." *Report of the Canadian Historical Association* (1953): 53–60.

– "The Impact of the Railway on a Pioneer Community." *Canadian Historical Association Reports* (1955): 1–12.

– "John Baptist Askin." In *Dictionary of Canadian Biography*. Vol. 9. Toronto: University of Toronto Press (1976): 8–9.

Taylor, Griffith. "Towns and Townships in Southern Ontario." *Economic Geography* 21 (April 1945): 88–96.

Taylor, Harry W., John Clarke, and W. Robert Wightman. "Contrasting Land Development Rates in Southern Ontario to 1891." In *Canadian Papers in Rural History*, vol. 5, edited by D.H. Akenson, 50–72. Gananoque, Ont.: Langdale Press 1986.

Taylor, M. Brook. "Reform Challenge in Upper Canada." Ch. 4 in *Promoters, Patriots and Partisans: Historiography in Nineteenth-Century English Canada*. Toronto: University of Toronto Press 1989.

Teeple, Gregory. "Land, Labour and Capital in Pre-Confederation Canada." In *Capitalism and the National Question*, edited by G. Teeple, 44–66. Toronto: University of Toronto Press 1972.

Thomas, Earl. *Sir John Johnson: Loyalist, Baronette*. Toronto: Dundurn Press 1986.

Thompson, C. Bradley. *John Adams and the Spirit of Liberty*. Lawrence, Kans.: University Press of Kansas 1998.

Thompson, Don W. *Men and Meridians: The History of Surveying and Mapping in Canada*. 2 vols. Ottawa: Queen's Printer 1966–67.

Thompson, Edward Palmer. *Whigs and Hunters: The Origins of the Black Act*. London: Allen and Lane 1975.

– *Customs in Common: Studies in Traditional Culture*. New York: New Press 1991.

Thompson, Francis M.L. "Landownership and Economic Growth in England in the Eighteenth Century." In *Agrarian change and economic Development*, edited by E.L. Jones and S.L. Woolf, 41–60. London: Methuen 1969.

Thompson, Samuel. *Reminiscences of a Canadian Pioneer for the Last Fifty Years*. Toronto: Hunter, Rose 1884. National Library of Canada, Ottawa. Microfiche.

Tierney, Brian. *The Crisis of Church and State, 1050–1300: With Selected Documents*. Englewood Cliffs, N.J.: Prentice Hall 1964.

Tomlins, Christopher L. *Law, Labor and Ideology in the Early American Republic*. Cambridge, U.K.: University of Cambridge 1993.

Toronto Public Library. *Landmarks of Canada: A Guide to the J. Ross Robertson Canadian Historical Collection in the Toronto Public Library*. 2 vols. in 1. Repr. ed., 1967.

Tousignant, Pierre, and Madelene Dionne-Tousignant. "François-Marie Picoté de Belestre." In *Dictionary of Canadian Biography*. Vol. 4. Toronto: University of Toronto Press (1979): 633–5.

Trail, Catherine Parr. *The Backwoods of Canada: Being Letters from the Wife of an Emigrant Officer*. London: Charles Knight 1846.

Trewartha, Glenn. "The Vegetal Cover of the Driftless Cuesta Hill Land." *Annals of the Association of American Geographers* 30, no.2 (1940): 109–42.

Trigger, Bruce G. *The Children of Aataentsic: A History of the Huron People to 1660*. Kingston and Montreal: McGill-Queen's University Press 1985.

Tulchinsky, Gerald. "George Moffatt." In *Dictionary of Canadian Biography*. Vol. 9. Toronto: University of Toronto Press (1976): 553–6.

– "John Redpath." In *Dictionary of Canadian Biography*. Vol. 9. Toronto: University of Toronto Press (1976): 654–5.

Tully, Alan. "The Political Development of the Colonies after the Glorious Revolution." In *The Blackwell Encyclopaedia of the American Revolution*, edited by J.P. Greene and J.R. Pole, 28–38. Oxford, U.K.: Blackwell 1991.

Tunis, Barbara. "William Holmes." In *Dictionary of Canadian Biography* Vol. 6. Toronto: University of Toronto Press (1987): 325–7.

Turner, Richard Walter. *The Equity of Redemption*. Cambridge, U.K.: Cambridge University Press 1931.

United Empire Loyalist Centennial Committee (Toronto). *The Centennial of the Settlement of Upper Canada by United Empire Loyalists, 1784–1884/...* Boston: Gregg Press 1972.

Upton, Leslie Francis Stokes. *The Loyal Whig: William Smith of New York and Quebec*. Toronto: University of Toronto Press 1969.

– "The Origins of Canadian Indian Policy." *Journal of Canadian Studies* 10, no.4 (1973): 51–61.

– "William Smith." In *Dictionary of Canadian Biography*. Vol. 4. Toronto: University of Toronto Press (1979): 714–18.

Vandall, Paul E. *An Atlas of Essex County*. Windsor, Ont.: Essex County Historical Association 1964.

Venturi, Franco. *The End of the Old Regime in Europe, 1768–1776: The First Crisis*. Princeton, N.J.: Princeton University Press 1979.

Veyne, Paul. "Where Public Life was Private." In *A History of Private Life: From Pagan Rome to Byzantium*, vol. 2., edited by Philippe Ariès and Georges Duby, 95–115. Cambridge, Mass.: Harvard University Press 1996.

Vincent, Andrew. *Theories of the State*. Oxford, U.K.: Blackwell 1987.

Walker, A.P. and R.W. Code. "Patrick McNiff." *Association of Ontario Land Surveyors Annual Report*, 100–4. Toronto: 1931.

Wallace, William Stewart. *The Family Compact: A Chronicle of the Rebellion of Upper Canada*. Toronto: Glasgow and Brook 1915.

– "Forsyth, Richardson and Company in the Fur-Trade." *Transactions of the Royal Society of Canada* 3, 34, sect. 2 (1940): 187–94.

Wallerstein, Immanuel. *Historical Capitalism*. London: Verso 1992.

Walsh, Lorena S. "The Development of Local Power Structures: Maryland's Lower Western Shore in the Early Colonial Period." In *Power and Status: Office Holding in Colonial America*, edited by B.C. Daniels, 53–74. Middleton, Conn.: Wesleyan University Press 1986.

Ward, Peter. *Courtship, Love and Marriage in Nineteenth-Century English Canada*. Kingston and Montreal: McGill-Queen's University Press 1990.

Watson, J.W. "Rural Depopulation in Southwestern Ontario." *Annals of the Association of American Geographers* 37, no.3 (1947): 145–54.

Watson, Stephen. *The Reign of George III 1760–1815.* Oxford, U.K.: Clarendon Press 1960.

Watt, Daryl. "A Historical Perspective of Lennox and Addington to 1825." Unpublished paper, Department of Geography: Carleton University 1994.

Weaver, John C. "While Equity Slumbered: Creditor Advantage, a Capitalist Land Market, and Upper Canada's Missing Court." *Osgoode Hall Law Journal* 28, no.4 (1990): 871–914.

Weaver, W.F. "Ontario Surveys and the Land Surveyor." *Canadian Geographical Journal* 32, no.4 (1946): 180–91.

– *Crown Surveys in Ontario.* Toronto: Ontario Department of Lands and Forest 1962.

Weber, Max. *The Protestant Ethic and the Spirit of Capitalism.* New York: Scribner's 1958.

Weldon, Jessie T. "The Salient Factors Contributing to the Earliest Settlement Patterns in East and West Hawkesbury Township, Upper Canada, 1788–1846." MA thesis, Carleton University 1980.

Westfall, William. "The Dominion of the Lord: An Introduction to the Cultural History of Protestant Ontario in the Victorian Period." *Queen's Quarterly* 83 (spring 1976): 47–70.

– "Order and Experience: Patterns of Religious Metaphor in Early Nineteenth Century Upper Canada." *Journal of Canadian Studies* 20, no.1 (1985): 5–24.

– *Two Worlds: The Protestant Culture of Nineteenth-Century Ontario.* Kingston and Montreal: McGill-Queen's University Press 1989.

Whebell, Charles F.J. "Corridors: A Theory of Urban Systems." *Annals of the American Association of Geographers* 59, no.1 (1969): 1–26.

White, J.H. and R.H. Hosie. *The Forests of Ontario.* Toronto: Ministry of Natural Resources 1973.

White, Richard. *The Middle Ground: Indians, Empires, and Republics in the Great Lakes Region, 1650–1815.* Cambridge, U.K.: Cambridge University Press 1991.

Whitfield, Carol (in collaboration with DCB). "Alexander Grant." In *Dictionary of Canadian Biography.* Vol. 5. Toronto: University of Toronto Press (1983): 363–7.

Whitfield, Carol and Robert Lochiel Fraser III. "John (Greenfield) Macdonnell." In *Dictionary of Canadian Biography.* Vol. 5. Toronto: University of Toronto Press (1983): 520–3.

Wickwire, Franklin B. "Richard England." In *Dictionary of Canadian Biography.* Vol. 5. Toronto: University of Toronto Press (1983): 306–7.

Widdis, Randy W. "A Perspective on Land Tenure in Upper Canada: A Study of Elizabethtown Township, 1790–1840." MA thesis, McMaster University 1977.

– "Motivation and Scale: A Method of Identifying Land Speculators in Upper Canada." *Canadian Geographer* 23, no.4 (1979): 337–51.

- "Tracing Property Ownership in Nineteenth-Century Ontario: A Guide to the Archival Sources." In *Canadian Papers in Rural History* vol. 2, edited by D.H. Akenson, 83–102. Gananoque, Ont.: Langdale Press 1980.
- "Speculation and the Surveyor: An Analysis of the Role Played by the Surveyors in the Settlement of Upper Canada." *Histoire Sociale/Social History* 15 (1982): 443–58.
- "Generations, Mobility and Persistence: A View from Genealogies." *Histoire Sociale/Social History* 25 (1992): 125–50.

Willey, Basil. *The Eighteenth Century Background: Studies on the Idea of Nature in the Thought of the Period.* London: Chatto and Windus 1949.
- *Nineteenth Century Studies.* London: Chatto and Windus 1949.

Williams, Basil. *The Whig Supremacy, 1714–1760.* Oxford, U.K.: Clarendon Press 1962.

Willis, L.P. *Canadian Scenery: Illustrated in a Series of Views by W.H. Bartlett* London: George Virtue, 1842.

Wilson, Alan. "The Clergy Reserves: Economic Mischief or Sectarian Issue." *Canadian Historical Review* 48 (1961): 281–99.
- *The Clergy Reserves of Upper Canada: A Canadian Mortmain.* Toronto: University of Toronto Press 1968.
- "John Colborne, 1st Baron Seaton." In *Dictionary of Canadian Biography.* Vol. 9. Toronto: University of Toronto Press (1976): 137–43.

Wilson, Bruce. "The Struggle for Wealth and Power at Fort Niagara 1775–1783." *Ontario History* 68, no.3 (1976): 137–54.
- *As She Began.* Toronto: Dundurn Press 1981.
- *The Enterprises of Robert Hamilton: A Study of Wealth and Influence in Early Upper Canada, 1776–1812.* Ottawa: Carleton University Press 1983.
- "Robert Hamilton." In *Dictionary of Canadian Biography,* Vol. 5. Toronto: University of Toronto Press (1983): 402–6.
- "Thomas Dickson." In *Dictionary of Canadian Biography.* Vol. 6. Toronto: University of Toronto Press (1987): 211–2.
- "William Dickson." In *Dictionary of Canadian Biography.* Vol. 7. Toronto: University of Toronto Press (1988): 250–2.

Wilson, Catherine A. *A New Lease on Life: Landlords, Tenants, and Immigrants in Ireland and Canada.* Kingston and Montreal: McGill-Queens University Press 1994.
- "The Scotch-Irish and Immigrant Culture on Amherst Island, Ontario." In *Ulster and North America: Transatlantic Perspectives on the Scotch-Irish,* edited by H.T. Bletchen and K.W. Woods, Jr, 134–45. Tuscaloosa and London: University of Alabama Press 1997.

Wilson, David A. *Paine and Cobbett: The Transatlantic Connection.* Kingston and Montreal: McGill-Queens University Press 1988.

Wilson, Emily S. "Fox Family Cemetery, Mersea." *Ontario Register* 4, no.2 (1971): 117–18.

Wilson, G.A. "The Political and Administrative History of the Upper Canada Clergy Reserves, 1790–1854." PHD thesis. University of Toronto 1979.

Wilson, Thomas B., ed. "Death Notices from the 'Patriot, Toronto.'" *Ontario Register* no.5 (1981): 39–60.

– "Marriages of the Western District Commencing in 1796." *Ontario Register* 2, no.1 (1969): 48–65.

– "Marriage Register of the Western District." *Ontario Register* 2, no.2 (1969): 65–83.

– "Marriage Register of the Western District." *Ontario Register.* 3, no.2 (1970): 65–106.

– "Marriage Register of the Western District." *Ontario Register.* 3, no.4 (1970): 241–7.

Winters, Donald L. *Farmers without Farms: Agricultural Tenancy in Nineteenth Century Iowa.* Ames: Iowa State University Press 1978.

– "Agricultural Tenancy in the Nineteenth Century Middle West: The Historiographical Debate." *Indiana Magazine of History* 78, no.2 (1982): 128–53.

Wise, Sidney F. "The Indian Diplomacy of John Graves Simcoe." *Canadian Historical Association Report* (1953): 36–44.

– "Tory Factionalism: Kingston Elections and Upper Canadian Politics, 1820–1836." *Ontario History* 57, no.4 (1965): 205–25.

– "Upper Canada and the Conservative Tradition." In *Profiles of a Province: Studies in the History of Ontario*, edited by E.G. Firth, 20–33. Toronto: Ontario Historical Society 1967.

– "Conservatism and Political Development: The Canadian Case." *South Atlantic Quarterly* 69 (spring 1970): 226–43.

– "Sir Francis Bond Head." In *Dictionary of Canadian Biography*. Vol. 10. Toronto: University of Toronto Press (1972): 342–5.

– "Liberal Consensus or Ideological Battleground: Some Reflections on the Hartz thesis." Canadian Historical Association, *Historical Papers* (1974): 1–14.

– "Robert Fleming Gourlay." In *Dictionary of Canadian Biography*. Vol. 9. Toronto: University of Toronto Press (1976): 330–6.

– "Thomas Gage." In *Dictionary of Canadian Biography*. Vol. 4. Toronto: University of Toronto Press (1979): 278–81.

– "The Annexation Movement and Its Effects on Canadian Opinion, 1837–1867." In *God's Peculiar Peoples: Essays on Political Culture in Nineteenth Century Canada*, edited by A.B. McKillop and P. Romney, 115–47. Ottawa: Carleton University Press 1993.

– "Canadians View the United States: Colonial Attitudes from the Era of the War of 1812 to the Rebellion of 1837." In *God's Peculiar Peoples: Essays on Political Culture in Nineteenth Century Canada*, edited by A.B. McKillop and P. Romney, 45–60. Ottawa: Carleton University Press 1993.

- "God's Peculiar People." In *God's Peculiar Peoples: Essays on Political Culture in Nineteenth Century Canada*, edited by A.B. McKillop and P. Romney, 19–43. Ottawa: Carleton University Press 1993.
- "The Rise of Christopher Hagerman." In *God's Peculiar Peoples: Essays on Political Culture in Nineteenth Century Canada*, edited by A.B. McKillop and P. Romney, 61–90. Ottawa: Carleton University Press 1993.
- "Sermon Literature and Canadian Intellectual History." In *God's Peculiar Peoples: Essays on Political Culture in Nineteenth Century Canada*, edited by A.B. McKillop and P. Romney, 1–17. Ottawa: Carleton University Press 1993.

Wood, Colin J. "Human Settlement in the Long Point Area." MA thesis, McMaster University 1966.

Wood, J. David. "The Historical Geography of Dumfries Township, Upper Canada, 1816–1852." MA thesis, University of Toronto 1958.
- "The Stage Is Set: Dumfries Township, 1816." *Waterloo Historical Society* 48 (1960): 40–50.
- "The Wood-Oak Transition Zone in the Settlement of W. Upper Canada." *Canadian Geographer* 5, no.1 (1961): 43–7.
- "Simulating Pre-Census Population Distribution." *Canadian Geographer* 18, no.3 (1974): 250–64.
- "The Settlers and the Land: Pioneer Experience in the Home District." *Families* 14, no.4 (1975): 108–25.
- "Population Change on an Agricultural Frontier: Upper Canada, 1796 to 1841." In *Patterns of the Past: Interpreting Ontario's History*, edited by R. Hall, W. Westfall, and L.S. MacDowell, 55–77. Toronto: Dundurn Press 1988.

Wood, J. David, Peter Ennals, and Thomas F. McIlwraith. "A New Agriculture: Upper Canada to 1851." Plate 14 in *Historical Atlas of Canada Volume II: The Land Transformed*, edited by R.L. Gentilcore. Toronto: University of Toronto Press 1993.

Wood, Leslie J. "Settlements in the Mount Elgin Ridges." MA thesis, Western University 1965.

Woodcock, George. *The Century That Made Us*. Toronto: Oxford University Press 1989.

Woodward, Herbert. *Canadian Mortgages*. Don Mills, Ont.: Collins 1959.

Wright, Esmond. *The Search for Liberty: From Origins to Independence: A History of the United States of America*. Oxford, U.K.: Blackwell 1995.

Wrigley, Edward Anthony. "Family Limitation in Pre-Industrial England." *Economic History Review* 19 (1966): 82–109.
- *Population and History*. New York: McGraw-Hill 1969.
- "The Process of Modernization and the Industrial Revolution in England." *Journal of Interdisciplinary History* 3 (1972): 225–9.

Wrong, Dennis Hume. *The Problem of Order: What Unites and Divides Society*. Cambridge, Mass.: Harvard University Press 1994.

Wulff, F. "Colonel Alexander McKee and British Indian Policy, 1735–1799."
MA, University of Wisconsin – Milwaukee 1969.

Wyckoff, William K. *The Developer's Frontier: The Making of the Western New York Landscape*. New Haven, Conn.: Yale University Press 1988.

Wynn Graeme. "Notes on Society and Environment in Old Ontario." *Journal of Social History* 13, no.1 (1979): 49–65.

Yeager, William R., ed. *Early Norfolk County Land Patents, 1795–1883*. 2 vols. Simcoe: Norfolk Historical Society 1981.

Young, A.H. "The Revd. Richard Pollard, 1752–1824." *Ontario Historical Papers: Papers and Records* 25 (1929): 455–80.

Index